4.19

$ 8.—

M O O N   H A   S0-BCL-905

ALBERTA
AND THE NORTHWEST TERRITORIES

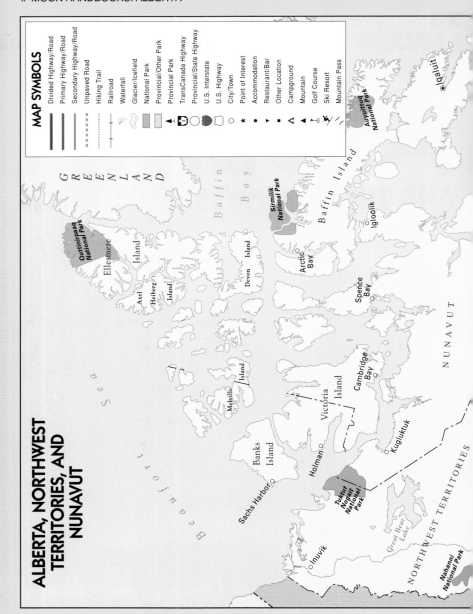

ALBERTA, NORTHWEST TERRITORIES, AND NUNAVUT

MAP SYMBOLS

- Divided Highway/Road
- Primary Highway/Road
- Secondary Highway/Road
- Unpaved Road
- Hiking Trail
- Railroad
- Waterfall
- Glacier/Icefield
- National Park
- Provincial/Other Park
- Provincial Park
- TransCanada Highway
- Provincial/State Highway
- U.S. Interstate
- U.S. Highway
- City/Town
- Point of Interest
- Accommodation
- Restaurant/Bar
- Other Location
- Campground
- Mountain
- Golf Course
- Ski Resort
- Mountain Pass

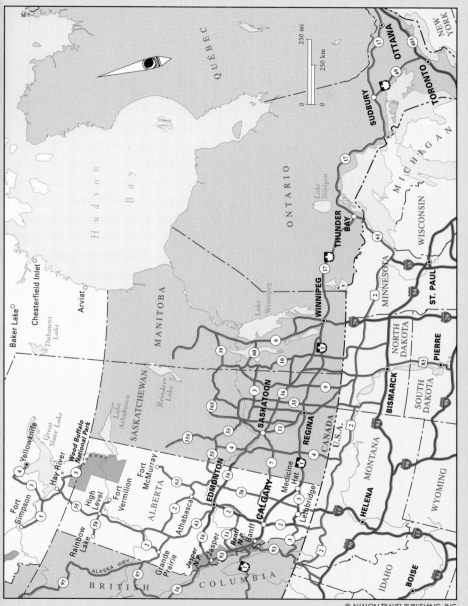

© AVALON TRAVEL PUBLISHING, INC.

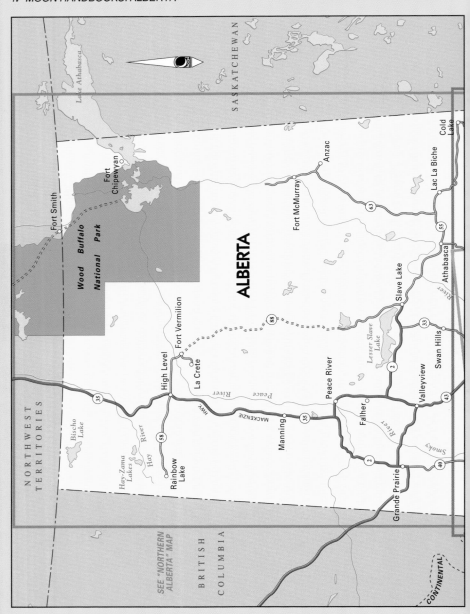

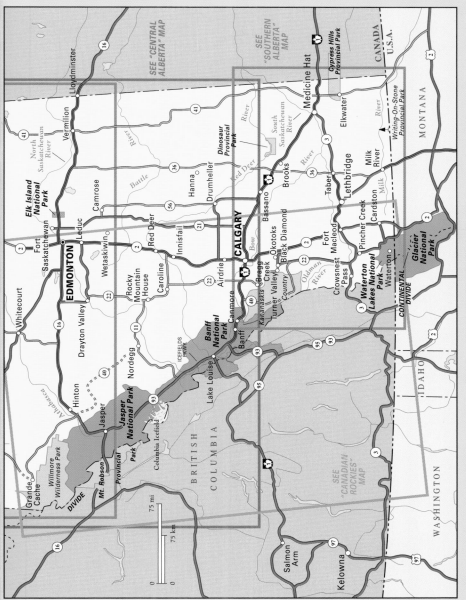

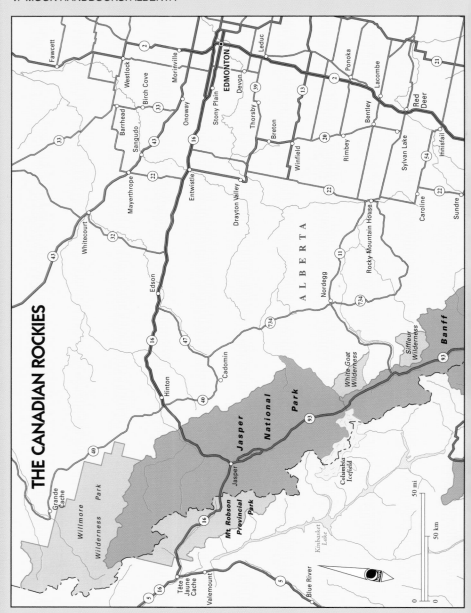

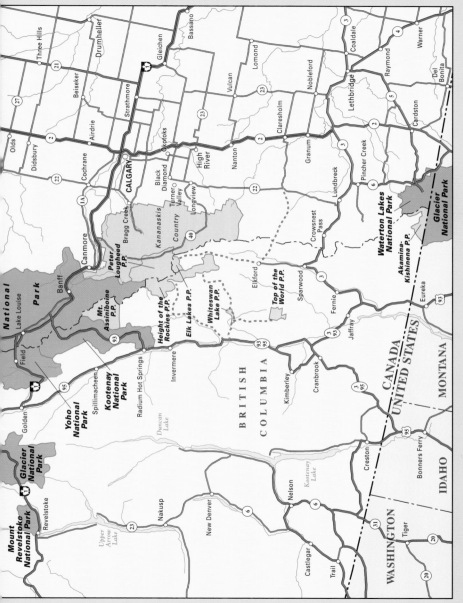

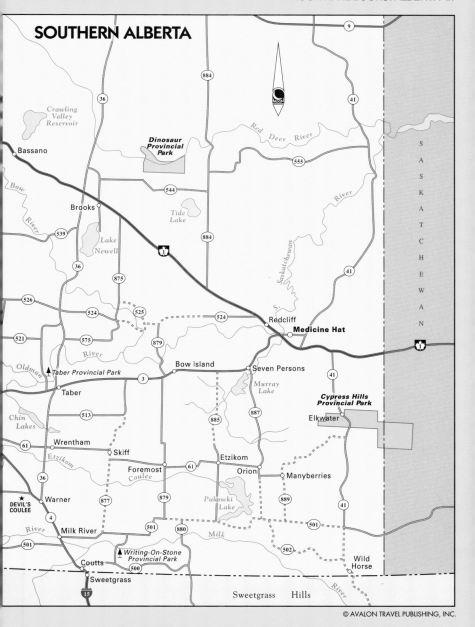

SOUTHERN ALBERTA

Crawling Valley Reservoir

Bassano

Dinosaur Provincial Park

Red Deer River

Brooks

Tide Lake

Lake Newell

Bow River

Saskatchewan River

Redcliff

Medicine Hat

Taber Provincial Park

Oldman River

Taber

Bow Island

Seven Persons

Murray Lake

Cypress Hills Provincial Park

Elkwater

Chin Lakes

Wrentham

Skiff

Etzikom Coulee

Foremost

Etzikom

Orion

Manyberries

DEVIL'S COULEE

Warner

Pakowki Lake

Milk River

Writing-On-Stone Provincial Park

Coutts

Sweetgrass

Milk River

Wild Horse

Sweetgrass Hills

SASKATCHEWAN

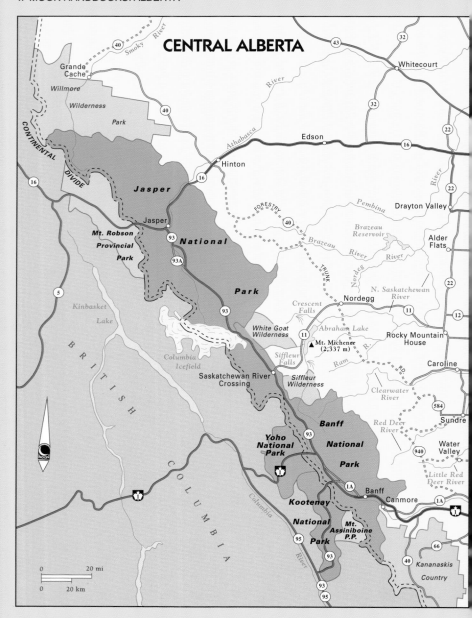

CENTRAL ALBERTA

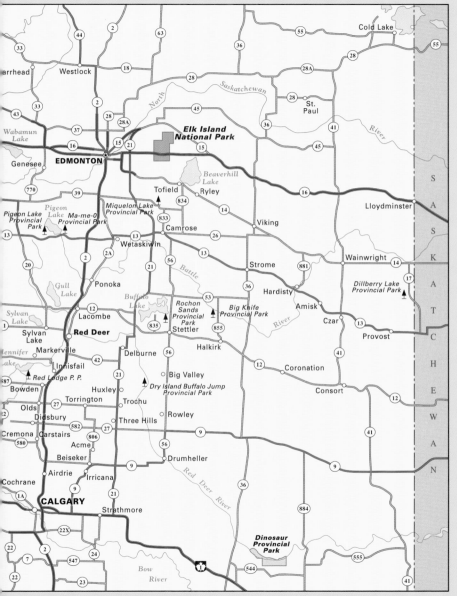

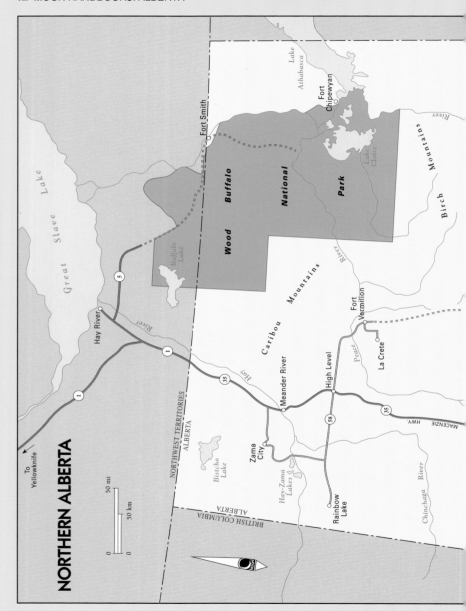

NORTHERN ALBERTA

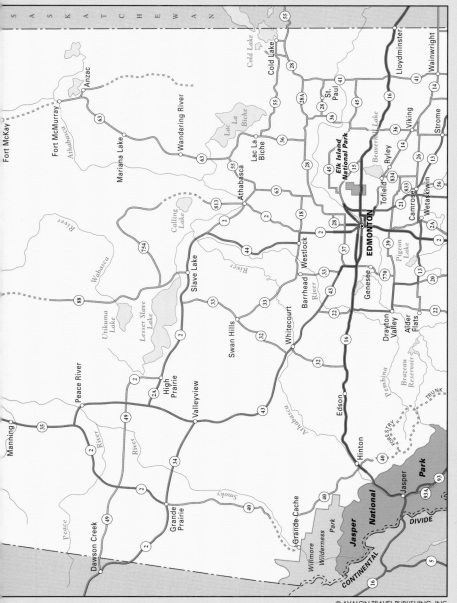

© AVALON TRAVEL PUBLISHING, INC.

NORTHWEST TERRITORIES AND NUNAVUT

Ward Hunt Island

Quttinirpaaq National Park

Ellesmere Island

ARCTIC OCEAN

Axel Heiberg Island

NORTH MAGNETIC POLE

Bathurst Island

Melville Island

Resolute

Beechey Island

Beaufort Sea

Banks Island

Sachs Harbour

Victoria Island

Holman

Cambridge Bay

Gjoa Haven

Boothia Pen

ALASKA

Herschel Island

Amundsen Gulf

Yukon River

UNITED STATES / CANADA

Aklavik

Fort McPherson

Tuktoyaktuk

Inuvik

Tsiigehtchic

Paulatuk

Tuktut Nogait National Park

Kugluktuk

Umingmaktok

Coppermine River

Queen Maud Bird Sanctuary

BATHURST INLET LODGE

Colville Lake

Dawson City

Fort Good Hope

Norman Wells

Deline

YUKON

Mackenzie River

Tulita

Great Bear Lake

Burnside River

NUNAVUT

Back River

Ross River

Rae Lakes

Snare Lake

Thelon Game Sanctuary

Mackenzie Mountains

Wrigley

NORTHWEST TERRITORIES

Whitehorse

Nahanni National Park

Wha Ti

Yellowknife

Dubawnt Lake

Watson Lake

Nahanni Butte

Fort Simpson

Lutselk'e

Great Slave Lake

Fort Liard

Hay River

BRITISH COLUMBIA

Fort Smith

Kasba Lake

ALBERTA

SASKATCHEWAN

MOON HANDBOOKS

ALBERTA
AND THE NORTHWEST TERRITORIES

FOURTH EDITION

ANDREW HEMPSTEAD

AVALON
TRAVEL

**MOON HANDBOOKS:
ALBERTA AND THE NORTHWEST
TERRITORIES
FOURTH EDITION**

Published by
Avalon Travel Publishing, Inc.
5855 Beaudry Street
Emeryville, CA 94608, USA

ISBN: 1-56691-270-9
ISSN: 1079-9338

Please send all comments,
corrections, additions,
amendments, and critiques to:

**MOON HANDBOOKS:
ALBERTA/NWT
AVALON TRAVEL PUBLISHING, INC.
5855 BEAUDRY ST.
EMERYVILLE, CA 94608, USA
e-mail: info@travelmatters.com
www.moon.com**

Printing History
1st edition—1995
4th edition—April 2001
5 4 3 2 1

Editor: Angelique S. Clarke
Series Manager: Erin Van Rheenen
Copy Editor: Ginjer Clarke
Map Editor: Mike Ferguson, Naomi Dancis
Production & Design: Marcie McKinley, Amber Pirker, Kelly Pendragon
Cartography: Mike Morgenfeld, Landis Bennett, Mark Stroud, Chris Folks, Allen Leech, Eurydice Thomas
Index: Vera Gross

Front cover photo: Mt. Robson, Mt. Robson Provincial Park, © Dick Dietrich

All photos by Andrew Hempstead unless otherwise noted.
All illustrations by Bob Race unless otherwise noted.

Distributed in the United States and Canada by Publishers Group West

Printed in the USA by Publishers Press

CONTENTS

MAPS

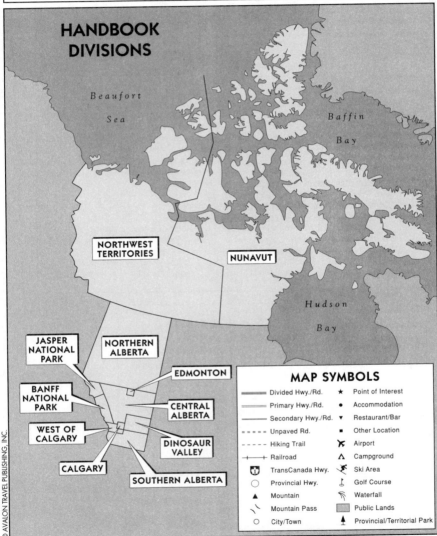

HANDBOOK DIVISIONS

Beaufort Sea

Baffin Bay

NORTHWEST TERRITORIES

NUNAVUT

Hudson Bay

JASPER NATIONAL PARK

NORTHERN ALBERTA

EDMONTON

BANFF NATIONAL PARK

CENTRAL ALBERTA

WEST OF CALGARY

DINOSAUR VALLEY

CALGARY

SOUTHERN ALBERTA

MAP SYMBOLS

Divided Hwy./Rd.	★ Point of Interest
Primary Hwy./Rd.	● Accommodation
Secondary Hwy./Rd.	▼ Restaurant/Bar
Unpaved Rd.	■ Other Location
Hiking Trail	✕ Airport
Railroad	∆ Campground
TransCanada Hwy.	Ski Area
Provincial Hwy.	Golf Course
Mountain	Waterfall
Mountain Pass	Public Lands
City/Town	Provincial/Territorial Park

© AVALON TRAVEL PUBLISHING, INC.

ABBREVIATIONS

APEX fare—advance-purchase excursion fare
B&B—bed-and-breakfast inn
BC—British Columbia
C.P.R.—Canadian Pacific Railway
d—double occupancy
4WD—four-wheel drive
GST—Goods and Services Tax
km—kilometer
kph—kilometers per hour

LRT—Light Rail Transit
NHL—National Hockey League
NWT—Northwest Territories
NWMP—North West Mounted Police
P.P.—Provincial Park
RCMP—Royal Canadian Mounted Police
s—single occupancy
T.P.—Territorial Park
UNESCO—United Nations Educational, Scientific, and Cultural Organization

DROP US A LINE

Although we have strived to produce the most up-to-date guidebook humanly possible, things change—restaurants and accommodations open and close, attractions come and go, and prices go up. If you come across a great out-of-the-way place, a new restaurant or lodging, or you think a particular hike warrants a mention, please write to us. Letters from tour operators and Albertan, NWT, and Nunavut people in the tourism and hospitality industries are also appreci-ated. When writing, be as accurate as possible; write notes on the road or even send brochures.

Write to:

Moon Handbooks: Alberta/NWT
c/o Avalon Travel Publishing, Inc.
5855 Beaudry St.
Emeryville, CA 94608 USA
e-mail: info@travelmatters.com

ACCOMMODATIONS RATINGS CHART

Ratings are based on high-season, double occupancy rates. Prices are in Canadian dollars.

Budget: up to $60
Inexpensive: $60–90
Moderate: $90–120
Expensive: $120–150
Premium: $150–180
Luxury: $180+

ACKNOWLEDGMENTS

Whether they're pumping gas, waiting tables, or whoopin' it up at the Stampede, Albertans are among the friendliest people you're likely to come across. So many have contributed to the book over the years, by pointing out town highlights, describing local hiking trails, or telling of favorite restaurants, which, in turn, makes this the most complete and up-to-date guide available to the province. For this, the fourth edition, thanks to the staff of information centers across Alberta (most of whom are volunteers), the national parks' staff, the Alberta Environment Information Centre, and all who contributed with written and spoken comments and suggestions; you know who you are.

ALBERTA

INTRODUCTION

The prosperous province of Alberta is the heart of western Canada, sandwiched between the mountains of British Columbia to the west and the prairies of Saskatchewan to the east. Edmonton, Alberta's capital, and Calgary, to the south, are Canada's fifth- and sixth-largest cities, respectively, between them holding more than half of the province's population. These boomtowns have been Canada's fastest-growing cities since World War II, centers for the staggering oil and gas reserves that have propelled Alberta to the forefront of world energy markets and technology. Edmonton is a modern, livable city boasting some of Canada's finest cultural facilities, as well as the world's largest shopping and amusement mall. Calgary, meanwhile, is home to the world-famous Calgary Stampede—a Western wingding of epic proportions—and the city received international attention as the host of the 1988 Winter Olympic Games. Its futuristic skyline rises from the prairie like the oil derricks that put the city on the map, and cattlemen in Caddies drive past gleaming skyscrapers on their way out to the ranch.

But for most visitors to Alberta, the great out-

doors, not the big cities or the fast bucks, is the main draw. The stunning mountain playgrounds of Banff, Jasper, and Waterton Lakes national parks show off the Canadian Rockies at their best, with pristine glaciers, rushing rivers, and snowcapped peaks reflected in hundreds of high-country lakes. The parks, and much of the rest of the province, are home to an abundance of wildlife such as moose, elk, bighorn sheep, wolves, bears, and an amazing array of birds; approximately 340 species of birds migrate through or nest in Alberta. And ancient wildlife thrived here, too; one of the world's greatest concentrations of dinosaur bones continues to be unearthed in the Red Deer River Valley outside Drumheller. The "Dinosaur Valley," as it's called, attracts tourist tyros and professional paleontologists alike to learn more about earth's once-dominant former tenants.

Throughout the province, wide-open spaces, endless blue skies, and accessible wilderness beckon, and big-city culture awaits when you come down from the hills. So whether your interests lean toward high peaks or high tea, you're sure to find plenty to suit you in Alberta.

THE LAND

Alberta is the fourth-largest province in Canada. With an area of 661,185 square kilometers, it's larger than all U.S. states except Alaska and Texas. The province lies between the 49th and 60th parallels, bordered on the south by Montana, USA, and on the north by Canada's Northwest Territories. To the west is British Columbia, and to the east is Saskatchewan. Along its roughly rectangular outline, the only natural border is the Continental Divide in the southwest. Here, from the International Boundary to Jasper, the lofty peaks of the **Canadian Rockies** rise to heights of more than 3,000 meters. The Canadian Rockies are only one small but exquisitely beautiful link in the Rocky Mountains chain, which forms the backbone of North America, extending from the jungles of central Mexico to the Arctic. Running parallel to the mountains along their eastern edge is a series of long, rolling ridges known as the **foothills.** This region is dominated by ranches in the south and undeveloped forests in the north. Finally, east of the foothills and across the rest of Alberta are **plains,** which cover almost three-quarters of the province. The plains provide practically all of Alberta's arable soil and natural resources. The term "plains" is very broad. Alberta's plains encompass three distinct vegetation zones: prairie, parkland, and boreal forest (see **Flora,** below).

GEOLOGY

The rocks of Alberta range in age from ancient to almost "brand-new," in geologic time. The 70-million-year-old Canadian Rockies, Alberta's most distinctive natural feature, are relatively young compared to the world's other major mountain ranges. By contrast, the Precambrian rock of the Canadian Shield, which is exposed in the province's northeast corner and underlying parts of the rest, was the progenitor of North America. It was the first land on the continent to remain permanently above sea level and is among the oldest rock on earth, formed more than 2.5 billion years ago.

Approximately 700 million years ago, in the Precambrian era, forces beneath the earth caused uplift, pushing the coastline of the Pacific Ocean—which then covered most of the province—westward. The ocean advanced, then receded, several times over the next half billion years. Each time the ocean flooded eastward, it deposited layers of sediment on its bed, and the layers built up with each successive inundation. This sediment is now a layer of sedimentary rock covering most of Alberta, up to seven kilometers deep in the southwest.

Alberta's Oil

Oil pools are created when oil globules—converted from decayed organic matter by the forces of heat and pressure beneath the earth's surface—are trapped in porous rock capped by nonporous rock. During the Middle Devonian period, 375 million years ago, with the Pacific Ocean once again covering Alberta, coral reefs formed. Over time, this coral would be trans-

ALBERTA AND CALIFORNIA

0   100 mi
0   100 km

The face of Banff's Temple mountain reveals horizontal layers of sedimentary rock.

formed into the porous rock that would hold the pools of oil. Also during this period, as well as in later years of the Paleozoic era, trillions of microscopic organisms in the sea died and sank to the bottom of the ocean, creating mass quantities of decaying organic matter in and around the coral. This organic matter would be transformed over time into the oil itself. Finally, approximately 300 million years ago, in the Carboniferous period, the Pacific Ocean extended as far as the foothills, and many rivers flowed into it from the east, carrying with them sediment that covered the porous reefs in nonporous layers. All of the elements necessary to eventually create and contain reserves of oil were then in place. A few hundred million years of "cooking" later, the primordial goo that fuels our modern, internal-combustion society is pumped nonstop from beneath Alberta. And one other huge source of oil in Alberta isn't pumped but *mined*. In the early Cretaceous period, 130 million years ago, the Arctic Ocean flooded Alberta from the north, laying down the **Athabasca Oil Sands** along the Arctic seaway. These sands hold more than one trillion barrels of heavy oil—more than all of the known reserves of conventional crude oil on the planet.

Birth of the Rockies
Also during the Cretaceous period, the Mackenzie Mountains began to rise, cutting off the Arctic seaway and forming an inland sea where marinelife such as ammonites, fish, and large marine reptiles flourished. Dinosaurs roamed the coastal areas, feeding on the lush vegetation as well as on each other.

Then, approximately 70 million years ago, two plates of the earth's crust collided. According to plate tectonics theory, the Pacific Plate butted into the North American Plate and was forced beneath it. The land at this subduction zone was crumpled and thrust upward, creating the Rocky Mountains. Layers of sediment laid down on the ocean floor over the course of hundreds of millions of years were folded, twisted, and squeezed; great slabs of rock broke away, and in some places, older strata were pushed on top of younger. By the beginning of the Tertiary period, approximately 65 million years ago, the present form of mountain contours was established and the geological framework of Alberta was in place. Then the forces of erosion went to work. The plains of the Late Tertiary period were at a higher altitude than those of today. The flat-topped Caribou Mountains, Buffalo Head Hills, Cypress Hills, Clear Hills, and Porcupine Hills are remnants of those higher plains.

The Ice Ages
No one knows why, but approximately one million years ago the world's climate cooled and ice caps formed in Arctic regions, slowly moving south over North America and Eurasia. These advances, followed by retreats, occurred four times.

The final major glaciation began moving southward 35,000 years ago. A sheet of ice up to 2,000 meters deep covered all but the highest peaks of the Rocky Mountains and Cypress Hills. The ice scoured the terrain, destroying all vegetation as it crept slowly forward. In the mountains, these rivers of ice carved hollows, known as **cirques,** into the slopes of the higher peaks. They rounded off lower peaks and reamed out valleys from their preglacial "V" shape to a trademark postglacial "U" shape. The retreat of this ice sheet, beginning approximately 12,000 years ago, was just as destructive. Rock and debris that had been picked up by the ice on its march forward melted out during the retreat, creating high ridges known as **moraines.** Many of these moraines blocked natural drainages, resulting in thousands of lakes across the north. And meltwater drained into rivers and streams, incising deep channels into the sedimentary rock of the plains.

The only remnants of this ice age are the scattered icefields along the Continental Divide—including the 325-square-kilometer **Columbia Icefield.** But wind and water erosion continues, uncovering dinosaur bones hidden among layers of sediment and carving an eerie landscape of badlands along the sides of many prairie river valleys.

Waterways

Alberta has three major watersheds draining 245 named rivers and 315 named creeks. More than half of the province drains into the **Mackenzie River System,** which flows north into the Arctic Ocean. The **Peace River,** which originates in the interior of British Columbia and flows northeast through Alberta, and the **Athabasca River,** whose initial source is the Columbia Icefield, are the province's two major tributaries in this system. They eventually meet to form the Slave River, which flows into the Mackenzie at Great Slave Lake in the Northwest Territories.

Central Alberta is drained mainly by the **Saskatchewan River System,** which is the major source of water for Alberta's farmers. This river system, which eventually flows into Hudson Bay, has three main tributaries: the **North Saskatchewan River,** originating from the Columbia Icefield; the **Red Deer River,**

originating in the heart of Banff National Park and flowing through "Dinosaur Valley" on its way east; and the **South Saskatchewan River.** The latter is fed largely by the **Bow River,** flowing down from Banff, and the **Oldman River,** which cascades out of the Rockies south of Kananaskis Country.

A small area in the south of the province is drained by the **Milk River,** which flows southeast into the Mississippi River System, ending up in the Gulf of Mexico.

The amount of water flowing into any one of Alberta's rivers depends on that particular river's source. Rivers originating from melt-out of the winter snowpack reach peak flow in midsummer and often run dry by late summer. Those that originate from glaciers run light in spring and reach a peak in midsummer but continue a light flow until winter. Those that rise in the foothills and higher areas of the plains have highly variable flows, depending entirely on precipitation.

CLIMATE

Alberta spans 11 degrees of latitude, and its varied topography includes elevations ranging from 170 to more than 3,700 meters above sea level. As a result, the climate of the province varies widely from place to place. In addition, the Canadian Rockies create some of Alberta's unique climatic characteristics. As prevailing, moisture-laden westerlies blow in from British Columbia, the cold heights of the Rockies wring them dry. This cycle makes for clear, sunny skies in southern Alberta; Calgary gets up to 350 hours of sunshine in June alone, which is good news, unless you're a farmer. In winter, the dry winds blasting down the eastern slopes of the Rockies can raise temperatures on the prairies by up to 40°C in 24 hours. Called **chinooks,** these desiccating blows are a phenomenon unique to Alberta.

Another interesting phenomenon occurring in southern Alberta's Rocky Mountain regions is the **temperature inversion,** in which a layer of warm air sits on top of a cold air mass. During these inversions, high- and low-country roles are reversed: prairie residents can be shivering and bundling up, while their mountain fellows are sunning themselves in shirtsleeves.

The Seasons

Overall, Alberta features cold winters and short, hot summers. May to mid-September is ideal for touring, camping out, and seeing the sights; one month on either side of this peak period and the weather is cooler but still pleasant; and the rest of the year the skiing and snowboarding are fantastic.

January is usually the coldest month, when Calgary's mean average temperature is −13°C and Fort McMurray's is −20°C. In winter, extended spells of −30°C are not uncommon anywhere in the province, and temperatures occasionally drop below −40°C. Severe cold weather is often accompanied by sunshine; the cold is a dry cold, unlike the damp cold experienced in coastal regions. Cold temperatures and snow can continue until mid-March.

Although March, April, and May are officially the months of spring, snow often falls in April, many lakes may remain frozen until May, and snow cover on higher mountain hiking trails remains until June. Late snowfalls, although not welcomed by golfers in Calgary, provide important moisture for crops.

The official months of summer are June, July, and August, with July being the hottest month and providing the most uniform temperatures throughout the province. On hot days, the temperature hits 30°C (usually every other summer day in the south) and occasionally climbs above 40°C. Again, because of the dry air, these high temperatures are more bearable here than in coastal regions experiencing the same temperatures.

The frost-free growing season is over by late September, when the air develops a distinct chill. October brings the highest temperature variations of the year, with the thermometer hitting 30°C but also dipping as low as −20°C. Mild weather can continue until early December, but the first snow generally falls in October, and by mid-November winter has set in.

FLORA

Alberta can be divided into two major geographical areas: the mountain-and-foothill region along its southwestern border and the plains covering the rest of the province. Within each of these two main areas are distinct vegetation zones, the boundaries of which are determined by factors such as precipitation, latitude, and altitude.

THE MOUNTAINS AND FOOTHILLS

In southwest Alberta, west of Highway 2 between the U.S. border and Edmonton, the land climbs through foothills to the high peaks of the Rockies. Along the way it gains more than 2,000 meters of elevation and passes through the montane, subalpine, and alpine vegetation zones. Although Banff and Jasper national parks are the obvious places to view these mountain biomes, the changes in vegetation are more abrupt and just as spectacular in less-visited Waterton Lakes National Park.

Montane

The foothills, along with most major valleys below an elevation of approximately 1,500 meters, are primarily cloaked in montane forest. Aspen, balsam poplar, and white spruce thrive here, and lodgepole pine dominates areas affected by fire. On dry, south-facing slopes, Douglas fir is the climax species. Where sunlight penetrates the forest, such as along riverbanks, flowers such as lady's slipper, Indian paintbrush, and saxifrage are common. Large tracts of fescue grassland are common at lower elevations.

The montane forest holds the greatest diversity of life of any vegetation zone in the province and is prime winter habitat for larger mammals. But much of this habitat has been given over to agriculture and development.

Subalpine

Subalpine forests occur where temperatures are lower and precipitation higher than the montane. Generally, this is 1,500–2,200 meters above sea level. The climax species in this zone are Engelmann spruce and subalpine fir, although extensive forests of lodgepole pine occur in areas that have been scorched by fire in the last 100 years. At higher elevations, stands of larch are seen. Larches are conifers, but unlike other evergreens, their needles turn a burnt-orange color each fall, producing a magnificent display for photographers.

Alpine

The alpine zone extends from the treeline to mountain summits. Vegetation at these high altitudes occurs only where soil has been deposited. Large areas of alpine meadows burst with color for a short period each summer as lupines, mountain avens, alpine forget-me-nots, moss campion, and a variety of heathers bloom.

THE PLAINS

Like the mountain-and-foothill region, Alberta's plains also are made up of three different vegetation zones. Across Highway 2, east of the mountains and foothills, southeast Alberta is dominated by the prairie—a vast, dry region of grasslands. Just north of the prairie is the aspen parkland, a belt of forest that runs across central Alberta to the foothills and covers approximately 10 percent of the province. Finally, Alberta's largest ecological zone by far, covering more than half of the province, is the boreal forest. It is located north of the aspen parkland and extends into the Northwest Territories to the treeline, where the tundra begins.

Prairie

Prairie is the warmest and driest ecological zone, with an annual precipitation less than 750 millimeters. This harsh climate can support trees only where water flows, so for the most part, the prairie is flat or lightly undulating open grassland. Irrigation has made agriculture possible across much of the south, and the patches of native grasses such as rough fescue and grama are rapidly disappearing. Among the cultivated pastureland and seemingly desolate plains, flowers punctuate the otherwise ochre-colored landscape. Alberta's floral emblem, the prickly wild rose, grows here, as do pincushion cactus, buckbrush (or yellow rose), and sagebrush. In river valleys, aspen, willow, and cottonwood grow along the banks.

The stands of large cottonwoods in Dinosaur Provincial Park were part of the reason this park was designated a UNESCO World Heritage Site. (The park is a good example of prairie habitat.) The Cypress Hills, which rise above the driest part of the province, contain vegetation not generally associated with the prairies, including spruce, aspen, a variety of berries, and the calypso orchid.

Aspen Parkland

Unique to Canada, this area is a transition zone between the prairie grassland to the south and the boreal forest to the north. As the name suggests, trembling aspen (named for light, flattened leaves that "tremble" in even the slightest wind) is the climax species, but much of this zone has been given over to agriculture—its forests burned and its soil tilled. Scattered stands of aspen, interspersed with willow, balsam poplar, and white spruce, still occur, whereas areas cleared by early settlers now contain fescue grass. Flowering plants such as prairie

VEGETATION ZONES

Boreal   Forest

Foothills

Mountains

o Edmonton

Parkland

o Calgary

Prairie

| 0 | 100 mi |
| 0 | 100 km |

© AVALON TRAVEL PUBLISHING, INC.

crocus, snowberry, prickly wild rose, and lily-of-the-valley decorate the shores of the many lakes and marshy areas found in this biome. Elk Island National Park, best known for its mammal populations, is an ideal example of this unique habitat.

Boreal Forest

Only a few species of trees are able to adapt to the harsh northern climate characteristic of this zone. The area is almost totally covered in forest, with only scattered areas of prairielike vegetation occurring in the driest areas. In the southern part of the boreal forest, the predominant species are aspen and balsam poplar. Farther north, conifers such as white spruce, lodgepole pine, and balsam fir are more common, with jack pine growing on dry ridges and tamarack also present. The entire forest is interspersed with lakes, bogs, and sloughs, where black spruce and larch are the dominant species. Like the trees, the ground cover also varies with latitude. To the south, and in the upland areas where aspen is the climax species, the undergrowth is lush with a variety of shrubs, including raspberries, saskatoons, and buffalo berries. To the north, where drainage is generally poor, the ground cover is made up of dense mats of peat.

Most areas of boreal forest accessible by road have been affected by fire or development, but some areas of old growth can still be found. Highway 63, which ends in Fort McMurray, runs through pristine northern boreal forest. Sir Winston Churchill Provincial Park, on an island in Lac La Biche, hasn't been burned for more than 300 years and supports stands of balsam fir up to 150 years old.

FAUNA

For 10,000 years, hundreds of thousands of bison roamed Alberta's plains, and wolves and grizzly bears inhabited all parts of the province, but this all changed with the coming of white men. Trappers and traders first devastated beaver and mink populations, then killed off all of the bison, wolves, and grizzlies on the prairies.

Today, because of the foresight of early conservationists, mammal populations have stabilized and Alberta's wilderness once again provides some of North America's best opportunities for viewing wildlife.

THE DEER FAMILY

Deer

Alberta's mule deer and white-tailed deer are similar in size and appearance. Their color varies with the season but is generally light brown in summer, turning dirty gray in winter. Both species are considerably smaller than elk. The **mule deer** has a white rump, a white tail with a dark tip, and large mulelike ears. It inhabits open forests bordering prairie. The **white-tailed deer's** tail is dark on top, but when the animal runs, it holds its tail erect, revealing an all-white underside. White-tails frequent thickets along the rivers and lakes of the foothills and aspen parkland.

Elk

The elk, or wapiti, is common throughout the Rockies and foothills. It has a tan body with a dark brown neck and legs, and a white rump. This second-largest member of the deer family weighs 250–450 kilograms and stands 1.5 meters at the shoulder. Stags grow an impressive set of antlers, which they shed each spring. Rutting season takes place between August and October; listen for the shrill bugles of the stags serenading the females. During the rut, randy males will challenge anything with their antlers and can be dangerous. In spring, females protecting their young can be equally dangerous.

Moose

The giant of the deer family is the moose, an awkward-looking mammal that appears to have been designed by a cartoonist. It has the largest antlers of any animal in the world, stands up to 1.8 meters at the shoulder, and weighs more than 450 kilograms. Its body is dark brown, and it has a prominent nose, long spindly legs, small eyes, big ears, and an odd flap of skin called a "bell" dangling beneath its chin. Apart from all that, it's good-looking. Each spring the bull begins to grow palm-shaped antlers that are fully grown by August. Moose are solitary animals that prefer marshy areas and weedy lakes. They forage in and around ponds on willows, aspen, birch, grasses, and all aquatic vegetation. Although they may appear docile, moose will attack humans if they feel threatened.

Caribou
Small populations of woodland caribou inhabit the alpine regions of the mountains and the boreal forests of northern Alberta. They are migratory but travel far less distances than the barren-ground caribou of the Arctic. Numbering approximately 5,000 within the province, diminishing habitat and declining numbers have led to their placement on Alberta's Threatened Wildlife List. These caribou are smaller than elk and have a dark brown coat with creamy patches on the neck and rump. Both sexes grow antlers, but those of the females are shorter and have fewer points. On average males weigh 180 kilograms, females 115 kilograms.

BEARS

Alberta's two species of bears—black bears and grizzlies—can be differentiated by size and shape. Grizzlies are larger than black bears and have a flatter, dish-shaped face and a distinctive hump of muscle behind their necks. Color is not a reliable way to tell them apart. Black bears are not always black. They can be brown or cinnamon, causing them to be confused with the brown grizzly.

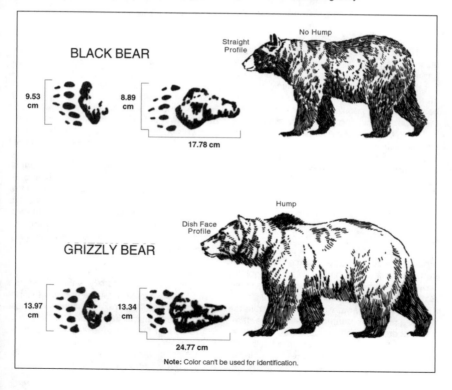

BLACK BEAR

Straight Profile

No Hump

9.53 cm

8.89 cm

17.78 cm

Dish Face Profile

Hump

GRIZZLY BEAR

13.97 cm

13.34 cm

24.77 cm

Note: Color can't be used for identification.

most common. On average, males weigh 200–250 kilograms. The bears eat small- and medium-sized mammals and supplement their diet with berries in fall. Like black bears, they sleep through most of the winter. When they emerge in early spring, the bears scavenge carcasses of animals that succumbed to the winter until the new spring vegetation becomes sufficiently plentiful.

WILD DOGS AND CATS

Foxes
The smallest of the North American wild canids is the **swift fox,** which had been eradicated from the Canadian prairies by 1928 but was reintroduced to the southeastern corner of Alberta in 1983. Today, a small population continues to thrive in this dry and desolate landscape, but the species is still considered endangered. It has a gray body with a long, black-tipped bushy tail, large ears, and smoky gray facial spots. The **red fox** is slightly larger than the swift fox and is common throughout Alberta.

Coyotes
The resilient coyotes have successfully survived human attempts to eradicate them from the prairies; today their eerie concerts of yips and howls can be heard across much of Alberta. A mottled mix of brown and gray, with lighter-colored legs and belly, the coyote is a skillful and crafty hunter that preys mainly on rodents. Both foxes and coyotes have the remarkable ability to hear the movement of small mammals under the snow, allowing them to hunt these animals without actually seeing them.

Wolves
Now inhabiting only the mountains and boreal forests, the wolf was once the target of a relentless campaign to exterminate the species. Wolves are larger than coyotes, resembling a large husky or German shepherd in size and stature. Their color ranges from snow white to brown or black. They are complex and intriguing animals that adhere to a hierarchical social order and are capable of expressing happiness, humor, and loneliness.

Wolves were once hunted to near extinction.

Black Bears
If you spot a bear feeding beside the road, chances are it's a black bear. These mammals are widespread throughout all forested areas of the province (except Cypress Hills Provincial Park), numbering approximately 40,000. Their weight varies considerably, but males average 150 kilograms and females 100 kilograms. Their diet is omnivorous, consisting primarily of grasses and berries but supplemented by small mammals. In winter, they can sleep for up to one month at a time before changing position.

Grizzly Bears
Most of Alberta's grizzlies are spread throughout the Rockies in Banff and Jasper national parks, Kananaskis Country, and Alberta's four designated wilderness areas. A small population inhabiting the Swan Hills is distinct from those found in the mountains and is probably related more closely to the grizzlies that once roamed the prairies.

Grizzlies are widespread but not abundant in the province, numbering approximately 800. The three mountain national parks hold an estimated 200 grizzlies; the remainder are found in the surrounding, undeveloped wilderness. Most sightings occur in alpine and subalpine zones, although sightings at lower elevations are not unusual, especially when snow falls early or late. The bears' color ranges from light brown to almost black, with dark tan being the

Wild Cats

The elusive **lynx** is identifiable by its pointy black ear tufts and an oversized "tabby cat" appearance. The animal has broad, padded paws that distribute its weight, allowing it to "float" on the surface of snow. It is uncommon but widespread through remote, forested regions of the province. **Bobcats** live in the coulees and caves of badlands such as in Writing-On-Stone and Dinosaur Provincial Parks.

Solitary and secretive, **cougars** (also called mountain lions) can grow to a length of 1.5 meters and can weigh 75 kilograms. These versatile hunters inhabit the mountain and foothill regions.

OTHER LARGE MAMMALS

Mountain Goats

The remarkable rock-climbing ability of these nimble-footed creatures allows them to live on rocky ledges or near-vertical slopes, safe from predators. They also frequent the alpine meadows and open forests of the Rockies, where they congregate around natural licks of salt. The goats stand one meter at the shoulder and weigh 80–130 kilograms. Both sexes possess black horns and a peculiar beard, or rather, goatee.

Bighorn Sheep

Bighorn sheep are found on grassy mountain slopes throughout the mountains. The males have impressive horns that curve backward up to 360 degrees. The color of their coat varies with the season; in summer it is brownish-gray (with a cream-colored belly and rump), turning grayer in winter.

Pronghorn

Found roaming the prairie grasslands of southeastern Alberta, the pronghorn, often called pronghorn antelope, is one of the fastest animals in the New World, capable of sustained speeds up to 80 kilometers per hour. Other remarkable attributes also ensure its survival, including incredible hearing and eyesight, and the ability to go without water for long periods.

Bison

Conservative estimates put the population of bison at approximately 60 million before the coming of Europeans. Within Alberta, these shaggy beasts are found in Elk Island and Wood Buffalo national parks and in several privately owned herds throughout the province. Two subspecies of bison inhabit Alberta, but they have mostly interbred. Wood bison are darker in color, larger (an average bull weighs 840 kilograms), and have long, straight hair covering the forehead. Plains bison are smaller, have shorter legs, a larger head, and frizzy hair. In summer they grow distinctive capes of woolly hair that cover their front legs, head, and shoulders.

RODENTS AND OTHER SMALL MAMMALS

Squirrels

Several species of squirrels are common in Alberta. The golden-mantled ground squirrel, found in rocky outcrops of subalpine and alpine regions, has black stripes along its sides and looks like an oversized chipmunk. The Columbian ground squirrel has reddish legs, face, and underside, and a flecked, grayish back. The bushy-tailed red squirrel, a bold chatterbox of the forest, leaves telltale shelled cones at the bases of

---

WILDLIFE AND YOU

Alberta's abundance of wildlife is one of its biggest drawing cards. To help preserve this unique resource, obey fishing and hunting regulations and use common sense.

• **Do not feed the animals.** Many animals may seem tame, but feeding them endangers yourself, the animal, and other visitors, as animals become aggressive when looking for handouts.

• **Store food safely.** When camping keep food in your vehicle or out of reach of animals. Just leaving it in a cooler isn't good enough.

• **Keep your distance.** Although it's tempting to get close to animals for a better look or photograph, it disturbs the animal and, in many cases, can be dangerous.

• **Drive carefully.** The most common cause of premature death for larger mammals is being hit by cars.

bighorn sheep

conifers. The lightly colored Richardson's ground squirrel, which chirps and flicks its thin tail when it senses danger, is found across much of Alberta; on the prairie, it is often misidentified as a "gopher." Another species, the nocturnal northern flying fox, glides through the montane forests of mountain valleys but is rarely seen.

Other Rodents

One of the animal kingdom's most industrious mammals is the **beaver.** Tipping the scales at approximately 20 kilograms, it has a flat, rudderlike tail and webbed back feet that enable it to swim at speeds up to 10 kilometers per hour. Beavers build their dam walls and lodges out of twigs, branches, sticks from felled trees, and mud. They eat the bark and smaller twigs of deciduous plants and store branches underwater, near the lodge, as a winter food supply. **Muskrats** also inhabit Alberta's waterways and wetlands. They are agile swimmers and are able to stay submerged for up to 12 minutes.

Closely related to muskrats are **voles,** which are often mistaken for mice. They inhabit the prairies and lower elevations of forested areas. **Kangaroo rats** live on the shortgrass prairie within the Palliser Triangle. They propel themselves with leaps of up to two meters. The furry **shrew** has a sharp-pointed snout and is closely related to the mole. It must eat almost constantly because it is susceptible to starvation within only a few hours of its last meal. The **pygmy**

shrew, widespread throughout Alberta, is the world's smallest mammal.

High in the mountains, **hoary marmots** are often seen sunning themselves in rocky areas at or above the treeline. When danger approaches, these large rodents emit a shrill whistle to warn their colony. **Porcupines** are common and widespread throughout all forested areas of the province.

Hares and Pikas

Hares and pikas are technically lagomorphs, distinguished from rodents by a double set of incisors in the upper jaw. Alberta's **varying hares** are commonly referred to as snowshoe hares because their thickly furred, wide-set hind feet mimic snowshoes. Unlike rabbits, which maintain a brown coat year-round, snowshoe hares turn white in winter, providing camouflage in the snowy climes they inhabit. One of their Albertan cousins, the **white-tailed prairie hare,** has been clocked at speeds of 60 kilometers per hour. Finally, the small, gray-colored pika, or rock rabbit, lives among the rubble and boulders of scree slopes above the treeline.

Weasels

The weasel family is composed of dozens of species of small, carnivorous mammals, many of which can be found in Alberta. Widely considered pests by farmers, they are highly prized for their furs. The smallest weasel, and the world's smallest carnivore, is the **least weasel,** widespread through lightly grassed areas and open meadows, which weighs just 70 grams. At the other end of the scale is the **wolverine,** largest of the weasels, weighing up to 16 kilograms. This solitary, cunning, and cautious creature inhabits northern forests and subalpine and lower alpine regions. Inhabiting the same environment are **fishers,** quick, agile hunters that feed at night. Also frequenting subalpine and lower alpine regions is the **marten,** which preys on birds, squirrels, mice, and voles as it moves through the trees. The **badger,** a larger member of the weasel family, inhabits the prairies and parkland, and although widespread is rare. It is endowed with large claws and strong forelegs, making it an impressive digger. Two other related species divide their time between land and water. **River otters** have round heads; short, thick necks; webbed feet; long facial whiskers; and grow larger than one meter in length. These playful characters are active both day and night and prey on both beaver and muskrat. They are widespread but not common throughout the northern half of Alberta. **Mink,** at home in or out of water, are smaller than otters and feed on muskrats, mice, voles, and fish. Mink are especially sought after for their pelts; they are raised in captivity for this purpose at mink farms throughout the province.

REPTILES AND AMPHIBIANS

Two species of **snakes,** the wandering garter snake and the red-sided garter snake (North America's northernmost reptile), are found as far north as the boreal forest. The other six species of snakes in the province, of which the plains garter snake is the most common, are restricted to the southern grasslands. Rattlesnakes are rarely encountered; their range is restricted to the badlands.

Three species of **frogs** and one species of **salamander** are present in Alberta.

FISH

Alberta's waters hold eight species of **trout;** rainbow, cutthroat, and brook trout are the predominant species in southern Alberta and the mountain regions, whereas lake trout, which grow to 20 kilograms, are common in the north. The bull trout, often confused with the brook trout but lacking black markings on the dorsal fin, is a unique species whose slow growth makes it prone to overfishing. Other fish inhabiting Alberta's waters include **arctic grayling,** two species of **whitefish, sturgeon** (largest of the freshwater fish), **burbot, northern pike,** and **walleye.**

BIRDS

Bird-watching is popular in Alberta, thanks to the 340 species of birds recorded in the province and the millions of migratory birds that follow the Central Flyway each year. All it takes is a pair of binoculars, a good book detailing species, and patience.

Shorebirds and Waterfowl

Alberta is home to 40 species of shorebirds, among them plovers, sandpipers, dowitchers, turnstones, gulls, terns, and herons. Of Alberta's ducks, **mallards** are present everywhere except the mountains, and **pintails** can often be seen feeding on grain in farmers' fields. The **wood duck** is much less common; identified by a distinctive crest, it can be spied around wetlands. Other widespread waterfowl species include **loons, grebes,** three species of **teal, geese,** and the threatened **trumpeter swan.**

Raptors

Raptors can be divided into two groups: those that hunt during daylight hours and those that hunt at night. Alberta's provincial bird, the **great horned owl,** is one of the latter. It is identified by its prominent "horns," which are actually tufts of feathers. Other nocturnal raptors in Alberta include the **pygmy owl, snowy owl,** and **great gray owl.**

Like owls, raptors that hunt during the day have adapted to specific environments—falcons to the prairies and hawks to forested areas. Falcons are easily distinguished among raptors for their long, pointed wings and narrow tails, allowing them to reach great speeds when in pursuit of prey. Most widespread of Alberta's falcons is the **prairie falcon,** whose territory extends from the prairies to the foothills. Other falcons present in Alberta include the **American kestrel,** which is commonly seen perched on fence posts and power poles throughout the prairies; the **merlin,** which tends to nest close to populated areas; and the rare **peregrine falcon,** which has been clocked at speeds of up to 290 kilometers per hour when diving for prey. Hawks have adapted to hunting in wooded areas by developing short, rounded wings and long tails. The rust-colored **ferruginous hawk,** the largest hawk in North America, inhabits the treed areas of the prairies. The **marsh hawk** is widespread through the prairies and parkland, and as the name suggests, lives around areas of wetland. Farther north, the **redtailed hawk** resides

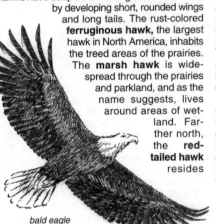

bald eagle

in the aspen parkland and southern extent of boreal forest. Two species of eagles are also present in Alberta. **Bald eagles** soar over the northern half of the province, the foothills, and mountains. **Golden eagles** rest in open and sparsely vegetated areas of grasslands and mountains. Both species are migratory. **Ospreys** are uncommon; look for them around mountain and parkland lakes and rivers. They migrate to Alberta for the summer nesting season, always returning to the same nest, which they build high up in tall dead trees, on telephone poles, or on rocky outcrops, but always overlooking water. They feed on fish, hovering up to 50 meters above water, watching for movement, then diving into the water, thrusting their legs forward and collecting prey in their talons.

Others
Birdwatchers will be enthralled with the diversity of eastern and western bird species in Alberta. Magpies, sparrows, starlings, grouse, ravens, and crows are all widespread in the region. Blackbirds, finches, thrushes, hummingbirds, woodpeckers, flycatchers, and 28 species of warblers are common in forested areas. The popular campground visitor, the cheeky gray jay, is similar in appearance to that of the curious Clark's nutcracker.

HISTORY

THE EARLIEST INHABITANTS

The first *Homo sapiens* probably arrived in North America approximately 15,000 years ago—migrating from northeastern Asia across a land bridge spanning the Bering Strait. At the time, most of what is now western Canada was covered by an ice cap, so these first immigrants headed south along the coast and into the lower, ice-free latitudes of North America (to what is now the United States). Other waves of similar migrations followed, and eventually these ancestors of today's Native American fanned out across North and South America.

Thousands of years later, the receding polar ice cap began to uncover the land north of the 49th parallel. Native hunters probably first ventured into what is now Canada approximately 11,000 years ago, in pursuit of large mammals at the edge of the melting ice mass. The people who ended up in what would become Alberta came from the south, and in much later waves from the east, and formed several broad groups, within which many tribes formed, each with a distinct culture and language.

Most of the natives who inhabited what is now Alberta relied on bison (misnamed buffalo by early Europeans) for almost all of their needs. They ate the meat, both fresh and dried, then pounded into a powder form known as pemmican; made clothing, blankets, and tepee covers from the hides; fashioned bones into tools and ornaments; and used the dung as a source of fuel. One of their most successful ways of killing the huge beasts was by stampeding a whole herd over a cliff, at places known today as "buffalo jumps." (The best example of such a site is Head-Smashed-In Buffalo Jump, northwest of Fort Macleod.) They lived in tepees, which are conical-shaped tents comprising a frame of poles covered in buffalo hides. All cooking was done inside the tepee, with weapons, clothing, and food hung on the inside. During large gatherings, such as a buffalo hunt or the midsummer Sun Dance religious ceremony, thousands of tepees dotted the landscape.

Blackfoot

The Blackfoot Confederacy was a group of traditional prairie dwellers and was the most warlike and feared of all native groups in Canada. Linguistically linked to the Algonkians, they were the "classic" Indian, depicted in story and film bedecked in costumes and headdresses and mounted on horses. (This perception is somewhat skewed, however, because the horse was a relatively modern addition to the plains, having been first introduced to North America by the Spanish in the mid-1600s and appearing north of the 49th parallel in the mid-1700s.) Before the arrival of Europeans, the Blackfoot Confederacy ruled the southern half of the province and comprised three allied bands, which hunted and camped together, intermarried, shared customs, and spoke dialects of the Algonkian language. They were the **Blackfoot** (best known today as **Siksika**), who lived along the North Saskatchewan River; the **Blood,** along the Red Deer River; and the **Peigan,** along the Bow River. As the Cree and Assiniboine to the north became armed with guns through their close links to the fur trade, the Blackfoot were pushed south, culminating in the last great intertribal battle in North America, which was fought against the Cree in 1870 within what is now Lethbridge city limits. By this time, the northernmost band of the once-powerful confederacy were the Siksika, who had been restricted to the land along the Bow River, while the Blood and Peigan lived to the south, with the Peigan territory extending well into Montana.

The **Sarcee** are also considered part of the Blackfoot nation but are of Athapaskan linguistic stock. This small tribe divided from the subarctic Beaver in the mid-1800s and integrated themselves with the Blackfoot in customs, lifestyle, and marriage but retained their original tongue.

Assiniboine

Circa 1650, the mighty Sioux nation, centered on the Great Lakes, began splintering, with many thousands of its members moving north into present-day Canada, obtaining guns and metal objects from Europeans. These people became known as the "Assiniboine," meaning the "people who cook with stones." (Stones would be heated in a fire and then placed in a rawhide or birchbark basket with water; meat and vegetables were added, cooking as the water heated.) Slowly, generation after generation, smaller groups pushed westward along the Saskatchewan River system, allying themselves with the Cree but keeping their own identity and pushing through Blackfoot territory of the plains to reach the foothills approximately 200 years ago. They split into bands, moving north and south along the foothills and penetrating the wide valleys where hunting was productive. A lifestyle very different to that of the plains Indians evolved. Moving with the seasons, they lived in small familylike groups, diversifying their skills, becoming excellent hunters of mountain animals and gathering berries in fall, and becoming less dependent on buffalo. They were a steadfast yet friendly people, and as Alexander Henry the Younger reported in 1811, "although [they are] the most arrant horse thieves in the world, they are at the same time the most hospitable to strangers who arrived in their camps." They knew themselves as the Nakoda, meaning "people." To the white man they were the Stoney, a shortening of the "Stone People," which in turn was an English interpretation of Assiniboine.

As the great buffalo herds were decimated, the Stoney were impacted less than the plains Indians because their reliance on the buffalo was almost nonexistent. But the effect of white man's intrusion on their lifestyle was still apparent. The missionaries of the day found that their teachings had more effect on the mountain people than those of the plains, so they intensified their efforts at converting the Stoney. Reverend John McDougall was particularly trusted, and in 1873 he built a small mission church by the Bow River at Morleyville. When the Stoney were presented with Treaty 7 in 1877, they chose to locate their reserve around the mission church at Morleyville. Abandoning their nomadic lifestyle, they quickly learned farming. Unlike the plains Indians, they were almost self-sufficient on the reserve, not needing government rations that the Blackfoot tribes survived on. Approximately 7,000 Stoney live on the Morley reserve today.

Cree

Before the arrival of Europeans, the Cree had inhabited most of eastern Canada for thousands of years. As the European fur traders pushed westward from Hudson Bay, the Cree followed, displacing enemies and adapting to new environments. By 1800, the Cree had moved as far west as the Peace River and to the northern slopes of the Rocky Mountains. They lived mostly in the forests fringing the prairies, acting as a middleman between Europeans and local natives, searching out furs

Native animals, such as this moose, were used for more than meat and clothing.

and trading buffalo hides obtained from plains natives for European goods. Although not related, the Cree and Assiniboine freely mixed together, camping, hunting, and fighting as a group.

Athapaskan

Athapaskan (often spelled Athabascan) is the mostly widely spread of all North American linguistic groups, extending from the Rio Grande to Alaska. It is believed that Athapaskan-speaking people moved into what is now Alberta approximately 7,000 years ago, following the receding ice cap and settling in forested areas throughout the subarctic. Athapaskans led a simple, nomadic life and were generally friendly toward each other and neighboring tribes. Although culturally diverse, the nature of this tribe's lifestyle left few archaeological remains; therefore, they are the least known of the natives who once lived within the boundaries of modern-day Alberta.

The southernmost Athapaskan group inhabiting Alberta was the **Beaver,** who were forced westward, up the Peace River watershed, by the warlike Cree in the late 1700s (the name Peace River originated after the two groups eventually made peace). Traditionally, the Beaver hunted caribou and bison that wandered north from the plains, but they were strongly influenced by the fur trade. Another distinct band of Athapaskans settled along the Mackenzie River watershed and are known today as the Dene (DEN-ay), meaning "the people." The Dene lived a simple life, depending on fish, birds, and game such as caribou and moose, and traveling in birchbark canoes. Further divisions within the Dene nation relate more to the area in which they lived rather than to distinct language or lifestyles. These groups include the **Slave** (known as the Slavey in the Northwest Territories) and the **Chipewyan,** both of whose traditional home was the upper watershed of the Mackenzie River.

Métis

The exact definition of Métis varies across Canada, but the term originated in the 1700s to describe those born of a mixed racial heritage as the result of relationships between French traders and native Cree women. The Métis played an invaluable role in the fur trade because they were able to perform traditional tasks and were bilingual. By the early 1800s, a distinct Métis culture developed, mostly along major trading routes. As the fur trade ended, and the great buffalo herds disappeared, many Métis found themselves drawn toward the familiarity of their own people and settled along Central Canada's Red River. Government threats to take their land along the Red River led to the 1869 Riel Rebellion and the 1885 North West Rebellion, after which the displaced Métis drifted back westward to the boreal forests, eking out food by hunting, trapping, and fishing. They were a people stuck between two cultures; they were excluded from treaties signed by full-blooded natives but were not a part of mainstream Canadian society.

EXPLORATION AND THE FUR TRADE

In 1670, the British government granted the Hudson's Bay Company the right to govern Rupert's Land, a vast area of western Canada that included all of present-day Manitoba, Saskatchewan, Alberta, and the Northwest Territories. The land was rich in fur-bearing mammals, which both the British and the French sought to exploit for profit. The Hudson's Bay Company first built forts around Hudson Bay and encouraged Indians to bring furs to the posts. Soon, however, French fur traders based in Montreal began traveling west to secure furs, forcing their British rivals to do the same.

In June 1754, Anthony Henday embarked on a journey up the North Saskatchewan River from York Factory on Hudson Bay, becoming the first white man to enter what is now Alberta on September 11, 1754. He returned to the east the following spring, bringing canoes loaded with furs and providing reports of snowcapped peaks.

In 1787, traders from Montreal formed the North West Company, whose men were known as Norwesters. One year later, Norwester Peter Pond built Fort Chipewyan on Lake Athabasca, which was the first fur-trading post in what is now Alberta. The Hudson's Bay Company built *its* first post in present-day Alberta—Buckingham House—right beside the North West Company's Fort George on the North Saskatchewan River. This practice of moving in right next to the competition—engaged in by both companies—

HISTORICAL BOUNDARIES OF ALBERTA

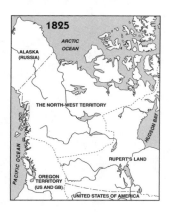

Turner Valley became a hive of activity when oil was discovered there in 1914

WHYTE MUSEUM OF THE CANADIAN ROCKIES

produced a rivalry between the two that continued unabated until they merged in 1821.

Trading posts were scattered over the entire west. Most were made of solid log construction and were located beside rivers, the main routes for transportation. Furs were the only reason white men came west for more than a century. Traders lived by their own rules and were opposed to settlement, which would have changed their lifestyle. But change was in the wind. In 1857, the British government sent Captain John Palliser west to Rupert's Land to determine whether the land was fit for agriculture. The Palliser Report, which he prepared upon his return to England, was unfavorable regarding an area in what is now southern Alberta (known as "Palliser Triangle"), but it encouraged settlement to the north.

The Dominion of Canada

By 1867, some of the eastern provinces were tiring of British rule, and a movement was abuzz to push for Canadian independence. The British government, wary of losing Canada as it had lost the United States, passed legislation establishing the Dominion of Canada. It created a central government with certain powers and delegated other powers to the provinces.

At that time, the North-West Territories, as

Rupert's Land had become known, was a foreign land to those in eastern Canada: life was primitive with no laws, and no post had more than a couple dozen residents. But in an effort to solidify the Dominion, the government bought the North-West Territories back from the Hudson's Bay Company in 1869, even as beaver stock was being depleted and the whiskey trade was having disastrous effects on the native population.

THE END OF AN ERA

Long before Europeans entered what is now Alberta, native populations felt their influence initially through the horse, which was a relatively modern addition to the plains, having been first introduced to North America by the Spanish in the mid-1600s and appearing north of the 49th parallel in the mid-1700s. Horses were followed by Europeans themselves, with their guns, alcohol, and diseases. From this time on, native lifestyle and the boundaries of the various tribes changed dramatically. For centuries, the buffalo population of the prairies had remained relatively constant. The Indians slaughtered many buffalo, but not enough to make a significant impact on total numbers. As beaver populations dwindled, however, traders turned to buffalo hides. Within 10 years, the once-prolific herds were practically eradicated. Without their traditional food source, the Indians of the plains were weakened and left susceptible to European-borne diseases such as smallpox and scarlet fever. The whiskey trade also took its toll on native populations. Living conditions among the Indians were pitiful, and frequent uprisings took place.

On June 6, 1874, a band of North West Mounted Police left Toronto under the command of Colonel James F. Macleod. Their task was to curb the whiskey trade and restore peace on the western prairies. They built a post on the Oldman River, and within one year, three other posts had been established in what is now southern Alberta.

Facing starvation, the chiefs had no choice but to sign treaties, relegating the tribes to reserves, which consisted of land set aside by the government for specific native bands, and changing their nomadic lifestyles forever. The chief of all chiefs, Crowfoot, of the powerful Blackfoot Confederacy, signed the first major treaty on September 22, 1877, followed by the chiefs of the Peigans, Stoneys, Sarcees, and Bloods. Their self-sufficiency taken away, the tribes were forced to accept what they were given. They were no longer free, they no longer hunted or fought, their medicine men could do nothing to stop the spread of the white man's diseases, and they slowly lost their pride.

EUROPEAN SETTLEMENT

An essential ingredient to the success of settling the West was the construction of a rail line across the continent, replacing canoe and cart routes. This idea was met with scorn by those in the east, who saw it as unnecessary and uneconomical. In 1879, a line reached Winnipeg. After much debate was waged about creating a route through the Canadian Rockies, the Canadian Pacific Railway line reached Fort Calgary and what is now Banff in 1883. Workers pushed on across the mountains, and on November 7, 1885, the final spike was laid, linking the fledgling province of British Columbia to the rest of the country. A northern route, through Edmonton and Jasper, was completed by the Grand Trunk Railway in 1914.

With two expensive rail lines in place, the government set about putting them to use by settling the land and encouraging tourists to visit the thriving resort towns of Banff and Jasper. The prairies were surveyed and homesteads were offered at $10 per quarter section (160 acres). People from diverse ethnic backgrounds flooded the western prairies, tending to settle in communities of their own people. Life was hard for the early settlers; those in the south found the land dry, whereas those in the north had to clear land.

The first to take advantage of the extensive grasslands that had once supported millions of bison was Senator Matthew Cochrane, who in 1881 secured a grazing lease on 189,000 acres west of Calgary. This homestead was the first of many ranches to be claimed in the foothills, and many herds of cattle were driven to their new homes by American cowboys.

Entering the Confederation

British Columbia had gained provincial status in 1871, four years after the Dominion of Canada was established, but the North-West Territories remained under federal control. This region had been divided into districts, of which Alberta—named after Princess Louise Caroline Alberta, the fourth daughter of Queen Victoria—was one. On September 1, 1905, Alberta and Saskatchewan were admitted as provinces of the Canadian Confederation, and Edmonton was named Alberta's capital.

For the years preceding World War I, the new province of Alberta led the way in Canadian agricultural export, but strict controls on wheat prices left many farmers in debt. After the war, the Canadian Wheat Board, later to become the Alberta Wheat Pool, was established to give farmers a fairer price and an incentive to stay on the land. The early 1930s were a time of terrible drought and worldwide depression, both of which hit especially hard in a province that depended almost entirely on agriculture. For the second time in 30 years, however, war bolstered the economy and agricultural production increased. For 50 years, agriculture was Alberta's primary industry and the main attraction for settlers, but this situation was to change dramatically.

OIL

Arguably the most important date in Canada's industrial history was February 13, 1947. Until that date, small discoveries of oil and gas beneath Alberta had been made, and the modest reserves under Turner Valley constituted the British Empire's largest oil field. But when Leduc Oil Well No. 1 belched black rings of smoke on that cold February morning, Alberta had hit the jackpot. A new economy for Alberta and all of Canada had begun.

American capitalists poured billions of dollars into Alberta as every valley, hill, and flat was surveyed. Seismic cut lines (lines cut through the forests by seismologists charting new oil fields) across northern Alberta are testimony to this frantic period. Early in 1948, a major field at Redwater was tapped, and farmers' fields throughout the province were soon littered with beam pumps bobbing up and down. Calgary became the financial and administrative headquarters of the industry, while Edmonton—at the center of many of the fields—became the technological, service, and supply center.

By 1954, the eight major fields had been proven to contain eight billion barrels of recoverable crude oil; the Leduc-Woodbend field alone had 1,278 wells, and Pembina had 1,700. But nothing came close to the staggering resources of the Athabasca Oil Sands in northern Alberta, where one trillion barrels of oil lay—more than all the proven reserves of conventional oil on earth. By 1967, Alberta was producing 67 percent of Canada's crude oil and 87 percent of its natural gas.

Each of the major fields needed services, and towns such as Drayton Valley, Swan Hills, High Level, and Rainbow Lake sprang up in otherwise unsettled areas. In less than a decade, the province's population doubled to more than one million.

The 1970s
In the early 1970s, despite abundant resources and frenzied activity in Alberta, the eastern Canadian provinces were importing oil from overseas, taking advantage of low prices obtained, most notably, from the oil-exporting countries of the Middle East. But then the Arab oil ministers got smart, banding together to form the Organization

of Petroleum Exporting Countries (OPEC). OPEC began demanding $6 a barrel—up from less than $2—and the price of oil quadrupled within three months. Suddenly, cheap, foreign oil was a thing of the past, and Alberta—after decades of feeling snubbed by the eastern provinces—held a trump card. With enormous reserves of oil and constitutional control over all of it, Alberta braced itself for the coming boom. The value of the province's petroleum resources tripled almost overnight; within another four years, it quadrupled again.

A change in government roughly coinciding with the oil boom also contributed to Alberta's success. For 36 years, the agricultural-based Social Credit party had controlled Alberta. But in 1971, the Conservative Party—led by Peter Lougheed—came to power. Lougheed was an uncompromising leader who cared little about what the powers in the eastern provinces thought of his policies. Described by many as an Albertan sheik, he tripled oil-royalty rates for the province, requiring Alberta's producers to pay the province 65 cents out of every dollar earned from the oil. The federal government refused to allow the oil companies to deduct those royalties on their federal income tax returns, and many major oil companies pulled out of Alberta. But not for long. Alberta had the goods, and with incentives from the government, the companies returned. This incident was only a slight hiccup in Lougheed's vision of a new and powerful west.

Revenues were flowing into the provincial coffers at $6,000 per minute; more millionaires were created than at any other time in Canadian history; and Calgary and Edmonton became two of North America's greatest boomtowns and the center of world oil technology. Calgary became the fastest-growing city in the country—a city of dreams, where no expense was spared and to where the power and wealth of eastern provinces moved.

AFTER THE BOOM

The latter part of the 20th century was a quiet time. World oil prices steadied in the late 1970s, and international oil companies spent money elsewhere. But the boom's impact on the province continued to be positive. The Heritage Savings

Trust Fund—a legacy of Lougheed's days—amassed fortunes in oil royalties to be spent on facilities for the people of Alberta. Kananaskis Country was the most grandiose creation of the fund, while other facilities, including interpretive centers, urban park systems, and museums, continue to preserve the province's natural and human history.

Self-made millionaires, who often came from humble beginnings, poured their enormous wealth back into the province that had made them rich. The philanthropies of oilman Eric Harvie, including the Glenbow Foundation, Banff Centre for the Arts, and Calgary Zoo, totaled at least $100 million. In 1978, Edmonton hosted the Commonwealth Games, and in 1988, Calgary hosted the Winter Olympic Games, both events providing boosts to Alberta's economy.

The New Millennium
Calgary and Edmonton have embraced the information technology boom, diversifying a resource-based economy and helping keep Alberta's economic growth well above the national average. Nonrenewable resources are still the back-bone of the economy, however, which was never more evident than through 2000, when OPEC decreased oil production and oil prices rose to more than $35 a barrel. Once again, Alberta experienced a surge in energy investments. Although royalties from the petroleum industry continue to pour into government coffers, impressive financial management is helping Alberta thrive economically. In turn, this growth is encouraging capital investment in resources, company relocation, and migration from eastern provinces (Alberta's annual population growth is two percent, more than double Canada's average). Albertans enjoy the benefits of the strong economy most directly because they pay a low rate of personal income tax and no provincial sales tax. Impressive financial management has allowed the government to consider unhooking Alberta from the federal tax system, which would further ease the tax burden on Albertans.

With a growing, relatively young, and well-educated population, a strong economy, and staggering resources still available in the ground, the future remains bright for this Western frontier made good.

ECONOMY AND GOVERNMENT

ECONOMY

Alberta's economy has traditionally been closely tied to the land—based first on the fur trade, then agriculture, and for the final 30 years of the 1900s on abundant reserves of oil and gas. The province's location away from main trade routes had always hindered economic diversity and fostered a boom-or-bust dependence on the land's resources. And although Alberta's industrial and commercial sectors would collapse without these resources, the province is at the forefront of the information technology tidal wave, making its economy less susceptible to ever-changing commodity prices. The Department of Resource Development promotes effective management of the province's mineral resources and collects royalties for the government. The Energy and Utilities Board administers the Conservation Act and regulates the production rate of wells.

Oil
Alberta lies above a vast basin of porous rock containing abundant deposits of oil, natural gas, and coal. The oil in Alberta occurs in three forms: crude oil, heavy oil, and oil sands. Conventional crude oil is recovered through normal drilling methods. More than 5,000 pools have been discovered, but half the oil production comes from just 25 of them. Most of this oil is refined for use as gasoline in cars, diesel for trucks, and heating fuel for homes. Heavy oil is more difficult to extract, and its uses are limited. In the future, however, as technology improves, recovering Alberta's estimated 300 million barrels of this oil will be viable. Oil sands consist of a tarlike mixture of sand and bitumen that is mined, then refined into synthetic crude for use in fuel products. The Athabasca Oil Sands, near Fort McMurray, are the world's largest such deposit. As conventional crude diminishes, Alberta's heavy oil and oil sands will play an increasingly important role in meeting

world energy demands. Alberta is already the world's largest producer of synthetic crude, and it is estimated that 60 percent of the province's oil production will be of this form by 2003.

Natural Gas

Natural gas was first discovered near Medicine Hat in 1883, but it wasn't seen as a viable source of energy until 1900. The price of gas tends to mirror that of oil, and when prices peaked in mid-2000, increased drilling took place. The province has always had more gas than it can use (currently, proven reserves stand at two trillion cubic feet), and 70 percent of it is exported, via pipelines to other provinces and the United States. Gas is mostly used for home heating but is also a source material for the petrochemical industry.

Coal

Large deposits of coal were mined early on in Crowsnest Pass, Drumheller, and the foothills, and by the 1920s, coal mining had developed into a major industry. Coal was first used to heat homes and provide fuel for steam locomotives, but oil took over those duties in the early 1950s. The industry was revived in 1962 when a coal-fired electric power plant opened at Wabamun, west of Edmonton. This market has since broadened, and today Alberta supplies 44 percent of Canada's coal, 70 percent of which is used for power production.

Minerals

Industrial, nonmetallic minerals such as limestone, shale, and salt are mined for consumption within Alberta. Sulphur, which is extracted as a coproduct of natural gas, is exported to the large agricultural markets of the United States, Europe, and Africa, for use in fertilizer. Metallic minerals such as copper, silver, and gold have all been mined at some stage, but compared to other areas of Canada, the province has been poorly explored.

Agriculture

Although oil and gas form the backbone of Alberta's economy, farms and ranches still dominate the landscape. More than 20 million hectares are used for agriculture, more than half of them cultivated—a back-breaking job that was started when the first homesteaders moved west. Approximately 75 percent of this land is irrigated, thanks to massive projects such as the Oldman River Dam, whereas the remainder is dryland farmed. Alberta produces about 20 percent of Canada's total agricultural output, directly employing 50,000 people in the process. The largest portion of the province's $4-billion annual farm income comes from cattle ($1.2 billion). Alberta has four million head of beef cattle—just under half of Canada's total—as well as 140,000 dairy cows. The largest crop is wheat, used mainly for bread and pasta. Barley, used for feeding livestock and making beer, accounts for more than $500 million in annual revenues. The other major crops are canola (recognizable by the bright yellow fields), oats, rye, and flax. The largest areas of vegetable production are east of Lethbridge, where the corn and sugar beet industries thrive.

Forestry

Although 60 percent of Alberta is forested, the forestry industry constitutes only one-tenth of one percent of the province's gross domestic product; current annual harvest is five million cubic meters. The main reason for such a small yield is the slow regrowth rate of the northern forests. The province has 300 sawmills, primarily producing dressed lumber. The forests are managed by the Department of Alberta Environment.

Tourism

Tourism is the second-most important industry to the economy, lagging only slightly behind the petroleum industry in revenues but employing twice as many people. The Tourism Development Branch of the government's Department of Economic Development markets the province worldwide as a tourist destination. The government has helped in other ways, too, investing millions of dollars of royalties from the oil-and-gas industry into improving facilities, building interpretive centers, and developing recreational playgrounds such as Kananaskis Country.

GOVERNMENT

Canada is part of the British Commonwealth, but the monarchy and the elected government of Great Britain have no control over Canada's political affairs. The British monarchy is represented in Canada by a governor general. The country's constitution is based on five important acts of British Parliament, the most recent being the Canada Act of 1982. That act gave Canada the power to amend its constitution, provided for recognition of the nation's multicultural heritage, and most important for Alberta, strengthened provincial ownership of natural resources.

The Canadian government operates through three main agencies: the Parliament (made up of the Senate and the House of Commons), which makes the laws; the Executive (Cabinet), which applies the laws; and the Judiciary, which interprets the laws. Elections are held every five years, and the leader of whichever political party is voted into power by Canadian citizens becomes the head of government, known as the prime minister. The prime minister then chooses a cabinet of ministers from members of his or her party. Each of the ministers is responsible for the administration of a department.

In Alberta, like the other nine provinces, the monarchy is represented by a lieutenant governor. Like the governor general, the position is mainly ceremonial. The members of the Alberta Legislature are elected on a party system for a maximum of five years. (The government's website is www.gov.ab.ca.) The Progressive Conservative Party, led by Ralph Klein, is currently in power. The other two major parties are the New Democratic Party and the Liberal Party. The leader of the party in power is known as a premier, who oversees the running of 18 departments. With so much control over the province's natural resources and, in turn, Alberta's future, many premiers have enjoyed a particularly high profile. One such premier, Peter Lougheed, initiated the Heritage Savings Trust Fund, which collects billions of dollars in oil royalties for the people of Alberta. Initiated in 1976, the fund changed direction in the mid-1990s, steering toward long-term financial returns as opposed to specific projects. Now, the General Reserve Fund holds monies for programs and services, but most of the fund's $12 billion is invested.

THE PEOPLE

For thousands of years before the arrival of Europeans to Alberta, several distinct indigenous peoples had lived off the land's abundant natural resources. With the coming of the white man, however, the native groups were overrun and reduced in numbers, today constituting only approximately 2.5 percent of Alberta's population. The Europeans came in droves—first drawn by game and arable land, and later by the oil-and-gas boom. People of many diverse cultures moved west, forming a melting pot of traditions. A census as early as 1921 noted 30 different languages in the province, in addition to the many distinct languages of the natives. Today, Alberta's population of three million is the fourth largest among the Canadian provinces and approximately 10 percent of the country's total. Alberta is Canada's fastest-growing province, with an annual population growth of two percent, which is double the national average.

Natives

As natives signed treaties, giving up traditional lands and settling on reserves (known as reser-vations in the United States), their lifestyles changed forever. They were no longer free, they no longer hunted or fought, their medicine men could do nothing to stop the spread of the white man's diseases, and they slowly lost their pride. The first Indian Act, drafted in 1876, attempted to prepare natives for "European" society, but it only ended up isolating them from the rest of society.

Natives who are registered as members of a band are known as "status" Indians; that is, they have the right to use designated reserve lands and have access to federal funding. Originally, the Indian Act sought to assimilate natives by removing their "status" when they were considered ready to assimilate, such as when they earned a university degree, or in the case of native women, when they married a nonnative man. The Indian Act has been rewritten many times, including as recently as 1985, when many antiquated sections were repealed. The most important recent change was that they didn't have to surrender their status to become a Canadian citizen and, therefore, vote and own property.

a Stoney family, photographed by Mary Schäffer in 1907

WHYTE MUSEUM OF THE CANADIAN ROCKIES

As a direct result of these changes, many natives who had lost their status, or in fact never had it, have been reclaiming it over the last 15 years. Therefore, the population of status Indians has grown considerably in recent years. Today, 65,000 "status" Indians live in Alberta, approximately 60 percent of them on reserves. Alberta has 93 reserves covering 6,598 square kilometers. The largest is a Blood reserve near Fort Macleod covering 136,760 hectares. Other major reserves include the Stoney reserve at Morley, the Sarcee (known officially as the Tsuu T'ina) reserve near Calgary, the Blackfoot reserve at Gleichen, and the Peigan reserve at Brocket. The reserves are administered by Indian and Northern Affairs Canada. The Congress of Aboriginal Peoples represents nonstatus Indians and status Indians living off reserves.

The First Nations are slowly but surely moving toward self-government, and in the process finding ways to have more involvement in decisions that affect their future. Some bands have already achieved self-government, along with a transfer of land ownership. Many reserves generate revenue from natural resources, and some bands have become wealthy owning factories, housing developments, and, in the case of the Sarcee near Bragg Creek, a golf course. A monthly magazine, *Sweetgrass,* focuses on native issues in the province. (For subscription information, write the Aboriginal Multi-media Society, 15001 112th Avenue, Edmonton, Alberta T5M 2V6, 780/455-2945.) The magazine is available online at www.ammsa.com/sweetgrass.

Alberta's Métis population established a form of self-government in 1990, with the signing of the Métis Settlement Accord. This accord gave them ownership of more than 1.2 million acres, which included eight existing settlements, while still receiving federal government funding. The Métis Settlements General Council represents these people on a provincial level, while the Canadian Métis Council represents all "mixed-blood, nonstatus Aboriginals" nationally.

Nonnatives

In the last 100 years, Alberta has seen a great influx of people from around the world. The Dominion census of 1881 recorded only 18,072 nonnatives in the province; Calgary had a population of only 75. The French, predominantly fur traders and missionaries, were the first permanent settlers and today constitute the fourth-largest ethnic group in the province. The first Asians to settle in the province were Chinese who came seeking gold in the 1860s and later settled, took up trades, and opened businesses.

One of the largest migrant influxes occurred between 1901 and 1906, when the Canadian government was selling tracts of land to homesteaders for $10. During this time, the population increased from 73,000 to 185,400; in another five years it doubled again. A large percentage of settlers during this period were British, and this group now constitutes Alberta's largest ethnic group. Germans also migrated to Alberta for various reasons and now constitute the province's second-largest ethnic group. Many people were lured by cheap land. Others, such as Hutterites, were persecuted in their homeland for refusing to fulfill military service. Hutterites have become the most successful of all ethnic groups at working the land. They live a self-sufficient lifestyle in tight-knit communities throughout southern and central Alberta. Ukrainians make up the third-largest ethnic group. They were also attracted by the province's agricultural potential, and today more than 130,000 residents of Ukrainian descent live mostly in Edmonton and to the east.

The oil-and-gas boom brought a population explosion similar to that of 1901–1906, but this time, with one exception, the immigrants came from eastern provinces rather than from other countries. The exception was a wave of Americans, whose oil-business acumen and technological know-how were vital to the burgeoning industry.

In the lead-up to the January 1, 1997 transfer of Hong Kong to the People's Republic of China, Canada saw a significant influx of immigrants from Hong Kong. Although Vancouver and Toronto have the largest Chinese communities in the country, those of Edmonton and Calgary both grew during this period. Calgary has a thriving pan-Asian population of about 50,000–60,000, and the pride of the city's Chinese community is well evidenced by such facilities as the Chinese Cultural Centre.

KAREN MCKINLEY

ON THE ROAD
RECREATION

The great outdoors is one of Alberta's prime attractions, and a diverse array of activities is available to those who seek them out. The mountains are the center of most activity. Raft and canoe tours operate on many mountain rivers, and the vast wilderness provides virtually limitless opportunities for camping, photography, and wildlife viewing. The national parks are a mecca for hikers and climbers in summer, downhill and cross-country skiers in winter. Fishing is good in almost all lakes and rivers in the province, and golfers can enjoy more than 230 courses. A comprehensive listing of all outfitters and tour operators is available from Travel Alberta (P.O. Box 2500, Edmonton, Alberta T5J 2Z1, 780/427-4321 or 800/661-8888, www.travelalberta.com).

HIKING

Hiking is, not surprisingly, the most popular outdoor activity in Alberta because it's free, anyone can participate, and the mountains offer some of the world's most spectacular scenery. **Banff National Park** holds the greatest variety of trails in the province. Here you can find anything from short interpretive trails with little elevation gain to strenuous slogs up high alpine passes. Trailheads for most of the best hikes are accessible by public transportation or on foot from the town of Banff. Those trails farther north begin at higher elevations, from which access to the high country is less painful. The trails in **Jasper National Park** are oriented more toward the experienced backpacker, offering plentiful routes for long backcountry trips. Other areas popular for hiking are **Kananaskis Country,** where crowds are minimal; **Waterton Lakes National Park,** where many trails lead to beautiful subalpine lakes; and the province's four wilderness areas, which are located in remote mountain regions accessible only on foot.

Heli-hiking is an out-of-the-ordinary way to experience the high alpine without making the elevation gain on foot. The day starts with a helicopter ride into the alpine, where short, guided hikes are offered and a picnic lunch is served. For details, contact **Alpine Helicopters,** 403/678-4802. Another option is hiking into backcountry lodges. The **Alpine Club of Canada** (403/678-3200, www.alpineclubofcanada.com) maintains a series of huts, each generally a full-day hike from the nearest road. Banff and Jasper National Parks have several privately owned backcountry lodges—great bases for day hiking—where on-site hosts provide hot meals; rates start at $120 per person per day including meals. Hikers must register at park information centers for all overnight hikes in national parks.

Topographic maps aren't required for the hikes detailed in this book, but they provide an interesting way to identify natural features. For extended hiking in the backcountry, they are vital. Several series of maps, in different scales, cover the entire province. You can purchase them from park information centers, some bookstores, and specialty map shops in Calgary and Edmonton.

CYCLING AND MOUNTAIN BIKING

Alberta is perfect for both road biking and mountain biking. On-road cyclists appreciate the wide shoulders on all main highways, whereas those on mountain bikes enjoy the many designated trails in the mountain national parks. One of the most challenging and scenic on-road routes is the **Icefields Parkway** between Lake Louise and Jasper, which has several well-placed hostels along its length.

Most large bookstores stock copies of cycling publications, such as the *Canadian Rockies Bicycling Guide,* which covers 60 routes through the mountains. Also, the **Alberta Bicycle Association** represents all touring clubs in the province and can provide further information. Write to 11759 Groat Road, Edmonton, Alberta T5M 3K6, 780/427-6352, www.albertabicycle.ab.ca.

Cycle Tours
Backroads (801 Cedar Street, Berkeley, CA 94710, USA, 800/462-2848, www.backroads.com) offers a wide variety of trips through the mountains. These excursions are designed to suit all levels of fitness and all budgets. An average of six hours is spent cycling each day, but the less ambitious always have the option of riding in the support van. There's also the option of camping each night (US$1,000 for six days) or staying in grand mountain lodges (US$1,800 for six days).

HORSEBACK RIDING

Horses are a traditional means of transportation in the Canadian West; many of the roads began as horse trails. Through the foothills, ranches still dominate the landscape, and at places like **Griffin Valley Ranch,** near Cochrane, 403/932-7433, unguided riding is permitted. Within the national parks, horse travel is restricted to certain areas, but trail riding is a popular way to enjoy the scenery.

If you really want to get a feeling for Western life, consider taking an overnight horseback pack-trip. In the mountains, many of these guides have been operating since before the parks were established. Outside the parks, riding is available at many ranches and outfitting operations in the foothills and at Grande Cache. On an overnight trip, expect to ride for up to six hours per day, with nights spent at a remote mountain lodge or a tent camp, usually in a scenic location where you can hike, fish, or ride further. Rates range $130–160 per person per day, which includes the riding, accommodations, and food. These trips are offered near Canmore by **Brewster Mountain Pack Trains** (403/762-5454 or 800/691-5085, www.brewsteradventures.com); in Banff National Park by **Warner Guiding and Outfitting** (403/762-4551 or 800/661-8352, www.horseback.com); and in Jasper National Park by **Skyline Trail Rides** (780/852-4215 or 888/852-7787); or **Tonquin Valley Adventures** (780/852-1188, www.tonquinadventures.com). The remote location of Willmore Wilderness Park makes it a popular destination for those on horseback. Contact the following outfitters for trips into the park: **Sherwood Guides and Outfitters,** 780/922-2266; **U Bar Enterprises,** 780/827-3641; and **Wild Rose Outfitting,** 780/693-2296.

Guest ranches, where accommodations and meals are included in nightly packages, include

PARKS AND PROTECTED AREAS

Alberta has five national parks and 66 provincial parks, as well as many recreation and protected areas, including wilderness areas, a wilderness park, wildland parks, a forest reserve covering much of the foothills, ecological reserves, natural areas, and provincial recreation areas. Combined, they encompass all of the province's most spectacular natural features, are home to many of Alberta's mammals, provide safe nesting areas for millions of birds, and protect areas that would otherwise be given over to agriculture or other resource-based industry.

National Parks
Created in 1885, **Banff National Park** was the founding member of Canada's grand national park system. As well as being home to the jewel of the Canadian national parks system, Alberta holds four other, equally unique parks. **Waterton Lakes,** to the south of Banff, and **Jasper,** to the north, are equally beautiful mountain parks. The others are **Elk Island National Park,** where mammal densities are similar to the Serengeti Plain, and **Wood Buffalo National Park,** the second-largest national park in the world, which is accessible by road only through the Northwest Territories.

Parks Canada manages Canada's national park system, which consists of 38 parks spread across every province and territory, combining to represent all of the country's natural landscapes. Provincial headquarters of Parks Canada is in the Harry Hays Building at 220 4th Avenue SE, Calgary, 403/992-2950, www.parkscanada.gc.ca.

Provincial Parks
Provincial parks, widespread throughout Alberta, protect areas of natural, historical, and cultural importance while providing ample recreational opportunities. All of the parks offer day-use facilities, and many more have campgrounds and summer interpretive programs. Those not to miss are **Writing-On-Stone Provincial Park,** so named for the abundant native rock art; **Dinosaur Provincial Park,** a UNESCO World Heritage Site with one of the world's highest concentrations of dinosaur bones; and **Cypress Hills Provincial Park,** a forested oasis that rises from the prairies. Provincial parks are man-

aged by Alberta Environment, which operates an excellent Information Centre at street level of the Great West Life Building at 9920 108th Street, Edmonton, 780/422-2079. Write Parks and Protected Areas Division, 2nd Floor, Oxbridge Place, 9820 106th Street, Edmonton, AB T5K 2J6, www.gov.ab.ca/env/parks.

Other Parks and Protected Areas
Alberta's Provincial Parks Act of 1930 has evolved into the Recreation and Protected Areas Network, which incorporates all of the following designations:

Wilderness areas and **wildland parks** are just that—totally wild and total wilderness, with no road access and remote locations, perfect for wilderness trips for those with backcountry experience.

Also offering a high level of protection are **ecological reserves.** These are generally remote tracts of land, and although open to the public, they have been established under the Ecological Reserves Program primarily for scientific research.

Pockets of land that represent the diversity of Alberta's natural habitats are protected by **natural areas.** Certain forms of recreation are permitted, but natural areas are generally left in their natural state, with no facilities.

Finally, dotted throughout the province are provincial recreation areas, typically roadside stops in scenic locations or staging areas beside rivers, but always very accessible. Picnic facilities are provided, and some offer basic camping facilities. All of these areas are managed by Alberta Environment; write Parks and Protected Areas Division, 2nd Floor, Oxbridge Place, 9820 106th Street, Edmonton, AB T5K 2J6.

Forest Reserves
Alberta Environment manages forested lands and associated waterways. Most of these lands are scattered throughout the foothills and northern Alberta. Basic recreational facilities such as day-use areas and rustic campgrounds are provided free of charge. The Forestry Trunk Road, extending 1,000 kilometers between the Crowsnest Pass and Grande Prairie, traverses much of the province's forest service land.

Brewster's Kananaskis Guest Ranch, east of Canmore (403/673-3737 or 800/691-5085, www.brewsteradventures.com); **Boundary Ranch,** in Kananaskis Country (403/591-7171 or 877/591-7177); and **Black Cat Guest Ranch,** on the eastern outskirts of Jasper National Park (780/865-3084 or 800/859-6840). Expect to pay $120–150 per person per day for accommodations, meals, and trail riding.

FISHING

Fishing is productive in almost all of Alberta's lakes, rivers, and streams, and the fly-fishing on the Bow and Crowsnest rivers is world-renowned. Although fishing is good throughout the province, northern Alberta is the destination of most dedicated anglers.

Rainbow trout are to western Canada what bass are to the eastern United States—a great fighting fish. They are found in lakes and rivers throughout Alberta and are the most common of the stocked fish because they are easy to raise and adapt to varying conditions. You can catch them on artificial flies, small spinners, or spoons. The largest species of trout is the lake trout, with Lake Athabasca yielding a 46-kilo-gram specimen. The largest "lakies" come from northern lakes. These fish live in the deep waters of the large lakes, so a motorboat is needed. In Banff National Park, **Lake Minnewanka** is an easily accessible lake trout fishing center, with boats and tackle for rent and guides offering their services. Cutthroat trout inhabit the cold and clear waters of the highest mountain lakes, which generally involves hiking in to reach them. Fishing for cutthroat requires using the lightest of tackle because the water is generally very clear; fly-casting is most productive on the still water of lakes, whereas spinning is the preferred river-fishing method. Brook trout aren't native to Alberta, but they are found in rivers and lake throughout the foothills and mountains. They are difficult to catch but grow to a decent size (two kilograms is not uncommon). Brown trout, introduced from Europe, are found in some streams in the foothills of Kananaskis Country as well as the Bow River. They are most often caught on dry flies, but they are difficult to hook onto. Golden trout, introduced from California,

have been stocked in lakes west of Pincher Creek. Walleye (also called pickerel) grow to 4.5 kilograms and are common in sandy-bottomed areas of lakes throughout the prairies. They are a popular catch with anglers, mostly because they taste so good. They feed only at night or in muddy waters, so catching them is more of a challenge than trout. They are most often caught using minnows or by jigging. The monster fish of Alberta is the northern pike (also known as jackfish), whose length can exceed one meter (the Canadian record is 20 kilograms). The largest specimens inhabit northern lakes and rivers, and fish from this area tend to be better tasting because they eat a different diet. Jigging with a large lure around the weedy extremes of large lakes gives the angler the best chance of hooking one of these monsters. Perch, at the other end of the size scale to pike but inhabiting the same shallow waters, are a fun, easy-to-catch fish—if you see kids fishing off a pier, chances are they're after perch. Arctic grayling, easily identified by a large dorsal fin, are common in cool clear lakes and streams throughout the far north of Alberta. These delicious-tasting fish are most often taken on dry flies, but their soft mouths make keeping them hooked somewhat of a challenge.

NATIONAL PARK PASSES

Passes are required for entry into all five of Alberta's national parks. A National Parks Day Pass is adult $5, senior $4, child $2 to a maximum of $10 per vehicle. The pass is interchangeable among parks and is valid until 4 P.M. the day following its purchase. An annual Great Western Pass, which is good for entry into five parks as well as those in British Columbia, Saskatchewan, and Manitoba, is adult $35, senior $27 to a maximum of $70 per vehicle ($53 for two or more seniors). This pass comes with a Great Western Passbook, which includes a wide variety of discount coupons. Both types of pass can be purchased at park gates, at all park information centers, and at campground fee stations. Annual passes can also be bought in advance by calling 800/748-7275 or online at the Parks Canada website, www.parkscanada.pch.gc.ca.

Each spring, approximately 200 lakes throughout the province are stocked with a variety of trout. "Stock stations" at Caroline and in the Crowsnest Pass maintain adult breeding stocks, which provide eggs to be hatched at Calgary's Sam Livingston Hatchery. These hatchlings are released each spring at lakes throughout the province (the fish's reproductive cycle is artificially reversed—they spawn in spring and the hatchlings are raised over winter—so that the released fish are of a decent size for a spring release). Rainbow trout, a hardy fish that tolerate wide-ranging habitats, constitute the largest percentage of stocked fish, with more than three million released in 2000, for example. Bull trout, an endangered species, have been incorporated into the stocking program and were released in Chain Lakes in 2000 and in Upper Kananaskis Lake in early 2001. Many other trout species are stocked, including brook, brown, cutthroat, and lake, bringing the total number of fish stocked annually to approximately 6.5 million.

Fishing Licenses
In 1998, Alberta introduced an automated licensing system, with licenses sold in sporting stores, hardware stores, and gas stations. To use the system, a **Wildlife Identification Number** (WIN) is needed. These numbers are sold by all license vendors and cost $8 (valid for five years). Your card is swiped through a vending machine, your name and number come up, and you're ready to purchase a license. An annual license for Canadian residents aged 16 and older is $18 (no license is required for those younger than 16 or for Albertans older than 64); for nonresidents aged 16 and older, it is $36, or $20 for a five-day license. The *Alberta Guide to Sportfishing Regulations,* which outlines all of the open seasons and bag limits, is available from outlets selling licenses, as well as from the Fisheries and Wildlife Management Division, Alberta Environment, Main Floor, South Tower, Petroleum Plaza, 9915 108th Street, Edmonton, Alberta T5K 2G8, 780/944-0313, www.gov.ab.ca/env/fw/fishing.

Fishing in national parks requires a separate license, which is available from park offices and some sport shops; $6 for a seven-day license, $13 for an annual license.

OTHER WATER-BASED RECREATION

Canoeing and Rafting
Canoeing, like horseback riding, has long been a form of transportation in the province, going back to the days of the voyageurs. Paddling provides an unparalleled opportunity for viewing wildlife around lakes that would otherwise be inaccessible. Canoes can be rented at all of the famous mountain lakes, but you can expect to pay for the experience—up to $30 per

Whitewater rafting is an exciting way to enjoy mountain scenery.

WILD WATER ADVENTURES

hour in the case of Lake Louise. Most provincial parks with lake systems also offer canoe rentals; expect to pay $8–12 per hour. The **Canadian Recreational Canoe Association** represents qualified guides and can recommend canoe routes. Contact them at 613/269-2910, www.crca.ca. The book *Canoeing Alberta,* by Lone Pine Publishing (currently out of print but most Albertan libraries have a copy), is a well-regarded source of information on all canoe routes.

Qualified guides operate commercial whitewater rafting trips on mountain rivers such as the **Sunwapta** and **Maligne rivers** in Jasper National Park, offering the biggest thrills, and the **Kicking Horse River,** on the British Columbia side of the Rockies. Guides also operate on larger, quieter rivers such as **Milk River,** through Writing-On-Stone Provincial Park; **Red Deer River,** through the foothills or badlands; **Athabasca River,** in Jasper National Park; and **Bow River,** in Banff National Park. Extended trips are possible along the Peace and Athabasca rivers in the northern part of the province, but wilderness trips should be attempted only by those with experience.

Scuba Diving

Being landlocked, Alberta is not renowned for scuba diving. A few interesting opportunities do exist, however, and rentals are available in Lethbridge, Calgary, and Edmonton. The old townsite of **Minnewanka Landing,** in Banff National Park, has been flooded, and although a relatively deep dive, the site is interesting. **Patricia Lake,** in Jasper National Park, has a sunken World War II barge, and because of the high altitude and clear water, visibility is exceptional. Another sunken boat is found at the bottom of Emerald Bay in Waterton National Park. Nearby are some wagons that fell through ice many winters ago. For a list of dive shops and sites, contact **Alberta Underwater Council,** 11759 Groat Road, Edmonton, Alberta T5M 3K6, 780/427-9125.

GOLFING

With beautiful scenery, long sunny days, more than 230 courses, and a golfing season that ex-

tends from April to October, Alberta is a golfer's hole-in-one. Getting a game can be difficult on city courses, however, especially on weekends. Rates range from $5 per round on the smaller municipal courses to more than $100 on a resort course in the mountains. Outside of Edmonton and Calgary, most courses are public or semi-private, and getting a game, with advance reservations, isn't a problem.

The best courses are **Kananaskis Country Golf Course,** a 36-hole, Robert Trent Jones–designed course built in the 1980s at a cost of $1 million per hole; **Silvertip** and **Stewart Creek,** two challenging resort-style golf courses at Canmore that opened in the summers of 1998 and 2000, respectively; Banff's **Stanley Thompson 18,** part of a 27-hole championship course strung out along the Bow River and rated one of the world's most scenic; **Jasper Park Lodge Golf Course,** a challenging par-73 course surrounded by spectacular mountain scenery; and **Wolf Creek Golf Resort,** an oasis on the prairies between Calgary and Edmonton.

WINTERTIME

Skiing and Snowboarding

Six world-class alpine resorts are perched among the high peaks of Alberta's Rockies. The largest in Alberta, and second-largest in all of Canada, is **Lake Louise,** overlooking the lake of the same name in Banff National Park. The area boasts 1,500 hectares of skiing and snowboarding on four distinct faces, with wide-open bowls and runs for all abilities. Banff's other two resorts are **Sunshine Village,** sitting on the Continental Divide and accessible only by gondola, and **Banff Mt. Norquay,** a resort with heart-pounding runs overlooking the town of Banff. Just outside Banff in Kananaskis Country is **Nakiska,** a resort developed especially for the downhill events of the 1988 Winter Olympic Games. Nearby **Fortress Mountain** is in a spectacular location and has runs for all abilities. **Marmot Basin,** in Jasper National Park, has minimal crowds with a maximum variety of terrain.

Nearly 50 other ski hills are scattered throughout the province, most with less than a 150-meter vertical drop. One area unique for its

The skiing is legendary in the Canadian Rockies.

ALBERTA TOURISM

proximity to the city center is the **Edmonton Ski Club** in the North Saskatchewan River Valley, overlooking downtown Edmonton. **Canada Olympic Park,** within the Calgary city limits, was built for the 1988 Winter Olympic Games and maintains some of the world's finest ski-jumping facilities. Most major resorts begin opening in early December and close in May or, in the case of Sunshine Village, early June.

Other Winter Activities

Many hiking trails provide ideal routes for **cross-country skiing,** and many are groomed for that purpose. The largest concentration of groomed trails is in Kananaskis Country. Other areas are Banff, Jasper, and Waterton national parks; the urban parks of Calgary and Edmonton; and the many provincial parks scattered throughout the province. Anywhere you can cross-country ski, you can also **snowshoe,** a traditional form of winter transportation that is making a comeback. **Ice fishing** for whitefish and burbot is good in all major rivers and those lakes large enough not to freeze to the bottom. **Sleigh rides** are offered in Banff, Lake Louise, and Jasper.

Winter travel brings its own set of potential hazards such as hypothermia, avalanches, frostbite, and sunburn. Necessary precautions should be taken. All park information centers can provide information on hazards and advice on current weather conditions.

ENTERTAINMENT

Museums

The best way to gain insight into Alberta's natural and human history is to visit one of its many museums. Not all of them are the crowded, stuffy kind, and many of the best ones are located outside the cities. The **Royal Tyrrell Museum of Palaeontology,** located in the dinosaur-rich badlands of the Red Deer River Valley, is the largest paleontological museum in the world. Inside you'll find more than 50 full-size dinosaurs on display. If you visit only one museum in Alberta, make it this one. Other major museums include the **Provincial Museum of Alberta** in Edmonton; **Glenbow Museum** in Calgary; **Remington-Alberta Carriage Centre** at Cardston, which houses more than 200 carriages, buggies, and wagons; and the **Reynolds-Alberta Museum** on the outskirts of Wetaskiwin, which catalogs the history of machinery in western Canada.

Performing Arts

For a province that prides itself on a Western heritage, Alberta has a surprising number of cultural diversions. Edmonton alone has a dozen professional theater companies, equal to any North American city of comparable size. Both Edmonton and Calgary have ballet troupes, an orchestra, and an opera company.

Country Music

For most of this century, singers and songwriters have found inspiration in the ranching lifestyle and mountain scenery of Alberta. In the 1930s, **Wilf Carter,** a cowboy by trade, began singing on Calgary radio. Within three years he had become a star in the United States as "Montana Slim," the yodeling cowboy. Most recently, **Terri Clark,** from Medicine Hat, and **Paul Brandt,** of Calgary, have hit the big time south of the border. They followed the path carved by **k.d. lang,** of Consort, who has more recently tended toward a mainstream dance/pop style of music, but who in the late 1980s became a country superstar with Grammy-winning albums pushing the boundaries of country music toward pop. **George Fox** and **Ian Tyson,** who both have ranches west of Calgary, have also made their mark on Canadian country music.

Large outdoor concerts that run over several days are popular venues for country music in Alberta. The biggest of these is the **Big Valley Jamboree** at Camrose in early August.

Nightlife

Although most cities have dance clubs and rock 'n' roll discos, Alberta's heritage lives on through the night in the country music bars. Bars like the **Ranchman's** in Calgary; **Cook County Saloon** in Edmonton; and dozens of small-town bars across the province keep the Western image alive. Many Western-style venues attract a more mainstream crowd by offering a wider variety of music, such as **Wild Bill's** in Banff, or a party atmosphere complete with scantily clad shooter girls, such as **Cowboys** in Edmonton and Calgary.

Spectator Sports

Lacrosse may be the national sport of Canada, but for most Albertans either **rodeo** or **ice hockey** is number one. Rodeo has its roots in the working lifestyle of cowboys. What began as friendly banter among cowboys as to who could ride the wildest horse and rope the fastest steer formed the basis of Wild West Shows that have evolved into a streamlined professional sport where cowboys and cowgirls compete for millions of dollars. Almost every town in Alberta hosts a rodeo. The smaller events are sanctioned by regional associations, whereas the Canadian Professional Rodeo Association (CPRA) controls more than 60 larger events throughout Canada (most in Alberta), from Calgary's Rodeo Royal in March to the national finals held in Edmonton in early November. For information and a schedule, contact the CPRA at 403/250-7440, www.rodeocanada.com.

The **ice hockey** season may be only seven months long, but to fans of the Edmonton Oilers and Calgary Flames—Alberta's National Hockey League (NHL) teams—it's a year-round obsession. The best seats are taken by die-hard season-ticket holders, but for $15–60 you can

WHYTE MUSEUM OF THE CANADIAN ROCKIES

Calgarian Wilf Carter, better known as "Montana Slim," was a country-music superstar in the 1930s.

usually score tickets through Ticketmaster a few days in advance. Both cities also have professional Canadian Football League (CFL) teams and AAA Pacific Coast League baseball teams.

SHOPPING

Arts and Crafts
The arts and crafts of Canada's indigenous people are available throughout the province. Jewelry, beaded moccasins, baskets, and leatherwork such as headdresses are favorite souvenirs. The stylistic art of the native people is also popular, but prints of the most recognizable works run into thousands of dollars. Two of the best outlets are the **Indian Trading Post** in Banff and **Northern Images** in West Edmonton Mall. The **Alberta Craft Council** (780/488-6611, www.albertacraft.ab.ca) represents craft shops throughout Alberta and lists exhibitions on its website.

Western Wear
You don't have to be able to ride a horse to dress like a cowboy—just ask the thousands of city folk who dress the part for the Calgary Stampede. Major department stores are the best places to find the basic Western accessories, whereas specialty shops are the places to go for gear that the real cowboys wear. Most of the latter sell handmade jewelry, authentic Stetsons, belt buckles

big enough to fry an egg on, and hundreds of pairs of boots in every style imaginable.

FESTIVALS AND EVENTS

Spring
The year's first major event for cowboys is the **Rodeo Royal,** part of the Roughstock celebration held at Calgary's Saddledome in late March, followed the next weekend by the **Spring Outdoor Rodeo** in Medicine Hat and in April by the **Makin' 8 Silver Buckle Rodeo** in Red Deer. The annual spring migration of birds through the province is celebrated during the Tofield **Snow Goose Festival** through April. Calgary hosts an **International Children's Festival** in May, with a wide variety of events for the younger generation. Alberta's winter resorts usually have snow on the ground until late spring, and many hold fun events at season's end, such as the **Slush Cup** at Sunshine Village.

Summer
Summer is the biggest event season in Alberta. Edmonton hosts a major festival just about every weekend, and something is almost always going on in the rest of the province as well.

    The Gathering comes to Pincher Creek in June . . . hear cowpokes read poems by the light of the, uh, stars? Stars of another type come to perform at the **Calgary International**

What's a parade without a local showband?

Jazz Festival, in late June. The festival draws famous jazz musicians from around the world.

Canada Day, July 1, is a national holiday celebrated in many towns with various events, often including a rodeo (Ponoka hosts the largest of the weekend's rodeos). Vegreville celebrates its multicultural past on this weekend with the **Ukrainian Folk Festival.**

The best known of Alberta's events is the **Calgary Stampede,** the world's richest rodeo, with 10 days of action and a winner-take-all format. This Western extravaganza is a not-to-be-missed event that takes place in early July. Equestrian events of a very different kind take place throughout summer just down the road from Stampede Park at **Spruce Meadows,** one of the world's finest international riding centers. The first event on the calendar, in early June, is the **National,** a show-jumping competition attracting thousands of enthusiasts.

In early July, the **International Street Performers Festival** offers more than 1,000 free performances at outdoor venues throughout Edmonton, and late July brings **Edmonton's Klondike Days,** a celebration centered around the city's tenuous connection to the Yukon goldfields; **Heritage Days,** a celebration of Edmonton's history; and the big **Medicine Hat Exhibition and Stampede,** held annually since 1887. The third Saturday in July is **Parks Day,** which is celebrated by pancake breakfasts, guided hikes, and interpretive events in national and provincial parks throughout Alberta. **Jazz Festival Calgary** takes place in late June, and then in July the city hosts a **Folk Music Festival.** July ends on a high note with the **Red Deer International Air Show** on the last weekend, featuring performances by some of the world's best stunt pilots. Meanwhile, the air over Grande Prairie is also alive with color when one of many **hot air balloon championships** takes place.

Lethbridge's **Whoop-Up Days** celebrates that city's past in early August. Also in early August is Canmore's popular **Folk Music Festival.** The **Edmonton Folk Music Festival** picks and strums its way into town in early August, and **The Fringe,** held in Edmonton mid-August, is North America's largest alternative theater festival. Calgary's cultural festivals are low-profile affairs compared to those in the capital, but the city does offer the **Afrikadey!** in August.

Fall
Just when all of the summer festivals are winding down, the action at Spruce Meadows equestrian center, outside Calgary, is heating up. **Spruce Meadows Masters** is the world's richest show-jumping event and the finale to a packed season. In late fall, the alpine resorts begin opening, and Banff hosts **Winterstart,** a six-week period of cheap deals and events held throughout the town. The first weekend of November is the **Banff Mountain Film Festival,** a gathering of the world's greatest adventure-film makers.

Winter
Most Albertan towns and cities have **winter carnivals** featuring weird and wonderful events that only people affected by the long winter could dream up. The largest ones, each lasting two weeks in January, are in Calgary, Banff, Jasper, and Edmonton. The one in Canmore, in late January, is held in conjunction with the **International Dog Sled Race. First Night** is an alcohol-free celebration of the New Year that takes place in downtown Calgary, Edmonton, and Banff.

ACCOMMODATIONS AND FOOD

ACCOMMODATIONS

For a list of all hotels, motels, lodges, and bed-and-breakfasts in Alberta, pick up a copy of *Alberta Accommodation Guide,* produced by the Alberta Hotel Association. It lists their facilities and room rates but gives no rating. The guide is available from tourist information centers, or from Travel Alberta (P.O. Box 2500, Edmonton, Alberta T5J 2Z4, 780/427-4321 or 800/661-8888, www.alberta-accommodations.com).

Hotels and Motels
Hotels and motels of some sort exist in just about every Albertan town. They range from sub-standard road motels advertising "Color TV"

Banff Springs Hotel

to sublime resorts, such as the Banff Springs Hotel and Chateau Lake Louise, high in the Canadian Rockies. The only time you'll have a problem finding a room is in Calgary during Stampede Week and in the national parks in July and August. In both cases, plan ahead or be prepared to camp. Accommodation prices in Banff and Jasper national parks are slashed by as much as 70 percent outside summer. In cities, always ask for the best rate available and check local tourist literature for discount coupons. Rates are usually lower on weekends. All rates quoted in this handbook are for the cheapest category of rooms during the most expensive time period (summer). To all rates quoted, you must add the 7 percent Goods and Services Tax (GST) and 5 percent provincial room tax. The former is refundable to nonresidents of Canada (keep receipts).

In many towns, you'll find older-style hotels where bathrooms are shared, the phone is in the lobby, and check-in is at the bar. Rooms are generally sparsely furnished, and what furniture there is dates to the 1960s. Expect to pay from $25 single, $30 double for a shared bathroom, and a few bucks more for a private bathroom.

Park-at-your-door, single-story road motels are located in all towns and on the outskirts of all major cities. In most cases, rooms are fine, but check before paying, just to make sure. Most motels have a few rooms with kitchenettes, but these fill fast. In the smaller towns, expect to pay $30–50 single, $35–60 double.

Most major towns and all cities have larger hotels, each of which typically has a restaurant, café, lounge, and pool. At these establishments, expect to pay from $60 single, $70 double for a basic room. Downtown hotels in Calgary and Edmonton begin at $80. A good deal can be suites or executive suites, with kitchenettes and one or two bedrooms for little more money than a regular room.

Finding inexpensive lodging in the mountain national parks is difficult in summer. By late afternoon the only rooms left are in the more expensive categories, and by nightfall all of these rooms are booked, too. Hotel rooms in Banff begin around $100; those in Jasper and Waterton are a little less.

Bed-and-Breakfasts

The bed-and-breakfast phenomenon is well entrenched in Alberta. Hosts are generally well-informed local people, and rooms are cozy. The establishments are often money-making ventures, so don't expect the bargains of European bed-and-breakfasts. The best way to find out about individual lodging is from local tourist information centers or listings in the back of the *Alberta Accommodation Guide*. The **Alberta Bed and Breakfast Association,** www.bbalberta.com, inspects and approves accommodations throughout the province. This association doesn't take bookings; for these, click on the links provided on their website, or contact

Alberta & Pacific B&B Reservation Service (P.O. Box 15477 M.P.O., Vancouver, BC V6B 5B2, 604/944-1793); **Bed and Breakfast Agency of Alberta** (410 19th Avenue NE, Calgary, Alberta T2E 1P3, 403/543-3900 or 800/425-8160); and **Canada-West Accommodations** (P.O. Box 86607, North Vancouver, BC V7L 4L2, 604/990-6730, www.b-b.com).

Backcountry Huts and Lodges

Scattered throughout the backcountry are 18 huts maintained by the Alpine Club of Canada. The huts are rustic—typically bunk beds, a woodstove, a wooden dining table, and an outhouse. Rates are $12–25 per person per night. Reservations should be made in advance by contacting the Alpine Club of Canada (403/678-3200, www.alpineclubof canada.ca).

Banff National Park has two privately operated backcountry lodges: **Shadow Lake Lodge,** northwest of Banff, and **Skoki Lodge,** east of Lake Louise. Jasper National Park is home to **Tonquin Amethyst Lake Lodge.** All three lodges require some degree of effort to reach—either by hiking or on horseback in summer, or by cross-country skiing in winter. The lodges are more than 10 kilometers from the nearest road. Rates begin at $120 per person including three meals. None have television, but all have running water and a congenial atmosphere.

Hostels

Hostelling International–Alberta operates 16 hostels in the province. They are located in Calgary, Edmonton, the town of Banff, at Lake Louise, all along the Icefields Parkway (which runs through Banff and Jasper National Parks), in the town of Jasper, Waterton Lakes National Park, Kananaskis Country, and the town of Nordegg. All hostels are accessible by road, and all but the Nordegg hostel are accessible by public transportation. During busy periods, males and females have separate dormitories. A sheet or sleeping bag is required, although these can usually be rented. All hostels are equipped with a kitchen and lounge room, and some have laundries. Those in Banff and Lake Louise are world-class, with hundreds of beds as well as libraries and cafés. The five rustic hostels along the Icefields Parkway are evenly spaced, perfect for a

bike trip along one of the world's great mountain highways. Rates for members are $10–22 per night, nonmembers $16–28. Whenever you can, make reservations in advance, especially in summer. The easiest way to do this is through Hostelling International's **International Booking Network** (IBN) through the Internet at www.ihyf.org or by contacting the individual hostel. Staying in hostels is an especially good bargain for skiers and snowboarders; packages including accommodations and a day pass at a local winter resort start at $48.

If you plan to travel extensively using hostels, join Hostelling International before you leave home. In the United States, write Hostelling International–American Youth Hostels, Inc. (133 1st St. NW, Suite 800, Washington, DC 20005, 202/783-6161, www.hiayh.org). In Canada, contact Hostelling International–Canada (400-205 Catherine Street, Ottawa, Ontario K2P 1C3, 613/237-7884, www.hostellingintl.ca). Hostelling International–Alberta has its own website, www.hostellingintl.ca/alberta. Membership in Canada is $24 per year.

Hostel Shops sell memberships and reasonably priced camping gear. They also provide general travel information and can book air, bus, and train trips for you. You'll find the shops in Edmonton at 10926 88th Avenue, 780/432-7798, and in Calgary at 1414 Kensington Road NW, 403/283-5551.

The **YMCA** and **YWCA** are other inexpensive lodging alternatives, often with prime locations. Calgary has a YWCA for women only; Banff has a YWCA open to both sexes with some family rooms (the Y Mountain Lodge); Edmonton has one of each. Rates begin at $16 per night, with reasonable weekly rates available.

Campgrounds

Those intending to camp or travel by RV are well catered for in Alberta. Calgary has a half dozen campgrounds spread around its outskirts, Edmonton has one near downtown, and almost every town, no matter its size, has a municipal campground. These facilities range in price from free to $16 for a tent site and up to $24 with hookups, depending on facilities and location. Often those campgrounds in smaller towns are a bargain—it's not uncommon to pay less than $10 for a site with hookups and hot showers.

Except in major cities, reservations aren't necessary—just roll up and pay the campground host or use the honor box. Each of Alberta's national parks has excellent campgrounds. At least one campground in each park has hot showers and full hookups. Prices are $10–24. All national park campgrounds operate on a first-come, first-served basis and often fill by midday in July and August. Banff, Jasper, and Waterton have winter camping but with limited facilities. Most provincial parks have a campground; prices are $9–17 depending on facilities available. Some have hookups, showers, boat rentals, and occasionally laundry facilities. In national and provincial parks, firewood is supplied, but at a cost. In the national parks, a nightly Fire Permit costs $6, which includes as much wood as you need. Throughout the foothills, campgrounds managed by Alberta Environment have pit toilets, picnic tables, and a supply of firewood. Most are accessed along the Forestry Trunk Road. These cost $6–10 per night.

Backcountry camping in the national parks is $6 per person per night to a maximum of $30 per person per trip. A $42 Annual Wilderness Pass is valid for unlimited backcountry travel and camping for 12 months from its purchase date. Before heading out, you must register at the respective park information center (regardless of whether you have an annual pass) and pick up a Wilderness Pass (for those without an annual pass, this costs the nightly camping fee multiplied by the number of nights you'll be in the backcountry). Many popular backcountry campgrounds have quotas, with reservations taken up to three months in advance. The reservation fee is $10 per party per trip. In 1998, Kananaskis Country also introduced a $6 per-person backcountry camping fee. Most campgrounds in the backcountry have pit toilets, and some have bear bins for secure food storage. Fires are discouraged, so bring a stove.

FOOD AND DRINK

If you're RVing it or camping, eating cheap in Alberta is easy. The two largest supermarkets, Safeway and I.G.A., generally have the least expensive groceries, but prices are still higher than in the United States. In most I.G.A. stores, you'll find an excellent bakery. If you're barbecuing, know that most urban campgrounds discourage open fires, and provincial and national parks charge up to $6 for a small bundle of firewood.

For a three-course meal in a family-style restaurant, including a steak dish, expect to pay $25–30 per person—double that in the better eateries. Edmonton, Calgary, and Banff have an astonishing array of ethnic restaurants; Banff, a town of 7,000, has more than 100 restaurants. Inexpensive options are Husky restaurants, located in gas stations of the same name along all major routes; Boston Pizza, a chain of Canadian family-style restaurants; and Tim Hortons, best known for donuts but with other meals offered. Calgary and Edmonton also have several excellent buffets where an all-you-can-eat Chinese or Western meal is $6–9 for lunch and $9–15 for dinner.

Local Produce

Fall is a wonderful time to pick up local produce. One of the local favorites is Taber corn, which is sold from pick-ups and "farm gate" stalls through September. The best way to purchase fresh produce is at a **farmer's market.** These take place throughout Alberta (often on a Saturday morning) and are denoted by a distinctive sign depicting a farmer with a hoe standing beside a pumpkin. By provincial law, sellers must have grown or their products contain at least 80 percent of what they are selling. This means you're guaranteed fresh and local produce. One of the best-known markets is held at the Millarville racetrack, west of Calgary, each summer Saturday morning.

Although Alberta isn't renowned for its culinary delights, the staple of the province—Alberta beef—is delicious and served in most restaurants. It is graded by the Alberta Cattle Commission, with Canada AAA—marbled with thin streaks of fat that melt through the meat during cooking—the finest. Bison meat, farmed throughout Alberta, is also popular but more expensive than beef. It's an extremely lean, low-fat meat that can be bought in most forms, including hamburger, jerky, and regular cuts such as T-bones.

Drink

Calgary and Edmonton each have specialty brewers that brew boutique beers for sale in the immediate area. Alberta's largest home-grown brewery is **Big Rock** in Calgary. The province's only winery, **Wolf Wineries,** is on the outskirts of Edmonton.

The minimum age for alcohol consumption in Alberta is 18. From the United States, visitors may bring 1.1 liters of liquor or wine or 24 cans or bottles of beer into Canada free of duty.

TRANSPORTATION

GETTING THERE

Air

Calgary and Edmonton have international airports served by major airlines from throughout the world. Many flights from the south are routed through Calgary before continuing to Edmonton, giving you a choice of final destinations for little or no price difference. Canada's national carrier is **Air Canada,** which took over troubled Canadian Airlines in 2000, forming an alliance that is one of the world's largest airlines. Air Canada now offers direct flights to Calgary from all major Canadian cities, as well as from Seattle, Los Angeles, San Francisco, Reno, Las Vegas, Phoenix, Chicago, Boston, Washington, Dallas/Fort Worth, New York, Atlanta, and St. Louis. Direct flights to Edmonton originate in all major Canadian cities west of Montreal, as well as Seattle, Denver, Minneapolis–St. Paul, and Chicago. From Europe, Air Canada flies direct from London to Calgary, and from Paris, Frankfurt, and Rome to either Calgary or Vancouver via Toronto. South Pacific and Asian cities served include Sydney, Melbourne, and Brisbane, as well as Auckland, Bangkok, Kuala Lumpur, Hong Kong, Taipei, Nagoya, Beijing, and Tokyo. Air Canada flights originating in the South American cities of Santiago, Buenos Aires, Sao Paulo, and Rio de Janeiro are routed through Toronto. For further information on Air Canada's routes and schedules, call 403/265-9555 or 888/247-2262, www.aircanada.ca.

Aside from Air Canada, many smaller airlines operate flights to Alberta from within Canada. These include **Air Transat,** 877/872-6728; **Canada 3000,** 403/509-3000 or 888/816-1166, www.canada3000tickets.com; **Royal Airlines,** 888/828-9797, www.royalairlines.com; and **WestJet,** 800/538-5696, www.westjet.com.

U.S. carriers offering service to Calgary and Edmonton are **American Airlines,** 800/443-7300, www.aa.com; **Delta Air Lines,** 800/221-1212, www.delta-air.com; **Horizon Air,** 800/547-9308, www.horizonair.com; and **Northwest Airlines,** 800/225-2525. **United Airlines,** 800/241-6522, www.ual.com, flies to Calgary but not Edmonton. Other international carriers serving the province include **Air New Zealand, Alitalia, Japan Airlines,** and **KLM.**

Cutting Flight Costs

Ticket structuring for air travel is so complex that often even travel agents have problems coming to grips with it. The first step when planning your trip to Alberta is to contact the airlines that fly to Calgary and Edmonton and ask for the best price that they have for the time of year you wish to travel. Then shop around the travel agencies; you should be able to save 30–50 percent of the price you were quoted by the airline. Check the Sunday travel section of most newspapers for an idea of current discount prices. The Internet is another good place to start searching out the cheapest fares.

Many cheaper tickets have strict restrictions regarding changes of flight dates, lengths of

---

DEPARTURE TAXES

The federal government imposes a tax of seven percent of the ticket price plus a Canadian International Transportation Tax of $6 to a maximum of $55 on all flights departing Canada for the United States. For all other international destinations, the departure tax is set at $55. These taxes are generally included in the ticket purchase price, but it pays to ask when booking.

Both Calgary and Edmonton International Airports charge an Airport Improvement Fee to all departing passengers. Since January 2000, the fee has been built into the price of the ticket.

Rail Travel is a great way to experience Alberta.

stay, and cancellations. A general rule is: The cheaper the ticket, the more restrictions. Most travelers today fly on advance-purchase excursion (APEX) fares. These are usually the best value, although some (and, occasionally, many) restrictions apply. These might include minimum and maximum stays, and nonchangeable itineraries (or hefty penalties for changes); tickets may also be nonrefundable, once purchased.

Within Canada, consolidator **Travel Cuts,** www.travelcuts.com, with offices in all major cities, consistently offers the lowest airfares available. In the United States, one of the largest consolidators is **Unitravel,** 800/325-2222, www.unitravel.com. The **Flight Centre,** 888/967-5331, www .flightcentre.com, with offices throughout the United States, guarantees to match any quoted airfare. In London, **Trailfinders,** 194 Kensington High Street, Kensington, tel. 020/7938-3939, www.trailfinders.com, always has good deals to Canada and other North American destinations.

When you have found the best fare, open a

frequent flyer membership with the airline; **Aeroplan** is a popular program administered by Air Canada that makes rewards easily obtainable.

Rail

VIA Rail provides transcontinental rail service from coast to coast. This form of transportation, which opened up the West to settlers and the Canadian Rockies to tourists, began to fade with the advent of efficient air services. Scheduled services to Calgary ended in 1991; the remaining transcontinental route passes through Edmonton and Jasper, terminating in Vancouver. The **Canadian,** as this train is known, operates three days a week in either direction and provides two classes of travel: Economy, which features lots of leg room, reclining seats, reading lights, pillows and blankets, and a Skyline Car complete with bar service; and Silver and Blue, which is more luxurious, featuring a variety of sleeping room configurations, daytime seating, a domed lounge and dining car reserved exclusively for passengers in this class, shower kits for all passengers, and all meals. At Jasper, the westbound transcontinental line divides, with one set of tracks continuing slightly north to Prince Rupert. Along this route, the **Skeena** makes three trips a week. It is a daytime-only service, with passengers transferred to Prince George accommodations for an overnight stay. It also offers first-class travel, in **Totem Class.** In all cases, discounts of 25 percent (40 percent if booked seven days in advance) apply to travel October through June (applicable to all classes). Those travelers older than 60 and younger than 25 receive a 10 percent discount, which can be combined with other seasonal fares. Check for advance-purchase restrictions on all discount tickets.

The **Canrailpass** allows unlimited travel anywhere on the VIA Rail system for 12 days within any given 30-day period. During high season (May 15–September 15) the pass is $639, and $399 the rest of the year. Extra days are $52.43 and $35.44, respectively. Even if you plan limited train travel, the pass is an excellent deal—but remember, if you travel on a service that, for example, departs at 10 P.M. and arrives at 2 A.M., it counts as two days of travel. VIA Rail has recently cooperated with Amtrak to offer a North American Rail Pass, with all of the same seasonal dates and discounts as the Canrailpass. The cost is CDN$965, US$659 for a high-season pass. (For Amtrak information, call 800/872-7245.)

Pick up a train schedule at any VIA Rail station or call 800/561-8630 within western Canada; in other Canadian locations, contact your local VIA Rail Station. In the United States, call any travel agent. The VIA Rail website, www.viarail.ca, provides route, schedule, and fare information as well as links to towns and sights en route.

Rocky Mountaineer Railtours, 604/606-2245 or 800/665-7245, www.rkymtnrail.com, operates a summer-only luxurious rail trip through the spectacular interior mountain ranges of British Columbia between Vancouver and Banff or Jasper. Travel is during daylight hours only, so you don't miss anything. Trains depart in either direction in the morning (every second or third day), overnighting at Kamloops. One-way travel in Signature Service, which includes light meals, nonalcoholic drinks, and Kamloops accommodations, costs $610 per person from either Banff or Jasper to Vancouver and $670 from Calgary. GoldLeaf Service is the ultimate in luxury. Passengers ride in a two-story, glass-domed car, eat in a separate dining area, and stay in Kamloops' most luxurious accommodations. GoldLeaf costs $1,110 from Banff or Jasper to Vancouver and $1,210 from Calgary. During value season (May and the first two weeks of October), fares are reduced by $100.

Bus

Greyhound (403/265-9111 or 800/661-8747, www.greyhound.ca) serves areas throughout Canada and the United States. From Vancouver, the main routes are along the TransCanada Highway to Banff and Calgary and a more northern route through to Jasper and Edmonton. From the east, buses depart Toronto daily for Calgary and Edmonton along two different routes. If you're traveling to Alberta from the United States, get yourself to Great Falls, Montana, from where regular services continue north to the Coutts/Sweetgrass port of entry. There you change to a Canadian Greyhound bus. Calgary buses depart from the port of entry daily at 12:10 P.M.

Travel by Greyhound is simple—just roll up at the depot and buy a ticket. No reservations are necessary. Greyhound bus depots in all major Albertan cities are close to inexpensive accommodations and other public transportation. Always check for any promotional fares that might be available at the time of your travel. Regular-fare tickets are valid for one year and allow unlimited stopovers between paid destinations.

The **Canada Coach Pass** is valid on all Greyhound routes in Canada. It is sold in periods of seven days ($249), 15 days ($379), 30 days ($449), and 60 days ($599). It must be purchased seven days in advance and is nonrefundable. You can buy the pass at any bus depot. In the United States, the pass can be bought from most travel agents. Outside of North America, it is sold as the **International Canada Coach Pass,** with a similar pricing structure except that gateway cities such as New York and Seattle can be visited.

GETTING AROUND

Air

Air B.C., a connector airline for Air Canada, 800/222-6596, offers scheduled flights to all cities and many larger towns within the province, including Lethbridge, Medicine Hat, Edmonton, Grande Prairie, and many British Columbia towns from Calgary; and to Grande Prairie, Peace River, High Level, Rainbow Lake, Fort McMurray, and northern British Columbia towns from Edmonton. Other intraprovincial carriers include **Capital City Air,** 877/935-9222, www.capitalcityair.com, and **Northern Sky Aviation,** 800/668-4037. Domestic flights are generally expensive, but discounts apply if tickets are purchased in advance or in conjunction with a long-haul flight. By buying a round-trip ticket seven to 14 days in advance and staying over a Saturday night, discounts of up to 50 percent apply.

Rail

The only scheduled rail service within the province is between Jasper and Edmonton. This thrice-weekly service is part of the transcontinental route. For further information on VIA Rail services, see the previous **Getting There** section, or call 800/561-8630 in Canada only.

Bus

Greyhound bus routes radiate from Calgary and Edmonton to points throughout the province. Service is regular, fast, and efficient. The only downside is that in larger centers, bus depots are often located in seedy parts of town. Many depots have cafeterias, some have lockers, but none of them remain open all night. For schedules and fares, call 403/265-9111 or in Canada only 800/661-8747, www.greyhound.ca.

Red Arrow (780/424-3339 or 800/232-1958, www.redarrow.pwt.ca) operates a more luxurious service that connects Calgary and Edmonton five to seven times daily, continuing twice daily to the oil sands city of Fort McMurray. All Red Arrow buses are equipped with fold-down tables, a row of single seats on one side of the bus, laptop plug-ins, and a range of complimentary refreshments.

Brewster provides coach service between Calgary and Banff and Jasper national parks. Brewster's advantage over Greyhound is that its service departs from Calgary International Airport and major Calgary hotels. One-way fare to Banff is $36, to Lake Louise $41, and to Jasper $71. You can book a trip at Brewster's booking desk on the arrivals level of Calgary International Airport or call 403/221-8242, www.brewster.ca.

Hostel Shuttle

Between mid-May and the end of October, a shuttle bus runs between Calgary and all hostels in the mountain national parks every second day. The route begins from the hostel in Calgary at 8 A.M. and ends at the Mt. Edith Cavell hostel at 4:30 P.M. that same day. The schedule is reversed the following day. Sample fares are Calgary to Banff, $23; Calgary to Lake Louise, $30; Calgary to Jasper, $65; Banff to Lake Louise, $14; Lake Louise to Jasper, $38. Book shuttle reservations through the hostels.

Car and RV Rental

All major car-rental agencies have outlets at Calgary and Edmonton International Airports; to ensure that a vehicle is available for you when you arrive, book in advance. Generally, vehicles can be booked through parent companies in the United States. Rates start at $60 per day for a small economy car, $75 for a mid-

size car, and $85 for a full-size car. Most major agencies now offer unlimited mileage, but not for rentals originating in Banff or Jasper national parks. Check to make sure about this policy. Cheaper cars are available from agencies such as **Rent-A-Wreck** (800/327-0116 in Canada, 800/535-1391 in the United States, www.rentawreck.ca), but each kilometer driven over 100 kilometers each day costs 15–30 cents. In all cases, insurance costs from $12 per day and is compulsory. Rates are often lower outside summer. Charges apply if you need to drop off the car at an agency other than the rental location. All agencies provide free pickup and drop-off at major city hotels. Major rental agencies include **Avis,** 800/879-2847, www.avis.com; **Budget,** 800/268-8900, www.budgetcanada.com; **Discount,** 800/263-2355, www.discountcar.com; **Dollar,** 800/800-4000, www.dollar.com; **Enterprise,** 800/325-8007, www.enterprise.com; **Hertz,** 800/263-0600, www.hertz.com; **National,** 800/227-7368, www.nationalcar.com; and **Thrifty,** 800/847-4389, www.thrifty.com.

Camper vans, RVs, and travel trailers are a great way to get around the Canadian Rockies without having to worry about accommodations each night. The downside is cost. The smallest vans, capable of sleeping two people, start at $100 per day with 100 free kilometers per day. Extra charges include insurance, a preparation fee (usually around $50 per rental), a linen/cutlery charge (around $60 per person per trip), and taxes. Major agencies, with rental outlets in Calgary, include **Cruise Canada** (403/291-4963 or 800/327-7799, or in the United States, 800/327-7778, www.cruiseamerica.com); and **Go West** (403/240-1814 or 800/240-1814). These two companies have depots in Vancouver, as do **Canadream** (604/572-3220 or 800/461-7368, www.canadream.com); and **C.C. Canada Camper** (604/327-3003, www.canadacamper .com). In most cases, a drop-off fee of $400 applies to drop-offs made in Vancouver from rentals originating in Calgary, or vice versa.

Driving in Alberta

Driving is the most practical and popular way to travel to and around Alberta. Driver's licenses from all countries are valid in the province for up to three months. An **International Driving**

Permit, available in your home country, is valid in Alberta for one year. You should also carry car registration papers or rental contracts. Proof of insurance must be carried, and you must wear seat belts. If coming from the United States, check that your American insurance covers travel in Canada. All highway signs in Alberta give distances in **kilometers** and speeds in **kilometers per hour** (kph). The speed limit on major highways is 100 kph (62 mph). U.S. motorists are advised to obtain a Canadian Non-resident Interprovincial Motor Vehicle Liability Insurance Card, available through U.S. insurance companies, which is accepted as evidence of financial responsibility in Canada. Members of the American Automobile Association (AAA) are entitled to services provided by the Canadian Automobile Association, including travel information.

Buying a car is relatively straightforward in Alberta. Proof of insurance in your home country lowers the standard liability insurance of $1,600 per year. Automobiles are cheaper in the United States, but insurance is higher, and unless you can convince customs that you won't be selling the car in Canada, you'll be up for hefty import charges.

Tours
Day tours are offered in Calgary, Banff, Jasper, and Edmonton. These tours are a great way to orient yourself to the region and are relatively inexpensive. The main tour operator is **Brewster** (403/762-6767, www.brewster.ca), which also offers tours to various parts of the province, as well as car rental and accommodation packages, overnight packages in Calgary and Edmonton, Calgary Stampede packages, golfing adventures, and round-trips to Alberta from Vancouver, British Columbia. Rocky Mountaineer Rail Tours (see Getting There) offer a wide variety of longer tours in conjunction with rail travel between Vancouver and Banff or Jasper.

OTHER PRACTICALITIES

VISAS AND OFFICIALDOM

Entry for U.S. Citizens
Citizens and permanent residents of the United States do not require a passport for entry to Canada. Although photo driver's licenses are acceptable forms of identification for entry, it is advisable to carry extra identification such as a birth certificate, passport, or alien card (the latter is essential for U.S. resident aliens to reenter the United States).

Other Foreign Visitors
Visitors from countries other than the United States require a valid passport and, in some cases, a visa for entry to Canada. Presently, citizens of the British Commonwealth and Western Europe do not require a visa, but check with the Canadian embassy in your home country. The standard entry permit is valid for six months; proof of onward tickets and/or sufficient funds are required in order to obtain the permit. Extensions are possible from the Employment and Immigration Canada offices in Calgary and Edmonton ($60 per person).

Employment and Study
Anyone wishing to work or study in Canada must obtain authorization *before* entering Canada. Authorization to work will be granted only if no qualified Canadians are available for the work in question. Applications for work and study are available from all Canadian embassies and must be submitted with a nonrefundable processing fee.

The Canadian government has a reciprocal agreement with Australia for a limited number of **holiday work visas** to be issued each year. Australian citizens under the age of 30 are eligible; contact your nearest Canadian embassy or consulate for more information.

Entry by Private Aircraft
For a list of Canadian airports with customs clearance facilities, request the *Canada Flight Supplement* from Canada Map Office (130 Bentley Ave., Ottawa, Ontario K1A 0E9, 613/952-7000). This office also sells aeronautical charts for $15 each. The publication *Air Tourist Information–Canada* (TP771E) lists all of Alberta's airports and other necessary information for visiting pilots; it's available from Transport Canada, AAN DHD, Ottawa, Ontario K1A 0N8, 613/990-2309.

Firearms

Handguns, automatic guns, and sawed-off rifles and shotguns are not allowed entry into Canada. Visitors must declare all firearms at the border, and those that are restricted will be held by customs for the duration of your stay. Those firearms not declared will be seized and fines may be imposed. It is also illegal to possess a firearm in a national park unless it is dismantled *and* carried in an enclosed case. Up to 5,000 rounds of ammunition may be imported but should be declared on entry. For further information on firearm regulations, call Canadian Customs Service at 613/954-7129 or 800/461-9999.

MONEY

As in the United States, Canadian currency is based on dollars and cents. Coins come in denominations of one, five, 10, and 25 cents, and one and two dollars. The one-dollar coin is the 11-sided, gold-colored "loonie," named for the bird featured on it. The unique two-dollar coin, introduced in 1996, is silver with a gold-colored insert. The most common notes are $5, $10, $20, and $50. A $100 bill does exist but is uncommon.

All prices quoted in this book are in Canadian dollars. American dollars are accepted at many tourist areas, but the exchange rate is more favorable at banks. Currency other than U.S. dollars can be exchanged at most banks, airport money-changing facilities, and foreign exchange brokers in Calgary, Banff, Jasper, and Edmonton. Traveler's checks are the safest way to carry money, but a fee is often charged to cash them if they're in a currency other than Canadian dollars. All major credit cards are honored at Canadian banks, gas stations, and most commercial establishments. Automatic teller machines (ATMs) can be found in almost every town.

Costs

The cost of living is lower in Alberta than in other provinces but higher than in the United States. By planning ahead, having a tent or joining Hostelling International, and being prepared to cook your own meals, it is possible to get by on less than $50 per person per day. Gasoline is sold in liters (3.78 liters equals one U.S. gallon), and like the rest of North America, its price spiralled skyward when the price of oil rose through the end of the 1990s. Gas currently costs 70–75 cents per liter for regular unleaded. North of Edmonton, the price is higher, up to 85 cents per liter.

Tips are not usually added to a bill, and in general 15 percent of the total amount is given. Tips are most often given to restaurant servers, taxi drivers, doormen, bellhops, and bar staff.

Taxes

Canada imposes a seven percent **goods and services tax (GST)** on most consumer purchases. Nonresident visitors can get a rebate for the GST they pay on short-term accommodations and on most consumer goods bought in the country and taken home. Items not included in the GST rebate program include gifts left in Canada, meals and restaurant charges, campground fees, services such as dry cleaning and shoe repair, alcoholic beverages, tobacco, automotive fuels, groceries, agricultural and fish products, prescription drugs and medical devices, and used goods that tend to increase in value, such as paintings, jewelry, rare books, and coins. The rebate is available on services and retail purchases that total at least $100 and were paid for within 60 days before your exit from the country. Rebates can be claimed any

---

CURRENCY EXCHANGE

The Canadian dollar lost value against the greenback through the late 1990s, but held steady through 2000. It currently trades at roughly **US$1 per CAD$1.45–1.49.**

Current exchange rates (into CAD$) for other major currencies are:

> AUS$1 = 91 cents
> DM1 = 72 cents
> EURO = $1.38
> HK$10 = $1.95
> NZ$1 = 70 cents
> UK£ = $2.25
> ¥100 = $1.39

time within one year from the date of purchase. You'll need to include with your claim all receipts and vouchers that prove the GST was paid. Most visitors apply for the rebate at duty-free shops (also called Visitor Rebate Centres) when exiting the country. The duty-free shops can rebate up to $500 on the spot. For rebates more than $500, you'll need to mail your completed GST rebate form directly to Revenue Canada, Customs and Excise, Visitors' Rebate Program, Ottawa, Ontario K1A 1J5. You can also submit rebate forms for amounts less than $500 directly to Revenue Canada. Rebate checks from Revenue Canada are issued in Canadian funds. For more information, call toll-free from anywhere in Canada 800/668-4748; from outside Canada, phone 902/432-5608, www.rc.gc.ca/visitors.

Alberta is the only province that doesn't impose a **Provincial Sales Tax,** which ranges from 5–12 percent throughout the country.

HEALTH

Compared to other parts of the world, Canada is a relatively safe place to visit. Vaccinations are required only if coming from an endemic area. That said, wherever you are traveling, carry a medical kit that includes bandages, insect repellent, sunscreen, antiseptic, antibiotics, and water-purification tablets. Good first-aid kits are available at most camping shops.

Taking out a travel-insurance policy is a sensible precaution because hospital and medical charges start at around $1,000 per day. Copies of prescriptions should be brought to Canada for any medicines already prescribed.

Giardia
Giardiasis, also known as beaver fever, is a real concern for those heading into the backcountry. It's caused by an intestinal parasite, *Giardia lamblia,* that lives in lakes, rivers, and streams. Once ingested, its effects, although not instantaneous, can be dramatic; severe diarrhea, cramps, and nausea are the most common symptoms. Preventive measures should always be taken, including boiling all water for at least 10 minutes, treating all water with iodine, or filtering all water using a filter with a small-enough pore size to block the *Giardia* cysts.

Winter Travel
Travel throughout the province during winter months should not be undertaken lightly. Before setting out in a vehicle, check antifreeze levels, and always carry a spare tire and blankets or sleeping bags. **Frostbite** is a potential hazard, especially when cold temperatures are combined with high winds (a combination known as **windchill**). Most often, frostbite leaves a numbing, bruised sensation, and the skin turns white. Exposed areas of skin, especially the nose and ears, are most susceptible.

Hypothermia occurs when the body fails to produce heat as fast as it loses it. It can strike at any time of the year but is more common during cooler months. Cold weather, combined with hunger, fatigue, and dampness, creates a recipe for disaster. Symptoms are not always apparent to the victim. The early signs are numbness, shivering, slurring of words, dizzy spells, and, in extreme cases, violent behavior, unconsciousness, and even death. The best way to dress for the cold is in layers, including a waterproof outer layer. Most important, wear headgear. The best treatment is to get the victim out of the cold, replace wet clothing with dry, slowly give hot liquids and sugary foods, and place the victim in a sleeping bag. Warming too quickly can lead to heart attacks.

SERVICES, COMMUNICATIONS, AND MEASUREMENTS

All **mail** posted in Canada must have Canadian postage stamps attached. First-class letters and postcards are 46 cents to destinations within Canada, 55 cents to the United States, and 96 cents to all other destinations. Post offices are open Monday–Friday only. If you would like mail sent to you while traveling, have it addressed to yourself, c/o General Delivery, Main Post Office, in the city or town you request, Alberta, Canada. The post office will hold all general delivery mail for 15 days before returning it to the sender.

Alberta has two **area codes.** All of Alberta south of Highway 16, including Calgary and Banff, is **403,** whereas the northern half of the province, including Edmonton and Jasper, is **780.** For the Northwest Territories and Nunavut,

HEADING FURTHER AFIELD?

Tourism British Columbia: 250/387-1642 or 800/435-5622; www.hellobc.com

Tourism Yukon: 403/667-5340; www.touryukon.com

Alaska Division of Tourism: 907/465-2010; www.dced.state.ak.us/tourism

Tourism Saskatchewan: 306/787-2300 or 800/667-7191; www.sasktourism.com

Travel Manitoba: 204/945-3777 or 800/665-0040; www.travelmanitoba.com

it is **867.** Unless otherwise noted, all numbers must be dialed with this prefix, including long-distance calls made within the province. The country code for Canada is 1, the same as the United States. Public phones accept five-, 10-, and 25-cent coins. Local calls are 25 or 35 cents, depending on the area, and most long-distance calls cost at least $2.50 for the first minute from public phones. Phone cards, which are available from drug and grocery stores, provide considerable savings for those using public phones.

Electrical voltage is 120 volts, the same as the United States. Alberta is on the metric system (see the **Metric System** chart at the back of this book), although many people talk in miles and supermarket prices are advertised in ounces and pounds.

Alberta is in the **mountain time zone,** one hour later than Pacific time, two hours earlier than eastern time.

Shops are generally open Monday–Friday 9 A.M.–5 P.M., Saturday 9 A.M.–noon, and are closed on Sunday. Major shopping centers and those in resort towns are often open until 9 P.M. and all weekend. **Banks** are open Monday–Friday 9:30 A.M.–3:30 P.M. and until 4:30 or 5 P.M. on Friday.

MAPS AND INFORMATION

Maps
Specialist map shops are the best source for accurate, high-quality maps; in Calgary, contact **Map Town** (400 5th Ave. SW, 403/266-2241), and in Edmonton, **Map Town** (10344 105th St., 780/429-2600). By request they can send out a catalog of maps designed specifically for hiking (topographical maps), camping (road/access maps), fishing (hydrographic charts of more than 100 lakes), and canoeing (river details such as gradients). They can also supply Alberta wall maps, Canada wall maps, thematic maps, historic maps, and aerial photography. These maps are also available over the counter at some sport and camping stores. **Gem Trek** maps are locally produced and of excellent quality. They are available at the aforementioned locations, or contact the company direct, 403/932-4208, www.gemtrek.ca.

Information
The best source of up-to-date information on all accommodations, attractions, and events is **Travel Alberta** (P.O. Box 2500, Edmonton, Alberta T5J 2Z4, 780/427-4321 or, from within North America, 800/661-8888, www.travelalberta.com). It also provides two excellent publications, *Alberta Accommodation Guide* and *Alberta Campground Guide,* and a road map. All major routes into the province have a **Travel Alberta Information Centre,** which are generally open in summer only with all the same information (except you must pay for the road maps). Each town has a **Tourist Information Centre,** each with its own hours, and usually open June–August. When these centers are closed, head to the chamber of commerce (year-round, Monday–Friday only) for information.

Alberta Environment manages parks and protected areas throughout the province. For information, visit the Alberta Environment Information Centre (9920 108th St., Edmonton, 780/922-2079), or write Parks and Protected Areas Division (9820 106th St., Edmonton, Alberta T5K 2J6, www.gov.ab.ca/env/parks). National parks are managed by **Parks Canada,** which operates a provincial headquarters in the Harry Hays Building at 220 4th Avenue SE, Calgary, 403/992-2950, www.parkscanada.gc.ca.

On the Internet

Alberta Tourism's website, www.travelalberta.com, is the best place to start planning your trip to Alberta. Many towns have developed their own websites, with links to local businesses. Only websites managed by tourism offices are listed in this book. Websites are also listed for accommodations, many of which now provide online booking forms. The best way to search the Internet for a particular business or attraction is by using a search engine; try www.alberta.com.

Found Locally is an Internet-based company that provides Web surfers with a wealth of information on Alberta's two largest cities, Calgary and Edmonton. The websites cover all aspects of entertainment and recreation, such as attractions, sporting events, concerts, movies, and hundreds of accommodations and restaurants. The restaurant listings are particularly comprehensive, with cuisine, price range, and business hours listed. The site also features daily weather information, transportation routings, and even where the police have set up their latest photo-radar speed traps. Access the sites at www.foundlocally.com/calgary and www.foundlocally.com/edmonton.

KAREN MCKINLEY

CALGARY

INTRODUCTION

Calgary's nickname, Cowtown, is cherished by the city's 795,000 residents, who prefer that romantic vision of their beloved home to the city's more modern identity as a world energy and financial center. The city's rapid growth, from a North West Mounted Police (NWMP) post to a large and vibrant metropolis in little more than 100 years, can be credited largely to the effects of resource development, particularly oil and natural gas.

Once run by gentlemen who had made their fortunes in ranching, Calgary is still an important cattle market. But the oil-and-gas bonanzas of the 1940s, 1950s, and 1970s changed everything. The resources discovered throughout western Canada brought enormous wealth and growth to the city, turning it into the headquarters for a burgeoning energy industry. Ignored by the eastern provinces, the city grew (at one time by 60 people per day) into a western dynamo, in constant conflict with the country's capital, Ottawa.

With the city's rapid growth came all the problems plaguing major cities around the world, with one major exception—the distinct lack of manufacturing and industrial sites has meant little pollution.

Today the city is home to 20,000 Americans, many of them big oilmen with Texas twangs. Downtown is a massive cluster of modern steel-and-glass skyscrapers, the legacy of an explosion of wealth in the 1970s. Set in this futuristic mirage on the prairie are banks, insurance companies, investment companies, and the head offices of hundreds of oil companies. But not forgetting its roots, each July the city sets aside all the material success it's achieved as a boomtown to put on the greatest outdoor show on earth—the Calgary Stampede, a Western extravaganza second to none.

HISTORY

In addition to being one of Canada's largest cities, Calgary is also one of the youngest; at 125 years old, it has a heritage rather than a history. Native Blackfoot people moved through the area approximately 2,000 years ago, but they had no particular interest in the direct vicinity of what is now Calgary. Approximately 300 years ago, Sarcee and Stoney natives moved down from the north and commenced continual warring between tribes. White settlers first arrived in the late 1700s. David Thompson wintered in the area, then the Palliser Expedition passed by on its way west to the Rockies. But it wasn't until the late 1860s that any real activity started. Buffalo had disappeared from the American plains, and as hunters moved north, so did the whiskey traders, bringing with them all the problems associated with this illegal trade.

Fort Calgary

The NWMP established a post at Fort Macleod soon after they came west to quell the whiskey trade. In 1875, a second fort was established on a terrace at the confluence of the Bow and Elbow rivers. It was named Fort Calgary after the Scottish birthplace of Inspector J.F. Macleod, who took over command of the fort in 1876. It is an apt name for a city that straddles the clear Bow River—*calgary* is Gaelic for "clear, running water," a fact of which Macleod was probably well aware.

The Coming of the Railway

For many years, the Canadian Pacific Railway had planned to build a northern route across the continent through Edmonton and Yellowhead Pass. But eventually the powers in the east changed their minds and decided on a southern route through Kicking Horse Pass. This meant that the line passed right through Fort Calgary. In 1883, a station was built on an alluvial plain between the Bow and Elbow rivers. A townsite was laid out around it, settlers streamed in for free land, and nine years after the railway arrived, Calgary acquired city status—something that had taken its northern rival, Edmonton, more than 100 years to obtain.

In 1886, a major fire destroyed most of the town's buildings. City planners decreed that all new structures were to be built of sandstone, which gave the fledgling town a more permanent look. The many sandstone buildings still standing today—the Palliser Hotel, the Hudson's Bay Company store, and the courthouse, for example—are a legacy of this early bylaw.

Ranching

An open grazing policy, initiated by the Dominion Government, encouraged ranchers in the United States to drive their cattle from overgrazed lands to the fertile plains around Calgary. Slowly, a

Sandstone buildings gave Calgary a "permanent" look, even in its earliest years, c. 1892.

PROVINCIAL ARCHIVES OF ALBERTA

ranching industry and local beef market developed. The first large ranch was established west of Calgary, and soon many NWMP retirees, English aristocrats, and wealthy American citizens had invested in nearby land. Calgary's first millionaire was Pat Burns, who developed a meat-packing empire that still thrives today. Linked to international markets by rail and sea, Calgary's fortunes continued to rise with those of the ranching industry, receiving only a minor setback in 1905 when Edmonton was declared the provincial capital. During the first 10 years of this century, the city's population increased 1,000 percent, and rail lines were built in all directions, radiating from the city like enormous spokes. Immigration slowed, and the economy spiraled downward as the effects of World War I were felt.

Oil

The discovery of oil at Turner Valley in Calgary's backyard in 1914 signaled the start of an industry that was the making of modern Calgary. The opening of an oil refinery in 1923 and further major discoveries nearby transformed a medium-sized cowtown into a world leader in the petroleum and natural-gas industries. At its peak, the city was the headquarters of more than 400 related companies. Calgary became Canada's fastest-growing city, doubling its population between 1950 and 1975. During the worldwide energy crisis of the 1970s, oil prices soared. Although most of the oil was extracted from farther afield, the city boomed as a world energy and financial center. Construction in the city center

during this period was neverending, as many corporations from around the world moved their headquarters to Alberta. During this period, Calgary had Canada's highest per capita disposable income and was home to more Americans than any other Canadian city. Much of the wealth obtained from oil and gas was channeled back into the city, not just for office towers but also for sporting facilities, cultural centers, and parks for citizens and visitors alike to enjoy. Calgary still has tremendous civic support today. Many of the city's self-made millionaires bequeath their money to the city, and the residents have always been willing to volunteer their time at events such as the Winter Olympic Games and the Calgary Exhibition and Stampede. This civic pride makes the city a great place to live and an enjoyable destination for the millions of tourists who visit each year.

1988 Winter Olympic Games

During the early 1980s, the province was hit by a prolonged downturn in the oil market. But good fortune prevailed when the International Olympic Committee announced that Calgary had been awarded the 1988 Winter Olympic Games. Life was injected into the economically ravaged city, construction started anew, and the high-spirited Calgarians were smiling once again.

The games are remembered for many things, but particularly the lack of snow, a bobsled team from Jamaica, the antics of English plumber/ski-jumper "Eddie the eagle," and most of all for their acclaimed success.

SIGHTS

GETTING ORIENTED

The TransCanada Highway (Highway 1) passes through the city north of downtown and is known as **16th Avenue North** within the city limits. Highway 2, Alberta's major north-south highway, becomes **Deerfoot Trail** as it passes through the city. Many major arteries are known as **trails,** named for their historical significance, not, as some suggest, for their condition. The main route south from downtown is **Macleod Trail,** a 10-kilometer strip of malls, motels, restau-

rants, and retail stores. If you enter Calgary from the west and are heading south, a handy bypass to take is **Sarcee Trail,** then **Glenmore Trail,** which joins Highway 2 south of the city. **Crowchild Trail** starts downtown and heads northwest past the university to Cochrane.

The street-numbering system is divided into four quadrants. At first it can be more confusing than the well-meaning city planner intended, but after initial disorientation, the system soon proves its usefulness. Basically, the four quadrants are geographically named—northwest, northeast, southwest, and southeast. Each street address has a corresponding abbreviation tacked onto it (NW, NE, SW, and SE). The north-south division is the Bow River. The east-west division is at Macleod Trail, and north of the downtown at **Centre Street.** Streets run north to south and avenues from east to west. Both streets and avenues are numbered progressively from the quadrant divisions (e.g., an address on 58th Avenue SE is the 58th street south of the Bow River, is east of Macleod Trail, and is on a street that runs east to west). Things don't get any easier in the many new subdivisions that dominate the outer flanks of the city. Many street names are *very* similar to one another, so check whether you want, for example, Mackenzie Lake Bay, Mackenzie Lake Place, Mackenzie Lake Road, or Mackenzie Lake Avenue. Fill the gas tank, pack a hearty lunch, and good luck!

DOWNTOWN

The downtown core is a mass of modern steel-and-glass high-tech highrises built during the oil boom of the 1970s and early 1980s. (Its ultramodern appearance was the setting for *Superman III* as well as the television series *Viper.*) Calgary's skyline was transformed during this period, and many historic buildings were knocked down to make way for a wave of development that has slowed considerably during the last 10 years. The best way to get around is on foot or on the C-train, which is free along 7th Avenue.

Crisscrossing downtown is the Plus 15 walkway system—a series of interconnecting, enclosed sidewalks elevated at least 15 feet above road level. In total, 47 bridges and 12 kilometers of public walkway link downtown stores, four large malls, hotels, food courts, and office buildings to give pedestrians protection from the elements. All walkways are well marked and wheelchair accessible. The following sights can be visited separately or seen on a walking tour (in the order presented).

Stephen Avenue Mall
The traditional center of the city is 8th Avenue, between 1st Street SE and 3rd Street SW—a traffic-free zone known as Stephen Avenue

Mall. This bustling, tree-lined pedestrian mall has fountains, benches, cafés, restaurants, and souvenir shops. In summer, the mall is full with shoppers and tourists, and at lunchtime, thousands of office workers descend from the buildings above. Many of Calgary's earliest sandstone buildings still stand along the mall on the block between 1st and 2nd streets SW. On the corner of 1st Street SW is the **Alberta Hotel,** one of the city's most popular meeting places until Prohibition in 1916.

Calgary Tower
Ninth Avenue south of the mall has banks, some of Calgary's best hotels, parking stations, the new convention center, the Glenbow Museum (see **Museums**), and one of the city's most famous landmarks, the Calgary Tower (at the corner of Centre St., 403/266-7171). Built in 1968 (known then as the Husky Tower), this 190-meter tower dominated the skyline until 1985, when the nearby Petro-Canada towers went up. The observation deck affords a bird's-eye view of the Canadian Rockies and the ski-jump towers at Canada Olympic Park to the west, the Olympic Saddledome (in Stampede Park) to the south, and the city below. The tower also houses the **Panorama Dining Room,** a casual bar and grill, a snack bar, and a gift shop. The one-minute elevator ride to the top costs adults $7, seniors $4.50, children $3. It runs daily 8 A.M.–midnight. At ground level are shops, Calgary's main Tourist Information Centre, and a currency exchange.

Olympic Plaza
This downtown park at the east end of Stephen Avenue Mall (on the corner of 2nd St. SE), which is filled with office workers each lunch hour, was used during the 1988 Winter Olympic Games for the nightly medal-presentation ceremonies. Plaques here commemorate medal winners, and the bricks on the ground are inscribed by members of the public who helped sponsor the Olympics by "purchasing" individual bricks before the Games. In summer, outdoor concerts are held here, and in winter, the shallow wading pool freezes over and is used as an ice-skating rink. Across 2nd Street SE from the plaza is **City Hall,** built in 1911. It still houses some city offices, although most have moved next door to the modern **Civic Complex.**

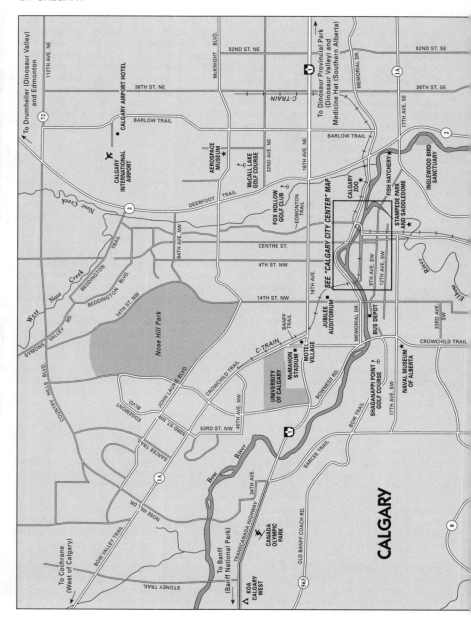

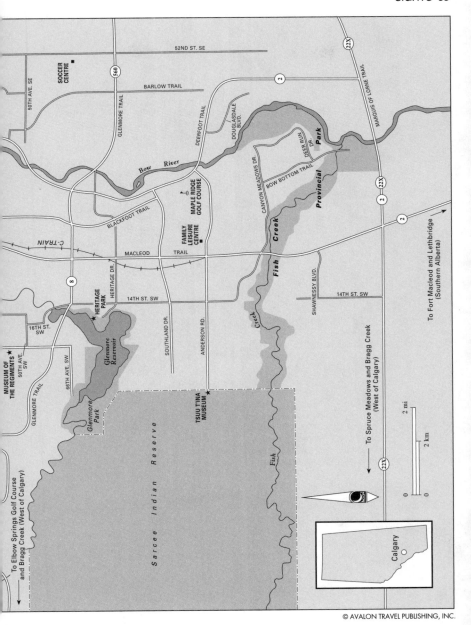

52ND ST. SE

SOCCER CENTRE

50TH AVE SE

560

BARLOW TRAIL

GLENMORE TRAIL

DEERFOOT TRAIL

2

22X

MARQUIS OF LORNE TRAIL

DOUGLASDALE BLVD.

Bow River

CANYON MEADOWS DR.

DEER RUN DR.

BOW BOTTOM TRAIL

BLACKFOOT TRAIL

MAPLE RIDGE GOLF COURSE

Fish Creek

Provincial Park

C-TRAIN

FAMILY LEISURE CENTRE

MACLEOD TRAIL

2   22X

2

To Fort Macleod and Lethbridge (Southern Alberta)

8

HERITAGE DR.

SHAWNESSY BLVD.

14TH ST. SW

HERITAGE PARK

14TH ST. SW

SOUTHLAND DR.

ANDERSON RD.

16TH ST. SW

50TH AVE. SW

Glenmore Reservoir

MUSEUM OF THE REGIMENTS

66TH AVE. SW

GLENMORE TRAIL

Glenmore Park

TSUU T'INA MUSEUM

Creek

Sarcee   Indian   Reserve

Fish

To Elbow Springs Golf Course and Bragg Creek (West of Calgary)

To Spruce Meadows and Bragg Creek (West of Calgary)

22X

2 mi

2 km

0

0

Calgary

© AVALON TRAVEL PUBLISHING, INC.

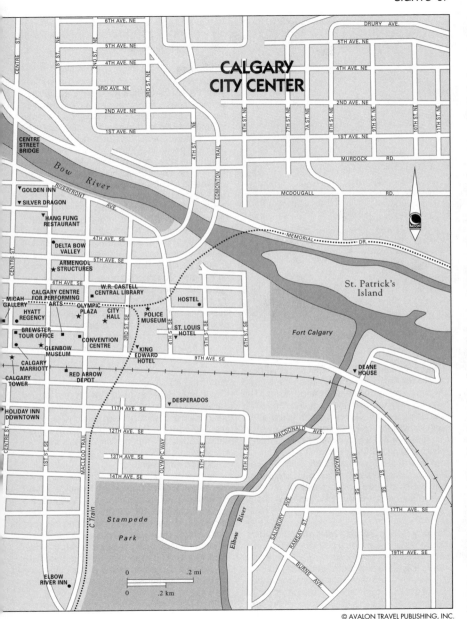

CALGARY
CITY CENTER

6TH AVE. NE
DRURY AVE.
5TH AVE. NE
5TH AVE. NE
4TH AVE. NE
4TH AVE. NE
3RD AVE. NE
2ND AVE. NE
2ND AVE. NE
1ST AVE. NE
1ST AVE. NE
CENTRE ST.
1ST ST.
2ND ST.
3RD ST. NE
4TH ST.
EDMONTON TRAIL
6TH ST. NE
7TH ST. NE
7A ST. NE
8TH ST. NE
9TH ST. NE
10TH ST. NE
11TH ST. NE

CENTRE
STREET
BRIDGE

MURDOCK   RD.

Bow   River

RIVERFRONT   AVE.

MCDOUGALL   RD.

▼ GOLDEN INN
▼ SILVER DRAGON

MOON

▼ HANG FUNG
RESTAURANT

MEMORIAL • • • • • • DR. • • • • • • •

4TH AVE. SE

● DELTA BOW
VALLEY

St. Patrick's
Island

5TH AVE. SE

CENTRE ST.

ARMENGOL
★ STRUCTURES

6TH AVE. SE

W.R. CASTELL
CENTRAL LIBRARY

CALGARY CENTRE
FOR PERFORMING
ARTS

HOSTEL
●

MICAH
GALLERY

OLYMPIC
PLAZA

CITY
HALL

Fort Calgary

HYATT
REGENCY

POLICE
MUSEUM

BREWSTER
TOUR OFFICE

ST. LOUIS
HOTEL

3RD ST. SE
4TH ST. SE
5TH ST. SE
6TH ST. SE

GLENBOW
MUSEUM

CONVENTION
CENTRE

KING
EDWARD
HOTEL

9TH AVE. SE

CALGARY
MARRIOTT

★

DEANE
▼ HOUSE

RED ARROW
DEPOT

CALGARY
TOWER

DESPERADOS

HOLIDAY INN
DOWNTOWN

11TH AVE. SE

MACDONALD   AVE.

12TH AVE. SE

CENTRE ST. SE
1ST ST. SE
MACLEOD TRAIL

OLYMPIC WAY
5TH ST. SE
6TH ST. SE

13TH AVE. SE

MAGGIE ST.
8TH ST. SE
11TH ST.

14TH AVE. SE

C Train

Stampede

17TH AVE. SE

Elbow River

SALISBURY AVE.
RAMSAY ST.

Park

19TH AVE. SE

BURNS AVE.

0   .2 mi

ELBOW
RIVER INN ●

0   .2 km

Olympic Plaza

Admission is $2. Open Monday and Wednesday 9 A.M.–4 P.M., Saturday 11 A.M.–4P.M., Sunday noon–4 P.M.

Chinatown

At the east end of town on 3rd Avenue is a small Chinatown of approximately 2,000 residents. Chinese immigrants came to Calgary in the 1880s to work on the railroads and stayed to establish exotic food markets, restaurants, and import stores here. Chinatown has seen its share of prejudice—from marauding whites gaining revenge for an outbreak of smallpox to bungling city bureaucrats who demanded that the streets be narrow and signs be in Chinese to give the area an authentic look. The **Calgary Chinese Cultural Centre** (197 1st St. SW, 403/262-5071) is one of the largest such centers in Canada. It's topped by a grand central dome patterned in the same style as the Temple of Heaven in Beijing. The centerpiece of its intricate tile work is a glistening golden dragon hanging 20 meters above the floor. Within the center is a museum and gallery displaying the cultural history of Calgarians of Chinese descent. One of the museum's most intriguing pieces is the world's first seismograph, which dates to A.D. 132. The museum is open daily 11 A.M.–5 P.M. Other facilities include a gift store and restaurant.

West on First Avenue

Eau Claire Market at the north end of 3rd Street SW is a colorful indoor market filled with stalls selling fresh fruit from British Columbia, seafood from the Pacific, Alberta beef, bakery items, and exotic imports. Under the same roof are specialty shops, an IMAX and regular theaters, and nine restaurants.

The northern limit of downtown is along the Bow River, where picturesque **Prince's Island Park** is linked to the mainland by a bridge at the end of 3rd Street SW. Jogging paths, tables, and grassy areas are scattered among the trees of this manmade island. To the east is the recently renovated **Centre Street Bridge,** which is still guarded on either side by large (restored) stone lions. For a good view of the city, cross the bridge and follow the trail along the cliff to the west.

From the north end of town, walk south along

Back across 2nd Street SE is the **Calgary Centre for Performing Arts,** incorporating two of Calgary's historic sandstone buildings. The complex houses three theaters and the 1,800-seat **Jack Singer Concert Hall.** Tours of the center are offered Monday and Saturday at 11 A.M. ($2). For more information or performance schedules, call 403/294-7455.

In front of the Education Building on 1st Street SE (between 5th and 6th avenues) are the **Armengol Structures**—expressionless, raceless, humanlike forms with outstretched arms, standing more than six meters tall.

Calgary Police Service Interpretive Centre

This small museum lies a couple of blocks east of Olympic Plaza (316 7th Ave. SE, 403/268-4566). Displays include memorabilia from all of western Canada's police services, mockups of famous crime scenes, a modern police car, and descriptions of the policing process.

Barclay Mall (3rd St. SW), then west on 5th Avenue (or take the Plus 15 walkway system from the Canterra Tower) to the Energy Resources Building.

Energeum and Vicinity

One of Calgary's many free attractions, the Energeum, located on the main floor of the Energy Resources Building (640 5th Ave. SW, 403/297-4293), outlines the history and development of Alberta's largest industry. Through interpretive and hands-on displays, the story of oil, natural gas, oil sands, coal, and electricity in Alberta unfolds. The facility is operated by the Energy Resources Conservation Board, a regulatory body overseeing virtually all energy-related projects in the province. Open 10:30 A.M.–4:30 P.M. Sun.–Fri. in summer, Mon.–Fri. the rest of the year.

Just across the road is the **McDougall Centre** (455 6th St. SW, 403/297-8687), a Renaissance Revival building that is the southern headquarters for the government of Alberta. It was declared an historic site in 1982. The center is open weekdays 8:30 A.M.–4:30 P.M.; call to arrange a tour.

Calgary Science Centre

This complex at 701 11th Street SW, 403/221-3700, is a little farther out (you could either walk the five blocks west from 6th Street or jump aboard the C-train that runs along 7th Avenue SW and walk the last block). The center's main attractions include **Discovery Hall,** featuring changing, often hands-on, science exhibits; **Discovery Circle,** a photographic display area; and **Discovery Dome,** where dynamic audiovisuals are projected onto a massive concave screen. Visitors can enjoy these attractions for the admission charge of adults $9, seniors $7, children $6.

The center also offers an **observatory,** which is open on clear nights, with the telescopes focused on the moon, planets, and clusters of stars. **Pleiades Theatre** has "mystery plays," which are presented throughout the year. For show details and ticket information, call 403/221-3700. The center is open daily in summer 10 A.M.–6 P.M., the rest of the year Tues.–Sun. 10 A.M.–5 P.M.

Devonian Gardens

The C-train will whisk you from the Calgary Science Centre back into the heart of the city to Devonian Gardens. A glass-enclosed elevator rises to the fourth floor of Toronto Dominion Square (8th Ave. and 3rd St. SW), where a one-hectare indoor garden features 16,000 subtropical plants and 4,000 local plants—138 species in all. Within the gardens are waterfalls, fountains, pools, and bridges. Lunchtime entertainers and art exhibits can often be enjoyed in this serene environment. Admission is free, and it's open year-round, daily 9 A.M.–9 P.M.

MUSEUMS

Glenbow Museum

This excellent museum, located at 130 9th Avenue SE (another entrance is on Stephen Avenue Mall), 403/268-4100, chronicles the entire history of western Canada through three floors of informative exhibits and well-displayed artifacts. The second-floor galleries display the museum's permanent collections of contemporary and Inuit art, as well as special exhibitions from national and international collections. The third floor presents historical displays on each aspect of the Canadian West. The stories and traditions of the native Indian peoples unfold through displays of clothing, jewelry, ceremonial objects, and art and crafts. Other displays chronicle the fur trade; the early pioneers; the NWMP; the ranching, oil, and agriculture industries; and the impact of the railway. On the fourth floor is a large collection of military paraphernalia, mineralogy displays (including a meteorite), and exhibits on the Warrior in Society and West Africa. The museum is open daily 9 A.M.–5 P.M.(until 9 P.M. Tues.–Fri. in summer and closed Monday in winter); adults $8, seniors $6, children $4. The library and archives are open Tues.–Fri. 10 A.M.–5 P.M.

AeroSpace Museum

This museum (beside McKnight Blvd. at 4629 McCall Way NE, 403/250-3752) traces the history of aviation in Canada through a large collection of aircraft scattered around the grounds, as well as through engines, uniforms, and old photographs dating back to the flight of one of Calgary's first airplanes, the *West Wind,* in 1914. The engine collection is one of the largest in North America. The museum also features an extensive library and archives, and a gift shop. It's open daily 10 A.M.–5 P.M.; adults $6, seniors $3.50. Take the Whitehorn C-train to Whitehorn and then bus number 57.

Nickle Arts Museum

This museum on the University of Calgary campus (off 32nd Ave. NW at 434 Collegiate Blvd., 403/220-7234) displays a collection of coins from the Ancient World. Throughout the year, more than 20 exhibitions of contemporary and historical art are displayed in one of three galleries. Hours are Tues.–Fri. 10 A.M.–5 P.M., Saturday 1–5 P.M.; admission is $2, free on Tuesday. From downtown, take the Brentwood C-train to the university or bus number 9 Varsity Acres.

Naval Museum of Alberta

Canada's second-largest naval museum is located in Calgary, more than 1,000 kilometers from the ocean. It honors those who served for Canada, many of whom were from the prairie provinces. The Royal Canadian Navy grew from humble beginnings in 1910 to become the Allies' third-largest navy in 1945. On display are three fighter aircraft that flew from the decks of aircraft carriers, as well as uniforms, models, flags, and photographs. The museum is open Tues.–Fri. 1–5 P.M., Sat.–Sun. 10 A.M.–6 P.M.; adults $5, seniors and children $3. It's beside HMCS *Tecumseh* at 1820 24th Street SW, 403/242-0002. Take bus number 2 (Killarney) from the corner of 7th Avenue and 8th Street SW.

Museum of the Regiments

Opened by Queen Elizabeth in 1990, this is the largest military museum in western Canada. It highlights four regiments—Lord Strathcona's Horse Regiment, Princess Patricia's Canadian Light Infantry, the King's Own Calgary Regiment, and the Calgary Highlanders—with realistic life-size figures, uniforms, badges, medals, photographs, and an audiovisual show. The museum is open daily (except Wednesday) 10 A.M.–4 P.M.; admission by donation. It's located on the old Canadian Forces Base at 4520 Crowchild Trail SW, 403/974-2869. Take bus number 13 (Mount Royal) from the Bay to 50th Avenue and walk north for five blocks.

Tsuu T'ina Museum

Commemorating the history of the Sarcee peoples, this small museum features a model tepee and two headdresses dating to the late 1930s. Many displays were donated by the Provincial Museum in Edmonton. The museum is open Mon.–Fri. 8 A.M.–4 P.M.; admission by donation. It's located on the eastern flanks of the Sarcee Reserve at 3700 Anderson Road SW, 403/238-2677. The closest public transportation is the Anderson C-train station.

HISTORIC PARKS

Fort Calgary Historic Park

In 1875, with the onset of a harsh winter, the newly arrived NWMP built Fort Calgary at the confluence of the Bow and Elbow rivers in less than six weeks. The original fort was replaced by a more permanent brick building in 1914, but this was later demolished and, by the 1970s, the area was an industrial wasteland. Much work has taken place on the 16-hectare site in the ensuing quarter century, including the construction of an excellent interpretive center and an ambitious program to construct an exact replica of the original fort using tools and techniques that are more than 100 years old. Until the completion of the fort, all of the activity happens in the interpretive center, which re-creates the earliest days of Canada's famous "Mounties"—the legacy of natives, hardy pioneers, and the wild frontier they tamed. Slide presentations about the NWMP are shown every 30 minutes. It's free to wander around the grounds, but to really appreciate the hardships of Calgary's earliest European settlers, visit the interpretive center and partially completed fort; it's worth the adults $5.75, seniors $5, children $3.25 admission. The grounds (at 750 9th Ave. SE) are open year-round. To get there, either walk along the river from downtown or hop aboard bus number 1 (Forest Lawn) or number 14 (East Calgary) from 7th Avenue. The interpretive center, 403/290-1875, is open daily 9 A.M.–5 P.M.

Across the Elbow River from the interpretive center stands **Hunt House,** the oldest structure on its original site in Calgary. The house was built in 1876 for a Hudson's Bay Company employee. On the same side of the Elbow River as Hunt House is the larger **Deane House,** with sweeping river views. Built in 1906 for a commanding officer of the NWMP, this is one of the oldest restored homes in the city. Over the years, it has been used as a stationmaster's house, boardinghouse, and artists' co-op. Since being restored in 1983, it has operated as a teahouse. The menu features light lunches, mainly salads, sandwiches, and traditional English desserts. Those with a hearty appetite should try the Captain's Tea Plate ($16.95 for two). The Deane House, 403/269-7747, is open daily 11 A.M.–2 P.M.; call for reservations.

Heritage Park

This 26-hectare park is located on a peninsula jutting into Glenbow Reservoir southwest of downtown. More than 100 buildings and exhibits help re-create an early-20th-century pioneer village. Many of the buildings have been moved to the park from their original locations. Highlights include a Hudson's Bay Company fort, a two-story outhouse, a working blacksmith's shop, an 1896 church, a tepee, and an old schoolhouse with original desks. A boardwalk links stores crammed with antiques, and horse-drawn buggies carry passengers along the streets. You can also ride in authentic passenger cars pulled by a steam locomotive or enjoy a cruise in a paddlewheeler on the reservoir. A traditional bakery sells cakes and pastries, and full meals are served in the Wainwright Hotel (including an excellent Sunday brunch served 10 A.M.–2 P.M. in winter). Park admission only is $11; admission with all rides is $18. General admission for children is $7; $14 with the rides. It's open mid-May to August, daily 9 A.M.–5 P.M., until 6 P.M. on weekends; breakfast is included with admissions before 9 A.M. Between September and early October, the park is open weekends only, 9 A.M.–5 P.M. The park is located at 1900 Heritage Drive SW, 403/259-1900. To

Irish-born Sam Livingston was Calgary's first official settler.

PROVINCIAL ARCHIVES OF ALBERTA

get there by bus, take number 53 south from downtown or take the Anderson C-train to Heritage Station and transfer to bus number 20 (Northmount).

CANADA OLYMPIC PARK

On the western outskirts of the city, beside the TransCanada Highway, is 95-hectare Canada Olympic Park, which was developed for the 1988 Winter Olympic Games. Ski-jumping, luge, bobsled, freestyle skiing, and disabled events were held here. Now the park offers activities year-round, including tours of the facilities, luge rides, summer ski-jumping, and sports training camps. In winter, the beginner/intermediate runs are filled with Calgarians who are able to hit the snow as early as November with the help of a complex snowmaking system. Many ski-jumping, bobsled, and luge events of national and international standard are held here throughout winter.

Olympic Hall of Fame

This is North America's largest museum devoted to the Olympic Games. Three floors catalog the entire history of the Winter Olympic Games through more than 1,500 exhibits, interactive video displays, costumes and memorabilia, an athletes timeline, a bobsleigh and ski-jump simulator, and highlights from the last three Winter Olympic Games held at Albertville (France), Lillehammer (Norway), and Nagano (Japan). A new addition to the museum is Pathways to Olympic Glory, which tells the stories of four Canadian Olympians. The museum is open daily 10 A.M.–5 P.M.; admission is $4.50.

Ski-Jumping, Luge, and Bobsleigh Facilities

Visible from throughout the city are the 70- and 90-meter ski-jump towers, synonymous with the Winter Olympic Games. These two jumps are

The ski jumps at Canada Olympic Park are a city landmark.

still used for national and international competitions and training. A glass-enclosed elevator rises to the observation level. The jump complex has three additional jumps of 15, 30, and 50 meters, which are used for junior competitions and training. All but the 90-meter jump have plastic-surfaced landing strips and are used during summer.

At the western end of the park are the luge and bobsled tracks. A complex refrigeration system keeps the tracks usable even on relatively hot days (up to 28°C). Summer luge rides are $15 per person, or the really adventurous can ride the **Road Rocket,** North America's only summer bobsleigh ride, which reaches speeds of up to 100 kilometers per hour; $45 per person.

Practicalities

A "Grand Olympic Tour" package that includes admission to the Hall of Fame, a trip to the observation deck of the 90-meter-ski-jump tower, a short bus ride to the luge and bobsled tracks, and a movie showing highlights from the 1988 Winter Olympic Games is adults $10, children $6, or take a self-guided tour for $7 and $4, respectively.

On the main level of the day lodge is a gift shop selling Olympic souvenirs, books, and clothing. The former start-house for the luge is now the **Naturbahn Teahouse,** open in summer Mon.–Fri. 10 A.M.–5 P.M. and year-round for Sunday brunch ($13.95), 11 A.M.–4 P.M.; reserva-

tions required, call 403/247-5465. For general information on the park, call 403/247-5452. A **Tourist Information Centre** is located on the main level of the day lodge; open summer only, daily 9 A.M.–5 P.M.

OTHER PARKS

Calgary Zoo

The Calgary Zoo, Botanical Gardens, and Prehistoric Park, to use its full name, is one of Canada's finest zoos. It was established in 1920 near the heart of downtown on St. Georges Island and has become noted for its realistic simulation of animal habitats. Unique viewing areas have been designed to allow visitors the best look at the zoo's 1,000-plus animals. For example, underwater observation points provide a look at swimming polar bears and seals, and a darkened room allows visitors to watch nocturnal animals during their active periods (lights are turned on at night, reversing night and day). Other highlights include a section on Australian animals, exotic mammals, greenhouses filled with tropical birds, and Canadian Wilds displays featuring animals of the aspen parkland in one and those of northern forests in the other. In the Prehistoric Park section, the world of dinosaurs is brought to life with 27 full-size replicas set amid plantlife and rock formations supposedly similar to those found in Alberta in prehistoric times, but looking more like badlands. The zoo also has a fast-food restaurant and several picnic areas. Admission is $10 for adults (half-price for seniors Tues.–Thurs.) and $5 for youths younger than 17. It's open in summer daily 9 A.M.–6 P.M., the rest of the year 9 A.M.–4 P.M. The Prehistoric Park section is only open June–Sept. and is free with general grounds admission. The zoo is located at 1300 Zoo Road NE. The main parking lot is off Memorial Drive, just west of the Deerfoot Trail. For more information, call 403/232-9300 or 403/232-9372 (recorded message). From downtown, take the Whitehorn C-train northeast.

Stampede Park

Best known for hosting the Calgary Exhibition and Stampede, these grounds south of downtown are used for many activities and events year-round. In the center of the park is the saddle-shaped 18,800-seat **Saddledome,** which boasts the world's largest cable-suspended roof and is one of Calgary's most impressive structures. It was used for the ice-hockey and figure-skating events during the 1988 Winter Olympic Games and is now home to the NHL Calgary Flames. "The Dome" is constantly in use for concerts, trade shows, and entertainment events. One-hour tours of the Saddledome are given on weekdays (nonevent days). Groups are preferred, but if you're interested, and don't have a family of 10, call ahead and ask anyway, 403/261-0400. The **Grain Academy** on the Plus 15 level of the **Roundup Centre,** 403/263-4594, is a museum cataloging the history of cereal-based agriculture in the province through working models and hands-on displays. It's open April–Sept. Mon.–Fri. 10 A.M.–4 P.M., Saturday noon–4 P.M. Admission is free. The Big Four Building and Agriculture Building also host trade shows and exhibitions, and thoroughbred and harness racing takes place on the grounds year-round. Stampede Park is located at 17th Avenue and 2nd Street SE. Take the C-train from downtown to Victoria Park/Stampede or Stampede/Erlton.

Sam Livingston Fish Hatchery

Pearce Estate Park, a pleasant spot for a picnic, is home to this hatchery. The facility produces approximately 3.5 million trout per year, which are used to stock 300 lakes and rivers throughout the province. A self-guided tour (grab a brochure at the main office) leads through the hatchery, from the incubation room to holding tanks and an area containing various displays. In summer the hatchery is open Mon.–Fri. 10 A.M.–4 P.M., Sat.–Sun. 1–5 P.M.; the rest of the year weekdays only. To reach the park and hatchery, 403/297-6561, take 17th Avenue east from the city and turn north onto 17th Street SE.

Inglewood Bird Sanctuary

More than 260 species of birds have been noted in this 32-hectare park on the bank of the Bow River, east of downtown. The land was originally owned by a member of the NWMP and was established as a park in 1929. Walking trails are open year-round, an interpretive center in summer only, Mon.–Thurs. 10 A.M.–8 P.M., Fri.–Sun. 10 A.M.–5 P.M. Take 9th Avenue SE to Sanctuary Rd., and follow the signs to a parking area on the south bank of the river, 403/269-6688. On weekdays, bus number 14 East turns off 9th Avenue at 17th Street SE, which is only a short walk from the park.

Nose Hill Park

This oasis of prairie surrounded by residential development lies northwest of downtown. The land was bought up in the late 1960s and remains in a totally natural state. The park has no

---

MIDNAPORE

The last rest stop for early travelers along the Macleod Trail, linking Fort Macleod to Fort Calgary, was just south of Fish Creek. A trading post and crude cabins constituted the town. The post office opened and was manned by a postmaster with dubious reading skills. One of the first parcels he received was addressed to Midnapore, India, and had been misdirected through him. Fear of losing his job kept him from asking too many questions, and as the community had no official name he directed that all mail to this post be addressed to Midnapore. The name stuck and that's how a suburb of Calgary came to have the same name as an Indian city on the opposite side of the world.

formed pathways or planted gardens, just 1,127 hectares of fescue grasslands bisected by wooded coulees and rough trails, much like natives would have encountered thousands of years ago. To get to the park, take 14th Street NW north out of downtown; this street forms the park's eastern boundary, and John Laurie Boulevard runs along its southern boundary.

Fish Creek Provincial Park
At the southern edge of the city, this 1,170-hectare park is one of the largest urban parks in North America. Many prehistoric sites have been discovered on its grounds, including campsites and buffalo jumps. In more recent times, the Calgary–Fort Benton Trail passed through the park. The site—much of which was once owned by Patrick Burns, the meat magnate—was officially declared a park in 1975. Three geographical regions meet in the area, giving the park a diversity of habitat. Stands of aspen and spruce predominate, but a mixed-grass prairie, as well as balsam, poplar, and willow can be found along the floodplains at the east end of the park. The ground is colorfully carpeted with 364 recorded species of wildflowers, and wildlife is abundant. Mule deer and ground squirrels are common, and white-tailed deer, coyotes, beavers, and the occasional moose are also present. An interpretive trail begins south of Bow Valley Ranch and leads through a grove of balsam and poplar to a shallow, conglomerate cave. An information display is located on the west side of Macleod Trail overlooking the site of Alberta's first woolen mill. To get to the main information center, turn east on Canyon Meadows Drive, then south on Bow River Bottom Trail. For more information, call 403/297-5293.

RECREATION

OUTDOOR ACTIVITIES

Calgary Parks and Recreation, 403/268-1311, operates a wide variety of recreational facilities, including swimming pools and golf courses, throughout the city. They also run a variety of excursions, such as canoeing and horseback riding, as well as inexpensive courses that range from fly-tying to rock-climbing. The **Calgary Area Outdoor Council,** www.calcna.ab.ca/cfns, is another good source of recreation information.

Walking and Biking
A good way to get a feel for the city is by walking or biking along the 210 kilometers of paved trails within the city limits. The trail system is concentrated along the Bow River as it winds through the city; other options are limited. Along the riverbank, the trail passes through numerous parks and older neighborhoods to various sights such as Fort Calgary and Inglewood Bird Sanctuary. From Fort Calgary, a trail passes under 9th Avenue SE and follows the Elbow River, crossing it several times before ending at Glenmore Reservoir and Heritage Park. Ask at tourist information centers for a map detailing all trails. Bicycle rentals ($20–25 per day) are available from **Rapid Rent** (903 Heritage Dr. SW, 403/253-2975). During summer at **Calgary Olympic Park,** west of downtown along the TransCanada Highway, chairlifts access 25 kilometers of mountain-biking trails; rentals and repairs are available at the day lodge.

Swimming
Calgary Parks and Recreation, 403/268-1311, operates nine outdoor pools (open June–early Sept.) and 12 indoor pools (open year-round). Facilities at each vary. Admission at indoor pools includes the use of the sauna, hot tub, and exercise room. Admission to all pools is $4.50.

The **YMCA** (101 3rd St. SW, 403/269-6701) is a modern fitness center beside Eau Claire Market at the north end of downtown. All facilities are first class, including an Olympic-size pool, a weight room, an exercise room, a jogging track, squash courts, a hot tub, and a sauna. It's open Mon.–Fri. 5:30 A.M.–10 P.M., Sat.–Sun. 7:30 A.M.–6:30 P.M.; admission is $8.

Golfing
More than 30 public, semiprivate, and private golf courses are located in and around the city

ballooning over Calgary

ALBERTA TOURISM

limits. Many courses begin opening in April for a season that extends for up to seven months. The courses operated by Calgary Parks and Recreation are all public. Those with 18 holes include **Maple Ridge** (1240 Maple Glade Dr. SE, 403/974-1825; greens fee $28); **McCall Lake** (1600 32nd Ave. NE, 403/974-1805; $28); and **Shaganappi Point** (1200 26th St. SW, 403/974-1810; $18). Each has a pro shop with club rentals. **Fox Hollow Golf Club** (at the corner of Deerfoot Trail and 32nd Ave. NE, 403/277-4653) is another public course, with greens fee of $31 and the longest season of all Calgary courses. It also features an indoor full-flight driving range, which is open year-round.

The aforementioned courses are all handy to downtown; although the following three are farther out, each offers a unique golfing experience. **Springbank Links** (125 Hackamore Trail NW, Springbank, 403/202-2000) offers nine holes of true target golf and nine holes of links-style play with knee-high rough; greens fee $45. **Elbow Springs Golf Club** (southwest of the city along Highway 8, 403/246-2800) is flatter, and a relatively easy 27-hole layout but still challenging from the back markers. One unique feature are the ponds stocked with *huge* rainbow trout; $51 per round. **Heritage Pointe Golf and Country Club** (south of downtown on Dunmore Rd., 403/256-2002) is generally regarded as one of Canada's best courses that allows public play. A stop on the Canadian Professional Tour,

this course comprises three distinct sets of nine holes; $90 includes a cart.

Ballooning

All summer, hot-air balloons can be seen floating peacefully over the city. Various companies offer flights, but be prepared to pay a lot for the experience (usually $160). One of the most professional companies is **Aero Dynamics** (4215 72nd Ave. SE, 403/287-9393). Launch sites vary depending on the wind direction, the basic aim being to float over the downtown area. After making a reservation, you will be contacted one hour before launch time and asked to meet at the Aero Dynamics office, from where you'll be ferried to the launch site and back. Flights generally last 90 minutes, and the cost includes all transportation, a champagne reception on landing, and a framed picture of your flight.

Calaway Park

This is western Canada's largest outdoor amusement park, with 24 rides, including a double-loop roller coaster. Other attractions include an enormous maze, a golf driving range, Western-themed mini-golf, a zoo for the kids, a trout-fishing pond, live entertainment in the Western-style "Showtime Theatre," and many restaurants and eateries. Admission to the park is $8, or $19.50 with unlimited rides. For children younger than seven and seniors, admission with unlimited rides is only $14.50. The park is located 10 kilometers west of the city limits on Springbank Road, 403/240-3822. It's open in summer daily 10 A.M.–8 P.M.; in May, June, and September, Friday 5–10 P.M. and weekends 10 A.M.–8 P.M.

Leisure Centers

The large **Family Leisure Centre** (11150 Bonaventure Dr. SE, 403/278-7542) is an excellent facility offering a giant indoor water slide, a wave pool, swimming pools, a steam room and sauna, a weight room, an ice-skating rink, a lounge, and a restaurant. It's open daily 9 A.M.–9 P.M., but the wave pool operates only during certain sessions; admission is $6–8. Similar facilities are **Village Square Leisure Centre** (2623 56th St. NE, 403/280-9714) and **Southland Leisure Centre** (just off Macleod Trail at 2000 Southland Dr. SW, 403/251-3505).

Kart Gardens (5202 1st St. SW, 403/250-9555) has one go-kart track where you can reach speeds of 80 kilometers per hour, and another slower, twisting one for first-time drivers. The park also has kiddy karts, mini-golf, and a snack bar. Open in summer only from 11 A.M. to dusk.

Winter Activities

When Calgarians talk about going skiing or snowboarding for the day, they are usually referring to the five world-class winter resorts in the Rockies, a 1.5-hour drive to the west. The city's only downhill facilities are at **Canada Olympic Park,** 403/247-3452. Although the park has world-class luge, bobsled, and ski-jumping facilities, snowmaking capabilities, one quad chair, two triple chairs, and a T-bar, its vertical rise is only 150 meters. On the plus side, however, are the extensive lodge facilities, excellent teaching staff, ski and snowboard rentals, and night skiing and snowboarding until 10 P.M. on weeknights. Lift tickets cost $22 per day or $17 for four hours.

SPECTATOR SPORTS

Ice Hockey

Calgary's favorite sports team is the **Calgary Flames,** the city's NHL franchise. The Olympic Saddledome in Stampede Park fills with 20,000 ice-hockey fans who follow every game with a passion; the atmosphere at a home game is electric. The season runs from October–April, and games are usually held in the early evening (7 P.M. weeknights, 8 P.M. Saturday, 6 P.M. Sunday). The Flames are among the most competitive of NHL Canadian franchises, although with the recent drop in exchange rates, like all other Canadian teams, the Flames find it difficult to compete with the U.S. teams when it comes to top-dollar player salaries. They last won the Stanley Cup in 1989. Tickets aren't cheap, starting at $18 for nosebleed seats during the regular season. For general information, call 403/777-2177, www.calgaryflames.com; for tickets, call 403/777-0000.

Baseball

The **Calgary Cannons** are the top affiliate farm team for the Chicago White Sox and play in the AAA Pacific Coast League during the regular baseball season (April–October). Tickets start at $7; seats closest to the home plate cost $10. The team plays at Burns Stadium on Crowchild Trail, across from the Banff Trail C-train station. For home-game dates and ticket information, call 403/284-1111.

Football

The **Stampeders** are Calgary's franchise in the Canadian Football League, an organization similar to the U.S. NFL, with slight modifications. The team's popularity fluctuates with its performance, but it usually does well enough to have a chance at finals time in November when the best teams compete for the Grey Cup. Later in the season, weather can be a deciding factor in both the games' results and attendance. At kickoff in the Stampeders' final game of 1993, the temperature was –20°C and –33°C with the windchill, but more than 20,000 Calgarians braved the weather to attend. The season runs from July–November. Home games are played at **McMahon Stadium** at the University of Calgary, 1817 Crowchild Trail NW. Take the C-train to Banff Trail Station. Tickets range from $25–45. For more information, call 403/289-0258, www.stampeders.com.

Soccer

Soccer is gaining popularity in North America, and Calgary is home to the first facility on the continent specially designed for playing soccer indoors. The **Calgary Soccer Centre** features six indoor fields (plus outdoor fields); games are played each evening and on weekends, but the building is always open (free admission). The complex is located off Glenmore Trail at 7000 48th Street SE, 403/279-8453.

Motor Racing

Race City Motorsport Park has three world-class tracks and is the premier motorsport facility in western Canada. It hosts national stock-car, motorcycle, and drag-racing events through summer Saturday at 7 P.M. and Sunday at 1 P.M. Prices vary according to event but generally run $10–21. The speedway is located at 68th Street SE and 114th Avenue. For upcoming events, call 403/272-7223.

ARTS AND ENTERTAINMENT

Calgary Straight and *ffwd* are weekly magazines available freely throughout the city that list theater events, cinema screenings, and art displays, to keep everyone abreast of the local music scene. Tickets to most major performances are available in advance from **Ticketmaster**, 403/777-0000, www.ticketmaster.ca.

Art Galleries

It may put a dent in Calgary's cowtown image, but the city does have a remarkable number of galleries displaying and selling work by Albertan and Canadian artisans. Unfortunately, they are not concentrated in any one area, and most require some effort to find. The **Micah Gallery** is the exception. It's right downtown on Stephen Avenue Mall (110 8th Ave. SW, 403/245-1340). The **Bearclaw Gallery** (1301 17th Ave. SW, 403/228-6533) features a wide variety of native arts and crafts, including Inuit soapstone carvings. In the same vicinity, the **Collectors Gallery** (829 17th Ave. SW, 403/245-8300) sells the work of prominent 19th- and 20th-century Canadian artists.

Theater

Calgary's Western image belies a cultural diversity that goes further than being able to get a few foreign beers at the local dance hall. In fact, the city has 10 professional theater companies,

an opera, an orchestra, and a ballet troupe. The main season for performances is September–May. For details on exact dates and prices, contact the companies directly or pick up a copy of *City Scope,* which is available free throughout the city.

Alberta Theatre Projects, 403/294-7475, is a well-established company based in the Calgary Centre for Performing Arts at 205 8th Avenue SE, beside the Glenbow Museum. Usual performances are of contemporary material. **Theatre Calgary,** 403/294-7440, is also based in Calgary Centre but performs in the city's other world-class facility, the Max Bell Theatre at 220 9th Avenue; tickets range from $10–40. **Lunchbox Theatre,** located on the second floor of Bow Valley Square (205 5th Ave. SW, 403/265-4292), usually features comedy productions Mon.–Sat. at noon. Tickets are $7. For adult-oriented experimental productions, head to **One Yellow Rabbit** (205 8th Ave. SW, 403/244-9177). **Storybook Theatre** (2140 9th Ave., 403/216-0808) specializes in children's productions.

Theatersports is a concept of improvisation-comedy theater that developed at the University of Calgary in the 1970s. The original performances led to the formation of the **Loose Moose Theatre Company,** which today offers this light-hearted form of entertainment Friday and Saturday nights at Garry Theatre (1229 9th Ave. SE, Inglewood, 403/265-5682).

Music and Dance

Calgary Opera, 403/262-7286, performs at the Jubilee Auditorium (1415 14th Ave. NW) Oct.–April. Tickets range from $20–80. The Jack Singer Concert Hall at the Calgary Centre for Performing Arts is home to the **Calgary Philharmonic Orchestra,** 403/571-0270, one of Canada's top orchestras. **Alberta Ballet** performs at locations throughout the city; for dates and ticketing details, call 403/245-4222.

Cinemas

Most major shopping malls—including Eau Claire Market, closest to downtown—have a **Cineplex Odeon** cinema. For information, call the 24-hour film line at 403/263-3166. Also in Eau Claire Market is an **IMAX Theatre,** 403/974-4629, with a screen that is five-and-a-half stories tall. Tickets are $7.25, or $10.50 for a double feature.

Uptown Stage & Screen (612 8th Ave. SW, 403/265-0120) is a newly restored downtown theater featuring alternative, art, and foreign films. Over the Bow River from downtown, the **Plaza Theatre** (1133 Kensington Rd. NW, Kensington, 403/283-3636) shows everything from mainstream to alternative.

Casinos

Calgary has a few low-key Alberta-style casinos that have little glitz and low maximum bets. They include **Elbow River Inn and Casino** (1919 Macleod Trail SE, 403/266-4355); **Stampede Casino** (Big Four Building, Stampede Park, 403/261-0422); **Frank Sisson's Silver Dollar Casino** (1010 42nd Ave. SE, 403/287-1183); and **Cash Casino** (4040 Blackfoot Trail SE, 403/287-1635). All casions open at noon and close sometime between midnight and 2 A.M.

Bars and Nightclubs

With a nickname like "Cowtown," it's not surprising that some of Calgary's hottest nightspots play country music. Along Macleod Trail are three favorites: **Ranchman's** (9615 Macleod Trail SW, 403/253-1100) is *the* place to check out first, especially during Stampede Week. Some of country's hottest stars have played this authentic honky-tonk. Food is served at a bar out front all day, then at 7 P.M. the large dance hall opens. The hall is a museum of rodeo memorabilia and photographs, with a chuck wagon hanging from the ceiling. Most nights feature live performances, and on Sunday mornings a church service is held. **Cowboy's** (826 5th St. SW, 403/265-0699) has a Western theme but attracts a young, hip crowd with country and rock bands, promotions, and a perky wait staff. A few blocks east, the famous Dusty's Saloon has been given new life as **Desperados** (1088 Olympic Way SE, 403/263-5343), with more than 40 televisions, a pool room, and a large dance floor.

The aforementioned three bars are open for lunch and offer a quiet atmosphere through the afternoon. All major downtown hotels have lounges, which is the best option for a drink away from the crowds. On Stephen Avenue Mall, in an old bank building, **James Joyce Irish Pub** (114 8th Ave. SW, 403/262-0708) has Guinness beer on tap and a menu of traditional British dishes. **The Garage** (in Eau Claire Market, 403/262-6762) is popular for its pool tables and afternoon happy hour. The **King Edward Hotel** (438 9th Ave. NE, 403/262-1680) and the **St. Louis Hotel** (at 8th Ave. NE and 4th St., 403/262-6341) are two old hotels that have survived the modernization of downtown.

Calgary's infamous Electric Avenue, a once-colorful strip of after-dark action, has lost its glitz and glamour in recent years. Most nightclubs have moved or closed, and the late-night set moved along with them. One of Calgary's most infamous nightspots is the **Back Alley** (4630 Macleod Trail SW, 403/287-2500), which has outlasted the other flash-in-the-pans of Electric Avenue. If you desire live music, head to the **Backstreet Bar** in the Smuggler's Inn (6920 Macleod Trail, 403/252-4365), open nightly except Sunday, or to **Buckingham's** (805 9th St. SW, 403/233-7550). Popular nightclubs include **The Palace,** an upmarket dance club (219 8th Ave. SW, 403/263-9980); **Mercury** (801 17th St. SW, 403/541-1175), attracting a young, hip crowd for its cocktail-bar ambience; **Crazy Horse** (downstairs at 1311 1st St. SW, 403/266-1133); **Concorde** (510 17th Ave. SW, 403/228-4757), with live music weeknights and DJs on weekends; and the alternative **Narcissus** (1213 Macleod Trail SE, 403/262-4242), where a DJ spins gothic and industrial tracks.

Jazz, Blues, and Comedy

The **Classic Jazz Guild of Calgary,** 403/244-8013, performs throughout the year at the Jack Singer Concert Hall. One of the most popular jazz clubs in town is **Kao's Jazz and Blues Bistro** (718 17th Ave. SW, 403/228-9997), with live performances Wed.–Sun. and a recently opened patio. **Beat Niq** (at the lower level of 811 1st St., 403/263-1650) is a New York–style jazz club that welcomes everyone.

The best place to listen to blues is the **King Edward Hotel** (438 9th Ave. SE, 403/262-1680), with live performances most nights and jazz jams on Saturday and Sunday. This place has hosted all of the legends, including Buddy Guy and Junior Wells.

Yuk Yuk's Komedy Kabaret is in the Blackfoot Inn (5940 Blackfoot Trail SE, 403/258-2028). Shows run Wed.–Sun. nights, and tickets are $7–12.

SHOPPING

Plazas and Malls

The largest shopping center downtown is **Calgary Eaton Centre,** on Stephen Avenue Mall at 4th Street SW. This center is linked to other plazas by the Plus 15 Walkway System, which provides shelter from the elements. Other downtown shopping complexes are **Eau Claire Market,** at the entrance to Prince's Island Park, where the emphasis is on fresh foods and trendy boutiques; **TD Square,** at 7th Avenue and 2nd Street SW; and **The Bay,** part of Alberta's history with its link to the Hudson's Bay Company. **Uptown 17** is a strip of more than 400 retail shops, restaurants, and galleries along 17th Avenue SW. **Kensington,** across the Bow River from downtown, is an eclectic mix of specialty shops.

Camping Gear and Western Wear

Mountain Equipment Co-op (830 10th Ave. SW, 403/269-2420) is Calgary's largest camping store. This massive outlet boasts an extensive range of high-quality clothing, climbing and mountaineering equipment (including a climbing wall), tents, sleeping bags, kayaks and canoes, books and maps, and other accessories. The store is a cooperative owned by its members, similiar to the American R.E.I. stores, except that to purchase anything you must be a member (a once-only $5 charge). To order a copy of the co-op's mail-order catalog, call 800/663-2667. Just down the road, a similar supply of equipment is offered at **Totem Outdoor Outfitters** (341 10th Ave. SW, 403/264-6363).

Smaller, yet with a good variety of equipment, is the **Hostel Shop** (1414 Kensington Rd. NW, 403/283-8311), operated by Hostelling International.

Alberta Boot Co. (614 10th Ave. SW, 403/263-4623), within walking distance of downtown, is Alberta's only Western boot manufacturer. This outlet shop has thousands of pairs for sale in all shapes and sizes, all made from leather. You'll find **Lammle's Western Wear** outlets in all the major malls, including the Eaton Centre. Another popular Western outfitter is **Riley & McCormick,** in Eau Claire Market.

FESTIVALS AND EVENTS

Spring

In conjunction with **Roughstock,** Calgary's rodeo season kicks off with **Rodeo Royal** at the Saddledome on the third weekend of March. **Calgary International Children's Festival** is the third week of May. Events include theater, puppetry, and performances by musicians from around the world. It's held in Jack Singer Concert Hall and Olympic Plaza; call 403/294-7414 for details. In late June, **Carifest** is a 10-day celebration of everything Carribean, including food, music and dancing, and a parade.

Calgary Stampede

Few cities in the world are associated as closely with an event as Calgary is with the Calgary Stampede. For details of the "Greatest Outdoor Show on Earth," held each summer in July, see the following section.

Summer

Jazz Festival Calgary features various jazz and blues artists at clubs and concert halls throughout the city during the last week of June. For locations, call 403/249-1119. **Canada Day** is celebrated on July 1 in Prince's Island Park and Heritage Park. The **Calgary Folk Music Festival,**403/233-0904, held the last week of July, is an indoor and outdoor extravaganza of Canadian and international performers. The second week of August is **Afrikadey!,**403/234-9110, with performances and workshops by African-influenced musicians and artists, and screenings of African-themed films.

Fall

In October, **hockey** and **skiing and snowboarding** fever hits the city as the **NHL Calgary Flames** start their season and the first snow flies. The first weekend of October is **Cody Snyder's Bull Bustin',** which brings together the world's top bull riders for two nights at the Saddledome. Early October also sees screenings of movies at the **Calgary International Film Festival,**403/283-1490. This is followed by **Wordfest,** where authors talk about their books, workshops are given, and many readings take place at venues throughout the city and in Banff. A good place for kids on Halloween is Calgary Zoo, where **Boo at the Zoo** celebrations take place.

Winter

Calgary has joined other major Canadian cities by celebrating New Year's Eve with a **First Night** festival. Although severely curtailed by the weather, Calgarians enjoy the winter with the opening of the theater, ballet, and opera seasons. National and international ski-jumping, luge, and bobsledding events are held at **Canada Olympic Park** November–March. The 11-day **Calgary Winter Festival** takes place in early February at locations throughout the city; call 403/543-5480 for details.

Spruce Meadows

This equestrian mecca, one of the world's greatest, is an oasis among the sprawling ranches that surround the city. An endless line of white paddock fencing surrounds the 120-hectare village, which has an international-events ring the size of a football field, two indoor arenas, six grassed warm-up rings, and a three-story tournament center. The name Spruce Meadows is marked on the calendars of all the world's best riders. Each year the site hosts four major events offering more than $26 million in prize money, drawing in 300,000 spectators, and attracting a television audience of millions. The four biggest tournaments are the **National,** during the first week of June; **Canada One,** on the last weekend of June; the **North American,** held early July, on the first weekend of the Stampede, and the **Masters,** the second week of September. The Masters is the world's richest show-jumping tournament. Up to 30,000 enthusiasts gather at the Masters each day. Admissionj is just $6, making it an affordable day out. For information on Spruce Meadows, call 403/254-3200, www.sprucemeadows.com. To get there, take Macleod Trail south to Highway 22X, and turn right toward the mountains.

CALGARY STAMPEDE

Every July, the city's perennial rough-and-ready Cowtown image is thrust to the forefront when a fever known as Stampede hits town. For 10 days, Calgarians let their hair down—business leaders don Stetsons, bankers wear boots, half the town walks around in too-tight denim outfits, and the rate of serious crime drops. Nine months later, maternity hospitals report a rise in business. For most Calgarians, it is known simply as The Week (always capitalized). The Stampede is many things to many people but is certainly not for the cynic. It is a celebration of the city's past—of endless sunny days when life was broncos, bulls, and steers, of cowboys riding through the streets, and saloons on every corner. But it is not just about the past. It's the Cowtown image Calgarians cherish and the frontier image that visitors expect. On downtown streets, everyone is your neighbor. Flapjacks and bacon are served free of charge around the city; normally staid citizens shout "Ya-HOO!" for no particular reason; Indians ride up and down the streets on horseback; and there's drinking and dancing until dawn every night.

The celebration epicenter is **Stampede Park,** immediately south of the city center, where more than 100,000 people converge each day. The nucleus of the Stampede, the park hosts the world's richest outdoor rodeo and the just-as-spectacular chuck wagon races, where professional cowboys from all over the planet compete in a winner-take-all $50,000 showdown. But Stampede Park offers a lot more than a show of cowboy skills. The gigantic midway takes at least a day to get around: a staggering number of attractions, displays, and free entertainment cost only the price of gate admission; some of the biggest stars in country music perform; and a glittering grandstand show, complete with fireworks, ends each day's shenanigans.

History

Earlier this century, Guy Weadick, an American cowpoke, got the idea that people would pay to see traditional cowboy skills combined with vaudeville showmanship. With the backing of four Calgarian businessmen who contributed $25,000 each, Weadick put on an inaugural show billed as "The Last and Best Great West Frontier Days." The name was a reference to the fact that many people thought the cattle industry in Alberta was near its end, and that wheat would soon be king. On September 2, 1912, the show kicked off with a parade of cowboys and more than 2,000 Indians in traditional dress. Its popularity proved so immense that the competition was extended two days. Canada's governor general, the Duke of Connaught, opened the show and enjoyed himself so much that he stayed for the duration. An estimated 60,000 people lined the streets for the parade, and 40,000 attended each day of rodeo events. This turnout was amazing, considering that barely more than 65,000 people lived in Calgary at the time. The prize money for the rodeo was an incredible $20,000. The highlight of the event was on the final day when Tom Three Persons, a little-known Blood Indian rider from southern Alberta, rode the legendary bronc "Cyclone" for eight seconds to collect the world-championship saddle and $1,000.

The following year, Weadick took the show to Winnipeg, then World War I intervened, and not until 1919 was the Calgary show revived with Weadick at the helm. In the era of popular Hollywood Westerns, Weadick convinced moviemakers down south that the event was worthy of screening. In 1925, *Calgary Stampede* was released, putting the city on the map. As it turned out, the inaugural show wasn't the first and last, but rather the beginning of an annual extravaganza that is billed, and rightly so, as "The Greatest Outdoor Show on Earth."

EVENTS

Stampede Parade

Although Stampede Park opens on Thursday evening for **Sneek-a-peek** (an event that alone attracts approximately 40,000 eager patrons), Stampede Week officially begins Friday morning with a spectacular parade through the streets of downtown Calgary. The approximately 150 parade participants include close to 4,000 people and 700 horses, and the procession takes two hours to pass any one point. It features an amazing array of floats, each cheered by 250,000 people who line the streets up to 10 deep. The

loudest "Ya-HOOs" are usually reserved for Alberta's oldest residents, Stampede royalty, and members of Calgary's professional sports teams, but this is the Stampede, so even politicians and street sweepers elicit enthusiastic cheers.

The parade proceeds west along 6th Avenue from 2nd Street SE, then south on 10th Street SW and east on 9th Avenue. Starting time is 9 A.M., but crowds start gathering at 6 A.M. and you'll be lucky to get a front-row spot much after 7 A.M.

Rodeo

The pinnacle of any cowboy's career is walking away with the $50,000 winner-take-all on the last day of competition in the Calgary Stampede. For the first eight days, heats are held each afternoon from 1:30 P.M., with finals held the last Saturday and Sunday. Although Stampede Week is about a lot more than the rodeo, everyone loves to watch this event. Cowboys compete in bronc riding, bareback riding, bull riding, calf roping, and steer wrestling, and cowgirls compete in barrel racing. Wild cow milking, a wild horse race, bull fighting, and nonstop chatter from hilarious rodeo clowns all keep the action going between the more traditional rodeo events.

Chuck Wagon Races

The **Rangeland Derby** chuck wagon races feature nine heats each evening starting at 8 P.M. At the end of the week, the top four drivers from the preliminary rounds compete in a winner-take-all, $50,000 dash-for-the-cash final. Chuck wagon racing is an exciting sport any time, but at the Stampede the pressure is intense as drivers push themselves to stay in the running. The grandstand in the infield makes steering the chuck wagons through an initial figure eight difficult, heightening the action before they burst onto the track for what is known as the Half Mile of Hell to the finish line. The first team across the finish line does not always win the race; drivers must avoid 34 penalties, ranging from one to 10 seconds added to the overall time.

Rope Square

During the Stampede, downtown's Olympic Plaza is known as Rope Square. Every morning, 8:30–10:30 A.M., free pancake breakfasts are served from the back of chuck wagons. For the rest of the morning, the square is the scene for a variety of entertainment, which might include country-music bands, native dance groups, marching bands, or mock gunfights. West along Stephen Avenue Mall, square dancing takes place each morning at 10 A.M. Also at 10, horse-drawn carriages leave the Palliser Hotel for an hour-long tour through town. Get there early to ensure that you get seats.

OTHER ENTERTAINMENT

The cavernous **Roundup Centre** holds various commercial exhibits and demonstrations (plenty of free samples), an International Photo Salon with prints submitted from around the world, Kitchen Theatre showcasing Calgary's culinary scene, and a Western Art Auction. At

RODEO EVENTS

For those watching for the first time, a rodeo can look like organized confusion. Although staying on the animals isn't as easy as professional cowboys make it look, learning the rules is, and it will make the events more enjoyable. The rodeo is made up of six basic events, three of which are judged on points and three of which are timed. Other team contests are included by the organizers to liven things up even more.

Bareback Riding
In this event, the rider doesn't use a saddle or reins. He is cinched to a handhold and leather pad attached to the horse's back. The idea is to stay on the wildly bucking horse for eight seconds. As the cowboy leaves the chute, he must keep both spurs above the horse's shoulders until the horse's front hooves hit the ground. Riders are judged on style

and rhythm, which is achieved by spurring effectively and remaining in control. The cowboy is disqualified if he doesn't last eight seconds, if he loses a stirrup, or if he touches the animal with his hand. Scores are given out of 100, with a possible 50 points allotted for the horse's power and bucking pattern and a maximum of 50 awarded to the rider, judged on his control and spurring action. Scores above 85 are usually good enough to win.

Saddle Bronc Riding
This event differs from bareback riding in that the horse is saddled and the rider, rather than being cinched to the animal, hangs onto a rein attached to the halter. Again, both spurs must be above the horse's shoulders after the first jump. Bronc riding is one of the classic rodeo events, and when performed properly is a joy to watch. Riders are judged by

saddle bronc riding

the front of the Roundup Centre is **Stampede Corral,** where you might find dog shows, the Calgary Stampede Show Band, or a talent show for seniors. **Stampede Square** is an outdoor entertainment venue where modern rides such as a reverse bungee are set up. Free phones are also provided here to call anywhere in Canada. A petting zoo and other activities keep the little ones entertained. A **midway** extends along the western edge of the park with the **Safeway Skyride** overhead.

The agricultural displays are situated in the center of Stampede Park. **Centennial Fair** is an outdoor stage with events for children such as duck races and magicians. In the **Agricultural Building,** livestock is displayed, and next door in the **John Deere Show Ring,** the World Blacksmith's Competition and horse shows take place.

spurring action and are disqualified for falling before eight seconds have elapsed. The highest score ever achieved in this event was a 95 by Australian Glenn O'Neill at the Innisfail Rodeo in 1996.

Bull Riding

Traditionally the last event in a rodeo, bull riding is considered to be the most exciting eight seconds in sport. The cowboy must hang onto an 1,800-pound bull for the required eight seconds with as much control as possible. No spurring is required (for obvious reasons), although if he gets the chance to do so, it earns the cowboy extra points. Disqualification occurs if the cowboy's loose hand touches either himself or the animal, or if he doesn't last the eight seconds, which is the case more often than not. Like bareback riding, the cowboy has one hand cinched to the animal in a handhold of braided rope. Riders are tied so tightly to the animal that if they are bucked off on the side away from their riding hand, they often become "hung up" and are dragged around like a rag doll until rescued by a rodeo clown. Scores are given out of 100; because of the difficulty in bull riding, just staying on for eight seconds ensures a good ride, but look for a score of around 85 to win.

Calf Roping

This timed event has its roots in the Old West, when calves had to be roped and tied down to receive a brand or medical treatment. The calf is released from a chute, closely followed by a mounted cowboy. The cowboy must lasso the calf, dismount, race to the animal, and tie a "pigging string" around any three of its legs. The cowboy then throws his hands into the air to signal the end of his run. After remounting his horse, the cowboy rides forward, slackening the rope. He's disqualified if the calf's legs don't remain tied for six seconds. The fastest time wins, with a 10-second penalty for breaking the gate. Any score under eight seconds is good.

Steer Wrestling

Also known as "bull-dogging," this timed event is for the big boys. The steer, which may weight up to five times that of a cowboy, jumps out of the chute, closely followed by a "hazer" (mounted cowboy), who rides alongside, jumps off his horse at full speed, and slides onto the steer's back, attempting to get hold of its horns. The cowboy slows down by digging his feet into the ground, using a twisting motion to throw the steer to the ground. The fastest time wins. Look for a winning score under four seconds (the world record is 2.2 seconds).

Barrel Racing

This is the only rodeo event for women. Riders must guide their horse around three barrels, set in a cloverleaf pattern, before making a hat-flying dash to the finish line. To do this requires great skill and an excellent relationship between the cowgirl and her horse. The fastest time wins, and there's a five-second penalty for knocking down a barrel.

Wild Cow Milking

Although not an official rodeo event, participants in the wild cow milking are greeted with just as much hootin' and hollerin' as those in the main events. At the Stampede, 20 two-man teams race into a herd of wild cows aiming to collect a few squirts of milk in a container and race with it to the judges' table.

Wild Horse Race

In this fun event, three-man teams select a horse from among a herd in the ring. Their aim is to saddle it and have one team member ride it across the finish line.

Mutton Busting

Mutton busting is for the little cowboys and cowgirls. Youngsters jump aboard a sheep for a wild and woolly ride across the ring.

At the far end of Stampede Park, across the Elbow River, is the **Indian Village.** Here, members of the five nations who signed Treaty Seven 100 years ago—the Blackfoot, Blood, Piegan, Sarcee, and Stoney—set up camp for the duration of the Stampede. Each tepee has its own colorful design; tours are available. Behind the village is a stage where native dance competitions are held.

Once you've paid gate admission, all entertainment (except the rodeo and chuck wagon races) is free. Well-known Canadian performers appear at the outdoor **Coca-Cola Stage** from 11 A.M.–midnight. **Nashville North** is an indoor venue with a bar, live country acts, and a dance floor; open until 2 A.M.

PRACTICALITIES

Food
There's no chance of anyone starving to death here. Within the grounds are three restaurants, two food courts, and an endless stream of fast-food stands. The **Saddledome Restaurant** offers an all-you-can-eat buffet. The selection isn't huge, but at $7.95 (less than a burger, fries, and a drink from a stand), it's the best deal on the grounds. Open daily 11 A.M.–9 P.M.; expect a wait after 4 P.M. **O'Reillys Pub,** upstairs in the Roundup Centre, serves typical pub grub throughout the day. Throughout the Stampede, look for free pancake breakfasts in shopping mall parking lots, at community centers, and on street corners.

Transportation
Parking around the grounds is limited; most people use public transport. The **C-train** runs at least every 10 minutes from 7th Avenue downtown to the Victoria Park/Stampede C-train station ($1.50 one-way). Many hotels and campgrounds run shuttle services to the park during Stampede Week; get details before making reservations because each service is different. Generally, they leave pickup points at 11 A.M. and 6 P.M., and return at 6 P.M. and midnight. A 7 A.M. shuttle to the city center for the parade on the opening Friday is usually also offered; expect to pay $10 round-trip per person. A taxi from downtown to Stampede Park runs approximately

$5. If you decide to drive, parking close to the grounds is possible, but the roads can be chaotic. Many local residents turn their gardens into parking lots—most stand out on the road waving at you as if to say that their month's rent depends on the $5–10 parking fee. The official parking lots nearby charge approximately $8 per day, rising to $10–12 in the afternoon, depending on how busy they are.

Tickets
Advance tickets for the afternoon rodeos and evening chuck wagon races/grandstand shows go on sale nearly one year ahead of time. The good seats are sold out by the time the event rolls around. The grandstand is divided into sections, each with a different price tag. The best views are from "A" section, closest to the infield yet high enough not to miss all the action. To either side are the "B" and "C" sections, also with good views. Above the main level is the Clubhouse level, divided into another four sections, all enclosed by glass and air-conditioned. These seats might not have the atmosphere of the lower or higher levels, but they are protected from the elements and patrons have access to a bar, full-service restaurant, and lounge area. At the top of the grandstand is the Balcony level, divided into two sections. Both are great for the chuck wagon races (you can see the wagons around the full circuit). Ticket prices for the first eight days of rodeo competition range $19–38 ($34 for section A). The evening chuck wagon races/grandstand shows run $23–46 ($39 for section A). Tickets to both the rodeos and chuck wagon races/grandstand shows include admission to Stampede Park (normally $10). Tickets for the final two days of competition are an extra $3–5.

To order tickets by phone, call 403/269-9822 or 800/661-1767. You can also buy tickets online at the Stampede website, www.calgary-stampede.com.

If you didn't purchase your tickets in advance, you'll need to pay the **general admission** at the gate. General admission was $9 in 2000, but it tends to go up $1 every year or so. Once inside the park, you can purchase tickets for the afternoon's rodeo or the chuck wagon race/grandstand show from the booths behind the grandstand. Tickets are about $10 to either event,

2001 CALGARY STAMPEDE TICKET INFORMATION

SECTION CODE	RODEO (1:30 P.M.)		EVENING SHOW (8 P.M.)	
	6-13 JULY	14-15 JULY	6-12 JULY	13-15 JULY
A	$34	$39	$39	$44
B	$31	$34	$37	$40
C	$23	$26	$28	$31
D	$28	$31	$37	$40
E	$21.50	$24.50	$30	$33
F	$38	$41	$46	$49
G	$28.50	$34.50	$38	$44
J	$28	$31	$34	$37
K	$19	$22	$23	$26
W	$20	$20	$21	$24

Sections A, B, and C:	Grandstand Main Level
Sections D and E:	Clubhouse Seats
Sections F and G:	Clubhouse Restaurant (in pairs only)
Sections J and K:	Balcony
Section W:	Wheelchair Accessible (one companion only; limited wheelchair seating in section D)

Tickets purchased in advance include the gate price; prices listed do not include tax. For information, write to P.O. Box 1060, Station M, Calgary, Alberta T2P 2K8; or call (403) 261-0101 or (800) 661-1260 anywhere in North America. To order tickets by phone, call (403) 269-9822 or (800) 661-1767. You can also visit the Stampede Web site at www.calgary-stampede.com.

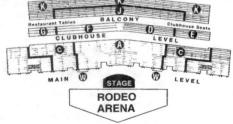

and you'll have access only to either an area of the infield with poor views or seats well away from the action.

Information
An Events Schedule and map are handed out at all park gates, and the *Calgary Sun* newspaper publishes a pull-out section each day during the Stampede with results of the previous day's competition and upcoming events throughout town. Thousands of volunteers (dressed in red and white) contribute to the Stampede's success. They can answer most questions or at least direct you to one of many **Howdy Folk Chuckwagons** for more information. The **Bank of Montreal** operates daily 11 A.M.–5 P.M. at the Agricultural Building, or you can use one of many ATMs located throughout the park.

In 2001, the Calgary Stampede will be held July 6–15; in 2002 it's July 5–14. For more information, write P.O. Box 1060, Station M, Calgary, Alberta T2P 2L8, or call 403/261-0101 or 800/661-1260 anywhere in North America. You can also visit the Stampede home page at www.calgary-stampede.com.

ACCOMMODATIONS

Accommodations in Calgary vary from campgrounds, hostels, and budget motels to a broad selection of high-quality hotels catering to top-end travelers and business conventions. Many of the older, cheaper downtown hotels were demolished in the 1990s to make way for office buildings, and several new upscale hotels are planned for early in the new millennium. Most of the downtown hotels offer drastically reduced rates on weekends—Friday and Saturday nights might be half the regular room rate. During Stampede Week, prices are higher than the rest of the year and accommodations are booked months in advance. (Rates quoted here are for a double room in summer, but outside of Stampede week.)

HOTELS AND MOTELS

Downtown—$50–100
Least expensive of Calgary's downtown hotels is the **Regis Plaza Hotel** (124 7th Ave., 403/262-4641). It is one of the few old hotels that has survived Calgary's ongoing construction boom. Of the 100 rooms, only 30 have ensuites—the rest share bathroom facilities—but all have televisions. Rates start at $62 single, $65 double. The only other downtown accommodation with rooms less than $100 is the **Lord Nelson Inn** (1020 8th Ave. SW, 403/269-8262 or 800/661-6017), with 56 air-conditioned rooms for $95 single or double.

Downtown—$100–150
Across the railway tracks from downtown, the **Best Western Suites Downtown** (1330 8th St. SW, 403/268-6900 or 800/981-2555) features more than 120 self-contained units, each with a kitchen and air-conditioning. Rates start at $125 single, $135 double. A few blocks west of the shopping district, and linked by the C-train, you'll find the **Sandman Hotel** (888 7th Ave. SW, 403/237-8626 or 800/726-3626, www.sandman.ca). This 300-room property features an indoor pool, a family-style restaurant, and large rooms from $112 single or double.

Downtown—$150–200
Least expensive of the hotels right downtown is the **Prince Royal Suites Hotel** (618 5th Ave. SW, 403/263-0520 or 800/661-1592, www.princeroyal.com), where each of the 300 one- and two-bedroom suites has kitchen facilities and costs $155–195 single or double.

The **Holiday Inn Calgary Downtown** (119 12th Ave. SW, 403/266-4611 or 800/661-9378, www.holiday-inn.com) is a new 12-story, 188-room accommodation on the south side of the railway tracks. It features a health club, a heated pool, a lounge, a restaurant, and downtown transfers. Rates are $179 single or double.

Downtown—More than $200
The **International Hotel of Calgary** (220 4th Ave. SW, 403/265-9600 or 800/661-8627, www.intlhocom) features 247 one- and two-bedroom suites, an indoor pool, a fitness room,

and a restaurant. Rates are from $210 single or double. Across from the Calgary Tower and on the same block as the Glenbow Museum is the **Calgary Marriott Hotel** (110 9th Ave. SE, 403/266-7331 or 800/228-9290), one of Calgary's newest and largest downtown hotels, with more than 300 rooms. It offers elegantly decorated rooms and a large indoor pool with a waterfall. Rates range from $219–489 single or double. One block north from the Marriott is the **Hyatt Regency Calgary** (700 Centre St., 403/717-1234, www.hyatt.com), Canada's fourth Hyatt, which opened in the summer of 2000. Incorporating an historic building along Stephen Avenue Mall in its construction, this 21-story hotel features an indoor swimming pool, a health club, a lounge, and a restaurant. Rooms are luxuriously appointed, from $270 single or double weeknights and $150 on weekends. The **Delta Bow Valley** (209 4th Ave. SE, 403/266-1980 or 800/268-1133, www.deltahotels.com) features 400 luxurious rooms with all the amenities for $245 single, $260 double. A few blocks west, in the heart of the shopping district, the **Westin Hotel** (320 4th Ave. SW, 403/266-1611 or 800/937-8461) has a wide range of facilities, including a rooftop indoor swimming pool, a café, a restaurant, a lounge, and more than 500 rooms. Standard rooms are $250 single or double, and "Tower" suites start at $280.

The gracious **Palliser Hotel** (133 9th Ave. SE, 403/262-1234 or 800/441-1414, www .fairmont.com) was built in 1914 by the Canadian Pacific Railway, the same company responsible for the Banff Springs Hotel and Chateau Lake Louise. The rooms may seem small by modern standards, and it lacks certain recreational facilities, but the elegance and character of this Calgary favorite are priceless. When the queen of England visits Calgary, she stays at this grande dame of hotels. Each of the 405 rooms has been restored. The cavernous lobby has original marble columns and staircases, a magnificent chandelier, and solid-brass doors that open onto busy 9th Avenue. As you'd expect, staying in this Calgary landmark isn't cheap, but it's a luxurious way to enjoy the city. Rates start at $280 single or double.

South on Macleod Trail

The following accommodations are lined up along Macleod Trail, the main route out of the city to the south. Those in the southwest sector of the city lie on the west side of Macleod Trail and those in the southeast sector to the east of it.

The **Elbow River Inn** (1919 Macleod Trail SE, 403/269-6771 or 800/661-1463, www. casino-hocom) is close to downtown and directly opposite Stampede Park, but don't even dream of staying here during Stampede Week unless you make reservations one year in advance. Within the motel are a restaurant, a pub, a popular casino, and 75 basic but comfortable rooms. Rates are $79 single, $89 double (which includes breakfast), rising to $159 single or double during the Stampede. The next motel to the south is the **Best Western Calgary Centre Inn** (3630 Macleod Trail SW, 403/287-3900 or 877/287-3900), which opened in 1999. Each of the rooms is decorated in a bright and breezy color scheme, and guests can use an indoor pool. Rates of $99–129 single or double include a buffet breakfast. Close by, the **Quality Hotel** (3828 Macleod Trail SW, 403/243-5531) is an older-style place with all facilities and similarly priced at $99 single or double. A few blocks farther south, with a C-train station on its back doorstep, stands **Holiday Inn Macleod Trail** (4206 Macleod Trail SW, 403/287-2700 or 800/661-1889, www.holiday-inn.com). Facilities here include a large indoor pool, a restaurant, and a lounge. Rooms cost $129 single or double.

The following accommodations lie south of Glenmore Trail, mingled with a strip of shopping malls and fast-food restaurants. The first of these is the **Travelodge Calgary South** (7012 Macleod Trail SW, 403/253-1111 or 800/578-7878); $90 single, $100 double. Nearby, and a better value, is the **Flamingo Inn** (7505 Macleod Trail SE, 403/252-4401 or 888/559-0559), with a large indoor pool and 73 comfortable rooms decorated in pastels; from $75 single, $80 double. The 10-story **Carriage House Inn** (9030 Macleod Trail SW, 403/253-1101 or 800/661-9566, www.carriagehouse.net) offers a wide range of facilities, including an indoor pool, a fitness room, a restaurant, and an English-style pub, but the rooms are pretty basic for $125 single or double. At the **Travelodge Calgary Macleod Trail** (9206 Macleod Trail SW, 403/253-7070 or 800/578-7878), guests enjoy an indoor pool and a restaurant; the recently renovated rooms are $109 single or double. It's also right across the road from the famous Ranchman's saloon. The 261-room **Best Western Hospitality Inn** (135 Southland Dr. SE, 403/278-5050 or 800/528-1234) features an array of facilities, including an indoor pool, two restaurants, a lounge, a pub, and a nightclub, for $124 single, $129 double. Southernmost of the motels on Macleod Trail is the **Stetson Village Inn** (10002 Macleod Trail SW, 403/271-3210), an older-style place tucked between shopping malls; $69 single, $73 double.

Motel Village

Motel Village is Calgary's main concentration of moderately priced motels. The "village" is not an official designation, just a dozen motels bunched together at the intersection of 16th Avenue NW and Crowchild Trail, and for a few blocks along Banff Trail, which parallels Crowchild Trail one block to the east. All of the accommodations in Motel Village are a $10 cab ride from downtown.

One of the least expensive is the **Holiday Inn Express** (2227 Banff Trail NW, 403/289-6600, www.holiday-inn.com), where rooms are $85 single, $95 double, including a light breakfast and use of a small outdoor pool. Further along is the **Quality Inn** (2359 Banff Trail NW, 403/289-1973 or 800/661-4667), which has an indoor pool, a fitness center, and a restaurant. Rates here are $89 single, $99 double. The adjacent **Comfort Inn** (2363 Banff Trail NW, 403/289-2581 or 800/228-5150) features an indoor pool and complimentary breakfast; $100 single, $110 double. Similarly priced are the **Econo Lodge–Banff Trail** (2231 Banff Trail NW, 403/289-1921 or 800/917-7779, www.econolodgecalgary.com); $80 single, $110 double; and the **Econo Lodge–Motel Village** (2440 16th Ave. NW, 403/289-2561 or 800/917-7779, www.econolodgecalgary.com), which offers well-equipped rooms, complete with coffee-makers and hair-dryers, as well as a fitness room, for $90 single, $100 double.

The **Best Western Village Park Inn** (1804 Crowchild Trail NW, 403/289-0241 or 800/774-7716) features 160 spacious rooms well equipped for the business traveler, and an indoor atrium containing a lounge with an adjoining restaurant. Rates are $117 single or double.

Next door is **Super 8 Motel** (1904 Crowchild Trail NW, 403/289-9211 or 800/800-8000, www.super8.com), which feature very large rooms, an outdoor heated pool, and complimentary breakfast; $130 single, $150 double.

East of the village proper is the imposing **Days Inn–Calgary West** (1818 16th Ave. NW, 403/289-1961 or 800/661-9564, www.daysinn.com), an older-style place (formerly the Highlander Hotel) that has recently undergone extensive renovations. It offers all of the usual eating and entertainment facilities along with an airport shuttle. Rates are $120 single, $130 double, including breakfast.

West of Downtown

Known as 16th Avenue N within city limits, a string of reasonably priced motels lines the TransCanada Highway heading west from the city toward the mountain parks. Usually not the best value, these accommodations offer the best location for visiting Canada Olympic Park or for day trips to the mountains. Closest to the city lies the **Budget Host Motor Inn** (4420 16th Ave. NW, 403/288-7115 or 800/661-3772), where the rooms are fairly standard, but the rates are right at $64 single, $69 double. Complimentary coffee is served in the lobby. Across the road is the **Travellers Inn** (4611 16th Ave. NW, 403/247-1388), which is nothing special but reasonably priced at $54 single, $58 double. On the same side of the road and similarly priced are the **Holiday Motel** (4540 16th Ave. NW, 403/288-5431), and the **Red Carpet Inn** (4635 16th Ave. NW, 403/247-9239). Directly opposite Canada Olympic Park is the new **Four Points Hotel Sheraton** (8220 Bow Ridge Crescent NW, 403/288-4441 877/288-4441), featuring a fitness room, an indoor pool, a water slide, and a restaurant; from $109 single, $139 double. Like other motels in the chain, the **Econo Lodge West** (west of Canada Olympic Park, 403/288-4436) provides 50 good-quality rooms from $99 single, $119 double. A little farther out is the **Westwind Inn,** 403/286-0333 or 800/665-0856; $85 single or double.

Northeast (Airport)

Many hotels lie in the northeast section of the city, near the airport, but **Delta Calgary Airport Hotel** (403/291-2600 or 800/268-1133, www.deltahotels.com) is the only one at the airport, and it's connected to the arrivals level of the main terminal, making it extremely handy for late arrivals or early departures. Many of the 296 rooms are smallish, but all are modern and well sound-proofed. Other facilities include an indoor pool, a fitness room, and a dining room. Rates are $170–240 single or double.

All of the dozen other motels in the northeast corner of the city have shuttles to the airport, and most can be contacted directly by courtesy phone from the airport. Of the bunch clustered near the intersection of 16th Avenue and 19th Street NE, the least expensive is the **Pointe Inn** (1808 19th St. NE, 403/291-4681 or 800/661-8164, www.pointeinn.com). It has basic rooms, a laundromat, a café, a restaurant, and a lounge; $70–80 single or double. Nearby, the **Best Western Airport Inn** (1947 18th Ave. NE, 403/250-5015 or 800/528-1234) charges $99 single, $109 double. Closer to the airport is the **Best Western Port O'Call Inn** (1935 McKnight Blvd. NE, 403/291-4600 or 800/661-1161, www.portocallinn .com), a full facility hostelry where rooms are $139 single or double. A step up in price is the **Radisson Hotel Calgary Airport** (2120 16th Ave. NE, 403/291-4666 or 800/333-3333, www .radisson.com), which features more than 180 renovated rooms, a large lobby filled with greenery and comfortable seating, and an indoor pool; from $189 single or double. But the pick of the crop is the **Sheraton Cavalier** (2620 32nd Ave. NE, 403/291-0107 or 800/325-3535). This full-service hostelry boasts a café, a restaurant, a lounge, a fitness room, Calgary's largest indoor waterpark, and a business center. The 306 rooms are modern, spacious, and well equipped. Rates are $250 single or double.

BED-AND-BREAKFASTS

The tourist information centers at the airport and downtown keep a list of places offering bed-and-breakfast accommodations and will make a booking for you. The **Bed & Breakfast Association of Calgary** represents 50 homes offering rooms to visitors. Prices are $35–80 single, $45–120 double. The association's website is www.bbassoc.calgary.ab.ca. One of the nicest options is **Inglewood B&B** (1006 8th Ave. SE,

403/262-6570), named for the historic neighborhood in which it lies. Its location is excellent—close to the river and Stampede Park, as well as a 10-minute stroll from downtown. The three rooms, each with private facilities, range $80–120 single or double, depending on the room configuration. Rates include a cooked breakfast.

BACKPACKER ACCOMMODATIONS

Calgary International Hostel
At 520 7th Avenue SE, 403/269-8239, this large hostel is ideally located only two blocks east of City Hall and Stephen Avenue Mall. It has 110 beds, many in eight-bed dormitories, some in private rooms. Other facilities include a fully equipped kitchen, laundry facilities, a large common room, an outdoor barbecue, a game room, a snack bar, lockers, and an information service. From the airport, shuttle buses stop two blocks away at the Delta Bow Valley Inn. A cab from the airport runs approximately $25. Rates are $16 for members and $22 for nonmembers. This place becomes crowded during summer, so book ahead.

CAMPGROUNDS

No camping is available within the Calgary city limits, although campgrounds can be found along all major routes into the city. Shuttle buses run to and from campgrounds into Stampede Park during the Calgary Stampede. Reservations are necessary for this week.

West
K.O.A. Calgary West, 403/288-0411 or 800/562-0842, is on a north-facing hill a short way west of Canada Olympic Park. The modern facilities include showers, a laundry room, an outdoor heated pool, a game room, and a grocery store. Unserviced sites are $24, hookups $26–28. It's open mid-April to mid-October.

Calaway Park, 403/249-7372, Canada's largest amusement park, is 10 kilometers farther west along the TransCanada Highway. It offers a large, open camping area. Trees are scarce, but on clear days the view of the Rockies is spectacular and prairie falcons often hover overhead. The toilets, showers, and laundry room are in a trailer but are of reasonable standard. The large overflow area is unserviced ($15) but is needed only during Stampede Week. Tent sites are $17, hookups $21–23. This campground closes in early September.

North
Northwest of the city is **Symons Valley R.V. Park,** 403/274-4574, which has showers, laundry facilities, and a restaurant. Unserviced sites are $11, hookups $18–20, and it's open year-round. To get there, take 14th Street NW north past Nose Hill Park to Symons Valley Road, continuing northwest along West Nose Creek to the campground at 144th Avenue NW. Also north of the city, right beside Highway 2, **Whispering Spruce Campground,**403/226-0097, is near the small town of Balzac. The campground has showers and a small grocery store. Tent sites are $15, unserviced sites $18, hookups $20–22.

East
Mountain View Farm Campground, three kilometers east of the city limits on the TransCanada Highway, 403/293-6640, doesn't have a view of the mountains, but it does have a small petting farm, mini-golf, and hay rides. The sites are very close together. Facilities include showers, a grocery store, and a laundry room. Tent sites are $18, hookups $22–26. Continuing east, on Chestermere Lake, is **Camp 'n' Water Park,** 403/273-5122, with plenty of activities for the kids, as well as an adults-only camping area. Sites range $18–22.

South
South of Calgary on the Bow River is **Nature's Hideaway Campground,** 403/938-8185. Although farther out than all of the others, it is located in a densely wooded floodplain. Birds are abundant, and deer and coyotes are seen often. Many guests stay here for the entire summer, and the facilities are a little rundown. There are showers, a grocery store, a dance hall (music on weekends), and a beach with swimming; unserviced sites $16, hookups $18–22. To get there, head south on Highway 2, then take Highway 552 east for 12 kilometers, then go north for one kilometer, then east for two more. It's open year-round.

FOOD

Calgary may lack the cultural trappings that Alberta's capital, Edmonton, boasts, but it gives that city a run for its money in the restaurant department. All of the major highrise buildings downtown have plazas with inexpensive food courts, coffeehouses, and cappuccino bars—the perfect places for people-watching. South of downtown, along 17th Avenue and 4th Street, a once-quieter part of the city has been transformed into a focal point for Calgary's restaurant scene, with cuisine to suit all tastes. Familiar North American fast-food restaurants line Macleod Trail south of the city center.

DOWNTOWN DINING

Eau Claire Market and Vicinity
At the entrance to Prince's Island Park, this expansive indoor market has a large food court and several restaurants. In the food court, you'll find a great seafood outlet, a bakery, and some Asian-food places. **Cajun Charlies,** opposite the food court, 403/233-8101, is a striking orange-and-black eatery serving Louisiana bayou dishes. For something more casual, head to **Good Earth Express,** 403/237-8684, for healthy snacks and a wide variety of teas and coffees.

Outside the market's western entrance is **Joey Tomato's Kitchen,** 403/263-6336, a trendy bistro-style restaurant serving moderately priced Italian food. Near the same entrance, you'll find **1886 Buffalo Cafe,** 403/269-9255, named for the year it was built. This restaurant oozes an authentic Old Calgary ambience. Breakfast attracts the most interesting group of diners, but the place is busy all day. Portions are generous, coffee refills are free, and when you've finished your meal, ask to see the museum downstairs. It's open weekdays from 6 A.M., weekends from 7 A.M., and it closes daily at 3 P.M.

Walk north from Eau Claire Market to the **River**

*1886 Buffalo Cafe,
Eau Claire Market*

Café on Prince's Island, 403/261-7670. More of a restaurant than a café, it features a wide range of North American dishes prepared with a modern flair. It's open daily 11 A.M.–10 P.M.

Steak

For the best steaks in the city that produces the best beef in Canada, head to **Caesar's Steak House** (512 4th Ave. SW, 403/264-1222). The elegant restaurant is decorated in a Roman-style setting. The chef is enclosed in a glass bubble, allowing diners to watch him at work. Although the menu is varied, Caesar's is famous for its juicy prime cuts. Entrées are $12–35. Open Mon.–Fri. noon–2 P.M. and daily 4:30 P.M.–midnight.

Buzzard's Cowboy Cuisine (140 10th Ave., 403/264-6959) offers inexpensive steaks and unique Canadian delights such as prairie oysters in a funky Western atmosphere. Open daily 11 A.M.–11 P.M.

Seafood

The city's best seafood is available at **Cannery Row** (317 10th Ave. SW, 403/269-8889) and directly upstairs at the aptly named **McQueens Upstairs** (317 10th Ave. SW, 403/269-4722). Cannery Row is a casual affair, with an open kitchen, an oyster bar, and the ambience of a San Francisco seafood restaurant. Typical fish dishes available are salmon, halibut, and shrimp, starting from $11 at dinner. A good choice of

southern-style entrées is also offered. The menu at McQueens Upstairs is more varied and more expensive (dinner entrées $18.50–35). Mc-Queens also features live jazz or blues Thurs.–Sat. evenings. Both restaurants are open Monday–Friday for lunch and daily for dinner and are busy during office lunch hours. Right downtown is the **Chowder House** (609 1st St., 403/269-1434). Dinner entrées are $11.50–19, with discounts for early diners.

Buy your fresh seafood at **Billingsgate Seafood Market,** over the C-Train line from downtown at 630 7th Avenue, 403/269-7717.

Calgary Tower

At the top of the Calgary Tower is the **Panorama Dining Room** (101 9th Ave. SW, 403/266-7171), a revolving restaurant that takes 45 minutes for a full rotation at lunch and one hour during dinner. As far as revolving restaurants go, the food is excellent; the menu features mainly local game, with dinner entrées ranging from $26–35. It's open daily for breakfast, lunch, and dinner. Breakfast is an especially good value—choose from a menu of dishes less than $12, which includes tea or coffee, juices, and a small selection of fruit. Sunday brunch, served 9 A.M.–11 A.M. is buffet-style for $18.

Japanese

Yuzuki Japanese Restaurant (510 9th Ave. SW, 403/261-7701) is a good downtown eatery where the most expensive lunch item is the assorted sushi for $14. Even this meal is an excellent value considering that it comes with 10 of those little rice packages and a bowl of miso soup. Less expensive items start at $8 and are priced only slightly higher at dinner.

More upscale is **Sushi Hiro** (727 5th Ave. SW, 403/233-0605). Sushi choices change regularly but generally include red salmon, yellowtail, sea urchin, and salmon roe. The tempuras ($14–16) are also excellent. If you sit at the oak-and-green-marble sushi counter, you'll be able to ask the chef what's best. Closed Sunday.

Chinese
Chinatown, along 2nd and 3rd avenues east of Centre Street, naturally has the best assortment of Chinese restaurants. **Hang Fung Restaurant** (119 3rd Ave. SE, 403/269-4646), tucked behind a Chinese grocery store, serves one-plate meals for less than $7. The barbecue pork is delicious and only $5. Just as inexpensive is **Golden Inn Restaurant** (107 2nd Ave. SE, 403/269-2211), which is popular with the local Chinese as well as with professionals, and late-shift workers appreciate its long hours (open until 4 A.M.). The menu features mostly Cantonese-style deep-fried food. Offering more atmosphere is the **Silver Dragon** (106 3rd Ave. SE, 403/264-5326), a large restaurant with subdued lighting and a relaxed and comfortable setting. For a Chinese buffet, head to **Regency Palace Restaurant** (328 Centre St., SE, 403/777-2288), a cavernous restaurant seating approximately 600 people. Open for lunch Monday–Friday and daily for dinner. The **Emperor Seafood Restaurant,** in the Chinese Cultural Centre, 403/265-4738, also offers a lunchtime buffet.

Hotel Dining
The **Owl's Nest** in the Westin Hotel (320 4th Ave. SW, 403/266-1611) is an upscale restaurant with elegant surroundings where ladies are presented with a rose and gentlemen with a cigar. Many entrées are low-cholesterol; others, such as turtle soup, quail, and beluga caviar, certainly aren't. Entrées are $19–38, but lunch is slightly less expensive. Open Monday–Friday for lunch and dinner and on Saturday for dinner only. In the Delta Bow Valley

Hotel is **The Conservatory** (209 4th Ave. SE, 403/205-5433), a fine-dining restaurant with a French chef. Enjoy a predinner drink in **The Lobby Lounge.** Other high-end restaurants in town include **Rimrock Restaurant** (133 9th Ave. SW, 403/262-1234), in the historic Palliser Hotel, and **Trader's** (110 9th Ave. SE, 403/266-7331), in the Calgary Marriott (where waiters wear white gloves and diners are entertained by a pianist).

KENSINGTON

Across the Bow River from downtown lies the trendy suburb of Kensington, which is home to several coffeehouses and restaurants. One of the nicest cafés is **Higher Ground** (1126 Kensington Rd. NW, 403/270-3780), a specialty coffee shop with a few windowfront tables. **Peppino,** a small deli-style café (1240 Kensington Rd., 403/283-5360), has a wide range of healthy sandwiches as well as gourmet meats and cheeses to go. Head to **Jugo Juice** (1154 Kensington Crescent NW, 403/270-0120) for freshly squeezed juices and a great variety of healthy smoothies.

Restaurants
The casual, two-story **Stromboli Inn** (1147 Kensington Crescent NW, 403/283-1166), featuring a few tables on private balconies, serves gourmet pizza and pastas (most less than $12). **Charly Chan's** (1140 Kensington Rd. NW, 403/283-6165) is a yuppie Chinese restaurant. You won't see many Chinese eating here, but the Peking-style dishes are well prepared and popular with Calgarians. Kensington's busiest intersection offers another bunch of eateries, namely **Tandoori Hut** (201 10th St. NW, 403/270-4012), serving a small lunch buffet for $6.95, and, at the same address, **Osteria de Medici,** 403/283-5553, a stylish Italian restaurant with main meals starting at $8 for lunch and $12 for dinner.

SOUTH OF THE RAILWAY TRACK

The area immediately south of downtown offers Calgary's best dining choices. In the 1980s, restaurants began springing up along 11th Avenue SW, but by 2000 the biggest concentration was south of 11th Avenue along 4th Street SW and along 17th Avenue SW, which is known locally as Uptown 17.

Breakfast

Nellie's, in an unassuming building at 738 17th Avenue SW, 403/244-4616, is a pleasant surprise. It's a small, low-key place with fast and friendly service and, most important, great food. Breakfasts claim the spotlight; a pile of bacon and eggs with all the trimmings, or a delicious omelette, will cost you just $7, and plenty of other lighter choices are offered as well. It's open daily for breakfast and lunch. Nellie's has recently opened a second location in the same vicinity (2308 4th St. SW, 403/209-2708). The **Galaxy Diner** (1413 11th St. SW, 403/228-0001) is an original 1950s diner where cooked breakfasts cost from $6, including bottomless coffee.

Italian

Few restaurants in the city are as popular as **Chianti** (1438 17th Ave. SW, 403/229-1600). More than 20 well-prepared pasta dishes are featured on the menu, and all of the pasta is made daily on the premises. Among many specialties are an antipasto platter ($13.50 for two) and Frutti Di Mare, a spicy seafood combination served on a bed of pasta; at $15.25, it's the most expensive entrée. All regular pasta entrées are less than $10. The restaurant is dark and noisy in typical Italian style. The owner often sings with an accordionist on weekends. It's open daily until midnight. Chianti has another restaurant at 10816 Macleod Trail SE, 403/225-0010. Another popular Italian eatery is **Il Giardino** (corner of 4th St. and 17th Ave. SW, 403/541-0088). Like Chianti, it's a fun, casual place, with a menu that runs the spectrum of Italian cooking styles. Most main dishes are less than $18, with all pastas less than $14. Closer to downtown is **Bonterra Restaurant,** in an historic building at 1016 8th Street SW, 403/262-8480. The décor has a distinctive look, with a vaulted ceiling, lots of exposed woodwork, and a Mediterranean-style patio. The menu is modern Italian, with dishes from $13.50.

French

For many years, **La Chaumiere,** one of North America's premier French restaurants, occupied an unpretentious building by Stampede Park, but in 1996 it moved to a location more befitting its prestige (139 17th Ave. SW, 403/228-5690). Dishes such as duck in brandy, flaming duck, and escargot are authentically prepared, and the formal service is meticulous. Reservations are required for dinner. It's open for lunch Monday–Friday noon–2:30 P.M. and for dinner Monday–Saturday from 5:30 P.M. Less expensive is **Entre Nous** (1800 4th St. SW, 403/228-5525), where a three-course lunch is less than $20 per person. The tin ceiling and glass-topped tables are a legacy of the way this restaurant began—as a French bistro. Entre Nous also has a small deck for summer dining.

Jojo Bistro Parisien, 917 17th Ave., 403/245-2382, is a small, subtly lit, and intimate eatery decorated simply with definitive provincial-French influence. Lunch items are mostly less than $10 while dinners range $15.50—22. The service is excellent. Open Mon.–Fri. 11:30 A.M.–2 P.M. and 5:30–10:30 P.M. and on Saturday for dinner only 5:30–11 P.M.

Moroccan

When you enter **Sultan's Tent** (909 17th Ave. SW, 403/244-2333), a server appears with a silver kettle and basin filled with orange-blossom-scented water with which to wash your hands. It's all part of Moroccan custom and part of the fun. The restaurant features swinging lanterns, hassocks, piped-in Arabic music, and, most important, delicious Moroccan delicacies. Try Guelli's Sultan Feast ($24.50), a six-course dinner.

Other Ethnic Restaurants

Restaurant Indonesia (1604 14th St. SW, 403/244-0645) is a busy, inexpensive eatery at the west end of 17th Avenue. Indonesian food is very similar to Chinese, although the sauces prepared here are usually richer and spicier, and vegetarian choices are more varied. Entrées are $6–11. On 4th Street SW between 17th and 25th avenues are several ethnic restaurants. **Rajdoot** (2424 4th St. SW, 403/245-0181) has an excellent lunchtime buffet ($9.95), with approximately 25 different Indian dishes, each rated mild, medium, or hot. The turnover of food is fast, ensuring that items stay fresh and hot. The Sunday brunch buffet ($11.95) has even more choices.

Macleod Trail South

This commercial strip from 36th Avenue to Anderson Road is crammed with all the familiar fast-food restaurants found everywhere in North America. Aside from these, a few family restaurants along this stretch are worth searching for. The **Cactus Club Cafe** (7010 Macleod Trail SE, 403/255-1088) has a yuppie Western atmosphere. The interior is absolutely crammed with cow-related artifacts, although the only thing that's authentic are the peanut shells on the floor.

The Ranche

This new restaurant is in an historic mansion that served as the headquarters of the Bow Valley Ranch in the late 1880s. The building has been restored to its Victorian-era glory, with the restaurant offering a menu of Canadian specialty cuisine. It's open daily for lunch and dinner. Access is from Bow Valley Trail, 403/225-3939.

NORTH OF DOWNTOWN

Italian

Mamma's (320 16th Ave. NW, 403/276-9744) is the most popular Italian eatery on the north side and has been around for decades. Start with the antipasto buffet, then try one of the many veal dishes, and finish with one of the spectacular desserts, all for less than $20 per person. Closed Sunday.

Nick's Steakhouse

Whether it's professional sportsmen, their managers, or their fans, chances are if they're from Calgary they've eaten at Nick's (2430 Crowchild Trail NW, 403/282-9278). Its prime location directly opposite McMahon Stadium, good food, and large-screen TV all contribute to the restaurant's success. Lunch specials are $7.95, dinner specials $11.95, and charbroiled steaks begin at $12. Open daily until 1 or 2 A.M. No reservations are taken.

TRANSPORTATION

GETTING THERE

Air

Calgary International Airport (YYC; www.calgaryairport.com) is within the city limits northeast of downtown. It is served by more than a dozen scheduled airlines and used by seven million passengers each year (Canada's fourth busiest). **Arrivals** is on the lower level, where passengers are greeted by White Hat volunteers who are dressed in traditional Western attire and answer visitors' questions about the airport, transportation, and the city. Among the baggage carousels is an information booth shaped like a chuck wagon (open daily 7 A.M.–10 P.M.). Also on the arrivals level are hotel courtesy phones and rental-car agencies. **Delta Calgary Airport Hotel,** connected by a skywalk, is the only hotel at the airport. A cab to downtown runs approximately $30, or you can catch the **Airport Direct** bus, 403/291-1991, to major downtown hotels for $9 per person

one-way. This service runs daily 5 A.M.–1 A.M. A couple of times daily, **Brewster,** 403/221-8242 or 800/661-1152, offers transfers between the airport and Banff ($36 one-way), Lake Louise ($41), and, in summer only, Jasper ($71).

Scheduled airlines using Calgary International Airport include **Air B.C.,** 403/265-9555; **Air Canada,** 403/265-9555 or 888/247-2262; **American Airlines,** 800/433-7300; **Canada 3000,** 403/509-3000 or 403/300-0669; **Capital City Air,** 877/935-9222; **Delta,** 800/221-1212; **Horizon,** 800/547-9308; **Northern Sky,** 800/668-4037;**Northwest Airlines,** 800/225-2525; **United Airlines,** 800/241-6522; and **WestJet,** 403/250-5839 or 800/538-5696.

Bus

The **Greyhound** bus depot (850 16th St. SW, 403/265-9111 or 800/661-8747) is two blocks away from the C-train stop ($1.50 into town), or you can cross the overhead pedestrian bridge at the terminal's southern entrance and catch a transit bus. To walk the entire distance to town would take 20 minutes. A cab from the bus depot to downtown runs $7, to Calgary International Hostel $8. The depot is cavernous. It has a restaurant, a Royal Bank cash machine, information boards, and lockers large enough to hold backpacks ($2).

Buses connect Calgary daily with Edmonton (3.5 hours, $37.12 one-way), Banff (two hours, $21.12 one-way), Vancouver (15 hours, $110.39 one-way), and all other points within the province. No reservations are taken. Just turn up, buy your ticket, and hop aboard. If you buy your ticket seven days in advance, discounts apply. If you plan to travel extensively by bus, the Canada Coach Pass is a good deal.

Red Arrow is a more luxurious bus service that shuttles passengers between downtown Calgary and downtown Edmonton with some services continuing to Fort McMurray in northern Alberta. To Edmonton it's $38 one-way. The Calgary office and pickup point is downtown at 205 9th Avenue SE (near the Calgary Tower), 403/531-0350 or 800/232-1958.

GETTING AROUND

Bus

You can get just about everywhere in town by using the Calgary Transit System, which combines three lightrail lines with extensive bus routes. Buses are $1.50 one-way to all destinations—deposit the exact change in the box beside the driver and request a transfer (valid for 90 minutes) if you'll be changing buses. A day pass, which is valid for unlimited bus and rail travel, is $4.50. The best place for information and schedules is the **Calgary Transit Customer Service Centre** at 240 7th Avenue SW (opposite the Bay department store). Open Mon.–Fri. 8:30 A.M.–5 P.M. An information line is available seven days a week; call 403/262-1000.

C-Train

C-train, the lightrail transit system, has three lines that converge downtown on 7th Avenue. The **Anderson C-train** parallels Macleod Trail south to Anderson Road; the **Whitehorn C-train** heads out of the city northeast; and the **Brentwood C-train** heads northwest past the university. The system is operated by Calgary

Transit, so fares are the same as buses: $1.50 one-way or $4.50 for a day pass. Transfers in the same direction are free, as is travel on the downtown route along 7th Avenue. For route information, call 403/262-7100. Route maps and ticket-vending machines are located at all C-train stations.

Passengers with Disabilities

Bus number 31 around downtown is wheelchair accessible, as are five other routes through the city. The Brentwood line (northwest) is the only fully accessible route on the C-train system. For information on all wheelchair-accessible services, call 403/262-1000. **Calgary Handi-bus** provides wheelchair-accessible transportation throughout the city. A book of eight tickets is $12, but visitors receive free service for a limited length of time. For more information, call 403/276-1212. A few manual wheelchairs are available for loan from the **Red Cross Society,** 403/205-3448.

Taxi

The flag charge for a cab in Calgary is $2.50, and it's $1.30 for every kilometer. Taxi companies include **Advance,** 403/777-1111; **Associated Cabs,** 403/299-1111; **Checker Cabs,** 403/299-9999; **Red Top,** 403/974-4444; and **Yellow Cab,** 403/974-1111.

Car Rental

If you've just arrived in Calgary, call around and compare rates. Lesser-known agencies are often cheaper, and all rates fluctuate with the season and demand. Many larger agencies have higher rates for unlimited mileage and built-in drop-off charges to nearby centers. (Drop-off charges to Banff are usually $50 extra, and to Edmonton $80 extra.) All agencies provide free pickup and drop-off at major Calgary hotels and have outlets at Calgary International Airport. Rental agencies include **Avis,** 403/269-6166 or 800/879-2847; **Budget,** 403/226-1550 or 800/268-8900; **Discount,** 403/299-1222 or 800/263-2355; **Dollar,** 403/221-1888 or 800/800-4000; **Economy,** 403/291-1640; **Enterprise,** 403/263-1273 or 800/325-8007; **Hertz,** 403/221-1300 or 800/263-0600; **National,** 403/227-7368 or 800/387-4747; **Rent-A-Wreck,** 403/237-6800 or 800/327-0116; and **Thrifty,**

403/262-4400 or 800/847-4389.

Tours
Brewster, 403/221-8242, runs a Calgary City Sights tour lasting four hours. Included on the itinerary are downtown, various historic buildings, Canada Olympic Park, and Fort Calgary. The tours run mid-May to mid-October and cost $47 per person. Pickups are at most major hotels. Brewster also runs day tours departing Calgary daily to Banff, Lake Louise, the Columbia Icefield, and Waterton Lakes National Park. Brewster's downtown office is located on Stephen Avenue Mall at the corner of Centre Street.

SERVICES AND INFORMATION

SERVICES

The downtown **post office** is located at 207 9th Avenue SW. All city libraries provide free Internet access, or you can head to **Wired** (1032 17th St. SW, 403/244-7070) or **Cyber Club Café** (1910 37th St., SW, 403/242-3965) for a cup of java and some online surfing. **Calforex** occupies 304 8th Avenue SW (Lancaster Building), 403/290-0330; as well as exchanging foreign currency, you can wire international payments. **American Express Travel Service** (421 7th Ave. SW, 403/261-5982) offers all of the same currency services with the advantages of also being a travel agency. Most major banks carry U.S. currency and can handle basic foreign-exchange transactions.

West Canadian Color (1231 10th Ave. SW, 403/244-2711) is the most efficient and reliable photo-developing lab in town. Turnaround time on print film is one hour; on E6 slide film, it's five hours. Drop any film off before closing time and it will be ready first thing the following day. It's open Mon.–Sat. 7 A.M.–5:30 P.M., Saturday 8 A.M.– 4 P.M.

For further travel arrangements, **Travel Cuts** (1414 Kensington Rd. NW, 403/531-2070) is the best place to start looking for inexpensive tickets.

Handy self-service laundromats are **Heritage Hill Coin Laundry,** 8228 Heritage Hill Road SE at the corner of Macleod Trail and Heritage Drive, and **The Great Canadian Cleaners,** 4949 Barlow Trail SE.

Emergency Services
For medical emergencies, call 911 or contact one of the following hospitals: **Foothills Hospital** (1403 29th Ave. NW, 403/670-1110); **Rockyview General Hospital** (7007 14th St. SW, 403/541-3000); or **Alberta Children's Hospital** (1820 Richmond Rd. SW, 403/229-7211). For the **Calgary Police,** call 403/266-1234.

INFORMATION

Libraries
The Calgary Public Library Board's 16 branch libraries are scattered throughout the city. The largest is **W.R. Castell Central Library** (616 Macleod Trail SE, 403/260-2600). Four floors of books, magazines, and newspapers from around the world are enough to keep most people busy on a rainy afternoon. Other main branches are **Nose Hill Library** (1530 Northmount Dr. NW) **Village Square Library** (2623 56th St. NE), and **Fish Creek Area Library** (11161 Bonaventure Dr. SE). Hours at each are generally Mon.–Thurs. 10 A.M.–9 P.M., Fri.–Sat. 10 A.M.–5 P.M. (and on Sunday in winter only).

Bookstores
Downtown, the **Book Company** in Bankers Hall (315 8th Ave. SW, 403/237-8344) is a good place to find books on western Canada as well as general travel writing and nonfiction works. **Chapters** has six outlets located throughout the city, including at 9631 Macleod Trail SW, 403/212-1442. The suburb of Kensington, immediately northwest of downtown, has a variety of new and used bookstores, including **Pages** (1135 Kensington Rd. NW, 403/283-6655), which sells new titles, and **Wee Book Inn** (1111 Kensington Rd., 403/283-3322), which stocks used books and is open daily until midnight.

The **Best Little Wordhouse in the West** (911 17th Ave. SW, 403/245-6407) is the best of many secondhand and collector bookstores along 17th Avenue SW. **Author Author** (223 10th St. NW, 403/283-9521) is one of a group of similar stores along 16th Avenue NW between 6th and 9th streets. Both recommended stores stock a good range of western Canada nonfiction.

For topographic, city, and wall maps, as well as travel guides, **Map Town** (400 5th Ave. SW, 403/266-2241) should have what you're looking for.

Information Centers

Within the city limits are two visitors service centers operated by the Calgary Convention and Visitors Bureau, 403/263-8510 or 800/661-1678. One is on the main floor of the **Calgary Tower Centre** at the corner of Centre Street and 9th Avenue SW. This small center is open year-round daily 8:30 A.M.–5 P.M. On the arrivals level at **Calgary International Airport** is another, which is open year-round daily 7 A.M.–10 P.M. If you're arriving in the city from the west, a small information desk operates at **Canada Olympic Park;** open June–Aug., daily 9 A.M.–5 P.M.

On the Internet

The official website of the Calgary Convention and Visitors Bureau is www.calgarytourism.com. For the latest news about Calgary's recreation and entertainment, along with a full listing of sights, accommodations, restaurants, and transportation, surf the Internet to **Found Locally** at www.foundlocally.com/calgary. The site is updated regularly, with many listings, such as weather forecasts. Another option is www.visitor.calgary.ab.ca.

KAREN MCKINLEY

DINOSAUR VALLEY

East of Calgary, the Red Deer River flows through some of the world's richest dinosaur fossil beds; hundreds of specimens from the Cretaceous period—displayed in museums throughout the world—have been unearthed along a 120-kilometer stretch of the river valley. One spot, **Dinosaur Provincial Park,** is the mother lode for paleontologists. This UNESCO World Heritage Site includes a "graveyard" of more than 300 dinosaurs of 35 species, many of which have been found nowhere else in the world. As a comparison, Utah's Dinosaur Natural Monument has yielded just 12 species. The valley has more than just dinosaur skeletons, though; paleontologists have unearthed skin impressions, eggshells, dung, and footprints, as well as fossilized insects, fish, amphibians, crocodiles, pterodactyls, and reptiles. And the valley's landforms are as enthralling as the prehistoric artifacts they entomb—spectacular badland formations make for a sight not easily forgotten.

Alberta's best-known dinosaur is the duck-billed hadrosaur. Remains of this creature have been found on all continents except South Amer-

ica and Australia, an item of interest to paleontologists. By comparing specimens found on different continents, they can prove that these ancient beasts roamed the greater part of the earth.

The major city in the valley, Drumheller, is home to the Royal Tyrrell Museum of Palaeontology. The museum is a research and display center with more than 50 full-size dinosaurs exhibited, more than in any other museum in the world.

The Great Canadian Dinosaur Rush

For generations, natives had regarded the ancient bones, which were always common in the valley, as belonging to giant buffalo. During early geographical surveys of southern Alberta by George Mercer Dawson, the first official dinosaur discovery was recorded. In 1884, one of Dawson's assistants, Joseph Burr Tyrrell, collected and sent specimen bones to Ottawa for scientific investigation. Their identification initiated the first real dinosaur rush. For the first century of digging, all of the dinosaur bones uncovered were transported to museums around the world for

DINOSAUR DIGS

Become involved in the actual digging of dinosaur bones by participating in the Royal Tyrrell Museum of Palaeontology's **Explorer Program.** The most popular part of the program is the **Day Dig.** These digs take place at a site close to Royal Tyrrell Museum, just outside of Drumheller. The adventure begins at 8:30 A.M. with a behind-the-scenes look at specimens already collected by museum staff, then it's out to the dig site. After a brief lesson in excavation techniques, the day is spent digging up dinosaur bones under the guidance of museum paleontologists. Lunch is provided, and you are returned to the museum by 4 P.M., free to wander around the displays. The work is not particularly strenuous, but it gets hot in the badlands, so bring plenty of sunscreen and a hat. Cost is $85 per person. Trips run July–August. Thre... want to watch the c... $12 per person.

For those with... trips allows intere... themselves in the... weeklong prograr...

Provincial Park. The week is spent prospecting for new finds, engaging in excavation work, and preparing specimens for further study. The program runs June–August, beginning each Sunday. The cost is $800 per person, which includes accommodations in trailers and all meals.

For further information on the Explorer Program, contact the Royal Tyrrell Museum at P.O. Box 7500, Drumheller, Alberta T0J 0Y0, 403/823-7707 or 888/440-4240, www.tyrrellmuseum.com.

further study. Just more than 100 years after Tyrrell's discovery, a magnificent museum bearing his name opened in the valley. The idea of the museum was promoted by dinosaur hunter Dr. Phil Currie, and since its opening the dinosaurs have stayed and the tourists have come.

DRUMHELLER AND VICINITY

Drumheller is one of Alberta's major tourist destinations. More than half a million people flock to this desolate part of Canada for one reason—dinosaurs. The city (pop. 6,600) is set in a spectacular lunarlike landscape in the Red Deer River Valley 138 kilometers northeast of Calgary. Ancient glacial meltwaters gouged a deep valley into the surrounding rolling prairie, and wind and water have continued the erosion process ever since. The city's proximity to some of the world's premier dinosaur fossil beds has made it a mecca for paleontologists. Scientists from around the globe come to Drumheller and its environs to learn more about the prehistoric animals that roamed the earth millions of years ago.

For all the dinosaurs' popularity, however, coal, not dinosaurs, was the catalyst for the area's first settlement. Coal deposits had been found in the area by early explorers, but the first mine didn't open until 1911. In 1913, when the rail link was completed with Calgary, the town's population exploded. The city was named after Samuel Drumheller, an early pioneer in the local coal industry. Coal dominated the economy until after World War II, when diesel replaced steam and demand for coal dwindled. Today, the town is an agricultural and oil center, with 3,000 oil wells perforating the farmland within a close radius of town.

SIGHTS

Royal Tyrrell Museum of Palaeontology

So many of the world's great museums are simply showcases for natural history, yet nestled in the badlands six kilometers northwest of Drumheller, the Royal Tyrrell Museum of Palaeontology, the world's largest museum devoted entirely to paleontology, is a lot more. It integrates display areas with fieldwork done literally on the doorstep (it lies within a few kilometers of that first "official" discovery), with specimens transported to the museum for research and

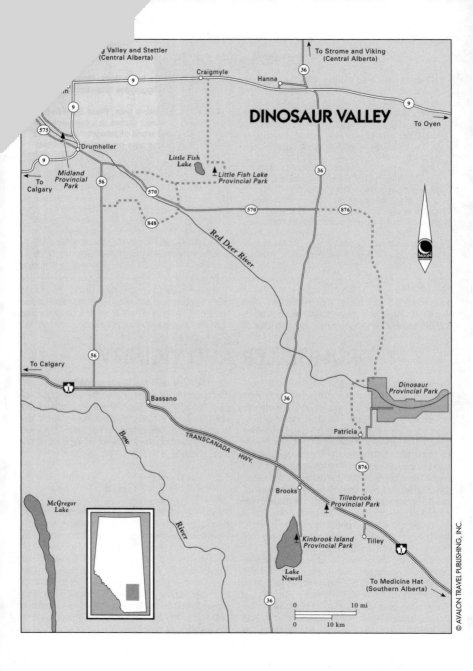

To Strome and Viking
(Central Alberta)

d Valley and Stettler
(Central Alberta)

Craigmyle   Hanna

DINOSAUR VALLEY

To Oyen

Drumheller

Little Fish
Lake

Little Fish Lake
Provincial Park

Midland
Provincial Park

To
Calgary

Red Deer River

To Calgary

Bassano

TRANSCANADA HWY.

Dinosaur
Provincial Park

Patricia

Brooks

Tillebrook
Provincial Park

McGregor
Lake

Kinbrook Island
Provincial Park

Tilley

Bow

River

Lake
Newell

To Medicine Hat
(Southern Alberta)

0   10 mi

0   10 km

© AVALON TRAVEL PUBLISHING, INC.

cataloging. Even for those visitors with little or no interest in dinosaurs, it's easy to spend half a day in the massive 11,200-square-meter complex. The museum holds more than 80,000 specimens, including 50 full-size dinosaur skeletons, the world's largest such display.

Beyond the lobby is a massive, slowly revolving model of the earth set against a starry night—a perfect introduction to the place this planet has in the universe. Beyond the globe, a "timeline" of exhibits covers 3.8 billion years of life on this planet, beginning with early life forms and the development of Charles Darwin's theory of evolution. Before the age of the dinosaurs, the Precambrian and Paleozoic eras saw life on Earth develop at an amazing rate. These periods are cataloged through numerous displays, such as the one of British Columbia's Burgess Shale, where circumstances allowed the fossilization of a community of soft-bodied marine creatures 530 million years ago. But the museum's showpiece is Dinosaur Hall, a vast open area where reconstructed skeletons and full-size replicas of dinosaurs are backed by realistic dioramas of their habitat. Another feature is the two-story paleoconservatory, featuring more than 100 species of plants, many of which flourished during the period when dinosaurs roamed the earth. Nearing the end of the tour, the various theories for the cause of the dinosaurs' extinction, approximately 64 million years ago, are presented. The coming of the ice ages is described in detail, and humanity's appearance on Earth is put into perspective.

The museum is also a major research center; a large window into the main preparation laboratory allows you to view the delicate work of technicians as they clear the rock away from newly unearthed bones.

The museum is in Midland Provincial Park (see following entry). It's open daily 9 A.M.–9 P.M. in summer, Tues.–Sun. 10 A.M.–5 P.M. the rest of the year. Admission is adults $7.50, seniors $5.50, children $3. For further information, call 403/823-7707 or 888/440-4240, www.tyrrellmuseum.com.

Other Dinosaur Sights
Towering above the Red Deer River at the north end of 2nd Street W is the world's biggest dinosaur. This 23-meter-high, steel-and-fiberglass *Tyrannosaurus rex* holds a gift shop and a flight of stairs that leads up to a viewpoint in its open mouth.

Also downtown, the **Drumheller Valley Interpretive Centre** (335 1st St. E, 403/823-2593) is a small museum with an interesting display of privately owned and donated prehistoric pieces, most of which have been collected from the Red Deer River Valley. Exhibits include interpretive boards explaining the geography of the ancient inland sea, the process of coal formation, and the fossilization process. Two items of particular interest are the mounted 10-meter-long skeleton of an edmontosaurus and the skull of a pachyrhinosaurus, the first of its species found. The museum is open in summer daily 10 A.M.–6 P.M., shorter hours in May and October. Admission is $3.50.

It's easy to spend hours in the many shops selling fossils, but the best in town is **The Fossil Shop** (61 Bridge St., 403/823-6774). Pieces start at $10 for chunks of unidentifiable dinosaur bones and go to thousands of dollars for magnificent ammonites from the United States. The owner is a knowledgable local man who has spent his life collecting fossils from around the world.

Midland Provincial Park
This 595-hectare park covers the lower part of Fox Creek Coulee on the northern bank of the Red Deer River. **McMullen Island**, created by an old river meander, is a secluded day-use area shaded by willows and cottonwoods. Pathways lead along the riverbank, and barbecues and a generous supply of wood are available. On the opposite side of the highway, the origins of the park become apparent. Slag heaps and building foundations are the only reminders of the three Midland Coal Mines that operated here until the late 1960s. The mine office is now the park visitors center, where interpretive boards explain the history of the area, and a short trail leads through the old mining sites. Many visitors to the park are not even aware that they're in it. The Royal Tyrrell Museum (see previous entry), from where rangers conduct short hikes during summer, is at the western end of the park. For more information on the park, call 403/823-1749.

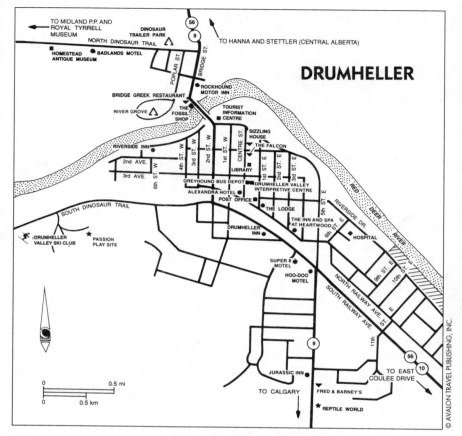

© AVALON TRAVEL PUBLISHING, INC.

Little Fish Lake Provincial Park

Undulating hills of northern fescue grassland and the clear waters of Little Fish Lake provide the backdrop for this small park located 40 kilometers east of Drumheller via East Coulee. (For sights along the way, see following section on **East Coulee Drive.**) The park is also accessible off Highway 9, 40 kilometers south from Craigmyle. Both access roads are gravel. The nearby **Hand Hills** were used by both Cree and Blackfoot as a viewpoint. Many indications of the area's prehistory—mainly tepee rings and campsites—have been found at the southeast end of the lake. The beach and cool water of the lake attract people from Drumheller, so the park can get busy on weekends. The lake is also popular with vacationing waterfowl en route to their summer arctic homes or returning in the fall. The primitive campground has pit toilets, a kitchen shelter, and firewood. Sites are $9.

Other Sights

The **Homestead Antique Museum,** featuring mostly pioneer artifacts, is housed in a Quonset hut two kilometers west of the city, 403/823-2600. The collection includes Indian relics, pioneer clothing, mining equipment, musical instruments, a two-headed calf, and re-creations of an early beauty parlor and barber shop. Outside is an array of farm machinery, automobiles, and a buffalo rubbing stone. The museum is open July–Aug. 9 A.M.–8 P.M., and May–June, September–October 10 A.M.–5:30 P.M. Admission is $4.

The country's largest collection of reptiles is housed at **Reptile World** (1222 Highway 9 S, 403/823-8623), where you can view and handle these much-maligned creatures. It's open in summer 10 A.M.–10 P.M., until 6 P.M. only in spring and fall. Admission is $5.

SCENIC DRIVES

The Dinosaur Trail

This 56-kilometer circular route to the west of Drumheller starts and finishes in town and passes many worthwhile stops, including two spectacular viewpoints. After passing the access road to Royal Tyrrell Museum, the first point of interest is the **Little Church,** often described as being able to seat thousands—but only six at a time. The road then climbs steeply out of the valley onto the prairie benchland. Take the first access road on the left—it doubles back to **Horsethief Canyon Lookout,** where you can catch spectacular views of the badlands and the multicolored walls of the canyons. Slip, slide, or somersault down the embankment here into the mysterious lunarlike landscape, and it's easy to imagine why early explorers the valley and how easy hide stolen horses along t 1900s.

The halfway point of th the Red Deer River on the **Bleriot** r the few remaining cable ferries in Alberta. It operates April–Nov. 8 A.M.–10:45 P.M. On the far side of the river is a primitive campground. Upstream from the campground, a major dinosaur discovery was made in 1923, when the fossilized bones of a duck-billed edmontosaurus were unearthed. The road continues along the top of the valley to **Orkney Hill Lookout** for more panoramic views across the badlands and the lush valley floor below. A "buffalo jump," where Indians once stampeded great herds of bison off the edge of the cliff, was located nearby, but centuries of erosion have changed the clay and sandstone landscape so dramatically that the actual position of the jump is now impossible to define.

East Coulee Drive

This 25-kilometer road, southeast from Drumheller, passes three historic coal-mining communities in an area dotted with mine shafts and abandoned buildings. The first town along this route is **Rosedale,** which at first looks prosperous. On closer inspection, however, you'll notice the distinct lack of businesses. In fact, the town's population dropped from 3,000 to

at the Royal Tyrrell
Museum

100 a few years ago. The community on the opposite side of the Red Deer around the Star Mine, but after the com-...ed car and rail bridge was washed out, town was moved to its present site. For many years, the mine still operated with workers crossing the river on a unique suspension bridge to get to work. The original bridge was built in 1931 but was later replaced by a cable-trolley system. Today, the bridge has been upgraded and is safe for those who want to venture across it.

A worthwhile detour from Rosedale is to **Wayne,** an almost-a-ghost town tucked up a valley alongside Rosebud Creek. It is nine kilometers south of Rosedale along Highway 10X, which spurs away from the river just south of the town and crosses the creek 11 times. In its heyday, Wayne had 1,500 residents, most of whom worked in the Rosedeer Mine. It was never known as a law-abiding town. During Alberta's Prohibition days, many moonshiners operated in the surrounding hills, safe from the nearest Royal Canadian Mounted Police (RCMP) patrol in Drumheller. By the time the mine closed in 1957, the population had dipped to 250 and then as low as 15 a few years back, but now the population stands at approximately 50. Many old buildings remain, making it a popular setting for film crews. The only operating business in the sleepy hamlet is the 1913 **Rosedeer Hotel,** 403/823-9189, where the walls are lined with memorabilia from the town's glory days. The hotel's back porch overlooking the creek is a great place to grab a beer and wallow in nostalgia.

From Rosedale, Highway 10 continues southeast, crossing the Red Deer River at the abandoned mining town of Cambria and passing

DINOSAURS OF ALBERTA

Dinosaur bones found in the Red Deer River Valley play an important role in the understanding of our prehistoric past. The bones date from the late Cretaceous period, around 70 million years ago; for reasons that have mystified paleontologists for over a century, dinosaurs disappeared during this period, after having roamed the earth for 150 million years. A recent theory, put together largely through work done in Alberta, suggests that while larger species disappeared, some of the smaller ones evolved into birds.

The bones of 35 dinosaur species—around 10% of all those currently known—have been discovered in Alberta. Like today's living creatures, they are classified in orders, families, and species. Of the two orders of dinosaurs, both have been found in the Red Deer River Valley. The bird-hipped dinosaurs (order Ornithischia) were herbivores, while the lizard-hipped dinosaurs (order Saurischia) were omnivores and carnivores. Apart from their sheer bulk, many herbivores lacked any real defenses. Others developed their own protection; the chasmosaurus had a bony frill around its neck, the pachycephalosaurus had a 25-centimeter-thick dome-shaped skull cap fringed with spikes, and the ankylosaurus was an armored dinosaur whose back was covered in spiked plates.

Among the most common herbivores that have been found in the valley are members of the family of duck-billed hadrosaurs. Fossilized eggs of one hadrosaur, the hypacrosaurus, were unearthed still encasing intact embryos.

Another common herbivore in the valley was a member of the horned ceratops family; over 300 specimens of the centrosaurus have been discovered in one "graveyard."

Of the lizard-hipped dinosaurs, the tyrannosaurs were most feared by herbivores. The 15-meter *Tyrannosaurus rex* is most famous among *Homo sapiens.* But the smaller albertosaurus, a remarkably agile carnivore weighing many tons, was the most common tyrannosaur found in the valley.

hoodoos to the left. These strangely shaped rock formations along the river valley have been carved by eons of wind and rain. The harder rock on top is more resistant to erosion than the rock beneath it, resulting in the odd, mushroom-shaped pillars.

East Coulee once had a population of 3,000, but now it's down to 250. Mining has taken place here since 1924, but building a rail line from Drumheller proved expensive. Eventually, part of the riverbank was blasted into the river, and the spur was completed in 1928. Full-time production at the main Atlas Mine ended in 1955, but the mine operated intermittently until the 1970s. Most buildings remain standing, but now only a hotel, a grocery store, and a garage are open. Through town is the **Historic Atlas Coal Mine,** 403/823-2220, a Provincial Historic Resource. A wooden ore-sorting tipple—the last one standing in Canada—towers above the mine buildings. It's a great place to just walk around, or you can take the guided tour ($2.50) to learn more about the mining process. It's open in summer daily 10 A.M.–6 P.M.. In the center of East Coulee is **East Coulee School Museum,** 403/822-3970, featuring a restored schoolroom, a coal-mining room, an art gallery, and a tearoom. It's open daily 9 A.M.–6 P.M., closed weekends in winter.

RECREATION

Drumheller's popularity as a tourist destination is only a recent change, but in the last few years many new facilities have been developed, including the expansion of **Dinosaur Golf and Country Club,** 403/823-5622, to 18 holes. The course is undoubtedly one of the most interesting in the province, with the back nine holes of lush fairways and greens winding through the arid badlands of the valley, on high ridges, and through narrow coulees. It is located past the Royal Tyrrell Museum and charges $34 per round.

In winter, skiing or snowboarding is good at the badlands at **Drumheller Valley Ski Club,** 403/823-2277, which boasts a vertical drop of 120 meters served by a chairlift. Lift tickets are $25 for a full day. Closed Monday and Tuesday. The hill is along South Dinosaur Trail.

Rosebud Opera House
Rosebud, located 32 kilometers southwest of Drumheller, is home to a live theater production that takes place year-round. The town's population dropped to only 10 in the early 1970s and has now grown to a respectable 70 residents, many of whom are involved in the production. The evening's entertainment starts in the old general store, where the actors and actresses serve up a buffet-style meal. Then everyone heads across the road for a lively theater production at the opera house. Tickets cost $35 at lunch and $39 at dinner. For details, call the Rosebud Theatre of the Arts at 403/677-2001 or 800/267-7555.

Canadian Badlands Passion Play
This Canadian version of the theatrical production of the life of Jesus Christ tells the story of his birth, his death, and his resurrection. The production is an enormous affair, with a cast of thousands in a natural amphitheater set among the badlands. It takes place seven times through the month of July. Tickets are $18 per person. To get to the site, take South Dinosaur Trail west from downtown and follow the signs south on 17th Street, 403/823-7750.

Drinking and Dancing
Drumheller has always been a hard-drinking coal-mining town, and the after-dark scene still reflects this tradition. Apart from the quiet lounge in the Drumheller Inn, there is nowhere respectable to go. The **Alexandra Hotel** (30 Railway Ave. W, 403/823-2642) is a lively rock 'n' roll bar where bands play most nights; cover charge Friday and Saturday. Go anywhere else and, if you're not careful, you'll finish up with more broken bones than an albertosaurus.

ACCOMMODATIONS

Outside of the cities and the Canadian Rockies, Drumheller is the province's next-largest tourist center, attracting more than half a million visitors annually. Yet fewer than 450 motel beds are available in town. Rooms are full by early afternoon every day and advance reservations are necessary in summer. Ask about off-season rates outside of summer.

Less than $50

No regular motels in Drumheller have rooms for less than $50. The only option in this price category is the old **Alexandra Hotel** (30 Railway Ave. W, 403/823-6337), which was extensively renovated in 1991. Even though the rooms were given a coat of paint, they remain basic. Shared facilities include bathrooms, a kitchen, a TV room, and a coin laundry. Rates are $24 single, $30 double for a room with a shared bathroom, $32 single, $40 double for a private bath.

$50–100

The two least expensive motels are at opposite ends of town. The **Hoo-doo Motel** (corner of highways 9 and 56, 403/823-5662) offers basic rooms at $60 single, $65 double, and on the road out to the museum, the **Badlands Motel** (801 N. Dinosaur Trail, 403/823-5155) has a great pancake house next door; $60 single, $65 double. The best asset of the **Lodge at Drumheller** (corner of North Railway Ave. and 1st St. E, 403/823-3322) is that it's right downtown; $60 single, $70 double includes a light breakfast. The two-story **Rockhound Motor Inn,** 403/823-5302, spreads out along the river over the bridge from downtown. It has large rooms of a reasonable standard for $65 single,

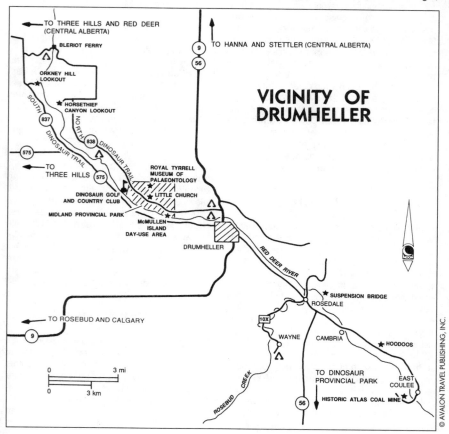

VICINITY OF DRUMHELLER

TO THREE HILLS AND RED DEER (CENTRAL ALBERTA)

BLERIOT FERRY

ORKNEY HILL LOOKOUT

HORSETHIEF CANYON LOOKOUT

SOUTH DINOSAUR TRAIL

NORTH DINOSAUR TRAIL

837

838

575

TO THREE HILLS

575

ROYAL TYRRELL MUSEUM OF PALAEONTOLOGY

LITTLE CHURCH

DINOSAUR GOLF AND COUNTRY CLUB

MIDLAND PROVINCIAL PARK

McMULLEN ISLAND DAY-USE AREA

DRUMHELLER

9

56

TO HANNA AND STETTLER (CENTRAL ALBERTA)

RED DEER RIVER

SUSPENSION BRIDGE

ROSEDALE

TO ROSEBUD AND CALGARY

9

10X

WAYNE

CAMBRIA

HOODOOS

ROSEBUD CREEK

TO DINOSAUR PROVINCIAL PARK

EAST COULEE

56

HISTORIC ATLAS COAL MINE

0   3 mi

0   3 km

hoodoos

$80 double. The **Drumheller Inn** (100 S. Railway Ave., 403-823-8400) is a large hostelry with 100 rooms, an indoor pool, a spa, and two restaurants; $90 single, $99 double.

$100–150

Two new motels provide modern, clean, and comfortable accommodations, and each has an indoor pool. The **Super 8 Motel** (680 2nd St., 403/823-8887 or 888/823-8882, www.super8. com) is situated at Drumheller's busiest intersection. The 49 rooms are each equipped with a small fridge and a microwave; other facilities include an indoor pool. Rates of $79 single, $129 double include a light breakfast. Farther up the hill, as the highway enters the river valley, **Best Western Jurassic Inn** (1103 Highway 9, 403/823-7700 or 888/823-3466, www.bestwestern.com) offers similar facilities as well as a fitness room, a lounge, and a restaurant; $99 single, $129 double.

Bed-and-Breakfasts

Each of the bed-and-breakfasts in town requires advance reservations. Right downtown is the brightly colored **The Inn and Spa at Heartwood** (320 N. Railway Ave., 403/823-6495 or 888/823-6495), surrounded by well-manicured gardens. It features 10 luxurious guest rooms, and the more expensive ones have a hot tub and a fireplace. Rates start at $89 for a room with shared bath, whereas those with ensuites range $120–189. The **Riverside Inn** (501 Riverside Dr. W, 403/823-4746) is also within walking distance of downtown, and five minutes west of Drumheller on South Dinosaur Trail is **Coles B&B,** 403/823-5844. Rates for both are $55 single, $60 double.

Campgrounds

Three campgrounds are located on the north side of the river. **River Grove Campground** (25 Poplar St., 403/823-6655) is in a well-treed spot beside the Red Deer River and offers welcome relief from the heat of the badlands. Serviced sites are semiprivate; tenters have more options and are able to disappear among the trees. The campground offers a nice beach (by Albertan standards), mini-golf, and an arcade, and town is just a short stroll away. Tent sites are $15, hookups $17–22. On the corner of Highway 9 and North Dinosaur Trail is **Dinosaur Trailer Park,** 403/823-3291. Also within walking distance of town, this private campground has unserviced sites for $15, hookups $16–21. On the north side of the river, four kilometers west of the Tyrrell Museum, is **Dinosaur Trail RV Resort,** 403/823-9333, which has a heated pool, groceries, a games room, a laundry room, and canoe rentals. Tent sites are $20, hookups $24–30. All three campgrounds are open April–October.

At the end of the Dinosaur Trail is **Bleriot Ferry Provincial Recreation Area,** with 35 sites, plenty of firewood, a kitchen shelter, and a small beach on the river; $7 per night. **Rosedale,** east of town, has a small, free campground with pit toilets and a kitchen. It's located at the back of town along the road to Wayne. **Wayne,** with a population of approximately 50, has two campgrounds: one beside the saloon, and the other over the green bridge. Each costs $9 and has limited facilities.

FOOD

Drumheller is probably the only place in the world where you can find a Chinese restaurant called **Fred & Barney's** (1222 Highway 9 S beside Reptile World, 403/823-3803). A regular Chinese menu is offered between 11 A.M.–10:30 P.M., but most people come for the excellent buffets served daily. Lunch is $7.95 and dinner (summer only) is $11.95. **The Falcon** (298 Centre St., 403/823-8441) is downstairs in a restored theater building. It also puts on a buffet spread, with lunch $7 and dinner $9. One block farther north is **Sizzling House** (160 Centre St., 403/823-8098), a popular and inexpensive eatery dishing up mostly Szechuan and Beijing cuisine but also some Thai dishes.

All dishes at the **Bridge Greek Restaurant** (71 Bridge St. N, 403/823-3225) are made from scratch, and everything is excellent. Appetizers are $3.50–7.50; try the lemon soup or large Greek salad. Greek entrées start at $11. The house specialty is Kleftiko, juicy spring lamb baked with herbs and spices; have it with the Greek salad for the full effect, or try the generous portion of moussaka. The atmosphere is informal, an abundance of greenery hangs from the ceiling, and later in the evening the chef can often be seen chatting with satisfied patrons. It's open 10:30 A.M.–midnight.

SERVICES AND INFORMATION

Transportation and Tours
Greyhound (308 Centre St., 403/823-7566 or 800/661-8747) has frequent service between Calgary and Drumheller. For a cab, call **Roy's Taxi,** 403/823-8883, or **Jack's Taxi,** 403/823-

2220. **National,** 403/823-3371 or 800/387-4747, is the only car-rental agency in town.

Drumheller Valley Tours, 403/823-7121, offer several tours through the valley; expect to pay from $30 per person for a half-day trip with a knowledgable guide.

Other Services
The **post office** is at 96 Railway Avenue E. You can wash your dusty clothes at the **laundromat** in the Esso gas station on Highway 9 on the south side of town. It's open until 8 P.M. **Drumheller Regional Health Complex** is at 665 Riverside Drive E, 403/823-6500. For the **RCMP,** call 403/823-2630.

Information
Drumheller Information Centre is in the local chamber of commerce building beside the Red Deer River at the corner of Riverside Drive and 2nd Street W (403/823-1331, www.dinosaurvalley.com). You can't miss it— look for the seven-story *Tyrannosaurus rex* in front. It's open daily 9 A.M.–9 P.M. during summer, Mon.–Fri. 9 A.M.–4:30 P.M. the rest of the year. **Drumheller Public Library** is at 224 Centre Street, 403/823-5382.

HIGHWAY 9 EAST

Hanna
This is the heart of goose country. Giant replicas of the Canada gray goose grace the entrances to this town of 2,800, and in fall the area is a mecca for hunters. **Hanna Museum** (east end of 4th Ave., 403/854-4244) is a recreation of a 19th-century village with a church, a railway station, a jail cell, a hospital, and a schoolhouse. It's open daily 10 A.M.–6 P.M. during summer; admission is $2.

Much of the bucking stock that throws the cowboys and woos the crowds at the Calgary Exhibition and Stampede is bred and raised at **Stampede Ranch,** located 50 kilometers south of Hanna. The ranch welcomes visitors (call ahead, 403/566-2206), but don't let anyone talk you into going on a trail ride.

Campers have a few choices. Beside the museum are some hookups ($15); three kilometers north of town is **Fox Lake Campground**

PRONGHORN

These agile and graceful animals (often mistakenly called antelope) that roam Alberta's shortgrass prairie have made a remarkable comeback after being hunted to near extinction in the first quarter of this century. They are easily recognized by their dark muzzles, tan bodies, and large white patches on the rump, cheeks, neck, and belly. Both sexes grow hollow, pronged horns that are shed annually.

Pronghorns have adapted well to life on the plains and are endowed with incredible attributes vital for their survival. Able to sustain speeds up to 80 kph over long distances, they are one of the fastest mammals in the New World. An oversized windpipe helps them to dissipate heat quickly as they breathe, allowing for large extended outbursts of energy. Telescopic eyesight enables them to detect movement from 1.5 km away. When a member of the herd senses danger, hairs on its white rump will stand erect, silently alerting comrades of the threat.

The pronghorn's diet consists primarily of sagebrush, but they'll eat weeds and sometimes grass as well. They obtain sufficient moisture from these plants to allow them to survive hot, dry summers without much to drink. And as a guard against the long and severe prairie winters, these amazing creatures have developed hollow body hairs to insulate against the cold.

($7–12); and 25 kilometers south is **Prairie Oasis Park** ($10), which has a good beach and swimming. The **Hanna Inn** (113 Palliser Trail, 403/854-2400 or 888/854-2401) is a recently renovated Best Western property where rooms are $69 single, $79 double; a restaurant, an indoor pool, a fitness center, and a laundromat are on the premises. The inn's restaurant is a popular place to eat, serving steaks, seafood, and pasta until midnight. The **information center** is in a train caboose on the highway beside Petro-Canada, 403/854-4494.

Oyen

From Hanna, Highway 9 continues east through many small communities to Oyen and into Saskatchewan. Pronghorn have been the most distinctive animal on this part of the prairies for thousands of years and have adapted remarkably well to the environment. Because of overhunting and particularly harsh winters in the early 1900s, their numbers were devastated until three national parks were created to protect them. When their numbers rebounded, the parks were abolished, and today many thousand live on the prairies. At the north end of Main Street is a replica of a pronghorn. **Oyen Crossroads Museum** (312 1st Ave. E, 403/664-2330) has many artifacts relating to the history of the area. It's open daily 9 A.M.–5 P.M. during summer. The campground in town is opposite the golf course; $8 for powered sites. At the junction of highways 9 and 41 is a **Travel Alberta Information Centre**, 403/664-2486, handy for those entering the province here (this highway is the most direct route between Calgary and Saskatoon). It's open mid-May–mid-June 10 A.M.–6 P.M., mid-June–August 9 A.M.–6 P.M.

HIGHWAY 56 NORTH

As Highway 56 passes out of the Red Deer River Valley on the north side of Drumheller, it climbs onto the prairie benchland and heads due north for 100 kilometers to Stettler. Along the route, the towns of Rowley and Big Valley are worth investigating, and **Morrin,** just off the highway, 22 kilometers north of Drumheller, has an interesting sod house, similar to those that many of Alberta's earliest pioneers lived in.

Rowley

The first time I visited Rowley was late one evening. The streets were empty (as they are most of the time), and yet within a few minutes I was in the community hall having coffee and apple pie with members of the town's rapidly shrinking population. It's just that sort of town. Like other prairie towns, many of its residents have moved to larger centers and their houses stand empty, but residents of Rowley have made good from bad. They actively promote the town and its empty buildings as a site for TV

The streets of Rowley are popular with visiting film crews.

commercials and movies. Most of the shopfronts along the main street are locked, but someone is always around to unlock them. In the back of the old café, you can watch videos of clips filmed in town. A small museum is near the rail line.

Big Valley

Located a few kilometers west of Highway 56, Big Valley is a quiet town of 300 with a restored railway station that houses a museum. Farther west, the Red Deer River has carved a canyon 120 meters into the surrounding prairie.

CALGARY TO DINOSAUR PROVINCIAL PARK

STRATHMORE AND VICINITY

From Calgary, the TransCanada Highway parallels the Bow River (although it's never in sight) 100 kilometers to Bassano. The only town along the way is Strathmore, which is home to large stockyards that are a major center for livestock auctions in southern Alberta. To catch the action, head down on Thursdays in summer (weekdays in fall). The yards are on the west side of town, 403/240-7694. The year's biggest event is **Strathmore Heritage Days,** on the August long weekend. Events include an afternoon rodeo (1 P.M.) and evening chuckwagon races (6:30 P.M.). For information, call 403/934-5811.

Wyndham-Carseland Provincial Park

Visit this 178-hectare park for the fishing. Rainbow and brown trout, up to 60 centimeters long, are caught in the Bow River where it flows through the park; the best fishing is in the deeper main channel. Also within the park is a large population of white pelicans, as well as prairie falcons, Canada geese, and great blue herons. This large, 200-site campground is spread out along the river, and all sites are $13. The park is located about 30 kilometers south of Strathmore via Highway 24 or 817.

BASSANO

Bassano is located on the TransCanada Highway midway between Calgary and Medicine Hat. It's a thriving agricultural town of 1,200 people.

Bassano Dam

Bassano Dam is situated six kilometers southwest of town at Horseshoe Bend on the Bow

River. It was built by the Canadian Pacific Railway between 1910 and 1914 to divert water from the Bow River into irrigation canals. Today, those canals provide water for more than 100,000 hectares of land, producing crops such as wheat, hay, potatoes, and beets. At the time of construction, the dam was known as the most important structure of its type in the world because of its great length and unique foundations. It consists of a 2.3-kilometer earthen embankment with 24 steel sluices controlling the river's flow. At the dam is a picnic area, and downstream are campsites.

BROOKS

Brooks (pop. 10,000) is in the heart of Alberta's extensive irrigated farmlands, 160 kilometers east of Calgary along the TransCanada Highway. The town began as a railway stop in the 1880s. Canadian Pacific Railway officials soon realized the potential for homesteading in the area and developed a major irrigation system. Today, the **Eastern Irrigation District** includes two dams, more than 2,000 kilometers of canals, and 2,500 control structures. Brooks offers all tourist services and is a good base for exploring Dinosaur Provincial Park (see following entry). From the TransCanada Highway, take the easternmost exit to access the museum and information center.

Sights
Brooks Aqueduct, seven kilometers southeast of town, was a vital link in the development of agriculture in southeastern Alberta and was used until the 1970s. It carried water across a shallow valley to a dry prairie on the other side, opening up a massive chunk of otherwise unproductive land to farming. At the time of its completion in 1914, the 3.2-kilometer aqueduct was the longest concrete structure of its type in the world and had been designed and built using unique engineering principles. Although now replaced by an earth-filled canal, the impressive structure has been preserved as a National Historic Site and now serves as a monument to those who developed the region. A small interpretive center, 403/362-4451, is open in summer daily 10 A.M.–6 P.M.

Brooks and District Museum (Sutherland Dr., 403/362-5073) catalogs the area's past from the era of dinosaurs to the heady days of a short-lived oil boom. Many restored buildings dot the grounds, including a log cabin built as an outpost for the North West Mounted Police (NWMP) in 1912, and the entrance is guarded by a five-meter-high replica of a hadrosaur. It's open in summer daily 10 A.M.–5 P.M.; admission by donation.

Budding gardeners won't want to miss the **Alberta Special Crops and Horticultural Research Centre** (east of town, 403/362-3391), where research is done on greenhouse crops, various fruits, ornamental flowers, vegetables, and weed control. The grounds are an oasis of flower beds and experimental plots, many of which are open to the public. Free, guided tours are offered through summer Mon.–Fri. 9 A.M.–4 P.M. and on weekends 1–5 P.M. At **Brooks Pheasant Hatchery** (beside Tillebrook Provincial Park east of town, 403/362-4122), ring-necked pheasants are hatched from breeding stock, raised, and released into the wild. A small visitors center is open in summer daily 9 A.M.–4 P.M., weekdays only the rest of the year.

Kinbrook Island Provincial Park
Part of this 48-hectare park, located 13 kilometers south of Brooks, is an island in **Lake Newell,** the largest manmade body of water in Canada. Naturally, most activities revolve around the water—swimming, fishing, and boating are all popular. The lake is home to northern pike, walleye, and whitefish, the latter two of which have been stocked in years gone by. The large expanses of freshwater attract many species of gulls, pelicans, and cormorants, which nest on the islands. The campground has firewood for sale and picnic shelters, and a concession with bike rentals operates during summer. Unserviced sites are $13, powered sites $15; reservations are taken, 403/362-2962. Open year-round.

Accommodations
Vacant motel rooms can be difficult to find in Brooks because it's the last major stop along the TransCanada Highway before Calgary. As usual, the **Super 8 Motel** (Cassils Rd., 403/362-8000 or 800/800-8000, www.super8.com) is a

good choice. This location features 61 air-conditioned rooms, each with a microwave. A continental breakfast is included in the rates of $70 single, $75 double. The best of the bunch of motels along 2nd Street W is **Tel-Star Motor Inn** (813 2nd St. W, 403/362-3466 or 800/260-6211). Each air-conditioned room has a microwave and fridge; $48 single, $54 double. Other options in town are the **Plains Motel** (1004 2nd St. W, 403/362-3367), $51 single, $57 double; the **Heritage Inn** (1303 2nd St. W, 403/362-6666 or 888/888-4374), with an indoor pool, a coffee shop, a restaurant, and more than 100 rooms at $78 single, $87 double; and the **Holiday Inn Express** (1302 2nd St. W, 403/362-7440, www.holiday-inn.com), a new motel where breakfast is included in the rate of $75 single, $85 double.

The **Douglas Country Inn,** 403/362-2873, is located seven kilometers north of Brooks on Highway 873. The seven large rooms are beautifully furnished, one with a fireplace and hot tub. Other amenities include a TV room, a solarium, and a lounge with a fireplace. Rates are $60–99 single or double, including a hearty country breakfast.

Halfway between Brooks and Tilley is **Tillebrook Provincial Park,** one of several campgrounds built along the TransCanada Highway during that road's construction. Tillebrook is an excellent base for exploring Dinosaur Provincial Park and Lake Newell and is one of the province's best developed parks. It has powered sites, enclosed kitchen shelters with gas stoves, showers, a laundromat, summer interpretive programs, and a trail to the aqueduct. Unserviced sites are $15, hookups $18–21. It's open April–October.

Information
The **Information Centre** is in a log building on Cassils Road (coming in from the west, take the second Brooks exit from the TransCanada Highway), 403/362-7641. It's open Wed.–Sun. 11 A.M.–6 P.M.

East to Medicine Hat
Continuing southeast from Brooks on the TransCanada Highway, it's approximately 100 kilometers across the prairies to Medicine Hat. For more information on Medicine Hat, see the **Southern Alberta** chapter.

DINOSAUR PROVINCIAL PARK

Badlands stretch along many river valleys throughout the North American plains, and some of the most spectacular sights are in 7,332-hectare Dinosaur Provincial Park, 200 kilometers east of Calgary. But the park is best known for being one of the most important dinosaur fossil beds in the world. Thirty-five species of dinosaurs—from every known family of the Cretaceous period—have been unearthed here, along with the skeletal remains of crocodiles, turtles, fish, lizards, frogs, and flying reptiles. Not only is the diversity of specimens great, but so is the sheer volume; more than 300 museum-quality specimens have been removed and are exhibited in museums around the world.

Originally established in 1955 to protect the fossil bonebeds, the park's environment is extremely complex and is unique within the surrounding prairie ecosystem. Stands of cottonwoods, a variety of animal life, and, most important, the extensive bonebeds, were instrumental in UNESCO's designation of the park as a World Heritage Site in 1979. In 1985, the opening of the **Royal Tyrrell Museum of Palaeontology,** 100 kilometers upstream in Drumheller, meant that bones that had previously been shipped to museums throughout the world for scientific analysis and display could now remain within the province. The Royal Tyrrell Museum operates a field station in the park, where many of the bones are cataloged and stored. The displays, films, and interpretive programs offered at the center will best prepare you to begin your visit to the park.

Prehistory
Seventy-five million years ago during Cretaceous times, the area was a low-lying marsh at the mouth of a river flowing into the Bearpaw Sea. The Bearpaw was the last in a succession of vast seas that covered the interior plains for 30 million years. Swamp grasses and reeds grew in

DINOSAUR PROVINCIAL PARK FACILITY AREA

RED DEER RIVER

COTTONWOOD FLAT

PARKING

DINOSAUR DISPLAY
PARKING

NOON

SERVICE CENTRE

JOHN WARE CABIN

FIELD STATION

PARKING

PUBLIC LOOP RD.

COULEE VIEWPOINT TRAIL

BADLANDS TRAIL

CREEK

SANDHILL

NATURAL PRESERVE (RESTRICTED ACCESS)

TO BROOKS AND DINOSAUR COUNTRY STORE

LOOKOUT

PARK BOUNDARY

LITTLE

0   0.25 mi

0   0.25 km

© AVALON TRAVEL PUBLISHING, INC.

DINOSAU...

104 DINOSAUR VA...

approximately 1...
hunters simply...
tons for mu...
of excava...
hecta...
tipl...

the wetlands, whereas on higher ground, giant redwoods and palms towered over a dense forest. Dinosaurs flourished in this subtropical environment.

More than millions of years ago, great quantities of silt and mud were flushed downriver, building up a delta at the edge of the sea. In time, this delta hardened, and the countless layers formed sedimentary rock. Soon after, great pressures beneath the earth's surface pushed the crust upward, forming a jagged mountain range that we know today as the Rocky Mountains. This event dramatically changed the climate of the plains region from tropical to temperate, probably killing off the dinosaurs approximately 64 million years ago. From then until one million years ago, the climate changed many times until the first of many sheets of ice covered the plains. As the final sheet receded, approximately 15,000 years ago, millions of liters of sediment-laden meltwater scoured the relative-

ly soft bedrock into an area we know as the badlands. The erosion process continues to this day, no longer by the action of glacial meltwater but by rain and wind. The carving action has created a dramatic landscape of hoodoos, pinnacles, mesas, and gorges in the sandstone here, which is 100 times softer than that of the Rockies. The hills are tiered with layers of rock in browns, reds, grays, and whites. Many are rounded, some are steep, others are ruddy and cracked, but they all have one thing in common—they are laden with dinosaur bones. As the Red Deer River curves through the park, it cuts deeply into the ancient river delta, exposing the layers of sedimentary rock and revealing the once-buried fossil treasures.

Fieldwork in the Park

Each summer, paleontologists from around the world converge on the park for an intense period of digging that starts in late June and lasts for

weeks. The earliest dinosaur
excavated whole or partial skele-
eum display. Although the basic
methods haven't changed, the types
vation have. "Bonebeds" of up to one
re are painstakingly excavated over mul-
summers. Access to much of the park is re-
tricted in order to protect the fossil beds. Digging takes place within the restricted areas.
Work is often continued from the previous season, or new sites are commenced, but there's
never a lack of bones. New finds are often discovered with little digging, having been exposed
by wind and rain since the previous season.

Excavating the bones is an extremely tedious
procedure; therefore, only a few sites are
worked on at a time, with preference given to
particularly important finds such as a new
species. Getting the bones out of the ground is
only the beginning of a long process that culminates with their scientific analysis and display by experts at museums around the world.

EXPLORING THE PARK

Much of the park is protected as a Natural Preserve and is off-limits to unguided visitors because current excavations are taking place. The
Natural Preserve protects the bonebeds and
the valley's fragile environment. It also keeps
visitors from becoming disoriented in the uniform landscape and ending up spending the
night among the bobcats and rattlesnakes. The
area is well marked and should not be entered
except on a guided tour. One other important
rule: *Surface collecting and digging for bones
anywhere within the park is prohibited.*

Interpretive Programs and Tours
Even though much of the actual digging of
bones is done away from public view, the **Field
Station of the Royal Tyrrell Museum,**
403/378-4342, organizes enough interesting
activities and tours to keep you busy for at least
a full day. The Field Station offers many interesting displays, including complete dinosaur
skeletons, murals, and models, and is the departure point for tours into the park. It's open
in summer daily 8:30 A.M.–9 P.M., September–mid-October daily 9 A.M.–4 A.M., and the
rest of the year, weekdays 9 A.M.–4 P.M. Admission is $2.

The **Badlands Bus Tour** takes you on a 90-
minute ride around the public loop road with
an interpretive guide who will point out the
park's landforms and talk about its prehistoric
inhabitants. The **Centrosaurus Bone Bed Hike**
takes visitors on a 2.5-hour guided hike into a
restricted area where more than 300 centrosaurus skeletons have been identified. Studies have been carried out in this area since the
early 1980s. The **Camel's End Coulee Hike** is
an easy 2.5-kilometer guided walk to discover

badlands at Dinosaur
Provincial Park

the unique flora and fauna of the badlands. Finally, a tour of the Field Station Laboratory is offered daily at 1:30 P.M. Space on all of these tours is limited. The laboratory tour is free. Each of the other tours costs $4.50. The tours are *very* popular, and this is reflected in the procedure for purchasing tickets. Tour tickets go on sale May 1 and must be picked up 30 minutes before the departure time. To reserve a seat, call 403/378-4344 Mon.–Fri. 9 A.M.–4 P.M. Some tickets are reserved for the day of the tour and sold as "rush" tickets (be at the Field Station when it opens at 8:30 A.M. to ensure that you get a ticket).

Movies are shown at the Field Station in the evenings, and special events are often staged somewhere in the park. The entire interpretive program operates in summer only, with certain tours offered in late May and September.

On Your Own
You may explore the area bounded by the public loop road and take three short interpretive trails on your own. The **loop road** passes through part of the area where bones were removed during the Great Canadian Dinosaur Rush. By staying within its limits, hikers are prevented from becoming lost, although the classic badlands terrain is still littered with fragments of bones, and the area is large enough to make you feel "lost in time." It's a fantastic place to explore. Of special interest are two dinosaur dig sites excavated earlier this century, one of which contains a still-intact skeleton of a duck-billed hadrosaur.

The **Badlands Trail** is a 1.4-kilometer loop that starts just east of the campground and passes into the restricted area. The **Coulee Viewpoint Trail,** which begins behind the Field Station, climbs steadily for 500 meters to a high ridge above Little Sandhill Creek. It's easy to ignore the nearby floodplains, but the large stands of cottonwoods you'll see were a con-

tributing factor to the park being designated as a UNESCO World Heritage Site. The **Cottonwood Flats Trail** starts 1.4 kilometers along the loop road, leading through the trees and into old river channels that lend themselves to good bird-watching.

The 1902 log cabin of black cowboy John Ware has been moved to the park and restored, and it is now open to the public. Many regard Ware—originally a southern slave who came north on an 1882 cattle drive—as the greatest horseman ever to ride in the Canadian West.

PRACTICALITIES

Accommodations and Camping
The park's campground is in a low-lying area beside Little Sandhill Creek. It has 128 sites, pit toilets, a kitchen shelter, and a few powered sites. Unserviced sites cost $15, powered sites $17. The campground fills up by early afternoon. To book a site, call 403/378-3700. Along the access road is **Dinosaur Corner Service,** which has a grassy spot for camping; tents $10, powered sites $14. The next closest alternative is in Brooks. **Patricia Hotel,** in Patricia, 15 kilometers from the park, 403/378-4647, is known for its Western atmosphere. Many of the cattle brands on the walls date back more than 50 years. The hotel has basic rooms with shared and private baths from $40 single, $45 double. The bar downstairs gets fairly lively, and there's a nightly cook-your-own barbecue.

Services and Information
The only commercial facility within the park is the **Dinosaur Service Centre,** a fast-food place open limited hours each day. Within the center are laundry facilities and coin showers. No groceries are available in the park.

For information, contact Dinosaur Provincial Park at 403/378-4342, www.gov.ab.ca/env/parks.

KAREN McKINLEY

SOUTHERN ALBERTA

We have passed through a country, dry, desolate, and barren, a very Sahara. It was the northern portion of the Great American Desert: but now we have fortunately come into a country that shows even in this late season, evidence of great fertility. We are just near the base of the Rocky Mountains; their snow-capped summits rise up to our left in jagged, rough peaks; the sun sinks behind them every night in one blaze of glory, making the most gorgeous sunsets that I have ever seen.

—R.B. Nevitt,
11 October 1874

Southern Alberta is bordered to the east by Saskatchewan, to the south by Montana, USA, and to the west by British Columbia. The Alberta/British Columbia border is along the Continental Divide, where the Canadian Rockies rise

dramatically from the prairies and are visible from up to 200 kilometers away. From high in these mountains, the Oldman, Crowsnest, Waterton, St. Mary, and Belly rivers flow east through the rolling foothills and across the shortgrass prairies into the South Saskatchewan River, which eventually drains into Hudson Bay. Among southern Alberta's rivers, only the Milk River is not part of this system; from its headwaters in northern Montana, the river flows north and east across southern Alberta before reentering the United States west of Wild Horse. From there, it joins the Missouri/Mississippi River System, eventually draining into the Gulf of Mexico. All of these rivers have carved deep gorges into the prairies, providing havens for many species of wildlife, including pronghorn, deer, foxes, coyotes, and bobcats.

For many people, a trip to southern Alberta starts in Calgary, from where they take Highway 2 south through Claresholm and Fort Macleod to Alberta's third-largest city, Lethbridge, a farming and ranching center 216 kilometers southeast of Calgary. Lethbridge offers many interesting things to see, including Fort Whoop-Up, a reconstruction of a notorious post where whiskey and guns were traded with the natives for buffalo hides.

East of Lethbridge, in an area declared "unsuitable for agriculture" by early explorer John Palliser, the city of Medicine Hat has grown up on top of vast reserves of natural gas. Traveling south from Medicine Hat, the Cypress Hills soon come into view, rising 500 meters above the prairies. The tree-covered plateau provides a refuge for many species of mammals, and mountain plants flourish here, far from the Rockies.

Southern Alberta reveals plentiful evidence of its history and prehistory. Thousands of years of wind and water erosion have uncovered the world's best-preserved dinosaur eggs near Milk River and have carved mysterious-looking sandstone hoodoos farther downstream at Writing-On-Stone Provincial Park—named for the abundant rock carvings and paintings created there by ancient artists. Head-Smashed-In Buffalo Jump, west of Fort Macleod, was used for at least 5,700 years by native peoples to drive massive herds of buffalo to their deaths.

The breathtaking mountainscapes of Waterton Lakes National Park are comparable to those of Banff and Jasper national parks, Waterton's two northern neighbors. The route to the park is scenic because the transition from prairie to mountain peaks is abrupt. Most activities in the park center around the park's namesake, but the park also offers some of the best wildlife-viewing opportunities in the province. One of the highlights of a visit to Waterton is an international cruise across the border to Goat Haunt, Montana.

The Municipality of Crowsnest Pass comprises several small communities that extend from the ranching center of Pincher Creek west to the British Columbia border. They were established to serve the pass's coal-mining industry, but after a series of disasters—some mining related, some not—the mines closed. Today the towns are only shadows of their former selves, and the entire corridor has been declared an ecomuseum. Here you can walk through the foundations of once-thriving communities, tour an underground mine, or climb infamous Turtle Mountain.

See color map of Southern Alberta, page ix.

CALGARY TO LETHBRIDGE

The trip between Alberta's largest and third-largest cities takes about two hours each way, with many worthwhile detours in between, including the ranching country southwest of Calgary (see **Ranchlands** in the West of Calgary chapter), the Porcupine Hills west of Claresholm, historic Fort Macleod, and Head-Smashed-In Buffalo Jump, one of the best-preserved sites of its type in North America.

NANTON AND VICINITY

This town of 1,800 people, located 70 kilometers south of Calgary, is a stop along busy Highway 2 and a supply center for nearby ranches. The highway divides through town, with the information center and many antique shops lining the northbound lanes. Nanton Spring Water Company bottles some of Canada's finest drinking water and distributes it throughout the world.

Sights
The **Nanton Lancaster Society Air Museum,** 403/646-2270, features one of the few Lancaster bombers still in existence. The Lancaster is a Canadian-built, four-engined, heavy bomber that played a major role in World War II air offensives on Nazi Germany. On the guided tour, you can sit in the plane's cockpit and look through the sight of the machine gun. A replica of another classic—a Vickers Viking biplane—sits outside. Other displays focus on Canada's role in World War II. The museum, on Highway 2 southbound, is open in summer daily 9 A.M.–8 P.M. and in spring and fall daily 9 A.M.–5 P.M.

An early-20th-century schoolhouse on the corner of Highway 2 northbound and 18th Avenue now holds the town's **Tourist Information Centre.**

Events
Every Friday and Saturday during July and August, the **Nanton Nite Rodeo** at the Rodeo

Grounds attracts local amateurs who are keen to test their skills. **Roundup Days,** the town's midsummer festival, held the last weekend of July, features a rodeo, beerfest, and road rally. Some of Canada's best musicians gather for the **Shady Grove Bluegrass Festival.** It takes place the third weekend of August at Broadway Farm, 13 kilometers east of Nanton; for more information, call 403/225-3845 or 403/652-5550.

Accommodations

The best place to stay in Nanton is the **Ranchland Inn** (on Highway 2 northbound, 403/646-2933), offering 26 basic but comfortable rooms for $50 single, $60 double. **Nanton Campground** is east of town on 18th Street, adjoining the local 18-hole golf course. Scattered among a grove of trees, the sites have picnic tables, and campers have the use of a covered cooking shelter and showers; $10 per night.

Willow Creek Provincial Park

South of Nanton, along the eastern edge of the Porcupine Hills and 14 kilometers west of the traffic roar on Highway 2, tree-lined Willow Creek flows through quiet Willow Creek Provincial Park. Generations of native tribes hunted and camped in the area; just outside the park you can find a buffalo jump and tepee rings well hidden in the grass. Visitors today swim in the creek and camp here. Up on the benchland is a campground with limited services; $13 per night. To reach the park, head west from Stavely.

Farther downstream on Willow Creek lies another historical site. **The Leavings** was a stopover on the Macleod Trail, aptly named to remind travelers they were leaving the last supply of water before Calgary. Later used as a North West Mounted Police (NWMP) post, the site was abandoned when the railway was laid farther to the east. Many sandstone foundations remain, as well as some log cabins and a sandstone barn with tree-trunk floorboards. By road the site is seven kilometers west of Highway 2 near Pultenay.

CLARESHOLM

When the Calgary and Edmonton Railway Line extended south from Calgary in 1891, a new town emerged at its southern terminus. As boomtown storefronts sprang up along the rail line and large landholdings were bought nearby, the town quickly gained a reputation as the hub of a leading grain-producing area and has prospered ever since. Clare Amundsen, the town's namesake, was one of its earliest settlers.

Most people stop at Claresholm (pop. 3,400), 100 kilometers south of Calgary, just long enough to fill up with gas, grab a burger, and stretch their legs. But it's worth more than a quick stop. Many of the buildings facing Highway 2 date to the early 1900s. The airbase at Claresholm was an aircrew training center during World War II and is still active today, hosting national and international soaring and gliding competitions. In town are two museums, and the Porcupine Hills to the west make an interesting detour.

Sights

The **Claresholm Museum** (5126 Railway Ave., 403/625-3131), in the Canadian Pacific Railway (CPR) station, holds an array of historical displays, including a dental clinic and a rail ticket office. The Claresholm **Tourist Information Centre** is also inside the museum. Both are open mid-May–mid-September daily 9:30 A.M.–5:30 P.M.; museum admission is $1. A brochure entitled *A Walking Tour of Claresholm,* available from the museum, details the town's historic buildings and sites.

The **Appaloosa Horse Club of Canada** has a small museum (4189 3rd St. E, 403/625-3326) that is one of only two such museums in the world. Native Americans brought the first Appaloosas over the border in the late 1800s. On display is a 200-year-old native saddle. The museum is open year-round Mon.–Fri. 8:30 A.M.–4:30 P.M.

Accommodations and Food

Motels and fast-food restaurants line Highway 2. The nicest of the accommodations is the **Bluebird Motel,** 403/625-3395 or 800/661-4891, at the north end of town. All rooms are air-conditioned and feature large TVs and coffeemakers; most also have refrigerators. Rates range $59–63 single or double. Two other motels along Highway 2 are similarly priced, but not as nice.

Centennial Park (4th St. W, north off Highway

520, 403/625-2751) is in a residential area close to the golf course. It offers powered sites, showers, and kitchen shelters; unserviced sites $8–11, hookups $15.

A&B Bakery (129 50th Ave. W) has delicious breads, pastries, and donuts. Along the highway you'll find a string of greasy-spoon restaurants. The **Old Fox Inn,** on Highway 2 south of the Tourist Information Centre, is worth investigating just for the effort put into the front doors; its inexpensive burgers and the fries with sour cream and chives are favorites.

Porcupine Hills

The Porcupine Hills, west of Claresholm on Highway 520, rest between the mountains and the plains, yet rise higher than the foothills to the west and support vegetation from four climatic zones: grassland, parkland, subalpine forest, and montane. They are bordered to the east by Highway 2, to the west by Highway 22, and extend south to Head-Smashed-In Buffalo Jump and north past Nanton. The Blackfoot call the area *Ky-es-kaghp-ogh-suy-is* (porcupine tails), describing how the forested ridges looked to natives. The heavily wooded Porcupine Hills are home to a variety of wildlife, including white-tailed and mule deer, elk, moose, coyote, lynx, beaver, pheasant, and wild turkey.

From Claresholm, Highway 520 climbs slowly west for 32 kilometers, passes through Burke Creek Ranch (one of Alberta's oldest ranches— look for classic buildings scattered by the creek), and continues into the **Rocky Mountain Forest Reserve.** It eventually crests a hill, affording breathtaking views of the Canadian Rockies before dropping down to Highway 22. At this hillcrest, **Skyline Road** branches off to the south into the Porcupine Hills, where rewarding hiking trails and sweeping views await explorers. Roads through this area can take you all the way to Cowley.

HIGHWAY 23 SOUTH

An eastern alternative to four-lane Highway 2 between Calgary and Lethbridge is Highway 23. From High River, it runs east past Frank Lake; after 35 kilometers, it turns south, skirting the western edge of the prairies. Along the way you'll pass the wheat-farming towns of Vulcan, Champion, Carmangay, and Barons. Highway 23 dead-ends at Highway 3, 17 kilometers west of Lethbridge.

Brant

After passing Frank Lake, Highway 23 east intersects with Highway 804, which detours south to Brant. The town was named for the Brant geese that rest in the area on their migration to and from the north. In 1915, Brant was a prosperous town of 125. But the Great Depression brought grain prices down, forcing farmers to make do with existing machinery. As a result, the dealerships, banks, and other businesses began to close, and many of the children of the 1940s and 1950s moved away. As the old-timers died and no one moved in to replace them, the town's population dwindled. The railway cut back services, the general store closed, and today only empty buildings and a grain elevator remain.

Vulcan

Halfway between Calgary and Lethbridge on Highway 23 lies Vulcan (pop. 1,600), named after the Greek god who lived on Mt. Olympus— the townsite sits on a not-so-Olympian rise above the surrounding prairie. Vulcan is also known as the "Wheat Capital of Canada" and has 12 grain elevators capable of holding more than two million bushels of grain.

Little Bow Provincial Park

On the banks of Travers Reservoir east of Champion is Little Bow Provincial Park, an extremely popular place for fishing, swimming, and boating, especially on summer weekends. Heavy irrigation creates the park's green lawns and lush vegetation—a welcome sight after driving through parched and scorched prairies. Some of the province's largest pike live in the reservoir, a feature that attracts anglers year-round. Canoe rentals are available from a lakeside concession. The large campground has a beach, kitchen shelter, showers, and firewood; $13 per night.

On the access road to the park, 1.5 kilometers from Highway 23, a stone cairn marks the site of Cleverville, a once-busy town forced to move when bypassed by the CPR. The new town, now at the junction of Highway 23 and the park access road, was named Champion and today serves as a center for nearby wheat farms. The **Champion Inn,** 403/897-3055, offers basic but clean rooms with shared bathrooms for $28 single or double, $35 with private bathroom. Downstairs is a restaurant (open daily 7 A.M.–10 P.M.) and a bar.

Tepee Rings in a Field
In an unimposing grassy field between Highway 23 and Little Bow River just north of Carmangay are nine circles of stone, mute testimony to the prehistoric people who roamed the plains of North America. Known as tepee rings, the stones were used to hold down the edges of natives' conical, bison-hide-covered tents. The lack of other artifacts, such as tools and bones, leads archaeologists to believe that this particular site was used for only a short time. A well-worn path leads from the parking lot to a ring that has been partially disturbed; better rings lay to the left of the path.

FORT MACLEOD

Southern Alberta's oldest permanent settlement is Fort Macleod (pop. 3,200), located 172 kilometers south of Calgary and 44 kilometers west of Lethbridge and just east of the junction of highways 2 and 3. In 1873, the West was in turmoil. Relations between American whiskey traders and natives had reached an all-time low, and intertribal wars were resulting in murder and massacre. That's when politicians in eastern Canada decided to do something about it. A paramilitary mounted police force, led by Colonel James F. Macleod, was sent west with orders to close down Fort Whoop-Up, a notorious whiskey-trading post located where the city of Lethbridge now stands. After finding it empty, they decided to push on farther west and build their own fort. The site chosen was an island in the Oldman River, one kilometer east of the present town of Fort Macleod. These early Mounties constructed the fort for the same reason as the whiskey traders—to prevent attacks by natives. But although the whiskey traders were encouraging natives to visit and trade their precious pelts, the police force was trying to drive the traders out of the region. These first troops of the NWMP

eventually put an end to the illicit whiskey trade, and with the help of Métis scout Jerry Potts—who ironically didn't mind a drop of the hard stuff himself—they managed to restore peace between the warring tribes. Potts stayed at Fort Macleod until he died and is buried in the local cemetery. The original fort had continual flooding problems. It was relocated to higher ground in the 1880s, and the town of Fort Macleod gradually grew up around it.

Historic Downtown
In 1906, a fire destroyed most of the wooden buildings on Main Street, so a bylaw was passed requiring any new structures to be built of brick or stone. The legacy of this bylaw remains in the 30 buildings of historical significance forming the downtown core, which has been declared an historic district. Many of the buildings function as they did during the town's boom years; the **Queen's Hotel** has rooms, the **Empress Theatre** is the oldest operating theater in the province, and Main Street comes alive with parades and dances during the summer months. Throughout summer, guided walking tours of town leave regularly from the Fort Museum. Or you can get the walking-tour brochure and do it at your own pace.

Fort Museum
The original fort on the Oldman River would have looked much like the Fort Museum does today, a crude structure approximately 40 meters wide and 50 meters long lined with buildings facing a central courtyard. The museum details the history of the NWMP and the early days of settlement in southern Alberta. Inside are various buildings reflecting aspects of frontier life, including a chapel, a blacksmith shop, an NWMP building, a law office, a tepee, and the Centennial Building, which is devoted to the history of the Plains tribes. Two corner blockhouses with panoramic views of the Oldman River were used as lookouts. In the arena during summer, riders dress in period costume and perform the **Mounted Police Musical Ride**—a spectacular display of precision riding—four times daily at 10 A.M., 11:30 A.M., 2 P.M., and 3:30 P.M. The museum is at 219 25th Street (westbound), 403/553-4703. It's open July–Aug. daily 9 A.M.–8:30 P.M.; May–June and September daily 9 A.M.–5 P.M.;

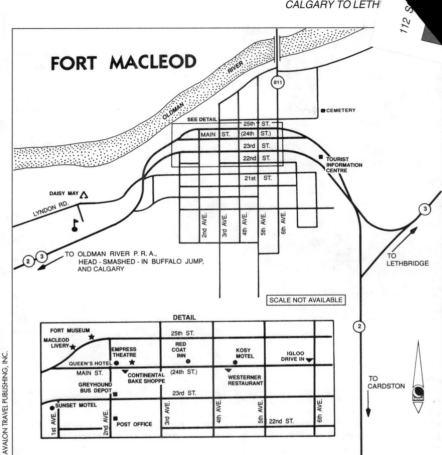

and the rest of the year weekdays 9:30 A.M.–4 P.M. Admission is \$4.50, which includes the Musical Ride.

Macleod Livery

Beside the museum is Macleod Livery, 403/553-4868, a reconstruction of pioneer buildings, with farm animals running around and a shaded picnic area. A small admission fee is charged. Horse-drawn carriage rides through town are \$7 per person, and rides down to the old fort site are \$10 per person. The carriages used are

beautifully restored and worth a look even if you don't plan on a tour.

Entertainment

The stage of the venerable 1912 **Empress Theatre** at 235 24th Street has been graced by acts from as far away as New York and Australia. Through its long history it has hosted vaudeville shows, opera and theater performances, political rallies, and film screenings—changing uses with the changing times. The theater has been renovated and returned to its former glory, and it

Many historic buildings line Fort Macleod's main street.

once again provides a venue for live shows and musical theater. Through the months of summer, three or four different productions are performed by the Great West Theatre Company. For schedule and ticket information, call 403/553-4404 or 800/540-9229. Most shows are less than $10. If nothing's happening at the Empress, check out the loud and boisterous **Midnight Lounge** in the Westerner Restaurant. It's open until 2 A.M. nightly, with a DJ on Saturday nights.

Accommodations
Motel rooms fill up fast every afternoon in summer, so book ahead or check in early. None of the motels offer rooms with kitchens, but all have air-conditioned rooms—a definite plus to combat the summer heat. Rates fluctuate with the season; expect to pay 20–30 percent less outside of summer. The least expensive rooms in town (with good reason) are at the **Queen's Hotel** (207 24th St., 403/553-4343); $28 single, $35 double. The strip of motels along the east end of

24th Street is the best place to start looking. At **Kosy Motel** (433 24th St., 403/553-3115, the 12 rooms are clean and comfortable and priced at a reasonable $45 single, $55 double. One step up is the **Red Coat Inn** (359 24th St., 403/553-4434 or 800/423-4434), offering an indoor pool; $54 single, $64 double. At the west entrance to town is the **Sunset Motel** (104 Highway 3 W, 403/553-4448 or 888/554-2784), where each of the 22 rooms has a small fridge. Coffee and toast are available in the morning; $54–60 single or double.

Daisy May Campground, 403/553-2455, is beside Alberta's oldest golf course and within walking distance of the museum and downtown. It provides showers, a camp kitchen, a heated pool, laundry facilities, and a game room. Tent sites cost $15, sites with hookups $19–22. North of the junction of highways 2 and 3 toward Calgary is **Oldman River Provincial Recreation Area,** with primitive campsites for $9 per night.

Food
In the heart of historic downtown Fort Macleod, the **Continental Bake Shoppe** (220 24th St., 403/553-4124) offers tasty cooked breakfasts from $4.50 and similarly priced sandwiches and bagels Monday–Saturday until 5:30 P.M. The **Westerner Restaurant** (404 Main St., 403/553-4066) has big breakfasts for $4–6; the omelettes are excellent. Lunch and dinner items range from $5.50–14 and all include soup or salad. It's open Mon.–Sat. 6 A.M.–midnight, Sunday 6 A.M.–10 P.M. For low-priced fast food, try **Igloo Drive In** (at the corner of 24th St. and 6th Ave., 403/553-4227), where you can get a burger, fries, and shake for $6.

Services and Information
Greyhound (1015 Hewiston Ave., 403/553-3383) leaves five times daily for Calgary and twice daily for Lethbridge. **Laundrette Kome Kleen** is behind the Sunset Motel and is open daily 8 A.M.–10 P.M. The **library** (264 24th St., 403/553-3880) is open Monday–Saturday 1–5 P.M. The museum gift shop has a large selection of local history and Canadiana books. The **Tourist Information Centre** is at the east end of town on 24th Street, 403/553-4955; open mid-May–August daily 9 A.M.–6 P.M.

HEAD-SMASHED-IN BUFFALO JUMP

Archaeologists have discovered dozens of buffalo jumps across the North American plains. The largest, oldest, and best preserved is Head-Smashed-In, which is located along a weathered sandstone cliff in the Porcupine Hills 19 kilometers northwest of Fort Macleod. At the base is a vast graveyard with thousands of years worth of bones from butchered bison piled 10 meters high. The jump represents an exceptionally sophisticated and ingenious hunting technique used by Plains natives at least 5,700 years ago—possibly up to 10,000 years ago—to cunningly outwit thousands of bison, once the largest mammal on the plains.

At the time white settlers arrived on the prairies, more than 60 million American bison (also known as buffalo) roamed the plains. The people of the plains depended almost en-tirely on these prehistoric-lo their survival. They ate the m it for pemmican; made tepe moccasins from the hides; ar and decorations from the horns. Several meth ods were used to kill the bison, but by far the most successful method was to drive entire herds over a cliff face. The topography of this region was ideal for such a jump. To the west is a large basin of approximately 40 square kilometers where bison grazed. They were herded from the basin east along carefully constructed stone cairns (known as drive lines) that led to a precipice where the stampeding bison, with no chance of stopping, plunged to their deaths below. Nearby was a campsite where they butchered and processed the meat.

The site has been well preserved. Although a small section of the hill has been excavated, most of it appears today the same as it has for thousands of years. The relative height of the cliff, however, drastically decreased with the buildup of bones. Along with the bones are countless numbers of artifacts such as stone points, knives, and scrapers used to skin the fallen beasts. Metal arrowheads found in the top layer of bones indicate that the jump was used up until the coming of whites in the late 1700s. In recognizing the site's cultural and historical importance, UNESCO declared the jump a World Heritage Site in 1981.

How the Jump Got Its Name
The name Head-Smashed-In has no connection to the condition of the bison's heads after tumbling over the cliff. It came from a Blackfoot legend: About 150 years ago, a young hunter wanted to watch the buffalo as they were driven over the steep cliff. He stood under a ledge watching as the stampeding beasts fell in front of him, but the hunt was better than usual, and as the animals piled up, he became wedged between the animals and the cliff. Later his people found him, his skull crushed under the weight of the buffalo—hence the name, Head-Smashed-In.

Interpretive Centre
As you approach the jump site along Spring Point Road, the Head-Smashed-In Interpretive Centre doesn't become visible until you've

Allow at least two hours in the interpretive center.

d your car and actually arrived at the entrance. The center—disguised in the natural topography of the landscape—is set into a cliff, part of which had to be blasted away to build it. A series of ramps and elevators marks the beginning of your tour as you rise to the roof from where a trail leads along the clifftop to the jump site. It isn't hard to imagine the sounds and spectacle of thousands of bison stampeding over the rise to the north and tumbling to their deaths below. To the east is the **Calderwood Buffalo Jump,** which can be seen farther along the cliff face.

Back inside you walk down floor by floor, passing displays and films explaining in an interesting and informative way the traditional way of life that existed on the prairies for nearly 10,000 years, as well as the sudden changes that took place when the first white men arrived. The lowest level describes the archaeological methods used to excavate the site and how the ancient cultures of the various Plains peoples are unraveled from the evidence found. A 10-minute movie, *In Search of the Buffalo,* cataloging the hunt, is shown every half hour on Level Four.

Outside the center is another trail that leads along the base of the cliff for a different perspective. Here a large aluminum building covers a recent dig site; the ground is littered with shattered bones. The center also has a gift shop and café selling, of all things, buffalo burgers. The year's largest event is **Head-Smashed-In Days** in mid-July, when a large tepee village is constructed on the grounds and native dance competitions, food tastings, and activities for all ages are presented. Each Saturday afternoon in July and August, a noted authority on a subject relevant to the jump presents a short show on his or her field of expertise.

The center is open in summer daily 9 A.M.–7 P.M., the rest of the year daily 9 A.M.–5 P.M. Admission is adults $6.50, seniors $5.50, children $3, half-price on Tuesday from October–April. For more information, contact the center at 403/553-2731, www.head-smashed-in.com.

LETHBRIDGE

An urban oasis on the prairies, this city of rich ethnic origins has come a long way since the 1860s when Fort Whoop-Up, the most notorious whiskey-trading fort in the West, was the main reason folks came to town. Today, Lethbridge is an important commercial center serving the surrounding ranch and farm country. With a population of 69,000, it is Alberta's third-largest city, and on any given day the downtown streets are busy with a colorful array of ranchers, cowboys, Hutterites, natives, and suited professionals. The city is also a transportation hub, with highways 3, 4, and 5 converging here. Calgary is 215 kilometers to the north, Medicine Hat 168 kilometers to the east, Waterton Lakes National Park 130 kilometers to the west, and the International Boundary 105 kilometers to the south.

In the last 20 years, Lethbridge has blossomed in a controlled way. Many of the city's sites of historical importance have been preserved, or in the case of Fort Whoop-Up, reconstructed. The Sir Alexander Galt Museum is one of the best museums in the province, and the Nikka Yuko Japanese Garden is symbolic of the culture from which many of the city's residents descended.

History

Lethbridge has always been a transportation and trade crossroads. Until the first half of the 19th century, it was the territory of various tribes of the powerful Blackfoot Confederacy. The tribes sheltered from the extreme winters at a site in the Oldman River Valley known to them as *Sik-ooh-kotoks* (black rocks) because of an exposed coal seam on the east bank of the river at that spot. The first white traders to the area arrived in the 1850s. Soon after came the whiskey traders who had been forced north by the U.S. Army. Fort Whoop-Up, built on the east bank of the Oldman River, became the most notorious of approximately 50 whiskey posts in southern Alberta.

The arrival of whiskey on the plains coincided with a smallpox epidemic and the dislocation of the Cree, who had been forced by the arrival of European settlers into the territory of the

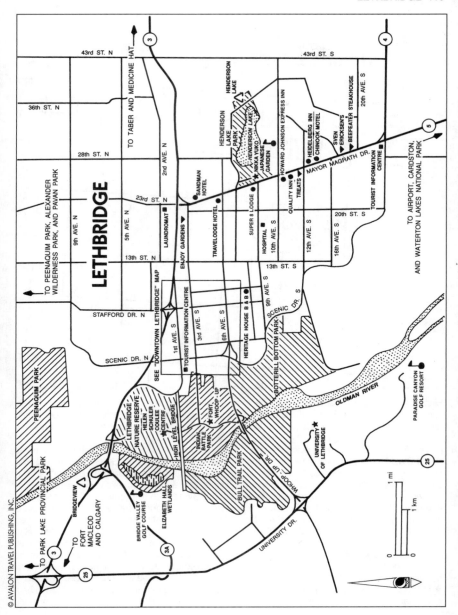

© AVALON TRAVEL PUBLISHING, INC.

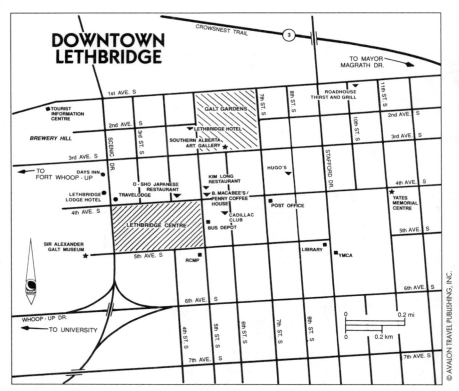

DOWNTOWN LETHBRIDGE

Blackfoot, their traditional enemies. These factors combined to create a setting for the last great intertribal battle to be fought in North America.

At dawn on October 25, 1870, a party of approximately 800 Cree warriors attacked a band of Blood Blackfoot camping on the west bank of the Oldman River. Unknown to the Cree, a large party of Peigan Blackfoot was camped nearby. Alerted by scouts, the Peigan crossed the river and joined the fray, forcing the Cree back into what is now known as Indian Battle Park. More than 300 Cree and approximately 50 Blackfoot were killed.

By 1880, the whiskey forts had been closed down by the NWMP, and the last of the natives had been resettled in reserves.

Nicholas Sheran, an Irish-American adventurer, was the first to realize the potential of the coal-bearing seams along the Oldman River. He established the first mine on the river, named Coalbanks. It was only a small operation, but it was large enough to attract the attention of English entrepreneur Elliot Galt. With the help of his father—Sir Alexander Galt—Elliot financed a large-scale drift mine in the east bank of the river, where the Coalbanks Interpretive Site now sits. By 1884, the hamlet of Coalbanks had sprung up around the mine entrance, and a sawmill was established. At first the Galts used sternwheel river steamers to transport the coal to Medicine Hat, but on many occasions, the current was so strong that the steamers required as much coal for the return trip as they were capable of hauling on the way out. So, after two years, a narrow-gauge railway was constructed to haul the coal. This advance shifted the community's focus away from the river's edge and up onto the prairie, where the town that took root came to be named Lethbridge. William Lethbridge was an Englishman who never set foot in Alberta, but being a friend of Galt, and a major financier in the Galts' coal mine, the town was named for him.

In 1909, the High Level Bridge—at that time the highest and longest structure of its type in the world—was constructed over the river valley, completing a more permanent link to Fort Macleod and Calgary. The last of the mines closed in 1942, and by 1960 the first of what is now a string of urban parks along the valley was established.

SIGHTS

With Lethbridge continuing to sprawl, particularly on the west side of the river, downtown businesses are trying their hardest to convince shoppers and visitors that "Downtown L.A." (Lethbridge, Alberta) really does have something to offer. Almost all sites downtown are within walking distance of each other. On market days, the many Hutterites who come to town are easy to recognize—the men wear black pants and those that are married have beards; the women wear colorful purple and red dresses and bonnets.

The **Southern Alberta Art Gallery** (601 3rd Ave. S in Galt Gardens, 403/327-8770) has contemporary and historical exhibitions that change throughout the year. It's open Tues.–Sat. 10 A.M.–5 P.M., Sunday 1–5 P.M.; admission by donation.

Sir Alexander Galt Museum

This excellent history-and-art museum is in a former hospital, named for Sir Alexander Galt, who helped finance the coal-mining operation that was fundamental in establishing the city. It was renovated in 1985 at a cost of $2.85 million and is now considered one of the best small-city museums in the country. The first gallery provides a view across the valley—in effect a panorama of the city's past. From this vantage point, you can see the site of the last major intertribal battle in North America, old coal mines, Fort Whoop-Up, and the High Level Bridge.

Other galleries contain exhibits explaining the history of the coal mines, the introduction of irrigation, the area's immigrants, and the city since World War II. Two additional galleries have rotating art exhibits of local interest. The museum is at the west end of 5th Avenue S off Scenic Drive. It's open July–Aug. Mon.–Thurs. 9 A.M.–8 P.M., Friday 9 A.M.–4 P.M., Sat.–Sun. 1–8 P.M.; the rest of the year Mon.–Fri. 10 A.M.–4 P.M., Sat.–Sun. 1–4 P.M. Admission is free. For more information, call 403/320-3898.

Fort Whoop-Up

This impressively palisaded structure in Indian Battle Park is a replica of the most notorious whiskey-trading post in the West. After the U.S. Army put a stop to the illicit trade in Montana, these traders of sorts simply began moving north into what is now Alberta. In December 1869, John Healy and Alfred Hamilton came north from Fort Benton, Montana, and established a fort on the Oldman River that soon became the whiskey-trading headquarters for southern Alberta. The story goes that its name was coined by someone who had returned to Fort Benton and, when asked how things were going at Hamilton's Fort, replied, "Oh, they're still whoopin' it up." Trading was simple. Natives pushed buffalo hides through a small opening in the fort wall. In return they were handed a tin cup of whiskey, which was often watered down. The success of the trade led to the formation of the NWMP, who rode west with orders to close down all whiskey-trading forts and end the lawless industry. The Mounties were preceded by word of their approach, and the fort was empty by the time they arrived in 1874. A cairn marks the fort's original location.

A reconstruction of the fort, complete with costumed staff, relives the days when "firewater" was traded for hides and horses. The fort looks much as it would have in 1869. A cannon used to defend the fort is on display, an audiovisual presentation is shown, and the Whoop-Up flag—now the official flag of Lethbridge—flies high above. To get there from the city center, turn west onto 3rd Avenue S and follow it down into the coulee. It's open mid-May to early September Mon.–Sat. 10 A.M.–6 P.M., Sunday noon–5 P.M.; admission is $3. For more information, call 403/329-0444.

Lethbridge Nature Reserve and Helen Schuler Coulee Centre

Lethbridge is unique in that it's built on the prairie benchlands and not beside the river that flows so close to town. The largely undisturbed Oldman River Valley has been developed into reserves and parks. One of these, the Lethbridge Nature Reserve, is an 82-hectare area of floodplain and coulees. It's home to the great horned owl—Alberta's provincial bird—porcupines, white-tailed deer, and prairie rattlesnakes. It's also home to the Helen Schuler Coulee Centre, which offers interpretive displays focusing on the entire urban park system. The center is the best place to start exploring the valley. From here, three short trails lead around the floodplain and through stands of cottonwood trees. To get there from downtown, head west on 3rd Avenue S, take a right just before Fort Whoop-Up, and pass under the High Level Bridge. It's open June–Aug. Sun.–Thurs. 10 A.M.–8 P.M., Fri.–Sat. 10 A.M.–6 P.M., the rest of the year Tues.–Sun. 1–4 P.M. For more information, call 403/320-3064.

Other Valley Parks

The most historically important urban park in Lethbridge is 102-hectare **Indian Battle Park.** It is named after the last great battle fought between the Cree and the Blackfoot, which took place on the west side of the river in 1870. Within the park, near Fort Whoop-Up, is a "medicine stone" that the Blackfoot believed had sacred significance—for many years they left offerings around it. Also in the park, the **Coalbanks Interpretive Site** is located at the site of the original mine entrance between Fort Whoop-Up and the Helen Schuler Coulee Centre. Coalbanks, founded in 1874, was the original settlement in the valley. Indian Battle Park extends from the Oldman River to behind the buildings on Scenic Drive. Many viewpoints can be found along the top of the coulee, which is accessible by timber steps leading up from the floodplain.

Botterill Bottom Park, adjacent to Indian Battle Park, houses underground utility lines and cannot be developed. Across the Oldman River is **Bull Trail Park,** an undeveloped area that extends south to the university. To the north is **Elizabeth Hall Wetlands,** a 15-hectare reserve of floodplain habitat that encompasses an oxbow pond. North of the Lethbridge Nature Reserve is **Peenaquim Park,** 97 hectares of floodplain that was formerly a stockyard. Access to **Alexander Wilderness Park** is from Stafford Drive N. This road descends into a coulee, and three short trails radiate out along the floodplain to viewpoints of the Oldman River. The northernmost river-valley park is **Pavan Park.** The entrance road winds down a narrow coulee to a day-use area by the Oldman River. Here a reclaimed gravel pit is stocked with trout, short walks lead along the floodplain, and a picnic area has firewood and fire rings.

High Level Bridge

High Level Bridge spans 1.6 kilometers and towers 100 meters above the Oldman River Valley—once the longest and highest trestle-construction bridge in the world. It was built by the CPR for $1.3 million in 1909, replacing 22 wooden bridges and drastically reducing the length of line between Lethbridge and Fort Macleod. More than 12,000 tons of steel were used in its construction, as well as 17,000 cubic yards of concrete and 7,600 gallons of paint. Of the many views of the bridge available along the valley, none is better than standing directly underneath it (walk down from the Tourist Information Centre on Brewery Hill).

Nikka Yuko Japanese Garden

This garden was established in 1967 by the City of Lethbridge and its Japanese residents as a monument "to the contribution made to Canadian culture by Canadians of Japanese origin." It has been designed as a place to relax and contemplate, with no bright flowers, only green shrubs and gardens of rock and sand. The buildings and bridges were built in Japan under the supervision of a renowned Japanese architect. The main pavilion is of traditional design, housing a *tokonoma* or tea ceremony room. Japanese women in traditional dress lead visitors through the gardens and explain the philosophy behind different aspects of the design. The best view of the garden is from the bell tower, whose gentle "gong" signifies good things happening in both countries simultaneously. A special presentation is made Sunday at 1:30 P.M., which may be anything from a bonsai pruning demonstration to a traditional Japanese sword fight. The garden is open June–mid-Sept. daily 9 A.M.–5 P.M., and a couple of weeks on either side of these dates Thurs. 208>Sun. noon–5 P.M.; admission is $4. The gardens are located in Henderson Lake Park on Mayor Magrath Drive, 403/328-3511.

RECREATION

Activities in **Henderson Lake Park** on Mayor Magrath Drive center around a 20-hectare lake that attracts residents year-round. The park features an outdoor swimming pool, tennis courts, demonstration gardens, boat rentals on the lake, and an 18-hole golf course. A paved trail for hikers and cyclists encircles the lake. Another popular recreation spot is **Park Lake Provincial Park,** located 17 kilometers north of Lethbridge on Highway 25. This once-arid prairie region has been transformed by irrigation. In summer, the lake is a good spot for swimming, windsurfing, fishing, and boating (boat rentals available).

There are five golf courses in the area. **Henderson Lake Golf Club,** 403/329-6767, is within walking distance of the lake's campground ($32); **Bridge Valley Golf Course,** 403/381-6363, is a par-three course on the west side of the High Level Bridge ($15); and **Paradise Canyon Golf Resort,** 403/381-4653 or 877/707-4653, near the university, is a championship course constructed on a reclaimed floodplain

along the Oldman River ($45). The other two courses are private.

Across from the library is the **YMCA** (515 Stafford Dr. S, 403/327-9622), which has a pool, a weight room, and a health club available for $3.75 per session. The $5.3-million **Max Bell Regional Aquatic Centre** (at the University of Lethbridge, 403/329-2583) is also open to the public; $4 for a swim.

Anderson Aquatics (314 11th St. S, 403/328-5040) is one of Alberta's few scuba-diving shops. Diving trips and lessons run throughout summer. The shop also rents equipment and fills tanks for those heading to Waterton Lakes National Park.

ENTERTAINMENT

A Little Bit of Culture
The Sterndale Bennett Theatre in the Yates Memorial Centre at 110 4th Avenue S is home to the **New West Theatre Society,** an amateur company whose popular summer performances sell out most nights. Productions are generally a combination of comedy, song, and dance appealing to everybody. For ticket information, call 403/381-9378. The **Lethbridge Symphony Orchestra** also has its office in Yates Centre but performs at locations throughout the city; call 403/328-6808 for dates and prices. The **Performing Arts Centre** at the

The High Level Bridge was once the highest and longest of its type in the world.

University of Lethbridge attracts national and international acts to its three theaters. For upcoming events, call 403/329-2656. The four **movie theaters** in town charge $6–8 and Tuesday is half-price night. One is in the Lethbridge Centre downtown, 403/329-3550.

A Little Less Culture

The **Cadillac Club** (420 6th St. S, 403/320-2233) "whoops it up" with live country music on Friday and Saturday nights. Another popular local venue is the **Roadhouse Thirst and Grill** (1016 1st Ave., 403/380-4210). If country music isn't your style, head to **Hugo's** (314 8th St. South, 403/320-0117), a newly renovated bar with hardwood décor and comfortable couches set around the fireplace. A popular nightclub is **Studio 54** (in the Lethbridge Hotel at 202 5th St. S, 403/328-6099) for Top 40, or have a beer with the boys in the public bar.

Festivals and Events

For a city of its size, Lethbridge offers surprisingly few festivals. The year's biggest event, **Whoop-Up Days,** is held at Fort Whoop-Up and at other locations in the city throughout the first week of August. The celebration features pancake breakfasts, a parade, a midway, a casino, a trade show, and grandstand events such as a rodeo. Nightly concerts and cabarets end each day's excitement. For more information, call 403/328-4491.

ACCOMMODATIONS

Downtown

Of the four downtown accommodations, the **Days Inn** (100 3rd Ave. S, 403/327-6000 or 800/329-7446) has the best-value rooms. Rates include a continental breakfast and use of an exercise room; $64 single, $69 double. Nearby is the **Lethbridge Travelodge** (207 4th Ave. S, 403/327-2104 or 800/578-7878), which has large rooms; $69 single, $79 double. **Lethbridge Lodge Hotel** (320 Scenic Dr. S, 403/328-1123 or 800/661-1232) is a modern, full-service hotel. Many of the 191 rooms have views of the Oldman River Valley, the others an enclosed tropical atrium. Amenities include a café, a restaurant, a cocktail lounge, and an indoor pool with a whirlpool; rooms from $109–119 single or double.

Mayor Magrath Drive

Approximately one dozen motels of varying standards but similar prices line Mayor Magrath Drive S (Highway 5). Many have restaurants, but those that don't are within walking distance of others that do. Also nearby is Nikka Yuko Japanese Garden and Henderson Lake Park. From north to south, the best-value motels are the nine-story **Sandman Hotel Lethbridge** (421 Mayor Magrath Dr. S, 403/328-1111 or 800/726-3626, www.sandman.ca), with an indoor pool and a 24-hour restaurant, $73 single, $76 double; the **Travelodge Hotel** (526 Mayor Magrath Dr. S, 403/327-5701 or 800/578-7878), with 105 rooms much nicer than the exterior suggests, $69 single, $79 double; the **Super 8 Lodge** (2210 7th Ave., 403/329-0100 or 800/800-8000, www.super8.com), featuring large rooms, a heated outdoor pool, and a laundry, $65 single, $67 double; the **Howard Johnson Express Inn** (1026 Mayor Magrath Dr. S, 403/327-4576 or 800/446-4656), where rates of $65 single, $70 double include a light breakfast; the **Quality Inn** (1030 Mayor Magrath Dr. S, 403/328-6636 or 800/561-9815), with rooms as good as anywhere along the strip for $72 single, $77 double; the **Heidelberg Inn** (1303 Mayor Magrath Dr. S, 403/329-0555 or 800/791-8488), a Best Western with a pool and a restaurant, $87 single, $92 double; and the **Chinook Motel,** next door to the Heidelberg Inn, $59 single, $64 double. Check into Chinook at the Heidelberg.

Heritage House B&B

The Heritage House B&B (1115 8th Ave. S, 403/328-3824) is an excellent alternative to the motels. The 1937 home is considered one of the finest examples of International–Art Deco design in the province. Its two guest rooms are spacious and tastefully decorated, a hearty breakfast is served downstairs in the dining room, and town is only a short walk along the tree-lined streets of Lethbridge's most sought-after suburb. The bathroom is shared, but for $40 single, $50 double, that is of little consequence.

Campgrounds

Henderson Lake Campground (7th Ave. S in Henderson Lake Park, 403/328-5452) has full hookups, showers, a laundry room, groceries, firewood, and fire rings. The serviced section is little more than a paved parking lot, but tenters and those with small vans enjoy the privacy afforded by trees at the back of the campground. Unserviced sites cost $16; those with hookups are $19–25. Open year-round. **Bridgeview RV Park** (on the west bank of the Oldman River at 910 4th Ave. S, 403/381-2357) has similar facilities to Henderson Lake Campground (as well as a heated pool), but the nearby highway can be noisy. Unserviced sites go for $18, hookups are $25–27. Another alternative is **Park Lake Provincial Park,** 17 kilometers northwest of town on Highway 25, which offers camping (no showers) for $13–15 per night.

FOOD

Downtown

Anton's, in the Lethbridge Lodge Hotel (320 Scenic Dr. S, 403/328-1123), is the only true fine-dining restaurant in town, serving dinner daily from 5 P.M. The menu is extensive, and the dishes using local produce are well prepared by a Swiss chef. Appetizers start at $5, entrées from $15. Also in the lodge is the **Garden Café,** open daily 6:30 A.M.–11:30 P.M. and always busy with guests and locals alike. Moderately priced meals are served amid much greenery. The dessert cabinet is strategically placed so that even the most health-conscious diner can't help but be tempted by it.

Good, inexpensive Vietnamese food is dished up at **Kim Long Restaurant** (329 5th St. S, 403/380-3866), open daily 10 A.M.–10 P.M., until midnight on Friday and Saturday. Most dishes are less than $10. If the menu looks Greek to you, ask to see the family photo album with color photographs of each dish.

Lethbridge has some fine coffee shops; the pick of the bunch is **Penny Coffee House** (331 5th St. S, 403/320-5282), where coffee is $1.50, refills are free, and a nice, thick, healthy sandwich with soup is $6.50. It's open Mon.–Fri. 7:30 A.M.–10 P.M., Saturday 7:30 A.M.–5:30 P.M., Sunday 10 A.M.–5 P.M.

Third Avenue South

The popular Chinese buffet at **Enjoy Gardens** (1903 3rd Ave. S, 403/328-8770) features lunch (daily 11 A.M.–2:30 P.M.) for $7 and dinner (5–8:30 P.M.) for $10.50. **O-Sho Japanese Restaurant** (311 4th St. S, 403/327-8382) serves authentic Japanese cuisine; you can sit at standard tables or dine in traditional style on mats in partitioned lounges. Lunch is $5–9.50, dinner $8.50–16. It's open for lunch Mon.–Fri. 11:30 A.M.–2:30 P.M. and for dinner Mon.–Fri. 4:30–10 P.M., Saturday 4–10:30 P.M.

Mayor Magrath Drive

As well as having the bulk of Lethbridge's accommodations, this road has many fast-food and family restaurants. **Treats Eatery** (1104 Mayor Magrath Dr. S, 403/380-4880) is a Western-style family-dining restaurant. It has an enormous gold-rimmed wagon wheel hanging from the ceiling—ask to sit away from it if you like. The menu is straightforward, basically burgers and beef, but is well-priced. Hours are Mon.–Sat. 11 A.M.–10 P.M., Sunday 4–10 P.M. The **Beefeater Steakhouse** (1917 Mayor Magrath Dr. S, 403/320-6211) is a traditional English restaurant offering traditional Albertan dishes; the prime rib of beef is especially good. Lunch is $7–12, and dinner specials start at $14. It's open Mon.–Sat. 11 A.M.–midnight, Sunday 11 A.M.–9 P.M. Farther up the road is the impressive **Sven Ericksen's Family Restaurant** (1715 Mayor Magrath Dr. S, 403/328-7756). The menu here is heavy on seafood, which seems odd for a place so far from the ocean, but enough beef and chicken dishes are offered for fishophobes to get by. It's open Mon.–Fri. 11 A.M.–10 P.M., Sat.–Sun. 11 A.M.–11 P.M.

TRANSPORTATION

Lethbridge Airport is eight kilometers south of town on Highway 5. It is served by **Air B.C.,** 888/247-2262, an Air Canada connector, which flies to Calgary four to seven times daily with connections to Edmonton and other national and international destinations. Some motels and car rental companies have courtesy phones at the airport. A cab to downtown is approximately $20.

Buses leave twice daily from the **Greyhound** bus depot (411 5th St. S, 403/327-1551 or 800/661-8747) for Fort Macleod, four times daily for Calgary, and twice daily to Medicine Hat and to the United States border at Coutts, where connections to Great Falls and Helena (Montana) can be made. The depot is open daily 7:30 A.M.–7:30 P.M. and has a small café and lockers.

L.A. Transit city buses run daily with limited service on Sunday. The main routes radiate from Lethbridge Centre on 4th Avenue S out to the university, Henderson Lake Park, and along Mayor Magrath Drive. The adult fare is $1.75. Call 403/320-3885 for schedules and information. The various car rental agency numbers are **Budget,** 403/328-6555; **Enterprise,** 403/328-3517; **Hertz,** 403/382-3470; **National,** 403/380-3070; and **Rent-A-Wreck,** 403/320-0707. For a taxi, call **Fifth Avenue Cabs,** 403/381-1111; **Lethbridge Cabs,** 403/327-4005; or **Royal Taxi,** 403/328-5333.

SERVICES AND INFORMATION

The **post office** (704 4th Ave. S) is in an historic stone building. Make a day of it at **Family Coin Laundry** (128 Mayor Magrath Dr. N), one block north of the highway, where there's a lounge, a TV, and free coffee; open daily 8 A.M.–9 P.M. Contact **Lethbridge Regional Hospital** (9th Ave. and 18th St. S, 403/382-6111) or the **RCMP** (403/329-5080) for emergency services or police assistance.

Lethbridge Public Library (810 5th Ave. S, 403/380-7310) is an excellent facility with a wide range of literature; open Mon.–Fri. 9:30 A.M.–9 P.M., Saturday 9:30 A.M.–5:30 P.M., and Sunday 1:30–5:30 P.M. The best bookstore in town is **B. Macabee's Booksellers** (333 5th St. S, 403/329-0771), which has a large selection of local history and Canadiana books. After browsing, why not let the smell from the Penny Coffee House lure you next door?

Lethbridge's main **Tourist Information Centre** (2805 Scenic Dr. at the corner of highways 4 and 5, 403/320-1222 or 800/661-1222, www.albertasouth.com) is open in summer daily 9 A.M.–8 P.M., the rest of the year Mon.–Sat. 9 A.M.–5 P.M. A second office near downtown is on Highway 3 W (1st Ave. S from the east, 403/320-1223) at Brewery Hill, beside the former site of the Lethbridge Brewery (a site known as **Brewery Gardens** for the thousands of vividly colored flowers that bloom there each summer). This small center is open in summer daily 9 A.M.–8 P.M., spring and fall Tues.–Sat. 9 A.M.–5 P.M.

EAST OF LETHBRIDGE

THE MILK RIVER

The Milk River is unique among western Canada's river systems. All of the others eventually drain east into Hudson Bay, but the Milk River flows south to the Missouri River, eventually draining into the Gulf of Mexico. The area itself is historically unique for western Canada because it has been under the jurisdiction of seven different governments and countries, as well as the Hudson's Bay Company. During the 1700s, France claimed all the lands of the Mississippi, so a small part of Alberta was under French rule. Later, the same area was part of the Spanish empire, and it's also, at one time or another, fallen under the rule of the Hudson's Bay Company, the British, and the Americans. It finally became part of the province of Alberta in 1905. A flag display and an historical cairn on the north bank of the river explain this complicated piece of Albertan history.

The town of Milk River (pop. 850) sits on the northern bank of its namesake, located 86 kilometers southeast of Lethbridge and 40 kilometers north of the Montana border.

Devil's Coulee
On May 14, 1987, an amateur paleontologist was exploring the coulees near her family's ranch outside of Milk River when she discovered some fossilized egg shells. The find sent waves of excitement around the scientific world, and the site became known as **Devil's Coulee Dinosaur Egg Site,** one of the most exciting

fossil discoveries ever made. What she had discovered were clutches of eggs that had been laid by hadrosaurs approximately 75 million years ago. Each prehistoric egg was about 20 centimeters long and contained the perfectly formed embryonic bones of unborn dinosaurs. No other find in the entire world has taught scientists more about this part of the dinosaur's life cycle.

Devil's Coulee Dinosaur Heritage Museum, 403/642-2118, is in the village of Warner, on Highway 4, 66 kilometers southeast of Lethbridge and 20 kilometers northwest of the small town of Milk River. It is only a small facility, but a display reconstructs the site. It's open in summer daily 9 A.M.–5 P.M., the rest of the year Monday and Wednesday 9 A.M.–5 P.M. The site has recently been opened to the public, but access is on a guided tour only. Tours leave from the museum daily throughout summer at 10 A.M. and 2 P.M. Tour cost is $10 per person and advance reservations are required.

Water Sports on the Milk River
The Milk River is popular with canoeists of all levels of expertise, although no rapids exceed Class I. What the river lacks in rapids, it more than makes up for in scenic beauty and rich history. The first section from the towns of Del Bonita to Milk River passes through shortgrass prairie, and the shallow river valley allows panoramic views of the landscape. This long section (103 kilometers) passes through mainly private property and has a few fence wires that cross the river. Past the town of Milk River, the river valley becomes deeper and enters the badlands of Writing-On-Stone Provincial Park (69 kilometers from Milk River).

Practicalities
The town of Milk River has basic services, including the following tourist facilities: The **Southgate Inn** (at the north end of town, 403/647-3733) has basic rooms for $55 single, $60 double. **Milk River Campground** in town is nothing more than a dusty parking lot with firewood and power; tents $8, RVs $13–15 per night. South toward Montana, 20 kilometers along Highway 4, **Gold Springs Park** is much nicer and the same price. A café/restaurant in the Milk River Inn, 403/647-2257, is open until 10 P.M., and

across the road is the **Delicia Bakery,** which lives up to its name.

Highway 4 is the main route into Alberta from the United States. The Coutts/Sweetgrass border crossing is open 24 hours a day year-round. A **Travel Alberta Information Centre** south of Milk River greets travelers crossing the border. It provides copious information and an interpretive center highlighting aspects of tourism within the province. The center, 403/647-3938, is open mid-May–mid-June 9 A.M.–6 P.M. and through summer 8 A.M.–7 P.M.

WRITING-ON-STONE PROVINCIAL PARK

This park located 43 kilometers east of the town of Milk River on Highway 501 has everything: a warm river for swimming, great canoeing, intriguing rock formations, abundant wildlife, and the largest concentrations of petroglyphs (rock carvings) and pictographs (rock paintings) found in North America. The native rock art lies hidden on sandstone cliffs along the banks of the Milk River, which has cut a deep valley into the rolling shortgrass prairie. The soft sandstone and shale cliffs here are capped with harder, iron-rich sediments. Years of wind and water erosion have carved out the softer, lower rock, leaving mushroom-shaped pinnacles and columns called **hoodoos.** Several plant and animal species here are found nowhere else in Alberta. Look for pronghorn on the grassland, bobcats and mule deer in the coulees, yellow-bellied marmots sunning themselves on sandstone outcrops. Don't look *too* hard for rattlesnakes, though, which are usually found in shady spots among the cliffs.

The Meaning of It All
Writing-On-Stone was a place of great spiritual importance to generations of natives, a place for contact with the supernatural. They attempted to interpret previous carvings and paintings, added their own artwork to the rock, and left gifts of tobacco and beads as a way of communicating with the spirits of the dead. Much of the cliff art remains visible today, providing clues to the region's early inhabitants.

Artifacts excavated from below the cliffs

hoodoos above the campground

suggest that the area had been inhabited for at least 3,000 years, but any rock art of that age would have been destroyed by erosion long ago. Dating the remaining petroglyphs and pictographs is difficult. They aren't covered in the layers of sediment usually used to date sites, nor can radiocarbon dating be applied because that technique requires wood or bone to test. The only way of dating the rock art is to estimate its age based on recognizable artistic styles or the depiction of certain historic events (such as the arrival of the white man). Of the carvings visible today, the earliest are thought to be the work of the Shoshoni, created approximately 700 years ago. Their work is characterized by warriors on foot carrying ornately decorated shields, while isolated images of elk, bears, and rattlesnakes appear as simple stylized outlines. During the 1730s, the Shoshoni were driven into the mountains by the Blackfoot, who had acquired horses and guns before other native bands. The valley's strange rock formations led the Blackfoot to believe that the area was a magical place—a place to be respected and feared—and that existing carvings were created by the spirits. The Blackfoot added their own artistry to the rocks, and many of the Blackfoot carvings are panels that tell a story. A striking change of lifestyle was documented on the rock faces, corresponding to the arrival of guns and horses to the Plains tribes. Mounted warriors armed with rifles dominate later artworks, the most famous being a battle scene containing more than 250 characters.

Into the 20th Century

An NWMP post was established at Writing-On-Stone in 1889 to stop the whiskey trade and curb fighting among natives. The Mounties passed time by using the petroglyphs for target practice and carving their names into a cliff that has become known as Signature Rock. The original NWMP post buildings were washed away by floodwaters, replaced, then destroyed by fire in 1918. In 1957, the area was officially designated a provincial park. Access to much of the park is restricted to prevent further damage to the carvings. A reconstructed NWMP post sits within this area at the mouth of **Police Coulee**. The best way to get a feel for the park and its history is by participating in the interpretive program; details are posted on notice boards throughout the park. The **Hoodoo Interpretive Trail** is a two-kilometer (one-way) hike along the cliffs, with numbered posts that correspond to a trail brochure available from the information center. Along the way are some examples of petroglyphs and pictographs (including the famous battle scene) that have been ravaged by time and vandals.

Accommodations and Information

The nearest motel rooms are in Milk River, but the park has an excellent campground nestled below the hoodoos in a stand of cottonwood trees. Showers are provided, and firewood costs $5 per bundle; unserviced sites $16, powered sites $19. For more information on the park, contact Writing-On-Stone Provincial Park, P.O. Box 395, Milk River, Alberta T0K 1M0, 403/647-2364.

THE DRY BELT

Not a tree in sight—just rolling shortgrass prairie, occasionally dissected by dried-up streams and eroded gullies. This is the sight that first greeted settlers to the area, and even with the help of complex irrigation systems, the land looks similar today. The far southeastern corner of Alberta has never been heavily populated, but

---

PALLISER TRIANGLE

On 4 July 1857, Capt. John Palliser set out west from Winnipeg on an assignment from the British government to make a comprehensive assessment of the agricultural potential, mineral reserves, soil quality, and timber resources of the prairies. Under his command were 20 men, two wagons, six Red River carts, and 29 horses. For three long years the expedition traveled the length and breadth of the prairies, before eventually submitting their findings in 1862. Palliser's report favored a band of territory stretching from Manitoba to the Peace River in northern Alberta. On the other hand, to the south he reported a vast land of shortgrass prairie that he called "an extension of the Great American Desert." He considered it unfit for agriculture: "[The land] is desert or semi-desert in character . . . [and] can never be expected to become occupied by settlers." This region—extending along the U.S. border and as far north as Red Deer— soon became known as the Palliser Triangle. Although the report wasn't favorable to the southern part of the province, it changed people's perception of the West. His report led to the settlement of southern Alberta, although it didn't happen overnight. Eventually the C.P.R. rail line was built across the prairies, and irrigation opened up arid parts of the land previously thought unsuitable for settlement.

---

not for a lack of trying. Before it was linked to the outside world by rail, settlers entered the area. Small villages emerged, but as was often the case, the CPR decided to bypass many of these fledgling settlements and create its own towns. Population bases moved, and towns slipped into oblivion. Highway 61 passes through this dry, unforgiving part of the province, past the towns of Wrentham and Skiff, with their boarded-up buildings and grim futures, to the town of Foremost and on through other small communities whose future hangs in the balance. The highway finally peters out at Manyberries. A gravel road (Highway 889) heads northeast from Manyberries to Highway 41 just south of Cypress Hills Provincial Park.

Foremost

In 1915, the CPR built a rail line east from Stirling through to Saskatchewan with great hopes of the area becoming heavily settled. But they hadn't counted on years of heavy drought, dust storms, and outbreaks of influenza that severely affected the populations of towns in the area. One of the few surviving towns was Foremost, whose population of 500 has remained relatively stable through trying times. Irrigation has played a major role in Foremost's longevity. The interpretive center at **Forty Mile Coulee Reservoir**, 23 kilometers north of town, explains the importance of irrigation to these farming communities. Nearby is a viewpoint and day-use area.

On the west side of town, a small campground with a covered cooking shelter has tent sites for $5, hookups $8–11.

Etzikom

The CPR built towns approximately every 16 kilometers along its lines, its strategy being that farmers would have access to a grain elevator within a day's haul of their farm, yet the towns would be far enough apart to survive independently. Between Foremost and Etzikom, the town of Nemiskam hasn't survived. The once-busy streets are quiet. The residents that remain head to the larger centers of Foremost and Medicine Hat to go shopping and do their business. The fate of Etzikom is similar. Once a thriving center with many businesses and two hotels, now fewer than 100 people live in town. Travel 16 kilometers east or west of Etzikom to see what the town's future holds. **Etzikom Museum,** 403/666-3737, relives the past—the railway, influenza, droughts, and the tenacity of its people. An outdoor display tells the story of wind power in Canada through a large collection of windmills. The museum is open during summer daily 10 A.M.–5 P.M.

Continuing East

The farmland east of Etzikom is particularly poor. The railway town of **Pakowki** slipped into oblivion long ago, its early residents preferring to do business in **Orion,** the next town to the east. Orion was once a thriving prairie town, but a terrible drought throughout much of the 1920s forced most farmers into bankruptcy. Those who survived were moved by the government to other parts of the province. A few residents still hang on, forever optimistic. And why not? The elevators still take in grain. To the south of Orion on Highway 887 are the **Manyberries Sandhills,** a prairie phenomenon well worth the detour, especially in the berry-picking season. From Orion, Highway 887 heads north to Seven Persons and Medicine Hat. Highway 61 jogs south and east from Orion to the small town of **Manyberries,** from where Highway 889 heads northeast to Cypress Hills Provincial Park or south then east to Saskatchewan; either way it's gravel.

HIGHWAY 3 EAST FROM LETHBRIDGE

Coaldale

The first town east of Lethbridge on Highway 3 is Coaldale, with a population of 5,700. The area was first settled in 1889 by Mennonites, and when the CPR built a rail line between Lethbridge and Medicine Hat in 1926, the company encouraged more Mennonite families to farm in the region. With their long agricultural traditions and doctrines of simple living, Mennonites were always welcome additions to prairie communities such as Coaldale. Today this rural community and its Mennonite population continue to prosper, mostly because of their proximity to Lethbridge.

The main reason to leave the highway here is to visit the **Alberta Birds of Prey Centre** (north of Highway 3 at 20th St., then left on 16th Ave., 403/345-4262). The aim of this off-the-beaten-path center is to ensure the survival of birds of prey such as hawks, falcons, eagles, and the great horned owl, Alberta's provincial bird. Many of the birds are brought to the center injured or as young chicks. They are nurtured at the center until they are strong enough to be released back into the wild. The interpretive building features the works of various wildlife artists and has displays cataloging human fascination with birds of prey through thousands of years. Behind the building, trails lead past birds that are recovering from injury, tame birds, and a cage where birds fly free (well, kind of, anyway). The center is open April–Oct. daily 10 A.M.–5 P.M. Admission is $6.

Accommodations are at **Coaldale Motor Inn** (913 19th Ave., 403/345-2555), which offers 16 air-conditioned rooms, a restaurant, and a lounge bar; $54 single or double.

Taber

Taber, 51 kilometers east of Lethbridge, is most famous for its deliciously sweet corn. It's also a base for the food-processing industry and a service center for the oil-and-gas industry. The original settlement began around Water Tank Number 77 (the site was 77 miles from Medicine Hat) along the CPR rail line. In 1901, the area was opened up to homesteaders, attracting settlers from eastern Canada and the United States, many of whom were Mormon. The name Taber was taken from Tabernacle, reflecting the religious influence of the Mormons. Local Blackfoot called the settlement *Itah Soyop* (Where We Eat From). Apparently, they mistook the name Taber for table.

Taber corn, as it is called, can be bought throughout western Canada and is the cornerstone of the town's economy. August is the best time to look for corn vendors along the road. Or find corn, along with other fresh, local produce, each Thursday at the farmers' market in the Taber Agriplex. On the last weekend of August, when the corn has ripened, the town's **Cornfest** celebration takes place, with a pancake breakfast, a midway, hot-air-balloon flights, a classic-car show, and, of course, plenty of corn to taste.

On the eastern outskirts of town is the **Taber**

Sugar Beet Factory, which processes more than 500,000 tons of sugar beets annually. During peak periods, enormous piles of beets sit beside the highway waiting to be processed into icing sugar, granulated sugar, and various powdered sugars. The factory does not offer tours, and judging by the smell *outside* the factory this is a good thing. One plant that does offer tours is **Lucerne Foods** (5115 57th St., 403/223-3566), which bottles fruit juices and cans vegetables at its Taber plant. Tours are available weekdays 9 A.M.–3 P.M.

The **Taber Motel,** 403/223-4411 or 877/232-2022, has the least expensive rooms in town. They are clean, but don't expect much; $45 single, $52 double. The much nicer and larger **Heritage Inn,** 403/223-4424 or 888/888-4374, offers a restaurant, café, and lounge; rooms start at $70 single, $79 double. **Taber Provincial Park,** on a floodplain above the Oldman River two kilometers west and three kilometers north of town, is a welcome relief from the surrounding prairie. Campsites are situated near a stand of large cottonwood trees. The unserviced sites are $15 per night.

On the north side of Taber's only traffic light (look for the giant corn husks) is the Taber Community Centre, home to an **information center,** 403/223-5550, and small museum; open in summer daily 9 A.M.–7 P.M.

Bow Island

This small town 58 kilometers east of Taber isn't on an island and isn't even near water. It's named for an island north of town on Grassy Lake, which isn't really a lake but part of the Bow River. (Go figure.) Vast reserves of natural gas in the area around Bow Island were first tapped in 1909 by a discovery well named "Old Glory," which soon developed into Alberta's first commercial

Petroglyphs are a record of early human history in the region.

gas field. The reserve of gas declined by the 1920s, and Bow Island's role in the industry changed; it became the first major gas-storage field in Canada. Today its storage reservoirs help meet southern Alberta's peak winter demand. Agriculture now plays an important role in the town's economy, as evidenced by large grain elevators and an alfalfa dehydrating and cubing plant two kilometers west of town (for tours, call 403-545-2293). On the east side of town are two inexpensive motels and an information booth, which is open in summer daily 9 A.M.–6 P.M. On the west side of town is a campground.

Red Rock Coulee

South of Seven Persons, the last community on Highway 3 before Medicine Hat, is a small area of badlands on a gentle rise in the surrounding plains. The bedrock here is relatively close to the surface, and wind and water erosion have cut through the topsoil to expose it. In some places, the erosion has extended into the bedrock itself, revealing varicolored strata laid down millions of years ago. This strange landscape is dotted with small hoodoos and red boulder-shaped concretions measuring up to 2.5 meters across. These intriguing rock formations formed under the surface of a prehistoric sea, when sand, calcite, and iron oxide collected on a nucleus of shells, bones, and corals. They became part of the bedrock as layers of sediment were laid down, but as erosion took its course, the surrounding bedrock disappeared and the concretions emerged. The formations here are believed to be the largest of their type in the world. To get there, follow Highway 887 south from Seven Persons for 23 kilometers. Where the road curves sharply to the east (left), continue straight ahead uphill on an unsealed road. You can't miss it.

MEDICINE HAT AND VICINITY

The prosperous industrial city of Medicine Hat (pop. 46,000) is in the southeastern corner of the province, 168 kilometers east of Lethbridge and 40 kilometers west of the Saskatchewan border. Known as "The Hat" to locals, the city straddles the South Saskatchewan River and is situated above some of western Canada's most extensive natural-gas fields. The gas was discovered by accident in 1883, by a CPR crew drilling for water. At first, nobody was particularly excited, except for the workers who got to heat their isolated homes. But eventually the word got out about the size of the reserves beneath the town, leading English writer Rudyard Kipling to describe Medicine Hat as "a city with all hell for a basement."

It wasn't long before industries developed around the gas fields; oil-and-gas extraction operations, petrochemical plants, mills, farms, and fertilizer factories today generate $1.5 billion annually. New housing estates, shopping centers, and an award-winning city hall are testimony to the success of these local industries. As an added bonus, a river that flows beneath the the city gives Medicine Hat an unlimited supply of water for its industries.

One other area resource is no longer exploited today but has left its mark on the face of the city. Nearby clay deposits led to a large pottery and brick industry that thrived from late last century until World War II. Many early-20th-century brick buildings have been restored and can be seen in the downtown core (where gas lamps still burn 24 hours a day).

Also of note is the **Saamis Archeological Site,** within the city limits, which is regarded as one of the most extensive and richest finds from the late prehistoric time period of native history. One hour south of the city is Cypress Hills Provincial Park, an upland plateau that survived the last ice age. This densely forested plateau rises abruptly from the surrounding prairie, is home to many species of mammals, and provides a variety of recreational opportunities. (See following section on **Cypress Hills Provincial Park.**)

The Name Medicine Hat

For centuries before white settlers came to the area, the Cree and the Blackfoot had battled each other over the right to claim this land as their own. Many tales recording these battles describe how the name Medicine Hat evolved. One of the most popular legends tells the story of the Cree chief who led his people to the cliffs above the South Saskatchewan River. Here, the Great Serpent told him that he must sacrifice his wife to the river in exchange for a *saamis* (medicine hat). This would give him magical powers and allow him to defeat the Blackfoot when they attacked later that night. Another story tells of how the Blackfoot were forced into the waters of the South Saskatchewan River by the Cree, who then fired an arrow into the heart of the Blackfoot medicine man. As he slowly sank below the water's surface, his hat was swept away into the hands of the Cree. The Blackfoot saw this as a terrible omen and retreated.

SIGHTS

Downtown

Many early-20th-century buildings located in the downtown area are still in active use, including private homes, churches, and businesses. The availability of local clay led to thriving brick-manufacturing plants here during the late 1800s; many original buildings still stand in mute testimony to the quality of the bricks. Near City Hall on 1st Street SE are three fine examples of this brickwork. The 1919 **Provincial Courthouse** has been restored and features an elaborately carved entrance, an interior marble-walled stairway, and a leaded-glass archway. Across the road is the 1887 **Ewart-Duggan Home,** which is the oldest brick residence still standing in Alberta and is topped by its original cedar shingles. On the corner of 4th Avenue is the **Kerr-Wallace Home,** the first of many early prestigious homes along 1st Street toward the TransCanada Highway (Highway 1).

Among other historical landmarks are the 1913 **St. Patrick's Church** (across the river

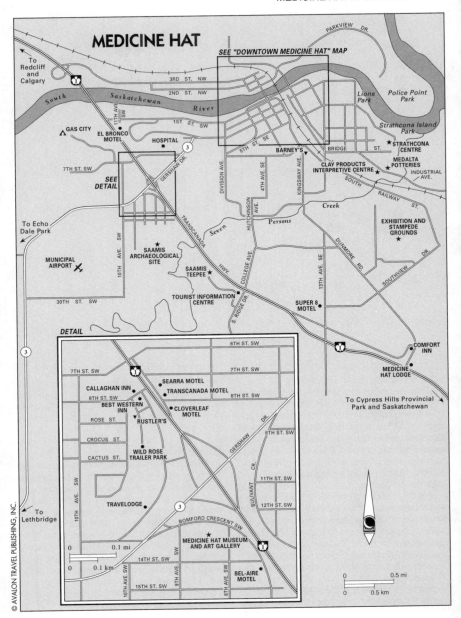

MEDICINE HAT

SEE "DOWNTOWN MEDICINE HAT" MAP

To Redcliff and Calgary

South Saskatchewan River

PARKVIEW DR.

3RD. ST. NW
2ND. ST. NW
1ST. ST. SW
5TH. ST. SE

Lions Park
Police Point Park

Strathcona Island Park

GAS CITY
EL BRONCO MOTEL
HOSPITAL

BARNEY'S
BRIDGE ST.
STRATHCONA CENTRE

CLAY PRODUCTS INTERPRETIVE CENTRE
MEDALTA POTTERIES
INDUSTRIAL AVE.

7TH. ST. SW
GERSHAW DR.

DIVISION AVE.
4TH AVE. SE
HUTCHINSON AVE.
KINGSWAY AVE.
SOUTH RAILWAY ST.

To Echo Dale Park

SEE DETAIL

TRANSCANADA HWY.

Persons
Seven
Creek

EXHIBITION AND STAMPEDE GROUNDS

MUNICIPAL AIRPORT

10TH AVE. SW

SAAMIS ARCHAEOLOGICAL SITE

SAAMIS TEEPEE

COLLEGE AVE.
S. RIDGE DR.

DUNMORE RD.
13TH AVE. SE
SOUTHVIEW DR.

30TH. ST. SW

TOURIST INFORMATION CENTRE

SUPER 8 MOTEL

COMFORT INN
MEDICINE HAT LODGE

To Lethbridge

DETAIL

6TH ST. SW
7TH ST. SW
7TH ST. SW
8TH ST. SW

SEARRA MOTEL
CALLAGHAN INN
TRANSCANADA MOTEL
8TH ST. SW
BEST WESTERN INN
ROSE ST.
RUSTLER'S
CLOVERLEAF MOTEL

CROCUS ST.
CACTUS ST.
WILD ROSE TRAILER PARK

10TH AVE. SW
TRAVELODGE

3

BOMFORD CRESCENT SW
MEDICINE HAT MUSEUM AND ART GALLERY

14TH ST. SW
9TH AVE. SW
8TH AVE. SW
BEL-AIRE MOTEL

15TH ST. SW
10TH AVE. SW

GERSHAW DR.
BULVANT CR.
8TH ST. SW
11TH ST. SW
12TH ST. SW

To Cypress Hills Provincial Park and Saskatchewan

0   0.1 mi
0   0.1 km

0   0.5 mi
0   0.5 km

N

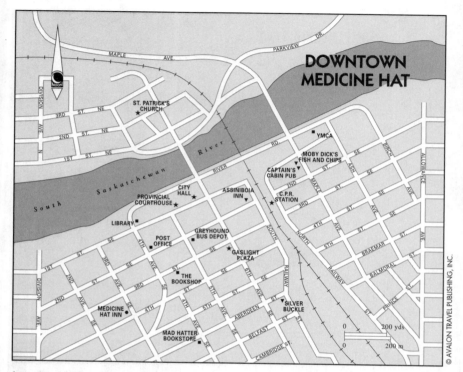

DOWNTOWN
MEDICINE HAT

from downtown on 2nd St.), said to be one of the finest examples of Gothic Revival architecture in North America; the **CPR station** (east of downtown), built shortly after the railway came to town in 1883; and the 1905 **Canadian Bank of Commerce** (corner of 6th Ave. and 2nd St.), a classic example of early bank architecture. These buildings and others are listed in the *Historic Walking Tour* brochure available from the Tourist Information Centre.

Another notable piece of architecture from a much later era is the **Medicine Hat City Hall,** which won the Canadian Architectural Award in 1986. Located on the banks of the South Saskatchewan River, it's open to the public on weekdays and contains many fine pieces of art.

Because of the abundance of natural gas in the area, city officials in the early days found it cheaper to leave the city's gas lamps on 24 hours a day rather than pay someone to turn them on and off. More than 200 copper replicas of the early gaslight fixtures were imported from England and now line the streets, burning 24 hours a day in the historical section of downtown.

Saamis Tepee

Standing more than 20 stories high beside the TransCanada Highway, with a base diameter of 50 meters and made entirely of steel (it weighs 1,000 tons), this is one sight you don't need directions to find. The Saamis Tepee was originally erected during the 1988 Calgary Winter Olympics to commemorate the cultural roles played by natives in the history of North America and has since been moved to its present site. It overlooks Seven Persons Creek Coulee, an archaeological site used in late prehistoric times as a native camp where buffalo were dried and processed. A self-guided interpretive trail, beginning at the tepee, leads to a bluff and into the valley where the camp was located. Native American ceremonial events are sometimes held here. The site is open year-round, but during the summer months free tours are offered, and a small interpretive center, which is open 9 A.M.–9 P.M., sells native arts and crafts. For more information, call 403/527-6773.

Medicine Hat Museum and Art Gallery
This large museum at 1302 Bomford Crescent SW, 403/527-6626, has a permanent collection of exhibits explaining the history of the natives that once inhabited the plains, the growth of the city, and the important role played by ranching and farming in southeastern Alberta, the NWMP, and the arrival of the railway. A military display catalogs the development of biological warfare through the ages from its earliest form—throwing snake-filled jars onto enemy ships! A large collection of photographs and manuscripts pertaining to the area's history is open by appointment only. The art gallery is a National Exhibition Centre hosting more than 20 national and international exhibitions annually. The complex is open Mon.–Fri. 9 A.M.–5 P.M., Sat.–Sun. 1–5 P.M.; admission $3.

Clay Products Interpretive Centre
Medicine Hat's early pottery industry relied on the same nearby clay deposits as the brick industry. For many years, the local Saskatchewan clay was mass-produced into high-quality china by three local companies, including Medalta Potteries at Medalta and Industrial avenues. For most of the middle period of this century, Medalta was a household name in Canada. The china was popular in homes and was used exclusively by CPR-owned hotels. During World War II, German prisoners of war worked in the factory making plates that were sent to Allied soldiers fighting in Europe. Since closing in 1954, fire, wind, and rain have taken their toll on the buildings, which have been declared a National Historical Site. The site is currently undergoing restoration, with one of four kilns open for inspection. Around the corner in the old Hycroft China Ltd. building (703 Wood St., 403/529-1070) is the Clay Products Interpretive Centre. The center displays the history of the clay and pottery industries in Medicine Hat,

Saamis tepee

has some fine examples of the now highly prized Medalta pieces, and is the start of a walking tour of the area. It's open mid-May–October daily 10 A.M.–5 P.M.

Redcliff
This small suburb of Medicine Hat bills itself as "Greenhouse Capital of the Prairies" because more than 10 hectares of greenhouses here are filled with brilliantly colored flowers and various vegetables such as cucumbers (12 million grown annually) and tomatoes (eight million grown annually). The greenhouses are open to the public year-round at 404 4th Street SW. To arrange a tour, call 403/548-3931. **Redcliff Museum** (23rd St. NE, 403/548-6260) depicts the area's history and has some interesting photographs and manuscripts. It's open in summer Tues.–Sat. 2–4 P.M., Sunday only the rest of the year. To get to Redcliff, follow the TransCanada Highway west of Medicine Hat and take the first exit to the north after the industrial estate.

City Parks

Medicine Hat's urban park system covers more than 400 hectares of open space and natural environment linked by 50 kilometers of multiuse trails developed for walking, biking, and cross-country skiing. **Strathcona Island Park,** on the banks of the South Saskatchewan River, is a heavily wooded area linked to the city center by a riverside trail that leads through **Lions Park.** From Lions Park, there's a viewpoint of the steep cliffs formed by the undercutting power of the river at a shallow point. Within Strathcona Island Park is the **Strathcona Centre,** which has a pool, rents paddleboats and canoes, and is the start of a short hiking trail. The park is at the end of 5th Street SE.

On the north side of the river, opposite Strathcona Island Park, is **Police Point Park** (turn off Parkview Dr. just past the golf club), which has many kilometers of trails that wind through stands of giant cottonwood trees and provide plentiful wildlife-spotting opportunities. White-tailed deer, foxes, and beavers are commonly seen. The **interpretive center,** 403/529-6225, outlines the area's natural and human history through exhibits and films; open in summer daily 1–9 P.M., the rest of the year weekends only 9 A.M.–5 P.M.

West of the airport on Holsam Road is **Echo Dale Park,** where the locals head on hot weekends to sunbake on the sandy beach and swim, fish, and boat in the manmade lake. Within the park is **Echo Dale Farm,** 403/527-7344, where you'll find farm animals, a two-story log house, and an interpretive center that's open in summer daily 9 A.M.–9 P.M.

FESTIVALS AND EVENTS

Medicine Hat holds one of the year's earliest rodeos, the **Spring Outdoor Rodeo.** The first weekend of June is the **Spectrum Festival,** a celebration of Medicine Hat's claim as the sunniest city in Canada. Kids' activities and street performers are plentiful, and tons of sand are dumped in a parking lot, transforming it into a beach for a volleyball tournament and beer garden. A mountain-bike race is held through the nearby river valley. A free pancake breakfast in Lions Park kicks off **Canada Day** (July 1) cel-

ebrations, which end with a spectacular fireworks display in the evening—watch it from Athletic Park or the Golf and Country Club off Parkview Drive.

The **Medicine Hat Exhibition and Stampede,** held on the last weekend of July, has been an annual event since 1887. It has grown to become Alberta's second-richest rodeo (behind the Calgary Stampede), guaranteeing three days of knuckle-clenching, bronc-riding, foot-stompin' fun. Various events are held throughout the city the preceding week, culminating Thursday–Saturday with the rodeo and chuckwagon races. The stampede also features many exhibitors displaying their wares, as well as a midway, a Pioneer Village, a trade show, and lots of free entertainment. Each night, top U.S. country-music stars strut their stuff. For more information, call the stampede office at 403/527-1234. Throughout summer, various other events are held at Stampede Park, including tractor pulls, sporting events, concerts, horse races, and smash-up derbies. For dates and prices, call the Tourist Information Centre at 403/527-6422.

ACCOMMODATIONS AND CAMPING

Less than $50

Medicine Hat is one of the only places in Alberta with a *choice* of motels offering rooms less than $50. These motels are bunched together along the downtown side of the TransCanada Highway around Gershaw Drive. The least expensive (and Alberta's cheapest motel) is the **TransCanada Motel** (780 8th St. SW, 403/526-5981), where rooms go for just $24 single, $28 double (as good a reason as any to check the room out before handing over your cash), and those with kitchenettes are $35. Surrounding motels include the **Searra Motel** (767 7th St. SW, 403/526-3355), with divey rooms for $32 single, $36 double, but free coffee; and the **Cloverleaf Motel** (773 8th St. SW, 403/526-5955 or 877/526-3319), with an indoor pool and laundry, $40 single, $50 double. A cheapie on the other side of the highway is the air-conditioned **Bel-Aire Motel** (633 14th St. SW, 403/527-4421), the best value of all Medicine Hat's bottom-end accommodations at $28 single, $36 double. The **El Bronco Motel,** is down toward the river (1177 1st St. SW, 403/526-5800), $34–42 single or double.

$50–100

A good value on the other side of the highway is the **Callaghan Inn** (954 7th St. SW, 403/527-8844 or 800/661-4440), with an indoor pool, a fitness room, and a restaurant; $55 single, $65 double. In the same vicinity is the **Best Western Inn** (722 Redcliff Dr. SW, 403/527-3700 or 800/528-1234), with more than 110 rooms of a higher standard and with fitness facilities and a pool; $79 single, $99 double.

Continuing east are two new motels that fall well within this price range on the TransCanada Highway. The **Super 8 Motel** (1280 Trans-Canada Hwy., 403/528-8888 or 800/800-8000), opened in 1996 with 70 modern rooms and an indoor pool. As with all Super 8 Motels, a continental breakfast is included in the room rate; $60 single, $70 double. Also new is the **Comfort Inn** (2317 TransCanada Hwy., 403/504-1700 or 800/228-5150). It features an indoor pool, an exercise room, and continental breakfast served in the downstairs restaurant; from $75 single or double.

The **Medicine Hat Inn** (530 4th St. SE, 403/526-1313 or 800/730-3887) is the only accommodation downtown. Although small (36 rooms), it is relatively modern, has a restaurant, and is within walking distance of most sights. Rooms are $75 single or double.

$100–150

The **Travelodge Medicine Hat** (1100 Redcliff Dr. SW, 403/527-2275 or 800/442-8729) features a large indoor waterslide complex, an indoor pool, a restaurant, and a lounge, but with so many other good-value accommodations in town, $95 single, $105 double is a little expensive. The only other accommodation in town more than $100 is the **Medicine Hat Lodge** (1051 Ross Glen Dr. SE, 403/529-2222 or 800/661-8095), which offers 190 well-appointed and spacious rooms, a wide range of recreational facilities, a lounge, a restaurant, and a casino; $95 single, $110 double.

Campgrounds

Gas City Campground, 403/526-0644, is on the edge of town, has nearly 100 sites, and is far enough away from the highway to be relatively quiet. From the back of the park, a trail heads to the river and into town. At night, this is a good spot to view the illumination of Medicine Hat's industrial core. It's open early May to late September; tent sites are $14, hookups $18–23. Good hot showers, laundry facilites, groceries, and full hookups make this the place to try first. To get there, turn off the highway at 7th Street SW and follow the signs down 11th Avenue. Another option, **Wild Rose Trailer Park** (28 Camp Dr., 403/526-2248), is in the same general area and has a large population of trailers. Unserviced sites go for $10, hookups $15–17. It's open year-round. Finally, west of town in Redcliff, a municipal campground offers showers and electrical hookups for just $7 per night, which makes this a good value.

FOOD AND DRINK

Downtown

Cafe Mundo (579 3rd St. SE, 403/528-2808) is the best of many downtown coffee shops. It's located in Gaslight Plaza, in a pleasant atmosphere away from busy downtown streets. Food is limited to bagels heaped with healthy fillings (from $2.75), but the coffee is good.

Moby Dick's Fish and Chips (140 Maple Ave. SE, 403/526-1807) has a delightful variety of English dishes. Fish in batter is from $2.40 per piece, fries $1.50. Also on the menu are other seafood specialties (from $10), traditional pub grub (from $3), and nine different meat pies (from $6). English draft beers are approximately $6 per pint. You can eat in the restaurant, the pub next door, or get it to go. Hours are Mon.–Sat. 11 A.M.–9 P.M., Sunday 3–8 P.M. **Season's Restaurant** in the Medicine Hat Inn (530 4th St. SE, 403/526-1313) is a typical hotel restaurant and is always busy. Dinner specials are approximately $14, menu items $11–21, and all dishes include a helping from a small salad bar. It's open daily 6 A.M.–10 P.M.

A long-time local favorite is **Barney's,** immediately south of downtown (665 Kingsway Ave. SE, 403/529-5663). The menu offers a wide variety of choices, but Barney's is best known for its steaks (from $15) and delicious Caesar salads.

Rustler's

Rustler's (901 8th St. SW, 403/526-8004), which is within walking distance of the strip motels along the TransCanada Highway, is one of the town's oldest eating establishments. Because it's in an historic house (see the menu for its amusing history), a real Wild West atmosphere prevails. Set out under the glass top of one table is a poker game complete with gun and bloodstained playing cards. The place is popular all day, but breakfast is especially crowded. Large portions of eggs, bacon, and hash browns begin at $4.25, omelettes at $4.95. For the rest of the day, the menu includes Southwestern-style cooking from $4.75, salads from $4, and pasta, steak, and chicken dishes from $9. It's open daily 6 A.M.–11 P.M.

Other Restaurants

Close to Rustler's and beside the TransCanada Highway are two excellent, inexpensive restaurants. **O'Rileys Restaurant and Bar** in the Callaghan Inn (7th St. SW, 403/527-8844) is a dimly lit, nostalgic place with gold-rimmed furniture and old posters on the walls. Monday is Mexican night (dishes from $7.50), Wednesday is pasta night (dishes from $6.50), and Friday and Saturday are rib nights (dishes from $14). Expect a wait on weekends. It's open daily 6 A.M.–11 P.M. Across the motel parking lot and beside the Best Western is the **Black Angus Restaurant** (925 7th St. SW, 403/529-0777), a family-style steakhouse specializing in Alberta beef. To the east along Dunmore Road is a smattering of chain restaurants including A&W and the more upmarket Earl's and Moxie's.

Drinking and Dancing

A large contingent of British soldiers spends summer training at the nearby Suffield military base. When they're given a night off, they head into downtown Medicine Hat to the **Assiniboia Inn** (680 3rd St. SE, 403/526-2801), known affectionately as the "Sin Bin," for a night of whoopee. This is as much of a warning as a recommendation. Around the corner is the **Silver Buckle,** a sports bar facing the railway tracks (687 S. Railway St. SE, 403/527-4043). Head across the tracks to **Captain's Cabin Pub** (140 Maple Ave. SE, 403/529-6629), which has English and Scottish draft beers on tap and

is decked out in the style of a traditional British pub. **O'Rileys** in the Callaghan Inn (7th St. SW, 403/527-8844) offers Mug Mondays, when all glass mugs, vases, and jars will be filled with beer for $1. Tuesday night is Yuk Yuk's Komedy Kabaret, admission $6.50. **Concerts** are often held at the Exhibition and Stampede Grounds; look for big-name country-music stars during Stampede Week at the end of July; call 403/527-1234 for details.

TRANSPORTATION

Medicine Hat Municipal Airport is five kilometers west of downtown on Highway 3 toward Lethbridge. Within the airport is a small café and courtesy phones for Budget and National rental cars. **Air B.C.,** 888/247-2262, flies daily between Medicine Hat and Calgary. No city bus serves the airport. Cabs meet all flights; expect to pay approximately $8 to get downtown.

The **Greyhound** bus depot (557 2nd St. SE, 403/527-4418) is in a convenient downtown location. The ticket office is open 5 A.M.–11 P.M. Inside the terminal are coin lockers and a popular café. Buses run twice daily to and from Calgary with a change in Fort Macleod. Buses also go east to Regina and Winnipeg four times daily. **Medicine Hat Transit** buses run from the terminal downtown throughout the suburbs. One-way fare anywhere on the route is $1.50; a day pass is $5. The following car-rental agencies have outlets in town: **Budget,** 403/527-7368; **Enterprise,** 403/526-8064; **Rent-A-Wreck,** 403/504-0047; and **National,** 403/527-5665. For a cab, call **Deluxe Central Taxi,** 403/526-3333.

SERVICES AND INFORMATION

The **post office** is at 406 2nd Street SE. **Kingsway Coin Laundry** is at 1039 Kingsway Avenue SE. The **YMCA** (150 Ash Ave. SE, 403/527-4426) has a pool, a weight room, and squash courts; $2.50 for a swim, $5 for use of all facilities, first visit free. The large **Medicine Hat Public Library** (414 1st St. SE, 403/502-8527) overlooks the river and has a free paperback exchange. It's open Mon.–Thurs. 10 A.M.–9 P.M., Fri.–Sat. 10 A.M.–5:30 P.M., Sunday 1–5:30 P.M.

The Bookshop (435 3rd St. SE, 403/527-7055) stocks a good selection of new books, whereas the **Mad Hatter Bookstore** (399 Aberdeen St. SE, 403/526-8563) has thousands of used books. **Medicine Hat Regional Hospital** is at 666 5th Street SW, 403/529-8000.

To get to the **Tourist Information Centre** (8 Gehring Rd. SE, 403/527-6422 or 800/481-2822), take the Southridge Drive exit from the TransCanada Highway just east of the big tepee. It's open in summer daily 8 A.M.–9 P.M., the rest of the year daily 9 A.M.–5 P.M. A good city website is www.city.medicine-hat.ab.ca.

CYPRESS HILLS PROVINCIAL PARK

Covering an area of 200 square kilometers, Cypress Hills is the third largest provincial park in Alberta. It occupies only a small section of an upland plateau that extends well into Saskatchewan. The hills rise as much as 500 meters above the surrounding grasslands, and at their highest elevation (1,466 meters, the same as Banff townsite), they are the highest point between the Canadian Rockies and Labrador. A forested oasis in the middle of the prairies, the park is thickly covered in lodgepole pine with stands of white spruce, poplar and aspen. The French word for lodgepole pine is *cyprès,* which led to the hills being named Les Montagnes de Cyprès, and in turn Cypress Hills, when in fact cypress trees have never grown in the park. Fall and spring are particularly pleasant times of year to visit the park—crowds are nonexistent and wildlife is more visible—but bring a jacket.

The park is located 70 kilometers southeast of Medicine Hat along Highway 41. It offers good hiking, fishing, or just plain relaxing and is popular as a place to escape the high summer temperatures of the prairies. The only commercial facilities within the park are in the townsite of **Elkwater,** which sits in a natural amphitheater overlooking **Elkwater Lake.** The facilities are limited (no bank, one restaurant, one motel, one gas station), so come prepared.

The Land

The hills are capped with a conglomerate composed of rounded pebbles carried east from the Rockies by a broad stream approximately 40 million years ago. When the massive sheets of ice moved slowly southward during the Ice Age, they thinned and split at the 1,400-meter level of the plateau. The top 100 meters remained unglaciated, forming a *nunatak* (an island of land surrounded by ice) of approximately 150 square kilometers. When the climate warmed and the sheet of ice slowly receded, its meltwaters rushed around and through the hills, slashing into the plateau and forming the narrow canyons and coulees that are visible today.

Flora

The park supports more than 400 recorded plant species in four ecological zones: prairie, parkland, foothills, and boreal forest. The best way to view the flora of the park is on foot; many trails pass through two or three zones in the space of a couple of kilometers. Sixteen species of orchids are found in the park—some are very common, whereas others, such as the sparrow's egg lady's slipper, are exceedingly rare. The book *A Guide to the Orchids of Cypress Hills,* by Robert M. Fisher, will tell you all you want to know. The Visitor Centre has a copy of the book you can look at.

Fauna

The unique environment of the hills provides a favorable habitat for 37 species of mammals, 400 species of birds, and a few turtles. Big game was once common throughout the hills, but in 1926 the last remaining large mammal—a wolf—was shot. Soon thereafter, elk were reintroduced to the park and now number more than 200. Moose, never before present in the park, were introduced in the 1950s and now number about 60. Other large mammals present in the park are mule deer, white-tailed deer, coyotes, and beavers.

Many bird species here are more typically found in the Canadian Rockies foothills, 250 kilometers to the west. About 90 species are transient, coming to the hills only to nest. Other species spend the entire year in the park. This is the only spot in the province with recordings of the common poorwill, which is rarely seen but occasionally heard. Wild turkeys were introduced in the 1930s, and their descendants can be heard warbling in certain parts of the park. Elkwater Lake and Spruce Coulee Reservoir are good

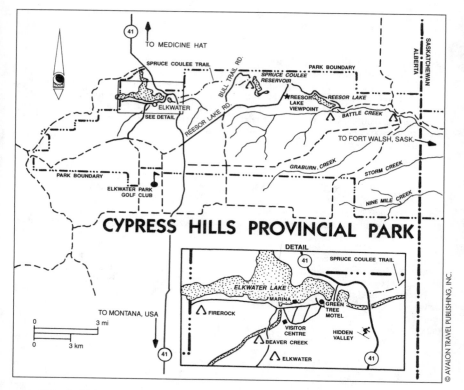

CYPRESS HILLS PROVINCIAL PARK

spots for waterbird-watching. Cormorants and trumpeter swans are common. A bird checklist is available at the Visitor Centre.

Cultural History

To the native bands of Cree, Blackfoot, and Assiniboine, this area was known as "Thunder Breeding Hills," a mysterious place that was home to plains grizzly bears, cougars, wolves, and kit foxes—all long since extinct in the area. These people followed the wandering herds of bison and had little need to visit the hills except to pick berries and collect various plants for medicinal and ceremonial uses. Little evidence of this early culture remains, although one archaeological site dating from 5000 B.C. has been studied. After the Cypress Hills Massacre, when 20 innocent Assiniboine were killed, the NWMP sent approximately 300 men to Fort Walsh (on the Saskatchewan side of the hills). The fort is now a National Historical Site.

Exploring the Park

Various roads link the townsite of Elkwater to lakes and viewpoints within the park. Because of glacial sediment called *loess,* the paved roads at higher elevations are terribly potholed. Unpaved roads are even worse and can become impassable after heavy rain. To access the center of the park, take Reesor Lake Road east from Highway 41, passing a herd of cattle and a viewpoint with spectacular vistas of the transition from grassland to boreal forest. The road then descends steeply to **Reesor Lake,** which has a campground, a picnic area, a short hiking trail to a viewpoint, and excellent fishing for rainbow trout. Bull Trail Road off Reesor Lake Road leads to **Spruce Coulee** and a reservoir stocked with eastern brook and rainbow trout. Unmarked gravel roads crisscross the park and head into Saskatchewan. Hiking within the park is limited. Most of the trails are easy to moderate, following the shores of Elkwater Lake (wheelchair accessible) and climbing out of the townsite into open fields and mixed forests. **Spruce Coulee Trail** (eight kilometers) is the longest hike. It starts behind the rodeo grounds and leads through woodland and past a few beaver ponds before reaching Spruce Coulee.

Just east of the marina, **Elkwater Boat & Bike Rentals**, 403/893-3877, rents mountain bikes ($5 per hour, $25 per day), canoes ($8 per hour, $40 per day), motorboats ($12 per hour), and jet skis ($45 per hour). **Elkwater Park Golf Club**, 403/893-2167, offers a nine-hole course at $18 per round. **Elkwater Landing**, 403/893-3930, opposite the marina, holds a restaurant, a grocery store, a post office, and a laundromat. The town has a gas station but no bank.

Wintertime

Although summer is the park's busiest time of year, many people are attracted by the range of winter activities possible. **Hidden Valley**, 403/893-3961, is a large ski hill (by prairie standards) with a vertical drop of 176 meters and two lifts and two rope tows that access a few beginner and intermediate runs, and a small snowboarding park. Lift tickets are $23. The hill is located three kilometers south of Elkwater. Equipment rentals are available at the hill or from **Lauder Cycles and Ski** (702 Kingsway Ave. SE, 403/526-2328) in Medicine Hat.

The park also offers 25 kilometers of cross-country ski trails for all levels of expertise, ice fishing in the lakes, toboggan hills, and winter camping for the brave.

orchid

Campgrounds and Lodging

Within the park are more than 500 campsites in 11 campgrounds. Closest to Elkwater are **Beaver Creek Campground** ($22) with full hookups and **Elkwater Campground** ($17–22) with unserviced and serviced sites. Both have showers. **Firerock Campground** ($15) on Elkwater Lake is particularly nice. It is linked to town by the Shoreline Trail.

Reesor Lake Campground ($15, no showers or hookups) at the eastern end of the park is much quieter—listen for bugling elk in the fall. An eight-kilometer hike from the rodeo grounds follows an abandoned road to **Spruce Coulee**, where you'll find 10 sites ($11) and good fishing in the reservoir. Reservations for campsites are taken; call 403/893-3782.

Green Tree Motel, 403/893-3811, is the only motel in the park. It offers 13 motel rooms from $50 single or double (kitchenettes an extra $5) and six self-contained log cabins ($70). During winter, ski packages are offered.

Services and Information

The large **Visitor Centre**, 403/893-3833, overlooks Elkwater Lake, a short walk from the townsite campgrounds and offers lots of information on the park and its history. Audiovisual programs explain the natural history and archaeological and historical resources of the park. It's open mid-May through Labor Day daily 9 A.M.–5 P.M. (until 9 P.M. Thurs.–Sat. in July and August). An interpretive program operates nightly during July and August; ask at the Visitor Centre for a program. For information in the off-season, try the park office along the first road to the left as you enter town from the east. It's open weekdays 8:15 A.M.–4:30 P.M. For more information, write to the office at P.O. Box 12, Elkwater, Alberta T0J 1C0, or call 403/893-3777.

CARDSTON

Cardston is a town of 3,500 at the base of the foothills 76 kilometers southwest of Lethbridge and 35 kilometers north of the United States border. Its rich heritage and many museums make it an interesting stop in itself, as well as a good base for exploring Waterton Lakes National Park (a half-hour drive to the west). The town was founded in 1887 by Charles Ora Card of the Church of Jesus Christ of Latter-day Saints (better known as the Mormon Church) after leading 11 families north from Utah in covered wagons. Card chose a spot to settle on Lee Creek and soon established a townsite, including a main street more than 30 meters wide, resembling those in Salt Lake City. These settlers developed Alberta's first irrigation system, which has grown to become the lifeblood of southern Alberta's economic base.

Cardston was also the birthplace of Fay Wray, a leading lady during the golden years of Hollywood. She appeared in 80 movies but is best known for her role as the leading-ape's love object in the 1933 classic *King Kong.*

SIGHTS

Remington-Alberta Carriage Centre
This world-class museum focusing on the era of horse-drawn transportation opened in 1993. It is one of North America's largest collections of carriages, buggies, and wagons—more than 200 at last count. The main exhibit galleries tell the story of the horse-and-buggy era through a life-sized early-20th-century townscape. You can transport yourself through time by watching blacksmiths at work in the carriage factory, listening to deals being made at the carriage dealer, or wandering over to the racetrack, where the rich liked to be seen on their elegant carriages. A program of equestrian events featuring Clydesdales and quarter horses takes place daily in the demonstration arena, and rides are offered on restored and replica carriages. The center also has a theater, a cafeteria, a gift shop, and an information booth. It's located at 623 Main Street, 403/653-5139; open May 15 to Labor Day 9 A.M.–8 P.M.,

the rest of the year 9 A.M.–5 P.M. Admission is adults $6.50, seniors $5.50, children $3, and carriage rides are $3 per person.

Alberta Temple
While living in simple log cabins, the early Mormon pioneers started planning the construction of the first Mormon temple built outside of the United States. The grand marble and granite structure was completed in 1923 and has become the town's centerpiece. Only members of the Mormon faith in good standing may enter the temple itself. (To be in good standing, a Mormon must neither smoke nor drink coffee or tea, and must pay 10 percent of his or her net annual income to the church.) A visitors center open to the public shows films and pictures depicting the interior of the temple and its history. The landscaped gardens are a good atmosphere for a pleasant stroll. The center is open May–Sept. 9 A.M.–9 P.M. You can see the temple from almost anywhere in town; it's at 348 3rd Street W, 403/653-1696.

Card Pioneer Home
When Charles Ora Card first arrived in 1887, he built a small log cabin on what would become Cardston's main drag. Today his humble home stands in its original location at 337 Main Street. It was the center of the community for many years. Town meetings were held inside, and travelers rested there until a hotel was built in 1894. The building is now a Provincial Historic Site, open June–Aug. Mon.–Sat. 10 A.M.–5 P.M.; admission by donation.

Courthouse Museum
This impressive courthouse (3rd Ave. just off Main St., 403/653-4322) was built in 1907 from locally quarried sandstone and was used longer than any other courthouse in the province before being refurnished as a museum. Exhibits include a pioneer home, artifacts from early settlers, and a geology display. In the basement are the original jail cells with graffiti-covered walls. The museum is open June–Aug. Mon.–Sat. 10 A.M.–5 P.M.

CARDSTON

To Waterton Lakes
National Park

1ST AVE.

HOSPITAL

2ND AVE.

POST OFFICE

MINGS GARDEN

COURTHOUSE MUSEUM

3RD AVE.

ALBERTA TEMPLE

CARD PIONEER HOME

CARRIAGE HOUSE THEATRE

4TH AVE.

CARDSTON SUPER 8

5TH AVE.

LIONS PARK

TOURIST INFORMATION CENTRE

6TH AVE.

REMINGTON-ALBERTA CARRIAGE CENTRE

COBBLESTONE MANOR RESTAURANT

7TH AVE.

LEE CREEK

HOWARD JOHNSON EXPRESS INN

8TH AVE.

FLAMINGO MOTEL

7TH AVE.

8TH AVE.

9TH AVE.

BUFFALO VIEW

SCALE NOT AVAILABLE

To International Boundary

Lee Creek

MACKENZIE ST.

MAIN ST.

© AVALON TRAVEL PUBLISHING, INC.

PRACTICALITIES

Accommodations

The choices are simple here—good-value motel rooms or camping downtown or in one of the nearby provincial parks. Least expensive of Cardston's motels is the **Flamingo Motel,** two blocks up the hill from the Remington-Alberta Carriage Centre (corner of Main St. and 8th Ave., 403/653-3952 or 888/806-6835), which has a small outdoor pool, a barbecue area, and a coin laundry; 50 single, $55 double. At the same intersection is the **Howard Johnson Ex-press Inn** (403/653-4481 or 800/446-4656), which has a fitness room, a laundry facility, and coffeemakers in each room. Rates are $64 single, $74 double, which includes a light breakfast. The **Cardston Super 8** (404 Main St., 403/653-8000 or 800/800-8000) is the town's newest motel. It features 45 rooms and an indoor pool; $70–81 single or double.

Within walking distance of the Remington-Alberta Carriage Centre is the **Lee Creek Campground** (at the end of 7th Ave. W, off Main Street, 403/653-3734), an excellent facility open May–Oct. with full hookups and showers. Tent sites are $10, hookups $15. Farther out you'll

...t **Woolford Provincial Park,** 16 ...o the east ($11); **Police Outpost** ...al **Park,** 33 kilometers south of town ...and **Payne Lakes Provincial Recre-** ...n **Area,** 24 kilometers southwest toward ...aterton ($13).

Food

The **Cobblestone Manor Restaurant** (173 7th Ave. W, 403/653-1519) is a unique place to indulge in some fine food. The original log structure was built in 1889, two years after the first Mormons arrived. In 1913, the house was bought by a Belgian immigrant who added more rooms, using cobblestones as building blocks. The interior wall panels and ceilings are inlaid with thousands of pieces of hard-wood, and the stained-glass bookshelves, Tiffany lights, and antique furniture give you the feeling of dining in an English manor. The food isn't too bad either. Light lunches start at $8, dinner entrées of steak, seafood, and chicken, all served with baked potato, fresh vegetables, and delicious homemade bread, start at $14. The restaurant is open daily for lunch 11 A.M.–2 P.M. and for dinner 5–9 P.M. It's located on a quiet residential street, across the road from Lee Creek Campground.

The only other dining choices in Cardston are along Main Street. The pick of the bunch among fast-food and pizza places is **Mings Garden** (262 Main St., 403/653-1682). A buffet is offered, but stick to the menu. The dishes are surprisingly good, mostly less than $10, and freshly prepared.

Entertainment and Events

The **Carriage House Theatre** (353 Main St., 403/653-1000) has a summer program of live theater productions, including musicals, comedy, and special events with a local theme. The performances are held July–Aug. Tues.–Sat. nights at 7:30 P.M.

On the third weekend of September is the **Combined Driving Event,** which is held in conjunction with the Remington-Alberta Carriage Centre. The meet consists of three events: carriage dressage, an obstacle course, and a marathon. With the exception of the marathon, all the excitement takes place at the Carriage Centre.

Services and Information

The **post office** is on 2nd Avenue. Laundromats are located at 165 Main Street and 77 3rd Avenue W. **Cardston Hospital** is at 144 2nd Street W, 403/653-4411. The **Tourist Information Centre** is beside Lee Creek at 490 Main Street, 403/653-3787. It's open June–Aug. daily 8 A.M.–8 P.M., or try the information booth at the Remington-Alberta Carriage Centre, which is open year-round, 403/653-1993.

Alberta Temple

VICINITY OF CARDSTON

Woolford Provincial Park

Original surveys of the area show this park as an island in the St. Mary River. A stand of large cottonwood trees here provides a pleasant, shaded area surrounded by prairie. A North West Mounted Police (NWMP) post was established in 1883 one kilometer northwest of the park to patrol the Canada/U.S. border but was short-lived, closing in 1908. Annual flooding after spring breakup is a continuing problem; the main river channel changes, and chunks of the island break off. To reach the park, travel three kilometers northeast of Cardston on Highway 3, then southeast for 13 kilometers along a gravel road. The campground is small, and facilities are limited to picnic tables, firewood, and pit toilets. Sites are $11 per night.

From the beginning of the park access road, Highway 5 runs northeast to Magrath and Lethbridge. **Magrath** has a "Buffalo Slope" grain elevator, the latest concept adopted by the Alberta Wheat Pool; open for tours Mon.–Fri. 8 A.M.–5 P.M., 403/758-3231.

South from Cardston

South of Cardston is the Old Mormon Trail that settlers from Utah used on their way north. The town of **Aetna**, just off Highway 2, was once a thriving Mormon community with a cheese factory, a school, and a store. A worthwhile stop in Aetna is **Jensen's Trading Post,** a general store with an interesting collection of antiques.

This is the beginning of the true prairie, and if you're heading east from here, it's hard not to keep glancing in the rearview mirror for glimpses of the Rocky Mountains you're leaving behind. From Aetna, Highway 501 skirts the International Boundary, passing the ruins of a community once known as Whiskey Gap. It crosses Highway 62 north of the Del Bonita port of entry (open June 1 to September 15 9 A.M.–9 P.M., the rest of the year 9 A.M.–6 P.M.) and continues east to Milk River through arid grassland not suitable for cultivation (see **Milk River** earlier in this chapter). Along much of the way the **Sweetgrass Hills** in Montana are visible rising high above the prairies south of Writing-On-Stone Provincial Park.

Beyond the turnoff to Aetna, Highway 2 continues to the International Boundary. **Police Outpost Provincial Park,** on a small lake beside the International Boundary, is accessible along a 23-kilometer gravel road 10 kilometers south of Cardston. The police outpost that gave the lake and park their name was set up in 1891 to control smuggling of whiskey north across the border, but the remote location led to its closure before the turn of the century. From the park, spectacular **Chief Mountain** can be seen to the southwest. Most of the park is grassland interspersed with isolated stands of aspen and wetlands, where birdlife is prolific. Fishing in Outpost Lake is good for rainbow trout. The park's campground has pit toilets and picnic tables; sites are $15.

The highway crosses into Montana at the Carway/Piegan port of entry (open daily 7 A.M.–11 P.M.).

WATERTON LAKES NATIONAL PARK

Everybody traveling to this rugged 526-square-kilometer park does so by choice. It's not on the way to anywhere else or on a major highway but is tucked away in the extreme southwestern corner of Alberta. The park is bounded to the north and east by the rolling prairies covering southern Alberta; to the south by the U.S. border and Glacier National Park in Montana; and to the west by the Continental Divide, which forms the Alberta/British Columbia border. The natural mountain splendor, a chain of deep glacial lakes, large and diverse populations of wildlife, an

unbelievable variety of day hikes, and a changing face each season make this park a gem that shouldn't be missed.

The route to Waterton is almost as scenic as the park itself. From whichever direction you arrive, the transition from prairie to mountains is abrupt, almost devoid of the foothills that characterize other areas along the eastern slopes of the Canadian Rockies. From the park gate, two roads penetrate the mountains to the west. One ends at a large glaciated lake, the other at a spectacular canyon.

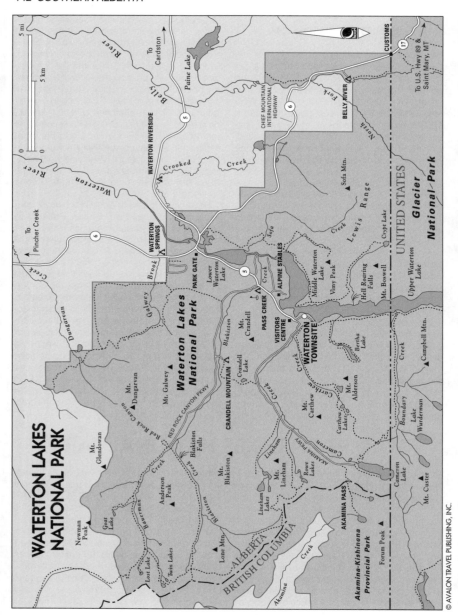

WATERTON LAKES NATIONAL PARK

© AVALON TRAVEL PUBLISHING, INC.

All visitors to the park are required to stop at the gate and buy a permit. Park entry for one day is adults $4, seniors $3, to a maximum of $8 per vehicle. A better deal for those traveling farther afield is the annual Great Western Pass, valid for all western Canadian national parks. It costs $35 per person to a maximum of $70 per vehicle ($27 to a maximum of $54 for seniors).

THE LAND

Geology

Major upheavals under the earth's surface that occurred approximately 85 million years ago forced huge plates of rock upward and began folding them over each other. One major sheet, known as the Lewis Overthrust, forms the backbone of Waterton's topography as we see it today. It slid up and over much younger bedrock along a 300-kilometer length extending north to the Bow Valley. Approximately 45 million years ago, this powerful uplift ceased, and the forces of erosion took over. About 1.9 million years ago, glaciers from the sheet of ice that once covered most of Alberta crept through the mountains. As these thick sheets of ice advanced and retreated with climatic changes, they gouged out valleys such as the classically U-shaped **Waterton Valley.** The three Waterton Lakes are depressions left at the base of the steep-sided mountains after the ice had completely retreated 11,000 years ago. The deepest lake is 150 meters. **Cameron Lake,** at the end of the Akamina Parkway, was formed when a moraine—the pile of rock that accumulates at the foot of a retreating glacier—dammed Cameron Creek. From the lake, Cameron Creek flows through a glaciated valley before dropping into the much deeper Waterton Valley at **Cameron Falls,** behind the town of Waterton. The town itself sits on an alluvial fan composed of silt and gravel picked up by mountain streams and deposited in Upper Waterton Lake.

Climate plays an active role in the park's natural landscape. This corner of the province tends to receive more rain, snow, and wind—much more wind—than other parts of Alberta. These factors, combined with the park's varied topography, create an environment where approximately 900 species of plants have been record-ed, more than half the known species in Alberta. Wind is the most powerful presence in the park. Prevailing winds from the south and west bring Pacific weather over the divide, creating a climate similar to that experienced farther west. These warm fronts endow the region with **chinooks,** dry winds that can raise temperatures in the park by up to 40°C in 24 hours. One of the nicest aspects of the park is that it can be enjoyed in all seasons. Summer for the sunny windless days, fall for the wildlife viewing, winter for the solitude, and spring for the long days of sunlight as the park seems to be waking up from its winter slumber. Be aware, however, that many of the park's best sights and hiking trails lie at high elevations; some areas may be snowed in until mid-June.

Flora

Botanists have recorded 1,200 species of plants growing within the park's several different vegetation zones. In the park's northeastern corner, near the park gate, a region of prairies is covered in semiarid vegetation such as fescue grass. As Highway 5 enters the park it passes **Maskinonge Lake,** a wetlands area of marshy ponds where aquatic plants flourish. Parkland habitat dominated by aspen is found along the north side of Blakiston Valley and near Belly River Campground, whereas montane forest covers most mountain valleys and lower slopes. This latter zone is dominated by a high canopy of lodgepole pine and Douglas fir, shading a forest floor covered with wildflowers and berries. An easily accessible section of this habitat is along the lower half of Bertha Lake Trail; an interpretive brochure is available at the Waterton Visitor Centre.

Above the montane forest is the subalpine zone, which rises as far as the timberline. These distinct forests of larch, fir, Engelmann spruce, and whitebark pine can be seen along the Carthew Lakes Trail. On the west-facing slopes of Cameron Lakes are mature groves of subalpine trees up to 400 years old—this oldest growth in the park has managed to escape fire over the centuries. Blanketing the open mountain slopes in this zone is bear grass, which grows up to one meter in height and is topped by a bright blossom often likened to a lighted torch. Above the treeline is the alpine zone where harsh winds and short summer seasons make trees a rarity. Only lichens and alpine wildflowers flourish at these high altitudes. Crypt Lake is a good place for viewing this zone.

Fauna

Two major flyways pass the park, and from September to November many thousands of waterfowl stop on Maskinonge and Lower Waterton lakes. On a power pole beside the entrance to the park is an active osprey nest—ask staff to point it out for you.

Wildlife viewing in the park requires patience and a little know-how, but the rewards are ample, as good as anywhere in Canada. Elk inhabit the park year-round. A large herd gathers by Entrance Road in late fall, wintering on the lowlands. By early fall many mule deer are wandering around town. Bighorn sheep are often seen on the north side of Blakiston Valley or on the slopes above the Waterton Visitor Centre; occasionally they end up in town. White-tailed deer are best viewed along Red Rock Canyon Parkway. The park has a small population of moose occasionally seen in low-lying wetlands. Mountain goats rarely leave the high peaks of the backcountry, but from Goat, Crypt, or Bertha lakes you might catch a glimpse of one perched on a cliff high above you.

The most common predators in the park are the coyotes that spend their summer days chasing ground squirrels around the prairie and parkland areas. For its size, Waterton has a healthy population of cougars, but these shy, solitary animals are rarely seen. Approximately 50 black bears live in the park. They spend most of the summer in the heavily forested montane regions. During August and September, scan the slopes of Blakiston Valley, where they can often be seen feasting on saskatoon berries before going into winter hibernation. Much larger than black bears are the grizzlies, which roam the entire backcountry but are rarely encountered.

Golden-mantled ground squirrels live on the Bear's Hump and around Cameron Falls. Columbian ground squirrels are just about everywhere. Chipmunks scamper about on Bertha Lake Trail. The best time for viewing beavers is dawn and dusk along the Belly River. Muskrats can be seen on the edges of Maskinonge Lake eating bulrushes. Mink also live in the lake but are seen only by those with patience.

HISTORY

Evidence found within the park suggests that the Kootenai (also spelled "Kootenay") people who lived west of the park made trips across the Continental Divide approximately 8,400 years ago to hunt bison on the plains and fish in the lakes. They camped in the valleys during winter, sheltering from the harsh weather. But by approximately 1,500 years ago, they were spending more time in the West and crossing the mountains only a few times a year to hunt bison. By the 1700s, the Blackfoot—with the help of horses—had expanded their territory from the Battle River throughout southwestern Alberta. They patrolled the mountains on horseback, making it difficult for the Kootenai hunting parties to cross, but their dominance was short-lived. With the arrival of guns and the encroaching homesteads of early settlers, Blackfoot tribes retreated to the east, leaving the Waterton Lakes Valley uninhabited.

"Kootenai" Brown

John George Brown was born in England in the 1840s and reputedly educated at Oxford University. He joined the army and went to India, later continuing to San Francisco. Then, like thousands of others, he headed for the Cariboo goldfields of British Columbia, quickly spending any of the gold he found. After a while he moved on, heading east into Waterton Valley, where his party was attacked by Blackfoot. He was shot in the back with an arrow and pulled it out himself. For a time he worked with the U.S. Army as a Pony Express rider. One day he was captured by Chief Sitting Bull, stripped, and tied to a stake until his fate could be decided, but he managed to escape during the night with his scalp intact. Brown acquired his nickname through his close association with the Kootenai people, hunting buffalo and wolves with them until they had all but disappeared. Even though Brown had been toughened by the times, he was a conservationist at heart.

After marrying in 1869, he built a cabin by the Waterton Lakes and became the valley's first permanent resident. Soon he started promoting the beauty of the area to the people of Fort Macleod. One of his friends, local rancher F.W. Godsal, began lobbying the federal government to establish a reserve. In 1895, an area was set aside as a Forest Reserve, with Brown as its first warden. In 1911, the area was declared a national park, and Brown, age 71, was appointed its superintendent. He continued to push for an expansion of park boundaries until his final retirement at age 75. He died a few years later. His grave along the main access road to the townsite is a fitting resting place for one of Alberta's most celebrated mountain men.

Oil City

Kootenai Brown was the first person to notice beads of oil floating on Cameron Creek. He and a business partner siphoned it from the water's surface, bottled it, and sold it in Fort Macleod and Cardston. This created much interest among the oil-starved entrepreneurs of Alberta, who formed the Rocky Mountain Development Co. to do some exploratory drilling. At this stage, the park was still a Forest Reserve; the trees were protected, but prospecting and mining were still allowed. A rough road was constructed through the Cameron Creek Valley, and in September 1901 the company struck oil at a depth of 311 meters. It was the first producing oil well in western Canada and only the second in the country. In the resulting euphoria, a townsite named Oil City was cleared and surveyed, a bunkhouse and dining hall were constructed, and the foundations for a hotel were laid, but the boom was short-lived. Drilling rigs kept breaking down, and the flow of oil soon slowed to a trickle. A monument along the Akamina Parkway stands at the site of the well, and a little farther up the road at a roadside marker a trail leads through thick undergrowth to the townsite. All that remains are the ill-fated hotel foundations and some depressions in the ground.

Waterton-Glacier International Peace Park

Shortly after Montana's Glacier National Park was created in 1910, the Canadian government set aside an area of land in the Waterton Valley as Waterton Lakes Dominion Park (later to be renamed a national park). Many people followed the footsteps of Kootenai Brown, and a small town named Waterton Lakes grew up on the Cameron Creek Delta. The town had no rail link, so unlike Banff and Jasper—its famous mountain neighbors to the north—it didn't draw large crowds of tourists. Nevertheless, it soon became a popular summer retreat with a hotel, a restaurant, and a dance hall. The Great Northern Railway decided to operate a bus service from its Montana rail line to Jasper, with a stop at Waterton Lakes. This led to the construction of the **Prince of Wales Hotel.** Boat cruises from the hotel across the International Boundary were soon the park's most popular activity. This brought the two parks closer together, and in 1932, after much lobbying from Rotary International members on both sides of the border, the Canadian and U.S. governments agreed to establish Waterton-Glacier International Peace Park, the first of its kind in the world. The parks are administered separately but cooperate in preserving this pristine mountain wilderness through combined wildlife management, interpretive programs, and search-and-rescue operations. Peace Park celebrations take place each year, and the **Peace Park Pavilion** by the lake is dedicated to this unique bond. In 1979, UNESCO declared the park a **Biosphere Reserve,** only the second such reserve in Canada. The park gained further recognition in 1995, when, along with Glacier National Park, it was declared a **World Heritage Site** by UNESCO.

SCENIC DRIVES

Akamina Parkway

This 16-kilometer drive starts in the townsite and switchbacks up into the Cameron Creek Valley, ending at Cameron Lake. The viewpoint one kilometer from the junction of the park road is on a tight curve, so park off the road. It looks out over the townsite and the **Bear's Hump,** which was originally part of a high ridge that extended across the lake to Vimy Peak until glacial action wore it down. This section of the road is also a good place to view bighorn sheep. From here to Cameron

Lake are several picnic areas and stops of interest, including the site of Alberta's first producing oil well, and a little farther along the road, the site of **Oil City,** the town that never was.

Cameron Lake, at the end of the road and 400 vertical meters higher than the townsite, is a subalpine lake in a large cirque carved approximately 11,000 years ago by a receding glacier. Mount Custer at the southern end of the lake is in Montana. Waterton has no glaciers, but Herbst Glacier on Mt. Custer can be seen from here. To the west (right) of Custer is **Forum Peak** (2,225 meters), whose summit has a cairn marking the boundaries of Alberta, Montana, and British Columbia. Canoes, rowboats, and paddleboats can be rented for $17 per hour, or you can walk along the lake's west shoreline. (Grizzlies often frequent the avalanche slope at the southwestern end of the lake.)

Red Rock Canyon Parkway
The best roadside wildlife viewing within the park is along this 13-kilometer road, which starts near the golf course and finishes at **Red Rock Canyon.** The transition between rolling prairies and mountains takes place abruptly as you travel up the Blakiston Valley. Black bears and occasionally grizzly bears can be seen feeding on saskatoon berries along the open slopes to the north. **Mount Blakiston** (2,920 meters), the park's highest summit, is visible from a viewpoint three kilometers along the road. The

road passes interpretive signs, picnic areas, and Crandell Mountain Campground. Red Rock Canyon, at the end of the road, is a water-carved gorge. The bedrock, known as argillite, has a high concentration of iron that oxidizes and turns red when exposed to air—it is literally rusting. A short interpretive trail leads along the canyon.

Chief Mountain International Highway
This 25-kilometer highway borders the eastern boundaries of the park and joins it to Glacier National Park in Montana. It starts east of the park gate at Maskinonge Lake and climbs for seven kilometers to a viewpoint where many jagged peaks and the entire Waterton Valley can be seen. The next stop, three kilometers farther south, has views of Chief Mountain, which has been separated from the main mountain range by erosion. The road then passes more spectacular viewpoints, Belly River Campground, and Chief Mountain. Hours of operation at the port of entry are mid-May to the end of May 9 A.M.–6 P.M., June 1 to August 7 A.M.–10 p.m, during early September 9 A.M.–6 P.M., and closed the rest of the year. When the post is closed, you must use the Carway/Piegan port of entry. It's on Alberta Highway 2 south of Cardston or Montana Highway 89 north of St. Mary (depending on your direction of travel). From the border it's 50 kilometers to St. Mary and the spectacular Going-to-the-Sun highway

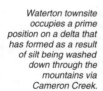

Waterton townsite occupies a prime position on a delta that has formed as a result of silt being washed down through the mountains via Cameron Creek.

through **Glacier National Park.** For more information on Glacier National Park, stop by the **St. Mary Visitor Centre** (406/888-7800, www.nps.gov/glac), which is open mid-May–mid-Oct. 8 A.M.–5 P.M. (until 9 P.M. in July and August).

HIKING

Although the park is relatively small, its trail system is extensive; 223 kilometers of well-maintained trails lead to alpine lakes and lofty summits affording spectacular views. One of the most appealing aspects of hiking in Waterton is that with higher trailheads than other parks in the Canadian Rockies, the treeline is reached quickly. Most of the lakes can be reached in a few hours. Once you've finished hiking the trails in Waterton, you can cross the international border and start on the 1,200 kilometers of trails in Glacier National Park.

The eight hikes detailed as follows make up only a small cross-section of Waterton's extensive trail system. Because most of the hikes climb to alpine lakes or viewpoints, the ratings that are given reflect the elevation gain. Anyone of reasonable fitness could complete them in the time allotted. Strong hikers will need less time, and if you stop for lunch it will take a little longer. Remember, all distances and times are one-way—allow yourself time at the objective and time to return to the trailhead. Topographic maps (one map covers the entire park) are available at various outlets in town. If you are planning to stay overnight in the backcountry, you must obtain a Wilderness Pass ($6 per person per night) from Waterton Visitor Centre or the administration office.

Don't underestimate the forces of nature. Weather can change dramatically anywhere in the park and at any time. That clear, sunny sky that looked so inviting during breakfast can turn into a driving snowstorm within hours. Ill-prepared hikers get lost in the park each year. Read the updated weather reports that are posted at all information centers before setting out, go prepared for all climatic conditions (always carry food, a sweater, and matches), and take plenty of water because open slopes can get very hot on sunny days.

Bear's Hump
- Length: 1.2 kilometers (40 minutes) one-way
- Elevation gain: 215 meters
- Rating: moderate

This is one of the most popular short hikes in the park, and although steep, it affords panoramic views of the Waterton Valley. The trailhead is at the Waterton Visitor Centre, opposite the Prince of Wales Hotel. The trail consists of switchbacks up the northern flanks of the Bear's Hump, finishing at a rocky ledge high above town. From this vantage point, the sweeping view extends across the prairies and down Upper Waterton Lake to the northern reaches of Glacier National Park.

Bertha Lake Trail
- Length: 5.8 kilometers (2 hours) one-way
- Elevation gain: 460 meters
- Rating: moderate

Bertha Lake is a popular destination with day-hikers and campers alike. The trail begins at the end of Evergreen Avenue near the far corner of Townsite Campground. For the first 1.5 kilometers, little elevation gain is made as the trail coincides with the Lakeshore Trail. Then the trail branches right and climbs steadily through a forest of lodgepole pine and Douglas fir along a well-maintained section to **Lower Bertha Falls.** Signs along this first, easier section correspond with the *Bertha Falls Self-Guiding Nature Trail* brochure available from the Visitor Centre. From here the trail passes **Upper Bertha Falls** and begins switchbacks steeply through a subalpine forest to its maximum elevation on a ridge above the hanging valley in which Bertha Lake lies. A trail encircles the lake. The backcountry campground on the lake's edge is one of the park's busiest.

Waterton Lakeshore Trail
- Length: 14 kilometers (4.5 hours) one-way
- Elevation gain: minimal
- Rating: easy to moderate

This trail follows the heavily forested western shores of Upper Waterton Lake across the International Boundary to **Goat Haunt, Montana,** linking up with more than 1,200 kilometers of trails in Glacier National Park. Many hikers take the **Inter-Nation Shoreline Cruise Co.** boat one-way ($11; 403/859-2362) and hike the other.

The boat dock at Boundary Bay, six kilometers from town, is a good place for lunch. Hikers heading south and planning to camp in Glacier National Park must register at Waterton Visitor Centre.

Crypt Lake Trail
• Length: 8.7 kilometers (3–4 hours) one-way
• Elevation gain: 680 meters
• Rating: moderate to difficult

This is one of the most spectacular day hikes in Canada. Access to the trailhead on the eastern side of Upper Waterton Lake is by boat. The trail switchbacks for 2.5 kilometers past a series of waterfalls and continues steeply up to a small, green lake before reaching a campground. The final ascent to Crypt Lake from the campground causes the most problems, especially for those who suffer from claustrophobia. A ladder on the cliff face leads into a natural tunnel that you must crawl through on your hands and knees. The next part of the trail is along a narrow precipice with a cable for support. The lake at the end of the trail, nestled in a hanging valley, is no disappointment. Its dark green waters are rarely free of floating ice, and the steep walls of the cirque rise more than 500 meters above the lake on three sides. The International Boundary is at the southern end of the lake. The **Crypt Lake Shuttle** leaves the marina at 9 A.M. and 10 A.M., returning from Crypt landing at 4 P.M. and 5:30 P.M. (A good way to avoid the crowds on this trail is to catch one of these afternoon shuttles over to the trailhead, camp at the landing, and set out on the trail before the first boat arrives in the morning.) The trip costs $12 round-trip. Reservations are necessary in summer; call 403/859-2362.

Crandell Lake
• Length: 2.4 kilometers (40 minutes) one-way
• Elevation gain: 120 meters
• Rating: easy

This easy hike to a subalpine lake from the Red Rock Canyon Parkway is popular with campers staying at Crandell Mountain Campground. The trailhead can be reached from within the campground or by noncampers along the Canyon Church Camp access road. The lake can also be accessed from a trailhead seven kilometers west of town along the Akamina Parkway. This trail is

shorter (0.8 kilometers) and follows a wagon road that was cut through the valley to Oil City.

Goat Lake Trail
• Length: 6.7 kilometers (2 hours) one-way
• Elevation gain: 500 meters
• Rating: moderate

The first hour of walking from the trailhead at Red Rock Canyon follows the Snowshoe Trail along **Bauerman Creek** before branching to the right and climbing switchbacks through a mixed forest. The steep gradient evens out as the trail enters the Goat Lake cirque. The lake is a welcome sight after the uphill slog, its emerald-green waters reflecting the towering headwalls that surround it. Look for the lake's namesake on the open scree slopes to the west of the lake.

Carthew-Alderson Trail
• Length: 20 kilometers (6–7 hours) one-way
• Elevation gain: 650 meters
• Rating: moderate to difficult

This hike linking Cameron Lake to Waterton townsite can be completed in one long strenuous day or done with an overnight stop at Alderson Lake, 13 kilometers from Cameron Lake. It leads through most of the climatic zones of the park and offers some of the best scenery to be had on any single hike. Most hikers begin at Cameron Lake. Transportation to the trailhead can be arranged through the **Park Transport Company** in the Tamarack Village Square ($7.50 one-way; 403/859-2378), which operates a hiker shuttle service to this and other trailheads in the park. From Cameron Lake, the trail climbs four kilometers to **Summit Lake,** a worthy destination in itself. The trail then forks to the left and climbs steeply to Carthew Ridge. After rising above the treeline and crossing a scree slope, the trail reaches its highest elevation of 2,310 meters at **Carthew Summit.** The views from here are spectacular, even more so if you scramble up to one of Mt. Carthew's lower peaks. To the north is a hint of prairie, to the southeast the magnificent bowl-shaped cirque around Cameron Lake, to the south directly below are the Carthew Lakes, and on the horizon are glaciated peaks in Montana. From this summit, the trail descends steeply to the Carthew Lakes, reenters the subalpine forest, and emerges at **Alderson Lake,** nestled under the headwalls of Mt. Alderson.

The trail then descends through the Carthew Creek Valley and finishes at Cameron Falls in the townsite.

Vimy Peak
- Length: 12 kilometers (5 hours) one-way
- Elevation gain: 825 meters
- Rating: moderate

Vimy Peak overlooks the townsite from across Upper Waterton Lake. It was once part of a ridge that extended across the Waterton Valley and was worn down by the relentless forces of glacial action. The trailhead is along the Chief Mountain International Highway, one-half kilometer from the Highway 5 junction. The first six kilometers are along the eastern bank of Lower Waterton Lake through forest and grassland. The trail then continues along the lake to Bosporus Landing opposite the town or climbs steeply to Vimy Peak (2,379 meters). The Vimy Peak trail actually ends at a basin short of the summit, which is still a painfully steep 40-minute scramble away.

OTHER RECREATION

Cruising to Goat Haunt, Montana
This is the most popular activity in Waterton. From the marina in downtown Waterton townsite, **Waterton Inter-Nation Shoreline Cruise Co.** runs scheduled cruises across the International Boundary to Goat Haunt, Montana, at the southern end of Upper Waterton Lake. The 45-minute trip along the lakeshore passes spectacular mountain scenery and usually wildlife. A half-hour stopover is made at Goat Haunt, which is located in a remote part of Glacier National Park and consists of little more than a dock, the Peace Park Pavilion, and a ranger station. You can return on the same boat or go hiking and return later in the day. If you are planning an overnight hike from here, you are required to register at the Waterton Visitor Centre. Another popular option is to take an early boat trip and walk back to town on the **Waterton Lakeshore Trail,** which takes about four hours. Boats leave the Waterton marina five times daily during summer. Fewer trips are made during May and September. The cruises operate until the end of September, but after the

Upper Waterton Lake is one of Alberta's premier scuba diving locations.

U.S. ranger station closes for the season in midmonth, the boats pass by Goat Haunt without stopping. Tickets cost $21 round-trip, $12 one-way, and you'll need to book ahead in summer; 403/859-2362. The same company operates a regular shuttle service to the Crypt Lake trailhead for $12 round-trip.

Other Water Activities
Fishing in the lakes is above average, with most anglers chasing brook and rainbow trout, pike, and whitefish. A national park fishing license is required and can be obtained from the Waterton Visitor Centre or any of the administration offices. The license costs $6 for seven days, or $13 for an annual permit.

Winds of up to 70 kilometers per hour attract hard-core windsurfers throughout summer and into fall. The winds are predominantly south to north, providing fast runs across Upper Waterton Lake from the beach at Cameron

SOUTHERN ALBERTA

Bay. The lake is deep, keeping the water temperature low and making a wetsuit necessary. Read the warning signs at the beach before heading out.

On any given summer day, scuba divers can be seen slipping into the frigid waters of Emerald Bay. A steamer was scuttled in the bay in 1918. It had been used to haul logs and as a tearoom but now sits on the lake's floor, attracting divers who find it a novelty to explore a sunken ship so far from the ocean. No equipment rental is available in the park. The closest is at **Anderson Aquatics** in Lethbridge (314 11th St. S, 403/328-5040), where you can also get your tanks filled. Full gear rental from Anderson is $50 per day, $75 for the weekend, including air fills. This shop also runs certification courses and field trips to Waterton Lakes throughout the spring and summer. Stop in on your way through for a rundown on all the dives, or ask at the Waterton Visitor Centre.

Golfing
The rolling fairways and spectacular mountain backdrop of **Waterton Lakes Golf Course** can distract even the keenest golfer's attention. The 18-hole course, designed by Stanley Thompson, is not particularly long (6,103 yards) or difficult, but the surrounding mountains and unhurried pace of play offer a pleasant environment. It is four kilometers north of the townsite on the main access road and is open June to early October. Its facilities include a rental shop, a clubhouse, and a restaurant serving sandwiches and snacks. A round of golf costs $28 during the day, dropping to $16 after 5 P.M. (which may have something to do with the healthy local bear population), or play as many rounds as you like in one day for $40. Club rentals are $7.50 and an electric cart is an additional $25 per round. For tee times, call 403/859-2114.

Horseback Riding
Just off the main park access road is **Alpine Stables**, 403/859-2462, which offers hour-long trail rides (starting on the hour 9 A.M.–5 P.M.) for $20. Two-hour Wildlife Habitat rides leave at 10 A.M. and 1 P.M. and cost $35. The three-hour ride, departing at 1:30 P.M., takes in the buffalo paddock on the edge of the prairies; $50.

When the Sun Goes Down
Interpretive programs are held nightly during the summer in Crandell Campground and at the **Falls Theatre** opposite Cameron Falls. Programs begin at 8:30 P.M. Ask at the Waterton Visitor Centre, or call 403/859-2445 for details.

Being the biggest bar in town, the **Thirsty Bear Saloon** in the Bayshore Inn gets crowded. It pours happy hour daily 3–6 P.M., and a band plays three or four nights a week. It's open 11 A.M.–2 A.M. In the Prince of Wales Hotel, the **Windsor Lounge** has panoramic views across the lake and live entertainment most nights. The **Rams Head Lounge** in the Kilmorey Lodge has a fireplace and an outside deck with views of the lake.

Waterton Lakes Opera House (309 Windflower Ave., 403/859-2466) shows movies nightly at 7:30 P.M. and 9:30 P.M.

Wintertime
Winter is a quiet time in the park. Traffic on the roads is light, a few trails are maintained for cross-country skiing, and the snowcapped peaks and abundant big game provide plenty of photographic opportunities. The main access road is plowed regularly, and the Akamina Parkway is cleared to allow access to ski trails. Skiing in the park is usually possible from December–March, but conditions can change dramatically. Arctic fronts scream down from the north, and chinook winds from the west can raise temperatures by up to 20°C in one hour. Ski trails are set on weekends, and the ski-touring opportunities are endless. Trails in the backcountry are not marked. Groups should carry avalanche beacons, be capable of self-rescue, and register with the warden before setting out. Ice climbing, snowshoeing, and backcountry winter camping are also popular. Winter camping is possible at Pass Creek, where a kitchen shelter, a woodstove, and pit toilets are provided. Three accommodations stay open year-round and offer all-inclusive winter packages. Gas may or may not be available in winter. Obtain trail information and weather forecasts at the park administration office on Mount View Road, open weekdays 8 A.M.–4 P.M., 403/859-2224. For information regarding backcountry skiing conditions and avalanche danger, contact the **Canadian Avalanche Association,** 800/667-1105.

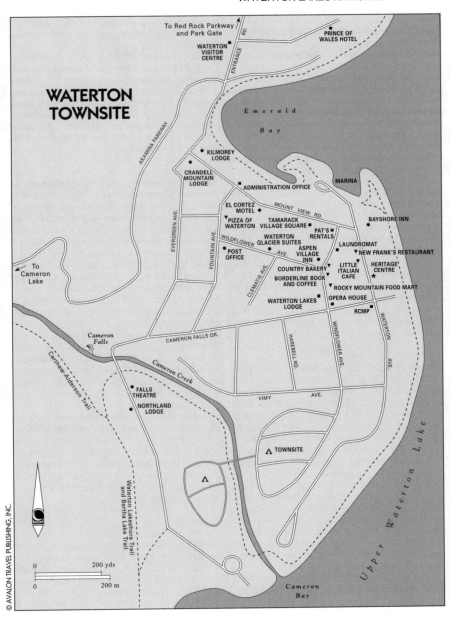

WATERTON TOWNSITE

To Red Rock Parkway
and Park Gate

ENTRANCE RD.

WATERTON
VISITOR
CENTRE

PRINCE OF
WALES HOTEL

Emerald
Bay

AKAMINA PARKWAY

KILMOREY
LODGE

CRANDELL
MOUNTAIN
LODGE

ADMINISTRATION OFFICE

MARINA

EL CORTEZ
MOTEL

MOUNT VIEW RD.

BAYSHORE INN

EVERGREEN AVE.

FOUNTAIN AVE.

WILDFLOWER

PIZZA OF
WATERTON

TAMARACK
VILLAGE SQUARE

PAT'S
RENTALS

WATERTON
GLACIER SUITES

ASPEN
VILLAGE
INN

LAUNDROMAT

NEW FRANK'S RESTAURANT

POST
OFFICE

AVE.

CLEMATIS AVE.

COUNTRY BAKERY

BORDERLINE BOOK
AND COFFEE

LITTLE
ITALIAN
CAFE

HERITAGE
CENTRE

To
Cameron
Lake

ROCKY MOUNTAIN FOOD MART

WATERTON LAKES
LODGE

OPERA HOUSE

RCMP

WATERTON AVE.

Cameron
Falls

CAMERON FALLS DR.

HAREBELL RD.

WINDFLOWER AVE.

Carthew-Alderson Trail

Cameron Creek

FALLS
THEATRE

NORTHLAND
LODGE

VIMY

AVE.

Waterton Lakeshore Trail
and Bertha Lake Trail

TOWNSITE

Upper Waterton Lake

Cameron
Bay

© AVALON TRAVEL PUBLISHING, INC.

MOON

0		200 yds
0		200 m

ACCOMMODATIONS AND CAMPING

Waterton has only a few accommodations. Most start opening in May and are full every night during July and August. By mid-October many are closed, with only the Kilmorey Lodge, Crandell Mountain Lodge, and Waterton Lakes Lodge open year-round. All accommodations are located within the townsite, so walking to the marina and shops isn't a problem. Although the standard of accommodations in Waterton is generally no lower than in Banff and Jasper national parks, the rates are considerably lower.

Less than $50
Hostelling International–Waterton is in the **Waterton Lakes Lodge** (corner of Windflower Ave. and Cameron Falls Rd., 403/859-2150 or 888/985-6343). Six rooms hold 21 beds, with a maximum of four beds in any one room. Guests have use of all lodge facilities, including the Waterton Spa and Recreation Centre (for a small fee), tennis, and bike rentals, as well as a shared kitchen and bathrooms. Beds are $19.55 for members, $23.55 for nonmembers—a great deal. Check-in is after 4 P.M., and it's open mid-April–October.

$50–100
The **Kilmorey Lodge** (Mount View Rd., 403/859-2334 or 888/859-8669, www.kilmoreylodge.com), an historic inn on the shores of Emerald Bay, provides excellent value for the money. From the lobby, a narrow stairway leads up to 23 rooms tucked under the eaves, many of which have spectacular lake views. Each is furnished with antiques, and the beds have down comforters to ensure a good night's sleep. Downstairs is one of the town's finest restaurants, along with a lounge and a gazebo for enjoying a quiet drink on those warm summer nights. The lodge stays open year-round. Rooms during summer start at $94 single or double, with more comfortable, larger rooms from $130. Some rooms have lake views, but book in advance for these. Inexpensive packages are offered in winter.

The **El Cortez Motel** is one block from the main street on Mount View Road, 403/859-2366. It's an older, park-at-your-door motel with basic

furnishings but no phones. Standard rooms are $70 single, $75 double, with some kitchenettes from $90.

Also in the same price bracket is the **Northland Lodge** (403/859-2353, www.northlandlodge.ab.ca), a converted house located 100 meters south of Cameron Falls along a road of the same name. It features nine guest rooms, a large lounge with a TV and fireplace, and free coffee and tea. The two rooms that share a bathroom are $75 single or double, and the remainder are $100 single or double.

$100–150
Across the road from the Kilmorey Lodge is **Crandell Mountain Lodge** (Mount View Rd., 403/859-2288, www.crandellmountainlodge.com), a country-style inn dating to 1940. The lodge has seen many changes since it first opened with shared bathrooms and wood-heated water. Today each of the 17 rooms has a private bath and is beautifully finished with country-style furnishings, and two rooms are wheelchair-accessible. Out back is a private garden area. Rates are $116–178 single or double in the height of summer with reduced rates (from $84) the rest of the year.

The **Aspen Village Inn** (Windflower Ave., 403/859-2255 or 888/859-8669) offers large rooms for $126 single or double but is best noted for self-contained cottages that sleep up to eight for $160, an excellent deal for small groups. Also on the property is a barbecue area and kids' playground.

A few dollars more than the Aspen Village Inn, the **Bayshore Inn** (Waterton Ave., 403/859-2211 or 888/527-9555, www.bayshoreinn.com) enjoys a prime waterfront location right on the main street. Amenities include private balconies, a hot tub, and an on-site restaurant and lounge. Rooms are $135 single or double for a basic room, $150 lake view.

$150–200
Two new accommodations, the first for many years, opened in the summer of 1998. The largest is the **Waterton Lakes Lodge** (corner of Windflower Ave. and Cameron Falls Rd., 403/859-2151 or 888/985-6343, www.watertonlakeslodge.com), which is set on a 1.5-hectare site in the heart of town. All 80 rooms

Prince of Wales Hotel

are large and modern, and each has mountain views. The lodge complex also holds the Waterton Spa and Recreation Centre (free entry for guests), a restaurant, a small café, and a lounge. Standard rooms are $155–185, whereas those with kitchenettes range $190–240. It's open year round.

The other new accommodation is **Waterton Glacier Suites** (Windflower Ave., 403/859-2004 or 888/527-9555, www.watertonsuites.com), featuring 26 luxurious rooms, each with a fireplace and whirlpool; $169–229 single or double.

More than $200

Waterton's most well-known landmark is the **Prince of Wales Hotel** (403/859-2231 or 602/207-6000 off-season), a seven-story gabled structure built in 1927 on a hill overlooking Upper Waterton Lake. It was another grand mountain resort financed by the railway, except, unlike those in Banff and Jasper national parks, it had no rail link. It was built as part of a chain of first-class hotels in Glacier National Park and is still owned by the company that controls those south of the border, Glacier Park, Inc. (www.glacierparkinc.com). Early guests were transported to the hotel by bus from the Great Northern Railway in Montana. After extensive restoration inside and out, the hotel has been returned to its former splendor. Guests from the United States travel to the park in vintage touring buses. Rooms start at $205 single, $245 double, but some are

fairly small. Lakeside rooms, with the best views, start at $285 single or double. The hotel is open mid-May–late September.

Campgrounds

The **Townsite Campground**, 403/859-2224, is in a prime location on the lake within walking distance of many trailheads, restaurants, and shops. Many of its more than 200 sites have power, water, and sewer hookups. The campground also has showers and kitchen shelters. Sites are available on a first-come, first-served basis and fill up by midafternoon most summer days. Open mid-May–mid-October; unserviced sites $15–17, hookups $20–23. **Crandell Mountain Campground** is located 10 kilometers from the townsite on Red Rock Canyon Parkway. It has unserviced sites, flush toilets, and kitchen shelters. It's open mid-May–August, sites $13. **Belly River Campground** is located 29 kilometers from the townsite on Chief Mountain International Highway and is the smallest and most primitive of the park's three developed campgrounds. It has pit toilets and kitchen shelters; sites are $10 per night. All of the campgrounds supply firewood but charge $4 per site to burn it. No reservations are taken at these campgrounds.

Waterton also has 13 backcountry campgrounds. Each has pit toilets, a cook shelter, and a water supply. Open fires are discouraged and are prohibited during periods of high fire danger; check with a warden. If you are planning to camp in the backcountry, you must obtain a permit from Waterton Visitor Centre or the administration office. Permits are $6 per person per night. Half of all sites can be reserved in advance ($10 per booking). Call 403/859-2224 for reservations. If your planned itinerary takes you over the border, ask at the information center about border-crossing regulations.

Outside of the park, two private campgrounds take up the nightly overflow. **Waterton Springs Campground,** three kilometers north of the park gate on Highway 6, 403/859-2247, has recently undergone massive renovations, including the construction of a large building holding modern bathroom facilities, a lounge, a general store, and a laundry room. Also on-site is a fishing pond stocked with rainbow trout. Tent sites are $15, trailers and RVs pay $17–21. On Highway 5, five kilometers east of the park gate, **Waterton Riverside Campground,** 403/653-2888, has powered sites, showers, and a barbecue on Saturday nights. Tent sites are $12, powered sites $15. Both of these campgrounds close by the middle of September.

FOOD

Restaurants range from pizza and fast food to elegant dining. If you plan on cooking your own food, stock up before you get to the park. Groceries are available at the **Rocky Mountain Food Mart** on Windflower Avenue (open 8 A.M.–10 P.M.) and in the Tamarack Village Square on Mount View Road. The Food Mart now sells hot chickens—an easy and inexpensive camping meal.

Cafés and Cheap Eats
For inexpensive breakfasts, homemade soups, delicious salads, and breads covered in homemade preserves, head to **Borderline Book and Coffee** (also known as Pearl's, 305 Windflower Ave., 403/859-2284), where the indoor/outdoor tables are always busy. Next door is the **Country Bakery,** a city-style deli serving meat and fruit pies as well as a wide range of pastries. In the theater building is **Waterton Bagel & Coffee Co.,** serving up exactly that. **Gazebo Cafe on the Bay** in the Kilmorey

Lodge serves light snacks and simple meals; seating is on an outdoor deck on the waterfront. It's open daily 10 A.M.–10 P.M.

For great pizza, try **Pizza of Waterton** (103 Fountain Ave., 403/859-2660), where they pile the dough with all kinds of meats, fresh vegetables, and a special savory sauce. It's open midday to midnight.

High Tea
Every afternoon between 2 P.M. and 4:30 P.M., the foyer of the Prince of Wales Hotel fills up as visitors descend on this historic landmark for high tea. Scrumptious pastries, tea, coffee, and other beverages are served on white linen at tables with the best view in town; $25 per person.

Restaurants
The **Little Italian Café** (Waterton Ave., 403/859-0003) is a great little restaurant serving inexpensive Italian delights. All basic pasta dishes are priced less than $10, but the Chicken Ranchesco, a delicious chicken dish cooked with ham and sun-dried tomatoes, is worth the extra bucks at $17.50. The Little Italian is also the best option for breakfast, with a full cooked breakfast offered for just $6.50. **New Frank's Restaurant** (106 Waterton Ave., 403/859-2240) serves inexpensive Chinese food (from $7.50) and Western food (from $9.50) and lays out a simple six-course buffet every night in summer ($12).

The **Kootenai Brown Dining Room** (in the Bayshore Inn, 403/859-2211) overlooks upper Waterton Lake and the mountains. Mule deer often feed within sight of diners. The food is excellent, especially the trout and beef dishes, which start at $15. The view is free. It's also open for breakfast and lunch. Hours are daily 7 A.M.–10 P.M. One of the most popular restaurants in town is in the Kilmorey Lodge. The **Lamp Post Dining Room,** 403/859-2334, has all the charm of the Prince of Wales Hotel but with a more casual atmosphere and lower prices to match. The mouthwatering menu has appetizers starting at $4, entrées ranging $12–22 (the French Rack of Lamb, $21, is a personal favorite), and you should leave room to finish with a delicious piece of homemade pie. It's open 7:30 A.M.–10 P.M.

The **Garden Court Dining Room** is a formal restaurant in the Prince of Wales Hotel with views of the lake through large windows. Its high ceiling and old-world elegance create a first-class ambience that is overshadowed only by the quality of the food. Prices are similar to any big-city restaurant of the same standard, so expect to pay approximately $100 for two full meals with a bottle of wine. If you are going to splurge, do it here. A large breakfast buffet served every morning (6:30–9:30 A.M.) is worth trying if you won't be coming for dinner. It's open for lunch 11:30 A.M.–1:30 P.M., dinner 5–9:30 P.M. Reservations are required; 403/859-2231.

TRANSPORTATION

Getting There
The nearest commercial airport is at Lethbridge, 140 kilometers away. Cars can be rented at the airport. The closest **Greyhound** buses come to the park is Pincher Creek, 50 kilometers away. From the depot there, at 1015 Hewetson Street, you'll need to get a cab, which costs approximately $55. Call **Crystal Taxi** at 403/627-4262.

Getting Around
The **Park Transport Company** operates hiker shuttle services to various trailheads within the park. Cameron Lake, the starting point for the Carthew-Alderson Trail (which ends back in town), is a popular drop-off point; $7.50 one-way. You could take one of these shuttles and return on the bus later in the day if driving the steep mountain roads doesn't appeal to you. The company also runs two-hour tours ($25 per person) through the park and a taxi service around town. Its office is in Tamarack Village Square on Mount View Road, 403/859-2378.

The **Crypt Lake Shuttle** leaves the marina regularly for Crypt landing; $12 round-trip. Reservations are necessary in summer; call 403/859-2362. **Pat's Rentals** (Mount View Rd., 403/859-2266) provides mountain bikes ($6.50 per hour, $32 per day) and motorized scooters ($18 per hour, $72 per day).

Tours
If you're in Calgary and interested in visiting the park but have a limited amount of time, consider a **Brewster** tour. The tour departs select Calgary hotels between 6:30 A.M. and 7 A.M., stop-ping at Head-Smashed-In Buffalo Jump before reaching the park. Approximately four hours is spent in the park, exploring town and its environs and traveling up to Cameron Lake. The return journey stops at an historic foothills ranch. The tours run 12 hours and cost $98 per person. For reservations, call 403/221-8242.

SERVICES AND INFORMATION

Shopping and Services
The proliferation of tourist-oriented gift shops along Waterton Avenue is worth browsing through when the weather isn't cooperating. In the **Tamarack Village Square** on Mount View Road, you'll find a sports store selling camping gear and fishing tackle, a good bookshop, and a currency exchange. The only **cash machine** in Waterton is in Pat's Rentals, also on Mount View Road. The **post office** is beside the fire station on Fountain Avenue. **Itussiststukiopi Coin-Op Launderette** at 301 Windflower Avenue is open daily 8 A.M.–10 P.M. The closest **hospitals** are in Cardston, 403/653-4411, and Pincher Creek, 403/627-3333. The park's 24-hour emergency number is 403/859-2636. For the **RCMP,** call 403/859-2244.

Books and Maps
Based in the Waterton Heritage Centre is the **Waterton Natural History Association,** which offers various educational programs and stocks every book ever written about the park as well as many titles pertaining to western Canada in general. The street address is 117 Waterton Ave., 403/859-2267. It's open May–Sept. 10 A.M.–5 P.M., longer hours in summer. Topographical maps of the park (one map covers the entire area) are available from the Waterton Visitor Centre, administration office, and Heritage Centre.

Information
On the main access road opposite the Prince of Wales Hotel is the **Waterton Visitor Centre,** 403/859-2445, which provides general information on the park, sells fishing licenses, and issues backcountry permits. Open June–Aug. 9 A.M.–8 P.M., May and early September 9 A.M.–5 P.M., closed the rest of the year. The park's

administration office (Mount View Rd., 403/859-2224) offers the same services as the Visitor Centre and is open year-round, weekdays 8 A.M.–4 P.M. For more information on the park, write to the Superintendent, Waterton Lakes National Park, Waterton Park, Alberta T0K 2M0, www.parkscanada.gc.ca/waterton. For general tourist information, www.discoverwaterton.com provides plenty of current information and links to accommodations.

CROWSNEST PASS AND VICINITY

The Municipality of Crowsnest Pass is located along Highway 3 between Pincher Creek and the Continental Divide in the southwestern corner of the province. The municipality encompasses a handful of once-bustling coal-mining communities, including Bellevue, Hillcrest, Frank, Blairmore, and Coleman. Many topographic features in the area are named "Crowsnest," including a river, a mountain, and the actual pass (1,396 meters) on the Continental Divide. From Pincher Creek, it is 62 kilometers to the pass. Continuing west from there, the highway (known as the Crowsnest Highway, of course) descends into British Columbia to the coal-mining and logging towns of Sparwood and Fernie, then on to the major population center of Cranbrook. The area is worth exploring for its natural beauty and recreation opportunities alone; the Crowsnest River reputedly offers some of Canada's best cutthroat, rainbow, brook, and bull trout fishing. But a trip through this area wouldn't be complete without visiting the historic towns and mines along the route. The Municipality of Crowsnest Pass is Alberta's only ecomuseum and was declared an Historic District in 1988, meaning that entire communities are preserved for future generations to explore.

History

The tumultuous history of the pass is one of strikes, disasters, and, in more recent times, unemployment, as the coal mines have closed one by one. Coal had been reported on the eastern slopes as early as 1845, but the area didn't begin attracting mining companies until the Canadian Pacific Railway (CPR) opened its southern line through the pass in 1898. Mines were opened and townsites laid out, attracting workers to the area. Many of them were immigrants who brought expectations of high wages and a secure future. But the area's entire economy revolved around just one industry—coal mining. Unfortunately for the miners, the coal here turned out to be of poor quality and located in seams at steep angles, making extraction difficult. In addition, most of the mining compa-

Buildings from the coal-mining days litter the pass. This is the remians of Leitch Collieries, just west of Pincher Creek.

nies were severely undercapitalized, leading to serious problems. The CPR was the mining companies' largest customer, but because the coal was inferior to that from the British Columbia mines, the price paid was considerably less. The first mine closed in 1915, and the others have followed suit one by one. Today, many of the local miners work in British Columbia, commuting over the Continental Divide each day. To the 6,500 residents of this job-starved valley, the tourism industry is new, but it's catching on quickly. At present, only Blairmore and Coleman have tourist services, but this situation will certainly change.

PINCHER CREEK AND VICINITY

This medium-size town of 4,200 is surrounded by some of the country's best cattle land. It is reputed to be the windiest spot in Alberta. The bitter winters are tempered by chinook winds that raise temperatures by up to 20°C in one hour. The town is located in a shallow valley in the southwest corner of the province, 211 kilometers south of Calgary and 70 kilometers north of the International Boundary. The town has many historic buildings, makes a good base for exploring the Crowsnest Pass, and is known as the gateway to Waterton Lakes National Park.

The NWMP established a horse farm at what is now known as Pincher Creek in 1876. They found that oats and hay, the horses' main source of sustenance, grew much better here in the foothills than at their newly built post at Fort Macleod. The story goes that a member of the detachment found a pair of pincers near the river—lost many years earlier by prospectors from Montana—and the name stuck. Word of this fertile agricultural land quickly spread, and soon the entire area was settled. As was so often the case for towns across the west, the CPR bypassed Pincher Creek and built a siding to the north called Pincher Station. Most towns either moved to the railway or struggled for a few

CHINOOK WINDS

On many days in the dead of winter, a distinctive arch of clouds forms in the sky over the southwestern corner of the province as a wind peculiar to Alberta swoops down over the mountains. The warm wind raises temperatures by up to 20° C in an hour and up to 40° C in a 24-hour period. The wind's impact on the environment is profound, its effect on the snowpack legendary. One story tells of a backcountry skier who spent the better part of a day traversing to the summit of a snow-clad peak on the front range of the Rockies. As he rested and contemplated skiing down, he realized that the slope had become completely bare!

Chinooks (a native word meaning "snow eater") originate over the Pacific Ocean as warm, moist air, which is pushed eastward by prevailing westerlies. As the air crosses British Columbia's rugged interior and climbs the western side of the Rockies, it releases moisture and picks up heat. The warm, dry air then descends the eastern slopes of the Rockies and blows across the prairies. The "chinook arch" is formed as the clear air pushes the cloud cover westward. The phenomenon is most common in southern Alberta but occurs to a lesser degree as far north as the Peace River Valley. Pincher Creek experiences around 35 chinooks each winter.

PACIFIC OCEAN   ROCKY MOUNTAINS   PRAIRIES

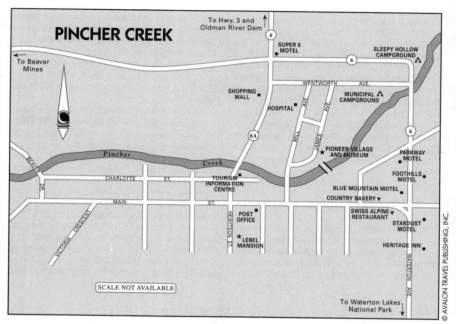

years and died, but not Pincher Creek; it stayed put and has thrived ever since.

Town Sights

The **Pincher Creek Pioneer Village and Museum,** 403/627-3684, is located in **Kootenai Brown Historic Park** on James Avenue. It houses many displays associated with early pioneers of the region, including extensive archives and a gift shop in the main log building by the entrance. Within the park are numerous historic buildings, including the cabin of Kootenai Brown, an early-20th-century folk hero (see previous **Waterton Lakes National Park** section). The cabin was moved from its original site on Waterton Lakes in 1969. It's open in summer daily, 10 A.M.–8 P.M., the rest of the year Wednesday and Sunday 1–5 P.M. Admission is $4. Overlooking Pincher Creek's main street is **Lebel Mansion** (696 Kettles St., 403/627-5272), a dignified 1910 brick house that has been restored by the Allied Arts Council. Inside is a small art gallery and cultural center open in summer daily 9 A.M.–5 P.M.

Oldman River Dam and Vicinity

Completed in 1991, the Oldman River Dam, north of Pincher Creek below the confluence of the Crowsnest, Castle, and Oldman rivers is the latest attempt to irrigate regions of southern Alberta not normally able to produce crops. The 25-kilometer-long reservoir is held back by one of Alberta's highest dam walls (76 meters); Highway 785, which branches north from Highway 3 three kilometers east of the Pincher Creek turn-off, crosses the wall and allows access to the base of the spillway, where there's camping, excellent fishing for rainbow trout, and a specially built kayaking course. The dam is also a popular recreation spot for windsurfing, boating, and fishing.

Two interesting museums lie in the vicinity of the dam. Beyond the dam wall, **Heritage Acres,** 403/627-5212, a museum run by the Heritage Acres Antique Equipment and Threshing Club, is signposted to the south. In addition to a large collection of antique farm machinery, it includes a schoolhouse, a grain elevator, a Doukhobor barn, and Crystal Village—

a collection of buildings (200,000 of them) made entirely from glass telephone insulators. It's open May–Sept. daily 8 A.M.–6 P.M.; admission is $1. At the turn-off to Heritage Acres, Highway 510 branches north then west along the reservoir, passing two great lakeside picnic and camping areas and a signposted road to **Three Rivers Rock and Fossil Museum,** 403/627-2206, a large private collection of shells, minerals, gems, rocks, and oddities of nature. It's open May–mid-October10 A.M.–5 P.M., closed Monday.

Beauvais Lake Provincial Park

Located deep in the foothills 24 kilometers southwest of Pincher Creek, Beauvais Lake Provincial Park is a wilderness area with a rich history of early settlement. Foundations of buildings are all that remain of the first homesteaders' efforts to survive in what was then a remote location. The park's most famous settler was James Whitford, one of General Custer's scouts at the famous Battle of Little Bighorn. He is buried at Scott's Point. A reservoir in the southeast corner of the park supplies water to Pincher Creek. The reservoir is also good for boating and is stocked annually with rainbow and brown trout. Wildlife is also prolific, with populations of beavers, white-tailed deer, elk, and moose present. The campground has limited services and costs $15 per night.

Castle Mountain Ski Resort

Alberta's fifth-largest ski area is also one of its best-kept secrets. Formerly known as Westcastle Park, the first lifts were installed in the late 1960s, and after 30 years of struggling to keep open, a consortium of keen local skiers bought it. Plans to turn this quiet ski area into a four-season resort have been in and out of court ever since. The only changes at this stage are a new double chairlift, which has doubled the vertical rise to an impressive 960 meters, and newly cut runs. Much of its 650-plus hectares are intermediate and advanced terrain above the treeline. The area is situated on a north-facing ridge 47 kilometers southwest of Pincher Creek along highways 507 and 774. Unfortunately, chinook winds—a ski area's worst nightmare—are prevalent in this part of the Rockies, and a 20°C temperature rise can turn hard-packed snow into slush very quickly.

Don't let this condition put you off, though, because the skiing is usually some of the best that a $34 lift ticket can buy. For more information, call the resort at 403/627-5101.

Events

Summer is busy in Pincher Creek. The town hosts two rodeos: the **Ranchers Rodeo** during the third weekend of June, and the **Pincher Creek Fair and Pro Rodeo** during the third week of August. The Ranchers Rodeo is part of a larger event—**The Gathering,** a celebration of cowboy poetry and Western art. The Gathering isn't a festival or competition—just a group of cowboys who come together each year to entertain each other. Poems are recited on Friday and Saturday; those known by heart are greeted with the most appreciation. On Saturday night, a huge barbecue takes place, with more beef than you could poke a brand at. This feast gets everyone in the mood to kick up their heels at the dance. Demonstrations and sales of traditional Western arts and crafts take place throughout the weekend. For more information, call 403/627-5855.

The **Children of the Wind Kite Festival,** which includes kite-flying demonstrations and competitions, fighting kites, events especially for the kids, fireworks, and telescope viewing, takes place during the third weekend of July at Oldman River Dam. Other annual events in Pincher Creek include **Heritage Days,** featuring working demonstrations of farm equipment, an antique tractor pull, a "parade of power," a free pancake breakfast, and a barn dance. This event is hosted by the Heritage Acres Antique Equipment and Threshing Club during the first weekend of August.

Accommodations and Camping

All except one of Pincher Creek's motels are spread along a four-block strip of Highway 6 east of downtown. The least expensive options are the **Parkway Motel** (1070 Waterton Ave., 403/627-3344 or 888/209-9902); the **Blue Mountain Motel** (981 Main St., 403/627-5335); and the **Stardust Motel** (979 Waterton Ave., 403/627-4366 or 800/268-5022). Each has basic rooms with coffeemakers, and all are within walking distance of the excellent Swiss Alpine Restaurant. Rooms start at $50 single,

$55 double. The **Foothills Motel** (1049 Waterton Ave., 403/627-3341 or 888/627-3340) is slightly more expensive but has a restaurant and a hot tub; $55 single, $58 double. The **Heritage Inn** (919 Waterton Ave., 403/627-5000 or 888/888-4374) is the nicest place to stay in town and has a coffee shop and a restaurant; $65 single, $75 double. The town's newest accommodation is the **Super 8 Motel,** at the north entrance to Pincher Creek (1307 Freebairn Ave., 403/627-5671 or 800/800-8000). It features 39 modern, air-conditioned rooms. A light breakfast is included in the rates of $63 single, $69 double. During winter, all of these motels offer ski packages to Castle Mountain for only slightly more than the price of a lift ticket.

The **Willowback B&B,** located southwest of Pincher Creek in the small mountain community of Beaver Mines, 403/627-2434, $50 single, $58 double, has shared bathroom facilities and a family room where you can relax with a cup of tea or coffee and a good book. On the premises is a wood-carving studio and gallery. Only a few minutes' walk away is the local general store, which sells excellent ice cream.

Pincher Creek Municipal Campground is located in a residential area on Wentworth Avenue just off Highway 6. It has no services but is central to town. A short path leads to Kootenai Brown Historic Park. The fee is $9 per night. On the northeast side of town on Highway 6 is the **Sleepy Hollow Campground,** 403/627-2033, with lots of permanent trailers, full hookups, and showers. Unserviced sites are $13, serviced $15–17. Much nicer than these two options, if you don't want hookups, is the **Cottonwood Campground,** situated 500 meters downstream of the Oldman River Dam 10 kilometers northeast of town. The 82 sites are spread throughout stands of towering cottonwood trees and all have easy river access. Fishing for rainbow trout is great in the river, but there's also a stocked trout pond. Camping is $13 per night. Along Highway 3 eight kilometers west of Pincher Creek is **Castle River Provincial Recreation Area** ($9), and to the southwest toward Beaver Mines is **Beauvais Lake Provincial Park** ($15). Both have pit toilets, kitchen shelters, and firewood.

Food
The **Swiss Alpine Restaurant** (988 Main St. at Waterton Ave., 403/627-5079) is a long-time favorite with locals and is the best dining choice in town, whether it's a casual lunch or an intimate dinner in a homey atmosphere. The lounge displays lots of taxidermy and a Western-style atmosphere, and the dining area has good food, including Alberta beef and lamb, delicious salads (the Alpine salad is especially good), and traditional Swiss dishes such as fondue. Most entrées are more than $12, but portions are generous. It's open 11 A.M.–10 P.M. for food, but the lounge stays open until the wee hours. The **Seasons Eatery** (in the Heritage Inn, 403/627-5000) is slightly cheaper but lacks the atmosphere of the Swiss Alpine. The Seasons is open for breakfast, lunch, and dinner. A good place for a light snack is the **Country Bakery** (967 Main St., 403/627-2532). You'll find a few Chinese restaurants along Main Street.

Services and Information
The **Greyhound** bus depot is at 1015 Hewetson Avenue, 403/627-2716. For a cab, call **Crystal Taxi** at 403/627-4262.

The **post office** is at 998 East Avenue. **Pincher Creek Hospital** is at 1222 Mill Avenue, 403/627-3333. The **Tourist Information Centre** (1041 Hewitson St., 403/627-5855 or 888/298-5855, www.pincher-creek.com) is contained in an imposing two-story building that is the town's namesake; it's open daily 9 A.M.–5 P.M. in summer and weekdays only the rest of the year.

PINCHER CREEK TO LEITCH COLLIERIES

The first worthwhile stop as Highway 3 begins its westward climb to the Crowsnest Pass from Pincher Creek is **Lundbreck Falls** (signposted from the highway), where the Crowsnest River plunges 12 meters into the canyon below. At the top of the falls is a viewpoint, with trails leading down to the base of the canyon and downstream along the river. This is a favorite fishing spot for rainbow and brown trout downstream of the falls and for rainbows and whitefish upstream. Below the falls is a campground with pit toilets, kitchen shelters, and firewood; $11 per night.

From the falls, Highway 3 passes the junction of Highway 22, which heads north to Kananaskis Country and Calgary. The next community west on Highway 3 is **Burmis,** which is well known for the **Burmis Tree,** a photogenic limber pine situated beside the highway on the west side of town.

Leitch Collieries

At the turn of the 20th century, Leitch Collieries was the largest mining and coking operation in Crowsnest Pass and the only one that was Canadian-owned. In 1915, it became the first operation to cease production. Now it's a series of picturesque ruins with one of the most informative interpretive exhibits in the area. The collieries opened in 1907, mining a steep coal seam south of the ruins. The Number 2 Mine, beside the highway, commenced operation in 1909. To house workers, a town named Passburg was built east of the mine. Today this site is the most accessible of the area's "ghost towns," although nothing more than a few depressions remains; most buildings were moved after the mine closed. The early development of the site included a sandstone manager's residence, a powerhouse used to supply electricity to Passburg, a row of 101 coke ovens, and a huge tipple. A boardwalk through the mine ruins leads to "listening posts" (where recorded information is played) and interpretive signs. The site is open year-round, with guided tours running daily 9 A.M.–5 P.M. in summer.

BELLEVUE

A French company, West Canadian Collieries, had been prospecting in the pass since 1898 and had bought 20,000 acres of land. Fortunately, the most impressive coal seams it found were right beside the main CPR line, which became the site of the **Bellevue Mine.** At 8 P.M. on December 9, 1910, an explosion rocked the mine and destroyed the ventilation fan. Thirty men died as a result of the accident. Most of them survived the initial blast but died after inhaling "afterdamp," a term used to describe the carbon dioxide and carbon monoxide left after fire has burned the oxygen from the air. The mine reopened soon after the tragedy, and at one time employed 500 men, but the gradual decline in the demand for coal led to the mine's closure in 1962.

The original town of Bellevue was built in 1905, before the mine disaster. The townsite centered around two streets: Front Street (now 213th St.) and Main Street (now 212th St.). The earliest single-story, wood-framed buildings had false facades to make them appear taller and more important than they really were. Two fires, in 1917 and 1921, destroyed many of the town's buildings, but these were soon replaced by more permanent structures, many of which still stand today.

On Highway 3 beside Bellecrest Campground is the **Wayside Chapel,** which seats eight people. Recorded sermons are held throughout summer, and the doors are always open. During the last weekend in June, the town celebrates Bellecrest Days with a parade, pancake breakfasts, a mud-bog race, and a Jell-O–eating contest.

Bellevue Mine Tour

The Bellevue Mine is the only mine on the pass that is open to the public. The tour is as realistic as possible without actually making you shovel dirt. The mine is cold, dark, and damp. Before entering you are given a hard hat and a headlamp, which you can attach to your hat or carry by hand. The guides carry blankets for those visitors who get cold—the average temperature in the mine is 7°C. The tour runs from mid-May–August 10 A.M.–5:30 P.M., every half hour and costs just $5.50. To get to the mine, follow the signs down the hill from the top end of 213th Street, 403/562-7388.

Practicalities

Downtown, the **Bellevue Inn** (2414 213th St., 403/564-4676) was built in 1921 to house business clients from the mine. Today it still operates as a bar and hotel, with renovated rooms for $40 single, $50 double. Next door is Bellevue's only restaurant and it's Chinese, with a limited Western menu (2438 213th St., 403/564-4801) and is open Tues.–Sun. 11 A.M.–9 P.M. A little farther up 213th Street, at 25th Avenue, is the **Old Dairy Ice Cream Shoppe.**

The **Bellecrest Campground** on Highway 3 at the east end of town has limited services but is

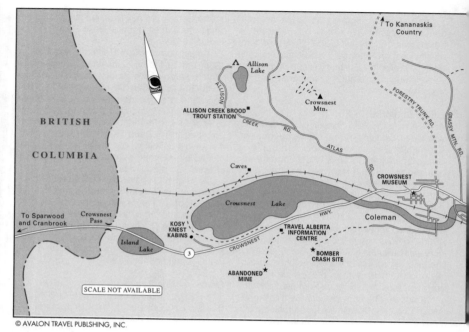

© AVALON TRAVEL PUBLISHING, INC.

free. Beside the campground, a small tepee-shaped **tourist information booth** is open during summer.

HILLCREST

Named after Charles Plummer Hill, one of the pass's earliest prospectors, Hillcrest is best remembered for Canada's worst mine disaster. The Hillcrest Coal and Coke Company began operations in 1905 and shortly thereafter laid out a townsite. Before long, the town had its own railway spur, school, hotel, and store. Then disaster struck. At 9:30 A.M. on June 19, 1914, with 235 men working underground, an explosion tore apart the tunnels of the Hillcrest Mine. The blast was so powerful that it destroyed a concrete-walled engine house located 30 meters from the mine entrance. Many of those who survived the initial explosion were subsequently asphyxiated by the afterdamp (residual carbon monoxide and carbon diox-

ide). Rescue teams from throughout the pass rushed to the mine but were forced back by gas and smoke. The final death toll was 189. The mine reopened and produced 250,000 tons of coal annually until closing in 1939 for economic reasons.

Many of the original miner residences still stand in Hillcrest, which is now a quiet town with a population of 1,000. The town has no services but two historically interesting sights. The **Hillcrest Mine** is accessible along a rough, unpaved road that branches left off 230th Street beyond the trailer court (it's easy to miss—the road runs along the trailer court's back fence). The ruins are extensive—look for the sealed mine entrance at the rear of the ruins, half hidden by trees. Through town to the west (this road joins back up to Highway 3) is the **Hillcrest Cemetery,** which is a Provincial Historic Site, off 8th Avenue. Many of the mine-disaster victims could not be identified. They were wrapped in white cloth and buried in the cemetery one foot apart in mass graves.

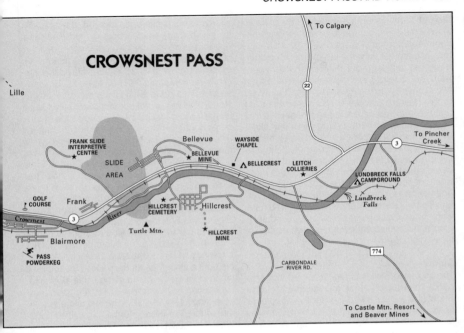

CROWSNEST PASS

Lille

To Calgary

22

FRANK SLIDE
INTERPRETIVE
CENTRE

SLIDE
AREA

Bellevue

BELLEVUE
MINE

WAYSIDE
CHAPEL

BELLECREST

LEITCH
COLLIERIES

To Pincher
Creek

3

LUNDBRECK FALLS
CAMPGROUND

Lundbreck
Falls

GOLF
COURSE

Frank

3

Crowsnest

River

HILLCREST
CEMETERY

Hillcrest

Turtle Mtn.

HILLCREST
MINE

Blairmore

PASS
POWDERKEG

CARBONDALE
RIVER RD.

774

To Castle Mtn. Resort
and Beaver Mines

FRANK

Frank, located two kilometers west of Bellevue, is probably the most famous (or infamous) town in the Crowsnest Pass area. In 1901, two Americans acquired mineral rights to the area directly below Turtle Mountain. Within months, their company, the Canadian-American Coal and Coke Company, had established a mine and laid out the townsite of Frank. The mine, when operational, became the first to sell coal in the pass and continued to thrive along with the town of Frank, whose population swelled to 600.

April 29, 1903

It was before dawn early in the 20th century. Everything in town was quiet, and the night shift was hard at work deep inside Turtle Mountain. Then, without warning, a gigantic chunk of the north face of the mountain sheared off, thundering into the valley below and burying part of Frank. It was the world's most destructive rock slide, burying 68 of the town's residents. Amazingly, none of the 20 working coal miners were killed. After being trapped for 14 hours, they dug themselves out.

In times of tragedy, there are usually heroes, and the hero of the Frank Slide was Sid Choquette. After realizing that the rail line had been covered, he scrambled over the still-moving mass of boulders and flagged down the morning express, stopping it before it reached the slide. As a token of appreciation, the CPR gave Choquette $25 and a letter of commendation. Within three weeks, the tracks were dug out and the railway reopened. One week later, the mine reopened. Most of Frank was intact, but fear of another slide led to the relocation of all the buildings across the railway line to a safer location. The mine closed in 1917.

It is impossible to calculate the amount of rock that fell from the mountain. It has been estimated at 82 million tons by some, 30 million cubic meters by others. Looking at the north face of Turtle Mountain will give you a visual idea of the slide, but the full extent doesn't become apparent until you actually drive through the slide area or view the fan of limestone boulders that spread more than three kilometers from the base of the mountain and more than two kilometers to the east and west. Scientists to this day puzzle over what caused the slide and the vast spread. Most experts believe that several factors contributed to the initial slide, and the weakening of the mountain by mining operations was only a small part of it. Regarding the spread of rock, one theory put forward by scientists is "air lubrication": as the huge mass of rock slid downward, it compressed and trapped air on which it rode across the valley. Today, Turtle Mountain is monitored daily with some of the world's most advanced seismographic equipment but has shown no sign of moving since.

Sights

The original townsite of Frank is now an industrial park. To get to it, cross the rail line at 150th Street (just west of the turn-off for the interpretive center). Take the first left and look for a rusty fire hydrant to the right. This landmark, which once stood on Dominion Avenue, Frank's main street, is all that remains of the ill-fated town. Directly behind it was the grand Imperial Hotel, which is now just a depression in the ground with a tree growing in it. This road then continues across Gold Creek and into the slide area. A memorial was erected here by Delbert Ennis, whose entire family survived the slide—and they lived on the south side of Gold Creek! This road was the main route through the area before the

slide and has since been cleared. It eventually joins up with the Hillcrest access road. The mine entrance is partially visible on the northern edge of the slide area, just above Frank Lake. For those with a sense of adventure, it is possible to climb Turtle Mountain (2,093 meters). The trailhead is located in East Blairmore on Pipeline Road. The trek to the summit is actually easier than it looks because the trail follows the mountain's northwest ridge. Only the last 20 meters along an exposed section are tricky. Allow two to three hours each way.

The **Frank Slide Interpretive Centre,** situated on a slight rise at the northern edge of the slide area, is an excellent place to learn more about the history of the valley, its settlers, and its tragedies. The audiovisual presentation *In the Mountain's Shadow* is a particularly moving account of the terrible working and social conditions in the valley. A 1.5-kilometer self-guided trail leads down into the slide. Better still, scramble up the slope behind the parking lot and walk along the ridge for a view of the entire slide area. Admission to the center is $6. It's open mid-May–August 9 A.M.–8 P.M., the rest of the year 10 A.M.–4 P.M. For more information, call 403/562-7388. No tourist services are available in Frank, but who wants to camp under Turtle Mountain anyway?

BLAIRMORE AND VICINITY

With a population of 1,900, Blairmore is the largest of the Crowsnest Pass communities. The town was originally known as Tenth Siding before being renamed in honor of A.G. Blair, the

Turtle Mountain
before the slide

PROVINCIAL ARCHIVES OF ALBERTA

Federal Minister of Railways. The town had only a small mine itself, but when the Frank Mine opened in 1901, Blairmore thrived. It became a main center for the surrounding mines and a supply point for the other towns. Real estate brokers, insurance agents, doctors, and barristers all made their homes here, and in 1907, West Canadian Collieries—which owned the Lille and Bellevue mines—relocated its offices to Blairmore. A brickyard opened, and many of the wooden-front buildings along the main street were replaced by impressive brick structures.

Coal mining still dictated the town's economy, however, and by the 1920s tensions between the workers and the mining companies had increased to the breaking point; in 1925, hundreds of miners protested on the streets of Blairmore. When the depression of 1929 set in, the companies cut wages, leading to further strikes. Communist labor leaders rallied local miners, and in February 1932 an election swept union representatives into power. The workers' town council had been elected with overwhelming support by their fellow miners. In an early act of rebellion, they renamed Blairmore's main street as Tim Buck Boulevard, honoring the leader of the Communist Party of Canada.

The Wayside Chapel is a unique little church on Blairmore's eastern outskirts.

Sights and Recreation

Many of Blairmore's original buildings still stand, including the brick structures on Main Street (20th Ave.). The three-story **Cosmopolitan Hotel** is the most impressive. It was built in 1912. The bar was always full of thirsty workers whom the manager obligingly served, even after hours (leading to the hotel's liquor license being revoked many times). Opposite the hotel is a **gazebo** that was a rallying point for miners during the 1920s.

Crowsnest Pass Golf and Country Club across Highway 3 from downtown Blairmore, 403/562-2776, is the only golf course in the pass. Greens fees are $15 for nine holes, $25 for 18. **Pass Powder Keg Ski Hill** features some runs ending right in town, but the main day lodge is accessed along a steep road spurring off 27th Street. The hill has a vertical rise of 400 meters and some surprisingly steep runs. Open for night skiing daily except Monday and all day on weekends; 403/562-8334.

The annual **Rum Runner Days** on the second weekend of July is a rip-roaring celebration of the town's seedy past. It kicks off with a pancake breakfast and parade on Saturday, followed by a barbecue and music in Bandstand Park. The weekend culminates at Leitch Collieries on Sunday with a picnic.

Accommodations

The historic **Cosmopolitan Hotel** (13001 20th Ave., 403/562-7321) has 16 guest rooms that have recently been renovated. They're still basic, and some share bathrooms, but the price is right—from $40 single, $44 double. Continuing west along the main street is the **Highwood Motel** (11373 20th Ave., 403/562-8888), which has a popular restaurant and pub on the premises; $44 single, $47 double. The nicest place to stay is the **Best Canadian Motor Inn**, right on the Crowsnest River at the far west end of town (11217 21st Ave., 403/562-8851). It has a sauna, a hot tub, a coin laundry room, and a restaurant. Rooms start at $59 single, $65 double.

Rather than paying $50 for a basic, boring motel room, however, you might consider the **Hearthside Bed and Breakfast** (12313 21st Ave., 403/562-7908). The former mine-manager's residence was built in 1915 and retains its historic charm. The rooms are cozy, and the coffeepot is always on in the large guest parlor. Rates are $50 single, $65 double, which includes a good, hot breakfast. **Lost Lemon Campground**, 403/562-2932, is across the railway tracks at the west end of town. It has showers, a swimming pool, and a laundry room and is situated right beside the Crowsnest River, making it the perfect overnight stop for anglers; tent sites are $17, hookups $21–23.

Food and Drink

The best place in Blairmore for a meal is the **Rende-vous Restaurant** (13609 20th Ave., 403/564-0000), which overlooks the Crowsnest River at the east entrance to town. It's open throughout the day, with a typical Canadian menu offered. Blairmore has a string of restaurants along 20th Avenue through downtown, none being particularly special. The **London Arms Pub** (in the Highwood Motel, 403/562-8888) provides glimpses of mountain scenery from the window tables. For breakfast, expect to pay $5, lunch $7, and dinner $8 and up. It's open Mon.–Sat. 6 A.M.–10:30 P.M., Sunday 7:30 A.M.–9 P.M. The **Cedar Gardens Restaurant,** in the Best Canadian Motor Inn (11217 21st Ave., 403/562-8851), is open daily 6 A.M.–10 P.M. Opposite the Greenhill Hotel is the **Yummy Inn,** 403/562-7357, for eat-in or take-out Chinese and a buffet for Tuesday lunch and Thursday dinner.

The bar in the Cosmopolitan Hotel is always busy, as is the Greenhill Hotel, which offers live country music on Friday and Saturday nights. Don't ask for an umbrella in your drink at either of these places. Both of the aforementioned motels also have a lounge.

Transportation, Services, and Information

Greyhound buses head to Pincher Creek and on to Calgary twice daily. They also go west into British Columbia. The depot is at 2020 129th Street, 403/562-2433. The **post office** is at 12537 20th Avenue. The only medical services available on the pass are at **Crowsnest Pass Hospital** (2001 107th Street, 403/562-2831). The best source of information about Blairmore, and the pass in general, is the Frank Slide Interpretive Centre (see previous entry).

In the Vicinity

The foundations of **Lille,** once a thriving community north of Highway 3, can be accessed only on foot. The hike is short, but the rewards are ample. The Lille mines and townsite were run by West Canadian Collieries, the same company that owned the Bellevue Mine. Its isolation from the pass and poor quality of coal forced the mines to close in 1913. The town's population of 400 moved out, and everything that could be salvaged was moved to Bellevue.

Two possible routes can be taken to Lille; the shortest is from Blairmore, whereas the other follows Gold Creek up a valley from east of Frank. To access the shorter trail, turn north just east of the Blairmore Golf Course on Grassy Mountain Road and follow it for eight kilometers to an intersection. The road to the right leads to Lille, but from here you're on foot; it's a three-kilometer (one-hour) hike along an old railway grade to the abandoned townsite in a grassy meadow.

Most of the building materials have been salvaged throughout the years, leaving only foundations. To the right of the path, you'll pass an impressive row of 50 coke ovens and the foundations of a once-grand hotel. Scattered through the meadow on the left-hand side of the trail lie the ruins of the miners' cottages, schools, and even a couple of rusty fire hydrants. A four-wheel-drive track leads east (left) through the meadow to two of the mines, which require some bushwhacking to find. On the south (right) side of this road are the foundations of the bakery, butcher shop, general store, and hospital.

COLEMAN

Westernmost of the Crowsnest Pass communities is Coleman, which is located 15 kilometers from the British Columbia border. The colliery in Coleman closed in December 1983, the last operation in the pass to do so. Many of the town's miners joined the ranks of the unemployed, some found work in the British Columbia mines, and others packed up their belongings and left the pass completely. The effect on the town has been devastating. A walk down Coleman's 17th Avenue is like what walking down the main street of Bellevue, Frank, Passburg, and Lille must have looked like after their respective mines had closed. Most of the buildings are boarded up, and all are dilapidated. Many businesses have relocated to the highway, hoping to catch passing trade. Those that remain are breathing their last gasp of air.

THE NOT-SO-GREAT TRAIN ROBBERY

It was August 1920, and the Lethbridge-Cranbrook train had just pulled out of Coleman toward the Crowsnest Pass, loaded with passengers. Suddenly, under orders from three gunwielding bandits, the train jerked to a halt. The trio, later identified as Aulcoff, Akroff, and Bassoff, had heard that successful local businessman Emilio Picariello—known to everyone as Emperor Pic—would be aboard carrying $10,000. The robbers' luck was short-lived from the start. They missed the wad of cash, fleeing with only $400 and several watches. After a night of drinkin' and dancin' in Coleman and evidently in no hurry, Akroff and Bassoff were spotted reading their "wanted" poster outside the Bellevue Cafe. The RCMP were alerted and confronted the pair. In the violent shoot-out that followed, Akroff and two policemen were killed. Bassoff was wounded and limped off in the direction of Frank Slide. On the run for several days, he was tracked to a Pincher Creek train yard where he sat passive and composed, eating lunch. Arrested and charged, he was hanged on 22 December 1920. Three and a half years later Aulcoff was apprehended in Montana, extradited, and sentenced, but he died in prison before the death sentence could be carried out. Although bullet holes were visible in booths at the Bellevue Cafe for many years after the incident, today the only reminder of this lawless episode is a plaque at the Frank Slide Interpretive Centre memorializing the slain officers.

History

Shortly after the land on which Coleman sat had been purchased by the International Coal and Coke Company, the town expanded rapidly. By 1904, it had two hotels, two churches, and several stores along Main Street. In 1918, the coal market collapsed and the mine closed. Still, the folks in Coleman were confident of the town's future, and concrete sidewalks were constructed before long. During the time leading up to World War II, the mine opened, but with a scaled-down operation. The 1950s were a time of amalgamation among the coal-mining companies in the pass, enabling the Coleman Colliery to remain open until 1983. Across the railway tracks at the west end of 17th Avenue are the remains of the coke ovens, the most complete in the pass. Many of the buildings that remain are of historical significance.

Museum

Located in the old Coleman High School building is the **Crowsnest Museum** (7701 18th Ave., 403/563-5434). The museum takes one complete hour to view because it has two floors crammed full with exhibits and artifacts from throughout the region. The schoolyard has displays of farming, mining, and firefighting equipment. It's open daily in summer 10 A.M.–6 P.M., the rest of the year Mon.–Fri. 10 A.M.–noon and 1–4 P.M. Admission is $4. Across the street is the *Coleman Journal* building. The *Coleman Journal* was a Pulitzer Prize–winning weekly newspaper that was published until 1970. After extensive restoration, the building has been opened to the public. Interpretive panels explain the slow process involved in early newspaper publishing. See the museum for hours of operation.

Bomber Crash Site

From Coleman, you can hike to the remains of a Royal Canadian Air Force Dakota that clipped the top of Andy Good Peak and crashed into the valley below in 1946. All seven airmen aboard died. The crash is on the south side of the Crowsnest River, nine kilometers from town. Cross the railway lines at 81st Street, then cross the river at 83rd Street and turn right (west) onto 13th Avenue. Because this road becomes gravel and fairly rough, it is recommended for four-wheel-drive vehicles only. At the wooden bridge located four kilometers from town, the road deteriorates, and it's five kilometers farther to the crash site (a 2.5-hour hike from town). Keep turning right at all intersections. The tail section, wing section, and the landing gear are all that remain of the plane.

The Forestry Trunk Road
The Forestry Trunk Road (Highway 40) is a well-graded gravel road that parallels the Canadian Rockies for more than 1,000 kilometers. The southernmost section starts in Coleman and heads north through the **Livingstone Range** to the Highwood Junction in Kananaskis Country, approximately 120 kilometers to the north of Coleman. Along the way are many hiking and fishing opportunities and plenty of primitive Forest Service campgrounds. Highlights include **Livingstone Gap** (48 kilometers north of Coleman), where the Oldman River flows through a narrow gorge, and **Livingstone Falls** (65 kilometers north of Coleman), which has a nearby campground.

Accommodations
Coleman has a few motels, but these certainly aren't your only option. An old hotel has been restored as a budget accommodation, and outside of town are cabins, a ranch, and a B&B. The **Stop Inn Motel** (on Highway 3 above downtown, 403/562-7381) has clean, basic rooms for $40 single, $46 double. Also on the highway, the newer **Valley View Motel,** 403/563-5600, has 25 small but modern rooms, some of which are air-conditioned; $52 single, $58 double. The **Grand Union Budget Hotel** (7719 17th Ave., 403/563-3433) was built in 1926. Early advertising for the hotel boasted of "thirty rooms with electric light and furnished in first-class style." Substantial restoration work has been undertaken in recent years, and although the rooms aren't first class anymore, they are of good standard. The hotel is also central within Coleman—17th Avenue was originally the town's main street. Rates are $20 single and from $28 double.

On Crowsnest Lake 12 kilometers west of town is **Kosy Knest Kabins,** 403/563-5155, where all 10 units have kitchenettes and TVs; $33 single, $48 double.

Food
Most of Coleman's businesses have relocated from the main street to Highway 3, which bypasses town to the north. **Chris & Irvin's Cafe,** 403/563-3093, is one of the few businesses hanging on downtown. It serves hamburgers, cheeseburgers, bacon burgers, and loaded burgers. The menu might be limited, but the burgers are good and start at $2. It's open Mon.–Sat. 6 A.M.–10 P.M., Sunday 8 A.M.–8 P.M. Up on the highway is **Popiel's,** 403/563-5555, which is surprisingly nice inside and with a reasonably priced steak, chicken, and seafood menu. It's open Tues.–Sat. 7 A.M.–midnight, until 10 P.M. on Sunday and Monday.

Services and Information
Greyhound stops at the Kananaskis Mohawk gas station on Highway 3. Beside Popiel's is a grocery store and laundromat. The **post office** on Main Street has recently closed and now houses only the residents' post boxes. The best source of information in town is the **Crowsnest Museum** (7701 18th Ave., 403/563-5434), open daily during summer 9 A.M.–6 P.M., the rest of the year Mon.–Fri. 10 A.M.–noon and 1–4 P.M.

WEST OF COLEMAN

Crowsnest Mountain
From Coleman, the British Columbia border is only 15 kilometers away, but there's no rush because you have a mountain to climb. Crowsnest Mountain (2,785 meters) is the symbol of the pass, and although it's a fairly difficult ascent with an elevation gain of 1,030 meters, it can be hiked by anyone with a good level of fitness. Snow may be encountered until July, and a certain amount of scrambling across scree slopes is required. For the most part, however, the trail is up the north-facing slope, so don't be perturbed by the cliff faces adjacent to the highway. Atlas Road spurs north three kilometers west of Coleman past one of Alberta's few outcrops of igneous rock (to the north just before the junction). Follow this road for 10.5 kilometers, staying right at the first fork. The trailhead is marked, and a little farther is the parking lot—well, a place to park your car anyway. At first the trail climbs steadily through a subalpine forest of

pine and spruce before crossing a stream. This is the last water source, so fill up. At the first scree slope, below the north face of the mountain, is an impressive view of the Seven Sisters to the northeast. The trail through the scree slope is not always obvious, but try to follow it anyway because it's the easiest route. At the base of the cliff, go right and climb up the wide gully to approximately 20 meters before the top of the rise, then veer sharply to the left. If you have difficulties scrambling up this section, turn back; if not, continue up three more gullies (the route is fairly obvious), from which the trail levels out and continues to the summit. The view from here is spectacular, extending well into British Columbia to the west and to the Porcupine Hills to the east. A canister attached to one of the summit markers contains a notepad in which to sign your name and prove you made it. It is only five kilometers to the summit, but you should allow between 3.5 and five hours each way. Check the weather forecast before heading out.

To the Border

Also accessed via Atlas Road (turn left onto Allison Creek Rd. after three kilometers) is the **Allison Creek Trout Brood Station,** 403/563-3385, where brown, brook, and rainbow trout are reared to provide eggs for trout hatcheries around the province. It's open to the public for a self-guided walk daily 9:30 A.M.–noon and 1–3:30 P.M. (closed weekends Sept.–May). Allison Creek Road continues to a recreation area on **Allison Lake,** which has good fishing and nearby camping. During winter, cross-country ski trails are set around the lake. The **Travel Alberta Information Centre,** 403/563-3888, on Highway 3 has a spectacular view of Crowsnest Mountain. The center is difficult to see coming from the east—look for a blue roof on the south side of the road opposite Crowsnest Lake. It's open mid-May–mid-June 10 A.M.–6 P.M. and mid-June–August 9 A.M.–6 P.M. Behind the information center, an old road now accessible only on foot leads three kilometers (one hour each way) to an abandoned mine. The road crosses a small creek several times before coming to an intersection. Continue straight ahead (follow the creek) past an old car and into a grassy meadow. Head one kilometer farther to the mine slag heap and scramble to the top for a view of the mine and some log cabins.

Nearby are some interesting caves, which are also accessible by a short walk; however, they are not marked, nor is there a set trail. The easiest way to get to them is from the roadside turnout on Crowsnest Lake (just west of the information center). Follow the lake's edge to the north, cross a small creek, and follow the railway tracks to a point nearly opposite the roadside turnout. Look for a small stream to the north. The caves are here, and their walls bear *petroglyphs* (native rock carvings).

Crowsnest Lake is popular for fishing and windsurfing. From here, Highway 3 crosses Island Lake and passes a small residential community known as **Crowsnest** before crossing the Continental Divide and entering British Columbia, which is another day and another book (*Moon Handbooks: British Columbia,* to be precise).

WEST OF CALGARY

Although most people driving west from Calgary head straight for the famous Banff and Jasper national parks, many other interesting detours are worth considering as well.

Although nonrenewable resources such as oil and gas are the basis of Alberta's economy today, ranching was the province's first major industry. The first ranch established in Alberta was at Cochrane, just west of Calgary, but the entire southern foothills have been used for running cattle for more than a century. Throughout the hills, many well-established towns with interesting histories, quaint teahouses, holiday ranches, and sprawling properties have the inspiring Canadian Rockies as a backdrop.

Kanmanaskis Country is a vast tract of land set aside by the Alberta government as a multiuse recreation area. It's located within easy day-trip distance west of Calgary. Although the region's emphasis is on the outdoors and camping, luxurious accommodations are available in Kananaskis Village. The village and the modern alpine resort of Nakiska nearby were built for the 1988 Winter Olympic Games. On the northern edge of Kananaskis Country, and at the entrance to Banff National Park, is the ever-growing mountain community of Canmore. The town provides an inexpensive alternative to staying deeper in the mountains and is an active outdoor center; many mountaineers, climbers, hikers, and skiers take advantage of the mountains surrounding the town.

RANCHLANDS

Between the snowcapped peaks of Kananaskis Country and the arid grassland of southern Alberta lies some of North America's best ranching country. From Cochrane in the north, throughout the ranching and farming communities of Oko-toks and High River, to the Porcupine Hills northwest of Fort Macleod, these low, rolling hills have been home to many of western Canada's cowboy heroes and the setting for movies such as the 2000 Jackie Chan hit *Shanghai Noon*,

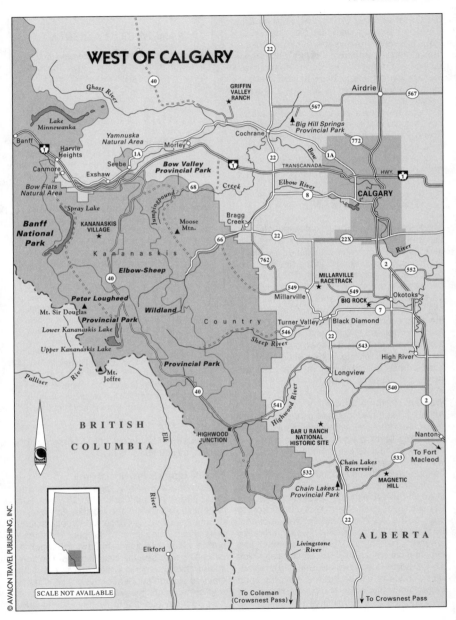

WEST OF CALGARY

Ghost River

GRIFFIN VALLEY RANCH ★

Airdrie

567

567

Big Hill Springs Provincial Park

Lake Minnewanka

Cochrane

772

Banff

1

Harvie Heights

Yamnuska Natural Area

Morley

Seebe

1A

Bow Valley Provincial Park

1

22

TRANSCANADA

Bow River

1A

Canmore

Exshaw

Bow Flats Natural Area

Creek

Elbow River

8

CALGARY

Spray Lake

Jumpingpound

68

KANANASKIS VILLAGE

Moose Mtn. ▲

Bragg Creek

22

22X

River

Banff National Park

K a n a n a s k i s

66

762

2

552

Elbow-Sheep

MILLARVILLE RACETRACK ★

40

549

549

Okotoks

Peter Lougheed

Millarville

BIG ROCK ★

7

Mt. Sir Douglas ▲

Provincial Park

Wildland

C o u n t r y

Turner Valley

Black Diamond

Lower Kananaskis Lake

546

22

543

Upper Kananaskis Lake

Sheep River

High River

Palliser River

Provincial Park

▲ Mt. Joffre

540

Longview

2

40

B R I T I S H

Elk River

541

Highwood River

C O L U M B I A

HIGHWOOD JUNCTION

BAR U RANCH NATIONAL HISTORIC SITE ★

Nanton

533

To Fort Macleod

Chain Lakes Reservoir

MoON

532

MAGNETIC HILL ★

Chain Lakes Provincial Park

Elkford

22

A L B E R T A

Livingstone River

SCALE NOT AVAILABLE

© AVALON TRAVEL PUBLISHING, INC.

To Coleman (Crowsnest Pass) ↓

↓ To Crowsnest Pass

the Oscar-winning *Unforgiven,* starring Clint Eastwood, and *Legends of the Fall,* starring Brad Pitt. Highway 2 follows the eastern flanks of these foothills south from Calgary. Other roads crisscross the region and lead to communities that are rich in heritage, many of which have recently been discovered by artisans and craftspeople who now call them home.

If you have ever dreamed of being a cowboy for a day or a week, this is the place to do it. The area also offers enough museums, teahouses, antique emporiums, and events to keep even the most saddle-sore city slicker busy all summer.

COCHRANE

The foundation of Alberta's cattle industry was laid down here in the 20th century, when Senator Matthew Cochrane established the first of the big leasehold ranches in the province. Today's town of Cochrane is situated 38 kilometers northwest of downtown Calgary along Highway 1A in the Bow River Valley and has a population of 11,000. Although ranching is still important to the local economy, Cochrane is growing as a "bedroom" suburb of Calgary. The business district, in the older section of town between Highway 1A and the rail line, is a delightful pocket of false-fronted buildings holding cafés, restaurants, and specialty shops.

Western Heritage Centre
Although Matthew Cochrane's 76,500-hectare ranch had almost everything going for it, several harsh winters in a row forced its closure in 1883. A 61-hectare site located one kilometer west of downtown Cochrane was once the headquarters of this historic ranch and today is the site of a heritage center. The facility has state-of-the-art exhibits cataloging western Canada's cattle industry from its earliest frontier days to the world of computerized auctions. Displays are indoors and out, with interpretive programs held each day during summer and events most weekends. The center also holds the Canadian Rodeo Hall of Fame and a restaurant with views across the property. It's open in summer daily 9 A.M.–8 P.M., the rest of the year 9 A.M.–5 P.M. Admission is adults $7.50,

RANCHING IN ALBERTA

The ranching tradition that Alberta so proudly claims started in the late 1800s. The massive herds of bison that once roamed the foothills had been devastated, the indigenous peoples had been moved to reservations, and the Canadian Pacific Railway had completed the link to the eastern provinces. A huge tract of land in the foothills now stood empty, and the Canadian government decided to lease it at a cent an acre. It didn't take long for word to get out. Cowboys from Montana, Wyoming, and Texas came hootin' and hollerin' as they drove thousands of head of cattle north. They brought with them a new spirit, craving the open spaces and the hardships associated with living on the land. Many of those who invested in the land were wealthy Americans and eastern Canadians who rarely, if ever, visited their holdings. Even English royalty became involved. Edward Prince of Wales, who abdicated the throne to marry Wallis Simpson, purchased a 10,000-hectare spread in 1919.

Ranching is still an important part of the province's economic base, with four million head of cattle worth $1.2 million annually to Alberta. Facts and figures aside, there's plenty of opportunity for visitors to experience ranching traditions, including at **Cochrane Ranche,** one of the first major landholdings and now home to the Western Heritage Centre commemorating the history of ranching in Alberta, and at **Bar U Ranch,** a National Historic Site where the traditions of life in the saddle live on through working displays and demonstrations of ranching skills.

seniors $5.50, children $3.50. For more information, call 403/932-3514.

Big Hill Springs Provincial Park
Protecting the end of a massive coulee, this small 26-hectare park is located 16 kilometers northeast of Cochrane and provides an example of vegetation that was once widespread across the prairies. The center of the park is a steep-walled valley with a stream flowing through it, cascading over several rocky terraces. The tree-lined banks of Big Hill Creek are an excellent place to escape the heat of the prairie and the roar of nearby highways. From artifacts found here, it is obvious that the valley was used by

prehistoric people as a habitation and buffalo-kill site. From where the park access road ends, continue on foot up Spring Creek.

Recreation
Immerse yourself in the Western lifestyle at **Griffin Valley Ranch,** 403/932-7433, one of the few places in Alberta that allows unguided horseback riding. Trails lead through this historic 1,800-hectare ranch along creeks, through wooded areas and open meadows, and to high viewpoints where the panorama extends west to the Canadian Rockies. Horse rentals are similarly priced to trail riding ($20 per hour); the only additional cost is an annual "membership" (simply sign a waiver and pay a $40 fee). To get to the ranch, follow Highway 1A west from Cochrane for 18 kilometers, take Highway 40 north, and then follow the signs.

Golfers shouldn't miss the **Links of Gleneagles,** 403/932-1100, one of the province's most challenging layouts (7,010 yards from the back markers). Lying high above the valley floor, the linkslike front nine winds through a subdivision, whereas the back nine provides the challenge of huge tee-to-green elevation changes; greens fee is $60.

Practicalities
The only accommodations right downtown are at the **Rocky View Hotel** (1st St., 403/932-2442), which has opened 15 rooms to guests. They're basic, with shared bathroom facilities, but go for just $30 single, $38 double per night. A better option is the **Bow River Inn,** on Highway 22 (near the Hwy. 1A intersection, 403/932-7900), which dates to the mid-1990s; $79 single, $89 double. Within walking distance of downtown is the **River's Edge Campground,** 403/932-4675, which has showers and charges $11 for unserviced sites, $18 for powered sites. **Ghost Reservoir Provincial Recreation Area,** located 22 kilometers west of town, has unserviced sites for $15 and powered sites for $18.

Of the many eateries lining Cochrane's downtown 1st Street, the most popular on a hot summer's afternoon is **Mackay's,** an ice cream parlor dating to 1948. **Cochrane Coffee Traders** (114 2nd Ave., 403/932-4395) has a wide range of specialty coffees. Back on 1st Street is the two-story wooden-fronted **Rocky View Hotel,** 403/932-2442, which houses the **Canyon Rose Restaurant,** a popular all-day dining spot, and the **Stageline Saloon.** Cochrane is the largest of three Albertan towns that has enacted a no-smoking policy in all of its restaurants.

In a log cabin between downtown and Highway 22 is **Cochrane Tourist Centre,** 403/932-2902, which is open in summer daily 9:30 A.M.–4:30 P.M. It's an easy walk from the center through Mathew Cochrane's historic ranch to the Western Heritage Centre.

BRAGG CREEK

Bragg Creek is a rural hamlet nestled in the Canadian Rockies foothills 40 kilometers west of Calgary. To the east is the Sarcee Indian Reservation and to the west is Kananaskis Country. The **Stony Trail,** an Indian trading route that passed through the area, had been in use for generations when the first white people arrived in the early 1880s. Much of the surrounding forest had been cleared by fire, encouraging farmers to settle in the isolated region and eke a living from the land. Improved road access in the 1920s encouraged families from Calgary to build weekender homes in town. Today many of Bragg Creek's 500 residents commute daily to nearby Calgary. The ideal location and quiet lifestyle have attracted artists and artisans—the town claims to have more painters, potters, sculptors, and weavers than any similarly sized town in Alberta.

Sights and Recreation
White Avenue, also known as **Heritage Mile** and originally the main commercial strip, is lined with craft shops, antique emporiums, and restaurants. The road continues southwest to 122-hectare **Bragg Creek Provincial Park,** a day-use area situated alongside the Elbow River, before continuing along the Elbow Valley into Kananaskis Country (see following **Kananaskis Country** section). North of Bragg Creek is the site of southern Alberta's first church. The earliest structure, built in 1873, was a crude cabin in which an Irish minister devoted his time ministering to the native Blackfoot people. A plaque marks this historic spot 12 kilometers north of town along Highway 22.

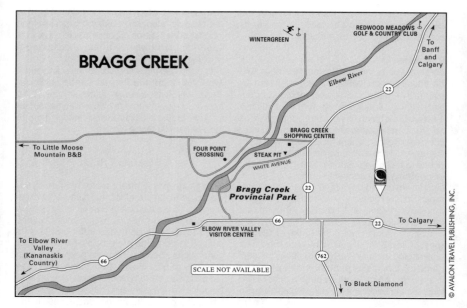

BRAGG CREEK

WINTERGREEN

REDWOOD MEADOWS
GOLF & COUNTRY CLUB

To
Banff
and
Calgary

Elbow River

22

← To Little Moose
Mountain B&B

FOUR POINT
CROSSING

BRAGG CREEK
SHOPPING CENTRE

STEAK PIT ▼

WHITE AVENUE

*Bragg Creek
Provincial Park*

22

To Calgary

ELBOW RIVER VALLEY
VISITOR CENTRE

66

22

To Elbow River
Valley
(Kananaskis
Country)

66

762

[SCALE NOT AVAILABLE]

To Black Diamond

© AVALON TRAVEL PUBLISHING, INC.

Wintergreen, 403/949-5105, is a four-season sporting facility located six kilometers north of town. Its immaculately manicured golf course features water hazards on 14 of the 18 holes and four sets of tees designed to fit all levels of golfer. Greens fees are $55 on weekends, $45 weekdays (the twilight rate of $50, which includes a cart and a steak dinner, is one of the better golfing deals in the Canadian Rockies), which includes use of an excellent practice facility. Immediately north of town is the **Redwood Meadows Golf & Country Club,** 403/949-3663, which is surprisingly flat considering its foothills location, but narrow fairways and a challenging design make it a favorite; $55 includes the use of a practice facility.

The huge log clubhouse at Wintergreen is the epicenter for a great variety of other activities, including swimming in the outdoor pool and mountain biking on the adjacent ski slopes ($7 for an all-day trail pass; lifts operate in summer Thurs.–Sun. 10:30 A.M.–8:30 P.M.), and a base of white-water rafting and horseback riding. In winter, a small ski area with five lifts and a vertical rise of 190 meters operates. Night

skiing is offered on Friday and Saturday. Lift tickets are $28.

Accommodations and Food
Although lacking motels and campgrounds (the closest camping is along the Elbow River in Kananaskis Country), Bragg Creek has bed-and-breakfasts and a restaurant that attracts folk from Calgary. **Four Point Crossing** (11 Elton Court, 403/949-2247) is a large, country-style house nestled among stands of trees, yet it is within walking distance of restaurants and shops. The home has a guest lounge with a fireplace and a sundeck, and a hearty breakfast is included in the rates of $55 single, $70 double. Another option, this one out of town, is **Little Moose Mountain B&B** (403/949-3564 or 877/949-3564, www.littlemoosemountain.com), which features two downstairs suites, each with separate entrances. Rates of $75 single, $85 double include a *huge* cooked breakfast of your choice served in your room. Call ahead for directions.

The **Steak Pit** (43 White Ave., 403/949-3633) is a fantastic restaurant. The décor is early Canadian, yet realistic and elegant. The dining room decorated with hand-hewn cedar furniture is only a small part of the restaurant, which also has a café, a lounge, a sports bar, and a gift shop. Eating here isn't cheap but *is* comparable to Calgary restaurants. The menu features mostly Alberta beef but has enough choices to please everyone. Open daily from 11:30 A.M. The Bragg Creek Shopping Centre has a wide variety of eateries as well as most services. **Pies Plus,** 403/949-3450, specializes in meat and fruit pies at reasonable prices. Also in the shopping center is the **Powderhorn Saloon,** 403/949-3946, which serves good food and has a few pool tables, including a Fusion pool table shaped like a double diamond and with 10 pockets. Ask the manager how to play and he'll probably buy you a game. Out at **Wintergreen,** across the river from town, the clubhouse is open in summer for Sunday brunch 10 A.M.–2 P.M.

BRAGG CREEK TO TURNER VALLEY

Millarville
From Bragg Creek, it's 70 kilometers southeast to Okotoks. The most scenic route south from Bragg Creek is along Highway 762 through Millarville. The local racetrack, located five kilometers northeast of the hamlet, is a hive of activity each Saturday morning 8:30 A.M.–noon, when huge crowds gather for the **Millarville Farmer's Market.** In addition to more than 150 local vendors, live entertainment and wagon rides are provided. The **Millarville Rodeo** was first held in 1997, but it has already gained a following among the local population. It's held the last weekend of May. The Canada Day (July 1) tradition of the **Millarville Races** goes back a lot farther, to 1905. The main race involves locals vying for a silver cup and belt buckle on stock horses. Head out to the racetrack to join the action.

TURNER VALLEY

Turner Valley, a quiet town of 1,600 straddling the Sheep River, is synonymous with the oil-and-gas industry in Alberta. In 1914, Canada's first major crude-oil discovery was made here,

but gas, not oil, first sparked interest in the valley. In 1903, a farmer named Bill Herron found gas seeping from fissures on his land. He had it tested and, to his surprise, was told it was petroleum gas. He was having trouble convincing anyone to back an oil-related enterprise and, so the story goes, he finally persuaded two oilmen to become involved by taking them to the site of the gas, lighting it, and cooking them a fried breakfast on the flame. Shortly after, the Calgary Petroleum Products Company was formed and started sinking wells, which was the beginning of an economic boom. During the oil boom, gas was burned off in an area known as "Hell's Half Acre" east of Turner Valley. It is estimated that 28 billion cubic meters of excess gas were flared off in the first 10 years.

Turner Valley Gas Plant
This National Historic Site is not set up as a tourist attraction, but the local information center runs interesting tours through the site each summer day 10 A.M.–5 P.M. The tour starts at the Municipal Centre, on Main Street, with an audiovisual presentation, then moves down to the gas plant for a casual but informative look at the one of Canada's most important historic industrial sites. If you don't take the tour, at least head over to **Hell's Half Acre Bridge,** which crosses the Sheep River southwest of downtown, from where gas flares that still burn 24 hours a day can be viewed. For further tour information, call 403/933-4944.

Practicalities
Turner Valley Hotel (112 Flare Ave., 403/933-7878) is the town's only motel; rooms are $50 single, $55 double. **Hell's Half Acre Campground,** downtown beside the information center, has showers and is in a central location; unserviced sites $8, powered sites $10. You'd be better off heading west into Kananaskis Country, though, for more enjoyable surroundings.

Just west of Turner Valley's only traffic light is the Quonset-shaped **Chuckwagon Café** (105 Sunset Blvd., 403/933-0003). It's a typical small-town diner, with the $2.99 breakfast special an especially good value, although the portion isn't huge (the record of three servings in one sitting is currently held by Ian Wallace of Canmore). The rest of the day, well-priced Canadian and

Chinese fare is served. The **Valley Rose Tea Room** (146 Main St., 403/933-2972) serves breakfast from $5 and lunch from $5–9, although most visitors stop for the daily afternoon ritual of tea and scones and to browse through the antiques. It's open daily 7 A.M.–5 P.M.

The **Tourist Information Centre** (Main St., 403/933-4944) is in the Municipal Centre. Open Mon.–Sat. 10 A.M.–6 P.M.

BLACK DIAMOND

This town of 1,700 on the banks of the Sheep River, four kilometers east of Turner Valley, was named for the coal once mined nearby. James A. McMillan, a government land surveyor, was digging an irrigation ditch when he uncovered a rich seam of coal. Within a few years, a mine had become operational, and the coal, which was of excellent quality, was used in households throughout the region. The coal mines have long since closed. Most residents work in the nearby oil fields or commute the 65 kilometers to Calgary.

Practicalities
The town has limited visitor services. The **Triple "A" Motel** (Hwy. 22, 403/933-4915) has basic rooms for $40 single, $50 double. A campground in **Centennial Park** by the Sheep River (access via 5th St.) has showers, a kitchen shelter, and firewood; unserviced sites $12, powered sites $14–18. The **Black Diamond Hotel** (Centre Ave., 403/933-4656) is a classic small-town pub that rocks with country music each weekend. Check out the building behind the hotel; originally a butcher shop, it now houses a small liquor store, complete with a chuck wagon on the roof. **Wonders,** a small gift shop (130 Goat Rd., 403/933-2347), is the unofficial tourist information center, but it's worth dropping by just to enjoy coffee on the outdoor deck.

HIGHWAY 22 SOUTH

Bar U Ranch National Historic Site
Established in 1882, the Bar U Ranch, located 31 kilometers south of Black Diamond, was one of western Canada's top ranches late last century. It was a corporate ranch, run by the Northwest Cattle Company and stocked with more than 3,000 cattle driven north from Montana. The company was renowned throughout North America as a leading breeder of Percherons, a type of draft horse that originated in the Perche region of France. Like most of the big ranches in North America, the Bar U was broken up over time. Today a 145-hectare parcel of the original spread has been preserved, with hundreds of Percherons running free through its rolling fields. Many of the old buildings have been restored; there's an interpretive center, a small theater, a blacksmith's shop, and a general store. Ranching skills are also demonstrated. In the **Roadhouse Restaurant,** the menu reflects the food that ranch hands of days gone by would have enjoyed after a long day in the saddle: buffalo burgers, sourdough breads, hearty soups, and stew are all offered. Bar U Ranch is open in summer Mon.–Fri. 10 A.M.–6 P.M., until 8 P.M. on weekends. For more information, call 403/395-2212 or 800/568-4996. Admission is $4.75.

Chain Lakes Provincial Park
Continuing south, the next worthwhile stop is Chain Lakes Provincial Park, sitting in the Willow Creek Valley between the Canadian Rockies and Porcupine Hills. The park was named for a series of spring-fed lakes that have since been dammed. The park is in a transition zone; therefore, plant and animal species are varied. Birdlife is especially prolific, with shorebirds, waterfowl, and osprey all present. In the north end of the park are some high bluffs, offering good views of the surrounding land. Fishing is excellent for rainbow trout, and in the spring of 2001 more than 60,000 bull trout were released as part of an ambitious program to restore the species to its once-prolific numbers. The campground and day-use area are at the southern end of the reservoir, close to a boat launch and beach. Camping is $13.

East to Nanton
Views of the Canadian Rockies in the rearview mirror are spectacular as you head east on Highway 533 from Chain Lakes Provincial Park through the northern reaches of the Porcupine Hills. At a high point in the hills is **Magnetic**

Hill, where an optical illusion creates a bizarre misimpression: put your car in neutral and it will slowly roll *up* the hill! As you descend into a valley east from the hill, you'll pass the old holdings of the A 7 Ranch, which was once one of Alberta's largest ranches. Its original owner, A.E. Cross, helped finance the first Calgary Stampede in 1912. The ranch has now been subdivided but remains in the same family. From this point, it's 35 kilometers to Nanton and Highway 2, where you can head north to High River, Okotoks, and Calgary, or south to Fort Macleod.

HIGH RIVER

In the heart of the province's ranching country, 45 kilometers south of Calgary, High River has grown steadily from its beginnings as a rest stop on the Macleod Trail. Originally it was known as "The Crossing" because it was the only possible place to ford the Highwood River. A period of severe drought at the turn of the 20th century was followed by many years of ample rainfall, and the community slowly grew to its current population of 8,000.

The **Museum of the Highwood** is housed in a restored Canadian Pacific Railway (CPR) station (406 1st St. W, 403/652-7156). Its displays portray early Western life. Of particular interest is the exhibit cataloging chuckwagon racing, a sport that has special significance to locals because the area boasts many champions. It's open in summer Mon.–Sat. 10 A.M.–5 P.M., Sunday 1–5 P.M. Admission is $2. Interesting shops downtown include **Eamor's Saddlery, Ltd.** and the **Olson Silver and Leather Company,** both on Centre Street. If you're in town on either of the middle weekends of June, don't miss the **North American Chuckwagon Championships** at the fairgrounds.

Of the three motels in town, the **Foothills Motel** (67 8th Ave., 403/652-1395) is the best value, with recently renovated rooms for $50 single, $60 double. Camping is allowed in **George Lane Memorial Park** off Macleod Trail at 5th Avenue W; unserviced sites $13, powered sites $18. In a restored rail car beside the museum is the **Whistle Stop Café,** 403/652-7026, which is open daily for lunch and on weekends for dinner.

OKOTOKS AND VICINITY

The fast-growing town of Okotoks is in the Sheep River Valley 34 kilometers south of Calgary and just minutes from Highway 2 to the east. It is the largest population base between Calgary and Lethbridge, and many of its 10,200 residents commute into Calgary to work. The name Okotoks came from the Blackfoot word *okatak* (rock), probably in reference to the

The Big Rock, west of Okotoks, is part of the Foothills Erratic Train, deposited across the foothills as the last ice age ended.

glacial erratics west of town. The town began as a rest stop along the Macleod Trail, which linked Fort Calgary to Fort Macleod last century. Many old buildings still stand and have been incorporated into a walking tour, with maps available at the Tourist Information Centre. **Okotoks Bird Sanctuary,** located east of town, attracts ducks, geese, and other waterfowl visible from a raised observation deck.

The Big Rock

The town's most popular attraction isn't a museum or a park—it's a rock, the Big Rock, the largest glacial erratic in the world. During the last Ice Age, a sheet of ice up to one kilometer thick crept forward from the north. A landslide in what is now Jasper National Park deposited large boulders on top of the ice. The ice continued moving south, carrying the boulders with it. Many thousands of years later, as temperatures warmed and the ice melted, the boulders were deposited far from their source (hence the name "erratic"). Big Rock, situated seven kilometers west of Okotoks, weighs 18,000 tons.

Practicalities

The best accommodations in town are provided at **Okotoks Country Inn** (on the main drag, 403/938-1999 or 877/938-3336). Opened in 1995, this motel features 40 climate-controlled rooms, modern facilities, and rates of $67 single, $72 double that includes a light breakfast. The **Ginger Room Restaurant and Gift Shop** (43 Riverside Dr., 403/938-2907) is a large Victorian-style mansion that has become a local landmark. Inside it's crammed with two floors of crafts and antiques. At the back is a tearoom that is always busy. Open daily 10 A.M.–8 P.M. Okotoks's original creamery is now a restaurant, bistro, and pub all under one roof called the **Foothills Cattle Co.** (35 Riverside Dr., 403/938-9955). Food in the bistro is served family style, and although the dining room is more expensive, it's still casual. The Sunday brunch is especially good. Open daily 11 A.M.–11 P.M.

An **information center** in a restored train station (53 N. Railway St., 403/938-3204) also has an interpretive display and art market. It's open in summer daily 8:30 A.M.–5 P.M.

KANANASKIS COUNTRY

During Alberta's oil-and-gas boom of the 1970s, oil revenues collected by the provincial government were channeled into various projects aimed at improving the lifestyle of Albertans. One lasting legacy of the boom is Kananaskis Country, a sprawling 4,250-square-kilometer area west of Calgary that has been developed with an emphasis on providing recreation opportunities for as many people as possible.

Within the area are two distinct ecosystems: the high peaks of the Continental Divide to the west, and the lower, rolling foothills to the east. The glacier-carved **Kananaskis Valley** separates the two. Although Kananaskis Country lacks the famous lakes and glaciated peaks of Banff and Jasper national parks, in many ways it rivals them. Wildlife is abundant, and opportunities for observation of larger mammals are superb. The region has large populations of moose, mule and white-tailed deer, elk, black bears, bighorn sheep, and mountain goats. Wolves, grizzly bears, and cougars are present, too, but are less likely to be seen.

Kananaskis Country can be geographically divided into several regions, each with its own distinct character, includeing **Bow Valley Provincial Park,** a small park beside the TransCanada Highway; **Kananaskis Valley,** home to a golf course, ski resort, and the accommodations of Kananaskis Village; **Peter Lougheed Provincial Park,** which rises from fish-filled lakes to the glaciated peaks of the Continental Divide; **Spray Lake,** which is named for a massive body of water nestled below the Continental Divide; **Sibbald,** an integrated recreation area where horseback riding is permitted; **Elbow River Valley** and the adjacent **Sheep River Valley,** sections of the foothills that rise to Elbow–Sheep Wildland Provincial Park; and in the far south, **Highwood/Cataract Creek,** where the rugged landscape ranges from forested valleys to snowcapped peaks. In total, Kananaskis Country contains four provincial parks, hundreds of kilometers of hiking trails, a complex network of bike paths, areas for horseback riding and some for all-terrain vehicles, a world-class 36-hole golf course, boat and bike rentals, and 40 lakes stocked with fish. The downhill-skiing events of the 1988 Winter Olympic Games were held at the specially developed Nakiska alpine resort, which is now open to the public. Fortress Mountain, located deeper in the mountains, provides more downhill skiing and snowboarding. Nordic skiers can glide over hundreds of cross-country skiing trails in the region. In addition to the areas set aside for recreation, large tracts of land, such as the Elbow–Sheep Wildland Provincial Park, provide full protection to wildlife.

Services within the recreation area include an information center at each of the main entrances, high-class accommodations in Kananaskis Village, camping at one of 3,000 campsites in 10 campgrounds, and accommodations for the physically challenged at William Watson Lodge.

The main access to Kananaskis Country is 80 kilometers west of Calgary off the TransCanada Highway (see "Old Banff Road" as follows). Other points of access are south from Canmore; at Bragg Creek on the region's northeast border; west from Longview in the southeast; or along the Forestry Trunk Road from the south. For more information, contact Kananaskis Country, Suite 201, Provincial Building, 800 Railway Avenue, Canmore, Alberta T1W 1P1, 403/678-5508, www.gov.ab.ca/env (and click on the "Parks" link).

Old Banff Road

The original route from Calgary into the mountains has long been bypassed, but for those with a little extra time, it remains as a pleasant alternative to the TransCanada Highway. Also known as Highway 1A, the easiest place to join it is at Cochrane, an important ranching center west of Calgary (see "Ranchlands'" earlier in this chapter). From there, Highway 1A follows the north side of the Bow River to Highway 40, the main entrance to Kananaskis Country. The first major junction is with Highway 940, which spurs northwest to **Ghost River Wilderness Area,** also accessible from Lake Minnewanka in Banff National Park. Soon after this junction, the highway passes **Ghost Lake,** which was created by damming the Bow River for hydroelectricity. Beyond the west end of the

lake is a white church built in 1875. For the next 30 kilometers, the road passes through the Stoney Reserve and the turn-off to the native settlement **Morley.** It then leaves the reserve and passes the turn-off to the TransAlta hamlet of **Seebe.** To the north is the impressive face of **Mt. Yamnuska,** a popular rock-climbing spot. From here, Highway 1A continues west, entering the mountains (views are marred by a cement plant and limestone quarry at Exshaw) and continuing to Canmore and Banff. Along this road, at a major junction 10 kilometers east of Seebe, Highway 40 crosses the Trans-Canada Highway and heads south into Kananaskis Country.

Bow Valley Provincial Park

This park, at the north end of Kananaskis Country, sits at the confluence of the Kananaskis and Bow rivers and extends as far south as Barrier Lake. The entrance to the park is four kilometers west of Highway 40 (the main access into Kananaskis Country), and Canmore is 28 kilometers to the west. It was originally part of Rocky Mountains Park (now Banff National Park), but the area became separated when park boundaries were reduced in 1930, excluding areas zoned for further industrial development.

The Bow Valley was gouged by glaciers during a succession of ice ages, leaving the typical U-shaped glacial valley surrounded by towering peaks. Three vegetation zones are found within the park, but evergreen and aspen forest predominates. To the casual motorist driving along the highway, the park seems fairly small, but more than 300 species of plants have been recorded, and 60 species of birds are known to nest within its boundaries. The abundance of wildflowers, birds, and smaller mammals can be enjoyed along four short interpretive trails. Other popular activities in the park include fishing for a variety of trout and whitefish in the Bow River, bicycling along the paved trail system, and attending interpretive programs presented by park staff.

Facilities at the two campgrounds within the park, **Willow Rock** and **Bow Valley,** are as good as any in the province. They both have showers, flush toilets, and kitchen shelters. Willow Rock also has powered sites and a coin

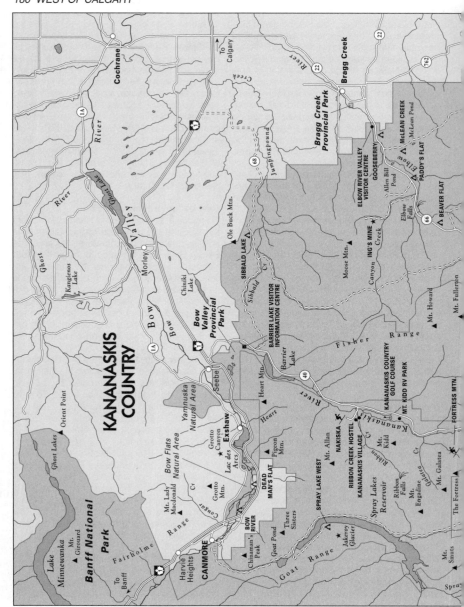

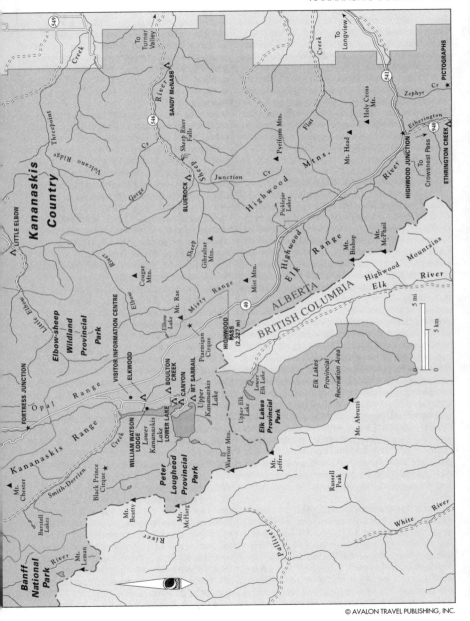

© AVALON TRAVEL PUBLISHING, INC.

laundry and is open for winter camping. Unserviced sites are $17–20, powered sites $20–23. Reservations can be made for both campgrounds at 403/673-2163, www.bowvalley campgrounds.com.

A **Visitor Information Centre** is at the park entrance on Highway 1X. It offers general information on the park and Kananaskis Country, as well as interpretive displays. A 2.2-kilometer hiking trail also begins here. The center is open in summer Mon.–Fri. 8 A.M.–8 P.M., the rest of the year Mon.–Fri. 8:15 A.M.–4:30 P.M.

KANANASKIS VALLEY

This is the most developed area of Kananaskis Country, yet summer crowds are minimal compared to Banff. Highway 40 follows the Kananaskis River through the valley to Peter Lougheed Provincial Park, and the Smith-Dorrien/Spray Trail parallels this road to the west. At the north entrance to the valley is the Barrier Lake Visitor Information Centre (open in summer daily 9 A.M.–6 P.M., the rest of the year daily 9 A.M.–4 P.M.), 403/673-3985, a good place to start your trip into Kananaskis Country. The epicenter of the valley is **Kananaskis Village,** comprising accommodations and restaurants. Nearby are two winter resorts; horseback riding at Boundary Ranch, 403/591-7171; a 36-hole golf course; and some spectacular mountain scenery. Although the best hiking is farther south in Peter Lougheed Provincial Park, there are a few trails around the village area. In the village, **Peregrine Sports,** 403/591-7453, rents a wide variety of sporting equipment, including mountain bikes (from $7 per hour, $30 per day), scooters ($13 per hour, $60 per day), fishing rods ($10 per day), canoes ($35 per day), and various downhill and cross-country skiing equipment.

Kananaskis Country Golf Course

This 36-hole resort-style course opened in 1983 at a cost of almost $1 million for each hole. Renowned golf-course architect Robert Trent Jones, who designed the layout, described the Kananaskis Valley as ". . . the best spot I have ever seen for a golf course." After marveling at the surrounding mountains, few will disagree with his statement. Just don't let the 136 sand

traps, water that comes into play on more than half the holes, or the large rolling greens distract you. The course is one of the best-value courses in North America; greens fees are only $50–75; for tee times, call 403/591-7272 or 877/591-2525.

Nakiska

This state-of-the-art winter resort was built on Mt. Allan as the host site for the alpine skiing events of the 1988 Winter Olympic Games. Originally, the events were to be held on existing ski slopes in Banff National Park. Environmentalists succeeded in keeping the games out of the park, but the victory soon turned sour when plans for a new area on the slopes of Mt. Allan were unveiled. This was the start of Nakiska's early problems. Anyone who had spent any time in this part of the mountains knew the effect chinook winds can have on the snow cover and how impractical it was to build a ski area there. The answer was snowmaking. A $5 million computerized snowmaking system covering 85 percent of the runs was installed, with 40 kilometers of piping and 343 hydrants capable of pumping 24 million liters of water per day. Great cruising and fast fall-line skiing on runs cut specially for racing will satisfy the intermediate-to-advanced crowd. For the less daring, the Bronze Chairlift accesses a novice area below the main area. The area has a total of 28 runs and a vertical rise of 735 meters. Lift tickets are adults $42, seniors and students $34, children $15. Packages are offered in Kananaskis Village, which is linked to Nakiska by shuttle from Canmore, 40 kilometers to the northwest.

For more ski resort information, call 403/591-7777 or the Snowphone at 403/229-3288. For accommodation reservations, call 800/258-7669.

Fortress Mountain

Fortress is a sleeping giant. It's a 30-minute drive farther into Kananaskis Country than Nakiska, but the rewards are uncrowded slopes, more snow, on-hill accommodations, and spectacular views. Runs are short, but with skiing and snowboarding permitted on three distinct faces, there's something for everyone. With a little hiking, experienced powderhounds can find untracked snow days after a storm. Facilities include three chairlifts and three T-bars serving a vertical rise of 330 meters, and a large day lodge with a cafeteria, a restaurant, and a bar. Lift tickets are $32 per day or $24 for the afternoon; seniors and students $25. For more information, call 403/264-5825 or the Snowphone at 403/245-4909. On-hill accommodations are at **Fortress Mountain Lodge,** 403/256-8473 or 800/258-7669, with rates from $120 per person for two nights' accommodation in a motel-style room and two lift tickets. The latest addition to the base area is a string of comfortable, self-contained three-bedroom chalets that cost $175 during the week and $225 on weekends.

Cross-Country Skiing
The most accessible of Kananaskis Country's 200 kilometers of cross-country trails are in the Ribbon Creek area. The trails radiating from Kananaskis Village and those around the base of the Nakiska ski area are the most heavily used. Most trails are easy to intermediate, including a five-kilometer track up Ribbon Creek. Rentals are available in the Village Trading Post in Kananaskis Village.

Kananaskis Village
This modern alpine resort 100 kilometers from Calgary was built for the 1988 Winter Olympic Games. Today it serves as headquarters for those who want to experience Kananaskis Country while enjoying the comforts of hotels and fine restaurants. The village is located on a narrow plateau overlooking the valley, with magnificent mountain vistas in all directions and two winter resorts a short drive away.

Of the two hotels in the village, the **Kananaskis Inn** (403/591-7500 or 888/591-7501, www.kananaskisinn.com) is the less expensive. Some of the 90 rooms are bedroom lofts with fireplaces, kitchenettes, and sitting rooms ($180); the others are standard hotel rooms that begin at $160. The inn also offers an exercise room and an indoor pool. The other hotel in the village, the upmarket **Delta Lodge at Kananaskis** (403/591-7711 or 800/268-1133, www.deltahotels.com), offers two distinctly different types of rooms. In the main lodge are 251 moderately large rooms, many with mountain views, balconies, and fireplaces as well as a shopping arcade. The John Palliser Manor holds 70 "Signature Club" (a Delta designation)

fresh tracks at Fortress

rooms, each boasting a mountain view, a luxurious bathroom complete with bathrobes, extra-large beds, and many extras, such as CD players. Guests in this wing also enjoy a private lounge. All guests have use of the Summit Spa and Fitness Centre, which comprises a full-facility health club, an indoor swimming pool, a whirlpool, a steam room, a sauna, and a beauty salon with tanning beds. Rooms in the main lodge start at $205 single or double, whereas those in the John Palliser Manor, where rates include a light breakfast, start at $295. Rates drop dramatically outside of summer; good ski packages are offered all winter.

The lodge contains six restaurants and bars. For a warm, relaxed atmosphere, head to the **Bighorn Lounge,** near the arcade's main entrance, which features a bistro-style menu. Also in the arcade is the **Peaks Restaurant,** with a casual Western-style atmosphere, floor-to-ceiling windows, and an adjoining outdoor patio used during summer. It's open daily 6 A.M.–10 P.M., with a buffet breakfast offered until 10 A.M. The country-style **Brady's Market** features seasonal produce prepared in traditional European dishes. **L'Escapade** (in the John Palliser Manor, 403/591-7711) is the village's most elegant restaurant. French-Canadian cuisine is served on sterling silver, as a pianist plays in the background. It's open for dinner only; expect to pay $18–30 for an entrée. Food is also available at the Alpine Garden Café, at Kananaskis Inn, or at the golf course, where the restaurant offers a casual atmosphere and stunning valley views.

Near the entrance to the village is the **Village Trading Post,** a post office, and an information center (open in summer daily 9 A.M.–5 P.M.).

Hostel
The **Ribbon Creek Hostel,** 403/762-4122, is situated along the access road to Kananaskis Village, within walking distance. The hostel has hot showers, a kitchen, family rooms, a lounge room with a fireplace, and an outdoor barbecue. Cost to members is $13, nonmembers $17.

Campgrounds
Mt. Kidd RV Park, 403/591-7700, is arguably the finest in Canada. It's nestled below the sheer eastern face of Mt. Kidd in a forest of spruce and lodgepole pine. The campground's showpiece is the Campers Centre. Inside are all of the usual bathroom facilities as well as whirlpools, saunas, a wading pool, a game room, a lounge, groceries, a concession, and laundry facilities. Outside are tennis courts, picnic areas by the river, and many paved trails. Tent sites are $19, hookups $23–29. It's open year-round.

Those who can survive without such luxuries have the choice of three other campgrounds along Highway 40 ($16).

PETER LOUGHEED PROVINCIAL PARK

This park, originally named Kananaskis Provincial Park, was renamed in 1986 after Peter Lougheed. Lougheed was the Albertan premier who, with the help of the oil-money–based Heritage Savings and Trust Fund, began the development of Kananaskis Country as a multiuse recreation area. The 500-square-kilometer wilderness is the second-largest provincial park in Alberta. The high peaks of the Continental Divide form the eastern and southern boundaries of the park, making a spectacular backdrop for the Kananaskis River and the Kananaskis Lakes. These lakes are the center of boating and fishing in the park, and opportunities abound for hiking and camping nearby.

Highway 40 is the main route through the park. In the southeastern corner, it climbs to **Highwood Pass** (2,227 meters), the highest road pass in Canada. South of the park administration office, **Kananaskis Lakes Trail** heads into the main recreation area. The **Smith-Dorrien/Spray Trail** is a gravel road that follows Smith-Dorrien Creek north from Lower Kananaskis Lake to Spray Lake and on to Canmore.

Recreation
Hiking is the most popular activity in the park (see following section) but by no means the only one. The **Bike Trail** is a 20-kilometer paved trail designed especially for bicycles that begins behind the Visitor Information Centre and follows Lower Kananaskis Lake to Mount Sarrail Campground. Many other trails are designated for mountain-biking use; inquire at the Visitor Information Centre, 403/591-6344. **Boulton Creek Trading Post,** 403/591-7058, rents mountain bikes during summer ($8 per hour, $32 per day). Upper and Lower Kananaskis Lakes have fair fishing for a variety of trout and whitefish. A nightly interpretive program takes place in campground amphitheaters throughout the park. Look for schedules posted on bulletin boards, or check with the Visitor Information Centre.

In winter, Highwood Pass is closed to traffic, but Highway 40 into the park is cleared, and cross-country skiing is excellent.

William Watson Lodge
This special facility is available to disabled persons and Albertan seniors. Guests stay in private cabins, but the lodge operates like a hostel, and you must supply your own bedding and food. The main lodge has a kitchen, a lounge, a library, a laundry room, and gas barbecues on the sundeck. Disabled guests may bring up to three family members or friends. The cost is $5–15 per person per night. Reservations are

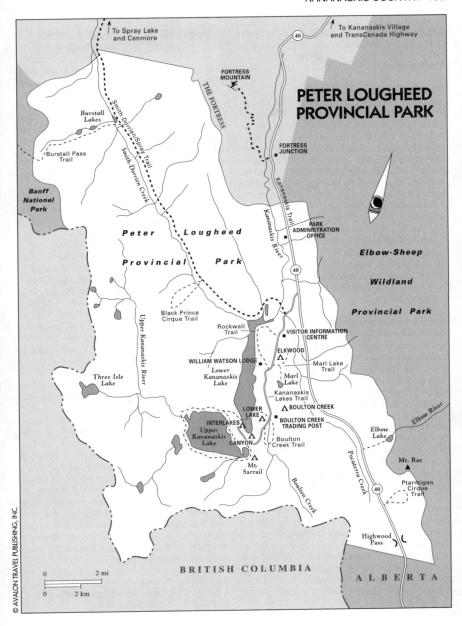

PETER LOUGHEED
PROVINCIAL PARK

To Spray Lake
and Canmore

To Kananaskis Village
and TransCanada Highway

FORTRESS
MOUNTAIN

THE FORTRESS

Burstall
Lakes

Smith Dorrien/Spray Trail

FORTRESS
JUNCTION

Burstall Pass
Trail

Smith-Dorrien Creek

Banff
National
Park

Kananaskis Trail

Kananaskis River

PARK
ADMINISTRATION
OFFICE

Peter   Lougheed

Provincial   Park

Elbow-Sheep

Wildland

Provincial   Park

Black Prince
Cirque Trail

Rockwall
Trail

VISITOR INFORMATION
CENTRE

ELKWOOD

Upper Kananaskis River

WILLIAM WATSON LODGE

Lower
Kananaskis
Lake

Marl Lake
Trail

Marl
Lake

Three Isle
Lake

Kananaskis
Lakes Trail

LOWER
LAKE

BOULTON CREEK

INTERLAKES

BOULTON CREEK
TRADING POST

Upper
Kananaskis
Lake

Elbow River

CANYON

Boulton
Creek Trail

Elbow
Lake

Mt.
Sarrail

Mt. Rae

Pocaterra Creek

Ptarmigan
Cirque
Trail

Boulton Creek

Highwood
Pass

BRITISH COLUMBIA

ALBERTA

0   2 mi

0   2 km

essential and can be made up to four months in advance. Write to William Watson Lodge, Peter Lougheed Provincial Park, P.O. Box 130, Kananaskis Village, Alberta T0L 2H0, or call 403/591-7227.

Camping

The nearest hotels are to the north in Kananaskis Village. Within the park are six auto-accessible campgrounds with a total of 507 sites. All are located on the Kananaskis Lakes Trail and are linked by bicycling and hiking trails. **Mount Sarrail,** at the southern end of Upper Kananaskis Lake, is for tenters only and has pit toilets; $13 per night. **Canyon, Lower Lake,** and **Interlakes** have pit toilets; $17 per night. **Elkwood** has showers ($1 for five minutes), flush toilets, powered sites, and an interpretive amphitheater; $17. **Boulton Creek** has showers, flush toilets, powered sites, an interpretive amphitheater, and a grocery store; $17 per night. Firewood is available at each campground for $6 per bundle. Boulton Creek is the only campground that takes reservations (403/591-7226, www.kananaskis camping.com).

Services and Information

Boulton Creek Trading Post, a grocery store selling basic supplies, fishing tackle, and souvenirs, as well as renting bikes, is located on the Kananaskis Lakes Trail. Next door is a small café serving hamburgers and light meals. The ice cream is good, although expensive.

The **Visitor Information Centre,** 403/591-6322, is an excellent facility located three kilometers along Kananaskis Lakes Trail. The staff is very knowledgable about the park and has hordes of literature hidden under the desk—but you have to ask for it. Ask them to put a movie or slideshow on in the theater; most tell about the park. The movie *Bears and Man* is a classic 1970s flick dealing with the public attitude toward bears, one of the first documentaries to do so. A large lounge that overlooks the valley is used mainly in winter by cross-country skiers but is always open for trip planning or relaxing on rainy afternoons. This center is the place to pick up fishing licenses and backcountry camping permits. It's open in summer daily 9 A.M.–7 P.M., the rest of the year Mon.–Fri. 9 A.M.–5 P.M. and Sat.–Sun. 9 A.M.–5 P.M.

HIKING IN PETER LOUGHEED PROVINCIAL PARK

The park has several interesting interpretive trails and more-strenuous hikes. Most trailheads are located along Kananaskis Lakes Trail. Many trails have interpretive signs along them, but others require an interpretive booklet available from the Visitor Information Centre. **Rockwall Trail,** from the Visitor Information Centre, and **Marl Lake Trail,** from Elkwood Campground, are wheelchair-accessible and barrier-free, respectively. Following are some of the park's more popular interpretive and day hikes.

Boulton Creek

- Length: 4.9 kilometers (90 minutes) round-trip
- Elevation gain: minimal
- Rating: easy

This trail starts where Kananaskis Lakes Trail crosses Boulton Creek. A booklet, available at the trailhead or at the Visitor Information Centre, corresponds with numbered posts along the trail. The highlighted stops emphasize the valley's human history. After a short climb, the trail reaches a cabin built in the 1930s as a stopover for forest ranger patrols. The trail then follows a high ridge and loops back along the other side of the creek to the trailhead.

Elbow Lake

- Length: 1.3 kilometers (30 minutes) one-way
- Elevation gain: 135 meters
- Rating: easy

The trailhead to this picturesque body of water lies along Highway 40 at the Elbow Pass day-use area, a few kilometers before Highwood Pass. The official trail is a wide road that climbs quickly into the bowl holding shallow Elbow Lake. The lake is a popular spot, especially for summer picnics; campsites are spread around the south shore. An interesting side trip is to Rae Glacier, a small glacier on the north face of Mt. Rae. The trail starts on the east shore of the lake, gaining 400 meters of elevation in just more than two kilometers.

Ptarmigan Cirque

- Length: 5.6 kilometers (2 hours) roundtrip
- Elevation gain: 230 meters

• Rating: moderate

The trailhead for this steep interpretive walk is across the road from Highwood Meadows, 17 kilometers south of Kananaskis Lakes Road on Highway 40. A booklet, available at the trailhead or at the Visitor Information Centre, corresponds with numbered posts along the trail. As it climbs into the alpine zone, magnificent panoramas unfold. Along the trail you are likely to see numerous small mammals, such as Columbian ground squirrels, pikas, least chipmunks, and hoary marmots. At higher elevations, the meadows are home to bighorn sheep, mountain goats, and grizzly bears. Another short walk, the **Rock Glacier Trail,** two kilometers north of Highwood Meadows, leads 150 meters to a unique formation of moraine rock.

Black Prince Cirque
• Length: 5.6 kilometers (90 minutes) round-trip
• Elevation gain: 210 meters
• Rating: easy to moderate

The trailhead is eight kilometers from Kananaskis Lakes Trail along the Smith-Dorrien/Spray Trail. Numbered posts along the trail correspond to a booklet available at the trailhead or at the Visitor Information Centre. The trail climbs steadily to an area that was logged in the early 1970s, then winds through a forest of Engelmann spruce and subalpine fir, crosses Old Creek, and emerges at a high mountain cirque scoured out by a glacier. Each spring the cirque fills with water, forming a small emerald-green lake.

Burstall Pass
• Length: 7.4 kilometers (2.5 hours) one-way
• Elevation gain: 480 meters
• Rating: moderate to difficult

The trailhead is on the west side of the Smith-Dorrien/Spray Trail at the south end of Mud Lake. For the first three kilometers, it climbs an old logging road to Burstall Lakes. After traversing the willow flats, it begins climbing again through heavy forest and avalanche paths to a large cirque. The final ascent to the pass is a real slog, but the view across the Upper Spray Valley (which is in Banff National Park) is worth it. From the pass, it is possible to continue to Palliser Pass (two days one-way) and Banff townsite (three days one-way).

COUGARS

Elusive and rarely encountered by casual hikers, cougars (also known as mountain lions, pumas, or catamounts) measure up to 1.5 meters long with the average male weighing 75 kilograms and the female 40-55 kilograms. Their athletic prowess puts Olympians to shame. They can spring forward over eight meters from a standstill, leap four meters into the air, and safely jump from a height of 20 meters.

Cougars are versatile hunters whose acute vi-

sion takes in a peripheral span in excess of 200 degrees. They typically kill a large mammal such as an elk or deer every 12—14 days, eating part of it and caching the rest. Their diet also includes chipmunks, ground squirrels, snowshoe hares, and occasionally porcupines. Although attacks on humans are rare, they do occur, usually if the cougar has been surprised or if it's particularly hungry. Cases have been recorded of the animal stalking human prey, but there have been no recorded cougar attacks in Alberta for 30 years.

The cougar is a solitary animal with distinct territorial boundaries. This limits its population density, which in turn means that its overall numbers are low. As is the case with all North America's large mammals, the cougar's biggest threat is man and the diminishing range of its habitat due to development and ranching. An extensive study of the cougar took place throughout the 1980s in Alberta, and the good news is that although its numbers are low they remain steady.

SPRAY LAKE

Massive Spray Lake can be accessed from Peter Lougheed Provincial Park to the south or from Canmore to the north. The Continental Divide and Banff National Park lie to the west. The dominant feature is Spray Lake Reservoir, a 16-kilometer-long body of water that is an integral part of a massive hydroelectric scheme. The Smith-Dorrien/Spray Trail is the only road through the zone. This 60-kilometer unpaved (and often dusty) road traverses the entire valley, from Peter Lougheed Provincial Park to Canmore.

From the south, the Smith-Dorrien/Spray Trail climbs up the Smith-Dorrien Creek watershed, passing Mud Lake and leaving Peter Lougheed Provincial Park just before Mount Engadine Lodge. Approximately three kilometers farther north is Buller Pond (on the west side of the road), from where the distinctive "Matterhorn" peak of Mt. Assiniboine can be seen on a clear day. The road then parallels Spray Lake, which is lined by three picnic areas and a campground.

Accommodations and Camping

Mount Engadine Lodge (403/678-4080, www.mountengadine.com) is a small lodge south of Spray Lake, near the Mt. Shark staging area. It comprises 12 rooms in the main lodge and two cabins set on a ridge overlooking an open meadow and small creek. The main lodge has a dining room and a comfortable lounge area. All meals are included in the nightly rate of $110–130 per person.

One campground is available along Spray Lake. It's spread out along the western shoreline of Spray Lake, with mostly private sites. Facilities are limited to picnic tables and pit toilets; $12 per night.

SIBBALD, ELBOW RIVER VALLEY, AND SHEEP RIVER VALLEY REGIONS

The northeastern section of Kananaskis Country spans the Sibbald, Jumpingpound, Elbow River, and Sheep River valleys. The valleys start in the west among the high peaks of the Opal Range. As they cut east through the foothills,

they gradually open up, ending at the prairie. At higher elevations, elk, bighorn sheep, and bears make their home. In the foothills, visitors are likely to see mule and white-tailed deer, elk, and moose. This area of Kananaskis Country also has a relatively high population of cougars, but these shy cats are rarely sighted.

Sibbald Creek Trail (Hwy. 68) traverses the rolling foothills of the Sibbald and Jumpingpound valleys and is accessible from the TransCanada Highway, intersecting Highway 40 south of the Barrier Lake Visitor Information Centre. Fishing is popular in **Sibbald Lake** and **Sibbald Meadows Pond.** A couple of short trails begin at the picnic area at Sibbald Lake, including the 4.4-kilometer **Ole Buck Loop**, which climbs a low ridge.

The main access road into the Elbow River Valley is Highway 66 west from Bragg Creek. It climbs steadily along the Elbow River, passing **McLean Pond** and **Allen Bill Pond** (both are stocked with rainbow trout) and six-meter-high **Elbow Falls,** before climbing through an area devastated by wildfire in 1981 before descending to a campground, 42 kilometers from Bragg Creek.

The Sheep River Valley lies immediately south of the Elbow River Valley, in an area of rolling foothills between open ranchlands to the east and the high peaks bordering Elbow–Sheep Wildland Provincial Park to the west. Access is from the town of Turner Valley (take Sunset Blvd. west from downtown), along Highway 546. The highway passes through **Sheep River Wildlife Sanctuary** (which protects the wintering ground of bighorn sheep), **Sheep River Falls,** and ends at a campground 46 kilometers west of Turner Valley.

Practicalities

At the entrance to the three areas listed previously are information centers that are open in summer only. The only other facilities are campgrounds, which are generally primitive and open mid-May–September. For camping information and reservations, call **Elbow Valley Campgrounds,** 403/949-3132, www.evcamp.com.

Sibbald Lake Campground offers 134 sites spread around five loops (Loop D comes closest to the lake). Amenities include pit toilets, drinking water, and a nightly interpretive program; $17 per site.

From Bragg Creek, Highway 66 passes five campgrounds along the Elbow River Valley. Each campground is close to the river and has kitchen shelters, firewood ($6 per bundle), and picnic tables; $17–23 per night. The most-developed is **McLean Creek Campground,** 12 kilometers west of Bragg Creek, which has a grocery store and showers.

Along Highway 546, west from Turner Valley, are two campgrounds. **Sandy McNabb Campround,** the larger of the two, is a short walk from the river right by the entrance to Kananaskis Country. All sites are $17 per night.

HIGHWOOD/CATARACT CREEK

The Highwood/Cataract region stretches from Peter Lougheed Provincial Park to the southern border of Kananaskis Country. This is the least developed area of Kananaskis Country. The jagged peaks of the Highwood Mountains are its most dominant feature; high alpine meadows among the peaks are home to bighorn sheep, elk, and grizzlies. Lower down, lush spruce and lodgepole pine forests spread over most of the valley floor, giving way to rich grazing lands along its eastern flanks. Access to the area is via Highway 40 from the north, Highway 541 from Longview to the east, and Highway

940 from Crowsnest Pass to the south. In winter, the only access is from Highway 541.

The main summer activities are hiking, horseback riding, climbing, and fishing. Winter use is primarily by snowmobilers. Only two formal hiking trails are signposted. The rest are a complex system of traditional routes that are not well traveled, and many require river crossings. One of the few marked trails, to **Picklejar Lakes** (4.2 kilometers one-way), accesses a popular fishing spot. The trailhead is across the road from the Lantern Creek day-use area (not the Picklejar day-use area).

Practicalities

All three campgrounds are south of Highwood Junction. **Etherington Creek** is seven kilometers south of the junction, whereas **Cataract Creek** is five kilometers farther south. In the far south of Kananaskis Country, along Highway 532, is **Indian Graves Campground. Each site has water, pit toilets, firewood, fire pits, and picnic tables; $17 per night.**

Highwood House is at Highwood Junction and has gas and a grocery store. It's open May–June Fri.–Sun. 9 A.M.–5 P.M., July–Sept. daily 9 A.M.–8 P.M., and Oct.–April weekends only 9:15 A.M.–5 P.M. The **Highwood Ranger Station,** 403/558-2151, also at the junction, is open in summer only Thurs.–Mon. 10 A.M.–6 P.M.

CANMORE

Canmore (pop.11,000) is nestled below the distinctive peaks of the Three Sisters in the Bow Valley between Calgary and Banff. It is the gateway to the mountain national parks and Kananaskis Country, and it provides inexpensive lodging and dining alternatives. Its ideal mountain location and the freedom it enjoys from the strict development restrictions that apply in the nearby parks have made the town one of the fastest-growing resort areas in the country. Downtown Canmore, on the southwestern side of the TransCanada Highway, has managed to retain much of its charm. Most of the development is taking place on the outskirts. Approximately $2.3 billion in resort and residential projects have been planned for the next two decades, and the town's population is

estimated to reach 20,000 by the end of that period. One of the largest and most controversial developments, still in its infancy, is the Three Sisters Resort. When completed, it will include 4,000 residential units, two hotels, and three golf courses on an 840-hectare parcel of land.

Apart from being a service center, the town has much to offer. As well as viewing the many historical buildings lining the downtown streets, the surrounding area, from Banff National Park east to Bow Valley Provincial Park is protected as 24,000-hectare **Bow Valley Wildland Park.** Hiking, fishing, and canoeing are excellent throughout the valley, and nearby Mt. Yamnuska is the most developed rock-climbing site in the Canadian Rockies. Canmore also

CANMORE

To Banff

TRAVEL ALBERTA
INFORMATION CENTRE

TRANSCANADA HWY.

MOUNTAIN AVE.

PALLISER TR.

SILVER TIP
RESORT

SILVER TIP RD.

CANMORE
GOLF COURSE

LARCH AVE.

POCATERRA INN

WESTRIDGE COUNTRY INN

RUNDLE MOUNTAIN
CAMPGROUND

BOW VALLEY TR.

AKAI MOTEL

SILVER TIP DR.

QUALITY RESORT
CHATEAU CANMORE

RUNDLE MOUNTAIN MOTEL

FAIRHOLME DR.

THE KABIN

17TH ST.

ROCKY MOUNTAIN SKI LODGE

BOSTON PIZZA

BEAMER'S COFFEE BAR

BEST WESTERN GREEN GABLES INN

WAPITI SPORTS

PATRINO'S

BACK OF
BEYOND B&B

HOWARD
JOHNSON
HOTEL

RAILWAY

CPR TRESTLE
BRIDGE

HOSPITAL

FOUR POINTS
HOTEL SHERATON

SEE "DOWNTOWN
CANMORE" MAP

MUSASHI

GEAR UP

LADY MACDONALD COUNTRY INN

AVE.

6TH

Bow River

CANMORE
NORDIC CENTRE

GEORGETOWN
INN

BENCHLANDS TR.

MCNEILL
HERITAGE INN

MAIN ST.

BEAR
COUNTRY
LODGE

HAMPSHIRE
INN

MINE
SHAREHOLDER'S
CABIN

8TH AVE.

CENTENNIAL
PARK

5TH ST.

COUGAR CREEK DR.

SUMMIT
CAFÉ

RUNDLEVIEW DR.

7TH AVE.

6TH AVE.

5TH AVE.

4TH AVE.

RADISSON
HOTEL

TRANSCANADA HWY.

THREE SISTERS DR.

RUNDLE DR.

2ND ST.

1ST ST.

RESTWELL
TRAILER
PARK

Policeman's Cr.

HOOLIGAN'S

Cougar Cr.

SPRAY LAKES RD.

Spring Cr.

HELIPORT

Bow Valley Tr.

Canmore Cr.

Quarry
Lake

MOON

To Grassi Lakes and
Kananaskis Country

To Alpine Club of Canada Clubhouse
and Grotto Canyon

1A

To Bow River Campground,
Stewart Creek Golf Course and Calgary

THREE SISTERS DR.

RESIDENCE
INN

Bow River

LAWRENCE GRASSI RIDGE

WALLACE WAY

THREE SISTERS PKWY.

SCALE NOT AVAILABLE

© AVALON TRAVEL PUBLISHING, INC.

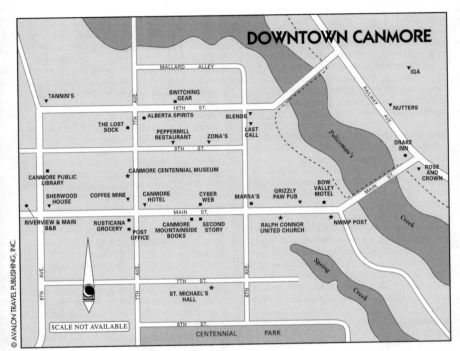

DOWNTOWN CANMORE

© AVALON TRAVEL PUBLISHING, INC.

SCALE NOT AVAILABLE

hosted the Nordic events of the 1988 Winter Olympic Games and is home to the Alpine Club of Canada.

History

The Hudson's Bay Company explored the Bow Valley corridor and attempted, without success, to establish a fur trade with the Stoney Indians for most of the 1840s. In 1858, an expedition from the east, led by John Palliser, sent back discouraging reports about the climate and prospects of agriculture in the valley. One of the conditions of British Columbian entry into the confederation of Canada was the completion of a rail line linking them to the east by 1881. The CPR chose the Bow Valley Corridor as the route through the mountains, and the first divisional point west of Calgary was established at what is now Canmore. Mining on the Three Sisters and Mount Rundle commenced soon after. Hotels and businesses were established, and a hospital, a North West

Mounted Police (NWMP) post, and an opera house were built. The Canmore Opera House—reputed to be the only log movie house in the world—still stands and has been relocated to the Calgary Heritage Park. In 1899, the CPR moved its divisional point to Laggan (now Lake Louise), but the mines continued to operate until 1979.

SIGHTS

Historic buildings from the coal-mining days are being preserved at their original locations around town. The best way to get downtown from the TransCanada Highway is to take Railway Avenue from Highway 1A and drive down 8th Street, the main drag. The first building of interest at the east end of 8th Street is Canmore's original NWMP post, built in 1892. The interior is decorated with period furnishings; open in summer, Mon.–Fri. 9 A.M.–5 P.M., Sat.–Sun.

noon–4 P.M., and admission is free. **Ralph Connor Memorial United Church,** opposite the bakery and a little farther down 8th Street, was built in 1890 and is now a Provincial Historic Site. **Canmore Hotel,** on the corner of 8th Street and 7th Avenue, was built in 1891 (at a time when four hotels already operated) and is still open for thirsty travelers. **Canmore Centennial Museum** (801 7th Ave., 403/678-2462) has a collection of artifacts from the area's early coal-mining days and a display from the 1988 Winter Olympic Games. Open daily noon–4 P.M., extended hours in summer.

Several historic sites lie across the Bow River from downtown. Reach them on foot by following the river north from Eighth Avenue and crossing at the old CPR trestle bridge, which once served the Cochrane Mine. Follow the paved trail downstream, past the **Mine Shareholders' Cabin,** a log structure built in 1914. In the same vicinity, a trail leads off from Three Sisters Drive up Canmore Creek, passing the remains of a mine site that was worked from 1891 to 1979. Continue up to small waterfalls and across Spray Lakes Road to **Quarry Lake.** This small lake lies in an open meadow and is a popular sunbathing and swimming spot.

HIKING

The hiking trails around Canmore are usually passed over in favor of those of its famous neighbors, but some interesting trails do exist. Paved paths around town are suitable for walking, bicycling, and, in winter, skiing. They link Policeman's Creek with the golf course, Nordic center, and Riverview Park on the Bow River.

Grassi Lakes
- Length: 2 kilometers (40 minutes) one-way
- Elevation gain: 300 meters
- Rating: easy to moderate

This historical trail climbs to two small lakes below Chinaman's Peak. To get to the trailhead, follow Spray Lakes Road past the Nordic center and take the first gravel road to the left after the reservoir. This road leads to a parking lot and trailhead. The trail forks to the left by a gate and climbs to **Grassi Falls.** Stairs cut into a cliff face lead up to a bridge over Canmore

Creek and to the lakes. A further scramble up a scree slope leads to four pictographs (native rock paintings) of human figures on the first large boulder in the gorge. Interpretive signs along the trail point out interesting aspects of the Bow Valley and detail the life of Lawrence Grassi, who built the trail back in the early 1920s.

Chinaman's Peak
- Length: 2.2 kilometers (90 minutes) one-way
- Elevation gain: 740 meters
- Rating: moderate to difficult

Chinaman's Peak is the impressive pinnacle of rock that rises high above Canmore to the southwest. Although the sheer eastern face is visible from town, this trail winds up on the back side of the mountain and ends with stunning views across the Bow Valley. The unmarked trailhead is along Spray Lakes Road. Leave your vehicle at the Goat Creek Trailhead, cross the road, then walk up to and over the canal to search out the trail, which begins from behind a small workshed. The trail winds mostly through subalpine forest of Engelmann spruce, climbing steadily until breaking out above the treeline, from where views north extend down the glacially carved Goat Creek Valley. The trail then forks; the left fork climbs unforgivingly to Chinaman's Peak, but hikers are rewarded with views no less spectacular by continuing to the left, along a lightly marked trail that ends at a saddle. On a clear day, the panorama afforded from this viewpoint is worth every painful step. Take care on the return journey, however, to stay high and to the right and watch for rock cairns and colored flagging to ensure that you enter the trees at the right spot.

Cougar Creek
- Length: 9.5 kilometers (four hours) one-way
- Elevation gain: 550 meters
- Rating: moderate

This unofficial trail follows a valley carved deeply into the Fairholme Range by Cougar Creek. To get to the trailhead from downtown, take the Bow Valley Trail over the TransCanada Highway and follow the Benchlands Trail to the parking lot beside Cougar Creek. The trail follows the northwestern bank of the creek past a housing estate and into a lightly forested area. Cross the creek just before the mouth of the canyon. The rough trail crosses the creek 10 times in the first three kilometers to a major fork. Stay left, continuing up the stony creekbed, which winds around the base of Mt. Charles Stewart. From this point, the valley walls close in, and it's a steep climb up to a high ridge, which forms the boundary of Banff National Park. On the return journey, continue beyond the parking lot to the Summit Café, and relax on the patio with a cool drink.

Grotto Canyon

- Length: 2 kilometers (40 minutes) one-way
- Elevation gain: 60 meters
- Rating: easy

This is one of the most interesting trails around Canmore. It begins from Grotto Pond, along Highway 1A east of town, following a power line road that winds behind the Baymag plant, then at a signed intersection takes off through the woods to the mouth of the canyon. No official trail traverses the canyon; hikers simply follow the creekbed through the towering canyon walls. Approximately 400 meters into the canyon, look for pictographs to the left. At the two-kilometer mark, the canyon makes a sharp left turn at Illusion Rock, where water cascades through a narrow chasm and into the main canyon. Many hikers return from this point, but through the next section of canyon, the valley opens up, passing hoodoos and a cave. It's 6.5 kilometers from the trailhead to the end of the valley, with most of the 680 meters of elevation gained in the last two kilometers.

Heart Creek

- Length: 2 kilometers (40 minutes) one-way
- Elevation gain: 80 meters
- Rating: easy

This well-formed trail is signposted from the Lac des Arcs interchange, 15 kilometers east of Canmore along the TransCanada Highway. The trail parallels the highway eastward until reaching a fork. The trail to the right follows Heart Creek for a little more than one kilometer, crossing the creek seven times via narrow log bridges, and ending at a cleared area below where Heart Creek is forced through a narrow cleft. Those tempted to continue farther can cross the creek, scramble up a steep-sided, forested ridge, then descend the other side to link up with the creek upstream of the gorge. Cross the creek again for views of another narrow chasm.

Heli-hiking

Heli-hiking is the summer alternative to heli-skiing—a helicopter does the hard work, and you get to hike in a remote, alpine region that would otherwise usually entail a long, steep hike to access. **Alpine Helicopters,** 403/678-4802, offers a variety of options starting at $225 per person, which includes 15 minutes of flight time and 2–3 hours hiking. The company is flexible, with ground-time and destinations depending on the group's choice. The heliport is located along Highway 1A south of downtown.

OTHER RECREATION

Canmore Nordic Centre

This remarkable complex was built at a cost of $15 million for the 1988 Winter Olympic Games. In 1998, it was designated a provincial park, adding 400 hectares to the protected areas of the

Wandering along the Bow River is a pleasant way to enjoy Canmore's natural surroundings.

Once a traditional form of transportation, dogsledding is now a popular winter sport.

Bow Valley. The cross-country skiing and biathlon (combined cross-country skiing and rifle shooting) events were held here, and today the center is a world-class training ground for Canadian athletes. Cross-country ski trails are set to all levels of expertise; a day pass is just $5. Even in summer, long after the snow has melted, the place is worth a visit. An interpretive trail leads down to the banks of the Bow River, where Georgetown, an old coal-mining town, once stood. Many other trails lead around the grounds, and it's possible to hike or bike to the Banff Springs Hotel. Mountain biking is extremely popular on the trails. Mountain bike and cross-country ski rentals are available at **Trail Sports,** 403/678-6764, at the center. The day lodge has an information rack with maps and brochures, lockers, a lounge area, and a cafeteria. It's open daily 8 A.M.–4:30 P.M. For more information, call 403/678-2400.

Fishing
The Bow River has good fishing for brown and brook trout; Gap Lake for brown and brook trout; Grotto Pond for rainbow trout; and Ghost Lake for lake, rainbow, and brown trout. **Wapiti Sports** (1506 Railway Ave., 403/678-5550) stocks bait and tackle and sells fishing licenses.

Climbing
Hundreds of climbing routes have been laid out around Canmore. **Mount Yamnuska,** east of town along Highway 1A, is the most developed site, but climbers also flock to Chinaman's Peak, Cougar Creek, and Grotto Canyon. Canmore is home to many qualified mountain guides. **Yamnuska** (403/678-4164, www.yamnuska.com) offers basic rock-climbing courses, as well as instruction for all ability levels on ice climbing, mountaineering, and trekking. A good introduction to rock climbing is the weekend-long Basic Rock course, which costs $185. Unique to the company are three-month-long courses that take in all aspects of mountaineering-oriented skills. Other local guiding companies are **Kiska Adventures,** 403/678-5657, and **M & W Guides,** 403/678-2642.

Golfing
Canmore has three golf courses. As with golfing elsewhere in the Canadian Rockies, book all tee times well in advance. **Canmore Golf Course,** 403/678-4784, built in 1929 as a nine-hole course, has developed into an 18-hole championship course with a clubhouse and a driving range. It is an interesting layout, with two holes beside the Bow River. Greens fee is $48, a cart is $28. The **Silvertip Resort** opened in the summer of 1998 on a wide bench between the valley floor and the lower slopes of Mt. Lady Macdonald, and it was quickly recognized as one of Canada's finest resort courses. The layout is very challenging (its Slope Rating is 153, the highest of any course in North America), with the most distinct feature being elevation changes of up to 40 meters on any one hole, and a total 200-meter elevation difference between the lowest and highest points on the course. Adding to this challenge are tight tree-lined fairways, numerous water hazards, 74 bunkers, and a course length of a frightening 7,300 yards from the back markers. Greens fee

is $125, which includes a mandatory cart (complete with global positioning system). Four hours before sunset, greens fee drops to $85. **Stewart Creek Golf Course,** 403/609-6360, which opened in 2000, lies across the valley in the Three Sisters development. It is shorter than Silvertip but still measures more than 7,000 yards from the back tees. The fairways are relatively wide, but positioning of tee shots is important, and the course is made more interesting by hanging greens, greenside exposed rock, and historic mine shafts. Greens fee is $105, with power carts an additional $30; twilight rates are just $55. These rates include use of a practice facility.

ARTS AND ENTERTAINMENT

Drinking and Dancing
Canmore doesn't have anywhere near the number of bars that nearby Banff is so famous for, but no one ever seems to go thirsty. The **Sherwood House** (838 8th St., 403/678-5211) has a beer garden that catches the afternoon sun and is especially busy on weekends. At the other end of the main street are the **Drake Inn** (909 Railway Ave., 403/678-5131) and the **Rose and Crown** (749 Railway Ave., 403/678-5168), both with a beer garden and live music on weekends. The **Grizzly Paw Pub** (622 8th St., 403/678-9983) brews its own beer, with six ales produced in-house. I'm not much of a drinker, but whenever I feel like a beer, I head down to the **Last Call** (637 10th St., 403/678-3934). I especially like Thursday night, when all bottled beer is $1.75, and Sunday, when pool is free and beer is $2.75.

Festivals and Events
Canmore's annual **Winter Carnival** is a two-week celebration including an ice-sculpture demonstration, ice-fishing derby, and pancake breakfasts. The highlight is the **International Dogsled Race** held at Canmore Nordic Centre, where teams of four, six, eight, and 10 dogs are harnessed up and compete in various heats. The festival is held the last two weeks of January.
Voices on the Wilderness, held every Saturday night through summer at St. Michael's Hall (709 7th St.) is a nature-oriented program of talks and audiovisual and slide presentations hosted by knowledgable locals. **Canada Day** (July 1) is celebrated with a parade, various activities in Centennial Park, and fireworks. Canmore Nordic Centre hosts one leg of mountain biking's **World Cup** each year, usually on the first weekend of July. Check dates at 403/678-2400. On the Heritage Day long weekend, the first weekend of August, Canmore hosts a **Folk Music Festival,** which starts on Sunday and runs through Monday evening. This event features national and international acts in Centennial Park.

On the first Sunday of September is the traditional **Canmore Highland Games,** a day of dancing, eating, caber tossing, and tug-of-war, culminating in a spectacular and noisy parade through the grounds of Centennial Park. The festival attracts more than 10,000 spectators.

ACCOMMODATIONS AND CAMPING

Hotels and Motels
Akai Motel (1717 Mountain Ave., 403/678-4664) is a little rundown, but each room has a kitchenette; $75 single, $85 double. In the heart of downtown is the **Bow Valley Motel** (610 Eighth St., 403/678-5085 or 800/665-8189, www.bowvalleymotel.com); $90 single, $95 double. Also downtown, **The Drake Inn** (909 Railway Ave., 403/678-5131 or 800/461-8730, www.drakeinn.com) is at the end of Canmore's main street. It has an outdoor hot tub, some rooms with a private balcony overlooking Policeman's Creek, and an adjoining bar is open daily for the best-value breakfast in town; $88 single, $98 double. The **Rundle Mountain Motel** (1723 Mountain Ave., 403/678-5322 or 800/661-1610, www.rundlemontain.com) has small but comfortable rooms, a small indoor pool, an outdoor whirlpool, and a small Swiss restaurant. Rates range $95–135 single or double.

The **Rocky Mountain Ski Lodge** (Bow Valley Trail, 403/678-5445 or 800/665-6111, www.rockymtnskilodge.com) has large, modern rooms and some loft apartments with kitchenettes; motel rooms are $95 single, $110 double, suites are from $160. The newest hotel along the "Strip" is the **Hampshire Inn** (815 Bow Valley Trail, 403/609-0075 or 877/609-6266), a small lodging with 29 comfortable rooms, some with private balconies; $119 single, $129 double. Across the road, the **Bear Country Lodge** (1002 Bow Valley Trail, 403/678-1000 or 888/678-1008) is another of Canmore's new motels. It features 44 medium-size rooms, each comfortable and with mountain views. Summer rates are $119 single, $129 double, which includes breakfast. The **Georgetown Inn** (1720 Bow Valley Trail, 403/678-3439 or 800/657-5955, www.georgetowninn.ab.ca) is run by a friendly English couple who have set the place up as a country inn of times gone by. Each of the 24 rooms has its own individual charm, and a delicious cooked breakfast is included in the rate of $129 double ($89 in winter). Next door, the **Lady Macdonald Country Inn** (1201 Bow Valley Trail, 403/678-3665 or 800/567-3919, www.ladymacdonald.com) exudes the same atmosphere. Its 11 rooms are all individually furnished, extending the Victorian-era charm that the exterior is styled after. The nicest of the rooms is the Three Sisters, which has a two-way fireplace and a hot tub. Rates range $130–185 single or double, which includes a delicious hot breakfast. The old Viscount Motor Inn is now the **Westridge Country Inn** (1719 Bow Valley Trail, 403/678-5221 or 800/268-0935, www.westridgecountryinn.com). The old rooms are still available ($90 single or double), but the much more comfortable rooms in a new section facing Bow Valley Trail are a better value at $145 single or double. Each has a balcony and fireplace. Similarly priced is the **Howard Johnson Hotel** (1402 Bow Valley Trail, 403/678-3625 or 800/263-3625), which features more than 200 rooms, a small indoor pool and waterslide, and a restaurant; $145 single or double.

The better of Canmore's two Best Western properties is the **Pocaterra Inn** (1725 Mountain Ave., 403/678-4334 or 888/678-6786, www.pocaterrainn.com), which features a large indoor pool, a fitness room, a sauna, and 83 guest rooms, each with a fireplace. Summer rates from $160 single or double include a light breakfast. The **Radisson Hotel** (511 Bow Valley Trail, 403/678-3625 or 800/333-3333, www.radissoncanmore.com) is a large complex that features an excellent restaurant (the Sunday brunch here is one of the best in the valley), an indoor pool, a fitness facility, and 232 spacious rooms set around landscaped gardens. Rooms range $159–209 single or double. Similarly priced, and of the same high standard, is the **Quality Resort Chateau Canmore** (1720 Bow Valley Trail, 403/678-6699 or 800/228-5151, www.chateaucanmore.com), where each room is fully self-contained; $165–205 single or double. The **Residence Inn** is a new hotel across the river from town (91 Three Sisters Dr., 403/678-3400, www.marriott.com). It offers 119 luxurious suites, each with a kitchen, as well as indoor and outdoor pools. A light breakfast is included in the rates of $175–245 single or double.

At the base of the Silvertip Resort, across the TransCanada Highway from all of the previous accommodations, is the **Four Points Hotel Sheraton Canmore** (Silvertip Trail, 403/609-4422 or 888/609-4422, www.fourpoints.com), Canmore's most luxurious lodging. It is a full-service hotel; from $240 single or double.

Harvie Heights

Lodging in Harvie Heights, located eight kilometers west of Canmore and 23 kilometers from Banff, may seem a little pricier than Canmore, but most units are self-contained. The least expensive option is the **Gateway Inn** (403/678-5396 or 877/678-1810), which charges from $70 single, $80 double for standard motel rooms. **Rundle Ridge Chalets** (403/678-5387 or 800/332-1299, www.chalets.ab.ca) offers 38 self-contained log cabins set in a pleasant wooded area. Rates range $99–139 single or double. Next door to Rundle Ridge, **Stockade Log Cabins** (403/678-5212 or 800/330-3824, www.stockadecabins.com) is a smaller but similar set up. Only some of the cabins have kitchens, but guests have use of barbecues; from $108 per unit. The newest of the Harvie Heights accommodations is the **Banff Boundary Lodge** (403/678-9555 or 877/678-9555, www.banffboundarylodge.com). The 42 units each have two bedrooms, a comfortable lounge area with TV and VCR, and a full kitchen. In summer, rooms are $189 per night, but the rest of the year, rates drop as low as $100 (an excellent value).

THE ALPINE CLUB OF CANADA

The Alpine Club of Canada, like similar clubs in the United States and Great Britain, is a nonprofit mountaineering organization whose objectives include the encouragement of mountaineering, the exploration and study of alpine and glacial regions, and the preservation of mountain flora and fauna.

The club was formed in 1906, mainly through the tireless campaign of its first president, Arthur O. Wheeler. A list of early members reads like a Who's Who of the Canadian Rockies—Bill Peyto, Tom Wilson, Byron Harmon, Mary Schäffer—names familiar to all Canadian mountaineers. The original clubhouse was near the Banff Springs Hotel, but in 1980 a new clubhouse was built in Canmore, serving as headquarters for over 3,000 members throughout Canada. The club's ongoing projects include operating the Lake Louise Hostel, maintaining a system of huts throughout the backcountry, and publishing the annual *Canadian Alpine Journal*—the country's only record of mountaineering accomplishments. A reference library of the club's history is kept at the Whyte Museum of the Canadian Rockies in Banff. For further information, membership details, and reservations contact Alpine Club of Canada: P.O. Box 8040, Canmore, AB T1W 2T8, tel. (403) 678-3200.

WHYTE MUSEUM OF THE CANADIAN ROCKIES

Deadman's Flats

Deadman's Flats, located seven kilometers southeast of Canmore, is little more than a truck stop but has three motels and dining at a Husky gas station. The best of the bunch is the **Big Horn Motel** (403/678-2290 or 800/892-9908, www.bighornmotel.com). It offers 24 clean and comfortable rooms, each with a balcony. Rates start at $65 single, $69 double. The other two choices are the **Pigeon Mountain Motel,** 403/678-5756, which charges $70 single, $75 double, and the **Green Acres Motel,** 403/678-5344 or 800/820-5344, which is decorated with colorful flowers each summer and offers spacious rooms for $75 single, $89 double.

Bed-and-Breakfasts

More than 40 bed-and-breakfasts operate in Canmore. Most are small, family-run affairs, with only one or two rooms. During summer, they fill up every night. For a full list of B&Bs in the area, ask at the Travel Alberta Information Centre or check the *Alberta Accommodation Guide.* A good, inexpensive choice is the **Back of Beyond B&B** (corner of Birchwood Place and Railway Ave., 403/678-6606), which is really quite central, linked to downtown by a pleasant creekside trail. The two rooms share a bathroom and are $55 single, $65 double. Right downtown is the **Riverview & Main B&B** (918 8th St., 403/678-9777), also with two rooms sharing a bathroom; $60 single, $75 double. Canmore's finest bed-and-breakfast is the **McNeill Heritage Inn,** across the Bow River from downtown (500 Three Sisters Dr., 403/678-4884 or 877/626-3455, www.mcneillinn. ab.ca). Set on a secluded one-hectare property set above the river, this property offers heritage-styled guest rooms, each with a private bathroom. Guests also enjoy full bar service, a comfortable lounge, a reading room, and outdoor seating set along a riverside verandah. Rates of $150–175 (reduced outside of summer) include a sumptuous breakfast and many special touches, such as chocolates upon arrival.

Brewster's Kananaskis Guest Ranch
This historic lodge, situated 10 minutes east of Canmore, has been owned and operated by five generations of the Brewster family—a name synonymous with tourism in Banff. The lodge is located on a picturesque lake in the Bow Valley, close to the mountain parks, yet a traditional Western atmosphere prevails. The emphasis is on horseback riding and the outdoors, although the lodge also has an indoor hot tub, a dining room, and a lounge. Chalets and cabins are basic but comfortable. Rates are $125 per person per day, which includes three meals and one hour of trail riding. For more information, call 403/673-3737 or 800/691-5085, www.brewsteradventures.com.

Hostel
The **Alpine Club of Canada Clubhouse** is an excellent hostel-style accommodation situated at the base of Grotto Mountain. The clubhouse overlooks the Bow Valley and can sleep 30 guests in the dormitories. It has a kitchen, an excellent library, a laundry room, a lounge area with a fireplace, a bar, and a sauna. Rates are $15 per night for Alpine Club members, $20 otherwise. Club membership is inexpensive and includes a discount at the Lake Louise Hostel. For reservations and more information, call 403/678-3200, www.alpineclubofcanada.ca. To get there from the east, take the first Canmore exit and follow Highway 1A toward Exshaw (to the northeast). The clubhouse is well-marked to the left after 400 meters.

Campgrounds
The **Restwell Trailer Park** enjoys a great creekside location off Eighth Street in downtown Canmore, 403/678-5111. It is mainly suited to RVs, but tents are allowed along a stretch of grass that parallels Policeman's Creek. Unserviced sites are $22, hookups $24–28, self-contained cabins $120 single or double. Along the Bow Valley Trail toward Banff is the **Rundle Mountain Campground**, opposite the motel of the same name, 403/678-1893. Like Restwell, it offers showers, laundry facilities, and hookups. Sites range $19–24.

East of Canmore are three government campgrounds operated by Bow Valley Campgrounds (403/673-2163, www.bowvalleycampgrounds.com). Each site has pit toilets, kitchen shelters, and firewood for sale at $6 per bundle. The **Bow River Campground** is three kilometers east of Canmore at the Three Sisters Parkway overpass; the **Three Sisters Campground** is accessed from Deadman's Flats, four kilometers farther east, and has a pleasant treed setting; and the **Lac des Arcs Campground** is a large lake of the same name seven kilometers farther toward Calgary. These campgrounds are open May–Sept., and all sites are $17.

FOOD

The **Drake Inn** (909 Railway Ave., 403/678-5131) has the best breakfast deals in town. A hearty breakfast of eggs, bacon, hash browns, and toast costs approximately $5, and you can finish off with a beer or shooter. Open from 7 A.M. Out on the Bow Valley Trail is **Beamer's Coffee Bar** (between Dairy Queen and Boston Pizza, 403/678-3988). Always busy, this place has a huge following because of its great coffee, a friendly owner, and a long, comfortable couch wrapped around a fireplace—the perfect place to relax with one of Beamer's complimentary daily papers. Downtown, the **Coffee Mine** (802 8th St., 403/678-2241) also has a strong local following. Away from downtown, near where Cougar Creek enters Canmore from the Fairholme Range (1001 Cougar Creek Dr., 403/609-2120), is the **Summit Café**. It features a health-conscious menu that includes lots of salads, but many guests come just to soak up the sun on the outside deck or relax with the daily paper and a cup of coffee. Open for breakfast, lunch, and dinner.

Restaurants
One block from the main street is **Zona's** (710 Ninth St., 403/609-2000), a great little bistro with a laidback atmosphere. The menu is small, but all dishes are healthy, freshly prepared, and delicious. It also serves homemade lemonade and a wide selection of wines and beers. Eat inside at the rustic tables or outside on tables spread around the yard. Open daily 11 A.M.–mid-

night. In the same vicinity, the **Peppermill** (726 9th St., 403/678-2292) serves excellent homemade pasta and lots of beef. Try daily specials such as lamb or arctic char, and finish with a bowl of delicious homemade ice cream. It's open daily 5–10 P.M. At the rustic **Sherwood House** (838 Eighth St., 403/678-5211), you can dine outdoors on a deck or inside in a simply furnished restaurant and lounge. The menu is mainly pasta and grills ranging from $14–24, but the bar menu is less expensive. Two blocks north of the Sherwood House is **Tannin's** (838 10th St., 403/609-9200), a city-style wine bar offering an extensive menu of appetizers that are perfect for sharing. Choices change with the season but usually include a cheese fondue and multiple seafood dishes. It's open for lunch Wed.–Sat. and for dinner Tues.–Sunday.

Other choices lay along the Bow Valley Trail. **Patrino's** (1602 Bow Valley Trail, 403/678-4060) is a large steakhouse with restaurant and lounge dining. Patrino's makes good pizza; eat-in or take-out from $14 for a medium. Two blocks east is Canmore's only Japanese restaurant, **Musashi** (1306 Bow Valley Trail, 403/678-9360), open Mon.–Sat. from 5:30 P.M. **The Kabin** (1712 Bow Valley Trail, 403/678-4878) is a two-story log structure at the eastern end of a strip of restaurants and motels. Although the menu is small, it is varied and should appeal to all tastes. Expect to pay $15–20 for a main meal. On Sunday, 10:30 A.M.–2 P.M., an appetizing brunch buffet is served for $16.95, which includes dessert.

TRANSPORTATION

Getting There
Brewster, 403/762-6767, and the **Banff Airporter,** 403/762-3330, both run between Calgary International Airport and Banff four to six times daily, stopping at Canmore's Radisson Hotel en route. Adjacent desks at the airport's Arrivals level take bookings. **Greyhound** stops behind Rusticana Grocery (801 8th St., 403/678-4465), with regular service to Calgary, Banff, and beyond. Local bus companies have come

and gone in recent years. The latest is **Link Transit,** 403/762-3795, which makes a loop through downtown and past the major hotels, then heads off to Banff. This is a summer-only service; $7 one-way.

Getting Around
The most enjoyable way to get around Canmore is on foot or bike, on the extensive trail network winding throughout the town. **Gear Up** (1302 Bow Valley Trail, 403/678-1636) rents mountain bikes, as well as canoes and kayaks. For a cab, call **Canmore Taxi,** 403/678-0888, or **Apex,** 403/609-0030. **Avis,** 403/678-9700, is Canmore's only rental-car outlet.

SERVICES AND INFORMATION

The **post office** is on 7th Avenue, beside Rusticana Grocery. **Mail Boxes Etc.** (743 Railway Ave., 403/678-1919) offers regular postal services, public Internet access, a courier service, faxing service (fax 403/678-1924), as well as a range of photocopying services. **The Lost Sock** laundromat, open 8 A.M.–9:30 P.M., is in the mall on 7th Avenue. **Canmore Hospital** is along Bow Valley Trail, 403/678-5536. For the **RCMP,** call 403/678-5516.

Canmore Public Library (700 9th St., 403/678-2468) is open Mon.–Thurs. 11 A.M.–8 P.M., Fri.–Sun. 11 A.M.–5 P.M. Send and receive email from the library (book in advance) or at **Cyber Web** down the alley (722 8th St., 403/609-3400). Across the road, **Canmore Mountainside Books** (721 8th St., 403/678-4482) stocks a small selection of local literature. Upstairs at **Second Story** (713 8th St., 403/609-2368) are thousands of used books, including a large selection of nonfiction Canadiana.

The best source of pretrip information is the www.tourismcanmore.com, which is maintained by the local chamber of commerce. A **Travel Alberta Information Centre,** 403/678-5277, on the west side of town, just off the TransCanada Highway, provides plenty of information on Canmore and Banff. Open May–Sept. 8 A.M.–8 P.M., and October 9 A.M.–6 P.M.

KAREN McKINLEY

BANFF NATIONAL PARK

INTRODUCTION

This 6,641-square-kilometer national park encompasses some of the world's most magnificent scenery. The snowcapped peaks of the Canadian Rockies form a spectacular backdrop for glacial lakes, fast-flowing rivers, endless forests, and two of North Americas's most famous resort towns, Banff and Lake Louise. The park's vast wilderness is home to deer, moose, elk, mountain goats, bighorn sheep, black and grizzly bears, wolves, and cougars. Many of these species are commonly sighted from roads in the park, others forage within town, and some remain deep in the backcountry. The human species is concentrated mainly in the picture-postcard town of Banff, located near the park's southeast gate, 128 kilometers west of Calgary. Northwest of Banff, along the TransCanada Highway, is Lake Louise, regarded as one of the seven natural wonders of the world, rivaled for sheer beauty only by Moraine Lake, just down the road. Just north of Lake Louise, the Icefields Parkway begins its

spectacular course alongside the Continental Divide to Jasper National Park.

Banff National Park is only one component of a complex geological and natural area consisting of four adjacent national parks that together have been declared a World Heritage Site by UNESCO. (The others are Jasper to the north and Kootenay and Yoho to the west in British Columbia.)

One of Banff's greatest drawcards is the accessibility of its natural wonders. Most highlights are close to the road system. For more adventurous travelers, an excellent system of hiking trails leads to alpine lakes, along glacial valleys, and to spectacular viewpoints where crowds are scarce and human impact has been minimal. Summer in the park is busy. In fact, the park receives nearly half of its four million annual visitors in just two months—July and August. The rest of the year, crowds outside the town of Banff are minimal. In winter, three world-class ski resorts—Banff Mt. Norquay, Sunshine Village, and Lake

Louise (Canada's second-largest ski area)—crank up their lifts. Being low season, hotel rates are reasonable. And if you tire of downhill skiing, you can try cross-country skiing, ice-skating, or snowshoeing; take a sleigh ride; soak in a hot spring; or go heli-skiing nearby.

The park is open year-round, although roads on mountain passes along the park's western boundary occasionally close in winter because of avalanche-control work and snowstorms.

Park Entry
Permits are required for entry into Banff National Park. A National Parks Day Pass is adults $5, seniors $4, children $2 to a maximum of $10 per vehicle. The pass is interchangeable among parks and is valid until 4 P.M. the day following its purchase. An annual Great Western Pass, good for entry into all 11 of western Canada's national parks, is adults $35, seniors $27 to a maximum of $70 per vehicle ($53 for two or more seniors). This pass comes with a Great Western Passbook, which includes a wide variety of discounts, including for camp fees. Both types of passes can be bought at the eastern park gate on the TransCanada Highway, the park information centers in Banff and Lake Louise, and campground kiosks. Day Passes can also be bought at the 24-hour Automated Pass Machines at strategic spots throughout the park. Annual passes can also be bought in advance by calling 800/748-7275 or online at the Parks Canada website, www.parkscanada.pch.gc.ca.

THE LAND

The park lies within the main and front ranges of the Rocky Mountains, a mountain range that extends the length of the North American continent. Although the mountains are composed of bedrock laid down up to one billion years ago, it wasn't until 100 million years ago that forces below the earth's surface transformed the lowland plain of what is now western Canada into the varied, mountainous topography we see today.

The **front ranges** lie to the east, bordering the foothills. These geographically complex mountains are made up of younger bedrock that has been folded, faulted, and uplifted. The **main ranges** are older and higher, lying mainly horizontal and not as severely disturbed as the front ranges. Here the pressures have been most powerful and the results most dramatic; these mountains are characterized by castlelike buttresses and pinnacles and warped waves of stratified rock. Most glaciers are found among these mighty peaks. Along the spine of the main range is the **Continental Divide.** To the east of the divide, all waters flow to the Atlantic Ocean, whereas those to the west flow into the Pacific.

Since rising above the surrounding plains, these mountains have been eroding. At least four times in the last million years, sheets of ice have covered much of the land, filling valleys and rounding off lower peaks such as **Tunnel Mountain.** As the ice retreated, meltwater carved deep channels into the valleys, rivers changed course, and U-shaped valleys were created, of which **Bow Valley** is the most distinctive.

Many factors combine to make these mountains so beautiful. They are distinctive because the layers of drastically altered sediment are visible from miles away, especially when accentuated by the angle of sunlight or a light fall of snow. Cirques, gouged into the mountains by glacial action, fill with glacial meltwater each spring, turning them their trademark translucent green color. And fantastic views of the wide, sweeping valleys are ensured by the climate, which keeps the treeline low and the vegetation sparse enough to not hide the view.

FLORA

Almost 700 species of plants have been recorded in the park, each falling into one of three distinct vegetation zones. The subalpine zone covers most of the forested area. Below it is the montane zone, which covers the valley floor, and above it is the alpine zone, where climate is severe and vegetation cover limited.

Montane-zone vegetation is usually found at elevations below 1,350 meters but can grow at higher elevations on sun-drenched, south-facing slopes. Because fires often affect this zone, lodgepole pine is the dominant species; its tightly sealed cones open only with the heat of a forest fire, thereby regenerating the species quickly after a blaze. Douglas fir is the zone's climax

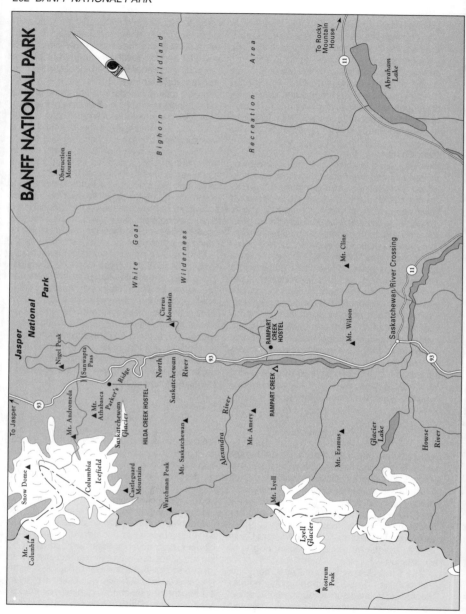

BANFF NATIONAL PARK

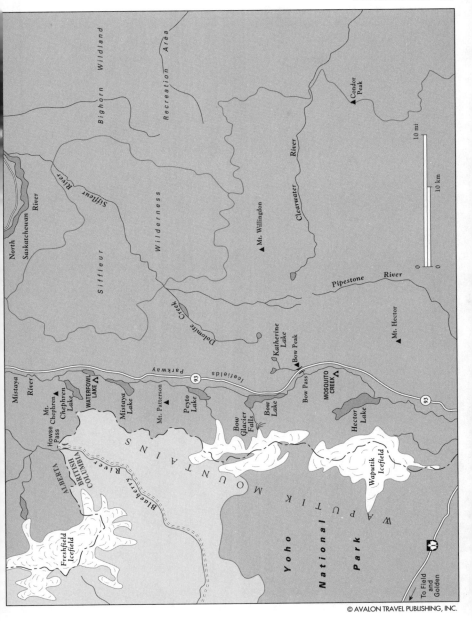

© AVALON TRAVEL PUBLISHING, INC.

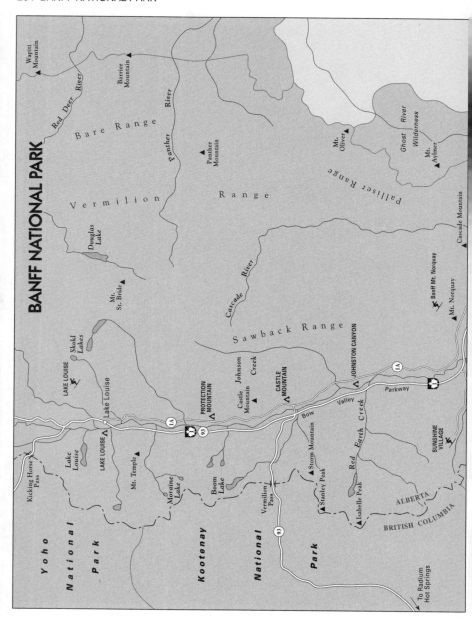

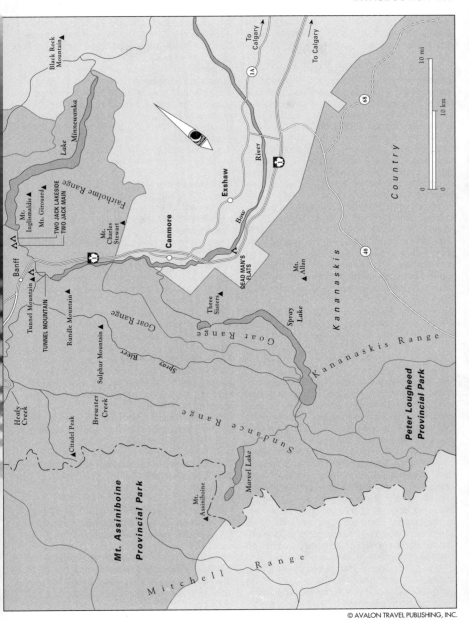

© AVALON TRAVEL PUBLISHING, INC.

species and is found in open stands such as on Tunnel Mountain. Aspen is common in older burn areas, whereas limber pine thrives on rocky outcrops.

Dense forests of white and Engelmann spruces typify the subalpine zone. White spruce dominates to 2,100 meters; above 2,100 meters to 2,400 meters, Engelmann spruce is most prevalent. In areas affected by fire, such as west of Castle Junction, lodgepole pine occurs in dense stands. In 1968, a fire burned 2,500 hectares near Vermilion Pass, a good area to view early stages of regeneration. Subalpine fir grows above 2,200 meters and is often stunted in growth, affected by the high winds experienced at such lofty elevations.

The transition from subalpine to alpine is gradual and usually occurs at approximately 2,300 meters. The alpine zone has a severe climate, with temperatures averaging below zero. Low temperatures, strong winds, and a very short summer force alpine plants to adapt by growing low to the ground with long roots. Mosses, mountain avens, saxifrage, and an alpine dandelion all thrive in this environment. The best place to view the brightly colored carpet of alpine flowers is Sunshine Meadows or Parker's Ridge.

FAUNA

Viewing the abundant and varied wildlife is one of the park's most popular activities. During summer, with the onslaught of millions of visitors, many of the larger mammals tend to move away from the more heavily traveled areas. It then becomes a case of knowing when and where to look for them. Spring and fall are the best times of year for wildlife viewing. The big-game animals have moved below the snow cover of the higher elevations, and the crowds have thinned out. Winter also has its advantages. Although bears are hibernating, a large herd of elk winters in the town of Banff, coyotes are often seen roaming around town, bighorn sheep have descended from the heights, and wolf packs can be seen along the Bow Valley Corridor.

One of the biggest changes in the park over the last 60 years has been in the way that the complex relationship among higher-order mammals has been perceived by, and presented to,

the visiting public. Only 20 years ago, hotels were taking guests to the Banff or Lake Louise dump to watch bears feeding on garbage; 30 years ago, a predator-control program led to the slaughter of nearly every wolf in the park; 30–50 years ago, it was deemed necessary to kill "surplus" elk; and only 60 years ago, Banff had a polar bear on display behind the Banff Park Museum. Amazingly enough, throughout these unsavory sagas, the park has remained a prime area for viewing the unique wildlife of the Canadian Rockies. It is hoped that these species will continue to thrive for a long time to come.

Small Mammals

One of the first mammals you're likely to come in contact with is the Columbian ground squirrel, seen throughout the park's lower elevations. The golden-mantled ground squirrel, similar in size but with a striped back, is common at higher elevations or around rocky outcrops. The one collecting Engelmann spruce cones is the red squirrel. The least chipmunk is striped but smaller than the golden-mantled squirrel. It lives in dry, rocky areas throughout the park.

Short-tailed weasels are very common, but long-tailed weasels are rare. Look for both varieties in higher subalpine forests. Pikas (commonly called rock rabbits) and hoary marmots (well known for their shrill whistles) live among rock slides near high-country lakes—look for them around Moraine Lake and along Bow Summit Loop. Porcupines are widespread and are most active at night.

Vermilion Lakes is an excellent place to view the beaver at work; the best time is dawn or dusk. Muskrats and mink are common in all wetlands within the park. Badgers and otters are rare but do occur in the lower reaches of the Bow River watershed.

Banff's Elk

Few visitors leave Banff without having seen elk, which are easily distinguished by their white rumps. Elk were reported passing through the park early this century but have never been indigenous. In 1917, 57 elk were moved to the park from Yellowstone National Park. Two years later, 20 more were transplanted, and the new herd multiplied rapidly. Coyotes, cougars, and wolves were being slaughtered under a predator-control program, leaving the elk relatively free from predators. The elk proliferated and soon became a problem because they took to wintering in the range of bighorn sheep, deer, moose, and beaver. Between 1941 and 1969, controlled slaughters of elk were conducted in an attempt to reduce the population.

Today, with wolf packs returning to the park, the elk population has stabilized at about 2,000. In summer, look for them in open meadows along the Bow Valley Parkway, along the road to Two Jack Lake, or at Vermilion Lakes. In fall, you'll find hundreds of elk grazing on the golf course until the first snow flies. Fall is rutting season, and the horny bull elk become dangerous as they gather their harems. In winter, small herds roam in and around town.

Other Hoofed Residents

Moose were once common around Vermilion Lakes, but competition from the expanding elk population caused their numbers to decline—now fewer than 100 live in the park. Look for them along the Icefields Parkway near Rampart Creek or at Waterfowl Lakes.

Mule deer, named for their large ears, are most common in the southern part of the park. Watch for them along the Mt. Norquay Road and Bow Valley Parkway. White-tailed deer are much less common but are seen occasionally at Saskatchewan River Crossing. The park has a population of approximately 25 woodland caribou. The small herd remains in the Dolomite Pass area and Upper Pipestone Valley and is rarely seen.

Mountain goats occupy all mountain peaks in the park, living almost the entire year in the higher subalpine and alpine regions. The most accessible place to view these high-altitude hermits is along Parker's Ridge in the far northwestern corner of the park. The park's 2,000 Rocky Mountain bighorn sheep have mostly lost their fear of humans and often congregate at certain spots to lick salt from the road. Look for them at the south end of the Bow Valley Parkway, between switchbacks on the Mt. Norquay Road, and just beyond Lake Minnewanka.

Predators

Coyotes are widespread along the entire Bow River watershed. They are attracted to Vermilion Lakes by an abundance of small game, and many have permanent dens there. The lynx population fluctuates greatly; look for them in the backcountry during winter. Cougars, the largest members of the cat family, are very shy and number less than 20 in the park. They are occasionally seen along the front ranges behind Cascade Mountain. Wolves had been driven close to extinction by the early 1950s, but today at least six wolf packs have been reported in the park. One pack winters close to the townsite and is occasionally seen on Vermilion Lakes during this period.

"Where Can I Go to See a Bear?"

This commonly asked question doesn't have an answer, but the exhilaration of seeing one of these magnificent creatures in its natural habitat is unforgettable. From the road, you're most likely to see black bears, which range in color from jet black to cinnamon brown. Try the Bow Valley Parkway at dawn or late in the afternoon. Farther north, they are often seen near the road as it passes Cirrus Mountain. Grizzly bears spend most of the year in remote valleys, often on south-facing slopes away from the Bow Valley Corridor. During late spring, they are occasionally seen in the area of Bow Pass.

The chance of encountering a bear face-to-face in the backcountry is remote. To lessen chances even further, several simple precautions should be taken. Never hike alone or at dusk, make lots of noise when passing through heavy vegetation, keep a clean camp, and read the pamphlet *Keep the Wild in Wildlife,* available at all park visitors centers. At the Banff Visitor Centre (224 Banff Ave.), daily trail reports list all recent bear sightings. Report any bears you see to the Warden's Office, 403/762-4506.

Reptiles and Amphibians

The wandering garter snake is rare and found only near the Cave and Basin, where warm water from the mineral spring flows down a shaded slope into Vermilion Lakes. Amphibians found in the park are the widespread western toad, the wood frog (commonly found along the Bow River), the rare spotted frog, and the long-toed salamander, which spawns in shallow ponds and spends summers under logs or rocks in the vicinity of its spawning grounds.

Fish

Many of Banff's lakes and rivers have at some time been stocked with a variety of fish, usually with a low rate of success. Rainbow trout are widespread throughout most deep lakes and large streams. Lake trout to 15 kilograms are found in Lake Minnewanka. Dolly Varden are also found in most lakes. Whitefish have been introduced, as have Atlantic salmon, Quebec red trout, brook trout, black bass, and golden trout.

Early residents of Banff released a variety of tropical fish into the marshes below the Cave and Basin, where they quickly multiplied. Today many thrive, but the extremely rare Banff longnose dace, found nowhere else in the world, is in danger of extinction.

Birds

Although more than 240 species of birds have been recorded in the park, most are shy and live in heavily wooded areas. One species that definitely isn't shy is the fearless gray jay, which haunts all campgrounds and picnic areas. Similar in color, but larger, is the Clark's nutcracker, which lives in higher, subalpine forests. Another common bird is the black and white magpie. Ravens are often encountered, especially around campgrounds.

Several species of woodpeckers live in subalpine forests. Several species of grouse are also in residence. Most common of the grouses is the downy ruffled grouse seen in montane

forest. The blue grouse and spruce grouse are seen at higher elevations, as is the white-tailed ptarmigan, which lives above the treeline (watch for them in Sunshine Meadows or on the Bow Summit Loop). A colony of black swifts in Johnston Canyon is one of only two in Alberta.

Good spots to view dippers and migrating waterfowl are Hector Lake, Vermilion Lakes, and the wetland area near Muleshoe Picnic Area. A bird blind has been set up below the Cave and Basin but is only worth visiting at dawn and dusk when the hordes of human visitors aren't around. Part of the nearby marsh stays ice-free during winter, attracting birds such as killdeer.

Although raptors are not common in the park, bald eagles and golden eagles are present part of the year, and the great horned owl, Alberta's provincial bird, lives in the park year-round.

HISTORY

Although the valleys of the Canadian Rockies became ice-free almost 8,000 years ago, and native people periodically hunted and traded in the area since that time, the real story of the park began with the arrival of the railroad to the area.

In 1871, Canadian Prime Minister John A. MacDonald promised to build a rail line linking British Columbia to the rest of the country as a condition of the new province joining the con-

Feeding bears was one of the park's early attractions.

WHYTE MUSEUM OF THE CANADIAN ROCKIES

federation. The line didn't reach Calgary until 1883, pushing through to **Laggan,** now known as Lake Louise, that fall. The rail line was one of the largest engineering jobs ever undertaken in Canada, eventually proving to also be one of the most costly.

On November 8, 1883, three young railway workers—Franklin McCabe and William and Thomas McCardell—went prospecting for gold on their day off. After crossing the Bow River by raft, they came across a warm stream and traced it to its source at a small log-choked basin of warm water that had a distinct smell of sulphur. Nearby, they detected the source of the foul smell coming from a hole in the ground. Nervously, one of the three men lowered himself into the hole and came across a subterranean pool of aqua-green warm water. The three men had found not gold but something just as precious—a hot mineral spring that in time would attract wealthy customers from around the world. Word of the discovery soon got out, and the government encouraged visitors to the Cave and Basin as an ongoing source of revenue to support the new railway.

A 25-square-kilometer reserve was established around the springs on November 25, 1885, and two years later the reserve was expanded and renamed **Rocky Mountains Park.** It was primarily a business enterprise centered around the unique springs and catering to wealthy patrons of the railway. At the turn of the 20th century, Canada had an abundance of wilderness; it certainly didn't need a park to preserve it. The only goal of Rocky Mountains Park was to generate income for the government and the Canadian Pacific Railway (CPR). Luxurious

hotels such as the Banff Springs were constructed, and golf courses, the hot springs themselves, and manicured gardens were developed. The park soon became Canada's best-known tourist resort, attracting visitors from around the world.

In 1902, the park boundary was again expanded to include 11,440 square kilometers of the Canadian Rockies. This dramatic expansion meant that the park became not just a tourist resort but also home to existing coal-mining and logging operations and hydroelectric dams. Government officials saw no conflict of interest, actually stating that the coal mine and township at **Bankhead** added to the park's many attractions. Many of the forests were logged, providing wood for construction, whereas other areas were burned to allow clear sightings for surveyors' instruments.

Most of the larger mammals were killed for food, and by 1915, game was scarce. The Victorian concept of wildlife was that it was either good or evil. Although an early park directive instructed superintendents to leave nature alone, it also told them to ". . . endeavor to exterminate all those animals which prey upon others."

As attitudes began to change, the government set up a Dominion Parks Branch, whose first commissioner, J.B. Hawkins, believed that land set aside for parks should be used for recreation and education. Gradually, resource industries were phased out. Hawkins's work culminated in the National Parks Act of 1930, which in turn led Rocky Mountains Park to be renamed Banff National Park. Its present boundaries, encompassing 6,641 square kilometers, were established in 1964.

TOWN OF BANFF

Many visitors to the national park don't realize that the town of Banff is a bustling commercial center with 7,000 permanent residents. The town's location is magnificent. It is spread out along the Bow River, extending to the lower slopes of Sulphur Mountain to the south and Tunnel Mountain to the east. In one direction is the towering face of Mt. Rundle, and in the other, framed by the buildings along Banff Avenue, is Cascade Mountain. Hotels and motels line the

north end of Banff Avenue, and a profusion of shops, boutiques, cafés, and restaurants hugs the south end. Also at the south end, just over the Bow River, is the Park Administration Building. Here the road forks—to the right is the historic Cave and Basin Hot Springs, to the left the Banff Springs Hotel and Sulphur Mountain Gondola. Some people are happy walking along the crowded streets or shopping in a truly unique setting, but those visitors who are more

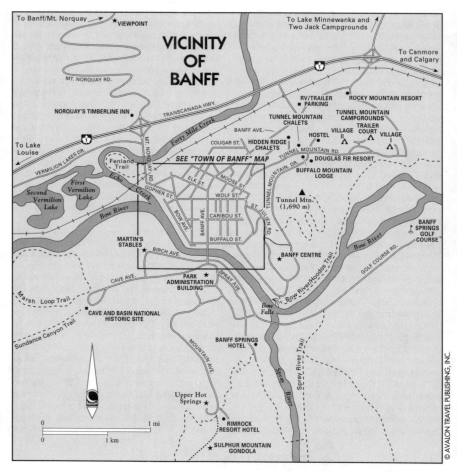

VICINITY OF BANFF

interested in some peace and quiet can easily slip into pristine wilderness just a five-minute walk from town.

History

After the discovery in 1883 of the Cave and Basin, just a few kilometers from the railway station then known as **Siding 29,** many commercial facilities sprang up along what is now Banff Avenue. William Cornelius Van Horne, the general manager of the CPR (later to become its vice president), was instrumental in creating a hotel business along the rail line. His most recognized achievement was the Banff Springs Hotel, the world's largest hotel at the time, which opened in 1888. Enterprising locals soon realized the area's potential and began opening restaurants and offering guided hunting and boating trips. By 1900, the bustling community of Banff had eight hotels. It was named after Banffshire, the Scottish birthplace of George Stephen, the CPR's first president.

After a restriction on automobiles in the park was lifted in 1916, Canada's best-known tourist resort also became its busiest. More and more commercial facilities sprang up, offering luxury and opulence amid the wilderness of the Canadian Rockies. Calgarians built summer cottages, and the town began advertising itself as a year-round destination.

For most of its existence, the town of Banff was run as a service center for park visitors by the Canadian Parks Service in Ottawa—a government department with plenty of economic resources but little idea about how to handle the day-to-day running of a midsized town. Any inconvenience this arrangement caused park residents was offset by cheap rent and subsidized services. In June 1988, Banff's residents voted to sever this tie, and on January 1, 1990, Banff officially became an incorporated town, no different than any other in Alberta (except that Parks Canada controls environmental protection within the townsite).

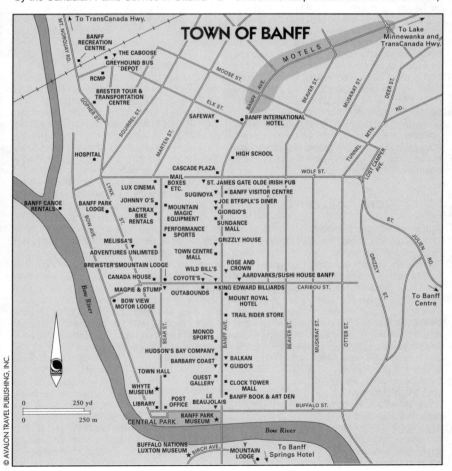

TOWN OF BANFF

Development and the Future

The town of Banff is the largest urban center in any national park in the world. Demand for housing continues to grow faster than development allows, real estate prices are high, and each summer, 50,000 visitors converge on the town daily, overloading existing facilities. On the surface, Banff's commercialism seems to work against the national park's mandate—visitors park in multistory car parks, shops sell bearskin rugs, and trees are logged for new housing estates—but because the park has grown from what was originally a money-making exercise, it is unique.

Another subject of often-heated debate is the high percentage of property in Banff owned by foreign interests, principally Japanese. Japanese investors bought into the area heavily in the 1980s, today owning approximately one third of Banff's hotel industry, including two of the three largest hotels. Non–English-speaking salespeople are common, and more than half of all jobs advertised locally require fluent Japanese.

These issues of continuing development, housing, and foreign ownership of property here in Canada's first national-park town will be debated well into the 21st century.

SIGHTS AND DRIVES

Sulphur Mountain Gondola

The easiest way to get high above town without raising a sweat is on this gondola, which rises 700 meters in eight minutes to an elevation of 2,285 meters. From the observation deck at the upper terminal, the breathtaking view includes the townsite, Bow Valley, Cascade Mountain, Lake Minnewanka, and the Fairholme Range. Bighorn sheep often hang around the upper terminal. The short **Vista Trail** leads along a ridge to a restored weather observatory. Between 1903 and 1931, long before the gondola was built, Norman Sanson was the meteorological observer who collected data at the station. During this period, he made more than 1,000 ascents of Sulphur Mountain, all in the line of duty.

If we can't export the scenery, we'll import the tourists.

—William C. Van Horne,
vice president of the
Canadian Pacific Railway

Summit Restaurant serves mediocre food, inexpensive breakfasts, and priceless views. The gondola, 403/762-5438, runs in summer 7:30 A.M.–9 P.M., shorter hours the rest of the year; closed in December. Adults pay $18, children $9. A 5.5-kilometer trail to the summit begins from the Upper Hot Springs parking lot. Although it's a long slog, views on the way up are good, and you'll be rewarded with a free gondola ride down—they don't check tickets at the top. From downtown, the gondola is three kilometers along Mountain Avenue. In summer, **Brewster,** 403/762-6767, provides shuttle service to the gondola from downtown hotels ($25 includes gondola ride).

Cave and Basin National Historic Site

At the end of Cave Avenue is this historic site, the birthplace of Banff National Park and of the Canadian national parks system. In 1883, three men employed by the CPR stumbled upon the hot springs now known as the Cave and Basin and were quickly lounging in the hot water—a real luxury in the Wild West. They built a fence around the springs, constructed a crude cabin, and began the long process of establishing a claim to the site. But the government beat them to it, settling their claims for a few thousand dollars and acquiring the hot springs. Bathhouses were installed in 1887, and bathers paid 10 cents for a swim. The pools were eventually lined with concrete, and additions were built onto the original structures. Ironically, the soothing minerals in the water that had attracted millions of people to bathe here eventually caused the pools' demise. The minerals, combined with chlorine, produced sediments that ate away at the concrete structure until the pools were deemed unsafe. After closing in 1975, the pools were restored to their original look at a cost of $12 million. They reopened in 1985, only to close again in 1993 for the same reasons, coupled with flagging popularity. Although the pools are now closed for swimming, the center is still one of Banff's most popular attractions. Interpretive displays describe the hows and whys of the springs. A narrow tunnel winds into the dimly lit cave, and short trails lead from the center to the entrance of the cave and through a unique environment created by the hot water from the springs. Interpretive tours are given four times daily in summer. The site is open in summer daily 9:30 A.M.–5 P.M., the rest of the year daily 11 A.M.–4 P.M. Admission to the center is $2.50. For more information, call 403/762-1566.

Upper Hot Springs

These springs on Mountain Avenue, toward Sulphur Mountain Gondola, were first developed in 1901. The present building was completed in 1935, with extensive renovations made in 1996. Once considered for privatization, these springs are still run by Parks Canada and are popular throughout the year. Swimming is $7, lockers and towel rental extra. Therapeutic massages are available for $45 (book at 403/760-2500). The facility, 403/762-1515, is open in summer daily 9 A.M.–11 P.M., shorter hours the rest of the year.

Bow Falls

Small but spectacular, Bow Falls is situated below the Banff Springs Hotel, only a short walk from downtown. The waterfall is the result of a dramatic change in the course of the Bow River brought about by glaciation. At one time, the river flowed north of Tunnel Mountain and out of the mountains via the valley of Lake Minnewanka. As the glaciers retreated, they left terminal moraines, forming natural dams and changing the course of the river. Eventually, the backed-up water found an outlet here between Tunnel Mountain and the northwest ridge of Mt. Rundle. The falls are most spectacular in late spring when the entire Bow Valley watershed is filled with meltwater.

To get there from town, cross the bridge at the south end of Banff Avenue, scramble down the grassy embankment to the left, and follow a pleasant trail along the Bow River to a point above the falls. This easy walk is one kilometer (30 minutes) each way. By car, cross the bridge and follow the Golf Course signs. From the falls, a paved road crosses the Spray River and passes through the Banff Springs Golf Course.

Cascade Gardens

One of the earliest entrepreneurs to take advantage of the hot springs was Dr. R.G. Brett. In 1886, he opened a private spa and hospital that became known as Brett's Sanatorium. It accommodated 90 guests, who were drawn to Banff by the claimed healing qualities of the hot springs' water. The hotel burned down in 1933 and was replaced in 1936 by the **Park Administration Building,** which stands today on the south side of the Bow River. Here you'll have a commanding view along Banff Avenue and of Cascade Mountain. And the surrounding gardens are immaculately manicured, making for enjoyable strolling on a sunny day.

Vermilion Lakes

This series of shallow lakes forms an expansive montane wetland supporting a variety of mammals and 238 species of birds. Vermilion Lakes Drive, paralleling the TransCanada Highway immediately west of Banff, provides the easiest access to the area. The level of **First Vermilion Lake** was once controlled by a dam. Since the removal of the dam, the level of the lake has dropped. This is the beginning of a long process that will eventually see the area evolve into a floodplain forest such as is found along the Fenland Trail. **Second** and **Third Vermilion Lakes** have a higher water level that is controlled naturally by beaver dams. Near First Vermilion Lake is an active osprey nest. The entire area is excellent for wildlife viewing, especially in winter, when it provides habitat for elk, coyote, and the occasional wolf.

Mount Norquay Road

One of the best views of town accessible by car is on this road, which switchbacks steeply to the base of Banff Mt. Norquay, the local skiing and snowboarding area. On the way up are several lookouts, including one near the top where bighorn sheep often graze.

To Lake Minnewanka

Lake Minnewanka Road begins where Banff Avenue ends at the northeast end of town. An alternative to driving along Banff Avenue is to take Buffalo Street, opposite the Banff Park Museum, and follow it around Tunnel Mountain, passing the hostel, campground, and several

Vermillion Lakes in winter

viewpoints of the north face of Mt. Rundle, rising vertically from the forested valley below. This road eventually rejoins Banff Avenue at the Rocky Mountain Resort. The first road to the right after passing under the TransCanada Highway leads to **Cascade Ponds,** a popular day-use area. The next turnout along this road is at **Lower Bankhead.** During the early 1900s, Bankhead was a booming mining town producing 200,000 tons of coal per year. The poor quality of the coal and bitter labor disputes led to the mine's closure in 1922. Soon after, all the buildings were moved or demolished. Although for many years the mine had brought prosperity to the park, people's perceptions changed. The National Parks Act of 1930, which prohibited establishing mining claims in national parks, was greeted with little animosity. From the parking lot at Lower Bankhead, a 1.1-kilometer interpretive trail leads through the industrial section of the town and past an old mine train. The town's 1,000 residents lived on the other side of the road at **Upper Bankhead.** Just before the Upper Bankhead turnoff, the foundation of the Holy Trinity Church can be seen on the side of the hill to the right. Not much remains of Upper Bankhead. It is now a day-use area with picnic tables, kitchen shelters, and firewood. Through the meadow to the west of here are some large slag heaps, concealed mine entrances, and various stone foundations.

Lake Minnewanka

Minnewanka (Lake of the Water Spirit) is the largest body of water in Banff National Park. **Mt. Inglismaldie** (2,964 meters) and the **Fairholme Range** form an imposing backdrop. The reservoir was first constructed in 1912, and additional dams were built in 1922 and 1941 to supply hydroelectric power to Banff. Minnewanka Landing was a resort village that was submerged when the most recent dam went in and is now a popular spot for scuba diving. **Lake Minnewanka Boat Tours,** 403/762-3473, has a 90-minute cruise to the far reaches of the lake. It departs from the dock three to five times daily and costs adults $26, children $11. Brewster, 403/762-6767, offers this cruise combined with a bus tour from Banff for $41 per person. Easy walking trails lead along the western shore. The lake is great for fishing (lake trout to 15 kilograms) and is the only one in the park where motorboats are allowed.

From Lake Minnewanka, the road continues along the reservoir wall—passing a herd of bighorn sheep and a commemorative plaque to the Palliser Expedition—to **Johnson Lake,** with good fishing and swimming, as well as lakeside picnic facilities.

BOW VALLEY PARKWAY

Two roads link Banff to Lake Louise. The TransCanada Highway is the quicker route, more popular with through traffic. The other is the more scenic 51-kilometer Bow Valley Parkway, which branches off the TransCanada Highway five kilometers west of Banff. Cyclists appreciate this road's two long, divided sections and low speed limit (60 kilometers per hour). Along this route are several impressive viewpoints, interpretive displays, picnic areas, good hiking, great opportunities for viewing wildlife, a hostel, three lodges, campgrounds, and one of the park's best restaurants.

As you enter the parkway, you pass the quiet **Fireside** picnic area beside a creek and an interpretive display describing how the Bow Valley was formed. At **Backswamp Viewpoint,** you can look upstream to the site of a former dam, now a swampy wetland filled with aquatic vegetation. Farther along the road is another wetland at **Muleshoe.** This wetland consists of oxbow lakes that were formed when the Bow River changed its course and abandoned its meanders for a more direct path. Across the parkway is a one-kilometer trail that climbs to a viewpoint overlooking the valley. (The slope around this trail is infested with wood ticks during summer, so be sure to check yourself carefully after hiking in this area.) To the east, **Hole-in-the-wall** is visible. This large-mouthed cave was created by the Bow Glacier, which once filled the valley and whose meltwater dissolved the soft limestone bedrock as it receded. It is known as a solution cave.

Beyond Muleshoe, the road inexplicably divides for only a few meters. A large white spruce stood on the island until it blew down in 1984. The story goes that while the road was being constructed, a surly foreman was asleep in the shade of the tree, and not daring to rouse him, workers cleared the roadway around him. The road then passes through particularly hilly terrain, part of a massive rock slide that occurred approximately 8,000 years ago.

Continuing down the parkway, you'll pass the following sights.

Johnston Canyon

Johnston Creek drops over a series of spectacular waterfalls here, deep within the chasm it has carved into the limestone bedrock. The canyon is not nearly as deep as Maligne Canyon in Jasper National Park (30 meters at its deepest, compared to 50 meters at Maligne), but the raised boardwalk that leads to the falls has been built through the depths of the canyon rather than along its lip, making it seem just as spectacular. The lower falls are one kilometer from Johnston Canyon Resort. Other falls are passed along the trail as it continues to weave its way through the canyon to the **Ink Pots,** mineral springs whose sediments reflect sunlight, producing a brilliant aquamarine color. While in the canyon, look for nesting great gray owls and black swifts.

Castle Mountain

Silver City

At the west end of **Moose Meadows,** a small plaque marks the site of Silver City. At its peak, this boomtown had a population of 2,000, more than Calgary had at the time. The city was founded by John Healy, who also founded the notorious Fort Whoop-Up in Lethbridge. During its heady days, five mines were operating, extracting not silver but ore rich in copper and lead. The town had a half dozen hotels, four or five stores, two real-estate offices, and a station on the transcontinental rail line when its demise began. Two men, named Patton and Pettigrew, salted their mine with gold and silver ore to attract investors. After selling 2,000 shares at $5 each, they vanished, leaving investors with a useless mine. Investment in the town ceased, mines closed, and the people left. Only one man refused to leave. His name was James Smith, but he was known to everyone as Joe. In 1887, when Silver City came under the jurisdiction of the National Parks Service, Joe was allowed to remain. And he did so, becoming a friend to everyone, including the Stoney Indians; Father Albert Lacombe, who occasionally stopped by; well-known Banff guide Tom Wilson; and, of course, to the animals that grazed around his cabin. By 1926, he was unable to trap or hunt because of his failing eyesight, and many people tried to persuade him to leave. In 1937, he finally moved to a Calgary retirement home, where he died soon after.

Castle Mountain to Lake Louise

Six kilometers farther northwest is **Castle Mountain Chalets** (403/762-3868, www.castlemountain.com). The older-style cabins have recently been replaced with 22 deluxe log chalets, which have high ceilings, beautifully handcrafted log interiors, three beds, a stone fireplace, a full kitchen with dishwasher, a bathroom with hot tub, and satellite TV; $175 for up to four people, $195 for five or six.

The road skirts the base of the mountain, passes **Castle Mountain Village,** and climbs a small hill to **Storm Mountain Viewpoint,** which provides more stunning views and a picnic area. The next commercial facility is **Baker Creek Chalets and Bistro,** an excellent spot for a meal, then another viewpoint at **Morant's Curve,** from where **Temple Mountain** is visible. After

passing another picnic area and a chunk of Precambrian shield, the road rejoins the Trans-Canada Highway at Lake Louise.

RAINY DAY BANFF

Banff Park Museum

Although displays of taxidermy are not usually associated with national parks, this museum (93 Banff Ave., 403/762-1558) provides an insight into the park's early history. Visitors during the Victorian era were eager to see the park's animals without actually having to venture into the bush. A lack of roads and scarcity of large game as a result of hunting meant that the best way to see animals was either in the game paddock, the zoo, or here in the museum. It was built in 1903, before the park had electricity—hence its "railroad pagoda" design with use of skylights on all levels. Between 1904 and 1937, the grounds behind the museum were occupied by the Banff Zoo and Aviary. The zoo kept more than 60 species of animals, including a polar bear.

Under the supervision of a keen naturalist, Norman Sanson, the museum's extensive collection of specimens continued to grow. As times changed, it was considered outdated, and plans for its demolition were put forward in the 1950s. Fortunately, this didn't occur, and the museum was restored for the park's 100th anniversary in 1985. The exhibits are an interesting link to the park's past and provide insight into the intricate workings of various park ecosystems. The museum is open in summer daily 10 A.M.–6 P.M., the rest of the year daily 1–5 P.M. Admission is $2.50. The museum also has a reading room stocked with books on the park.

Buffalo Nations Luxton Museum

Looking like a stockade, this museum, located to the west of the Banff Bridge (1 Birch Ave., 403/762-2388), is dedicated to the heritage of the Indians who once inhabited the Canadian Rockies and surrounding prairies. It was named for prominent Banff resident Norman Luxton, who had a close relationship with the natives of the area and was involved in the Banff Indian Days. He operated a trading post on the site for many years before opening the museum in

1952 with the help of the Glenbow-Alberta Institute. The museum contains memorabilia from Luxton's 60-year relationship with the Stoney Indians, as well as an elaborately decorated tepee, hunting equipment, a few taxidermy exhibits, a realistic diorama of a buffalo jump, peace pipes, and traditional clothing. The Indian Trading Post is now one of Banff's better gift shops and is definitely worth a browse. The museum is open in summer daily 9 A.M.–7 P.M., the rest of the year 11:30 A.M.–4:30 P.M. Admission is $6.

Whyte Museum of the Canadian Rockies
The Whyte Foundation was established in the mid-1950s by local artists Peter and Catherine Whyte to help preserve artistic and historical material relating to the Canadian Rockies. Their museum opened in 1968 and has continued to grow ever since. It now houses the world's largest collection of Canadian Rockies literature and art. Included in the archives are more than 4,000 volumes, oral tapes of early pioneers and outfitters, antique postcards, old cameras, manuscripts, and a large photographic collection.

WILD BILL PEYTO

" . . . rarely speaking—his forte was doing things, not talking about them." These words from a friend sum up one of Banff's earliest characters. These attributes, combined with his knowledge of the Canadian Rockies, earned Bill Peyto status as one of Banff's greatest guides. In 1886, at the tender age of 18, Ebenezer William Peyto left England for Canada. After traveling extensively he settled in Banff and was hired as an apprentice guide for legendary outfitter Tom Wilson. Wearing a tilted sombrero, fringed buckskin coat, cartridge belt, hunting knife, and a six-shooter, he looked more like a gunslinger than a mountain man. As his reputation as a competent guide grew, so did the stories. While guiding clients on one occasion, he led them to his cabin. Before entering, Peyto threw stones in the front door until a loud snap was heard. It was a bear trap that he'd set up to catch a certain trapper who'd been stealing his food. One of the guests commented that if caught, the trapper would surely have died. "You're damned right he would have," Bill replied. "Then I'd have known for sure it was him."

In 1900 Peyto left to fight in the Boer War and was promoted to corporal for bravery. This was revoked before it became official after they learned he'd "borrowed" an officer's jacket and several bottles of booze for the celebration. Returning to a hero's welcome in Banff he established an outfitting business and continued prospecting for copper in Simpson Pass. Although his outfitting business thrived, the death of his wife left him despondent. He built a house on Banff Avenue. Its name, "Ain't it Hell," summed up his view of life. In his later years, after being wounded in WW I, he became a warden in the Healy Creek–Sunshine district where his

exploits during the 1920s added to his already legendary name. After 20 years of service he retired, and in 1943, at the age of 75, he passed away. One of the park's most beautiful lakes is named after him, as is a glacier and one of Banff's popular watering holes, Wild Bill's, a designation that he would have appreciated. His face also adorns the large signs welcoming visitors to Banff.

WHYTE MUSEUM OF THE CANADIAN ROCKIES

The highlight is the photography of Byron Harmon, whose black-and-white studies of mountain geography have shown people around the world that the Canadian Rockies are one of the most beautiful mountain destinations in the world. The downstairs gallery features changing art and photographic exhibitions. The museum also houses the library and archives of the Alpine Club of Canada. On the grounds are several heritage homes formerly occupied by local pioneers. The Whyte Museum (beside the library, 111 Bear St., 403/762-2291) is open in summer Tues.–Sat. 10 A.M.–9 P.M. and Sun.–Mon. 10 A.M.–6 P.M., the rest of the year 10 A.M.–5 P.M. Admission is adults $4, seniors $2. Don't miss this one.

The Whyte Museum hosts a variety of interesting walking tours throughout summer. The most popular of these is the Historic Banff Walk, which departs from the museum daily at 11 A.M. and 3 P.M., taking approximately 90 minutes.

Natural History Museum

Banff's smallest museum, located upstairs in the Clock Tower Mall (112 Banff Ave., 403/762-4747), is crammed with exhibits displaying the geological evolution of the Canadian Rockies. Highlights include a replica of Castleguard Cave (one of the largest caves in North America), an interesting slideshow, rock and fossil displays, and a tacky life-size model of Bigfoot—just what you came to Banff for. It's open daily midday–5 P.M., until 10 P.M. in summer.

Banff Centre

Located on the lower slopes of Tunnel Mountain is the Banff Centre for the Arts, whose surroundings provide inspiration for some of Canada's finest postgraduate artists. Banff Centre, as it's usually called, first opened in the summer of 1933 as a theater school and has grown to become a prestigious institution attracting artists of many disciplines from throughout Canada. The center's **Walter Phillips Gallery** (St. Julien Rd., 403/762-6281) has changing exhibits of visual arts from throughout the world. Open Tues.–Thurs. noon–5 P.M., Fri.–Sat. noon–8 P.M., and Sunday noon–5 P.M. Activities are held on the grounds year-round. Highlights include concerts, displays, live performances, the Banff Arts Festival, the Banff Television Festival, the Banff Mountain Book Festival, and the Banff Mountain Film Festival, to name a few (see **Festivals and Events**). Call 403/762-6100 for a program or check the *Crag and Canyon* (published weekly on Wednesday).

Banff Springs Hotel

On a terrace above a bend in the Bow River is one of the largest, grandest, and most opulent mountain-resort hotels in the world. What better way could there be to spend a rainy afternoon than to explore this turreted 20th-century castle? You can even find a writing desk overlooking one of the world's most photographed scenes and pen a long letter to the folks back home.

"The Springs" has grown with the town and is an integral part of its history. William Cornelius Van Horne, vice president of the CPR, decided that the best way to encourage customers to travel on the newly completed rail line across the Rockies was to build a series of luxurious mountain accommodations. The largest of these resorts was begun in 1886, as close as possible to Banff's newly discovered hot springs. The location chosen had magnificent views and was only a short carriage ride from the train station. Money was no object, and architect Bruce Price began designing a mountain resort the likes of which the world had never seen. At some stage of construction, his plans were misinterpreted, and much to Van Horne's shock the building was built back to front. The best guest rooms faced the forested slopes of Sulphur Mountain, whereas the kitchen had panoramic views of the Bow Valley.

On June 1, 1888, it opened as the largest hotel in the world, with 250 rooms beginning at $3.50 per night, including meals. Water from the nearby hot springs was piped into the hotel's steam baths. Rumor has it that when the pipes blocked, water from the Bow River was used, secretly supplemented with bags of sulphur-smelling chemicals. Overnight, the quiet community of Banff became a destination resort for wealthy guests from around the world, and the hotel soon became one of North America's most popular accommodations. Every room was booked every day during the short summer seasons. In 1903, a wing was added, doubling the hotel's capacity. The following year, a tower was added to each wing. Guest numbers reached 22,000 in 1911, and construction of a new hotel, designed by Walter Painter, began that year. The original design—an 11-story tower joining two wings in a baronial style—was reminiscent of a Scottish castle mixed with a French country chateau. This concrete-and-rock-faced, green-roofed building was completed in 1928 and stands to this day.

Don't let the hotel's opulence keep you from spending time here. Sightseeing is actually encouraged. Visit the hotel between 11:30 A.M. and 1:30 P.M., and enjoy a huge buffet lunch combined with a 30-minute **Historical Hotel Tour** for $19.95 per person. Call 403/762-2211 for details. Otherwise, wander through on your own (maps are available in the lobby), admiring the 5,000 pieces of furniture and antiques (most "antiques" in public areas are reproductions), paintings, prints, tapestries, and rugs. Take in the medieval atmosphere of Mt. Stephen Hall with its lime flagstone floor, enormous windows, and large oak beams, or relax in one of 13 eateries or four lounges.

The hotel is a 15-minute walk southeast of town along Spray Avenue, or via the trail along the south bank of the Bow River. Horse-drawn buggies take passengers from the Trail Rider Store at 132 Banff Avenue to the Springs for $35; **Banff Transit** buses leave downtown twice an hour, $1.

HIKING

After experiencing the international thrills of Banff Avenue, many people want to see the *real* Banff—the reason that millions of visitors flock here, thousands take low-paying jobs just to stay here, and those who become severely addicted cut ties with the outside world, raise families, and live happily ever after here. Although many landmarks can be seen from the roadside, to really experience the park's personality, you'll need to go for a hike. One of the best things about Banff's approximatley 80 hiking trails is the variety. From short interpretive walks originating in town, to easy hikes rewarded by spectacular vistas, to a myriad of overnight backcountry opportunities, Banff's trails offer something for everyone. Before attempting any hikes, however, you should visit the **Banff Visitor Centre** (224 Banff Ave., 403/762-1550), where staff can advise you on the condition of trails and closures. If you are planning an overnight trip into the backcountry, you *must* pick up a Wilderness Permit from here before heading out; $6 per person per night.

Most of the trails listed as follows start in or near town; the last four start out of town, on the way toward Lake Louise.

Fenland
- Length: 2 kilometers (30 minutes) round-trip
- Elevation gain: none
- Rating: easy

This short interpretive trail begins at the Forty Mile Creek Picnic Area 300 meters north of the rail line along Mt. Norquay Road. A brochure, available at the trailhead, explains the various stages in the transition between wetland and a floodplain forest of spruce as you progress around the loop. This fen environment is prime habitat for many species of birds. The work of beavers can be seen along the trail, and elk winter here. This trail is also a popular shortcut for joggers and cyclists heading for Vermilion Lakes.

Tunnel Mountain
- Length: 2.3 kilometers (30–60 minutes) one-way
- Elevation gain: 300 meters
- Rating: easy to moderate

Accessible from town, this short hike is an easy climb to one of the park's lower peaks. The trailhead is on St. Julien Road, 350 meters to the south of Wolf Street. The trail ascends the western flank of Tunnel Mountain through a forest of lodgepole pine, switchbacking past some viewpoints before reaching a ridge just below the summit. Here the trail turns northward, climbing through a forest of Douglas fir to the summit, which is partially treed, preventing 360-degree views.

Bow River/Hoodoos
- Length: 4.8 kilometers (60–90 minutes) one-way
- Elevation gain: minimal
- Rating: easy

From the Bow River Viewpoint on Tunnel Mountain Drive, the trail descends to the Bow River, passing under the sheer east face of Tunnel

Mountain. It then follows the river for a short distance before climbing into a meadow where deer and elk often graze. From this perspective, the north face of Mt. Rundle is particularly imposing. As the trail climbs, you'll hear the traffic on Tunnel Mountain Road long before you see it. The trail ends at **hoodoos,** strange limestone-and-gravel columns jutting mysteriously out of the forest. An alternative to returning the same way is to catch the **Banff Explorer** bus from Tunnel Mountain Campgrounds. It leaves every half hour ($1.50).

Sundance Canyon
- Length: 4.4 kilometers (90 minutes) one-way
- Elevation gain: 100 meters
- Rating: easy

Sundance Canyon is a rewarding destination accessed from the Cave and Basin National Historic Site. Unfortunately, the first three kilometers are along a paved road that is closed to traffic (but not bikes) and hard on your soles. Occasional glimpses of the Sawback Range are afforded by breaks in the forest. The road ends at a shaded picnic area, from where the 2.4-kilometer Sundance Loop begins. Sundance Creek was once a larger river whose upper drainage basin was diverted by glacial action. Its powerful waters have eroded into the soft bedrock, forming a spectacular overhanging canyon whose bed is strewn with large boulders that have tumbled in.

Spray River
- Length: 6 kilometers (2 hours) one-way
- Elevation gain: 70 meters
- Rating: easy to moderate

This trail follows one of the many fire roads in the park. It is not particularly interesting, but it's accessible from Banff and is a pleasant way to escape the crowds. For serious hikers, this trail provides access to the rugged and remote southern reaches of the park. From the Bow Falls parking lot walk, cross the Spray River and follow Golf Course Road to the green of the first hole on the right. From there, a trail heads uphill into the forest. It follows the Spray River closely—when not in sight, the river can always be heard. For those so inclined, a river crossing one kilometer from the golf course allows for a shorter loop. Continuing south, the trail

climbs a bluff for a good view of the Banff Springs Hotel and Bow Valley. The return journey is straightforward, with occasional views, ending at a locked gate behind the Banff Springs Hotel, a short walk to Bow Falls.

Western Slope of Mount Rundle
- Length: 5.4 kilometers (2 hours) one-way
- Elevation gain: 480 meters
- Rating: moderate

At 2,950 meters, Mt. Rundle is one of the park's dominant peaks. Climbing to its summit is possible without ropes, but previous scrambling experience is advised. An alternative is to ascend the mountain's western slope along an easy-to-follow trail that ends just more than 1,000 vertical meters before the summit. The trail follows the Spray River Trail (see previous entry) before branching off left 700 meters from Golf Course Road and climbing steadily, breaking out of the enclosed forest after 2.5 kilometers. The trail ends in a gully, from where the undefined route to the summit begins.

Stoney Squaw
- Length: 2.4-kilometer loop (1 hour round-trip)
- Elevation gain: 180 meters
- Rating: easy

Stoney Squaw's 1,884-meter summit is dwarfed by Cascade Mountain, situated directly behind it. To get to the trailhead, follow Mt. Norquay Road to a parking lot at the ski area. Immediately to the right of the entrance, a small sign marks the trail. The narrow trail passes through a thick forest of lodgepole pine and spruce before breaking out into the open near the summit. The sweeping panorama includes Vermilion Lakes, the Bow Valley, Banff, the Spray River Valley, Mt. Rundle, Lake Minnewanka, and the imposing face of Cascade Mountain (2,998 meters). The return trail follows the northwest slope of Stoney Squaw to an old ski run at the opposite end of the parking lot.

Cascade Amphitheatre
- Length: 6.6 kilometers (2–3 hours) one-way
- Elevation gain: 610 meters
- Rating: moderate to difficult

This enormous cirque and the subalpine meadows directly behind Cascade Mountain are one of the most rewarding destinations for hiking in the Banff area. The demanding trail begins by the Banff Mt. Norquay day lodge at the end of Mt. Norquay Road. From parking lot number 3, the trail skirts the base of severak ski lifts, following an old road to the floor of Forty Mile Valley. Keep right at all trail junctions. One kilometer after crossing Forty Mile Creek, the trail begins switchbacking up the western flank of Cascade Mountain through a forest of lodgepole pine. Along the way are breathtaking views of Mt. Louis's sheer east face. After the trail levels off, it enters a magnificent U-shaped valley, and the amphitheater begins to define itself. The trail becomes indistinct in the subalpine meadow, which is carpeted in colorful wildflowers during summer. Farther up the valley, vegetation thins out as the boulder-strewn talus slopes cover the ground. If you sit still long enough on these rocks, marmots and pikas will slowly appear, emitting shrill whistles before disappearing again.

The most popular route to the summit of 2,998-meter Cascade Mountain is along the southern ridge of the amphitheater wall. It is a long scramble up scree slopes—made more difficult by a false summit—and should be attempted only by experienced scramblers.

C Level Cirque
- Length: 4 kilometers (90 minutes) one-way
- Elevation gain: 455 meters
- Rating: moderate

This trail begins from the Upper Bankhead Picnic Area on Lake Minnewanka Road and is named for an abandoned mine along its route. It climbs steadily through a forest of lodgepole pine, aspen, and spruce to a pile of tailings and broken-down concrete walls. Soon after is a panoramic view of Lake Minnewanka, then the trail reenters the forest before ending in a small cirque where there are views down the Bow Valley to Canmore and beyond. The cirque is carved into the eastern face of Cascade Mountain, where snow often lingers until July. When the snow melts, the lush soil is covered in a carpet of colorful wildflowers.

Aylmer Lookout
- Length: 12 kilometers (4 hours) one-way
- Elevation gain: 810 meters
- Rating: moderate to difficult

The first eight-kilometer stretch of this trail follows the northern shore of Lake Minnewanka from the day-use area to a junction. The right fork leads to a campground, and the left climbs steeply to the site of an old fire tower on top of an exposed ridge. The deep blue waters of Lake Minnewanka are visible, backed by the imposing peaks of Mt. Girouard (2,995 meters) and Mt. Inglismaldie (2,964 meters). Bighorn sheep are often seen grazing in this area. From here, a trail forks left and continues climbing to the alpine tundra of Aylmer Pass.

Cory Pass
- Length: 5.8 kilometers (2.5 hours) one-way
- Elevation gain: 920 meters
- Rating: moderate to difficult

This strenuous hike from the Fireside Picnic Area at the Banff end of the Bow Valley Parkway has a rewarding objective—a magnificent view of dogtoothed Mt. Louis. The towering slab of limestone rises more than 500 meters from the valley below. Just more than one kilometer from the trailhead, the trail divides. The left fork climbs steeply across an open slope to an uneven ridge that it follows before ascending yet another steep slope to Cory Pass—a wild, windy, desolate area surrounded in jagged peaks dominated by Mt. Louis. An alternative to returning along the same trail is descending into **Gargoyle Valley,** following the base of Mt. Edith before ascending to Edith Pass and returning to the junction one kilometer from the picnic area. Total distance for this trip would be 13 kilometers, a long day considering the steep climbs and descents involved.

Bourgeau Lake
- Length: 7.6 kilometers (2.5 hours) one-way
- Elevation gain: 730 meters
- Rating: moderate

This trail follows Wolverine Creek from a parking area three kilometers west of Sunshine Village Junction on the TransCanada Highway to a small subalpine lake nestled at the base of an impressive limestone amphitheater. Although the trail is moderately steep, plenty of distractions along the way are worthy of a stop (and rest). Across the Bow Valley, the Sawback Range is easy to distinguish. As the forest of lodgepole pine turns to spruce, the trail passes under the cliffs of Mt. Bourgeau and crosses Wolverine Creek (below a spot where it tumbles photogenically over exposed bedrock). After strenuous switchbacks, the trail climbs into the cirque containing Bourgeau Lake. As you continue around the lake's rocky shore, you'll hear the colonies of noisy pikas, even if you don't see them.

Rock Isle Lake

- Length: 8 kilometers (2.5 hours) one-way
- Elevation gain: 590 meters
- Rating: moderate

Sunshine Meadows, straddling the Continental Divide, is a unique and beautiful region of the Canadian Rockies. Large amounts of precipitation create a lush cover of vegetation during the short summer season—more than 300 species of wildflowers alone have been recorded. For 60 years, the meadows have been a favorite area for downhill skiing, but summer activities were not promoted until 1984. Suddenly, instead of a few hundred adventurous souls willing to hike the 6.5-kilometer road into the meadows, tens of thousands of visitors were whisked onto the fragile alpine tundra by gondola. In 1992, Sunshine Village terminated its summer gondola service, and the meadows are quiet once again.

To get to the base station from Banff, follow the TransCanada Highway nine kilometers west to Sunshine Village Road, which continues another nine kilometers to the Gondola Base Station. The road to the meadows is closed to public traffic and climbs steadily for 6.5 kilometers to Sunshine Village. From there, the Rock Isle Lake Trail passes the Strawberry Chairlift and climbs out of the valley into an alpine meadow covered in a colorful carpet of fireweed, glacier lilies, mountain avens, white mountain heather, and forget-me-nots. Mount Assiniboine (3,611 meters), known as the "Matterhorn of the Rockies," is easily distinguished to the southeast. On the descent to the lake are various viewpoints, and around the shoreline are benches and an observation deck.

In summer, **White Mountain Adventures,** 403/678-4099 or 800/408-0005, offers a shuttle service for a few hikers from Banff (daily at 8:45 A.M., $35 round-trip) and the Sunshine Village parking lot (daily at 9:30 A.M., 10:30 A.M.,

11:30 A.M., and 1:30 P.M.; $18 round-trip) to the village itself. Included in the fare are a variety of guided walks.

Shadow Lake

- Length: 14.3 kilometers (4.5 hours) one-way
- Elevation gain: 440 meters
- Rating: moderate

Shadow is one of the many impressive subalpine lakes along the Continental Divide but is also popular as a base for a great variety of day trips. The trail begins at the Redearth Creek Parking Area, 20 kilometers west of Banff on the TransCanada Highway. It follows the old Redearth fire road for 11 kilometers before forking right and climbing into the forest. The campground is located two kilometers beyond this junction, and 500 meters farther is Shadow Lake Lodge. The lake is nearly two kilometers long, and from its southern shore, trails lead to Ball Pass, Gibbon Pass, and Haiduk Lake.

Castle Lookout

- Length: 3.7 kilometers (90 minutes) one-way
- Elevation gain: 520 meters
- Rating: moderate

However you travel through the Bow Valley, you can't help but be impressed by Castle Mountain rising proudly from the forest below. This trail takes you above the treeline on the mountain's west face to the site of Mt. Eisenhower fire lookout, which was abandoned in the 1970s and burned in the 1980s. The trailhead is on the Bow Valley Parkway, five kilometers northwest of Castle Junction. The trail follows a wide pathway for 1.5 kilometers to an abandoned cabin in a forest of lodgepole pine and spruce. It then becomes narrower and steeper, switchbacking through a meadow before climbing through a narrow band of rock and leveling off near the lookout site. From here a magnificent panorama of the Bow Valley is afforded in both directions. Storm Mountain can be seen directly across the valley.

Rockbound Lake

- Length: 8.4 kilometers (2.5 hours) one-way
- Elevation gain: 760 meters
- Rating: moderate to difficult

The trailhead for this strenuous hike is located just east of Castle Junction on the Bow Valley

Parkway. For the first five kilometers, it follows an old fire road along the southern flanks of Castle Mountain. Early in the season or after heavy rain, this section can be boggy. Glimpses of surrounding peaks ease the pain of the steady climb as the trail narrows. **Tower Lake** is reached after eight kilometers. The trail skirts it to the right and climbs a steep slope. From the ridge, Rockbound Lake comes into view, and the reason for its name immediately becomes apparent. Good views can be achieved by scrambling up any of the nearby slopes.

OTHER RECREATION

Mountain Biking
Whether you have your own bike or you rent one from the many bicycle shops in town, cycling in the park is for everyone. The roads to Lake Minnewanka, Mt. Norquay, and along the Bow Valley Parkway are all popular. Severak trails radiating from Banff townsite and ending deep in the backcountry have been designated as bicycle trails, including Sundance (3.7 kilometers one-way), Rundle Riverside (eight kilometers one-way), Spray River Loop (43 kilometers round-trip), and Cascade Trail (nine kilometers one-way). Other trails are at Redearth Creek, Lake Louise, and in the northeastern reaches of the park near Saskatchewan River Crossing. Before heading into the backcountry, pick up the *Trail Bicycling Guide* from the Banff Visitor Centre. Riders are particularly susceptible to sudden bear encounters. Be alert and make loud noises when passing through heavy vegetation.

Bactrax Bike Rentals (225 Bear St., 403/762-8177) rents front- and full-suspension mountain bikes for $6–10 per hour and $20–38 per day, the best deal in town. Rollerblade rentals are $15 per day. Bactrax also offers mountain-bike tours, including to Vermilion Lakes and along Sundance Canyon. Tours cost $15 per person per hour. The shop is open daily 8 A.M.–8 P.M.

Horseback Riding
Jim and Bill Brewster led Banff's first paying guests into the backcountry on horseback more than 100 years ago. Today, visitors are still able to enjoy the park on this traditional form of transportation. **Warner Guiding & Outfitting**, based at the Trail Rider Store (132 Banff Ave., 403/762-4551), offers a great variety of trips. Trips depart from **Martin's Stables**, 403/762-2832, behind the recreation grounds on Birch Avenue, and **Banff Springs Corral**, 403/762-2848, along Spray Avenue. One-hour rides are $27, two hours $40, three hours $64. Other day trips include the three-hour Mountain Morning Breakfast Ride, which includes a hearty breakfast along the trail, for $61; the Explorer, a seven-hour ride up the Spray River Valley, $115; and the Evening Steak Fry, a three-hour ride with a steak dinner along the trail, $61. Overnight trips to established backcountry camps and lodges are also available; rates begin at $437, including all meals, one night's accommodation at Sundance Lodge, and the horse, of course.

White-water Rafting and Canoeing
Anyone looking for white-water–rafting action

Horseback riding is a traditional form of transportation through the mountains.

will want to run the Kicking Horse River, which flows down the western slopes of the Canadian Rockies into British Columbia. Many operators based in Banff offer exhilarating trips down this river, all of which include transportation from Banff. Operators are **Alpine Rafting,** 888/599-5299;

Hydra River Guides, 403/762-4554 or 800/644-8888; **Kootenay River Runners,** 403/762-5385 or 800/599-4399; **Rocky Mountain Raft Tours,** 403/762-3632; and **Wet 'n' Wild Adventures,** 800/668-9119. The cost of a full-day trip is $90–130, which includes transportation and lunch. Driving yourself to Golden saves a few bucks and allows the option of a half-day trip.

Rocky Mountain Raft Tours, 403/762-3632, offers one-hour ($24) and two-hour ($39) float trips down the Bow River, beginning just below Bow Falls.

Banff Canoe Rentals, (on the corner of Wolf St. and Bow Ave., 403/762-3632) rents canoes for use on the Bow River or Vermilion Lakes; $16 per hour or $40 for a full day.

Fishing and Boating

The finest fishing in the park is in Lake Minnewanka, where lake trout as large as 15 kilograms have been caught. One way to ensure a good catch is through **Lake Minnewanka Guided Fishing,** 403/762-3473, which offers 3.5-hour guided fishing expeditions; $200 for one or two persons. Fishing boats and tackle are also for rent. **Adventures Unlimited** (211 Bear St., 403/762-4554 or 800/644-8888) offers a wide variety of fishing trips, including drifting down the Bow River in a boat, fishing high alpine lakes from a belly boat, or simply fly-casting from the banks of a river or stream favored by your guide. Rates of $115–165 per person for a full day include guiding, gear, and lessons. Before fishing anywhere in the park, you need a National Park fishing license ($6 per week, $13 per year), available from the Banff Visitor Centre and sport shops around town.

Golfing

Spread out along the Bow River between Mt. Rundle and Tunnel Mountain is a golf course considered one of the world's most scenic. The first golf holes were laid out in 1911, but not until 1928, when Stanley Thompson was brought in,

were the original 18 championship holes designed. In 1989, the Tunnel Nine opened, completing the 27-hole course. The original 1911 clubhouse still stands, but it has been replaced by a modern, circular-design building situated in the heart of the course. Between 1997 and 1999, no expense was spared in rebuilding the entire original 18 holes. The order of play on these holes has been changed, and the course is now known as the **Stanley Thompson 18.** Not only is the course breathtakingly beautiful, but it's also challenging for all levels of golfer. Pick up a copy of the book *The World's Greatest Golf Holes,* and you'll see a picture of the fourth hole on the Rundle Nine. It's a par three, over Devil's Cauldron 70 meters below, to a small green backed by the sheer face of Mt. Rundle rising vertically more than 1,000 meters above the putting surface. Another unique feature of the course is the abundance of wildlife. There's always the chance of seeing elk feeding on the fairways, or coyotes, deer, or black bears scurrying across in front of you as you putt.

Greens fee is $125 for 18 holes including a cart (through the first and last months of operation, May and mid-September through mid-October, greens fee is reduced to $70). Free shuttle buses run from the Banff Springs Hotel to the clubhouse, where you'll find club rentals ($25), three putting greens, a driving range, a pro shop, a café, and a restaurant. Booking tee times well in advance is essential; 403/762-6801.

Indoor Recreation

Banff Springs Hotel, 403/762-2211, has a four-lane, five-pin bowling center; games are $3.75 per person. **King Edward Billiards** (upstairs at 137 Banff Ave., 403/762-4629) is a large, clean pool hall. Tables are $12 per hour. The **Lux Cinema Centre** (229 Bear St., 403/762-8595) shows new releases for $8.

Banff's only water slide is in the Douglas Fir Resort (Tunnel Mountain Dr., 403/762-5591). The two slides are indoors, and the admission price of $7.50 (children under five free) includes use of a hot tub and exercise room. It's open Mon.–Fri. 2–9:30 P.M., Sat.–Sun. 10 A.M.–9:30 P.M.

The **Solace** (in the Banff Springs Hotel, 403/762-2211) is the place to pamper yourself. In the grand traditions of the hotel, this 3,000-square-meter facility offers a great variety of spa

The steep slopes of Banff Mt. Norquay can be seen from town.

services, including facials, body wraps, massage therapy, salon services, and hydrotherapy. Additionally, there are indoor and outdoor pools, a large fitness room, spas, a sauna, an exercise room, personal trainers, fitness classes, and luxurious bathroom facilities. The Solace is open daily 6 A.M.–10 P.M. General admission is $50 per day, with almost 100 services available at an additional cost.

WINTERTIME

Of Alberta's six world-class alpine resorts, three are in Banff National Park. Banff Mt. Norquay is a small but steep hill overlooking the town of Banff; Sunshine Village is located high in the mountains on the Continental Divide, catching more than its share of fluffy white powder; and Lake Louise, Canada's second-largest alpine resort, is spread over four distinct mountain faces, providing something for everyone (see **Lake Louise**). Apart from an abundance of snow, the resorts have something else in common—spectacular views—which are worth the price of a lift ticket alone.

In fact, the entire park transforms itself into a winter playground covered in an impossibly white blanket of snow from November until May. You'll always find something to do: cross-country skiing, ice-skating, snowshoeing, dogsledding, or just relaxing. Crowds are nonexistent, and hotels

reduce rates by up to 70 percent (except Christmas holidays), which is reason enough to venture into the mountains. Lift and lodging packages begin at $60 per person.

Banff Mt. Norquay

The steep eastern slopes of Mt. Norquay had been attracting local skiers for 20 years before Canada's first chairlift was installed on its face in 1948. Ever since then, the resort has had an experts-only reputation, mainly because of the terrain serviced by the North American Chair, including the famous double-black-diamond Lone Pine run. But an express quad installed in 1990 opened up new intermediate terrain and made the resort—located only six kilometers from Banff—a favorite with shredders and cruisers alike. Lift tickets are $42 per day; lift, lesson, and rental packages cost about the same. Night skiing is offered on Wednesday. A shuttle bus picks skiers up from Banff hotels for the short ride up the hill; $5 one-way. For more information on the resort, call 403/762-4421, or in Calgary call the 24-hour Snowphone, 403/221-8259.

Sunshine Village

The skiing and boarding at Sunshine has lots going for it—more than six meters of snow annually (no need for snowmaking up here), wide-open bowls, a season stretching for almost 200 days, skiing in two provinces, and the only slope-side accommodations in the park.

The first people to ski the Sunshine Meadows were two local men, Cliff White and Cyril Paris, who got lost going over Citadel Pass in the spring of 1929 and returned to Banff with stories of deep snow and ideal slopes for skiing. In the following years, a CPR cabin was used as a base for skiing in the area. In 1938, the Canadian National Ski Championships were held here, and in 1942 a portable lift was constructed. The White family was synonymous with the Sunshine area for many years, running the lodge and ski area while Brewster buses negotiated the steep, narrow road that led to the meadows. In 1980, a gondola was installed to whisk skiers six kilometers from the parking area in Bourgeau Valley to the alpine village. More recently, new high-speed quads have opened up the north face of Goats Eye Mountain and made the trip to the summit of 2,730-meter Lookout Mountain much quicker. One of Canada's most infamous runs, Delirium Dive, off the northeast-facing slope of Lookout Mountain, opened after a 20-year closure for the 1998–1999 season. To ski this up-to-50-degree run, you must be equipped with a transceiver, shovel, probe, and partner, but you'll have bragging rights that night at the bar (especially if you've skied the Bre-X line).

The area has a remarkable variety of terrain serviced by a gondola and nine lifts, including five high-speed quads and the fastest chairlift in the Canadian Rockies. Lift tickets are $52 per day, seniors $42, and children under six free. Two days of skiing and one night's lodging at the slopeside Sunshine Inn costs from $125 per person per day. The inn has a restaurant, a lounge, a game room, and a hot tub. For lodging information, call 403/762-5561 or 800/661-1676. For general resort information, call 403/762-6500 or the Snowphone at 403/760-7669. Transportation from Banff to the hill is $10 round-trip; call the hill or inquire at major hotels for the timetable.

Ski and Snowboard Rentals

Each resort has rental facilities, but getting your gear in town is often easier. Try **Abominable Ski** (229 Banff Ave., 403/762-2905); **Adventures Unlimited** (211 Bear St., 403/762-4554); **Clock Tower Sports** (110 Banff Ave., 403/760-3525); **Monod Sports** (129 Banff Ave., 403/762-4571); **Mountain Magic Equipment** (224 Bear St., 403/762-2591); or **Snow Tips** (225 Bear St., 403/762-8177). Basic packages—skis, poles, and boots or snowboard and boots—are $20–25 per day, whereas high-performance packages range $20–40. **Rude Boys Snowboard Shop,** downstairs in the Sundance Mall (215 Banff Ave., 403/762-8480), is *the* snowboarder hangout.

Heli-Skiing

Although no heli-skiing is allowed in Banff National Park, **R.K. Heli Ski Panorama** (250/342-3889 or 800/661-0252, www.rkheliski.com) books trips to areas outside the park. Each morning during winter, the company's bus leaves Banff to take skiers to Panorama in British Columbia for a day of helicopter skiing high in the Purcell Mountains. Banff is also headquarters for the world's largest heli-skiing operation, **Canadian Mountain Holidays** (403/762-7100 or 800/661-0252, www.cmhski.com), founded by Hans Gmoser. Seven-day packages in British Columbia's interior mountain ranges begin at approximately $5,600 per person.

Cross-Country Skiing

No better way of experiencing the park's winter delights exists than skiing through the landscape on cross-country skis. Many summer hiking trails are groomed for winter travel. The most popular areas are Johnson Lake, Golf Course Road, Spray River, Sundance Canyon, on Lake Louise, Moraine Lake Road, and in Skoki Valley at the back of the Lake Louise Ski Area. The booklet *Cross-country Skiing—Nordic Trails in Banff National Park,* is available for $1 from the Banff and Lake Louise visitor centres. Weather forecasts (403/762-2088) and avalanche hazard reports (403/762-1460) are posted at both centers.

Rental packages are available from **Performance Sports** (208 Bear St., 403/762-8222); Travellers Inn; and **Mountain Magic Equipment** (224 Bear St., 403/762-2591). Expect to pay $12–20 per day. **White Mountain Adventures,** 403/678-4099, offers lessons for $50 per person.

Ice-Skating

Rinks are located at **Banff High School** on Banff Avenue at Wolf Street; on the **Bow River** along Bow Street; and on the golf course side of the

Banff Springs Hotel. The latter rink is lit after dark, and a raging fire is built beside it—the perfect place to enjoy a hot chocolate. Rent skates from **The Ski Stop** (in the Banff Springs Hotel, 403/762-5333) for $5 per hour.

Other Winter Activities

Without the tourists, dogsledding probably wouldn't take place in the park, but there are tourists and there is dogsledding. **Mountain Mushers,** 403/762-3647, offers half-hour ($75), one-hour ($130), and half-day ($275) tours (rates are for two people) around the Banff Springs Golf Course.

Located beside the Banff Springs Hotel ice-skating rink is an unofficial toboggan run; ask at your hotel for sleds or rent them from **The Ski Stop** in the Banff Springs Hotel for $4 per hour.

Banff Fishing Unlimited, 403/762-4936, offers ice-fishing trips on nearby lakes.

Anyone interested in ice climbing must register at the national park desk in the Banff Visitor Centre or call 403/762-1550. The world-famous (if you're an ice climber) **Terminator** is located just outside the park boundary. Curling bonspiels take place at the Banff Recreation Centre on Mt. Norquay Road.

If none of these activities appeals to you, head to **Upper Hot Springs** for a relaxing soak; open Mon.–Fri. noon–9 P.M., Sat.–Sun. 10 A.M.–11 P.M. ($7). Camping might not be everyone's idea of a winter holiday, but Tunnel Mountain Village II remains open year-round.

NIGHTLIFE

Similar to other resort towns around the world, Banff has more than its fair share of bars and nightclubs. **Wild Bill's Legendary Saloon** (upstairs at 201 Banff Ave., 403/762-0333) is named for Banff guide Bill Peyto and is truly legendary. The music is mostly country, but bands usually play a bit of everything. The food here is excellent. Just as popular is the **Barbary Coast** (119 Banff Ave., 403/762-4616), which also serves good food and has live music in a clean, casual atmosphere. Across the road from Wild Bill's is the **Rose and Crown** (202 Banff Ave., 403/762-2121), an English-style pub serving British beers

and typical pub meals. It also features a rooftop patio. Two newer British-style pubs are the **Pump and Tap Tavern,** in the lower level of the Sundance Mall (215 Banff Ave., 403/760-6610), and **St. James Old Irish Pub** (205 Wolf St., 403/762-9355). Below the Mount Royal Hotel is the **Buffalo Paddock** (138 Banff Ave., 403/762-3331), with pool tables. The lounge in the **Voyager Inn** (555 Banff Ave., 403/762-3301) has drink specials every night. Just past the Voyager Inn is **Bumpers,** with a small bar and pool table upstairs.

One of the more stylish places for a quiet drink is **Outfitters,** in Brewster's Mountain Lodge (208 Caribou St., 403/762-2900), a casual yet elegant lounge that exudes a stylish Western atmosphere. The lounge at the **Buffalo Mountain Lodge** (Tunnel Mountain Rd., 403/762-2400) has a similar atmosphere.

Banff's newest night spot is the cavernous **Aurora,** downstairs in the Clock Tower Mall (110 Banff Ave., 403/760-5300). Formerly the infamous Silver City, this place has tried to add some class to Banff's clubbing scene (and is respectable early in the evening), but becomes one obnoxiously loud, overpriced, smoky pickup joint after midnight. The other option is **Outabounds** (137 Banff Ave., enter from Caribou St., 403/762-8434). It's open daily 8 P.M.–2 A.M.

Police patrol Banff all night, promptly arresting anyone who even looks like trouble, including anyone drunk or drinking on the streets.

SHOPPING

It may seem a little strange, but city folk from Calgary actually drive into Banff National Park to shop for clothes. This trend reflects the many clothing shops in Banff rather than a lack of choice in one of Canada's largest cities. About the only clothing store that Banff lacks is an army-surplus outlet.

One of the best places to shop for outdoor apparel is **Outdoor Access** at 201 Banff Avenue; downstairs is a factory outlet with big savings. Other recommended stores are **Monod Sports** at 129 Banff Avenue, and **Helly Hansen,** in the back of the mall at 119 Banff Avenue. Pick up your Canadian-made Tilley Hat and other Tilley Endurables from **Piccatilley Square** on the main floor of the Cascade Plaza at 317 Banff Avenue. The **Rude Boys,** on the lower level of the Sundance Mall at 215 Banff Avenue, is, well, rude. Take a look—the T-shirts are hilarious (and, unlike anything else on Banff Avenue, original), but don't expect to find anything for your grandparents here.

Camping equipment and supplies can be found in **Home Hardware** at 208 Bear Street and **The Hudson's Bay Company** at 125 Banff Avenue (downstairs). More specialized needs are catered to at **Mountain Magic Equipment** (224 Bear St., 403/762-2591), which has a large range of top-quality outdoor and survival gear including climbing equipment and rents tents ($17 per day), sleeping bags ($10), backpacks ($8), and boots ($7.50).

Gifts and Galleries

Banff has a great selection of galleries displaying the work of mostly Canadian artists. **Canada House** (201 Bear St., 403/762-3757) features Canadian landscape and wildlife works and native art. The **Quest Gallery** (105 Banff Ave., 403/762-2722) offers a diverse range of affordable Canadian paintings and crafts as well as more exotic pieces such as mammoth tusks from prehistoric times and Inuit carvings from Nunavut. Across the Bow River from downtown, browse through traditional native arts and crafts at the **Buffalo Nations Luxton Museum Shop** (1 Birch Ave., 403/762-2388).

FESTIVALS AND EVENTS

Spring

Most of the major spring events take place at local ski areas, including a variety of snowboard competitions that make for great spectator viewing. At Lake Louise, a half pipe and jump are constructed right in front of the day lodge for this specific purpose. One long-running spring event is the **Slush Cup,** which takes place at Sunshine Village in late May. Events include kamikaze skiers who attempt to jump an ice-cold pit of water. Although keen skiers are found at higher elevations, swooshing down the slopes of some of North America's latest-closing resorts, late spring sees the Banff Springs golf course open for the season.

The **Jasper to Banff Relay** footrace, attracting 120 teams along the 300-kilometer route, is held on the weekend falling closest to June 1. Call 780/497-4680 for entry details.   During the second week of June, the **Banff Television Festival** attracts the world's best television directors, producers, writers, and even actors for meetings, workshops, and awards, with many show screenings open to the public. For information, call 403/678-9260.

Summer

Summer is a time of hiking and camping, so festivals are few and far between. The main event is the **Banff Arts Festival,** a summer-long extravaganza presented by professional artists studying at the Banff Centre. They perform dance, drama, opera, and jazz for the public at locations around town. Look for details in the *Crag and Canyon* or call 403/762-6300 or 800/413-8368.

On July 1, Banff celebrates **Canada Day** with a parade, fireworks, and events for the whole family in Central Park.

Each summer, the national park staff presents an extensive **Park Interpretive Program** at locations in town and throughout the park, including downstairs in the visitors center daily at 8:30 P.M. All programs are free and include guided hikes, nature tours, slideshows, campfire talks, and lectures. For details, consult *The Mountain Guide* available at the Banff Visitor Centre, 403/762-1550, or look for postings on campground bulletin boards.

Fall

Fall is the park's quietest season but busiest in terms of festivals and events. First of the fall events, on the last Saturday in September, **Melissa's Mini-marathon** attracts more than 2,000 runners in 3-, 10-, and 22-kilometer races. The following weekend is **Taste of Banff/Lake Louise,** when visitors can take advantage of the park's varied dining opportunities by "testing" samples of cuisine from local restaurants. In the same vein is a **wine and food festival** hosted by the Banff Springs Hotel at the end of October. To encourage tourism during the quietest time of the year, **Winterstart** features cheap lodging and many fun events. This festival coincides with the opening of local ski hills.

Banff Mountain Film Festival

One of the year's biggest events is the Banff Mountain Film Festival, held on the first weekend of November. Mountain-adventure filmmakers from around the world submit films to be judged by a select committee. Films are then shown throughout the weekend to an enthusiastic crowd of thousands. Exhibits and seminars are also presented, and top climbers and mountaineers from around the world are invited as guest speakers.

Tickets go on sale one year in advance and sell out in advance. Tickets for daytime shows start at $40 (for up to 10 films). Night shows are from $25, and all-weekend passes cost approximately $120 (weekend passes with two nights' accommodations and breakfasts start at a reasonable $250). Films are shown in the two theaters of the Banff Centre. For more information, call the Banff Centre for Mountain Culture, 403/762-6675; for tickets, call the Banff Centre box office, 403/762-6301 or 800/413-8368. Tickets can also be purchased online at www.banffcentre.ab.ca/cmc. If you miss the actual festival, it hits the road on the Best of the Festival World Tour. Look for it in your town, or check out the website for venues and dates.

Starting in the days leading up to the film festival, then running in conjunction with it, is the **Banff Mountain Book Festival,** which showcases the work of publishers, writers, and photographers whose work revolves around the world's great mountain ranges. Tickets can be bought to individual events ($15–30), as well as a Book Festival Pass and a pass combining both festivals.

Winter

By mid-December, all local ski areas are operating. **Santa Claus** makes an appearance on Banff Avenue at noon on the last Saturday in November; if you miss him there, he usually goes skiing at each of the local resorts on Christmas Day. Events at the resorts continue throughout the long ski season, among them **World Cup Downhill** skiing. **First Night** is an alcohol-free New Year's celebration held downtown. The **Banff/Lake Louise Winter Festival** is a 10-day celebration held at the end of January that has been a part of Banff's history for more than 75 years. Look for ice sculpting, the

Lake Louise Loppet, barn dancing, and the Town Party, which takes place in the Banff Springs Hotel. The long-running **Lake Louise Loppet,** a Nordic-skiing competition, comprises races run at 10-kilometer and 20-kilometer distances, with prizes in 29 age categories. For details, call the Calgary Ski Club at 403/245-9496.

HOTEL AND MOTEL ACCOMMODATIONS

Finding a room in Banff in summer is nearly as hard as trying to justify its price. By late afternoon, just about every room and campsite in town is occupied, and basic hotel rooms begin at approximately $100. Fortunately, many alternatives are available. Rooms in private homes begin at approximately $50 single, $60 double. Canmore, just outside the park boundary, has many hotels and motels. Banff International Hostel has dormitory-style accommodations from $19 per night. Bungalows or cabins can be rented, which can be cost-effective for families or small groups. And approximately 1,000 campsites close to town accommodate campers. Wherever you decide to stay, it is vital to book well ahead during summer and the Christmas holidays. The park's off-season is from October–May, and hotels offer huge rate reductions during this period. Shop around and you'll find many bargains.

Banff Central Reservations (403/705-4020 or 877/542-2633, www.banffreservations.com) represents most hotels in the park and can make reservations for you.

All rates quoted as follows are for a standard room in the high season (June–Sept.).

Less than $50

The only beds in town less than $50 are at the Banff International Hostel (see **Other Accommodations**) and at the **Y Mountain Lodge** (102 Spray Ave., 403/762-3560 or 800/813-4138, www.ywcabanff.ab.ca). Along with a recent name change, this accommodation has undergone massive renovations, and although still a part of the YWCA organization, it is an excellent choice for budget travelers. Facilities include a casual restaurant open throughout the day, a laundry facility, and the Great Room, a huge living area where the centerpiece is a massive stone fireplace with writing desks and shelves stocked with books scattered throughout. A bed in the dormitory is $21 per person, a private room that shares bathroom facilities is $55 single or double, and an ensuite is $72–79 single or double. These rates are reduced outside of summer.

$50–100
Banff's only motel rooms less than $100 are at the **Spruce Grove Motel** (545 Banff Ave., 403/762-2112), the last park-at-your-door–style motel left in town. This orange, green, and white dinosaur from the past offers basic rooms for $75; kitchenettes are $95 but are larger and sleep four (you can get rooms for $55 in the off-season).

$100–150
The **Elkhorn Lodge** (124 Spray Ave., 403/762-2299) is halfway up the hill to the Banff Springs Hotel. The small sleeping rooms are $100, whereas larger rooms with kitchens are $155.

Most Banff Avenue accommodations fall in the next higher price bracket, but for less than $150, a few choices are available within walking distance of downtown. The best value is **Rundle Manor**, six blocks along the motel strip from downtown (348 Marten St., 403/762-5544 or 800/661-1272), offering one-bedroom suites for $135, two-bedroom suites for $205, each with a full kitchen.

Near the far end of the motel strip, the **Banff Voyager Inn** (555 Banff Ave., 403/762-3301 or 800/879-1991) has an outdoor swimming pool, a restaurant, a bar renowned for the cheapest beer in town, and a liquor store; $120 single or double. One block farther from town, **Bumper's Inn** (603 Banff Ave., 403/762-3386 or 800/661-3518) is best known for its steakhouse, but behind the restaurant are 39 older-style rooms for $135 single or double. Closer to downtown are the **Red Carpet Inn** (425 Banff Ave., 403/762-4184 or 800/563-4609), which offers rooms for $120 single, $140 double; **Irwin's Mountain Inn** (next door at 429 Banff Ave., 403/762-4566 or 800/661-1721, www.irwinsmountaininn.com), $140 single or double; and the **Homestead Inn** (217 Lynx St., 403/762-4471 or 800/661-1021), a fairly basic hostelry charging $145 single or double.

If you have your own transportation, consider **Norquay's Timberline Inn,** away from downtown on the north side of the TransCanada Highway (403/762-2281 or 877/762-2281, www.bannfftimberline.com). Standard rooms are $133–153; those on the second floor have private balconies, and those on the south-facing side have excellent views. Out in back are chalets that sleep six to eight in three bedrooms. Each chalet has a kitchen and fireplace; $280 per night.

$150–200
Across the road from the river and two blocks from Banff Avenue is the **Bow View Motor Lodge** (228 Bow Ave., 403/762-2261 or 800/661-1565, www.bowview.com); rooms are $150 or, with a view of the river, $175.

Along Banff Avenue are many choices in this price range. At the **Dynasty Inn** (501 Banff Ave., 403/762-8844 or 800/667-1464), each of the 99 rooms has a log-trimmed balcony, and the facade is Rundlestone (quarried locally and named for Mt. Rundle). Rooms are $155 single or double. Also a good value is the **Rundlestone Lodge** (537 Banff Ave., 403/762-2201 or 800/661-8630, www.rundlestone.com), which features an indoor pool, a whirlpool, and a sauna, and many of the elegantly furnished rooms have balconies, fireplaces, and kitchenettes. Rooms begin at $170; some are wheelchair accessible. Toward downtown is the **High Country Inn** (419 Banff Ave., 403/762-2236 or 800/661-1244, www.banffhighcountryinn.com), which has an indoor pool, hot tubs, and a popular Swiss/Italian restaurant and pool, $150 per room; and **Charlton's Cedar Court** (513 Banff Ave., 403/762-4485 or 800/661-1225, www.charltonresorts.com), where standard rooms are $180 single or double, loft suites with a fireplace $205. **Banff Traveller's Inn** (401 Banff Ave., 403/762-4401 or 800/661-0227, www.banfftravellersinn.com) has larger rooms, many with mountain views; $180 single or double. After undergoing a massive renovation program, the **Banff Ptarmigan Inn** (337 Banff Ave., 403/762-2207 or 800/661-8310) has reopened as a full-service hotel with tastefully decorated rooms, down comforters on all beds, a restaurant, and a variety of facilities to soothe sore muscles, including a spa, a whirlpool, and a sauna. Rooms start at $178 single, $193 double. Within easy walking distance of downtown is the **Banff Caribou Lodge** (521 Banff Ave., 403/762-5887 or 800/563-8764, www.banffcaribouproperties.com); $180 single, $195 double. The impressive log entrance is not easily missed. The **Best Western Siding 29 Lodge** (453 Marten St., 403/762-5575 or 800/528-1234, www.siding29.com) is a good value for small groups; rooms are $195 for up to four people.

In the heart of downtown Banff, the venerable **Mount Royal Hotel** (138 Banff Ave., 403/762-3331 or 800/267-3035, www.mountroyalhotel.com) first opened in 1908. Since its purchase by the Brewster Transport Company in 1912, this distinctive red-brick building has seen various expansions and a disastrous fire in 1967, which destroyed the original wing. Today, guests are offered 136 tastefully decorated rooms and the use of a large health club with a newly renovated hot tub. Also on the premises are a restaurant and a small lounge. Rates are from $195 single or double.

The following three accommodations are located on Tunnel Mountain. Although falling in the same price range as many of those on Banff Avenue, all have self-contained units, making them good for families, small groups, or those who want to cook their own meals. Town is a 15-minute walk away. The **Douglas Fir Resort** (403/762-5591 or 800/661-9267, www.douglasfir.com) has 133 large condo-style rooms. Each has a fully equipped kitchen and a lounge with a fireplace. Facilities include an indoor pool, two water slides, a hot tub, a weight room, squash and tennis courts, a grocery store, and a laundromat. Rates begin at $195 single or double. Across the road is **Tunnel Mountain Chalets** (403/762-4515 or 800/661-1859, www.tunnelmountain.com). Each modern unit is fully self-contained; one-bedroom units go for $195, two-bedrooms $235. **Hidden Ridge Chalets** (403/762-3544 or 800/661-1372, www.banffhiddenridge.com) is just that—hidden—with 83 self-contained cabins spread among stands of Douglas fir and spruce, behind Tunnel Mountain Chalets. Rates start at $195 per night.

$200–250

More than 100 years since Jim and Bill Brewster guided their first guests through the park, their descendants are still actively involved in the tourist industry, having opened Banff's most central and stylish accommodations in 1996. **Brewster's Mountain Lodge** (208 Caribou St., 403/762-2900 or 888/762-2900, www.brewsteradventures.com) features an eye-catching log exterior with an equally impressive lobby and adjoining lounge in a prime downtown location. The Western theme is continued in the 71 upstairs rooms. Superior rooms feature two queen-size beds or one king-size bed ($200), deluxe rooms offer a private balcony ($220), and suites have private hot tubs ($290–400). All rates include breakfast. Rates here in the off-season are slashed up to 50 percent.

The **Banff International Hotel,** close to downtown (333 Banff Ave., 403/762-5666 or 800/665-5666, www.banffinternational.com), is a full-service hotel that underwent extensive renovations inside and out in 1999. Guests enjoy extensive in-room facilities, as well as a comfortable lounge area, a fitness room, and dining choices; $209–259 single or double. One of Banff's larger hotels, but only a 10-minute walk into town, is **Inns of Banff** (600 Banff Ave., 403/762-4581 or 800/661-1272, www.innsofbanff.com), which offers a wide range of guest facilities; $210–285 single or double.

The first thing you'll notice at **Buffalo Mountain Lodge,** which is a 15-minute walk from town (Tunnel Mountain Rd., 403/762-2400 or 800/661-1367, www.crmr.com/bml.com), is the impressive log entrance. The rooms, chalets, and bungalows all have fireplaces, and many have kitchens. Rooms start at $225. The lodge takes its name from Tunnel Mountain, which early park visitors called Buffalo Mountain, for its shape.

Also away from the main strip of accommodations is the **Banff Rocky Mountain Resort,** located at the northeast end of Banff Avenue on the corner of Tunnel Mountain Road (403/762-5531 or 800/661-9563, www.rockymountainresort.com), an ideal alternative for groups or families. Many units have kitchens, and guest facilities include a restaurant, a pool, an exercise room, and tennis courts. Rates range $225–300 single or double. A free shuttle runs into town from the resort each hour.

Located just two blocks from the heart of downtown Banff, the **Banff Park Lodge** (222 Lynx St., 403/762-4433 or 800/661-9266, www.banffparklodge.com) is a modern, full-service luxury hotel with more than 200 rooms. Rooms begin at $240, suites with bedside hot tubs are $285.

More than $250

Banff's newest hotel is **Charlton's Royal Canadian Lodge** (459 Banff Ave., 403/762-3307 or 800/661-1379, www.charltonresorts.com), which opened in the summer of 2000. It features 99 luxuriously appointed rooms, heated underground parking, a lounge and a restaurant, a large spa-pool complex, and a landscaped courtyard. Rates start at $290 single or double.

On Mountain Avenue a short walk from the Upper Hot Springs is the **Rimrock Resort Hotel** (403/762-3356 or 800/661-1587, www.rimrockresort.com). The original hotel was constructed in 1903 but was fully rebuilt and opened as a 346-room full-service luxury resort in the mid-1990s. Each well-appointed room has a king-size bed, a comfortable armchair, a writing desk, a mini-bar, and a hair dryer. This hotel caters to disabled persons as well as any in the park. Because it's set high above the Bow Valley, views for the most part are excellent. Prices range from $265–$345 depending solely on the views. Regular shuttle buses make the short run to town during summer.

Banff Springs Hotel

This famous landmark, one of the world's great mountain resort hotels, has been undergoing massive renovations in recent years, cementing its position as Banff's premier accommodation. More than $30,000 has been spent installing air-conditioning, updating furnishings, and replacing beds in each of the 840 rooms. Other major changes include moving the lobby to a more accessible side of the hotel, reopening the old lobby as a cavernous lounge area, and changing many of the in-house dining facilities. Throughout the massive changes, the hotel came under the ownership of Fairmont Hotels and Resorts, losing its century-old tag as a Canadian Pacific hotel and, in the process, its ties to the historic railway company that constructed the original hotel back in 1888.

Even though the rooms have been modernized, many date to the 1920s, and as is common in older establishments, these rooms are small. But room size is only a small consideration when staying in this historic gem. With 16 eateries, a luxurious spa facility, a huge indoor pool, an elegant library, a 27-hole golf course, tennis courts, horseback riding, and enough twisting, turning hallways, boardwalks, towers, and shops to warrant a detailed map, you won't want to spend much time in the room. Unless, of course, you're in the presidential suite, which is located in the central tower and has eight rooms, a canopy bed, a hot tub, a baby grand piano, a private pool, and a glass elevator linking each of the three floors.

Banff Springs Hotel

In the process of changing ownership and undergoing the renovations, the manner in which rooms are charged has also changed. Staying at the Banff Springs is now *very* expensive through summer because rooms are charged as part of a package. Guests have the choice of two packages, the **Castle Experience** and the **Canadian Rockies Experience.** The Castle Experience is the least expensive of the two and includes golfing and golf lessons, horseback riding, guided hiking and climbing, tennis, mountain bike rental, canoeing, unlimited entry to the Solace and one spa treatment, and three meals daily in any of the hotel restaurants. This package taken in a Canadian Pacific room costs $979 double, but these rooms are fairly small, and for an extra $100 you can stay in a much larger Heritage room. The Canadian Rockies Experience includes all that the Castle Experience does, as well as guided fishing, white-water rafting, and all Brewster tours. This package starts at $1,079 double with accommodations in the smallest rooms. (Although you may not want to take full advantage of all the activities offered, if you do, for example, a golf lesson followed by a round on the hotel's course, an afternoon horseback ride, and an evening at the Solace while also dining in the hotel, the actual room works out to about $300 for the night. Between October and May, rooms are sold on a bed-and-breakfast basis and cost from $190 single, $210 double.

The hotel is located at the end of Spray Avenue. For reservations, call 403/762-2211 or 800/441-1414, or click on the relevant link at www.fairmont.com.

OTHER ACCOMMODATIONS

Lodges Along the Bow Valley Parkway

The Bow Valley Parkway is the original route between Banff and Lake Louise. It is a beautiful drive in all seasons, and along its length are three lodges, each a viable alternative to staying in Banff.

The **Johnston Canyon Resort** (403/762-2971 or 888/378-1720, www.johnstoncanyon.com) is located 26 kilometers west of Banff at the beginning of a short trail that leads to the famous canyon. The rustic cabins are older, and some have kitchenettes. On the grounds are tennis courts, a barbecue area, and an excellent new restaurant. Basic two-person cabins are $109, two-person cabins with a fireplace are $149, and they go up in price all the way to $245 for a "Classic" cabin complete with cooking facilities and luxurious Heritage-style furnishings. It's open mid-May to early October.

Six kilometers farther northwest is **Castle Mountain Chalets** (403/762-3868, www.castlemountain.com). A variety of accommodations are available here; small summer cottages with kitchenettes are $58 single or double, $75 with two double beds. Log chalets that sleep four and have kitchenettes and a fireplace are $120. The 22 newly built deluxe log chalets are one of the park's best bargains. They have high ceilings, beautifully handcrafted log interiors, three beds, a stone fireplace, a full kitchen with dishwasher, a bathroom with a hot tub, and satellite TV; $175 for up to four people, $195 for five or six.

Baker Creek Chalets, 403/522-3761, is the next resort along the parkway, 40 kilometers from Banff and 10 kilometers from Lake Louise. Each of the 25 log cabins has a kitchenette, a fireplace, and an outside deck (complete with cute wood-carvings of bears climbing over the railings). Basic one-room cabins are $140 for two; one-bedroom cabins with loft (sleeps six) are $185; two-bedroom cabins (sleeps six) are $240. A new wing has eight luxurious suites, each with a kitchen and a hot tub, for $200 single or double. Each additional person is $15. The restaurant here is highly recommended.

Bed-and-Breakfasts

The Banff/Lake Louise Tourism Bureau in the Banff Visitor Centre (224 Banff Ave., 403/762-8421) has a list of bed-and-breakfasts and private homes that rent rooms or cabins. Standards range from fair to good, but the prices are lower than those of the hotels.

The **Blue Mountain Lodge** (137 Muskrat St., 403/762-5134, www.bluemtnlodge.com) has rooms for $75 and small cabins from $90. All guests have use of shared kitchen facilities. A better value is **Beaver St. Suites and Cabins** (220 Beaver St., 403/762-5077), with rooms beginning at $65 and cabins at $75. Without a doubt, the best bed-and-breakfast in town is **Eleanor's House** (125 Kootenay Ave., 403/760-2457, www.bbeleanor.com), a lovely guesthouse on a quiet residential street. It has a library, and each luxuriously furnished room has a private bathroom. Rates are $135 single, $145 double, which includes a gourmet breakfast and evening cocktails.

Hostels

The **Banff International Hostel,** 403/762-4122, is located just off Tunnel Mountain Road three kilometers from downtown. This large, modern hostel sleeps 154 in small two-, four-, and six-bed dormitory rooms. The large lounge area has a fireplace, and other facilities include a recreation room, a bike and ski workshop, a large kitchen, a self-service café, and a laundry room. Members of Hostelling International pay $20 per night, nonmembers $24. During July and August, reserve space at least one month in advance to be assured of a bed. To get there from town, ride the **Banff Transit** bus ($1), which passes the hostel twice an hour during summer. The rest of the year, the only transportation is by cab, which is approximately $6 from the bus depot. The hostel is open all day, but check-in isn't until 3 P.M.

Thirty-two kilometers along the Bow Valley Parkway is the **Castle Mountain Hostel,** which is near several interesting hikes. This hostel sleeps 36 and has a kitchen, a common room, hot showers, and bike rentals; members $13, nonmembers $17. Make reservations through the Banff Hostel.

Backcountry Huts and Lodges

In the backcountry of the national park are two distinct types of accommodations—rustic mountain huts and lodges. Each of the often historic huts has a stove, a lantern, kitchen utensils, and foam mattresses. The extensive system of huts is managed by the Alpine Club of Canada. For locations and reservations, contact the club at 403/678-3200, www.alpineclubofcanada.ca. No huts are located in the southern end of the park.

Shadow Lake Lodge, 403/762-0116 or 800/691-5085, is 14 kilometers from the nearest road. Access is on foot, or in winter on skis. The lodge is near a picturesque lake of the same name, and many hiking trails are nearby. The oldest structure here has been restored as a dining area. Guests sleep in newer, cozier cabins. All meals and afternoon tea are included in the rate of $170 single, $264 double. The trailhead is along the TransCanada Highway, 19 kilometers from Banff, at the Redearth Creek parking area.

CAMPGROUNDS

Although Banff has seven campgrounds with approximately 1,500 sites in its immediate vicinity, all of them fill by early afternoon. Reservations are not taken at any national park campgrounds. Therefore, the best way to ensure a site is to arrive in the morning, when other campers are leaving. When the main campgrounds fill, visitors unable to secure a site are directed to an "overflow" area, which provides few facilities and no hookups but at less cost.

Open fires are permitted in designated areas throughout all campgrounds, but you must purchase a Firewood Permit ($4 per site per night) to burn wood, which is provided at no cost.

Closest to town are **Tunnel Mountain Village II** and **Tunnel Mountain Trailer Court,** 3.5 kilometers along Tunnel Mountain Road. The former has electrical hookups and is the only campground in the park that is open year-round. The latter has full hookups. Both have hot showers but little privacy between sites. Sites are $21–24 and no tents are allowed (except when Tunnel Mountain Village I is closed). Less than one kilometer farther along the road is **Tunnel Mountain Village I,** which has hot showers, private sites, and kitchen shelters, but no hookups. Sites are $17. Toward Lake Minnewanka northeast of town is **Two Jack Lakeside,** which has showers and lots of trees; $17 per night. In the same vicinity is **Two Jack Lake Main;** $13. Along the Bow Valley Parkway, you'll find **Johnston Canyon Campground, Castle Mountain Campground,** and **Protection Mountain Campground.** Generally, these don't open until June, and they fill up later than those in Banff; $13–17 per night.

FOOD

Banff has more than 100 dining establishments. That's more restaurants per capita than any town or city across Canada. From lobster to linguine, alligator to à la carte, and fajitas to fudge—

anyone who spends time in the park will find something that suits his or her taste and budget, although not necessarily at the same place. Many eateries have been around for decades and attract diners from as far away as Calgary (some of whom have been known to stay overnight just to eat at their favorite haunt). An eclectic mix of restaurants lines Banff Avenue, most of which have menus posted out front. The less adventurous can try one of the options at the major hotels. The Banff Springs Hotel tops the list with a choice of 13 restaurants. In July and August, the most popular restaurants don't take reservations, and you can expect to wait at most spots. Various dining guides are available throughout town.

Budget Stretchers

The best place to begin looking for cheap eats is the Food Court in the lower level of Cascade Plaza at 317 Banff Avenue. Here, you'll find two bakeries and **Edo Japan,** which sells simple Japanese dishes for approximately $6, including a drink. A local bylaw prohibiting obtrusive signs and neon lights means that the fast-food chains are easily missed. For the most expensive Big Macs this side of the Toronto Skydome, **McDonald's** is at 116 Banff Avenue. **KFC** is at 202 Caribou Street, and **Harvey's** is at 304 Caribou Street. A good spot for breakfast is **Craig's Way Station** (461 Banff Ave., 403/762-4660).

    Café Alpenglow, in the Banff International Hostel (Tunnel Mountain Rd., 403/762-4122) is open to everyone. It features all the usual café-style dishes, such as a pile of nachos for $7; no entrée is more than $10.

Coffee Shops

The **Cake Company** (220 Bear St., 403/762-2330) serves great coffee, as well as a delicious range of pastries, muffins, and cakes baked daily on the premises. Another Cake Company outlet is on the lower level of Cascade Plaza; a muffin and coffee is $2.50. **Evelyn's,** on Banff Avenue in the Town Centre Mall, has good coffee and huge sandwiches, and is a super place for socializing and people-watching. **Jump Start** (206 Buffalo St., 403/762-0332) has a wide range of coffee concoctions, as well as delicious homemade soups ($5) and sandwiches ($6).

    Bruno's Café & Grill (304 Caribou St.,

403/762-8115)—named for Bruno Engler, renowned photographer, ski instructor, and mountain man—is a cozy little café with a great "mountain" ambience and comfortable couches. It's open daily 7 A.M.–10 P.M.

Canadian

A town favorite that has faithfully served locals for many years is **Melissa's** (218 Lynx St., 403/762-5511), housed in a log building that dates from 1928 (the original Homestead Inn). For breakfast, the hotcakes piled high on your plate ($5.50) can't be beat. Or try the bran muffins made from scratch each morning. Lunch and dinner are casual affairs—choose from a wide variety of generously sized burgers, freshly prepared salads, and mouth-watering Alberta beef. Melissa's also features a small outside patio and a rustic bar with well-priced drinks. Open daily 7 A.M.–10 P.M.

    Even though **Bumper's** (603 Banff Ave., 403/762-2622) is away from the center of Banff, it is one of the town's busiest restaurants. And not just in summer; locals and visitors alike flock to this popular steak house year-round. Large cuts of Alberta beef, efficient service, and great prices keep people coming back. Favorite choices are the prime rib Pile-o-bones, Barbecue Beef Ribs, and, of course, slabs of juicy beef cooked to your taste. Main entrées are $10.50–27 and include a fresh salad bar. Upstairs is the **Loft Lounge,** a good place to wait for a table or relax afterward with an inexpensive drink. It's open 4:30–10 P.M.

    Closer to town in the Banff Caribou Lodge is **The Keg** (521 Banff Ave., 403/762-4442), part of a western Canada chain noted for its consistently good steak, seafood, and chicken dishes at reasonable prices. All entrées include a 60-item salad bar. Open daily 7 A.M.–2 A.M. Another Keg location is downtown (117 Banff Ave., 403/760-3030). The familiar **Earl's** (upstairs at 229 Banff Ave., 403/762-4414) has more of the same at slightly higher prices.

    The **Buffalo Mountain Lodge Restaurant** has a distinctive interior of hand-hewn cedar beams and Old World elegance—the perfect setting for a moderate splurge. Expect to pay approximately $30 per person for soup, an entrée, and a dessert. Breakfast is also good. It's open daily 7 A.M.–11 P.M. Most of Banff's motels have restaurants, all similarly priced. The better ones include **Churchill's** (Mount Royal Hotel, 138 Banff Ave., 403/762-7180); the **Chinook Restaurant**, with a great Sunday brunch (Banff Park Lodge, 222 Lynx St., 403/762-4433); and the **Big Horn Steakhouse** (Norquay's Timberline Inn, Mt. Norquay Rd., 403/762-2285). All feature a menu that combines Canadian and continental cuisine.

One of Banff's only bistro-style restaurants is **Coyote's** (206 Caribou St., 403/762-3963). Meals are prepared in full view of diners, and the menu emphasizes health-conscious, Southwestern-style dishes (lots of chilies); the salmon, broiled chicken, and tempting desserts are favorites. Entrées are $10–19.50. Coyote's is open daily 8 A.M.–10 P.M.

The romantic era of the railway is relived in the **Caboose Steak and Lobster Restaurant,** in the old Canadian Pacific Railway (CPR) station (corner of Elk and Lynx Streets, 403/760-9199). Although not the original station, kings, queens, and millions of other visitors have passed through the building. The walls are lined with railway memorabilia, and the elegant atmosphere creates a memorable dining experience. Seafood and steak dominate the menu; expect to pay $18–35 for entrées and approximately $5 for dessert. All meals include the self-service salad cart that is wheeled to your table. The Caboose is open daily 5–10 P.M.

Mexican and Cajun
The **Magpie & Stump** (203 Caribou St., 403/762-4067) serves no-frills authentic Mexican food at reasonable prices. Lunch is from $5.50, dinner from $9, and a few outside tables catch the afternoon sun. It's open 11 A.M.–midnight.

Italian
Banff is blessed with fine Italian restaurants. **Guido's** (116 Banff Ave., 403/762-4002) is known for its homemade pasta, which is cooked to perfection in a variety of sauces that appeal to all tastes and diets. Entrées are $9.50–19. It's open daily from 5 P.M. More trendy (reflected in the prices) is **Giorgio's** (219 Banff Ave., 403/762-5114), which was fully remodeled in 1994 with stylish décor and a casual Old World atmosphere. Pasta dishes begin at $11. It's open from 4:30 P.M. The **Old Spaghetti Factory** (upstairs in the Cascade Plaza on Banff

Ave., 403/760-2779) is a family favorite, with a casual rustic décor, and a few tables spread along a balcony. The most you'll pay for any meal is $16, which includes soup or salad and dessert.

If you are staying on Tunnel Mountain (or even if you're not), the **Cilantro Mountain Café** (Buffalo Mountain Lodge, 403/762-2400) is well worth trying. The menu is limited to a few Italian-style dishes, but each is well prepared, and the outside deck is perfect for those hot summer nights. The wood-fired oven pizza is a personal favorite.

Greek
The **Balkan** (120 Banff Ave., 403/762-3454) is run by Greeks, but the menu blends their heritage with the cuisines of Italy, China, and Canada. Select from Greek ribs (pork ribs with a lemon sauce) for $15.95, the Greek chow mein (stir-fried vegetables, fried rice, and your choice of meat) for $10.50, or Greek spaghetti for $9.50. But the most popular dishes are souvlaki ($12.95) and an enormous Greek platter that includes a leg of lamb ($39 for two). The Balkan is open daily 11 A.M.–11 P.M.

Swiss-Italian
Once one of Banff's busiest restaurants, **Ticino** has moved from downtown to the High Country Inn (415 Banff Ave., 403/762-3848). It's named for the southern province of Switzerland, where the cuisine has a distinctive Italian influence. The Swiss chef is best known for his beef and cheese fondues, veal dishes, and juicy steaks. Expect to pay approximately $6 for appetizers and from $14 for entrées; open daily 5–11 P.M.

Japanese
The many Japanese visitors in Banff have created the need for good Japanese restaurants. **Shiki Japanese Noodles,** in the back of the Clock Tower Mall (110 Banff Ave., 403/762-0527), has a choice of *donburi,* various meat cakes, teriyaki, and sushi. Dishes are $5–10 each. There are only a few tables, and it's a casual place, popular for lunch (there's a take-out window). It's open daily 11 A.M.–9 P.M. More expensive is **Suginoya** (225 Banff Ave., 403/762-4773), which has a relaxed atmosphere. Choose from the sushi bar, *ozashiki*

booths, or regular tables. Traditional *shabu-shabu* and seafood teriyaki are popular. The many Japanese diners here are indicative of the quality. Expect to pay at least $13 for entrées, $19–25 for one of the combination dinners. Open daily 11 A.M.–10:30 P.M. **Sushi House Banff** (304 Caribou St., 403/762-2971) is a unique little restaurant where diners sit around a moving miniature railway, picking sushi and other delicacies from a train as it circles the chef, who loads the carriages as quickly as they empty. Banff's best Japanese restaurant is the **Samurai,** in the Banff Springs Hotel (see following section).

French

Le Beaujolais (212 Buffalo St., 403/762-2712) is a Canadian leader in French cuisine and has been one of Banff's most popular fine-dining restaurants for more than a decade. Its second-floor location ensures great views of Banff, especially from window tables. The dishes feature mainly Canadian ingredients, prepared and served with a French flair. Entrées begin at $18, but the extent of your final tab depends on whether you choose à la carte items or the four- or six-course table d'hôte menu ($50 and 66, respectively)—and also on how much wine you consume (at $20–250 a bottle). The restaurant is open daily from 6 P.M.; reservations are necessary.

The Grizzly House

This unique fondue restaurant (207 Banff Ave., 403/762-4055) provides Banff's most unusual dining experience. The décor is, to say the least, eclectic (or should that be eccentric?). Each table has a phone for across-the-table conversation, or you can call your waiter, the bar, a cab, diners in the private booth, or even those who spend too long in the bathroom. Through all this playfulness, the food is good and the service professional. Although traditional Swiss fondues are on the menu, the buffalo, seafood, oriental, rattlesnake, and alligator dishes are the most popular. Of course, it wouldn't be right to leave without having a chocolate fondue dipped with fresh fruit. Individual fondues are $18–34 (lunch a little cheaper), and complete three-course dinners start at $40. Open 11:30 A.M.–midnight.

Baker Creek Bistro

Along the Bow Valley Parkway, toward Lake Louise, are the Baker Creek Chalets. The intimate restaurant here, 403/522-2182, housed in a log building, is definitely worth the drive from Banff. Next to the restaurant is a rustic lounge and a large outdoor patio. The bistro is open in summer daily 7 A.M.–10 P.M., shorter hours the rest of the year.

Banff Springs Hotel

Whether staying there as guests or not, most visitors to Banff drop by to see one of the town's biggest tourist attractions. And a meal here might not be as expensive as you think. The hotel has more eateries than most small towns—from a deli serving pizza to the finest of fine dining in the Banffshire Club.

If you are in the mood for a light snack or sandwiches to go, head downstairs to the Arcade Level and the **Delicatessen**, which is open 24 hours daily. Named for the adjacent spa facility, **Solace Lite** has a corresponding menu of health-conscious salads and light meals. This café-style eatery also offers stunning mountain views. In the same vicinity of the hotel, the **Bow Valley Terrace** features outdoor summer lunch dining between 11:30 A.M. and 6 P.M.

The **Bow Valley Grill,** with seating for 275, is the hotel's largest dining room. Each morning, a large buffet of hot and cold delicacies, including freshly baked bread and seasonal fruits, is laid out for the masses. Lunch is served from 11:30 A.M.–5:30 P.M., with a wide-ranging menu featuring everything from salads to seafood. Throughout the busiest months of summer, a buffet lunch is offered from 11:30 A.M.–1:30 P.M., with a free Historical Hotel Tour included in the rate of $19.95 per person. The hotel's Sunday brunch, served in the Bow Valley Grill, is legendary, with chefs working at numerous stations scattered around the dining area, and an enormous spread not equaled for variety anywhere in the mountains. Dinner is served nightly until 10 P.M., with entrées running $15–26.50. Reservations are required for Sunday brunch (as far in advance as possible) and dinner.

Throughout the recent hotel renovations, the **Alhambra Room** retained its Old World atmosphere and reputation as an elegant yet casual dining choice. The à la carte dinner menu features a wide variety of beef and seafood dishes. In July and August, this restaurant features Van Horne's Grand Buffet, with chef-attended dining stations offering dishes prepared to order from around the world. Open nightly for dinner, **Castello Ristorante** serves pasta at good prices as well as a wide range of other Italian specialties and a mouthwatering antipasto bar. The **Samurai Restaurant** is the most expensive of Banff's many Japanese restaurants but is also the most traditional (and busiest); open for dinner only.

Two restaurants lie within the grounds surrounding the hotel, and both are worthy of consideration. Originally the golf course clubhouse, the **Waldhaus Restaurant** is nestled in a forested area of lodgepole pine directly below the hotel. Open daily 6–10 P.M., it features German specialties, with entrées from $17. Below this restaurant is a pub of the same name, with a pub-style dinner menu offered in a casual atmosphere. The **Clubhouse Dining Room** is a seasonal restaurant on the golf course proper that serves light breakfasts, casual lunches, and more formal dinners. A shuttle bus runs every 30 minutes between the main lobby and the clubhouse.

The **Rundle Lounge** is a long, narrow piano bar, where most tables offer views down the Bow Valley. It's open 11 A.M.–midnight, with an à la carte menu offered. Smoke-free **Grapes** is an intimate yet casual wine bar noted for its fine cheeses and pâtés. More substantial meals, such as fondues, are also offered. It's open for lunch and dinner.

The hotel's most acclaimed restaurant is the **Banffshire Club,** which seats just 76 diners and requires men to wear a jacket. Like its predecessor, the Rob Roy Room, this fine-dining restaurant has quickly become renowned for its excellently prepared Alberta beef. (Try the beef strip loin for two, broiled to order then carved at your table.) Many lighter dishes, such as chicken and seafood ($18–34), are also offered. It's open daily 6–10 P.M.

For all Banff Springs Hotel dining reservations, call 403/662-6860, or after 5 P.M., call 403/762-2211. During the summer months, a desk in the main lobby has all menus posted and takes reservations.

TRANSPORTATION

Getting There

Banff has no airport and no scheduled rail service. The closest airport is 1.5 hours away in Calgary. **Brewster,** 403/762-6767, operates an airporter service that leaves Calgary International Airport four times daily; $36 each way. This service terminates in Banff at the large **Brewster Tour and Transportation Centre** at 100 Gopher Street. The depot has a ticket office, lockers, a café, and a gift shop. It is open daily 7:30 A.M.–10:45 P.M. Other airporter buses are **Banff Airporter,** 403/762-3330 or 888/449-2901; **Laidlaw,** 403/762-9102 or 800/661-4946; and **Skyshuttle,** 403/762-1010 or 888/220-7433. All charge $36 one-way to Banff.

Brewster is the only company with a bus service between Banff and Jasper. From Jasper, Brewster offers an express service to Banff ($51), departing the railway station on Connaught Drive mid-April to mid-October daily at 1:30 P.M. A longer alternative is the nine-hour Jasper-to-Banff tour, which stops at the Columbia Icefield and Lake Louise; $89 one-way, $124 round-trip. In spring and fall, the fare is $67 one-way, $89 round-trip. No bus service runs between Banff and Jasper in winter.

Greyhound, 403/762-1092 or 800/661-8747, offers scheduled service from the Calgary bus depot at 877 Greyhound Way SW five times daily to the Brewster Banff Terminal. Greyhound buses also leave Vancouver from the depot at 1150 Station Street, three times daily for the scenic 14-hour ride to Banff.

Getting Around

Most of the sights and many trailheads are within walking distance of town. **Banff Transit,** 403/760-8294, runs along two routes: one from the Banff Springs Hotel to the RV and trailer drop-off at the far end of Banff Avenue, and the other from the Luxton Museum to the hostel and Tunnel Mountain Campgrounds. Mid-May to September, buses run twice an hour between 7 A.M. and midnight. From October to December, the two routes are merged as one, with buses running hourly midday to midnight. No local buses run the rest of the year. Travel costs $1 per sector.

THE BREWSTER BOYS

Few guides in Banff were as well known as Jim and Bill (pictured) Brewster. In 1892, aged 10 and 12, respectively, they were hired by the Banff Springs Hotel to take guests to local landmarks. As their reputation as guides grew, they built a thriving business. By 1900, they had their own livery and outfitting company, and soon expanded operations to Lake Louise. Other early business interests included a trading post, the original Mt. Royal Hotel, the first ski lodge in the Sunshine Meadows, and the hotel at the Columbia Icefield.

Today, a legacy of the boys' savvy, **Brewster,** a transportation and tour company, has grown to become an integral part of many tourists' stays. The company operates some of the world's most advanced sightseeing vehicles, including a fleet of Snocoaches on Athabasca Glacier.

WHYTE MUSEUM OF THE CANADIAN ROCKIES

Cabs around town are reasonably priced—flag drop is $2.75, then it's $1.50 per kilometer. From the bus depot to the farthest hotel, the Banff Springs, runs approximately $6. Companies are **Banff Taxi,** 403/762-4444; **Taxi Taxi,** 403/762-3111; and **Mountain Taxi,** 403/762-3351.

The days when a row of horse-drawn buggies eagerly awaited the arrival of wealthy visitors at the CPR station have long since passed, but the era is relived by the **Trail Rider Store** (132 Banff Ave., 403/762-4551), offering visitors rides around town in a beautifully restored carriage ($9 per person for 15 minutes). Expect to pay approximately $38 per carriage between downtown and the Banff Springs Hotel.

As you'd expect, rental cars in the park aren't cheap. The other catch is that none offer unlimited mileage. The most you'll get is 150 kilometers free, and then expect to pay 20–25 cents per kilometer. **Banff Rent-a-Car** (230 Lynx St., 403/762-3352) rents used cars for $50 per day with 150 free kilometers. Other agencies are **Avis,** 403/762-3222 or 800/879-2847; **Budget,** 403/762-4565 or 800/268-8900; **Hertz,** 403/762-2027 or 800/263-0600; and **National,** 403/762-2688 or 800/227-7368. Reservations for cars in Banff should be made well in advance.

Persons with Disabilities

The **Banff Visitor Centre** is wheelchair accessible; its washrooms, information desks, and theater are all barrier free. Once inside, use the handy Touchsource monitor for a full listing of all barrier-free services within the park. An all-terrain wheelchair is available at the Cave and Basin National Historic Site for use on park trails. To reserve it, call 403/762-1566.

Tours

Brewster, 403/762-6767, offers a three-hour Discover Banff bus tour that takes in downtown Banff, Tunnel Mountain Drive, the hoodoos, the Cave and Basin, and Sulphur Mountain Gondola (gondola fare not included). This tour runs in summer only and departs from the bus depot daily at 8:30 A.M.; call for hotel pickup times. Adult fare is $44, children half-price. Brewster also has a four-hour tour departing select Banff hotels daily 1:15–1:40 P.M. to Lake Louise; $40 one-way, $49 round-trip. In winter, this tour departs in the morning, runs five hours, and includes Banff sights; $38 one-way, $44 round-trip. During summer, other tours available are Upper Hot Springs ($20; includes pool admission), Sulphur Mountain Gondola ($25; includes gondola ride), Lake Minnewanka ($41; includes two-hour boat cruise), and Columbia Icefield ($89). From Calgary, Brewster has nine-hour tours out to Banff ($88) and Lake Louise ($92).

SERVICES

The **post office** is on the corner of Buffalo and Bear streets opposite Central Park; open Mon.–Fri. 9 A.M.–5:30 P.M. The general-delivery service here is probably among the busiest in the country, with the thousands of seasonal workers in the area, no home mail-delivery service, and a two-year wait for a P.O. box. Address all mail to General Delivery, Banff, Alberta T0L 0C0. For all other postal services, try the small and friendly full-service postal outlet in **Cascade Plaza Drug,** located in the Cascade Plaza at 317 Banff Avenue. **Mail Boxes Etc.** (226 Bear St.) is a privately run postal outlet and can send and receive faxes. Public Internet access is free at the library, but advance bookings are needed. For instant access, head to **Cyber-web,** downstairs in the Sundance Mall (215 Banff Ave., 403/762-9226).

Major banks can be found along Banff Avenue and are generally open 9 A.M.–4 P.M. The **Bank of Montreal** (107 Banff Ave.) allows cash advances with MasterCard, and the **C.I.B.C.** (98 Banff Ave.) accepts Visa.

Freya's Currency Exchange is in the Clock Tower Mall at 108 Banff Avenue and has offices in the Cascade Plaza and Banff Springs Hotel.

Downtown laundromats are **Johnny O's,** 223 Bear Street, open Mon.–Sat. 8 A.M.–11 P.M., Sunday 10 A.M.–10 P.M.; and **Cascade Coin Laundry,** on the lower level of the Cascade Plaza, open daily 7:30 A.M.–10 P.M. Located on Tunnel Mountain Road at the Douglas Fir Resort, and within walking distance of the hostel, is **Chalet Coin Laundry;** open daily 8 A.M.–10 P.M. Along Banff Avenue is a handful of one-

hour film labs; check around for the cheapest price because many of them have special offers. The most competitive and reliable is **Miles High Image Center** (119 Banff Ave., beneath the Barbary Coast, 403/762-5221). Drop slide film here on Wednesday and it will be ready for pickup Friday morning. Get photographic supplies from **Wolf Street Cameras** at 203 Bear Street.

Mineral Springs Hospital is at 301 Lynx Street, 403/762-2222. **Cascade Plaza Drug,** on the lower level of the Cascade Plaza at 317 Banff Avenue, is open until 9 P.M., as is **Harmony Drug** at 111 Banff Avenue. (Harmony Drug was once owned by noted Banff photographer Byron Harmon, whose prints, circa 1915, adorn the walls and adjacent mall.) **Gourlay's Pharmacy** at 229 Bear Street is open until 8 P.M. For the **RCMP,** call 403/762-2226.

INFORMATION

Banff Public Library

Banff's library is located opposite Central Park (101 Bear St., 403/762-2661). The extensive collection of nonfiction books, many about the park and its environs, makes it an excellent rainy-day hangout. It also has a large collection of magazines and newspapers. Internet access is free, but book ahead. Hours are Mon.–Thurs. 10 A.M.–8 P.M., Friday 10 A.M.–6 P.M., Saturday 11 A.M.–6 P.M., and Sunday 1–5 P.M.

Books and Bookstores

The Canadian Rockies are one of the most written about, and definitely the most photographed, regions in Canada. As a walk along Banff Avenue will confirm, there is definitely no lack of postcards, calendars, and books on the subject. For general reading, the guides and coffee-table books produced by **Altitude Publishing** in Canmore are the best. Look for them in all Banff bookstores. Ben Gadd's *Handbook of the Canadian Rockies* is the best all-around source of information for those interested in the geology, climate, ecology, flora, and fauna of the Canadian Rockies.

Banff Book & Art Den (94 Banff Ave., 403/762-3919) stocks a large collection of park literature, wilderness guides, coffee-table books, travel guides, and relevant topographical maps for backcountry trips within the park. Open in summer daily 10 A.M.–9 P.M., until 7 P.M. the rest of the year. Another bookstore is **Cascade Mountain Books,** downstairs in the Cascade Plaza, 403/762-8508.

Look for the *Crag and Canyon* each Wednesday. It's been keeping residents and visitors informed about park issues and town gossip for more than 90 years.

Banff Visitor Centre

This large complex, at 224 Banff Avenue, houses information desks for **Parks Canada** and the **Banff/Lake Louise Tourism Bureau.** The national park staff will answer all of your questions regarding Banff's natural wonders and advise of trail closures. Anyone planning an overnight backcountry trip should register here and obtain a permit ($6 per person per night). The brochure *Banff and Vicinity Drives and Walks* is a compact guide to things to see and do around Banff. At the back of the center is a free slideshow, videos, updated trail reports, and copies of the best hiking books. Across the floor is the tourism bureau, 403/762-8421, which represents businesses and commercial establishments in the park. Here you can find out about accommodations and restaurants and have any other questions answered. To answer the most-often-asked question, the washrooms are downstairs. The center is open July–Aug. daily 8 A.M.–8 P.M., June and September daily 8 A.M.–6 P.M., the rest of the year daily 9 A.M.–5 P.M. For more information on the park, contact The Superintendent, Banff National Park, P.O. Box 900, Banff, Alberta T0L 0C0, 403/762-1550, www.parkscanada.gc.ca/banff. The **Warden Office** is located in the industrial park, 403/762-1470 or 403/762-4506. For general tourism information, try Banff/Lake Louise Tourism Bureau, P.O. Box 1298, Banff, Alberta T0L 0C0, www.banfflakelouise.com.

Call the **weather office** at 403/762-2088 for updated forecasts. A full weather synopsis is available by calling 403/762-3091. Tune into Channel 10 on the television for park information.

LAKE LOUISE

As the first flush of morning sun hits Victoria Glacier, and the impossibly steep northern face of Mt. Victoria is reflected in the sparkling emerald-green waters of Lake Louise, you'll understand why this lake is regarded as one of the world's seven natural wonders. Overlooking the lake is one of the world's most photographed hotels, Chateau Lake Louise. Apart from staring, photographing, and videoing, the area has plenty to keep you busy. Some of the park's best hiking, canoeing, and horseback riding are nearby. And only a short distance away is Moraine Lake, not as famous as Lake Louise but rivaling it in beauty.

Lake Louise is located 51 kilometers northwest of Banff along the TransCanada Highway, or a little bit farther if you take the quieter Bow Valley Parkway. The hamlet of Lake Louise, composed of a small mall, hotels, and restaurants, is located in the Bow Valley, just west of the TransCanada Highway. The lake is 200 vertical meters above the valley floor, along a winding four-kilometer road. Across the valley is Canada's second-largest ski area, Lake Louise, a world-class facility renowned for its diverse terrain, abundant snow, and breathtaking views.

From Lake Louise, the TransCanada Highway continues west, exiting the park over Kicking Horse Pass (1,647 meters) and passing through Yoho National Park to Golden. Highway 93, the famous Icefields Parkway, also begins at the townsite and heads northwest through the park's northern reaches to Jasper National Park.

History

During the summer of 1882, Tom Wilson, an outfitter, was camped near the confluence of the Bow and Pipestone rivers when he heard the distant rumblings of an avalanche. He questioned Stoney Indian guides and was told the noises originated from the "Lake of Little Fishes." The following day, Wilson, led by a native guide, hiked to the lake to investigate. He became the first white man to lay eyes on what he named Emerald Lake. Two years later, the name was changed to Lake Louise, honoring Princess Louise Caroline Alberta, daughter of Queen Victoria.

A railway station known as Laggan was built where the rail line passed closest to the lake, six kilometers away. Until a road was completed in 1926, everyone arrived by train. The station's name was changed to Lake Louise in 1913 to prevent confusion among visitors. In 1890, a modest two-bedroom wooden hotel replaced a crude cabin that had been built on the shore of the lake as word of its beauty spread. After many additions, a disastrous fire, and the addition of a concrete wing in 1925, the chateau of today took

"The lakes are such marvelous colors. What kind of chemicals do you use?"
—Anonymous, Lake Louise Visitor Centre

WHYTE MUSEUM OF THE CANADIAN ROCKIES

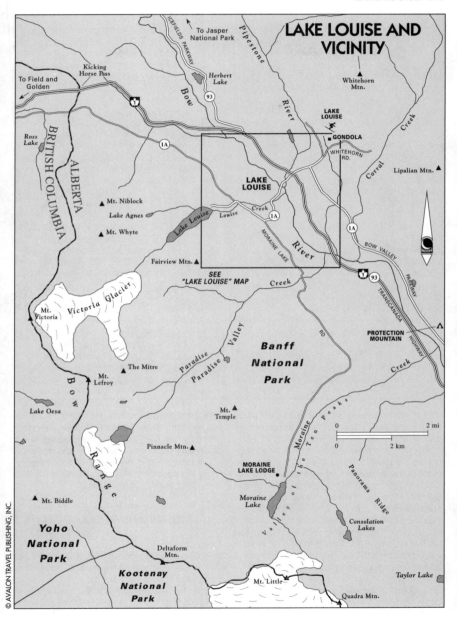

LAKE LOUISE AND VICINITY

To Jasper National Park

Kicking Horse Pass

To Field and Golden

Herbert Lake

Whitehorn Mtn.

Bow

Pipestone

River

LAKE LOUISE

GONDOLA

WHITEHORN RD.

Lipalian Mtn.

Corral

Creek

Ross Lake

BRITISH COLUMBIA

ALBERTA

LAKE LOUISE

Mt. Niblock

Lake Agnes

Mt. Whyte

Lake Louise

Louise

Creek

BOW VALLEY

PARKWAY

TRANSCANADA HIGHWAY

Fairview Mtn.

Moraine Lake

River

SEE "LAKE LOUISE" MAP

Creek

PROTECTION MOUNTAIN

Victoria Glacier

Mt. Victoria

The Mitre

Paradise

Paradise Valley

Banff National Park

RD

Creek

Mt. Lefroy

Lake Oesa

Mt. Temple

2 mi

2 km

Bow

Pinnacle Mtn.

Range

Valley of the Ten Peaks

Moraine

Panorama Ridge

MORAINE LAKE LODGE

Mt. Biddle

Yoho National Park

Moraine Lake

Consolation Lakes

Deltaform Mtn.

Kootenay National Park

Mt. Little

Quadra Mtn.

Taylor Lake

© AVALON TRAVEL PUBLISHING, INC.

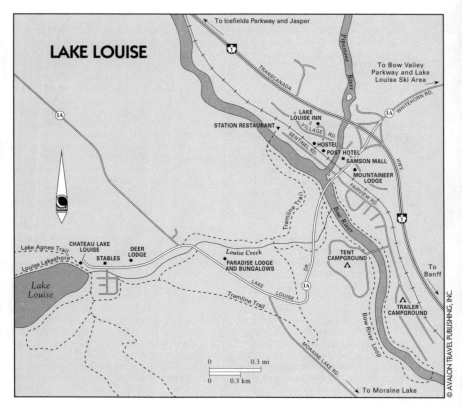

LAKE LOUISE

To Icefields Parkway and Jasper

TRANSCANADA

Pipestone River

To Bow Valley Parkway and Lake Louise Ski Area

WHITEHORN RD.

LAKE LOUISE INN

STATION RESTAURANT

VILLAGE RD.

SENTINEL RD.

HOSTEL

POST HOTEL

SAMSON MALL

HWY.

MOUNTAINEER LODGE

FAIRVIEW RD.

Bow River

Tramline Trail

CHATEAU LAKE LOUISE

Lake Agnes Trail

DEER LODGE

STABLES

Louise Lakeshore

Louise Creek

PARADISE LODGE AND BUNGALOWS

Lake Louise

LAKE LOUISE DR.

TENT CAMPGROUND

To Banff

Tramline Trail

Bow River Loop

TRAILER CAMPGROUND

MORAINE LAKE RD.

© AVALON TRAVEL PUBLISHING, INC.

0   0.3 mi
0   0.3 km

To Moraine Lake

shape. A 51-square-mile reserve was set aside around the lake, and this was incorporated as part of Rocky Mountains Park in 1902.

Recreational mountaineering has been popular in the park for more than 100 years, and most of the early climbing was done on peaks around Lake Louise. In 1893, Walter Wilcox and Samuel Allen, two Yale schoolmates, spent the summer climbing in the area, making two unsuccessful attempts to reach the north peak of Mt. Victoria. The following summer, they made the first ascents of Mt. Temple and Mt. Aberdeen, extraordinary achievements considering their lack of experience and proper equipment.

During the summer of 1896, P.S. Abbot slipped and plunged to his death attempting to climb Mt. Lefroy. In doing so, he became North

America's first mountaineering fatality. Following this incident, Swiss mountain guides were employed by the CPR to satisfy the climbing needs of wealthy patrons of the railway and make the sport safer. During the period of their employment, successful climbs were made of Mt. Victoria, Mt. Lefroy, and Mt. Balfour.

SIGHTS AND RECREATION

Lake Louise

In summer, approximately 10,000 visitors per day make the journey from the Bow Valley floor up to Lake Louise. By noon, the tiered parking lot is often full. An alternative to the road is one of two trails that begin at the townsite and end at the public parking lot (see **Hiking**). From here, several paved trails lead to the lake's eastern shore. From these vantage points, the dramatic setting can be fully appreciated. The lake is 2.4 kilometers long, 500 meters wide, and up to 90 meters deep. Its cold waters reach a maximum temperature of 4°C in August.

Chateau Lake Louise is a tourist attraction in itself. Built by the CPR to take the pressure off the popular Banff Springs Hotel, the chateau has seen many changes in the last 100 years and is still one of the world's great mountain resorts. No one minds the hordes of camera-toting tourists who traipse through each day, and there's really no way to avoid them. The immaculately manicured gardens between the chateau and the lake make an interesting foreground for the millions of photographs taken each year of Lake Louise.

The snow-covered peak at the back of the lake is **Mt. Victoria** (3,459 meters), which sits on the Continental Divide. Amazingly, its base is more than 10 kilometers from the eastern end of the lake. Mount Victoria, first climbed in 1897, is one of the park's most popular peaks for mountaineers. Although the difficult northeast face (facing the chateau) was first successfully ascended in 1922, the most popular and easiest route to the summit is along the southeast ridge, approached from Abbot Pass.

Moraine Lake

Although less than half the size of Lake Louise, Moraine Lake is just as spectacular and worthy of just as much film. It is located up a winding road 12.5 kilometers off Lake Louise Drive. Its rugged setting, nestled in the Valley of the Ten Peaks among the towering mountains of the main ranges, has provided inspiration for millions of people from around the world since Walter Wilcox became the first white man to reach its shore in 1899. Wilcox's subsequent writings, such as "no scene has given me an equal impression of inspiring solitude and rugged grandeur." guaranteed its future popularity. Although Wilcox was a knowledgable man, he named the lake on the assumption that it was dammed by a glacial moraine deposited by the retreating Wenkchemna Glacier. In fact, the large rockpile that blocks its waters was deposited by major rockfalls from the Tower of Babel to the

south. The lake often remains frozen until June, and the access road is closed all winter.

Lake Louise Sightseeing Gondola

During summer, the Friendly Giant quad chairlift at Lake Louise Ski Area whisks visitors up the face of Mt. Whitehorn to Whitehorn Lodge, at an altitude of more than two kilometers above sea level. The view from the lodge—of the Bow Valley, Lake Louise, and the Continental Divide—is among the most spectacular in the Canadian Rockies. Short trails lead through the forests, across open meadows, and, for the energetic, to the summit of Mt. Whitehorn more than 600 vertical meters above. After working up an appetite, head to the teahouse in the Whitehorn Lodge or try the outdoor barbecue. The lift operates July–August daily 8:30 A.M.–6 P.M., shorter hours June and September; adults $14, seniors $12, children $8. For more information, call 403/522-3555. Free shuttles run from Lake Louise accommodations to the lift.

White-water Rafting

Wild Water Adventures, 403/522-2211 or 888/647-6444, operates rafting adventures on the Kicking Horse River. Half-day trips depart from Lake Louise daily at 8:30 A.M. and 1:30 P.M.; $68 per person includes a light snack.

Horseback Riding

Brewster Lake Louise Stables, 403/522-3511, has hour-long rides (departing on the hour) for $30, rides to the end of Lake Louise for $45, half-day rides for $60, and all-day rides up Paradise Valley for $120.

HIKING

The variety of hiking opportunities in the vicinity of Lake Louise and Moraine Lake is surely equal to any area on the face of the earth. The region's potential for outdoor recreation was first realized in the late 1800s, and it soon became the center of hiking activity in the Canadian Rockies. This popularity continues today; trails here are among the most heavily used in the park. Hiking is best early or late in the short summer season. Head out early in the morning to miss the strollers, high heels, dogs, and bear-bells that

Chateau Lake Louise

you'll encounter during the busiest periods.

The two main trailheads are Chateau Lake Louise and Moraine Lake. Two trails lead from the village to the chateau (a pleasant alternative to driving the steep and very busy Lake Louise Drive). Shortest is the 2.7-kilometer **Louise Creek Trail.** It begins on the downstream side of the point where Lake Louise Drive crosses the Bow River, crosses Louise Creek three times, and ends at the Lake Louise parking lot. The other trail, **Tramline,** is 4.5 kilometers—longer but not as steep. It begins behind the railway station and follows the route of a narrow-gauge railway that once transported guests from the CPR line to Chateau Lake Louise.

Bow River Loop

- Length: 7 kilometers (1.5–2 hours)
- Elevation gain: minimal
- Rating: easy

This loop follows both banks of the Bow River, northwest from where Lake Louise Drive crosses the river to the railway station and southeast past both campgrounds and the Louise Creek and Tramline trails to Lake Louise. Interpretive signs along its length explain the ecosystem of the Bow River. It's used by joggers and cyclists to access various points in the village.

Louise Lakeshore

- Length: 2 kilometers (30 minutes) one-way
- Elevation gain: none
- Rating: easy

Probably the park's busiest trail, it follows the north shore of Lake Louise, beginning in front of the chateau and ending at the west end of the lake. Numerous braided glacial streams empty their silt-filled waters into Lake Louise. Along its length are benches to sit and ponder what English mountaineer James Outram once described as "a gem of composition and of coloring . . . perhaps unrivalled anywhere."

Plain of the Six Glaciers

- Length: 5.3 kilometers (90 minutes) one-way
- Elevation gain: 370 meters
- Rating: easy to moderate

Hikers along this trail are rewarded not only with panoramic views of the glaciated peaks of the main range, but also with homemade goodies baked on a wooden stove served at a rustic teahouse at the end of the trail. For the first two kilometers, the trail follows Louise Lakeshore Trail to the western end of the lake, from where it begins a steady uphill climb through a forest of spruce and alpine fir. It enters an open area where an avalanche has come tumbling down (now a colorful carpet of wildflowers), then passes through a forested area into a vast wasteland of moraines produced by the advance and retreat of Victoria Glacier. Views of surrounding peaks continue to improve until the trail switchbacks through a stunted forest before arriving at the teahouse.

Built by the CPR at the turn of the 20th century, the teahouse operates as it has since it was first built. Supplies are packed in by horse, and all cooking is done in its rustic kitchen. It's open July through early September. After resting, it's worthwhile continuing one kilometer to the end of the trail at the top of a narrow ridge of lateral moraine. From here, the trail's namesakes are visible. From left to right the glaciers are Aberdeen, Upper Lefroy, Lower Lefroy, Upper Victoria, Lower Victoria, and Pope's. Between Mt. Lefroy (3,441 meters) and Mt. Victoria (3,459 meters) is Abbot Pass, where it's possible to make out Abbot Hut on the skyline. When constructed in 1922, this stone structure was the highest building in Canada. The pass and hut are named for Phillip Abbot, who died attempting to climb Mt. Lefroy in 1896.

Lake Agnes

- Length: 3.6 kilometers (90 minutes) one-way
- Elevation gain: 400 meters
- Rating: moderate

This strenuous hike is one of the park's most popular. It begins in front of the chateau, branching right near the beginning of the Louise Lakeshore Trail. For the first 2.5 kilometers, the trail climbs steeply, switchbacking through a forest of alpine fir and Engelmann spruce, crossing a horse trail, passing a lookout, and leveling out at tiny **Mirror Lake.** Here, the old, traditional trail veers right (use if it's wet or snowy underfoot), whereas a more direct route veers left to the Plain of the Six Glaciers. Take a sharp right along a trail that climbs steeply below the Big Beehive. The final elevation gain along both trails is made easier by a flight of steps beside **Bridal Veil Falls,** ending beside a rustic teahouse that overlooks Lake Agnes, a subalpine lake nestled in a hanging valley carved out by a receding glacier. The teahouse offers homemade soups, healthy sandwiches, and a wide assortment of teas. From the teahouse, a one-kilometer trail leads to **Little Beehive** and impressive views of the Bow Valley. Another trail leads around the northern shore of Lake Agnes, climbing to Big Beehive (see following entry) or to the Plain of the Six Glaciers Trail (see previous entry) 3.2 kilometers from the chateau and 2.1 kilometers from the teahouse at the end of that trail.

Big Beehive

- Length: 5 kilometers (2 hours) one-way
- Elevation gain: 520 meters
- Rating: moderate

The lookout atop the larger of two "beehives" is one of the best places to admire the uniquely colored waters of Lake Louise, more than half a kilometer directly below. The many variations in trails to the summit have one thing in common—all are steep, but the rewards are worth every drop of sweat along the way. The most popular route follows the Lake Agnes Trail for the first 3.6 kilometers to Lake Agnes. From the teahouse, a trail leads to the western end of the lake, then switchbacks steeply up an exposed north-facing ridge. At the crest of the ridge, the trail forks. To the right, it descends to the Plain of the Six Glaciers Trail, and to the left, it continues 300 meters to a log gazebo. This trail is not well defined, but scrambling through the large boulders is easy. Across Lake Louise is Fairview Mountain (2,745 meters), and behind this peak is the distinctive shape of Mt. Temple (3,549 meters). Views also extend up the lake to Mt. Lefroy and northeast to the Lake Louise Ski Area. Views from the edge of the cliff are spectacular, but be very careful becuase it's a long, long way down. By returning down the Lake Louise side of the Big Beehive, the loop is 11.5 kilometers (4–5 hours).

Saddleback

- Length: 3.7 kilometers (90 minutes) one-way
- Elevation gain: 600 meters
- Rating: moderate

This trail climbs the lower slopes of Fairview Mountain from beside the boat shed on Lake Louise, ending in an alpine meadow with a view of Mt. Temple from across Paradise Valley. Four hundred meters from the trailhead, the trail forks. Keep left and follow the steep switchbacks through a forest of Englemann spruce and alpine fir until reaching the flower-filled meadow. The meadow is actually a pass between Fairview Mountain (to the northwest) and Saddle Mountain (to the southeast). Although most hikers are content with the awesome views from the pass and return along the same trail, it is possible to continue to the summit of Fairview (2,745 meters), a further climb of 400 vertical meters. The barely discernible, switchbacking trail to the summit begins near a stand of larch trees above the crest of Saddleback. As you would expect, the view from the top is stupendous; Lake Louise is more than one kilometer directly below. This option is for strong, experienced hikers only. From the Saddleback, the trail descends into **Sheol Valley**, then into **Paradise Valley**. The entire loop would be 15 kilometers.

Paradise Valley

- Length: 18 kilometers (6 hours) round-trip
- Elevation gain: 380 meters
- Rating: moderate

This aptly named trail makes for a long day hike, but it can be broken up by overnighting at the backcountry campground at the far end of the loop. The trailhead is located 3.5 kilometers along the Moraine Lake Road in a heavily forested area on the right. The trail climbs steadily for the first five kilometers, crossing **Paradise Creek** numerous times and passing the junction of a trail that climbs the Sheol Valley to Saddleback (see previous entry). After five kilometers, the trail divides again, following either side of the valley, forming a 13-kilometer loop. **Lake Annette** is 700 meters along the left fork. It is a typical subalpine lake in a unique setting—nestled against the near-vertical 1,200-meter north face of snow- and ice-capped **Mt. Temple** (3,549 meters), one of the 10 highest peaks in the Canadian Rockies. This difficult face was successfully climbed in 1966, relatively late for mountaineering "firsts." The lake is a worthy destination in itself; allow yourself four hours round-trip from the trailhead. For those completing the entire loop, continue beyond the lake into an open avalanche area that affords views across Paradise Valley. Look and listen for pikas and marmots among the boulders. The trail then passes through **Horseshoe Meadow,** crosses Paradise Creek, and begins back down the valley. Keep to the left at all trail crossings, and you'll quickly arrive at a series of waterfalls known as the **Giant Steps.** From the base of these falls, it is eight kilometers back to the trailhead.

Consolation Lakes

- Length: 3 kilometers (1 hour) one-way
- Elevation gain: 65 meters

- Rating: easy to moderate

This short trail begins from the bridge over Moraine Creek near the Moraine Lake parking lot and ends at a pleasant subalpine lake. The first section of the trail traverses a boulder-strewn rock pile—the result of rock slides on the imposing Tower of Babel (3,101 meters)—before entering a dense forest of Engelmann spruce and alpine fir and following **Babel Creek** to the lower lake. The wide valley affords 360-degree views of the surrounding jagged peaks, including Mt. Temple back down the valley and Mt. Bident and Mt. Quandra at the far end of the lakes. After eating lunch while perched on one of many boulders, you could continue to Upper Consolation Lake by crossing Babel Creek and following a usually wet and muddy trail along the lake's eastern shore.

Larch Valley

- Length: 2.9 kilometers (60–90 minutes) one-way
- Elevation gain: 450 meters
- Rating: moderate

In fall, when the larch trees have turned a magnificent gold and the sun is shining, few spots in the Canadian Rockies can match the beauty of this valley. But don't expect to find much solitude. Although the most popular time for visiting the valley is fall, it is a worthy destination all summer. The trail begins just past Moraine Lake Lodge and climbs fairly steeply with occasional glimpses of Moraine Lake below. After reaching the junction of the Eiffel Lake Trail, keep right, passing through an open forest of larch and into the meadow beyond. The range of larch is restricted within the park, and this is one of the few areas where they are prolific. Mount Fay (3,235 meters) is the dominant peak on the skyline, rising above the other mountains that make up the Valley of the Ten Peaks.

Keen hikers should continue through the meadows to **Sentinel Pass** (2,608 meters), one of the park's highest passes. From the end of the meadow, the trail switchbacks for 1.2 kilometers up a steep slope to the pass, which is sandwiched between Pinnacle Mountain (3,067 meters) and Mt. Temple (3,549 meters). From the pass, most hikers opt to return along the same trail, although it is possible to continue into Paradise Valley.

Eiffel Lake

- Length: 5.6 kilometers (2 hours) one-way
- Elevation gain: 400 meters
- Rating: moderate to difficult

Eiffel Lake is small and looks even smaller in its rugged and desolate setting, surrounded by the famed Valley of the Ten Peaks. For the first 2.4 kilometers, follow the Larch Valley Trail (see previous entry), then fork left. Most of the elevation gain has already been made, and the trail remains relatively level before emerging onto an open slope from where each of the 10 peaks can be seen, along with Moraine Lake far below. From left to right, the peaks are Fay, Little, Bowlen, Perren, Septa, Allen, Tuzo, Deltaform, Neptuak, and Wenkchemna. The final two peaks are divided by **Wenkchemna Pass** (2,605 meters), four kilometers farther and 360 vertical meters above Eiffel Lake. The lake soon comes into view. It lies in a depression formed by a rock slide from Neptuak Mountain. The lake is named for **Eiffel Peak** (3,085 meters), a rock pinnacle behind it, which (with a little imagination) could be compared to the Eiffel Tower.

Skoki Lodge

- Length: 14.4 kilometers (5 hours) one-way
- Elevation gain: 775 meters
- Rating: moderate to difficult

The trail into historic Skoki Lodge is only one of the endless hiking opportunities tucked behind Lake Louise Ski Area, across the valley from all previously detailed hikes. Access to the Skoki Valley is from a parking lot on a gravel road that branches right from the ski area access road. The first four kilometers of the trail are along a gravel access road leading to Temple Lodge, part of the Lake Louise Ski Area. From here, the trail climbs to **Boulder Pass,** passing a campground and Halfway Hut, above Corral Creek. The pass harbors a large population of pikas and hoary marmots. The trail then follows the north shore of Ptarmigan Lake before climbing again to **Deception Pass,** named for its false summit. It then descends into Skoki Valley, passing the Skoki Lakes and eventually reaching Skoki Lodge (see **Accommodations**). Just more than one kilometer beyond the lodge is a campground, an excellent base for exploring the region.

WINTERTIME

Lake Louise is an immense winter playground offering one of the world's premier ski resorts, hundreds of kilometers of cross-country-ski trails, ice-skating, sleigh rides, nearby heli-skiing, and more. Between November and May, accommodation prices are reduced by up to 70 percent (except Christmas holidays). Lift and lodging packages begin at $56 per person, and you'll always be able to get a table at your favorite restaurant.

The most popular cross-country skiing areas are on Lake Louise, along Moraine Lake Road, and in Skoki Valley at the back of the Lake Louise ski area. For details and helpful trail classifications, pick up a copy of *Cross-country Skiing—Nordic Trails in Banff National Park* ($1) from the Lake Louise Visitor Centre. Before heading out, check the weather forecast at the visitors center or call 403/762-2088 for a recorded message. For avalanche reports, call 403/762-1460. On the first Sunday in March, the long-running **Lake Louise Loppet,** a Nordic-skiing competition, is held. Races are run at 10- and 20-kilometer distances, with prizes in 29 age categories. For details, call the Calgary Ski Club at 403/245-9496.

Of all the ice-skating rinks in Canada, the one on frozen Lake Louise, in front of the chateau, is surely the most spectacular. Spotlights allow skating after dark, and on special occasions, hot chocolate is served. Skates are available in the chateau at **Monod Sports,** 403/522-3837; $12 for two hours.

Brewster Lake Louise Sleigh Rides, 403/522-3511, ext. 1210, or 403/762-5454, offers rides in traditional horse-drawn sleighs along the shores of Lake Louise beginning from in front of the chateau. Although blankets are supplied, you should still bundle up. The one-hour ride is adults $16, children $11. Reservations are necessary. The rides are scheduled hourly from 11 A.M. on weekends, and from 3 P.M. weekdays.

Lake Louise

Canada's answer to the United States' megaresorts such as Vail and Killington is Lake Louise. The nation's second-largest ski area comprises

40 square kilometers of gentle trails, mogul fields, long cruising runs, steep chutes, and vast bowls filled with famous Rocky Mountain powder.

The earliest skiing undertaken in the Lake Louise area was in the 1920s, when groups from Banff went backcountry touring in the Skoki Valley. In 1930, Cliff White and Cyril Paris built a small ski chalet in the valley. The location of this chalet, 20 kilometers from the nearest road, turned out not to be practical, so another, closer one was built on the site of today's Temple Lodge. In 1954, a lift was constructed next to Temple Lodge's back door, opening the slopes of Larch Mountain to the ever-increasing number of downhill enthusiasts in the area. A young Englishman who had inherited a fortune from his father saw the potential for a world-class ski resort here and made the completion of his dream a lifelong obsession. Norman Watson, known as the "Barmy Baronet," pulled together a group of financiers and constructed a gondola up the slopes of Whitehorn in 1958. More lifts were constructed, and two runs—Olympic Men's Downhill and Olympic Ladies' Downhill—were cut on the south face of Whitehorn in anticipation of a successful bid for the 1968 Winter Olympics. The bid eventually failed because of opposition from environmentalists (for the same reason that the alpine events of the 1988 Calgary Winter Olympics were held on a specially built hill outside of the park boundary). Huge development plans for the base area that included rooms for 6,500 guests were scuttled in 1972, but, under the supervision of one-time local mountain guide Charlie Locke, the area has continued to improve and grow and often hosts World Cup skiing events.

The resort is made up of four distinct faces. The front side has a vertical drop of 1,000 meters and is served by eight lifts, including two high-speed quads. The four back bowls are each as big as many midsize ski areas and are all well above the treeline. The Larch and Ptarmigan faces have a variety of terrain, allowing you to follow the sun as it moves across the sky or escape into trees for protection on windy days.

Each of the three day lodges has a restaurant and a bar. Ski rentals, clothing, and souvenirs are available at the base area. Lift tickets are $54 adults, seniors $43, children $15. Lifts

Paradise Lodge and Bungalows

are open from early November to early May, 9 A.M.–4 P.M. Free, guided tours of the mountain are available three times daily—inquire at customer service. Free shuttle buses run regularly from Lake Louise accommodations to the hill. From Banff, you pay $15 round-trip for transportation to Lake Louise. For more information on the ski area, call 403/522-3555.

ACCOMMODATIONS AND CAMPING

In summer, accommodations at Lake Louise are even harder to come by than in Banff, so it's essential to make reservations well in advance. Any rooms not taken by early afternoon will be the expensive ones.

$100–150

Aside from the Chateau, the **Lake Louise Inn** (210 Village Road, 403/522-3791 or 800/661-9237, www.lakelouiseinn.com) is the village's largest lodging, sprawling over two hectares within easy walking distance of Samson Mall. Its 232 rooms start at $148 single or double.

$150–200

Not right in the village, but a good deal for families, small groups, and those who like privacy, is **Paradise Lodge and Bungalows** (403/522-3595, www.paradiselodge.com). Spread out around well-manicured gardens are 21 self-contained cabins beginning at $165 per night. Bungalows with kitchens are $175 for one bedroom and $185 for two bedrooms. A few self-contained two-room units with large balconies boast views across the Bow Valley for $195. Twenty-four newly built suites, each with a fireplace, a TV, one or two bedrooms, and fabulous mountain views, start at $235, or $255 with a kitchen. Honeymoon suites, with all of the aforementioned amenities, as well as a hot tub, are $280. The lodge is open mid-May to mid-October. To get there from the valley floor, follow Lake Louise Drive toward Chateau Lake Louise for two kilometers.

The historic **Deer Lodge** (403/522-3747 or 800/661-1595, www.crmr.com/dl) began life in 1921 as a teahouse, with rooms added in 1925. Facilities include a rooftop hot tub, a games room, a restaurant, and a bar. Rooms range from $160–220. It's along Lake Louise Drive, up the hill from the village, and just below the lake itself.

The **Mountaineer Lodge,** which is close to everything (101 Village Rd., 403/522-3844, www.mountaineerlodge.com), charges from $160 single or double for large rooms, each with separate sleeping areas. It's open only May–October.

More than $200

Originally called Lake Louise Ski Lodge, the **Post Hotel** (403/522-3989 or 800/661-1586, www.posthotel.com) is bordered to the east and south by the Pipestone River. It may lack views of Lake Louise, but it is as elegant, in a modern, woodsy way, as the Chateau. Each bungalow-style room is furnished with Canadian pine and has a balcony. Many rooms have whirlpools and fireplaces, and some have kitchens. Other facilities include an indoor pool, a steam room, and a library. High tea is served in the lobby each afternoon. The hotel has 17 different room types, with 26 different rates depending on the view. Rates start at $300 single or double.

Overlooking its famous namesake lake, 11 kilometers from the valley floor, is luxurious **Moraine Lake Lodge** (403/522-3733 or 800/661-8340, www.morainelake.com). Rooms in the main lodge are spacious and well-appointed; guests are pampered with afternoon tea and evening liqueurs. It's open only June–September, with rooms in the lodge going for $350 or more and cabins from $410 in the height of summer.

Chateau Lake Louise

This historic 500-room hotel on the shore of Lake Louise has views equal to any mountain resort in the world, but this historic charm and mountain scenery comes at a price. During the summer season (June to mid-October), rooms must be booked as a Canadian Rockies Experience or Castle Experience package, costing from $1,079 double for a wide range of activities (many of them, such as golf, are back in Banff). This rate is for a standard room, and it rises exponentially for mountainside and lakeside rooms. Rates drop as low as $219 single, $238 double outside of summer, with ski packages often advertised. Children under 17 sharing a room with parents are free, but if you bring a pet, it'll be an extra $20. For reservations—and you'll need one—call 403/522-3511 or 800/441-1414, www.fairmont.com.

Skoki Lodge

Skoki is a rustic lodge, situated deep in the backcountry, north of the Lake Louise Ski Area. Getting there requires an 11-kilometer hike or ski, depending on the season. The lodge is an excellent base for exploring nearby valleys and mountains. It dates to 1930, when it operated as a lodge for skiers. Today it comprises a main lodge and three cabins, sleeping a total of 22 people. Accommodations are rustic—there is no electricity or indoor plumbing—but comfortable, and the lodge has a reputation for excellent meals, which are included in the nightly rate of $131.40 per person. For information and reservations, contact the lodge 403/522-3555, www.skilouise.com/skoki.

Hostel

At approximately $100 less than any other bed in town, the **Canadian Alpine Centre,** 403/522-2200, fills up quickly each day. Made of log construction, with large windows and high vaulted ceilings, the hostel is a joint venture between the Alpine Club of Canada and the Southern Alberta Hostelling Association. It opened early in the summer of 1992, with extensions in 1995 bringing the total number of beds to 150. Downstairs is a large reception area and Bill Peyto's Café, the least expensive place to eat in Lake Louise. Upstairs is a large lounge area and guides room—a quiet place to plan your next hike or browse through the large collection of mountain literature. Hostel members pay $22 per night in a two-, four-, or six-bed dorm, and nonmembers pay $26. The hostel is open year-round. In summer and on weekends during the ski season, advance bookings (up to six months) are essential. The hostel is located along Village Road, one kilometer from Samson Mall.

Campgrounds

Lake Louise Campground, within easy walking distance of the village, is divided into two areas by the Bow River. One side has unserviced sites, the other serviced. Individual sites are close together, but some privacy and shade are provided by towering lodgepole pines. The unserviced (tent camping) sites have showers, flush toilets, kitchen shelters, fire rings, and firewood ($4); $17 per night. Serviced (trailer camping) sites have power, showers, and flush toilets; $21. A dump station is located near the entrance to the campground ($5 per use). An interpretive program runs throughout summer, nightly at 9 P.M. in the outdoor theater. The **Bow River Loop** leads into the village along either side of the Bow River, crossing at the southern end of the serviced sites and again behind Samson Mall. To get to the campground, take Lake Louise Drive under the railway bridge, turn left on Fairview Drive, and continue past the impressive log-built staff accommodations to the fee station. The campground is open year-round.

FOOD AND DRINK

On the Cheap

Samson Mall is the center of much activity each afternoon as campers descend on the grocery store to stock up on supplies for the evening meal. Prices are high, and by the end of the day, stocks are low. **Laggan's Mountain Bakery** (in the mall, 403/552-2017) is *the* place to hang out with a coffee and one of their delicious freshly baked pastries, cakes, or muffins. If the tables are full and you manage to somehow reach the cake cabinet, order takeout and enjoy your feast on the grassy bank behind the mall. The chocolate brownie ($1.60) is delicious. Order two slices to save having to line up again. It's open daily 6 A.M.–7 P.M.

Forget the Bar and Grill in the mall—much better is **Bill Peyto's Café** in the hostel on Village Road. The food is consistent, and although prices have been creeping upward in the last couple of years, it's still well priced compared to other options in the village. You don't have to be staying in the hostel to eat there. Open daily 7 A.M.–9 P.M. **Legends** (in the Lake Louise Inn, 403/522-3791) is more expensive, but the choices are varied and the atmosphere enjoyable.

Lake Louise Station Restuarant

One hundred years ago, visitors departing trains at Laggan Station were keen to get to the Chateau Lake Louise as quickly as possible to begin their adventure. Today, guests from the chateau, other hotels, and even people from as far away as Banff return to the restored station to dine in this unique restaurant. Although the menu is not extensive, the ample variety satisfies most tastes. Open for lunch and dinner. For reservations, call 403/522-2600.

Chateau Lake Louise

Within this famous hotel are a choice of eateries and an ice-cream shop. The **Poppy Room** has obscured lake views and is the most casual place for a meal. A continental buffet breakfast is served 7–9 A.M. for $10.50. For dinner, a pizza and pasta buffet is offered ($16), or you can order off the menu. It's open until 8:30 P.M. The **Walliser Stube** is an elegant two-story wine bar decorated with oak furniture. It offers a simple menu of German dishes from $15.95 as well as cheese fondue. The **Lakeside Lounge** is an open-front grill. Victorian afternoon tea of crumpets, sandwiches, desserts, and drinks is served each afternoon for $16.95. The **Victoria Din-**

ing Room is a relaxed but stylish restaurant open for breakfast, a buffet lunch, and evening dining with live entertainment. The **Edelweiss Dining Room** has the best view of Lake Louise and offers the chateau's most elegant dining. Appetizers start at $4.75 while entrées from the fish, game, chicken, and meat menu start at $19.50. For all reservations, call 403/522-3511.

Post Hotel

In 1987, the Post Hotel was expanded to include a luxurious new wing. The original log building was renovated as a rustic, timbered dining room, linked to the rest of the hotel by an intimate bar. Although eating here is not cheap, it's a favorite of locals and visitors alike. The chef specializes in European cuisine—preparing several Swiss dishes (such as veal Zurichois) to make owner George Schwarz feel at home—but he's also renowned for his presentation of Alberta beef, Pacific salmon, and Peking duck. Main meals start at $25. The restaurant is open daily 7 A.M.–2 P.M. and 6–8:30 P.M. Reservations are essential for dinner; call 403/522-3989.

TRANSPORTATION

Getting There

Calgary International Airport is the closest major airport to Lake Louise. **Brewster,** 403/762-6767, operates a bus service leaving the airport four times daily, stopping at Banff, Samson Mall, and the chateau. Lake Louise to Banff is $15, to Calgary and Jasper is $41.

Greyhound, 403/522-2121 or 800/661-8747, leaves the Calgary Bus Depot at 877 Greyhound Way SW five times daily for Banff and Lake Louise. Banff to Lake Louise is less than $10. Buses leave Vancouver from 1150 Station Street, 604/662-3222, three times daily for the 13-hour haul to Lake Louise.

Getting Around

The campground, hostel, and hotels are all within easy walking distance of Samson Mall. Chateau Lake Louise is a 2.7-kilometer walk from the valley floor. The only car-rental agency in the village is **National,** 403/522-3870 or 800/387-4747. The agency doesn't have many cars, so you'd be better off picking one up in

Banff or at Calgary International Airport. **Lake Louise Taxi & Tours** is located in Samson Mall, 403/522-2020; flag drop is $2.50, then $1.35 per kilometer. From the mall to Chateau Lake Louise runs approximately $10, to Moraine Lake $18, and to Banff $97. **Wilson Mountain Sports** (in Samson Mall, 403/522-3636) rents mountain bikes for $8 per hour or $34 per day (includes a helmet, bike lock, and water bottle). Inquire here about canoe rentals for float trips along the Bow River to Banff.

Tours

No tours of the area are offered for visitors staying in Lake Louise. For those staying in Banff, **Brewster,** 403/762-6767, has a four-hour tour departing select Banff hotels daily 1:15–1:40 P.M. to Lake Louise for $49. In winter, this tour departs in the morning, runs five hours, and includes Banff sights for $44.

SERVICES AND INFORMATION

Services

Located in Samson Mall is a small postal outlet serving as a bus depot and car-rental agency. Although Lake Louise has no banks, there's a currency exchange in the Chateau Lake Louise and a cash machine in the grocery store. The mall also has a laundromat that's always busy. Camping supplies are available from **Wilson Mountain Sports** and photographic supplies from **Pipestone Photo,** 403/522-3617. Pipestone has a one-hour photo-developing service and is the only place in the park offering overnight slide developing. The closest **hospital** is in Banff, 403/762-2222. For the **RCMP,** call 403/522-3811.

Information

Woodruff & Blum (in the Samson Mall, 403/522-3842) has an excellent selection of books on the natural and human history of the park, animal field guides, hiking guides, and general western Canadiana.

The **Lake Louise Visitor Centre,** 403/522-3833, is beside Samson Mall on Village Road. This excellent facility has interpretive displays, slide and video displays, and park staff on hand to answer questions, issue backcountry camping permits, and recommend hikes suited to your ability. Look for the stuffed (literally) female grizzly and read her fascinating, but sad, story. It's

open mid-June–August daily 8 A.M.–8 P.M., mid-May to mid-June and September daily 8 A.M.–6 P.M., the rest of the year daily 9 A.M.–4 P.M.

ICEFIELDS PARKWAY—BANFF

The 230-kilometer Icefields Parkway, between Lake Louise and Jasper, is one of the most scenic, exciting, and inspiring mountain roads ever built. From Lake Louise, it parallels the Continental Divide, following in the shadow of the highest, most rugged mountains in the Canadian Rockies. The first 122 kilometers to Sunwapta Pass (the boundary between Banff and Jasper national parks) can be driven in two hours, and the entire parkway in four. But you'll probably want to spend at least one day, and probably more, stopping at each of the 13 viewpoints, hiking the trails, watching the abundant wildlife, and just generally enjoying one of the world's most magnificent landscapes. Along the section within Banff National Park are two lodges, three hostels, three campgrounds, and one gas station.

Although the road is steep and winding in places, it has a wide shoulder, making it ideal for an extended bike trip. Allow seven days to pedal north from Banff to Jasper, staying at hostels or camping along the route. This is the preferable direction to travel by bike because the elevation of Jasper townsite is more than 500 meters lower than either Banff townsite or Lake Louise.

History

Natives and early explorers found the swampy nature of the Bow Valley difficult for foot and horse travel. Instead, they used the Pipestone River Valley, farther east, when heading north. Banff guide Bill Peyto led American explorer Walter Wilcox up the Bow Valley in 1896, to the high peaks along the Continental Divide northeast of Lake Louise. The first complete journey along this route was made by Jim Brewster in 1904. Soon after, A.P. Coleman made the arduous journey, becoming a strong supporter for the route aptly known as "The Wonder Trail." During the Great Depression of the 1930s, as part of a relief-work project, construction began on what was to become the Icefields Parkway. It was completed in 1939, and the first car traveled the

route in 1940. In tribute to the excellence of the road's early construction, when upgraded to its present standard in 1961, the original roadbed was followed nearly the entire way.

The parkway remains open year-round, although winter brings with it some special considerations. The road is often closed for short periods for avalanche control, so check road conditions in Banff or Lake Louise before setting out. And fill up with gas because no services are available between November and April.

SIGHTS

The Icefields Parkway forks right from the TransCanada Highway just north of Lake Louise. The impressive scenery begins immediately. Just three kilometers from the junction is **Herbert Lake,** formed during the last Ice Age when retreating glaciers deposited a pile of rubble—known as a moraine—across a shallow valley and water filled in behind it. The lake is a perfect place for early morning or evening photography when the **Waputik Range** and distinctively shaped **Mt. Temple** are reflected in its waters.

Traveling north, you'll notice numerous depressions in the steep, shaded slopes of the Waputik Range across the Bow Valley. The cooler climate on these north-facing slopes makes them prone to glaciation. Cirques were cut by small "local glaciers." On the opposite side of the road, **Mt. Hector** (3,394 meters), easily recognized by its layered peak, is soon visible.

Hector Lake Viewpoint is 16 kilometers from the junction. Although the view is partially obscured by trees, the emerald-green waters nestled below a massive wall of limestone form a breathtaking scene. **Bow Peak,** seen looking northward along the highway, is only 2,868 meters high but is completely detached from the Waputik Range, making it a popular destination for mountain climbers. As you leave this viewpoint, look across the northeast end of Hector

Lake for glimpses of **Mt. Balfour** (3,246 meters) on the distant skyline.

Crowfoot Glacier

The aptly named Crowfoot Glacier can best be appreciated from north of Bow Lake. From the viewpoint, 17 kilometers north of Hector Lake, it is easy to see how this and other glaciers are formed. It sits on a wide ledge near the top of Crowfoot Mountain, from where its glacial "claws" cling to the mountain's steep slopes. The retreat of this glacier has been dramatic. Only 50 years ago, two of the claws extended to the base of the lower cliff.

Bow Lake

The sparkling, translucent waters of Bow Lake are among the most beautiful that can be seen from the Icefields Parkway. The lake was created when moraines, left behind by retreating glaciers, dammed subsequent meltwater. On still days, the water reflects the snowy peaks, their sheer cliffs, and the scree slopes that run into the lake. You don't need to take a photography class to take good pictures here! At the southeast end of the lake is a day-use area with waterfront picnic tables and a trail that leads to a swampy area at the lake's outlet. At the upper end of the lake is a lodge and the trailhead for a walk to Bow Glacier Falls (see **Hiking**).

The road leaves Bow Lake and climbs to **Bow Summit.** Looking back, the true color of Bow Lake becomes apparent, and the Crowfoot Glacier reveals its unique shape. At an elevation of 2,069 meters, this pass is one of the highest points crossed by a public road in Canada. It is also the beginning of the Bow River, the one you camped beside at Lake Louise, photographed flowing through the town of Banff, and strolled along in downtown Calgary.

Peyto Lake

From the parking lot at Bow Summit, a short, paved trail leads to one of the most breathtaking views you could ever imagine. Far below the viewpoint is Peyto Lake, an impossibly intense green-colored lake whose hues change according to season. Before heavy melting of nearby glaciers begins (June to early July), the lake is dark blue. As summer progresses, meltwater flows across a delta and into the lake. This water is laden with fine particles of ground-rock debris known as "rock flour," which remains suspended in the water. The mineral content of the rock flour is not responsible for the lake's unique color, but rather the particles reflecting the blue-green sector of the light spectrum. Therefore, as the amount of suspended rock flour changes, so does the color of the lake.

The lake is one of many park landmarks named for early outfitter Bill Peyto. In 1898, he was part of an expedition camped at Bow Lake. Seeking solitude (as he was reportedly wont to do), he slipped off during the night to sleep near

spectacular Bow Lake and Crowfoot Glacier

NADINA PURDON

this lake. Other members of the party coined the name "Peyto's Lake," and it stuck.

Three kilometers farther along the parkway is a viewpoint from where **Peyto Glacier** is visible at the far end of Peyto Lake Valley. This glacier is part of the extensive **Wapta Icefield,** which straddles the Continental Divide and extends into the northern reaches of **Yoho National Park** in British Columbia.

Beside the Continental Divide

From Bow Pass, the parkway descends to a viewpoint directly across the Mistaya River from **Mt. Patterson** (3,197 meters). **Snowbird Glacier** clings precariously to the mountain's steep northeast face, and the mountain's lower, wooded slopes are heavily scarred where rock and ice slides have swept down the mountainside.

As the parkway continues to descend and crosses **Silverhorn Creek,** the jagged limestone peaks of the Continental Divide can be seen to the west. **Mistaya Lake** is a three-kilometer-long body of water that sits at the bottom of the valley between the road and the divide, but it can't be seen from the parkway. The best place to view this panorama is from the **Howse Peak Viewpoint** at Upper Waterfowl Lake. From here, the high ridge that forms the Continental Divide is easily distinguishable. Seven peaks can be seen from here, including, of course, **Howse Peak** (3,290 meters). At no point along this ridge does the elevation drop below 2,750 meters. From Howse Peak, the Continental Divide makes a 90-degree turn to the west. One dominant peak that can be seen from Bow Pass to the north of the Saskatchewan River Crossing is **Mt. Chephren** (3,268 meters). Its distinctive shape and position away from the main ridge of the Continental Divide make it easy to distinguish (directly north of Howse Peak).

To Saskatchewan River Crossing

Numerous trails lead around the swampy shores of **Upper** and **Lower Waterfowl Lakes,** providing one of the park's best opportunities to view moose, who feed on the abundant aquatic vegetation that grows in Upper Waterfowl Lake. Rock and other debris that has been carried down from nearby valley systems has built up, forming a wide alluvial fan, nearly

blocking the **Mistaya River** and creating Upper Waterfowl Lake.

Continuing north is **Mt. Murchison** (3,337 meters), on the east side of the parkway. Although not one of the park's highest mountains, this gray-and-yellow massif of Cambrian rock includes 10 individual peaks, covering an area of 30 square kilometers.

From a parking lot 14 kilometers northeast of Waterfowl Lake Campground, a short trail descends into the montane forest to **Mistaya Canyon.** Here, the effects of erosion can be appreciated as the Mistaya River leaves the floor of Mistaya Valley, plunging through a narrow-walled canyon into the North Saskatchewan Valley. The area is scarred with potholes where boulders have been whirled around by the action of fast-flowing water, carving deep depressions into the softer limestone bedrock below.

The **North Saskatchewan River** posed a major problem for early travelers and later the builders of the Icefields Parkway. This swiftly running river eventually drains into Hudson Bay. In 1989, it was named a Canadian Heritage River. A panoramic viewpoint of the entire valley is located one kilometer past the bridge. From here, the Howse and Mistaya rivers can be seen converging with the North Saskatchewan at a silt-laden delta. This is also a junction with Highway 11 (also known as David Thompson Highway), which follows the North Saskatchewan River to Rocky Mountain House and Red Deer. From this viewpoint, numerous peaks can be seen to the west. Two sharp peaks are distinctive: **Mount Outram** (3,254 meters) is the closer, and the farther is **Mt. Forbes** (3,630 meters), the highest peak in Banff National Park (and the sixth-highest in the Canadian Rockies).

To Sunwapta Pass

On the north side of the North Saskatchewan River is the towering hulk of **Mt. Wilson** (3,261 meters), named for Banff outfitter Tom Wilson. The Icefields Parkway passes this massif on its western flanks. A pullout, just past Rampart Creek Campground, has good views of Mt. Amery to the west and mounts Sarbach, Chephren, and Murchison to the south. Beyond here is the **Weeping Wall,** a long cliff of gray limestone where a series of waterfalls tumbles more than 100 meters down the steep slopes of **Cirrus Mountain.** In winter, this wall of water freezes, becoming a mecca for ice climbers. After climbing quickly, the road drops again, before beginning the long climb to Sunwapta Pass. Before ascending to the pass, the road makes a sweeping curve over an alluvial plain of the North Saskatchewan River. Halfway up the 360-vertical-meter climb is a viewpoint well worth stopping for. Cyclists will definitely appreciate a rest. From here, views extend down the valley to the slopes of Mt. Saskatchewan and, on the other side of the parkway, Cirrus Mountain. Another viewpoint, farther up the road, has the added attraction of **Panther Falls** across the valley. A cairn at **Sunwapta Pass** (2,023 meters) marks the boundary between Banff and Jasper national parks. It also marks the divide between the North Saskatchewan and Sunwapta rivers, whose waters drain into the Atlantic and Arctic oceans, respectively.

HIKING

Helen Lake
- Length: 6 kilometers (2.5 hours) one-way
- Elevation gain: 455 meters
- Rating: moderate

The trail to Helen Lake is one of the easiest ways to access true alpine environment from the southern end of the Icefields Parkway. The trailhead is opposite Crowfoot Glacier Lookout, 33 kilometers from the junction with the TransCanada Highway. The trail climbs steadily through a forest of Engelmann spruce and alpine fir for the first 2.5 kilometers to an avalanche slope, reaching the treeline after three kilometers. The view across the valley is spectacular, with Crowfoot Glacier visible to the southwest. As the trail reaches a ridge, it turns 180 degrees and descends into the glacial cirque where Helen Lake lies. Listen and look for hoary marmots around the scree slopes along the lakeshore.

For those with the time and energy, it's possible to continue an additional three kilometers to **Dolomite Pass;** the trail switchbacks steeply up a further 100 vertical meters in less than one kilometer, then descends steeply for a further one kilometer to Katherine Lake and beyond to the pass.

Bow Glacier Falls
- Length: 3.4 kilometers (1 hour) one-way
- Elevation gain: 130 meters
- Rating: easy to moderate

This hike skirts one of the most beautiful lakes in the Canadian Rockies before ending at a narrow but spectacular waterfall. The trail begins beside Num-ti-jah Lodge at the north end of Bow Lake and follows the shore through Willow Flats to a gravel outwash area at the end of the lake. Across the lake are reflected views of Crowfoot Mountain and, farther west, a glimpse of Bow Glacier among the jagged peaks of the Waputik Range. The trail then begins a short but steep climb up the rim of a canyon before leveling out at the edge of a vast moraine of gravel, scree, and boulders. This is the end of the trail, although it's possible to reach the base of Bow Glacier Falls by picking your way through the 800 meters of rough ground that remains.

Peyto Lake
- Length: 1.4 kilometers (30 minutes) one-way
- Elevation loss: 100 meters
- Rating: easy

Without a doubt, the best place to view Peyto Lake is from the popular viewpoint accessible via a short trail from Bow Summit. From here, a trail drops nearly 300 meters in 2.4 kilometers to the lake. For those wanting to reach the lake's shore, however, there is an easier alternative. From a small parking lot 2.4 kilometers north of Bow Summit, an unmarked trail leads 1.4 kilometers to the shore of this famous lake. The pebbled beach, strewn with driftwood, is the perfect setting for picnicking, painting, or admiring the lake's quieter side.

Chephren Lake
- Length: 4 kilometers (60-90 minutes) one-way
- Elevation gain: 100 meters
- Rating: easy to moderate

This pale-green body of water is hidden from sight of those traveling the Icefields Parkway. The trailhead is located within **Waterfowl Lakes Campground,** where the Mistaya River flows into the lake. The trail crosses the Mistaya River, 400 meters from the trailhead, then dives headlong into a subalpine forest until reaching the lake, nestled under the buttresses of Mt. Chephren. To the left is Howse Peak. The trail to **Cirque Lake** (4.5 kilometers from the trail-head) branches left after 1.7 kilometers and is less heavily used.

Glacier Lake
- Length: 9 kilometers (2.5-3 hours) one-way
- Elevation gain: 220 meters
- Rating: moderate

This three-kilometer-long lake is one of the largest backcountry lakes in the park. Although not as scenic as the more accessible lakes along the parkway, it's a pleasant destination for a full-day or overnight trip. The trailhead is in an old gravel pit on the west side of the highway, one kilometer north of the Saskatchewan River Crossing service center. For the first kilometer, the trail passes through an open forest of lodgepole pine to a fancy footbridge across the rushing North Saskatchewan River. It then climbs gradually to a viewpoint overlooking Howse River and the valley beyond before turning away from the river for a long slog through a dense forest to Glacier Lake. A primitive campground is located just more than 300 meters from where the trail emerges at the lake.

Saskatchewan Glacier
- Length: 7.3 kilometers (2 hours) one-way
- Elevation gain: 150 meters
- Rating: moderate

The Saskatchewan Glacier, a tongue of ice from the great Columbia Icefield, is visible from various points along the Icefields Parkway. This hike takes you right to the toe of the glacier. The trailhead is an old concrete bridge located on the gravel flats just before the road begins its "big bend," 35 kilometers north of the Saskatchewan River Crossing service center. The trail begins across the bridge, disappearing into the forest to the right, joining an old access road, and continuing up the valley along the south bank of the river. When the toe of the glacier first comes into sight, it looks deceptively close, but it is still a long hike over rough terrain to the glacier.

Nigel Pass
- Length: 7.4 kilometers (2.5 hours) one-way
- Elevation gain: 365 meters
- Rating: moderate to difficult

On the east side of the Icefields Parkway, 2.5

kilometers north of the switchback on the "big bend," is a gravel road that leads to a locked gate. Turn right here and cross Nigel Creek on the bridge. The trail is obvious, following open avalanche paths up the east side of the valley. In a stand of Engelmann spruce and alpine fir two kilometers from the trailhead is an old campsite used first by native hunting parties, then by mountaineers exploring the area around the Columbia Icefield. Look for carvings on trees recording these early visitors. From here, the trail continues to climb steadily, only increasing in gradient for the last one kilometer to the pass. The pass (2,195 meters) marks the boundary between Banff and Jasper national parks. For the best view, scramble over the rocks to the left. To the north, the view extends down the Brazeau River Valley, surrounded by a mass of peaks. To the west (left) is **Nigel Peak** (3,211 meters), and southwest are views of Parker's Ridge and the glaciated peaks of Mt. Athabasca.

Parker's Ridge
- Length: 2.4 kilometers (1 hour) one-way
- Elevation gain: 210 meters
- Rating: easy to moderate

This short trail into the alpine begins from a parking lot at the north end of the park, just four kilometers south of Sunwapta Pass. From the trailhead on the west side of the road, the wide path gains elevation quickly through open meadows and scattered stands of alpine fir. This fragile environment is easily destroyed, so it's important that you stay on the trail. During the short alpine summer, these meadows are carpeted with red heather, white mountain avens, and blue alpine forget-me-nots. From the summit of the ridge, you can see the two-kilometer-wide Saskatchewan Glacier spreading out below. Beyond is **Castleguard Mountain,** renowned for its extensive cave system.

ACCOMMODATIONS

Lodging
Pioneer guide and outfitter Jimmy Simpson built **Simpson's Num-ti-jah Lodge** on the north shore of Bow Lake in 1920. In those days, the route north from Lake Louise was nothing more than a horse trail. The desire to build a large

structure when only short timbers were available led to the unusual octagonal shape of the main lodge. Simpson remained at Bow Lake, a living legend until his death in 1972 at age 95. Today the lodge continues to offer facilities for travelers along the highway. Rooms here cost $140 single or double with shared bathrooms, $160 single or double with private bathrooms, and $185 with views. A small coffee shop is open daily 9 A.M.–5:30 P.M., and the **Elkhorn Dining Room** is open for dinner. Horseback rides are offered for guests and nonguests. A one-hour ride along Bow Lake is $25, a three-hour ride to Peyto Lake is $52, and a full-day ride to Helen Lake is $100. Book at 403/522-2167 or online at www.num-ti-jah.com. Closed in November.

Just north of Saskatchewan River Crossing, 45 kilometers south of the Columbia Icefield, is **The Crossing**, 403/761-7000, with rooms for $84 single, $89 double (40 percent discount in spring and fall), a restaurant, a cafeteria, a lounge, a large gift shop, and gas. It's open late March–October.

Hostels

From Lake Louise, hostels are located at kilometers 24, 88, and 118 of the Icefields Parkway. The first is **Mosquito Creek Hostel,** which has good hiking nearby, accommodations for 38 in four cabins, and a large common room with a fireplace, a kitchen, and a wood-heated sauna.

Rampart Creek Hostel is located 12 kilometers north of the Saskatchewan River Crossing, a long day's bike ride from Mosquito Creek. Accommodation for 30 is in two cabins, and there's a kitchen, a sauna, and good hiking nearby. After the long climb up to Sunwapta Pass, **Hilda Creek Hostel** is a welcome sight for cyclists. This hostel is located just below the glacial moraines left by the retreating Columbia Icefield and has a variety of hikes beginning from the doorstep. It has 21 dorm beds, a kitchen, a sauna, and a common room. Members $12–13, nonmembers $16–17. Mosquito Creek is open year-round; the latter two, nightly mid-May to mid-October and weekends only mid-December to mid-May (closed the rest of the year). You should book ahead during July and August because these hostels fill each night. Rampart Creek requires reservations between November and May. Reservations can be made at the hostels in Banff (403/762-4122), Lake Louise (403/522-2200), or Calgary (403/237-8282).

Campgrounds

Campgrounds are found at **Mosquito Creek** (kilometer 24; $10), **Waterfowl Lake** (Kilometer 57; $13), and **Rampart Creek** (kilometer 88; $10). Each has pit toilets, kitchen shelters, firewood, and fire rings, but no showers or hookups, and each is open from mid-June to early September. Mosquito Creek also remains open for winter camping.

KAREN MCKINLEY

JASPER NATIONAL PARK

INTRODUCTION

Snowcapped peaks, vast icefields, beautiful glacial lakes, soothing hot springs, thundering rivers, and the most extensive backcountry trail system of any Canadian national park make Jasper a stunning counterpart to its sister park, Banff. A 3.5-hour drive west of Alberta's provincial capital of Edmonton, Jasper extends from the headwaters of the Smoky River in the north to the Columbia Icefield (and Banff National Park) in the south. To the east are the foothills, and to the west is the Continental Divide, which marks the Alberta/British Columbia border. This 10,900-square-kilometer wilderness is a haven for wildlife; much of the park is traveled only by wolves and grizzlies.

The park's most spectacular natural landmarks can be admired from two major roads. The **Yellowhead Highway** runs east-west from Edmonton to British Columbia through the park. The **Icefields Parkway,** which is regarded as one of the world's great mountain drives, runs north-south, connecting Jasper to Banff. The main service center in the park is the town of Jasper, a smaller, less-commercial version of Banff, where

you'll find several motels and restaurants. Many of the park's campgrounds are accessible by road, whereas others are located throughout the backcountry. Also popular in the park are fishing, boating, downhill skiing, golfing, horseback riding, and white-water rafting.

The park is open year-round, although roads on the Icefields Parkway do close during winter months because of avalanche-control work and snowstorms.

Permits are required for entry into the park; they're available from all park gates as well as the Park Information Centre in Jasper. A one-day permit is $5 per person, and an annual Great Western Pass, good for entry to all 11 of western Canada's national parks, is $35 per person to a maximum of $70 per vehicle.

THE LAND

The Rocky Mountains, extending from the Arctic to the jungles of central Mexico, form the backbone of

North America. Although the peaks of Jasper National Park are not particularly high, they are among the most spectacular along the range's entire length. Approximately 100 million years ago, layers of sedimentary rock—laid down here up to one billion years ago—were forced upward, folded, and twisted under tremendous pressure into the mountains seen today. The land's contours were further altered during four ice ages that began approximately one million years ago. The last Ice Age ended approximately 10,000 years ago, and the vast glaciers began to retreat. A remnant of this final sheet of ice is the huge Columbia Icefield; approximately 325 square kilometers and up to 400 meters deep, it's the most extensive icefield in the Rocky Mountains. As the glaciers retreated, piles of rock melted out and were left behind. Meltwater from the glaciers flowed down the valleys and was dammed up behind the moraines. **Maligne Lake**, like many other lakes in the park, was created by this process. The glacial silt suspended in the lake's waters produces amazing emerald, turquoise, and amethyst colors; early artists who painted these lakes had trouble convincing people that their images were real.

In addition to creating the park's gemlike lakes, the retreating glaciers carved out the valleys that they ever-so-slowly flowed through. The Athabasca River Valley is the park's largest watershed, a typical example of a U-shaped, glacier-carved valley. The Athabasca River flows north through the valley into the Mackenzie River System and ultimately into the Arctic Ocean. The glacial silt that paints the park's lakes is also carried down streams into the Athabasca, giving the river a pale-green "milky" look. Another beautiful aspect of the park's scenery is its abundance of waterfalls. They vary from the sparkling tumble of Mountain Creek as it cascades down a limestone cliff into a picturesque pool at Punchbowl Falls, to the roar of Athabasca Falls where the river is forced through a narrow gorge.

FLORA

Vegetation zones in the park range from montane in the valleys, through subalpine evergreen forests higher up, to alpine tundra above the treeline.

Only a small part of the park is montane. It is characterized by stands of Douglas fir, as well as savannahlike grasslands that occur on drier sites in valley bottoms. Well-developed stretches of montane can be found along the floors of the Athabasca and Miette River valleys, providing winter habitat for larger mammals such as elk.

The subalpine zone, heavily forested with evergreens, extends from the lower valley slopes up to the treeline. The dominant species in this zone is lodgepole pine, although Engelmann spruce, alpine fir, poplar, and aspen grow here. Lodgepole pine has adapted to make use of fire. Its hard seed cones are sealed by a resin that is melted only at high temperatures. When fire races through the forest, the resin melts and the cones release their seeds. As a result, these are the first conifers to regenerate in burned-out areas. The park's extensive stands of lodgepole pine are inhabited by few large mammals because the understory is minimal. Wildflowers are common in this zone and can be found by the roadside, in clearings, or on riverbanks.

Timberline here lies at an elevation between 2,050 and 2,400 meters above sea level. At this height, only a few stunted trees survive. Above this point is the alpine zone, where the climate is severe; the average yearly temperature is below freezing, and summer is brief. The zone's plant species grow low to the ground, with extensive root systems to protect them during high winds and through the deep snow cover of winter. During the short summer, these open slopes and meadows are carpeted with a profusion of flowers such as golden arnicas, bluebells, pale columbines, and red and yellow paintbrush. Higher still are brightly colored heathers, buttercups, and alpine forget-me-nots.

FAUNA

Wildlife is abundant in the park and can be seen throughout the year. During winter, many larger mammals move to lower elevations where food is accessible. February and March are particularly good for looking for animal tracks in the snow. By June, most of the snow cover at lower elevations has melted, the crowds haven't arrived, and animals can be seen feeding along the valley floor. In fall, tourists move to warmer

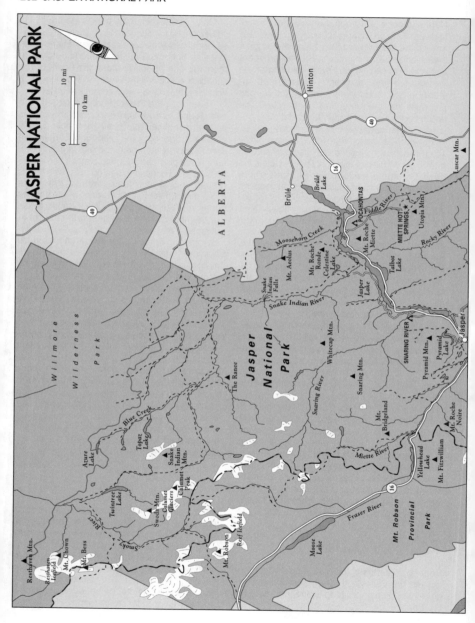

JASPER NATIONAL PARK

10 mi

10 km

Hinton

40

16

Brûlé

Brûlé Lake

A L B E R T A

Moosehorn Creek

POCAHONTAS

Fiddle River

Mt. Roche Miette

MIETTE HOT SPRINGS ★

Utopia Mtn.

Mt. Aeolus

Mt. Roche Ronde

Celestine Lake

Rocky River

Lascar Mtn.

Snake Indian Falls

Snake Indian River

Jasper Lake

Talbot Lake

Jasper

SNARING RIVER

Whitecap Mtn.

Pyramid Mtn.

Pyramid Lake

The Ranee

Snaring River

Snaring Mtn.

Willmore

Wilderness

Park

Jasper

National

Park

Blue Creek

Azure Lake

Topaz Lake

Snake Indian Mtn.

Mt. Bridgeland

Mt. Roche Noire

Miette River

Yellowhead Lake

Mt. Fitzwilliam

Twintree Lake

Swoda Mtn.

Calumet Glaciers

Calumet Peak

Smoky River

Reef Icefield

Mt. Robson

Fraser River

Moose Lake

Mt. Robson

Provincial

Park

Resthaven Mtn.

Resthaven Icefield

Mt. Chown

Mt. Bess

16

40

40

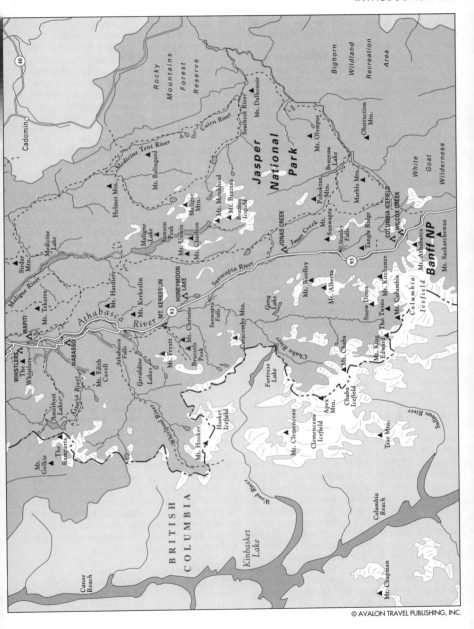

climates, the rutting season begins, bears go into hibernation, and a herd of elk moves into Jasper townsite for the winter.

Although the park provides ample opportunities for seeing numerous animals in their natural habitat, it also leads to human/animal encounters that are not always positive. For example, less than 10 percent of the park is made up of well-vegetated valleys. These lower areas are essential to the larger mammals for food and shelter but are also the most heavily traveled by visitors. Game trails used for thousands of years are often bisected by roads, and hundreds of animals are killed each year by speeding motorists. Please drive slowly in the park.

Campground Critters
Several species of small mammals thrive around campgrounds, thanks to an abundance of humans who are careless with their food. Columbian ground squirrels are very bold and will demand scraps of your lunch. Golden-mantled ground squirrels and red squirrels are also common. The least chipmunk (often confused with the golden-mantled ground squirrel because of its similar stripes) can also be seen in campgrounds; they'll often scamper across your hiking trail, then sit boldly on a rock waiting for you to pass.

Aquatic Species
Beaver dams are common between the townsite and the park's east gate. Dawn and dusk are the best times to watch these intriguing creatures at work. Also common in the park's wetlands are mink and muskrat.

Hoofed Residents
Five species of deer inhabit the park. The large-eared mule deer is commonly seen around the edge of the townsite or grazing along the road. White-tailed deer can be seen throughout the park. A small herd of woodland caribou roams throughout the park; they are most commonly seen during late spring, feeding in river deltas. The town of Jasper is in the home range of approximately 500 elk, which can be seen most of the year around the townsite or along the highway northeast and south of town. Moose, although not common, can be seen along the major drainage systems feeding on aquatic plants.

In summer, mountain goats can often be seen feeding in alpine meadows. A good place for goat watching is Goat Lookout on the Icefields Parkway. Unlike most of the park's large mammals, these surefooted creatures don't migrate to lower elevations in winter but stay sheltered on rocky crags, where wind and sun keep the vegetation snow free. Often confused with the goat is the darker bighorn sheep. The horns on the males of this species are very thick and often curl 360 degrees. Bighorns are the most common of all large mammals in the park; look for them in the east of the park at Disaster Point.

Reclusive Residents
Several of the park's resident species keep a low profile, usually out of sight of humans. Populations of the shy and elusive lynx fluctuate with that of their primary food source, the snowshoe hare. The largest of the big cats in the park is the cougar (also called the mountain lion), a solitary carnivore that inhabits remote valleys. Jasper's wolves are one of the park's success stories. After being driven to near extinction, the species has rebounded. Five packs now roam the park, but they are rarely seen—keeping to the deep wilderness rarely traveled by people. Although not common in the park, coyotes can be seen in cleared areas alongside the roads, usually at dawn and dusk.

Bears
Black bears number approximately 80 in the park and occasionally wander into campgrounds looking for food. They are most commonly seen along the Icefields Parkway in spring, when they first come out of hibernation.

Grizzly bears are occasionally seen crossing the Icefields Parkway at higher elevations early in summer. For the most part, they remain in remote mountain valleys, and if they do see, smell, or hear you, they'll generally move away. Read the pamphlet *Keep the Wild in Wildlife*, which is available at campgrounds and information centers throughout the park, before setting out into the woods.

Other Mammals
The pine marten is common but shy; look for them in subalpine forests. The short-tailed weasel—a relative of the marten—is also com-

mon, whereas the long-tailed weasel is rare. At higher elevations, look for pikas in piles of fallen rock. Hoary marmots live near the upper limits of vegetation growth, where their shrill warning whistles carry across the open meadows. Porcupines are widespread in all valleys and are most active at night.

Birds

The extensive tree cover in the lower valleys hides many species of birds, making them seem less abundant than they are. A total of 248 species have been recorded. The two you're most likely to see are the gray jay and Clark's nutcracker, which regularly joins picnickers for lunch. Also common are black-and-white magpies, raucous ravens, and several species of ducks, which can be seen around lakes in the Athabasca River Valley. Harlequin ducks nest in the park during early summer. A stretch of the Maligne River is closed during this season to prevent human interference.

The colony of black swifts in Maligne Canyon is one of only two in Alberta. Their poorly developed legs make it difficult for them to take off from their nests in the canyon walls—they literally fall before becoming airborne. High alpine slopes are home to white-tailed ptarmigans, a type of grouse that turns white in winter. Also at this elevation are flocks of rosy finches, which live under overhanging cliffs. In subalpine forests, the songs of thrushes and the tapping of woodpeckers can be heard.

At dusk, great horned owls swoop silently through the trees, their eerie call echoing through the forest. Golden eagles and bald eagles can be seen soaring high above the forests, and 12 pairs of ospreys are known to nest in the park, many along the Athabasca River between town and the east park gate.

HISTORY

The first white man to enter the Athabasca River Valley was David Thompson, one of Canada's greatest explorers. He was looking for a pass through the mountains to use as access to the Pacific Ocean. The gap he eventually found—**Athabasca Pass,** south of Mt. Edith Cavell—became famous as the route used by the North West and Hudson's Bay companies to cross the Rockies.

Meanwhile, the North West Company built a post named Jasper's House near the present townsite of Jasper. In time, an easier passage through the mountains was discovered farther north (at what is now called **Yellowhead Pass**), displacing Thompson's original, more difficult route to the south.

Leading up to the end of the fur-trading era, many visitors to the area returned home with accounts of the region's natural splendor. In 1858, Irish-Canadian artist Paul Kane published the book *Wanderings of an Artist,* which gave the outside world its first glimpse of the Jasper area.

At the turn of the 20th century, only seven homesteaders lived in the valley, but the Grand Trunk Pacific Railway was pushing westward, bringing with it the possibility of multitudes of settlers coming to live there. In 1907, the federal government officially declared the boundaries of Jasper Forest Park and bought all the land within it, except for one homestead owned by Lewis Swift. (This parcel remained privately owned until 1962, long after the stubborn Mr. Swift had passed away.) The threat of oversettlement of the valley had been abated, but as a designated forest park, mining and logging were still allowed. In 1908, Jasper Park Collieries staked claims in the park. By the time the railway came through in 1911, mining activity was centered at **Pocahontas** (near the park's east gate), where a township was established and thrived. During an extended miners' strike, the men spent their spare time constructing log pools at Miette Hot Springs, which were heavily promoted to early park visitors. The mine closed in 1921, and many families relocated to Jasper, which had grown from a railway camp into a popular tourist destination. Jasper was officially designated as a national park in 1930. This was followed by the construction of many roads, including the Icefields Parkway, which opened in 1940.

ICEFIELDS PARKWAY—JASPER

Sunwapta Pass, at the boundary between Banff and Jasper national parks, is situated just more than halfway between Lake Louise and Jasper townsite along the 230-kilometer Icefields Parkway, one of the world's great mountain drives. From the pass, it is 108 kilometers to Jasper, passing first the Columbia Icefield, then following the Athabasca River for the rest of the way. The scenery along this stretch of road is no less spectacular than the other half through Banff National Park, and it's easy to spend a few days en route. Along this section of the parkway are lodges, hostels, campgrounds, and a gas station.

SIGHTS

Columbia Icefield

The largest and most accessible of 17 glacial areas along the Icefields Parkway is 325-square-kilometer Columbia Icefield at the south end of the park. It's a remnant of the last major glaciation that covered most of Canada 20,000 years ago, and it has survived because of the elevation (1,900–2,800 meters above sea level), cold temperatures, and heavy snowfalls. From the main body of the ice cap, which sits astride the Continental Divide, glaciers creep down three main valleys. Of these, **Athabasca Glacier** is the most accessible and can be seen from the Icefields Parkway. A path to the toe of the glacier traverses a mixture of rock, sand, and gravel, known as "till," deposited by the glacier as it retreats. The speed at which glaciers advance and retreat varies with the long-term climate. Athabasca Glacier has retreated to its current position from across the highway, a distance of more than 1.5 kilometers, in 100 years. Currently, it retreats two to three meters per year.

The icefield is made more spectacular by the impressive peaks that surround it. **Mt. Athabasca** (3,491 meters) dominates the skyline, and three glaciers cling to its flanks. **Dome Glacier** is also visible from the highway. Although part of Columbia Icefield, it is not actually connected. It is made of ice that breaks off the icefield 300

meters above, supplemented by the large quantities of snow the area receives each winter.

Exploring the Icefield

The icefield can be very dangerous for unprepared visitors, especially the broken surface of Athabasca Glacier where often-deep crevasses are uncovered as the winter snows melt. The safest way to experience it firsthand is on specially developed vehicles with balloon tires that can travel over its crevassed surface. These Snocoaches are operated by **Brewster,** 403/762-6767. The 90-minute tour of Athabasca Glacier includes time spent walking on the surface of the glacier. The tour, which begins with a bus ride from the Columbia Icefield Centre, is adults $26, children $13 and operates from late May to early October 9 A.M.–5 P.M. Early in the season, the glacier is still covered in a layer of snow and is, therefore, not as spectacular as during the summer months. Brewster operates a day trip to Columbia Icefield from Banff (10 hours; $89 per person, excluding Snocoach) and Calgary (15 hours; $112 per person).

Icefield Centre

The magnificent Icefield Centre, which opened in the summer of 1996, is nestled at the base of Mt. Wilcox, overlooking the Athabasca Glacier. It is the staging point for Snocoach tours, but before heading out onto the icefield, don't miss the **Glacier Gallery.** Located on the lower floor, this large display area details all aspects of the frozen world, including the story of glacier formation and movement. It explains everything you've ever wanted to know about glaciers. The centerpiece is a scaled-down fiberglass model of the Athabasca Glacier, which is surrounded by hands-on displays and audiovisual presentations. On the main floor of the center, you'll find a Parks Canada desk, a Snocoach booking area, and a reception for the upstairs hotel rooms. Upstairs is a cavernous snack bar, with the option of sitting outside, and the Glacier Dining Room, which is open daily for dinner. The complex (including display area) is open daily 9 A.M.–11 P.M.

To Sunwapta Falls

Sunwapta Lake—at the toe of the Athabasca Glacier—is the source of the **Sunwapta River,** which the Icefields Parkway follows for 48 kilometers to Sunwapta Falls. Eight kilometers north from the Icefield Centre, the road descends to a viewpoint for **Stutfield Glacier.** Most of the glacier is hidden from view by a densely wooded ridge, but at its toe, till left by the glacier's retreat litters the valley floor. The main body of the Columbia Icefield can be seen along the clifftop high above. To the south of the glacier is **Mt. Kitchener.** Six kilometers farther down the road is **Tangle Ridge,** a grayish-brown wall of limestone over which Beauty Creek cascades. At this point, the Icefields Parkway runs alongside the Sunwapta River, following its course through the **Endless Range,** the eastern wall of a classic glacier-carved valley.

An additional 40 kilometers along the road, a one-kilometer gravel spur to the left leads to **Sunwapta Falls.** Here, the Sunwapta River changes direction sharply and drops into a deep canyon. Two kilometers downstream, the river flows into the much wider Athabasca Valley.

Goat Lookout

After following the Athabasca River for 17 kilometers, the road ascends to a lookout. Below the lookout is a steep bank of glacially ground material containing natural deposits of salt. The local mountain goats spend most of the year on the steep slopes of Mt. Kerkeslin, to the northeast, but often cross the road in spring and can be seen searching for the salt licks along the riverbank.

Athabasca Falls

At Athabasca Falls, the Athabasca River is forced through a narrow gorge and over a cliff into a cauldron of roaring water below. Old river channels can be seen along the west bank. As the river slowly erodes the center of the riverbed, the falls move upstream. Trails lead from a day-use area to various viewpoints above and below the falls.

Continuing north, the Icefields Parkway passes **Horseshoe Lake,** a picturesque body of water reached via a 300-meter-long trail. Two kilometers farther north are a couple of lookouts with spectacular views across the Athabasca River to the Athabasca Pass, which was discovered by David Thompson in 1808. To the north of the pass lies the distintive eastern face of Mt. Edith Cavell. From this lookout, it is 26 kilometers to Jasper townsite. For information on Mt. Edith Cavell, see the following section.

HIKES ALONG ICEFIELDS PARKWAY

Wilcox Pass
- Length: 4 kilometers (90 minutes) one-way
- Elevation gain: 340 meters

Brewster's Snocoaches drive right onto the icefield for a close look.

BREWSTER

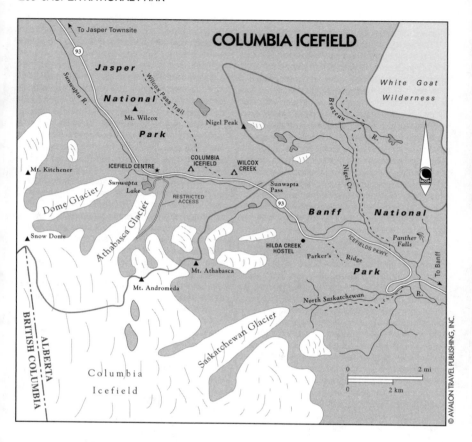

COLUMBIA ICEFIELD

© AVALON TRAVEL PUBLISHING, INC.

• Rating: moderate

This trail was once used by northbound outfitters because, 100 years ago, Athabasca Glacier covered the valley floor and had to be bypassed. The trail begins from the north side of Wilcox Creek Campground, three kilometers south of the Icefield Centre. It climbs through a forest of Engelmann spruce and alpine fir to a ridge with panoramic views of the valley, Columbia Icefield, and surrounding peaks. Ascending gradually from there, the trail enters a fragile environment of alpine meadows. From the pass, most hikers return along the same trail, although it is possible to continue north, descending to the

Icefields Parkway at Tangle Ridge, 11.5 kilometers from the trailhead.

Fortress Lake
• Length: 24 kilometers (7–8 hours) one-way
• Elevation gain: minimal
• Rating: moderate

The trail to this seldom-visited lake straddling the Continental Divide begins from the Sunwapta Falls parking lot. For the first 15 kilometers, the trail meanders along the east bank of the Athabasca River, then crosses it. Beyond the main bridge, you'll need to ford the braided Chaba River, then continue southwest along the river flats for six kilometers to the east end of Fortress Lake. The lake lies within British Columbia in Hamber Provincial Park. Its shores are difficult to traverse because they lack established trails.

Geraldine Lakes
- Length: 5 kilometers (2 hours) one-way
- Elevation gain: 410 meters
- Rating: moderate

The first of the four Geraldine Lakes is an easy two-kilometer hike from the trailhead (located 5.5 kilometers along the Geraldine Fire Road, which spurs south off Highway 93A west of Athabasca Falls). The forest-encircled lake reflects the north face of Mt. Fryatt (3,361 meters). The trail continues along the northwest shore, climbs steeply past a scenic 100-meter waterfall, and traverses some rough terrain where the trail becomes indistinct; follow the cairns. At the end of the valley is another waterfall. The trail climbs east of the waterfall to a ridge above the second of the lakes, five kilometers from the trailhead. Although the trail officially ends here, it does continue to a campground at the south end of the lake. Two other lakes, accessible only by bushwhacking, are located farther up the valley.

ACCOMMODATIONS

Lodging
Accommodations are strung out along the Icefields Parkway, generally open only between late April and early October. **Columbia Icefield Chalet** (780/852-6550, www.brewster.ca), part of the Icefield Centre, lies in a stunning location high above the treeline and overlooking the Columbia Icefield, 103 kilometers south of Jasper townsite. It features 29 standard rooms, 17 of which have glacier views, and three larger, more luxurious corner rooms. Rates June–September range $175–195 single or double, whereas the last week of May and the first few days in October, rates start at $90. The facility is closed the rest of the year. Continuing north, the next lodging is **Sunwapta Falls Resort** (780/852-4852, www.sunwapta.com), 53 kilometers south of Jasper townsite. It has 52 units, two restaurants, and a gift shop; from $175 single or double. It's open early May to mid-October.

Spread along a picturesque bend on the Athabasca River six kilometers south of town is **Becker's Chalets** (780/852-3779, www.beckerschalets.com). This historic lodging took in its first guests more than 50 years ago and continues to be a park favorite, with many guests coming back every year. The original cabins still stand, with one-bed sleeping rooms for $80, chalets with kitchenette, fireplace, and double bed $125 (or $145 for those on the riverfront). The new units feature all the modern conveniences, including a color TV; from $205 per night. Becker's also boasts one of the park's finest restaurants. Continuing north, just four kilometers south of Jasper townsite, **Jasper House Bungalows,** 780/852-4535, offers basic sleeping units for $120; those with cooking facilities begin at $190.

Hostels
Along this section of the Icefields Parkway, hostels are located at kilometers 144 and 198 (from Lake Louise). **Beauty Creek Hostel,** 17 kilometers north of Columbia Icefield, is nestled in a small stand of Douglas fir between the Icefields Parkway and the Sunwapta River. It has separate male and female cabins, each of which sleeps 12 and has a woodstove. A third building holds a well-equipped kitchen and dining area. Members of Hostelling International pay $10, nonmembers $15. Open May–September. **Athabasca Falls Hostel** is 60 kilometers farther north and 32 kilometers south of Jasper townsite. It is larger and has electricity. Athabasca Falls is only a few minutes' walk away; members $11, nonmembers $16. Reservations for these hostels can be made at all major hostels or by calling 780/852-3215.

Campgrounds
Wilcox Creek and **Columbia Icefield campgrounds** are within two kilometers of each other at the extreme southern end of the park. Both are primitive campgrounds with toilets, cooking shelters, and fire rings; sites are $10. Traveling north, **Jonas Creek, Honeymoon Lake,** and **Mt. Kerkeslin campgrounds** are within 50 kilometers of each other. Each is $10 per site, per night. **Wabasso Campground** is located along Highway 93A, 16 kilometers south of Jasper townsite; $13.

JASPER TOWNSITE

The townsite of Jasper is Banff's northern counterpart, linked to its neighbor by a similar history and, today, by the Icefields Parkway. The town, which is run by Parks Canada, has a little more than half the population of Banff, and its setting is less dramatic. But it's also less commercialized than Banff and its streets a little quieter. Part of the town's charm is its location at the confluence of the Athabasca and Miette rivers, surrounded by the rugged, snowcapped peaks of Jasper National Park. From town, it's a 3.5-hour drive to Edmonton, the closest city. The town of Banff is 280 kilometers to the southeast, and to the west is the vast wilderness of the Monashee, Cariboo, and Columbia ranges of the British Columbia interior.

Connaught Drive, the town's main street, parallels the rail line as it curves through town. Along here, you'll find the Park Information Centre, the bus depot, the rail terminal, restaurants, motels, and a parking lot. Behind Connaught Drive is Patricia Street (one-way), which has more restaurants and services and leads to more hotels and motels on Geikie Street. Behind this main core are rows of neat houses—much less pretentious than those in Banff—and all the facilities of a regular town, including a library, a school, a post office, a museum, a swimming pool, and a hospital.

History

In the winter of 1810–1811, when David Thompson was making the first successful crossing of the Continental Divide, some of his party remained in the Athabasca River Valley and constructed a small settlement east of the present townsite. The settlement was named Henry House and was used for many years by the North West Company as a supply depot for fur traders. The post was run by a clerk named Jasper Hawes, and in time the settlement became known as Jasper's House. Over the years, stories of the area's natural beauty filtered east. Gold seekers commonly stopped by on their way to the Cariboo goldfields. But when the fur-trading era ended in the mid-1880s, the post closed.

In 1911, a construction camp was established

for the Grand Trunk Pacific Railway near the present townsite of Jasper. The company had dreamed of a transcontinental rail line to rival the Canadian Pacific Railway (CPR) line that crossed the Rockies farther south. When the northern line was completed, visitors flocked into the remote mountain settlement, and its future was ensured. The first accommodation for tourists was 10 tents on the shore of Lac Beauvert, which became known as Jasper Park Camp. In 1921, the tents were replaced, and the original Jasper Park Lodge was constructed. By the summer of 1928, a road was completed from Edmonton, and a golf course was built. As the number of tourists to the park continued to increase, existing facilities were expanded. In 1940, the Icefields Parkway opened, and in the 1960s, Marmot Basin Ski Area opened and the downtown core of the townsite was developed.

SIGHTS AND DRIVES

Downtown

With all the things to do and see in the park, it's amazing how many people hang out in town. July and August are especially busy; much-needed improvements to the parking problem have had little impact on the traffic. The best way to avoid the problem is to avoid town during the day. The Park Information Centre, on Connaught Drive, is the only real reason to be in town. The shaded park in front of the center is a good place for people-watching, but you may get clobbered by a wayward Hacky Sack.

At the back of town is the excellent **Jasper-Yellowhead Museum and Archives** (400 Pyramid Lake Rd., 780/852-3013). A new gallery opened in 1998, featuring exhibits that take visitors through a timeline of Jasper's human history. The museum also features extensive archives, including photographs, documents, maps, videos, and a small gift shop. Admission is $3. It's open mid-June to September daily 10 A.M.–9 P.M., the rest of the year Thurs.–Sun. 10 A.M.–5 P.M.

If you like taxidermy, visit **The Den Wildlife Museum,** which exhibits stuffed animals in

JASPER VICINITY

Pyramid Mountain

Pyramid Lake

To Edmonton and Miette Hot Springs

SIXTH BRIDGE

PYRAMID LAKE RESORT

MALIGNE CANYON HOSTEL

Maligne River

Patricia Lake

PATRICIA LAKE BUNGALOWS

PYRAMID RIDING STABLES

To Maligne Lake

Edith Lake

Annette Lake

Cottonwood

Slough

PINE BUNGALOWS

Jasper National Park

SEE "JASPER TOWNSITE" MAP

JASPER PARK LODGE

HWY.

Lac Beauvert

OLD FORT POINT

YELLOWHEAD

Miette River

To Prince George, BC

JASPER INTERNATIONAL HOSTEL

ALPINE VILLAGE

93A

Athabasca

Jasper National Park

JASPER TRAMWAY

WHISTLERS

JASPER HOUSE BUNGALOWS

WAPITI

The Whistlers

BECKER'S CHALETS

Valley of the Five Lakes

0   1 mi
0   1 km

MARMOT BASIN

To Mt. Edith Cavell and Banff National Park

ICEFIELDS PARKWAY

River

93A

93

To Banff National Park

© AVALON TRAVEL PUBLISHING, INC.

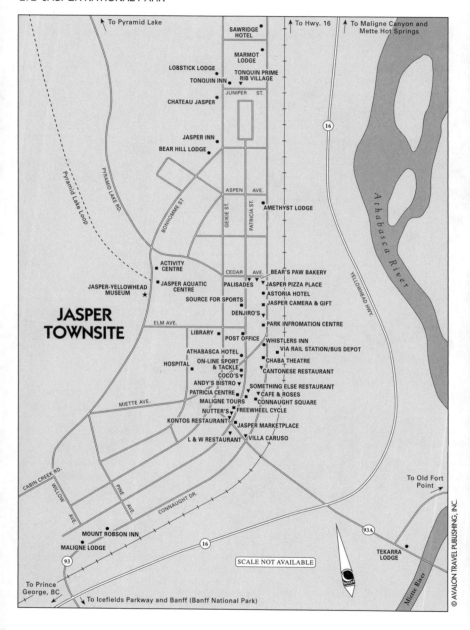

To Pyramid Lake

SAWRIDGE HOTEL

MARMOT LODGE

LOBSTICK LODGE

TONQUIN INN

TONQUIN PRIME RIB VILLAGE

CHATEAU JASPER

JUNIPER ST.

JASPER INN

BEAR HILL LODGE

BONHOMME ST.

ASPEN AVE.

GEIKIE ST.

PATRICIA ST.

AMETHYST LODGE

To Hwy. 16

16

To Maligne Canyon and Miette Hot Springs

Athabasca River

JASPER-YELLOWHEAD MUSEUM

JASPER TOWNSITE

ACTIVITY CENTRE

JASPER AQUATIC CENTRE

CEDAR AVE.

BEAR'S PAW BAKERY

PALISADES

JASPER PIZZA PLACE

ASTORIA HOTEL

SOURCE FOR SPORTS

JASPER CAMERA & GIFT

DENJIRO'S

ELM AVE.

PARK INFROMATION CENTRE

LIBRARY

POST OFFICE

WHISTLERS INN

YELLOWHEAD HWY.

ATHABASCA HOTEL

VIA RAIL STATION/BUS DEPOT

HOSPITAL

ON-LINE SPORT & TACKLE

CHABA THEATRE

COCO'S

CANTONESE RESTAURANT

ANDY'S BISTRO

MIETTE AVE.

PATRICIA CENTRE

SOMETHING ELSE RESTAURANT

CAFE & ROSES

MALIGNE TOURS

CONNAUGHT SQUARE

NUTTER'S

FREEWHEEL CYCLE

KONTOS RESTAURANT

JASPER MARKETPLACE

L & W RESTAURANT

VILLA CARUSO

CABIN CREEK RD.

WILLOW AVE.

PINE AVE.

CONNAUGHT DR.

To Old Fort Point

93A

MOUNT ROBSON INN

MALIGNE LODGE

93

16

SCALE NOT AVAILABLE

MOON

TEKARRA LODGE

Miette River

To Prince George, BC

To Icefields Parkway and Banff (Banff National Park)

© AVALON TRAVEL PUBLISHING, INC.

their "natural setting." It's located down a dark stairway beneath the Whistlers Inn. Yep, they even charge you for it. Open year-round daily 9 A.M.–10 P.M.

Patricia and Pyramid Lakes

A winding road heads through the hills at the back of town to these two picturesque lakes, which were formed when glacial moraines dammed shallow valleys. The first, to the left, is Patricia; the second, farther along the road, is Pyramid, backed by **Pyramid Mountain** (2,765 meters). Both lakes are popular spots for picnicking, fishing, and boating. Boat rentals are available at **Pyramid Lake Boat Rentals** (at Pyramid Lake Resort, 780/852-3536). Canoes, rowboats, paddleboats, and kayaks are $15 for the first hour and $10 for each additional hour. The resort also rents motorboats ($30 per hour). From the resort, the road continues around the lake to a bridge, which leads to an island that is popular with picnickers. The road ends at the quieter end of the lake.

Jasper Tramway

This tramway climbs more than 1,000 vertical meters up the steep north face of **The Whistlers,** which is named after the hoary marmots that live on the summit. The tramway operates two 30-passenger cars that take seven minutes to reach the upper terminal, during which time the conductor gives a narrated lecture about the mountain and its environment. From the upper terminal, a one-kilometer trail leads to the summit (2,470 meters). The view is breathtaking; to the south is the Columbia Icefield, and on a clear day you can see Mt. Robson (3,954 meters)—the highest peak in the Canadian Rockies—to the northwest. Round-trip fare is $18; allow two hours on top and, on a clear summer's day, two more hours in line at the bottom. The tramway is located three kilometers south of town on Highway 93 (Icefields Parkway) and then three kilometers up Whistlers Road. It operates in summer daily 8 A.M.–10 P.M., shorter hours April–May and Sept.–Oct., closed the rest of the year. For more information, call 780/852-3093.

Mount Edith Cavell

The original Icefields Parkway (Highway 93A), which followed the southeast bank of the Athabasca River, has been bypassed by a more direct route on the other side of the river. Along the original route, known also as the Athabasca Parkway, a 14.5-kilometer road leads to a parking area below the northeast face of Mt. Edith Cavell (3,363 meters). This peak can be seen from many vantage points in the park, including the townsite, but none is more impressive than directly below it. On this face, **Angel Glacier** lies in a saddle on the mountain's lower slopes. From the parking area, the **Path of the Glacier Trail** (one hour round-trip) traverses moraines deposited by the receding Angel Glacier and leads to some great viewpoints. For other hiking opportunities in the vicinity of Mt. Edith Cavell, see **Hikes near Mount Edith Cavell.**

Edith and Annette Lakes

These two lakes along the road to Jasper Park Lodge—across the Athabasca River from town—are perfect for a picnic, a swim, or a pleasant walk. They are remnants of a much larger lake that once covered the entire valley floor. The lakes are relatively shallow; therefore, the sun warms the water to a bearable temperature. In fact, they have the warmest waters of any lakes in the park. The 2.5-kilometer **Lee Foundation Trail** encircles Lake Annette and is wheelchair accessible. Both lakes have day-use areas with beaches and picnic areas.

Jasper Park Lodge

Accommodations are not usually considered "sights," but then this is the Rockies, where three grand railway hotels attract as many visitors as the more legitimate natural attractions. Jasper Park Lodge has been the premier accommodation in the park since it opened in 1921. Back then, it was a single-story structure, reputed to be the largest log building in the world. It burned to the ground in 1952 but was rebuilt. Additional bungalows were erected along Lac Beauvert, forming a basis for today's lodge. Rows of cabins radiate from the main lodge, which contains restaurants, lounges, and the town's only covered shopping arcade. Today, up to 900 guests can be accommodated in 442 rooms. A large parking area for nonguests is located on Lodge Road, behind the golf clubhouse; you're welcome to walk around the resort, play golf, dine in the restaurants, and, of course, browse through the shopping promenade, even if you're not a registered guest. From the main lodge, a hiking trail follows the shoreline of Lac Beauvert and links up with other trails from Old Fort Point. To walk from town takes one hour.

Maligne Canyon

To get here, head northeast from town and turn right onto Maligne Lake Road. The canyon access road veers left 11 kilometers from Jasper. This unique geological feature has been eroded out of the easily dissolved limestone bedrock by the fast-flowing Maligne River. Surface water here is augmented by underground springs; therefore, it seems that more water flows out of the canyon than into it. The canyon is up to 50 meters deep, yet so narrow that squirrels often jump across. At the top of the canyon, opposite the teahouse, are large potholes in the riverbed. These potholes are created when rocks and pebbles become trapped in what begins as a shallow depression, and under the force of the rushing water the rocks carve jug-shaped hollows into the soft bedrock.

An interpretive trail winds down from the parking lot, crossing the canyon six times. The most spectacular sections of the canyon can be seen from the first two bridges, at the upper end of the trail. In summer, a teahouse operates at the top of the canyon. To avoid the crowds at the upper end of the canyon, an alternative would be to park at Sixth Bridge, near the confluence of the Maligne and Athabasca rivers, and walk *up* the canyon (see **Hiking around Town**). The **Maligne Lake Shuttle** stops at the canyon eight times daily. For reservations, call 780/852-3370; fare is $8 one-way from town. In winter, guided tours of the frozen canyon are an experience you'll never forget (see **Wintertime**).

Medicine Lake

From the canyon, Maligne Lake Road climbs to Medicine Lake, which does a disappearing act each year. The water level fluctuates because of an underground drainage system known as karst. At the northwest end of the lake, where the outlet should be, the riverbed is often dry. In fall, when runoff from the mountains is minimal, the water level drops, and by November the lake has almost completely dried up. Early

Indians believed that spirits were responsible for the phenomenon, hence the name.

Maligne Lake

At the end of the road, 48 kilometers from Jasper, is Maligne Lake, the largest glacier-fed lake in the Canadian Rockies and the second largest in the world. The first paying visitors were brought to the lake in 1929, and it has been a mecca for camera-toting tourists from around the world ever since. Once at the lake, activities are plentiful. But other than taking in the spectacular vistas, the only thing you won't need your wallet for is hiking one of the numerous trails in the area.

The most popular tourist activity at the lake is a 90-minute narrated cruise on a glass-enclosed boat up the lake to oft-photographed **Spirit Island.** Cruises leave in summer, every hour on the hour from 10 A.M.–5 P.M., with fewer sailings in May and September; $32 per person. Many time slots are block-booked by tour companies, so reservations are suggested. Rowboats and canoes can be rented at the Boat House for $10 per hour or $45 per day. The lake also has excellent trout fishing (Alberta's record rainbow trout was caught here), horseback riding, and white-water rafting on the Maligne River (for details on all of these activities, see **Other Recreation**). The cruises, boat rentals, and all activities are operated by **Maligne Tours** (627 Patricia St., 780/852-3370). At the lake, Maligne Tours operates a souvenir shop and large café with outdoor seating overlooking the lake.

The **Maligne Lake Shuttle** runs from the Maligne Tours office and from various hotels out to the lake three to six times daily. The fare to Maligne Canyon is $8 one-way, or $12 out to the lake.

Miette Hot Springs

Near the park's east gate is Miette Hot Springs Road, which leads to the warmest springs in the Canadian Rockies. One kilometer along the road is **Punchbowl Falls,** where a small river cascades through a narrow crevice in a cliff to a pool of turbulent water. After curving, swerving, rising, and falling many times, the road ends at the hot springs. In the early 1900s, the springs were one of the park's biggest attractions. In 1910, a packhorse trail was built up the valley, and the government constructed a bathhouse. The original hand-hewn log structure was replaced in the 1930s with pools that remained in use until new facilities were built in 1985. Water that flows into the pools is artificially cooled from 54°C to a soothing 39°C. A swim in the pools is $5.50, a towel $1, and lockers 25 cents. It's open mid-May to mid-Oct. 10:30 A.M.–9 P.M., with extended hours in the peak summer months. For more information, call 780/866-3939.

Many hiking trails begin from the hot springs complex; the shortest is from the picnic area to the source of the springs (200 meters), and the longest crosses the front ranges to Whitehorse Wildland Park near Cadomin. Below the springs is a restaurant and lodging.

HIKING AROUND TOWN

The 1,000 kilometers of hiking trails in Jasper are significantly different than those in the other mountain national parks. The park has an extensive system of interconnecting backcountry trails that, for experienced hikers, can provide a wilderness adventure rivaled by few areas on the face of this earth. For casual day-hikers, on the other hand, opportunities are more limited. Most trails in the immediate vicinity of the townsite have little elevation gain and lead through montane forest to lakes. The trails at the base of Mt. Edith Cavell, in the Tonquin Valley, around Maligne Lake, and along the Icefields Parkway have more rewarding objectives and are more challenging.

The most popular trails for extended back-country trips are the **Skyline Trail,** between the townsite and Maligne Lake (44.5 kilometers, three days each way); the trails to **Amethyst Lakes** in the Tonquin Valley (19 kilometers, one day each way) and **Athabasca Pass** (50 kilometers, three days each way), which was used by fur traders for 40 years as the main route across the Rockies; and the **South Boundary Trail,** which traverses a remote section of the front ranges into Banff National Park (160 kilometers, 10 days each way).

Before setting off on any hikes, whatever the length, go to the **Park Information Centre** in Jasper townsite for trail maps, trail conditions, and trail closures. To prevent overuse, many longer trails operate on a quota system and you *must* pick up a Wilderness Pass before heading out; $6 per person per night.

BIGHORN SHEEP

Bighorn sheep are some of the most distinctive mammals of the Canadian Rockies. Easily recognized by their impressive horns, they are often seen grazing on grassy mountain slopes or at salt licks beside the road. The color of their coat varies with the season; in summer it is a brownish gray with a cream-colored belly and rump, turning lighter in winter. At seven years of age, males are fully grown and can weigh up to 120 kilograms. Females generally weigh around 80 kilograms.

Both sexes possess horns, rather than antlers like moose, elk, and deer. Unlike antlers, horns are not shed each year and can grow to astounding sizes. The horns of rams are larger than those of ewes and curve up to 360 degrees. The spiraled horns of an older ram can measure 115 centimeters and weigh as much as 15 kilograms. As the horns grow, they become marked by an annual growth ring. By counting the rings it is possible to determine the approximate age of the animal. In fall, during the mating season, a hierarchy is established among them for the right to breed ewes. As the males face off against each other to establish dominance, their horns act as both a weapon and a buffer against the head-butting of other rams. The skull structure of the bighorn, rams in particular, has become adapted to these clashes, avoiding heavy concussion.

These animals are particularly tolerant of humans and often approach parked vehicles; although they are not dangerous, as with all mammals in the park, you should not approach or feed them.

Pyramid Lake Loop

- Length: 17 kilometers (5 hours) round-trip
- Elevation gain: 150 meters
- Rating: easy to moderate

Myriad official and unofficial hiking trails are located on the benchland immediately west of Jasper townsite. From the parking lot opposite the Aquatic Centre on Pyramid Lake Road, a well-marked trail climbs onto the benchland. Keep right, crossing Pyramid Lake Road, and you'll emerge on a bluff overlooking the Athabasca River Valley. Bighorn sheep can often be seen grazing here. If you return to the trailhead from here, you will have hiked seven kilometers. The trail continues north, disappearing into the montane forest until arriving at Pyramid Lake. Various trails can be taken to return to town; ask at the Park Information Centre for a map of the entire area before setting out.

Patricia Lake Circle

- Length: 5-kilometer loop (90 minutes round-trip)
- Elevation gain: minimal
- Rating: easy

This trail begins across the road from the riding stables on Pyramid Lake Road. It traverses a mixed forest of aspen and lodgepole pine, prime habitat for a variety of larger mammals such as elk, deer, and moose. The second half of the trail skirts Cottonwood Slough, where you'll see several beaver ponds.

The Whistlers

- Length: 8 kilometers (2.5–3 hours) one-way
- Elevation gain: 1,220 meters
- Rating: difficult

This steep ascent, one of the most arduous in the park, is unique in that it passes through three distinct vegetation zones in a relatively short distance. From the trailhead on Whistlers Road, 200 meters below the hostel, the trail begins climbing and doesn't let up until you merge with the crowds getting off the tramway at the top. The trail begins in a montane forest of aspen and white birch, climbs through a subalpine forest of Engelmann spruce and alpine fir, then emerges onto the open, treeless tundra, which is inhabited by pikas, hoary marmots, and a few hardy plants. Carry water with you because none is available before the upper tramway terminal.

Old Fort Point

- Length: 6.5-kilometer loop (2 hours round-trip)
- Elevation gain: 60 meters
- Rating: easy

Old Fort Point is a moderately sized knoll above the Athabasca River, to the east of Jasper townsite. Although it is not likely that a fort was ever located here, the first fur-trading post in the Rockies, Henry House, was located just downstream, and it is easy to imagine fur traders and early explorers climbing to this summit for 360-degree views of the Athabasca and Miette rivers. To get to the trailhead from town, take Highway 93A and turn left to Lac Beauvert. The trail begins just over the Athabasca River. Climb the wooden stairs, take the left trail to the top of the knoll, then continue back to the parking lot along the north flank of the hill.

Valley of the Five Lakes

- Length: 2.3 kilometers (1 hour) one-way
- Elevation gain: 60 meters
- Rating: easy

These lakes, nestled in an open valley, are small but make a worthwhile destination. From the trailhead, 10 kilometers south of Jasper townsite along the Icefields Parkway, the trail passes through a forest of lodgepole pine, crosses a stream, and climbs a ridge that affords a panoramic view of surrounding peaks. As the trail descends to the lakes, turn left at the first intersection to a point between two of the lakes. These lakes are linked to Old Fort Point by a tedious 10-kilometer trail through montane forest.

Maligne Canyon

- Length: 3.7 kilometers (90 minutes) one-way
- Elevation gain: 125 meters
- Rating: moderate

Maligne Canyon is one of the busiest places in the park, yet few visitors hike the entire length of the canyon trail. By beginning from the lower end of the canyon, at the confluence of the Maligne and Athabasca rivers, you'll avoid starting your hike alongside the masses, and you'll get to hike downhill on your return (when you're tired). To get to the trailhead, head east from the townsite, turn right on Maligne Lake Road, and follow it 2.5 kilometers to the warden's office, from where a one-kilometer access road leads to Sixth Bridge. Crowds will be minimal for the first three kilometers, to Fourth Bridge, where the trail starts climbing. By the time you get to Third Bridge, you start encountering "adventurous" hikers coming down the canyon, and soon thereafter you'll meet the real crowds, bear-bells and all. Upstream of here, the canyon is deepest and most spectacular. See **Sights and Drives** for details of the hike starting from the *top* of the canyon.

HIKES NEAR MOUNT EDITH CAVELL

Mount Edith Cavell Road begins from Highway 93A and winds through a subalpine forest, ascending 300 meters in 14.5 kilometers. Trailheads are located at the end of the road (Cavell Meadows Trail and a short interpretive trail) and across from the hostel two kilometers from the end (Astoria River Trail). A third trailhead is on Marmot Basin Road where it crosses Portal Creek (Maccarib Pass Trail).

Cavell Meadows
• Length: 4 kilometers (1 hour) one-way
• Elevation gain: 350 meters
• Rating: easy to moderate
This trail, beginning from the parking lot beneath Mt. Edith Cavell, provides easy access to an alpine meadow and panoramic views of Angel Glacier. The trail climbs steadily through a subalpine forest of Engelmann spruce and alpine fir to emerge facing the northeast face of Mt. Edith Cavell and Angel Glacier. The trail continues to higher viewpoints and an alpine meadow that, in mid-July, is filled with wildflowers.

Astoria River
• Length: 19 kilometers (6–7 hours) one-way
• Elevation gain: 450 meters
• Rating: moderate
Beginning opposite the hostel on Mt. Edith Cavell Road, this trail descends through a forest on the north side of Mt. Edith Cavell for five kilometers, then crosses the Astoria River and begins a long ascent into spectacular Tonquin Valley. Amethyst Lakes and the 1,000-meter cliffs of the Ramparts first come into view after 13 kilometers. At the 17-kilometer mark, the trail divides. To the left, it climbs into Eremite

Valley, where there is a campground. The right fork continues following Astoria River to Tonquin Valley, Amethyst Lakes, and a choice of four campgrounds.

Maccarib Pass
• Length: 21 kilometers (7–8 hours) one-way
• Elevation gain: 730 meters
• Rating: moderate
This trail is slightly longer and gains more elevation than the trail along the Astoria River but is more spectacular. From 6.5 kilometers up Marmot Basin Road, the trail strikes out to the southwest. It follows Portal Creek and passes under Peveril Peak before making a steep approach to Maccarib Pass, 12.5 kilometers from the trailhead. The full panorama of the Tonquin Valley can be appreciated as the path gradually descends from the pass. At Amethyst Lakes, it links up with the Astoria River Trail, and many options for day hikes head out from campgrounds at the lakes.

HIKING IN THE MALIGNE LAKE AREA

Maligne Lake, 48 kilometers from Jasper townsite, provides more easy hiking with many opportunities to view the lake and explore its environs. The first two hikes detailed are along the access road to the lake; the others leave from various parking lots at the northwest end of the lake.

Watchtower Basin
• Length: 10 kilometers (3.5 hours) one-way
• Elevation gain: 630 meters
• Rating: moderate to difficult
Watchtower is a wide, open basin high above the crowds of Maligne Lake Road. The trailhead is 24 kilometers from Jasper townsite. All the elevation gain is made during the first six kilometers, through a dense forest of lodgepole pine and white spruce. As the trail levels off and enters the basin, it continues to follow the west bank of a stream, crossing it at kilometer 10 and officially ending at a campground. To the west and south the **Maligne Range** rises to a crest three kilometers beyond the campground. From the top of this ridge, at the intersection with the Skyline Trail, it is 17.5 kilometers northwest to

Maligne Canyon, or 27 kilometers southeast to Maligne Lake. By camping at Watchtower Campground, day trips can be made to a small lake in the basin or to highlights of the Skyline Trail, such as the Snowbowl, Curator Lake, and Shovel Pass.

Jacques Lake

• Length: 12 kilometers (3–3.5 hours) one-way
• Elevation gain: 100 meters
• Rating: moderate

The appeal of this trail, which begins from a parking lot at the southeast end of Medicine Lake, is its lack of elevation gain and the numerous small lakes it skirts as it travels through a narrow valley. On either side, the severely faulted mountains of the Queen Elizabeth Ranges rise steeply above the valley floor, their strata tilted nearly vertical.

Lake Trail (Mary Schäffer Loop)

• Length: 3.2-kilometer loop (1 hour round-trip)
• Elevation gain: minimal
• Rating: easy

This easy, pleasant walk begins from beside the Boat House, following the eastern shore of Maligne Lake to a point known as **Schäffer Viewpoint,** named for the first white person to see the valley. After dragging yourself away from the spectacular panorama, follow the trail into a forest of spruce and subalpine fir before looping back to the middle parking lot.

Opal Hills

• Length: 8.2-kilometer loop (3 hours round-trip)
• Elevation gain: 455 meters
• Rating: moderate

Turn left into the parking area beside Maligne Lake, then left again and continue to the top parking lot; this trail begins from behind the information board in the north corner. The trail climbs steeply for 1.5 kilometers to a point where it divides. Both options end in the high alpine meadows of the Opal Hills; the trail to the right is shorter and steeper. Once in the meadow, the entire Maligne Valley can be seen below. Across Maligne Lake are the rounded Bald Hills, the Maligne Range, and to the southwest, the distinctive twin peaks of Mt. Unwin (3,268 meters) and Mt. Charlton (3,217 meters).

Bald Hills

• Length: 5.2 kilometers (2 hours) one-way
• Elevation gain: 495 meters
• Rating: moderate

From a picnic area at the very end of Maligne Lake Road, this trail follows an old fire road for its entire distance, entering an open meadow near the end. This was once the site of a fire lookout. The 360-degree view includes the jade-green waters of Maligne Lake, the Queen Elizabeth Ranges, and the twin peaks of Mt. Unwin and Mt. Charlton. The Bald Hills extend for seven kilometers, their highest summit not exceeding 2,600 meters. A herd of caribou summers in the hills.

MARY SCHÄFFER

In the early 1900s, exploration of mountain wilderness areas was considered a man's domain. However, a spirited and tenacious woman entered that domain and went on to explore areas of the Canadian Rockies that no white man ever had. Mary Sharples was born in 1861 in Pennsylvania and raised in a strict Quaker family. Mary was introduced to Dr. Charles Schäffer on a trip to the Rockies, and in 1889 they were married. His interest in botany drew them back to the Rockies, where Charles collected, documented, and photographed specimens until his death in 1903. Mary also became apt at these skills. After hearing Sir James Hector (the geologist on the Palliser Expedition) reciting tales of the mountains, her zest

to explore the wilderness returned. In 1908, with Billy Warren guiding, Mary, her dog, and a small party set out for a lake that no white man had ever seen but that the Stoney Indians knew as Chaba Imne, or "Beaver Lake." After initial difficulties, they succeeded in finding the elusive body of water now known as Maligne Lake. In Mary's words, "there burst upon us . . . the finest view any of us have ever beheld in the Rockies . . ." In 1915 Mary married Billy Warren, continuing to explore the mountains until her death in 1939. Her success as a photographer, artist, and writer were equal to any of her male counterparts. But it was her unwavering love of the Rockies—her "heaven of the hills"—for which she is best remembered.

Moose Lake
- Length: 1.4 kilometers (30 minutes) one-way
- Elevation gain: minimal
- Rating: easy

This trail begins 200 meters along the Bald Hills trail, spurring left along the Maligne Pass Trail (signposted). One kilometer along this trail, a rough track branches left, leading 100 meters to Moose Lake—a quiet body of water where moose are sometimes seen. To return, continue along the trail as it descends to the shore of Maligne Lake, a short stroll from the picnic area.

OTHER RECREATION

Several booking agents represent the many operators in Jasper. **Jasper Adventure Centre,** in the lobby of the Chaba Theatre (604 Connaught Dr., 780/852-5595), takes bookings for all of the following activities, as well as for accommodations and for transportation to various points in the park and beyond. **Jasper Travel Agency** (in the railway station, 780/852-4400) offers a similar service. **Maligne Tours** (627 Patricia St., 780/852-3370) operates all activities in the Maligne Lake area, including the famous lake cruise.

Mountain Biking
Bicycling in the park continues to grow in popularity—the ride between Banff and Jasper, along the Icefields Parkway, attracts riders from around the world. In addition to the paved roads, many designated unpaved bicycle trails radiate from the town. One of the most popular is the Athabasca River Trail, which begins at Old Fort Point and follows the river to a point below Maligne Canyon. Cyclists are particularly prone to sudden bear encounters. (A couple of years ago, a rider was pulled from his bike by a grizzly, within screaming distance of Jasper Park Lodge.) Fit bear-bells to your bike, or make noise when passing through heavily wooded areas. The brochure *Trail Bicycling Guide* lists designated trails and is available from Freewheel Cycle (618 Patricia St., 780/852-3898).

White-water Rafting
The Athabasca, Sunwapta, and Maligne rivers are run by a half dozen outfitters. On the Athabasca River, the Mile 5 Run is an easy float that appeals to all ages, taking two hours. Farther upstream, some operators offer a trip that begins from below Athabasca Falls, on a stretch of the river that passes through a narrow canyon; this run takes three hours. The boulder-strewn rapids of the Sunwapta and Maligne rivers offer more thrills and spills; these trips are for the more adventurous and last approximately three hours. Most companies offer a choice of rivers and provide transportation to and from downtown hotels. Expect to pay $40–55 for trips on the Athabasca and $55 for the Sunwapta and Maligne. The following companies run at least two of the three rivers: **Maligne Rafting Adventures,** 780/852-3370; **Raven Adventures,** 780/852-4292; **Rocky Mountain River Guides,** 780/852-3777; and **White Water Rafting,** 780/852-7238 or 800/557-7238. **Jasper Raft Tours,** 780/852-2665, floats the Athabasca River in large, stable inflatable rafts; adults $40, children $15.

For a different, more relaxing, and historically linked adventure, try a trip down the Athabasca River in a stable 10-meter voyageur canoe, similar to those used by early explorers and fur traders. These trips are offered by **Rocky Mountain Voyageur,** starting at Old Fort Point and floating downstream for two to three hours. The cost, including transfers, is $50. For reservations, call 780/852-3343 or drop by Jasper Adventure Centre in the Chaba Theatre.

Fishing
Fishing in the many alpine lakes—for rainbow, brook, Dolly Varden, cutthroat, and lake trout, as well as pike and whitefish—is excellent. Guided fishing trips are offered by many outfitters. Whether you fish with a guide or by yourself, you'll need a National Park fishing license ($6 per week, $13 per year), available from the Park Information Centre or On-line Sport & Tackle at 600 Patricia Street. Maligne Lake is the most popular fishing hole; in 1981, a 10-kilogram rainbow trout was caught in its deep waters, a provincial record. Small motorboats are available from the Boathouse at Maligne Lake, 780/852-3370, for $70 per day, with rod and reel rentals extra. Guided fishing trips on the lake are offered by **Maligne Tours,** 780/852-3370; half day $125 per person, full day $170 per person for two or more people. **Currie's Guided Fishing,**

780/852-5650, offers trips to Maligne Lake (full day $160 per person) and other lakes requiring a 30- to 60-minute hike to access (from $140). Currie's shop on Connaught Drive sells and rents tackle, canoes, and boats. **On-line Sport & Tackle** (600 Patricia St., 780/852-3630) offers similar trips, sells tackle, and rents canoes and boats (from $30 per day).

Golfing
The world-famous **Jasper Park Lodge Golf Course** was designed by renowned golf-course architect Stanley Thompson. The 18-hole championship course takes in the contours of the Athabasca River Valley as it hugs the banks of turquoise-colored Lac Beauvert. The 6,670-yard course is a true test of accuracy, and with holes named "The Maze," "The Bad Baby," and "The Bay," you'll need lots of balls, literally. Greens fee for 18 holes varies with the season; $109 in summer, $89 mid-May through June and mid-Sept. to mid-October. Golfing after 5 P.M. is $79, which includes a cart—a great deal during the long days of June and July. Club rentals are $28–42, and an electric cart is $32. Tee times can be reserved by calling 780/852-6090.

Indoor Recreation
Jasper Aquatic Centre (401 Pyramid Lake Rd., 780/852-3663) has an Olympic-size swimming pool; admission $4.75. **Jasper Activity Centre** (next door, 780/852-3381) has squash courts, indoor and outdoor tennis courts, and a weight room; admission $6.

WINTERTIME

Winter is certainly a quiet time in the park, but that doesn't mean there's a lack of things to do: Marmot Basin offers world-class downhill skiing and snowboarding; many snow-covered hiking trails are groomed for cross-country skiing; portions of Lac Beauvert and Pyramid Lake are cleared for ice-skating; horse-drawn sleighs travel around town; and Maligne Canyon is transformed into a magical, frozen world. Hotels reduce rates by 40–70 percent through winter, and many offer lodging and lift tickets for less than $70 per person.

Marmot Basin
The skiing at Marmot Basin is highly underrated; the terrain is good, there's plenty of the dry fluffy stuff, and the mountain scenery is breathtaking, to say the least. A fellow by the name of Joe Weiss saw the potential for skiing in the basin in the 1920s and began bringing skiers up from the valley. A road was constructed from the highway in the early 1950s, and the first paying skiers were transported up to the slopes in a Sno-Cat. The first lift, a 700-meter rope tow, was installed on the Paradise face in 1961, and the area has continued to expand ever since. Marmot Basin now has eight lifts servicing 400 hectares of terrain and a vertical rise of 701 meters. This hill doesn't get the crowds of Banff, so lift lines are uncommon. The season runs from early December to late April. Lift tickets are adults $44, seniors $32, children $18. Lift tickets in January are $31. Rentals are available at the resort or in town at **Totem Ski Shop** (408 Connaught Dr., 780/852-3078). For more information on the resort, contact Marmot Basin Ski-lifts, 780/852-3816 or, from Edmonton, 780/488-5909.

Buses depart three times daily for Marmot Basin (the first departure is 8–8:30 A.M.) from most Jasper hotels; $7 one-way, $12 round-trip.

Cross-Country Skiing
For many visitors, traveling Jasper's hiking trails on skis is just as exhilarating as on foot. An extensive network of summer hiking trails is groomed for cross-country skiing. The four main areas of trails are along Pyramid Lake Road, around Maligne Lake, in the Athabasca Falls area, and at Whistlers Campground. The booklet *Cross-country Skiing in Jasper National Park,* available at the Park Information Centre, details each trail and its difficulty. Weather forecasts and avalanche-hazard reports are also posted here.

Rental packages are available from **Source for Sports** (406 Patricia St., 780/852-3654); **Spirit of Skiing** (in the Jasper Park Lodge, 780/852-3433); and **Totem Ski Shop** (408 Connaught Dr., 780/852-3078), offering rentals, repairs, and sales.

Maligne Canyon
By late December, the torrent that is the Maligne River has frozen solid. Where it cascades

ALBERTA TOURISM

Maligne Canyon in winter

down through Maligne Canyon, the river is temporarily stalled for the winter, creating remarkable formations through the deep limestone canyon. **Maligne Tours** (626 Connaught Dr., 780/852-3370) offers exciting two-hour guided tours into the depths of the canyon throughout winter, daily at 9 A.M. and 1 P.M.; adults $28, children $12.50.

ARTS AND ENTERTAINMENT

Theater
A local theater company, the Heritage Production Co. (98 Geikie St., 780/852-4204), puts on two productions of historical interest in the Jasper Inn. The brave exploits of nurse Edith Cavell, for whom the park's best-known peak is named, come alive in a theater performance of *Edith Cavell Returns* each Sunday, Tuesday, and Thursday. Captured by German soldiers while assisting Allied troops in German-occupied Belgium during World War I, Edith Cavell was executed in 1915. The *David Thompson Story* tells the tale of one of North America's great geographers and his links to the Canadian Rockies. The plays cost adults $14, children $7 and are performed June–Sept., daily (except Saturday) at 8:30 P.M.

Bars and Nightclubs
The most popular nightspot in town is the **Atha-b**, in the Athabasca Hotel (510 Patricia St.,

780/852-3386). Bands play some nights, and it gets pretty rowdy with all the seasonal workers but is still enjoyable; minimal cover charge. This hotel also has a large lounge, a bar with a pool table, and a popular 5–7 P.M. happy hour. **Pete's**, upstairs, beside the Patricia Centre (614 Patricia St., 780/852-6262), has a jam on Tuesday night and bands playing Friday–Sunday. The music varies; it could be blues, rock, or Celtic. The **De'd Dog Bar and Grill,** in the Astoria Hotel (404 Connaught Dr., 780/852-3351), is a large, dimly lit bar with pool tables and plenty of locals drinking copious amounts of beer, especially during the 5–7 P.M. happy hour. Right downtown, **The Whistle Stop Pub,** in the Whistlers Inn (105 Miette Ave., 780/852-3361), has great atmosphere with a classic wooden bar and memorabilia everywhere. You don't need to be a guest of Jasper's finest hotel to enjoy its ambience. The **Tent City Sports, Emerald,** and **Palisade lounges,** in Jasper Park Lodge, 780/852-3301, are stylish, relaxing spots to relax. Most of Jasper's other larger hotels, including the Amethyst Lodge, Jasper Inn, and Marmot Lodge, have lounges, too.

Shopping
Jasper certainly doesn't provide the shopping experience found in Banff, but there are several interesting shops for those rainy days. **Our Native Land** (601 Patricia St., 780/852-5592) is a large shop chock-full of Indian arts and crafts

produced by artisans from throughout western Canada. It also stocks Inuit soapstone carvings from the Canadian Arctic. **Bearberry** (612 Connaught Dr., 780/852-1112) features a good cross-section of Canadiana. Beyond the information center, **Pine Cones & Pussy Willow** (308 Connaught Dr., 780/852-5310) is a little less tacky than your average souvenir shop, with furry toys and plastic rulers complemented by the works of local artists.

Within 100 meters of the information center is **Totem Sports** (408 Connaught Dr., 780/852-3078), with a good stock of camping gear.

Festivals and Events

Summer is prime time on the park's events calendar. The first weekend of June is the **Jasper to Banff Relay. Canada Day** celebrations begin with a pancake breakfast, then everyone congregates in front of the information center for a flag-raising ceremony, which is followed by a parade along Connaught Drive. Live entertainment and a fireworks display end the day. The **Jasper Lions Pro Indoor Rodeo,** on the second weekend of August, dates from 1933 and attracts professional cowboys from across Canada. Apart from the traditional rodeo events, the fun includes dances, a casino, pancake breakfasts, a good ol' Western shoot-out, and the Miss Jasper contest. All of the action takes place at the Jasper Activity Centre on the corner of Pyramid Avenue and Pyramid Lake Road.

On the other side of the calendar, winter is not totally without parties—**Jasper in January** is a two-week celebration that includes fireworks, special evenings at local restaurants, a chili cook-off, discounted skiing and snowboarding at Marmot Basin ($30 lift tickets), and all the activities associated with winter.

Park Interpretive Program

Parks Canada offers a wide range of interpretive talks and hikes throughout summer. Each summer night in the **Whistlers Campground Theatre,** a different slide and movie program is shown. The theater is located near the shower block. The **Wabasso Campfire Circle** takes place each Saturday evening at dusk; hot tea is supplied while wardens and various speakers talk about the park. Many different free, guided hikes are offered throughout summer; check

bulletin boards at the Park Information Centre and campgrounds, or call 780/852-6176.

HOTELS AND MOTELS

Motel and hotel rooms here are expensive. Most of the motels and lodges are within walking distance of town and have indoor pools and restaurants. Luckily, alternatives to staying in $100-plus places do exist. In the following section are several less-expensive options, including "bungalow camps" that open only in summer, rooms that can be rented in private residences, hostels, and camping in the good ol' outdoors.

Aside from the famous Jasper Park Lodge, all hotels and motels discussed here are within a five-minute walk of downtown Jasper. Rates quoted are for a standard room in summer. Outside the busy June–September period, most lodgings reduce rates drastically (also ask about ski packages during winter).

$50–100

Jasper's least expensive rooms can be found right downtown in the **Athabasca Hotel** (510 Patricia St., 780/852-3386). The cheapest of the hotel's 61 rooms share bathrooms and are above a noisy bar, but the price is right at $55 single, $65 double. This hotel also has more expensive rooms, each with a private bathroom; $139 single or double.

$100–150

Right downtown is the 35-room **Astoria Hotel** (404 Connaught Dr., 780/852-3351 or 800/661-7343, www.astoriahotel.com), a European-style lodging built in 1924 and kept in the same family since. All rooms have a small fridge; from $145 single or double.

$150–200

On Connaught Drive southwest of downtown, the **Mount Robson Inn** (780/852-3327 or 800/587-3327, www.mountrobsoninn.com) was extensively renovated in the late 1990s; $163 single or double. Adjacent to the Mount Robson Inn is the **Maligne Lodge** (780/852-3143 or 800/661-1315), with an indoor pool and a restaurant; rates range $169–189 single or double. The **Whistlers Inn** is right downtown (105 Miette

Ave., 780/852-3361 or 800/282-9919, www. whistlersinn.com), the rooms are spacious, and the rates are reasonable at $171 single or double. The **Tonquin Inn,** at the northern edge of the townsite (on Juniper Street, 780/852-4987 or 800/661-1315, www.tonquininnrockies.com), features luxurious rooms, a beautiful indoor pool, an outdoor hot tub, and laundry facilities; from $174 single or double. In the same vicinity, the **Marmot Lodge** (86 Connaught Dr., 780/852-4471 or 888/852-7737) offers more than 100 rooms, many with mountain views. Rates begin at $179 single or double.

A few kilometers north of town is the **Pyramid Lake Resort** (Pyramid Lake Rd., 780/852-4900 or 888/852-4900, www.pyramidlakeresort.com), the only lodging away from town, besides Jasper Park Lodge, open year-round. Plenty of water-based activities and rentals, an interpretive program, and a large barbecue area make the resort a good choice for families; $149–239 per unit.

$200–250

The **Lobstick Lodge** (94 Geikie Ave., 780/852-4431 or 888/852-7737, www.mtn-park-lodges.com) has 139 extra-large, simply furnished rooms and a range of modern amenities, including an indoor pool and an outdoor hot tub; from $204 single or double. The **Amethyst Lodge,** in a central location (200 Connaught Dr., 780/852-3394, www.mtn-park-lodges.com), offers large air-conditioned rooms, an outdoor hot tub, and a restaurant; $204 single or double. The **Jasper Inn** (98 Geikie St., 780/852-4461 or 800/661-1933, www.jasperinn.com) is a modern chateau-style lodging of brick and red cedar. Many rooms have private balconies, and more than 100 are self-contained suites with kitchenettes and fireplaces. Other features include a large indoor pool and an outdoor sundeck overlooking a Japanese rock garden. Rates range $210–260 single or double.

More than $250

The **Sawridge Hotel** (82 Connaught Dr., 780/852-5111 or 800/661-6427, www.sawridge.com/jasper) has rooms built around a large atrium and indoor pool; rooms start at $259 single or double, discounted to $109 in the off-season. **Charlton's Chateau Jasper** (96 Geikie St., 780/852-5644 or 800/661-9323, www.charltonresorts.com) is one of Jasper's nicest lodgings. The rooms are large, and the low ceilings give them a cozy feel. Downstairs is an excellent restaurant, and up top is a roof-top sundeck; $300 single or double.

The **Jasper Park Lodge** (780/852-3301 or 800/441-1414, www.jasperparklodge.com) lies along the shore of *Lac Beauvert* (beautiful green, in French). This is the park's original resort and its most famous. It has four restaurants, three lounges, horseback riding, tennis courts, a championship golf course, and Jasper's only covered shopping arcade. The main lodge features stone floors, carved wooden pillars, and a high ceiling. The 446 rooms vary in configuration; some are modern, whereas others are elegantly rustic. Most are in cottages spread around Lac Beauvert, each with a porch or balcony. Basic rooms start at $479 single or double, off-season rates begin at $149.

OTHER JASPER ACCOMMODATIONS

Summer Lodging

The following lodgings all open for the summer months only (generally May to late September). The **Bear Hill Lodge** (100 Bonhomme St., 780/852-3209, www.bearhilllodge.com) offers the only accommodation of this type in the townsite. Cabins are basic, but each has a TV, a bathroom, and coffee-making facilities; $119–189 single or double.

Patricia Lake Bungalows (780/852-3560, www.patricialakebungalows.com) is beside the lake of the same name, a five-minute drive north from Jasper along Pyramid Lake Road. Comfortable cottages with kitchens are $145–200 depending on the size. Several basic motel-style rooms are $75. Other facilities include a barbecue area and an outdoor hot tub. Beyond this accommodation is the **Pyramid Lake Resort,** open year-round and covered under "Hotels and Motels."

With your own transportation, you can seek out several good options along the Athabasca River, which parallels the Icefields Parkway and flows past town to the east of the Yellowhead Highway. The least expensive accommodation along this stretch of river is also the closest to

284 JASPER NATIONAL PARK

town. **Pine Bungalows,** 780/852-3491, is located on a secluded section of the Athabasca River opposite the northern entrance to town. Sparse but comfortable motel-style units with kitchenettes are $95 single or double, individual cabins with kitchens and fireplaces begin at $105. The **Tekarra Lodge** (780/852-3058 or 888/404-4540, www.tekarralodge.com) is located 1.5 kilometers southeast of the townsite at the confluence of the Miette and Athabasca rivers. Rooms in the lodge are $139 single or double; cabins, each with a kitchenette and a wood-burning fireplace, begin at $159. Beyond the Tekarra Lodge, at the junction of highways 93 and 93A, is **Alpine Village** (780/852-3285, www.alpinevillagejasper.com). Cabins are spread around grassed gardens, just across the road from the Athabasca River; all have kitchens and fireplaces. Rates range $140–180.

Other summer-only choices lie east of the townsite. **Pocahontas Bungalows,** 780/866-3732 or 800/843-3372, is near the park's east gate at the bottom of the road that leads to Miette Hot Springs; $80–170 single or double. **Miette Hot Springs Bungalows,** 780/866-3750, is within walking distance of the park's only hot springs. Motel units are $125; bungalows begin at $145.

Tonquin Amethyst Lake Lodge

The only backcountry accommodation in the park is the Tonquin Amethyst Lake Lodge (780/852-1188, www.tonquinadventures.com). The lodge is located southwest of Jasper in the spectacular Tonquin Valley. Getting there involves a 23-kilometer hike or horseback ride or, in winter, a cross-country ski trip, from a trailhead opposite Mt. Edith Cavell Hostel. The original lodge was built in 1939, with more modern additions made in 1990, including a rustic dining room. Private cabins have wood-burning heaters, bunk beds, oil lanterns, and a spectacular view. The rate, $125 per person per night, includes accommodations, three meals, and use of small boats and fishing gear. Tonquin Adventures offers several well-priced packages, including riding into the lodge on horses. Rates are reduced in winter.

Private Home Accommodations

At last count, Jasper had more than 80 residential homes offering accommodations. They often

supply nothing more than a room with a bed (and, officially, park bylaws prohibit them from serving breakfast), but the price is right at $40–80 single or double. The bathroom is usually shared with other guests or the family, few have kitchens, and only some supply breakfast. The positive side, apart from the price, is that your hosts are usually knowledgable locals, and town is only a short walk away. The Jasper Tourism and Commerce Information Centre has a board listing private home accommodations with rooms available for the upcoming night. For a full listing that includes the facilities at each, write to Jasper Home Accommodation Association, P.O. Box 758, Jasper, Alberta T0E 1E0, or check out the www.bbcanada.com/jhaa.html. A couple of readers have written me complaining of overbooking and the lack of professionalism of some of these operators, so it's important to remember that, in most cases, you are simply renting a bed in someone else's home (which is reflected in the low price), and that they are not officially bed-and-breakfasts.

Hostels

Hostelling International operates three hostels in the vicinity of Jasper townsite but none right downtown; the closest is seven kilometers away. A summer-only shuttle service runs between Calgary and Jasper, stopping at all hostels en route. To ride the shuttle, you must have advance reservations for both the bus and the hostel. A couple of privately owned shuttle services link the hostels in the immediate vicinity of Jasper. Make bookings for both accommodations and transportation through Jasper International Hostel, 780/852-3215.

On the road to the Jasper Tramway, seven kilometers from town, is the **Jasper International Hostel,** which has 80 beds in men's and women's dorms, a large kitchen, a common room, showers, an outdoor barbecue area, and mountain bike rentals. Members of Hostelling International pay $16, nonmembers $21. For hostel reservations, call 780/852-3215. In the summer months, this hostel fills up every night. A cab between downtown Jasper and the hostel is $15.

The **Maligne Canyon Hostel** is on Maligne Lake Road, beside the Maligne River and a short walk from the canyon. Although rustic, it is in a beautiful setting. The 24 beds are in two cabins; other facilities include electricity, a kitchen, and a dining area. Rates are members $11, nonmembers $16. For reservations, call 780/852-3215. The hostel is closed Wednesday Oct. –April.

The **Mt. Edith Cavell Hostel** has a million-dollar view for the price of a dorm bed. It's located 13 kilometers up Mt. Edith Cavell Road. Because of the location, there's usually a spare bed. Opposite the hostel are trailheads for hiking in the Tonquin Valley, and it's just a short walk to the base of Mt. Edith Cavell. The hostel is rustic but has a kitchen, a dining area, and an outdoor wood sauna. Members pay $11 per night; nonmembers pay $16. It's closed November to mid-June. For reservations, call 780/852-3215.

Campgrounds
Whistlers Campground, at the base of Whistlers Road, three kilometers south of Jasper townsite, has 781 sites, making it the largest campground in the Canadian Rockies. It is divided into three sections; prices vary with the services available—walk-in sites $15, unserviced sites $17, powered sites $21, full hookups $24. Each section has showers. The campground is open May to mid-October. Two kilometers farther south is **Wapiti Campground,** which is the park's only campground that is open year-round and has showers; in summer, unserviced sites are $16, powered sites $19; winter camping is $15.

East of the townsite, along Highway 16, are two smaller, more primitive campgrounds. **Snaring River Campground,** 17 kilometers from Jasper on Celestine Lake Road, is $10; **Pocahontas Campground,** 45 kilometers northeast, is $13. Both are open mid-May to early September.

FOOD

Coffeehouses and Cafés
The **Soft Rock Internet Cafe,** in Connaught Square (622 Connaught Dr., 780/852-5850), starts the day by dishing up plates of waffles topped with cream and your choice of fresh fruit for $4.50. If the cinnamon buns are still in the oven, you'll have to come back later in the day—

they're gigantic! The variety of coffee concoctions here is mind-boggling, and the prices are reasonable. It's open 7 A.M.–11 P.M. Nearby (614 Connaught Dr., 780/852-4445), is **Café & Roses,** a small coffee shop away from the busy main street that proudly advertises itself as an outlet for Starbucks coffee. **Truffles & Trout,** in Jasper Marketplace (corner of Patricia and Hazel streets, 780/852-9676), is a popular local hangout, with all the usual coffees, as well as boxed picnic lunches on offer. Across the road, **Nutter's** (622 Patricia St., 780/852-5844) is another good prehiking stop, with a wide choice of goodies in bulk bins. **Spooner's,** in the Patricia Centre (610 Patricia St., 780/852-4046), is a second-floor café with stunning mountain views and a good range of coffees and light meals. **Dano's** (604 Patricia St., 780/852-3322) will satisfy any ice cream or cappuccino cravings you may be having.

Cool and Casual
For pizza, you won't be able to miss **Jasper Pizza Place** (402 Connaught Dr., 780/852-3225). It's a large and noisy restaurant with bright furnishings and walls lined with photos from Jasper's earliest days. Pizza from the wood-fired oven starts at $10.50, whereas smaller pita pizzas, perfect for a lunchtime snack, cost just $4.50. **Papa George's** (406 Connaught Dr., 780/852-3351) is a locals' favorite and one of Jasper's oldest restaurants. Breakfast is $4–8, and lunch and dinner feature burgers, pasta, and steaks; daily specials are $11–17 and include soup and salad. Hours are 7 A.M.–11:30 P.M.

The best Greek meals in town are served at **Something Else Restaurant** (621 Patricia St., 780/852-3850). The portions are generous, the service is friendly, the prices are right, and you'll find plenty of alternatives if the Greek dishes don't appeal to you. Greek favorites are $10–15, pasta dishes $10–13, pizza from $10. It's open daily 11 A.M.–midnight.

Kontos Restaurant (622 Patricia St., 780/852-3444) is a new addition to the Jasper dining scene. The menu is fairly standard, family-style dining with inexpensive lunch specials for $5 and dinner entrees ranging from $10–21. The bathrooms here are worthy of a special mention—they contain everything from sunscreen to singing birds. The **Treeline Restaurant,** 780/852-5352, situated high above town on The Whistlers, undoubtedly has the best views in town. Daily lunch and dinner buffets complement the à la carte menu. Also out of town is the **Pyramid Lake Resort Restaurant,** overlooking Pyramid Lake, 780/852-4900, with a small outdoor patio for lunchtime dining.

Middle of the Road

Miss Italia Ristorante (610 Patricia St., 780/852-4002), upstairs in the Patricia Centre, features mountain views from tables indoors and out. Pastas average $12, whereas Taste of Italy choices, featuring a sampling of cuisines from three regions, run $18.

The place to go for Alberta beef is the **Tonquin Prime Rib Village** (Juniper St. beside the Tonquin Inn, 780/852-4966), which specializes in charbroiled steaks and prime rib but also offers a good choice of seafood. Upstairs (640 Connaught Dr., 780/852-3920) is another popular steakhouse, **Villa Caruso,** which has a lot more than steak to offer, with all the usual chicken, seafood, and pasta.

The Cantonese Restaurant (608 Connaught Dr., 780/852-3559) offers a wide variety of Chinese dishes; combo specials are $9–13, and set menus for two start at $23. It's open daily noon–10 P.M. **Denjiro** (410 Connaught Dr., 780/852-3780) features a traditional sushi bar and eight tatami booths for eating the very best Japanese cuisine; combination dinners average $17 per person. It's open 5–11:30 P.M.

Top End

Most of the larger accommodations have restaurants. **Walter's Dining Room,** in the Sawridge Hotel (82 Connaught Dr., 780/852-5111), features a menu of Alberta beef, Rocky Mountain trout, and British Columbia salmon in an elegant but relaxed atmosphere. Walter's also does a breakfast buffet. The **Inn Restaurant,** in the Jasper Inn (98 Geikie St., 780/852-3232), sits within a glass-enclosed atrium and features a menu of Alberta beef, ribs, fondue, and seafood. Entrées start at $15. Diners are offered complimentary limousine service to the restaurant. The same menu is served in the just-as-elegant lounge for half the price. The award-winning **Beavallon Dining Room** (Chateau Jasper, 780/852-5644, ext. 179) offers an extensive menu emphasizing Continental cuisine prepared by a Swiss chef. All of the chairs are upholstered, and the blue tablecloths and wood-trimmed crimson walls provide an air of elegance, which you pay handsomely for. The Sunday brunch here is worth the splurge.

Five kilometers south of town is **Becker's Gourmet Restaurant,** 780/852-3535, where the atmosphere is intimate and relaxing, the views of Mt. Kerkeslin and the Athabasca River are inspiring, and the steak and seafood dishes are well prepared. With a bottle of wine, expect to pay $100 for two.

The **Fiddle River Seafood Company** (620 Connaught Dr., 780/852-3032), upstairs in Connaught Square, has fresh seafood, but expect to pay approximately $40 per person for a three-

Early guests to the Jasper Park Lodge, then a remote mountain retreat, were treated to all the luxuries of the day.

WHYTE MUSEUM OF THE CANADIAN ROCKIES

course meal. If you can't afford to eat here, at least stick your head in the door and admire the décor.

Jasper Park Lodge

The lodge offers a choice of casual or elegant dining in a variety of restaurants and lounges. **Obsessions,** in the Beauvert Shopping Promenade, has tempting French pastries, gourmet coffee, and homemade truffles and chocolates. Drinks and light snacks are served at the **Spike Lounge** overlooking the golf course. At lunchtime, the smell of sizzling steaks from **La Terrasse** wafts across Lac Beauvert; this outdoor eatery is open only in summer. The **Meadows Café,** downstairs in the shopping arcade, is open for a breakfast buffet 8–11:30 A.M., then in the evening for a dinner buffet 5:30–9 P.M. The **Beauvert Dining Room** is a casual 500-seat eatery. It features a daily buffet breakfast and an eclectic dinner menu. The Sunday brunch, served between 10:30 A.M. and 1:30 P.M. and costing $20, is especially popular. The **Moose's Nook,** with a rustic atmosphere, is a good place to enjoy traditional Canadian fare such as buffalo steak and salmon. It's open for dinner only, with entrées from $18. The **Edith Cavell Room** is the finest fine-dining restaurant in Jasper. Its dark oak walls contrast with the white linens and large, bright windows overlooking Lac Beauvert and the mountains beyond. The classic cuisine is served with a French flair and price tag; if you need to ask the price, you can't afford it (the five-course table d'hôte menu is $62 per person). For all lodge restaurant reservations, call 780/852-6052. Food is also available in each of the lodge's three lounges.

TRANSPORTATION

Getting There

Getting to Jasper by public transportation is easy, although the closest airport handling domestic and international flights is at Edmonton, 360 kilometers to the east. The **VIA rail station** and the **bus depot** (used by both Greyhound and Brewster) are in the same building, central to town at 607 Connaught Drive. The building is open 24 hours daily in summer, the

rest of the year Mon.–Sat. 7:30 A.M.–10:30 P.M., Sunday 7:30–11 A.M. and 6:30–10:30 P.M. Lockers are available for $1 per day. A travel agent and car-rental agencies are also located in this building.

Jasper is on the "Canadian" route, the only remaining transcontinental passenger rail service in the country. Trains run either way three times weekly. To the west, the line divides going to both Prince Rupert and Vancouver; to the east, it passes through Edmonton ($116 one-way from Jasper) and all points beyond. For all rail information, call 800/561-8630. Another rail option is offered by **Rocky Mountaineer Railtours,** 800/665-7245, which operates a luxurious summer-only rail service between Vancouver and Jasper with an overnight in Kamloops (British Columbia). The one-way fare is $610 per person, with a $100 discount for travel in May and October.

Greyhound buses, 780/852-3926 or 800/661-8747, depart Jasper for all points in Canada, including Vancouver (three times daily, 12–13 hours), Edmonton (five times daily, 4.5 hours), with connections to Calgary, and Prince Rupert (once daily, 18 hours).

The only bus service between Jasper and Banff runs mid-April to the end of October, with buses continuing on from Banff to Calgary International Airport mid-May to mid-October. Buses depart the airport daily at 12:30 P.M. ($71 one-way to Jasper), pick up passengers in Banff at 3:15 P.M. ($51 one-way) and Lake Louise at 4:15 P.M. ($44 one-way), and arrive in Jasper at 8:20 P.M. The return service departs daily from Jasper Park Lodge at 12:50 P.M. and from the downtown bus depot at 1:30 P.M., arriving at Calgary airport at 9:30 P.M. Brewster also runs a nine-hour (one-way) tour between Banff and Jasper departing daily mid-April through October from the Banff and Jasper depots at 8 A.M.; if the bus picks you up at your lodging, departure time is earlier. The tour costs $89 one-way ($67 in spring and fall), $124 round-trip ($89 in spring and fall). The round-trip requires an overnight in Jasper. All of these bus services are operated by **Brewster,** 780/852-3332.

Getting Around

The **Maligne Lake Shuttle,** 780/852-3370, runs out to Maligne Lake three to six times daily ($24 round-trip) and makes drop-offs at Maligne Canyon and Maligne Canyon Hostel ($8 one-way).

Rental cars start at $65 per day with 100 free kilometers. The following companies have agencies in town: **Avis**, 780/852-3970 or 800/879-2847; **Budget**, 780/852-3222 or 800/610-3222; and **National**, 780/852-1117 or 800/227-7368.

Mountain bikes can be rented from **On-line Sport & Tackle** (600 Patricia St., 780/852-3630); **Source for Sports** (406 Patricia St., 780/852-3654); **Freewheel Cycle** (618 Patricia St., 780/852-3898); and **Beauvert Boat & Cycle** (Jasper Park Lodge, 780/852-5708). Expect to pay $5–8 per hour or $15–28 per day. Freewheel Cycle leads a five-hour bike tour along Maligne Lake Road, but most of the hard work is done for you because transportation is provided to the lake, allowing a two-hour downhill run on the bikes; $85 per person.

Cabs in town are not cheap; most drivers will take you on a private sightseeing tour or to trailheads if requested: try **Jasper Taxi**, 780/852-3600 or 852-3146. **Heritage Cabs**, 780/852-5558, has a fleet of antique cars.

Tours

Brewster, 780/852-3332, offers a three-hour Discover Jasper tour taking in Patricia and Pyramid lakes, Maligne Canyon, and Jasper Tramway (ride not included in fare). It departs April–Oct. daily at 8:30 A.M. from the main bus depot; $42. **Maligne Tours** (627 Patricia St., 780/852-3370) has a variety of tours, including one to Maligne Lake ($56, includes cruise). **Jasper Adventure Centre,** in the Chaba Theatre at 604 Connaught Drive in summer (at 306 Connaught Dr. in winter), 780/852-5595, operates several well-priced tours, including the following at $40 per person per tour: Mount Edith Cavell (departs 2 P.M.; three hours), Maligne Canyon (spring and fall only; departs 9:30 A.M. and 1 P.M.; three hours), and Miette Hot Springs (departs 6 P.M.; four hours). The company also offers similar-priced tours taking in historical sites or local wildlife, as well as a mystery tour. The Jasper Adventure Centre is also an agent for rafting trips, guided hikes, heli-hiking, fishing trips, and just about everything else; open in summer daily 7:30 A.M.–9 P.M.

Air Jasper, 780/865-3616, offers customized air tours from Hinton Airport, 69 kilometers east of Jasper townsite; the cost is $110 per person per hour. Typically, 90 minutes of airtime will get you as far as Columbia Icefield.

SERVICES AND INFORMATION

Services

The **post office** is at 502 Patricia Street, behind the Park Information Centre. Mail to be picked up here should be addressed General Delivery, Jasper, Alberta T0E 1E0. Public Internet access is available at two locations within Connaught Square Mall: **More than Mail,** 780/852-3151, and **Soft Rock Internet Café,** 780/852-5850. The former offers a wide range of other communication services, including regular post, fax and copying facilities, a work area for laptops, international calling, and currency exchange. Internet access is also offered at the local library and at Jasper International Hostel. The two laundromats on Patricia Street are open 6 A.M.–11 P.M. and offer showers that cost $2 for 10 minutes (quarters). **Jasper Travel Agency** (in the VIA rail station, 780/852-4400) exchanges currency, sells phone cards, and is a good place to make onward travel plans. The **hospital** is at 518 Robson Street, 780/852-3344. For the **RCMP,** call 780/852-4848.

Books and Bookstores

The small **Jasper Municipal Library** (Elm Ave., 780/852-3652) holds just about everything ever written about the park. It's open Mon.–Thurs. 2–5 P.M. and 7–9 P.M., Friday 2–5 P.M., Saturday 10 A.M.–3 P.M.

Head to the Park Information Centre or the museum for a good selection of books about the park's natural and human history. Another good selection of literature can be found at **Jasper Camera and Gift** (412 Connaught Dr., 780/852-3165).

Information

A beautiful old stone building dating to 1913, which was the residence of Jasper's first superintendent, is now used by Parks Canada as the **Park Information Centre.** It's right downtown in Athabasca Park (Connaught Dr., 780/852-6176). The staff provides general information on the park and can direct you to hikes in the immediate vicinity. They also handle questions for those going into the backcountry. **Jasper Tourism and Commerce,** 780/852-3858, also staffs a desk in the building, and the friendly staff never seems to tire of explaining that all the rooms in town are full. They will happily call around to find accommodations for you and can provide general information on the town. They also have a large collection of brochures on activities, shopping, and restaurants in town. In the far corner is a **Parks and People** outlet selling maps, books, and local publications. Look for notices posted out front with the day's interpretive programs. The center is open in summer daily 8 A.M.–7 P.M., the rest of the year daily 9 A.M.–5 P.M.

Jasper's weekly newspaper, *The Booster,* is available throughout town on Wednesday.

For a list of park-related items, including publications and topographic maps, write to Parks and People, P.O. Box 992, Jasper, Alberta T0E 1E0, or call 780/852-4767. For more information on the park, contact The Superintendent, Jasper National Park, P.O. Box 10, Jasper, Alberta T0E 1E0, www.parkscanada.gc.ca/jasper. For general tourist information, write to Jasper Tourism and Commerce, P.O. Box 98, Jasper, Alberta T0E 1E0, or call 780/852-3858. The best commercial website related to the park is www.explorejasper.com, with lists of current events, current weather conditions, and loads of helpful links. A similar website is www.visit-jasper.com. **Jasper National Park Radio** is on the AM band at 1490. For weather conditions in the park, call 780/852-3185.

KAREN MCKINLEY

CENTRAL ALBERTA

The central sector of the province is a diverse region extending from the peaks of the Canadian Rockies in the west through the foothills and aspen parkland to the prairies in the east. **Rocky Mountain Forest Reserve** occupies much of the heavily forested western foothills, nestled against the folded and faulted front ranges of the Canadian Rockies. Most of this large coniferous forest is committed for nonrenewable resource development, although two designated wilderness areas in the reserve are totally protected from development. The entire reserve is a recreation playground: perfect for camping, fishing, hiking, and other outdoor activities. Rocky Mountain House, a medium-size town on Highway 11, is the gateway to the foothills. The North West and Hudson's Bay companies once used trading posts here as a jumping-off point into the mountain wilderness to the west.

See color map of Central Alberta, page x–xi.

The 290-kilometer route between Calgary and Edmonton through central Alberta on Highway 2 takes about three hours to drive straight through. Those with a little more time can explore the many historic towns along the way or visit a buffalo jump used by natives to stampede herds of bison to their deaths. Halfway between Calgary and Edmonton is Red Deer, a city of 65,000 that was once an important way station for travelers on the Calgary Trail (or Edmonton Trail, depending on which direction they were going).

North and east of Red Deer is the aspen parkland, a biome with characteristics unique to Canada's prairie provinces. Long, straight country roads link primarily agricultural towns along three main highways that extend east into the neighboring province of Saskatchewan. Highlights of this section of parkland include five provincial parks, one of Canada's last remaining passenger steam trains at Stettler, and a fantastic museum dedicated to machinery at Wetaskiwin.

WEST-CENTRAL ALBERTA

Highway 2 between Calgary and Edmonton skirts the edge of the prairie—just west of the highway, a region of foothills begins. The hills rise gradually, eventually reaching the lofty peaks of the front ranges adjoining Banff and Jasper national parks. Several rivers—among them the North Saskatchewan, Red Deer, Clearwater, and Brazeau—slice through the foothills on their cascading descent from sources high in the Canadian Rockies. Fur trading was once a booming industry here, but the greatest human impact on the area came from coal mining early in the 20th century. Rocky Mountain House, located on the bank of the North Saskatchewan River, is the largest town in the region and a good base for exploring.

This little-traveled region of the Canadian Rockies attracts outdoor enthusiasts year-round. Here you can hike in two wilderness areas, camp in many Alberta Environment campgrounds, fish in abundantly populated lakes and rivers, explore historic sites, run the North Saskatchewan River, take horseback trips into the hills, cross-country ski in winter, or just admire the spectacular mountain scenery.

HIGHWAY 22 NORTH

This highway follows the eastern flanks of the foothills from Cochrane, northwest of Calgary, through the small communities of Cremona, Sundre, and Caroline, and the larger town of Rocky Mountain House. The Canadian Rockies dominate the western horizon for much of the route and are especially imposing around Sundre.

Sundre

This town of 2,300, on the banks of the Red Deer River, is the quintessential Albertan town. Surrounded in rolling foothills that are historically tied to the ranching industry, oil and gas now keep the local economy alive. Sundre has a popular Sunday farmers' market, a good golf course, and is also a jumping-off point for trips into the Rocky Mountain Forest Reserve. Nearby rivers provide excellent white-water–rafting

opportunities for those with their own craft. Highway 584, heading west from town, links up with Forestry Trunk Road, providing access to many campgrounds and fishing spots.

In town, Sundre's **Pioneer Museum and Village** (130 Centre St., 403/638-3233) displays a large collection of artifacts from early pioneer days, including farm machinery, a blacksmith shop, and an old schoolhouse. It's open in summer Mon.–Sat. 10 A.M.–4 P.M. and Sunday noon–4 P.M. A canoe race is held on the Red Deer River on the last weekend of May, and the **Sundre Pro Rodeo** comes to town on the third weekend of June.

Sundre has four motels, all on Main Avenue. The least expensive is the **Bulldog Inn,** on the town's western outskirts, 403/638-4748; $38 single, $42 double. The best is the **Chinook Country Inn,** 403/638-3300, where the rates of $50 single, $58 double include a light breakfast. The **Greenwood Park Campground,** 403/638-2680, on the west bank of the Red Deer River, has clean facilities that include showers and a covered cooking shelter complete with a wood stove; unserviced sites $12, hookups $15–20. East of town is the **Tall Timber Leisure Park,** 403/638-3555, a full-service RV park where tenters aren't welcome; $18–25. **Outlaw's Bar and Grill** (250 Main Ave., 403/638-2882) is the only place in town to get a decent meal. Lunch specials are $5–7, including a salad bar, and the weekend hot breakfast buffet, served until noon, is $7.95. The **Tourist Information Centre** is located on the east bank of the Red Deer River; open in summer Thurs.–Mon. 10 A.M.–8 P.M.

Caroline

Named after the daughter of one of the town's earliest settlers, Caroline depended on agriculture and forestry to support its economy until recently, when Alberta's largest sour gas discovery was made south of town. Now Shell Canada's plant at the site also contributes to the area's livelihood.

Four-time World Men's Figure Skating champion (and four-time professional champion)

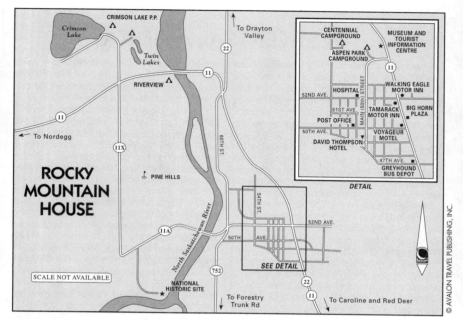

Kurt Browning was born and raised on a ranch just west of town. His portrait adorns local tourist literature, and the town's Kurt Browning Arena, on 48th Avenue, houses Kurt's Korner, a display of personal memorabilia. It's open Mon.–Fri. 8 A.M.–4 P.M.

The two motels in town are inexpensive, and **Caroline Municipal RV Park,** at the east end of town, 403/722-2210, has showers and powered sites; $10–12 per night.

Forestry Trunk Road
At regular intervals along Highway 22, gravel roads lead west to the Forestry Trunk Road—a well-graded gravel road that parallels the Rockies for more than 1,000 kilometers. Along the route are plenty of campgrounds, beautiful scenery, and a degree of solitude not found along roads through the national parks farther west. The middle section of the trunk road begins at its intersection with Highway 1A, 13 kilometers west of Cochrane. Heading north from there, the first services available are 265 kilometers away at Nordegg, on Highway 11.

Opportunities to exit and enter the road are found west of Cremona, Sundre, Caroline, and Rocky Mountain House.

ROCKY MOUNTAIN HOUSE

This town of 6,100, best known simply as "Rocky," straddles the North Saskatchewan River and is surrounded by gently rolling hills in a transition zone between aspen parkland and mountains. Highway 11 (also known as David Thompson Highway) passes through town on its way east to Red Deer (82 kilometers) and west to the northern end of Banff National Park (170 kilometers).

History
Between 1799 and 1875, four fur-trading posts were built at the confluence of the Clearwater and North Saskatchewan rivers, west of the present townsite. The forts were used not only for trading but also as bases for exploring the nearby mountains. David Thompson, one of

western Canada's greatest explorers, was a regular visitor. In 1821, after the two major fur-trading companies merged, the community that had grown around the forts was christened Rocky Mountain House. In the early 1900s, settlers began arriving. Today, the town's economy relies on forestry, natural-gas processing, agriculture, and tourism.

Rocky Mountain House National Historic Site

This National Historic Site commemorates the important role fur trading played in Canada's history. The first trading post, or fort, was built on the site in 1799. By the 1830s, beaver felt was out of fashion in Europe, and traders turned to buffalo robes. By the 1870s, the massive herds of buffalo that had roamed the plains for thousands of years were gone. This signaled an end to the fur trade, an industry that had opened up the West and had been the Indians' main source of European goods, such as clothing, horses, and guns. The last post at Rocky Mountain House closed soon after and, by the early 1900s, was reduced to two brick chimneys. In 1926, the forts were declared National Historic Sites. Today, the protected areas include the sites of four forts, a buffalo paddock, and a stretch of riverbank where the large voyageur canoes would have come ashore to be loaded with furs bound for Europe.

The **visitors center** is the best place to begin

a visit to the site; its interpretive displays detail the history of the forts, the fur trade, and exploration of the West. Two trails lead along the north bank of the river. The longer of the two, a 3.2-kilometer loop, passes the site of the two original forts. Frequent "listening posts" along the trail play a lively recorded commentary on life in the early 1800s. All that remains of the forts are depressions in the ground, but through the commentary and interpretive displays, it is easy to get a good idea of what the forts looked like. To the north of the fort site is an observation deck for viewing a herd of 25 buffalo that may or may not be visible. The other trail leads one kilometer to two chimneys, remnants of the later forts.

The park is open year-round on weekdays 10 A.M.–6 P.M., although the visitors center is only open mid-May to Sept., daily 10 A.M.–5 P.M. It's five kilometers west of Rocky Mountain House on Highway 11A, 403/845-2412. Admission is adults $2.50, seniors $2, children $1.50.

Other Sights

In the summer of 2000, the **Rocky Mountain House Museum,** 403/845-2332, moved from a 1927 schoolhouse on 49th Avenue to a new building on Highway 22 that also houses the information center. Exhibits include an array of pioneer artifacts, including an early Forest Service cabin, and an interesting rope-making machine. It's open in summer July and August

First Nations people built dome-shaped sweat lodges out of brush and covered them in buffalo robes.

daily 9 A.M.–8 P.M., June and September daily 9 A.M.–6 P.M., the rest of the year weekdays only. The Canadian chapter of the **Rocky Mountain Elk Foundation** (Big Horn Plaza, 403/845-6492) is based in Rocky. The foundation's main objective is to preserve critical wildlife habitat by buying large chunks of land; members are mostly hunters.

Recreation and Events

The best way to appreciate the history of the area, see some great river scenery, and generally have a good time is to take a float trip with **Voyageur Adventure Tours,** 403/845-7878, on the North Saskatchewan River. The voyageur canoes used are replicas of those used by early explorers; they are large and stable, requiring little paddling skill. Half-day trips, which include a stop at the National Historic Park and lunch, are $40; a full day with cooked lunch—prepared along the riverbank while you take a short hike or rest in the sun—is $60. Overnight tours start at $150, and a five-day trip, including three days on horseback, is $425.

Another center of water-based activities is **Crimson Lake Provincial Park,** northwest of town. Crimson Lake is great for boating and canoeing (rentals available), whereas nearby Twin Lakes, also in the park, is stocked with rainbow trout. The undeveloped northwest side attracts many species of waterfowl, including loons, herons, grebes, sandhill cranes, and a variety of ducks.

Pine Hills Golf Course, 403/845-7400, offers linksters an 18-hole course eight kilometers west of town, with one par-5 measuring more than 600 yards; greens fee is $32.

If you're passing through town on the third weekend of August, check out the **Rocky Mountain Lumberjack,** where participants compete in events such as woodchopping, axe throwing, and logrolling.

Accommodations and Camping

Many motels are spread out along Highway 11 east of town. The newest and most comfortable is the **Tamarack Motor Inn** (403/845-5252 or 877/845-5252, www.tamarackmotorinn.com), with 66 rooms, the best restaurant in town, and a lounge. This place is a good value at $59 single, $67 double. Other options include the **Voyageur Motel** (403/845-3381 or 888/845-5569, www.voyageurmotel.com), which has large, clean rooms from $44 single, $52 double (rooms in the new wing are $54 single, $62 double); the **Big Horn Motel** (in the Big Horn Plaza, 403/845-2871), $50 single, $55 double; and the **Walking Eagle Motor Inn,** 403/845-2804, which is easily recognized by its striking log exterior, $62 single, $68 double. **Old Town Cottages** (4203 62nd St., 403/844-4442, www.oldtowncottages.com) offers basic, self-contained two-bedroom cottages from $65.

Both of the municipal campgrounds are behind the information center and have toilets, showers, and firewood; unserviced sites $10. **Aspen Park** is the larger of the two and has powered sites ($16). The other, **Centennial Park,** is accessed from 54th Street. **Riverview Campground,** 403/845-4422, on the North Saskatchewan River, is the only commercial facility in town. The unserviced sites are tucked in among a grove of trees on the riverbank, and above them are serviced sites, with spectacular views along the valley. The campground has a small grocery store, a laundromat, showers, and free firewood; unserviced sites $13, hookups $16–18.

In **Crimson Lake Provincial Park,** northwest of town along an access road off Highway 11, you'll find two campgrounds; sites along the bank of Crimson Lake are $19–21, whereas those beside Twin Lakes are $16.

Food and Drink

The only restaurants in town are those in the strip of family-style and fast-food places along Highway 11 and 52nd Avenue. The restaurant in the **Tamarack Motor Inn,** 403/845-5252, offers a large range of choices, including hearty cooked breakfasts for $5–8 and a Friday night buffet and Sunday brunch. The **Walking Eagle Motor Inn,** on the east side of the highway, also has a restaurant.

A wild honky-tonk bar in the **David Thompson Hotel** (4834 50th St., 403/845-3123) cranks out live music most nights.

Services and Information

The **Greyhound** bus depot is in the Shell gas station (4504 47th Ave., 403/845-2650). Greyhound operates a daily service between Calgary and Rocky, but you must change buses in Red Deer. For a taxi, call **Rocky Cabs,** 403/845-4000.

The **post office** is downtown at 5011 50th Avenue. **Maytag Homestyle Laundry** is at 4647 47th Avenue. **Rocky Mountain House General Hospital** is at 5016 52nd Avenue, 403/845-3347. For the **RCMP**, call 403/845-2881, and if you spot a forest fire, call 403/845-8211.

The **Tourist Information Centre** is located beside Highway 11 north of downtown (54th Ave., 403/845-5450 or 800/565-3793, www. rockymtnhouse.com). Don't buy the town map because many shops in town give them away. The center is open in July and August daily 9 A.M.–8 P.M., June and September daily 9 A.M.–6 P.M., the rest of the year weekdays only.

NORDEGG

Westbound Highway 11 climbs slowly from the aspen parkland around Rocky Mountain House into the dense forests on the eastern slopes of the Canadian Rockies. The only community between Rocky and Banff National Park is Nordegg, 85 kilometers west of Rocky. Nordegg was once a booming coal-mining town of 3,500, but the town was abandoned when the mines closed. Now fewer than 100 hardy souls call the town home. Below the old townsite, just off Highway 11, various tourist facilities have sprung up, including an excellent interpretive center. And the town is near many fine fishing rivers and the Forestry Trunk Road.

History

Early in the 20th century, Martin Nordegg staked a claim at a site near where his namesake town is today. Soon after, he established **Brazeau Collieries** and struck a deal with the Canadian National Railway; if they would extend the line to his mines, he would have 100,000 tons of coal waiting. He kept his side of the deal and the railway kept theirs, completing the rail line in 1914. Until then, miners had been housed in makeshift quarters. But the railway brought construction supplies, and permanent structures were soon erected. The town of Nordegg became the first "planned" mining town in Alberta. The streets were built in a semicircular pattern, centered around the railroad station and shops. Fifty miners' cottages were built, all painted in pastel colors. Gardens were planted, and two churches and a modern hospital were built; miners had never had it better. In 1923, production peaked at nearly half a million tons of coal. By the 1930s, most of the coal was being converted to briquettes, which were easy to handle and burned better than raw coal. By the early 1940s, with four briquette presses, Nordegg had one of the largest such operations in North America. But the success soon turned to ash. In 1941, an explosion killed 29 men, and in 1950, fire destroyed many structures. Then trains began converting to diesel fuel and home heating went to natural gas. Brazeau Collieries ceased operations in January 1955. Many miners had spent their entire lives working the mine and had raised families in the remote mining community. By the summer of 1955, the town had been abandoned. A minimum security prison has operated on the site since 1963, and only a few of the original buildings remain.

The **Nordegg Historical Society,** made up of many former residents of the mining community, has commenced restoration of some of the buildings. The townsite is not open to the general public. To visit the area, you must either take a guided tour or do a short stint in the slammer. I recommend the tour.

In Town

Tourist services are on an access road south of Highway 11. The **Nordegg Heritage Centre** is housed in the old schoolhouse, just up the hill from "downtown." Among many interesting displays are newspaper articles telling of the town's ups and downs. The center also holds a café. Tours of the abandoned townsite and mine leave from here in summer, daily at 1 P.M. They last about 2.5 hours and cost $6. The heritage center, 403/721-2625, is open in summer daily 9 A.M.–5 P.M. and is a good source of information about the area. The Natural Resources Service office, 403/721-3965, has information on current road conditions; open year-round Mon.–Fri. 8:30 A.M.–midday.

Practicalities

Nordegg Resort Lodge (403/721-3757, www.nordegg.com) is the town's only motel, but if there's any mineral exploration in the area, the 38 rooms are full. It has a restaurant (open daily 7 A.M.–9 P.M.), a lounge, and a laundry room, and the front-desk staff can organize horseback riding with a local operator. The rooms go for $70–80 single or double. If you must have a roof over your head, another option is the **Shunda Creek Hostel,** a huge log chalet in a bush setting that has a fully equipped kitchen, a dining room, a fireplace, hot showers, and some private rooms. Members of Hostelling International pay $17 per night, nonmembers $21. For reservations, call 403/721-2140, or book through the Edmonton Hostel at 780/988-6836. The hostel is along Shunda Creek Recreation Area Road, just west of Nordegg. If you've never stayed in a hostel, check this one out.

Campers here have many choices, with provincial recreation area campgrounds north and south along the Forestry Trunk Road, and provincial recreation areas east and west along Highway 11. All sites are primitive but have pit toilets, firewood, and kitchen shelters and are usually beside a creek or lake. Expect to pay $9–11 per night. Closest to town is **Upper Shunda Creek,** three kilometers west of Nordegg.

WEST FROM NORDEGG

The **Forestry Trunk Road** crosses Highway 11 three kilometers west of Nordegg. This road, used mainly to maintain the forest, is well traveled by those going fishing, hiking, and camping. From Highway 11, it is 190 kilometers north to Hinton and 265 kilometers south to Cochrane. No services are available along either route, but the scenery is spectacular, the fishing great, and the crowds nonexistent.

From this junction, Highway 11 veers southwest. Twenty-three kilometers from Nordegg, it passes a gravel parking area at the trailhead for **Crescent Falls** and **Bighorn Canyon.** Five kilometers farther, a gravel road leads south to the eastern end of **Abraham Lake** on the North Saskatchewan River, one of

Alberta's largest reservoirs. An information center at the dam, 403/721-3952, is open in summer daily 8:30 A.M.–4:30 P.M. Back on the highway, the main body of Abraham Lake quickly comes into view, its brilliant turquoise water reflecting the front ranges of the Canadian Rockies. Don't stop for a photo session just yet, though, because the views improve farther west. Across the lake is **Michener Mountain** (2,337 meters).

The **David Thompson Resort** (403/721-2103, www.davidthompsonresort.com) provides the only services along the highway west of Nordegg. Its full-service RV park charges $15 for unserviced sites, $17–19 for hookups. Motel rooms are available for $70 single, $75 double. A café serves hearty breakfasts from $4, lunch and dinner from $6. The resort also rents bikes for $12 per day and has a heated pool and a Frisbee golf course. It's open mid-May to early October.

Kootenay Plains EcologicalReserve/ Siffleur Falls

Located at the south end of Abraham Lake, this reserve protects a unique area of dry grasslands in the mountains. The climate in this section of the valley is unusually moderate, the warmest in the Rockies. June grass and wheat grass, usually associated with the prairies of southeastern Alberta, thrive here. The valley is a prime wintering area for elk, but because of the dry microclimate and its associated vegetation, mammals are not abundant in summer.

Two kilometers farther west along the highway is the trailhead for a hike to spectacular Siffleur Falls. Along the first section, the trail crosses the North Saskatchewan River via a swinging bridge, then at the two-kilometer mark crosses the Siffleur River, reaching the falls after four kilometers (allow 70 minutes one-way). These are the official "Siffleur Falls," but others lie farther upstream at the 6.2- and 6.9-kilometer marks.

Highway 11 then continues climbing, past a parking area (from where a trail leads to a whirlpool on the North Saskatchewan River) and on into Banff National Park at Saskatchewan River Crossing. From here, it is 153 kilometers north to Jasper and 127 kilometers south to Banff.

DAVID THOMPSON

David Thompson, one of Canada's greatest explorers, was a quiet, courageous, and energetic man who drafted the first comprehensive and accurate map of western Canada. He arrived in Canada from England as a 14-year-old apprentice clerk for the Hudson's Bay Company. With an inquisitive nature and a talent for wilderness navigation, he quickly acquired the skills of surveying and mapmaking. Natives called him Koo-koo-sint, which translates as "The Man Who Looks at Stars."

Between 1786 and 1808 Thompson led four major expeditions into what is now Alberta—the first for the Hudson's Bay Company and the last three for its rival, the North West Company. The most important one was the fourth, from 1806 to 1808, during which he traveled up the North Saskatchewan River and discovered the Athabasca Pass through the Continental Divide. For many years, this was the main route across the Canadian Rockies to the Pacific Ocean.

In 1813 Thompson began work on a master map covering the entire territory that the North West Company controlled. It was four meters long and two meters wide, detailing over 1.5 million square miles. On completion it was hung out of public view in the council hall of a company fort in the east. It was years later, after his death in 1857, that the map was "discovered" and Thompson became recognized as one of the world's greatest land geographers.

White Goat Wilderness Area

The region's three designated wilderness areas—White Goat, Siffleur to the south, and Willmore to the north—afford hikers the chance to enjoy the natural beauty and wildlife of the Canadian Rockies away from the crowds associated with the mountain national parks. No horses or motorized vehicles are allowed within wilderness area boundaries, and hunting and fishing are prohibited, as is all construction. This, ironically, gives these lightly traveled regions (an unnamed 15-year resident of adjoining Banff National Park had never heard of them) more protection than the national parks. The drawback, however, and the reason so few people explore these areas, is that wilderness really means *wilderness*, sans roads, bridges, or campsites. With one exception at Willmore, no roads even lead to the areas' boundaries; the only access is on foot.

White Goat is the largest of the three wilderness areas, comprising 445 square kilometers of high mountain ranges, wide valleys, hanging glaciers, waterfalls, and high alpine lakes. The area's vegetation zones are easily recognizable: subalpine forests of Engelmann spruce, subalpine fir, and lodgepole pine, followed by alpine tundra higher up. Large mammals here include a large population of bighorn sheep, as well as mountain goats, deer, elk, woodland caribou, moose, cougars, wolves, coyotes, black bears, and grizzly bears.

The most popular hike is the **McDonald Creek Trail,** which first follows the Cline River, then McDonald Creek to the creek's source in the heart of the wilderness area. McDonald Creek is approximately 12 kilometers from the parking area on Highway 11, but a full day should be allowed for this section because the trail crosses many streams. From where McDonald Creek flows into the Cline River, it is 19 kilometers to the McDonald Lakes, but allow another two full days because the total elevation gain for the hike is 1,224 meters. Other hiking possibilities include following the Cline River to its source and crossing Sunset Pass into Banff National Park, 17 kilometers north of the Saskatchewan River Crossing, or heading up Cataract Creek and linking up with the trails in the Brazeau River area of Jasper National Park. White Goat Wilderness Area has no services and is for experienced hikers only. For more information, contact Alberta Environment, Main Floor, 9945 108th Street, Edmonton, Alberta T5K 2A6, 780/944-0313, www.gov.ab.ca/env.

Siffleur Wilderness Area

Siffleur, like White Goat Wilderness Area, is a remote region of the Canadian Rockies, completely protected from any activities that could have an impact on the area's fragile ecosystems, including road and trail development. No bridges have been built over the area's many fast-flowing streams, and the few old trails that do exist are not maintained. Elk, deer, moose, cougars, wolverines, wolves, coyotes, black bears, and grizzly bears roam the area's four main valleys, whereas higher, alpine elevations harbor mountain goats and bighorn sheep.

The area is located on the opposite (south) side of Highway 11 from White Goat Wilderness and borders Banff National Park to the west and south. The main trail into the 412-square-kilometer wilderness begins from a parking area two kilometers south of the Two O'-clock Creek Campground at Kootenay Plains (see previous entry). The area's northeastern boundary is a seven-kilometer hike from here. Once inside the wilderness area, the trail climbs steadily alongside the Siffleur River and into the heart of the wilderness. Ambitious hikers can continue through to the Dolomite Creek Area of Banff National Park, finishing at the Icefields Parkway, seven kilometers south of Bow Summit. The total length of this trail is 68 kilometers (five to seven days). Another access point for the area is opposite Waterfowl Lakes Campground in Banff National Park. From here, it is six kilometers up Noyes Creek to the wilderness area boundary; the trail peters out after 4.5 kilometers and requires some serious scrambling before descending into Siffleur. This trail—as with all others in the wilderness area—is for experienced hikers only. For more information, write to Alberta Environment, Main Floor, 9945 108th Street, Edmonton, Alberta T5K 2A6, 780/944-0313, www.gov.ab.ca/env.

NORTH FROM ROCKY MOUNTAIN HOUSE

Alder Flats

Alder Flats is located 61 kilometers north of Rocky and six kilometers west of Highway 22. Through town, along a gravel road, is Alberta's only privately owned ghost town, **Em-te Town.** It was built completely from scratch and includes a saloon, a jailhouse, a harness shop, stables, a bank, an emporium, and a church. Rose's Cantina serves meals throughout the day. A campground at the ghost town has hot showers, but sites are unserviced; $10 per night. Admission to Em-te is $5; 403/388-2166.

Pigeon Lake

East of Alder Flats along Highway 13, this lake is a popular recreation area for residents of Edmonton (60 kilometers to the northwest). The lake is reputed to be the best swimming lake in Alberta and offers good fishing for walleye, pike, and whitefish. At the southeastern end of the lake is the little hamlet of **Ma-me-o,** where the streets are lined with a colorful array of summer cottages. The beach here is good and is backed by a few shops, including a restaurant. In the heart of the town is Alberta's smallest provincial park, **Ma-me-o Provincial Park** (1.5 hectares). It is a day-use area only. Along the western shoreline is **Pigeon Lake Provincial Park.** At the main campground, you'll find a beach, showers, kitchen shelters, firewood sales, and the start of a short hiking trail; unserviced sites $13, powered sites $15. **Zeiner Campground,** a little farther north, has powered sites, kitchen shelters, firewood sales, groceries, canoe rentals, and showers; unserviced sites $17, powered sites $19. Reservations are taken for both these campgrounds; call 403/586-2644.

Drayton Valley and Vicinity

Drayton Valley is a town of 5,200 at the base of the foothills and at the western edge of Alberta's extensive oil and gas fields, 110 kilometers north of Rocky Mountain House. It is located on what is known as the **subcontinental divide:** a high point of land dividing the Arctic Ocean–bound Pembina River System from the Atlantic Ocean–bound North Saskatchewan River System. To the southwest, along Highway 620, is **Brazeau Reservoir,** whose waters are used to supply hydroelectric power to nearby industry. To the east, 40 kilometers along Highway 39, then 25 kilometers north on Highway 770, are the **Genesee Fossil Beds.** Each year the North Saskatchewan River erodes its banks here, exposing often perfectly preserved 60-million-year-old fossilized plants. To get to the site from the hamlet of Genesee, head west three kilometers, south 1.5 kilometers, then west again 1.5 kilometers to a small creek. A partially defined trail leads down to the much larger river and to the fossil beds.

CALGARY TO RED DEER

The main route out of Calgary is the Deerfoot Trail, which becomes Highway 2 as it heads through outlying suburbs and onto the prairies. To the west are the foothills and, more than 100 kilometers away, dominating the horizon, the Canadian Rockies. They remain in view for much of the 145-kilometer run to the city of Red Deer, located halfway to Edmonton. The Calgary and Edmonton Railway Company built the first permanent link between Alberta's two largest centers in 1891, following a trail that had been used for generations by natives, early explorers, traders, and missionaries. With the coming of the automobile, a road was built. The original road (Highway 2A) is now paralleled the entire length by Highway 2, a four-lane, divided highway that makes the trip an easy three-hour drive. Highway 2A is still maintained in some sections, passing through small ranching and farming communities. A longer but more interesting alternative is to take highways 9 and 21, to the east of Highway 2, passing through the southern edge of the aspen parkland to a buffalo jump used by natives 2,000 years ago.

VIA HIGHWAY 2A

Airdrie

This fast-growing city (population 19,000) is mostly residential. Folks from Calgary who become disenchanted with city living need only move to this rural town—only 10 minutes from Calgary International Airport—to escape the hustle. It began as the first stopping house on the Calgary and Edmonton Railway and has grown ever since. The town's **Nose Creek Valley Museum** (1701 Main St. S, 403/948-6685) has an interesting exhibit of artifacts from the Blackfoot and Shoshoni tribes, who fought many battles in the area, vying for dominance as buffalo herds declined. Admission $2. It's open in summer daily 9 A.M.–5 P.M.

Beside the main highway is the **Best Western Regency Inn** (121 Edmonton Trail, 403/948-3838 or 800/558-4844), convenient to Calgary International Airport and a handy alternative to

Calgary lodgings during Stampede Week. Rooms are $109 single, $119 double, and there is a restaurant on site. West of Airdrie is **Big Springs Estate Bed & Breakfast** (403/948-5264 or 888/948-5851, www.bigsprings-bb.com), a luxurious accommodation set on 14 hectares. Each of the four rooms is well appointed, and the rates include a gourmet breakfast and light evening snacks, such as homemade chocolate fudge. The nightly cost is $90–160 single or double, depending on the room (the Grand Executive Room is huge).

Carstairs

Carstairs is a small farming, dairy, and ranching center 67 kilometers north of Calgary. The town's tree-lined streets are dotted with grand old houses, and the grain elevators associated with all prairie towns stand silhouetted against the skyline. Although a small museum is located at 1138 Nanton Street, the main attractions are outside of town. **PaSu Farm**, 403/337-2800, 10 kilometers west of town (follow the signs), is a working farm with a dozen breeds of sheep. It also displays a wide variety of sheepskin, Albertan wool products, and weavings from Africa. The farm's Devonshire Tea Room serves scones, homemade apple pie, and various teas each afternoon. The farm is open year-round Tues.–Sat. 10 A.M.–5 P.M., Sunday noon–5 P.M.

Much of the wool from PaSu Farm is sold to **Custom Woollen Mills,** on the other side of Carstairs, 20 kilometers east on Highway 581 and 4.5 kilometers north on Highway 791, 403/337-2221, open Mon.–Fri. 8 A.M.–5 P.M. At this working museum, the raw wool is processed on strange-looking machines—some of which date to the mid-1800s—into the finished product ready for knitting. A self-guided tour is offered.

Olds

Olds is located a little more than halfway between Calgary and Red Deer. Surrounded by rich farmland, it's home of **Olds Agriculture College,** which has been a leader in the development of Canadian agriculture for most of the 20th century and beyond. The school's landscaped gardens provide a welcome break from the seemingly endless farms surrounding the town. The 600-hectare campus is located between highways 2 and 2A.

Red Lodge Provincial Park

This small park is located 14 kilometers west of **Bowden** on the **Little Red Deer River.** An English settler built a large log house on the river's edge and then painted the logs red, hence the name. The park is situated within a heavily wooded strip of land that extends east from the foothills well into central Alberta, an ideal habitat for deer and moose. The campground has a kitchen shelter, coin-operated showers, and firewood sales, and the river is good for swimming and fishing. It can get busy on weekends; $15.

Innisfail

Innisfail (pop. 6,000) is the largest town between Calgary and Red Deer. From Antler Ridge, north of town, Anthony Henday (in 1754) became the first white man to see the Canadian Rockies. Highway 54, named the Anthony Henday Highway in his honor, begins in town and branches west, passing the turnoff to Markerville and continuing to Caroline and the Forestry Trunk Road. **Innisfail Historical Village** (in the fairgrounds at 42nd St. and 52nd Ave., 403/227-2906) has re-created historic buildings, including a stopping house, a school, a store, a Canadian Pacific Railway (CPR) station, and a blacksmith's shop, on a one-hectare site. It's open in summer daily 11 A.M.–5:30 P.M. The Royal Canadian Mounted Police (RCMP) **Dog Training Kennels,** four kilometers south of town on the east side of the highway, is the only one of its type in Canada. Canine cops receive training here in obedience, agility, and criminal apprehension. Tours of the facility are given year-round, weekdays 1–3 P.M.; book in advance by calling 403/227-3346.

Innisfail has two inexpensive motels, and just west of town is **Anthony Henday Campground,** with showers and kitchen shelters; unserviced sites $8, powered sites $12.

Markerville

This town, 16 kilometers west then three kilometers north of Innisfail, was originally settled by Icelandic people in the late 1800s; today their heritage lives on through the work of the local

Icelandic Society. In town is the **Historic Markerville Creamery,** 403/728-3006. Between 1897 and the time of its closure in 1972, the creamery won many awards for its fine-quality butters. Tours of the factory explain how butter is made. A café serves Icelandic specialties. Admission is $2. It's open in summer daily 10 A.M.–5:30 P.M.

Just north of Markerville is the distinctive pink-and-green colored **Stephansson House,** once home to Stephan A. Stephansson, one of the Western world's most prolific poets. He spent the early part of his life in Iceland, but most of his poetry was written here. The house has been restored with displays about the man and his work. Open May–Sept. daily 10 A.M.–6 P.M. For more information, call 403/728-3929.

THE BACK WAY

The area east of Highway 2, immediately north of Calgary, was once covered in aspen. But over time, the trees have given way to cereal agriculture and large dairy farms. Stands of trees are now limited to the valleys of tributaries of the Red Deer River, the region's main watershed. The landscape is generally flat, but along the main route north (via highways 9 and 21) are interesting towns and a buffalo jump.

To Three Hills

Highway 9 intersects Highway 1 approximately 31 kilometers east of Calgary and heads north to **Irricana.** Two kilometers northwest of town, **Pioneer Acres of Alberta** displays a large collection of working farm machinery and holds a festival the second weekend each August, with demonstrations of pioneer farming and homemaking activities. It's open May–Sept. daily 9 A.M.–5 P.M. Admission is $3. For more information, call 403/935-4357.

North of Irricana is **Beiseker,** where a CPR station, built in 1910, has been restored and now houses a museum, 403/947-3774. From here, Highway 9 heads east, passing the junction with Highway 21 and continuing on to Drumheller (see the **Dinosaur Valley** chapter). North up Highway 21 is **Three Hills,** home of **GuZoo Animal Farm,** 403/443-7463, which keeps a collection of approximately 90 exotic animals such as Siberian tigers, as well as cougars and bob-

THE CANADA GOOSE

Each spring and fall the skies of central Alberta come alive with the honking of the Canada goose, a remarkable bird whose migatory path takes it clear across the North American continent. Each spring family units migrate north to the same nesting site, year after year. These are spread throughout Canada, from remote wetlands of northern Alberta to desolate islands in the Arctic Ocean. Groups of families migrate together in flocks, the size of the flock varying according to the region, subspecies, and season. Preparation for long flights includes hours of preening and wing-flexing. Once in the air they navigate by the sun, moon, and stars, often becoming disoriented in fog or heavy cloud cover. They are intensely aware of air pressure and humidity. In spring Canada geese hitch a ride north on the strong winds produced by low-pressure systems rolling up from the southwest. In fall they take advantage of Arctic fronts that roar south. If weather conditions aren't right, the geese will rest for a while, usually in farmers' fields (taking advantage of freshly sown crops). The "V" formation, for which the geese are famous, serves a very specific purpose: Each bird positions itself behind and slightly to the side of the bird immediately ahead. In this way every goose in the flock has a clear view, and all but the leader benefit from the slipstream of the birds ahead.

If, during migration, a goose becomes ill or is crippled by a hunter's bullet, family members will remain with the bird, delaying their flight and leaving the injured bird only if it dies or if their own survival is in jeopardy.

---

cats—native to Alberta but rarely seen. It's open year-round daily from 9 A.M. Admission is $5. To get there from Three Hills, head 1.5 kilometers west, then six kilometers north.

Torrington

Torrington, on Highway 27, 25 kilometers west of Highway 21, has more gophers than residents. This normally wouldn't be unusual for a prairie town, except that Torrington's gophers are all stuffed. The town made world headlines in 1997 with the opening of the **Gopher Hole Museum** (208 1st St., 403/631-2133), which, as the brochure describes, is "a whimsical portrayal of daily life in our tranquil village." Approximately 40 dioramas house stuffed gophers in various poses, including gophers in love, gophers playing sports, trailer court gophers, and even gophers wearing shirts declaring that animal rights activists, who were incensed at the idea of the museum, should "Go stuff themselves." Open in summer daily 10 A.M.–5 P.M. The admission price of $2 includes a copy of the words to the *Torrington Gopher Call Song,* which wafts through the quiet streets of the village whenever the museum is open.

Trochu

Continuing north along Highway 21 is Trochu, which is worth a stop for the following two sights. The **Arboretum** (just off Highway 21 on North Rd., 403/442-2111) showcases the flora of southern Alberta. Pathways lead through the gardens, where more than 100 different plant species attract a variety of birds. The arboretum is open in summer daily 9 A.M.–8 P.M. **St. Ann Ranch** was established in 1905 by a group of aristocratic French settlers and is now a Provincial Historic Site. A French settlement, including a school, a church, and a post office, grew around it. The thriving community suffered a blow during World War II when many townsmen returned to France to defend their country. Descendants of one of the men now operate the ranch, which has been partly restored. A small museum displays many historic items, and a large tearoom serves, among other delicacies, delicious fruit pies; open in summer daily 2–5 P.M. Seven rooms are available for guest use; rates run $45–55 single, $55–75 double, including breakfast. For information or room reservations, call 403/442-3924.

Dry Island Buffalo Jump
This 1,180-hectare park is named for both an isolated mesa in the Red Deer River Valley and the site where natives stampeded bison over a cliff approximately 2,000 years ago. The buffalo jump—a 50-meter drop—is much higher than other jumps in Alberta and is in an ideal location; the approach to the jump is uphill, masking the presence of a cliff until the final few meters. Below the prairie benchland, clifflike valley walls and banks of sandstone have been carved into strange-looking badlands by wind and water erosion. A great diversity of plantlife grows in the valley; more than 400 species of flowering plants have been recorded. The park is a day-use area only; apart from a picnic area and a few trails, it is undeveloped. Access is along a gravel road east from Huxley on Highway 21. From the park entrance, at the top of the buffalo drop, the road descends steeply for 200 vertical meters into the valley. (It can be extremely slippery after rain.)

RED DEER

This city of 65,000 (Alberta's fourth-largest) is on a bend of the Red Deer River, halfway between the cities of Calgary and Edmonton, which are 145 kilometers south and 148 kilometers north, respectively. From the highway, Red Deer seems to be all industrial estates and suburban sprawl, but an extensive park system runs through the city, and many historic buildings have been restored.

History
The name Red Deer was mentioned on maps by explorer David Thompson in the early 1800s. The Cree name for the river is *Waskasoo* (elk); scholars believe that Thompson translated the word incorrectly, confusing these animals with the red deer of Scotland.

Permanent settlement began in 1884 at a site where the busy trail linking Calgary to Edmonton crossed the Red Deer River. Most of the early settlement was centered around Fort Normandeau, at the river crossing. But the Calgary and Edmonton Railway Company built its line and a station farther east, and the town slowly grew in around it. Initially, the economy was based on agriculture, but it profited from the oil-and-gas boom after World War II. By the 1970s, Red Deer was one of Canada's fastest-growing cities, and things haven't slowed down yet, with surrounding tracts of land being broken up for residential and industrial subdivisions.

SIGHTS AND RECREATION

If you're arriving in Red Deer from either the north or south, stay on Highway 2 until the large red-and-white **Red Deer Visitor and Convention Bureau** building comes into view (from the north, take the 32nd Street exit and loop back onto Highway 2 northbound). In addition to being a good source of information about the city, it is home to an interesting sports museum. From this complex, duck through the Heritage Ranch parking lot to get downtown.

Alberta Sports Hall of Fame and Museum
Being halfway between Calgary and Edmonton, Red Deer is a good home for a museum that highlights the feats of Alberta's sporting heroes, including hockey legend Wayne Gretzky and multiple-time World Figure Skating Champion Kurt Browning. In addition to a "Highlights of History" exhibit, the museum has a computerized honor roll, film footage of great sporting moments, and a variety of interactive sports booths. Admission is $3 and it's open in summer 9 A.M.–6 P.M., the rest of the year 10 A.M.–5 P.M. The museum is located on Highway 2 in the same building as the Red Deer Visitor and Convention Bureau.

Waskasoo Park and Fort Normandeau
Red Deer's sights are spread out along the Red Deer River, connected by 11-kilometer-long, 1,000-hectare Waskasoo Park. The park has a 75-kilometer trail system, which is good for walking or biking in summer and cross-country skiing in winter. If you've stopped at the highway-side information center, it's possible to drive through the one-way gate to adjacent **Heritage Ranch,** 403/347-4977, but there's no access from the ranch back out to the highway. The

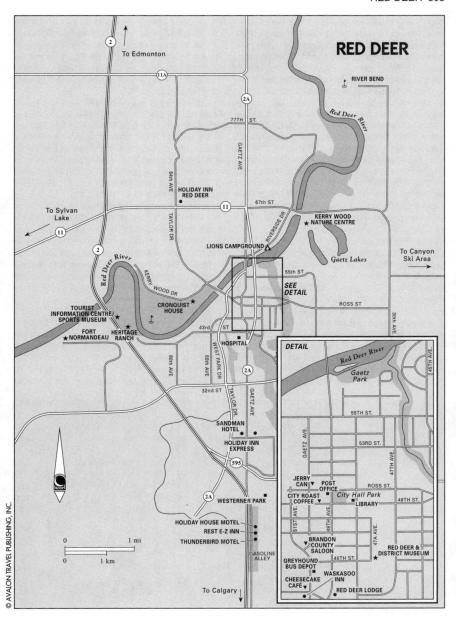

ranch is primarily an equestrian center offering trail rides ($18 per hour). From the ranch, walk upstream through the wooded river valley, or drive back out along 32nd Street, crossing Highway 2, to Fort Normandeau. This replica is built on the site of the original fort, constructed in the spring of 1885 in anticipation of the Reil Rebellion—a Métis uprising led by Louis Reil. As protection against marauding natives, a hotel by the river crossing was heavily fortified. Its walls were reinforced, lookout towers were erected, and the entire building was palisaded. The fort was never attacked and was moved to an outlying farm in 1899. Beside the fort is an interpretive center with displays depicting early settlement at the crossing. The center, 403/347-7550, is open mid-May through June daily 10 A.M.–5 P.M., July–Aug. noon–8 P.M.

Other Sights
The **Red Deer and District Museum** (4525 47A Ave., 403/309-8405) tells the story of the area from prehistoric times to the present, with emphasis on the growth and development of the last 100 years. It's open July–Aug. Mon. –Fri. 10 A.M.–5 P.M. and Sat.–Sun. 1–5 P.M., the rest of the year daily 1–5 P.M. The museum is also the starting point for two historical walking tours—ask here for a map—and a guided evening cemetery walk. Adjacent to the museum is **Heritage Square,** a collection of historic structures, including the Stevenson-Hall

Block, Red Deer's oldest building, and a re-created Norwegian log and sod farmhouse, typical of those lived in by many early settlers in Alberta. One block west, on Ross Street, in front of City Hall, is **City Hall Park,** where 45,000 flowering plants create the perfect spot for a relaxing rest.

On the opposite side of the river from downtown (take 55th St., then Taylor Dr.) is **Cronquist House,** 403/346-0055. This 1911 three-story Victorian farmhouse overlooks Bower Ponds. When it was threatened with demolition, enterprising locals waited until winter and moved it piece by piece across the frozen lake to its present site. Open Mon.–Fri. 9 A.M.–4 P.M. and Sunday 1–4 P.M.

Kerry Wood Nature Centre is north of downtown (6300 45th Ave., 403/346-2010), open daily 10 A.M.–5 P.M. The center has various exhibits and videos on the natural history of the river valley and provides access to the adjacent 118-hectare **Gaetz Lakes Sanctuary,** an area of spruce and poplar interspersed with marshes that is home to 128 species of birds and 25 species of mammals.

Recreation
The city's park system provides a range of recreational facilities. Paddleboats and canoes can be rented at Bower Ponds, 403/347-9777. At Heritage Ranch, 403/347-4977, trail riding, horseback-riding lessons, and wagon and

Cronquist House

sleigh rides are offered. **River Bend Golf Course,** 403/343-8311, is a 6,700-yard course where water comes into play on 11 holes, with a driving range, a pro shop, and club rentals; green fees are $33. To get there, follow 30th Avenue four kilometers north of the city.

Canyon Ski Area, nine kilometers east of town along Highway 11 (403/346-5589, Snowphone 403/346-5588), has 11 runs on a 164-vertical-meter slope and night skiing and snowboarding on weekday nights. Lift tickets are $25 adults, $19 children six to 12, and $6.50 toddlers five and under.

Sylvan Lake

This lake, 22 kilometers west of Red Deer, has been one of Alberta's most popular summer resorts since the turn of the 20th century. It has more than five kilometers of sandy beaches, clean warm water, a large marina, and plenty of recreation facilities. **Wild Rapid Waterslides** (Lakeshore Dr., 403/887-3636) offers two 110-meter-long water slides, nine other slides, a heated pool, and sailboard and paddleboat rentals; $15 adults, $11 children under 12. Other facilities at the lake include boat rentals from **Sylvan Marina,** 403/887-2950; three golf courses; and a greyhound racetrack (racing each Saturday), 403/887-5782.

Festivals and Events

Most city events take place at **Westerner Park,** a sprawling complex at the far south end of the city. The park is also home to the Red Deer Rebels hockey team, who play in the Western Hockey League. The **Makin' 8 Silver Buckle Rodeo,** held in late April, kicks off Red Deer's festival season and attracts rodeo stars from throughout North America. **Westerner Days** begins in mid-July, the weekend that the Calgary Stampede ends; festivities include a parade, a midway, livestock displays, chuckwagon races, an art display, and a casino. In early November, Red Deer hosts a large **Farm Expo.** For information about all of these events, contact Westerner Park (403/343-7800, www.westerner.ab.ca). The **Red Deer International Air Show,** held on the weekend closest to August 1, is one of Canada's most spectacular aerial events. For information, call 403/340-2333.

ACCOMMODATIONS AND CAMPING

Red Deer's location between Alberta's two largest cities makes it a popular location for conventions and conferences, so the city has a lot of hotels. The larger hotels are generally full of conventioneers during the week; ask about reduced rates on weekends.

$50–100

The **Thunderbird Motel** is in "Gasoline Alley," the southernmost commercial strip (403/343-8933 or 800/268-7132), and as you can guess from the name, it's an older place. The 40 rooms are set around an outdoor pool and barbecue area. Rates are $55 single, $60 double. In the same vicinity is the **Rest E-Z Inn** (403/343-8444 or 800/424-9454), $57 single, $65 double, where a continental breakfast is included in the price; and the **Holiday House Motel** (403/346-4188), a real cheapie with rooms from $50 single or double.

The least expensive accommodation within walking distance of downtown is the **Waskasoo Inn** (4124 Gaetz Ave., 403/342-6969), with basic rooms for $48 single, $59 double. A much nicer downtown choice is the **Red Deer Lodge** (4311 49th Ave., 403/346-8841 or 800/661-1657), a seven-story hostelry with more than 200 rooms. This full-service establishment has rooms set around a huge tropical atrium where there's an indoor pool, a garden restaurant, and two lounges. Rates start at $95 single or double.

One of the few motels north of downtown is the **Holiday Inn Red Deer** (6500 67th St., 403/342-6567 or 800/661-4961, www.holidayinnreddeer.com), which has larger rooms, an indoor pool, an exercise room, and a restaurant; $85 single or double.

$100–150

Red Deer's **Holiday Inn Express** is south of downtown on the northbound side of the road (2803 Gaetz Ave., 403/343-2112 or 800/223-1993, www.hiexpress.com). The rooms are spacious, modern, and well furnished; $105 single or double. Directly across the road is the **Sandman Hotel Red Deer** (2828 Gaetz Ave., 403/343-7400 or 800/726-3626, www.sandman.ca), which opened in summer of 2000. It features 143 modern rooms, an indoor pool, a fitness center, a lounge, and a restaurant; $105 single, $115 double.

Campgrounds

Red Deer has excellent city camping at the **Lions Campground,** on the west side of the river (4723 Riverside Dr., 403/342-8183). To get there, follow Gaetz Avenue north through town and turn right after crossing the Red Deer River. The campground has showers, full hookups, and a laundry room; unserviced sites $14, hookups $18. Open in May–Sept. only.

OTHER PRACTICALITIES

Food and Drink

Downtown, head to **City Roast Coffee** (4940 Ross St., 403/347-0893). It's a big-city–style coffeehouse offering coffees from around the world and light snacks. It's open Mon.–Sat. 7:30 A.M.–6 P.M. Around the corner, a very different type of eatery, the **Jerry Can** (5005 50th Ave., 403/347-9417), attracts a strange collection of locals who come for the inexpensive meals and to catch up on gossip. Fast-food restaurants line Highway 2 as it passes by town; Gaetz Avenue has additional fast-food choices, as well as a range of family-style dining places. One of these, the **Cheesecake Café,** which is close to downtown (4320 Gaetz Ave., 403/341-7818), is part of a restaurant chain but a cut above the rest. It features a health-conscious menu of soups, sandwiches, and freshly squeezed juices. It's open daily for lunch and dinner and from 10:30 A.M. for Sunday brunch. Farther south, **Willy's Hamburgers** (on the east side of Highway 2 S, 403/347-5444) has daily breakfast specials and is open from 6:30 A.M. **Snifters Dining Lounge,** in the Red Deer Lodge, opens daily at 5 P.M. for fine dining.

The **Brandon County Saloon** (4608 50th Ave., 403/341-6060) plays country music seven nights a week.

Transportation

Two scheduled bus services link Red Deer to Calgary and Edmonton. **Greyhound** departs from the depot (4303 Gaetz Ave., 403/343-8866) throughout the day for both cities. **Red Arrow** offers a more luxurious service, with complimentary beverages and snacks. Their buses depart the **Holiday Inn Red Deer,** north of downtown at 6500 67th Street up to four times daily for Calgary and Edmonton; call 800/232-1958.

For a cab, call **City Cabs,** 403/346-4444, or **Central Alberta Gold Taxi,** 403/341-7777.

Services and Information

The **post office** is at 4909 50th Street. The **Lost Sock Laundromat** (6350 67th St.) is open daily 9 A.M.–9 P.M. **Red Deer Regional Hospital** is at 3942 50th Ave., 403/343-4422. For the **RCMP** call 403/341-2000.

Red Deer Library is an excellent facility housed in a single-story, red-brick building behind City Hall (4818 49th St., 403/346-4576); open Mon.–Thurs. 9:30 A.M.–8:30 P.M., Fri.–Sat. 9:30 A.M.–5:30 P.M., Sunday 1:30–5 P.M. **Chapters** (5250 22nd Street, 403/309-2427) is part of a chain of Canadian mega-bookstores. The **Red Deer Book Exchange** (6791 50th Ave., 403/342-4883) features a wide variety of used books and magazines. The Red Deer Visitor and Convention Bureau operates an excellent **Tourist Information Centre** on Highway 2 between the main north and south entrances to the city. It's on the city-side of the highway (if you're arriving from the north, take the 32nd Street exit and loop back onto Highway 2 northbound). In addition to providing a load of information, the center has a gift shop, a concession area, restrooms, and is adjacent to a picnic area. It's open year-round Mon.–Fri. 9 A.M.–5 P.M., Sat.–Sun. 10 A.M.–5 P.M. and until 6 P.M. in summer. Phone numbers for the information center are 403/346-0180 or 800/215-8946, www.tourism.reddeer.net.

EAST OF HIGHWAY 2: THE ASPEN PARKLAND

The aspen parkland lying east of Highway 2, between Red Deer and Edmonton, is a transition zone between the prairies to the south and the boreal forest to the north. Here, groves of aspen and, to a lesser degree, balsam poplar grow around sloughs and pothole-like depressions left by the retreating ice sheet at the end of the last Ice Age. Much of the original vegetation was burned by native peoples in order to attract grazing bison. In the last 100 years, the land has been given over to agriculture, changing its ecological makeup forever. Although much of the forest has been cleared and cultivated, the region is still home to mammals such as fox, coyote, lynx, white-tailed deer, beaver, and muskrat. The lakes and sloughs attract more than 200 species of birds, including literally millions of ducks that can be seen in almost all bodies of water.

From Red Deer, halfway between Calgary and Edmonton, Highway 2 continues north, providing access to outdoor recreation opportunities along the way. Sylvan, Gull, and Pigeon lakes are popular summer resort areas west of the highway. To the east are the historic towns of Lacombe, Ponoka, and Wetaskiwin, home of the large Reynolds-Alberta Museum. Highways 12, 13, and 14 are the main routes east. Along each are many small towns with interesting museums and quiet provincial parks. Camrose, on Highway 13, hosts one of North America's largest gatherings of country-music superstars each August.

HIGHWAY 12 EAST

Lacombe

Lacombe, 30 kilometers north of Red Deer and three kilometers east of Highway 2, is an historic town of 7,800 that is the site of provincial and federal agricultural stations. At the turn of the 20th century, the town was a bustling commercial center of 1,000, where an important spur of the Calgary and Edmonton Railway headed east. After a devastating 1906 fire, the town implemented a bylaw dictating that all new buildings were to be constructed using brick or stone. Today, many Edwardian-era buildings stand in the main business district. One block from the main street (50th Ave.), at 5036 51st Street, is **Michener House,** the birthplace of Roland Michener, Canadian governor-general between 1967 and 1974. Dating to 1896, this small wooden house is open in summer Mon.–Fri. noon–4 P.M., 403/782-3933. Between the highway and downtown is a golf course, a campground, and an information center.

Rochon Sands Provincial Park

This small 99-hectare park is located on a peninsula on the south shore of Buffalo Lake, 14 kilometers north of Erskine. The lake is used by migrating waterfowl each spring and fall and supports a large population of northern pike. Camping is $13 per night. The west side of the lake is part of the Buffalo Lake Moraine, a hummocky area created by receding ice during the last Ice Age.

Stettler

Stettler (pop. 4,900) is located along Highway 12, 72 kilometers east of Highway 2 in the middle of a farming and ranching area well known for its purebred livestock. One of Canada's last remaining passenger steam trains operates from an historic railway station at the end of the main street. **Alberta Prairie Steam Tours** runs these trains each weekend May through October (and Thurs.–Fri. in July and August) between Stettler and small prairie towns such as Big Valley, Rowley, Donalda, and Halkirk. Onboard entertainment is provided, and a hearty smorgasbord lunch or dinner is served at the destination. The fare is adults $60, seniors $57, children $29.50. For more information, call 403/742-2811. Stettler also offers the **Town and Country Museum** (44th Ave., 403/742-4534), comprising a courthouse, a railway station, and a schoolhouse spread over three hectares. Admission $3. Open summer only, daily 9 A.M.–5 P.M.

The nicest of four accommodations in town is the newly renovated **Super 8 Motel** (5720 44th Ave., at the south end of town, 403/742-3391 or 888/742-8008); $69 single, $76 double. The **Stettler Lions Campground** is adjacent to the golf course on the west side of town (off Hwy. 12 on 62nd St.). It has showers and hookups for $9–14 per night. Most restaurants are along Highway 12; try **White Goose Restaurant**, 403/742-2544, a family-style eatery with inexpensive seafood dishes. **Kalamata** (4920 50th St., 403/742-3520) is a pleasant downtown Greek restaurant; entrées are $10–13. A tepee-shaped **Tourist Information Centre** is located at the junction of highways 12 and 56.

Big Knife Provincial Park
Legend has it that Big Knife Creek was named after a fight between two long-standing enemies—one Cree, the other Blackfoot—that resulted in the death of both men. Recent history is no less colorful. A local farmer named One-eyed Nelson ran a moonshine operation here. His hooch was in demand throughout the prairies; he even exported the popular brew to Montana. Thirty years after he'd left the area, park rangers found the remains of his still in the side of the creek bank.

The small campground at the park has no services, but the Battle River flows through the park, making for good swimming and canoeing. Sites are situated among towering cottonwood trees; $13. To get to the park from Stettler, head east along Highway 12 approximately 40 kilometers to Halkirk, then north on Highway 855 another 29 kilometers.

northern phalarope

Gooseberry Lake Provincial Park
This small park, 14 kilometers north of Consort, is on the shore of a tree-encircled lake and is made up of rolling grassland and a series of alkaline ponds. Many birds, including the northern phalarope, use the lake as a staging area along their migratory paths. The campground is between the lake and a nine-hole golf course and has powered sites, a kitchen shelter, and firewood sales. Unserviced sites are $12, powered sites $16. To the north are the **Neutral Hills**, which, according to legend, the Great Spirit raised to prevent the Cree and Blackfoot from fighting.

Nearby **Consort** is the birthplace of Katherine Dawn Lang, best known to the country/pop/dance music world as Grammy-winning star k.d. lang.

WETASKIWIN

This town, halfway between Red Deer and Edmonton on Highway 2A, was founded as a siding on the Calgary and Edmonton Railway and has developed into a wheat-farming and cattle-ranching center of 11,000. In the language of the Cree, *Wetaskiwin* (Where Peace was Made) is a reference to nearby hills where a treaty between the Cree and Blackfoot was signed in 1867.

Reynolds-Alberta Museum
Usually, museums of this caliber are located in major cities. But here in the rolling hills two kilometers west of Wetaskiwin, a world-class facility cataloging the history of all types of machinery rises like a mirage from the rural prairie landscape. Surrounding the main exhibition hall, the complete history of transportation in Alberta is recreated, from horse-drawn carriages to luxurious 1950s automobiles. Most have been fully restored, but some, such as the handmade snowmobile, are in their original condition. At the end of the display, you can peer into a large hall where the restoration takes place. The transportation displays encircle a large area where traditional farm machinery is on show, from the most basic plow to a massive combine harvester. The museum is open year-round daily 9 A.M.–5 P.M. Admission is adults 6.50, seniors $5.50, children $3. For further information, call 780/361-1351.

Behind the museum lies an airstrip and a large hangar that houses **Canada's Aviation Hall of Fame.** The Hall of Fame recognizes those who have made contributions to the history of aviation and contains several vintage aircraft. Admission is included with a ticket to the Reynolds-Alberta Museum. Hours are also the same. Operating out of the Hall of Fame, **Central Aviation**, 780/352-9689, offers a 10-minute flight in an old biplane for $42; weekends only.

The display at the Reynolds-Alberta Museum shows the amount of work it takes to restore an antique vehicle.

Reynolds Antique Machinery Museum

After donating one collection of antique machinery to the government for display in the Reynolds-Alberta Museum, Stan Reynolds went right on pursuing his favorite hobby. A legacy of his work is this outdoor museum containing hundreds of old cars, tractors, military vehicles, aircraft, steam engines, and assorted farm machinery strewn about in varying states of repair. The collection is halfway between town and the Reynolds-Alberta Museum (4110 57th St., 780/352-6201). Open in summer daily 10 A.M.–5 P.M.; admission is $2.

Accommodations and Food

Wetaskiwin's best lodging is provided at the **Super 8 Motel** (3820 56th St., 780/361-3808 or 800/800-8000), a new place that is within walking distance of the two museums. Rooms are $69 single or double. The other two options are the **Fort Ethier Lodge** (3802 56th St., 780/352-9161), $49–59 single or double; and the **Wayside Inn** (4103 56th St., 780/352-6681), which has a restaurant, $65 single or double. The **Wetaskiwin Lions RV Campground**, 2.5 kilometers east of town along Highway 13, has free showers, a laundry room, a cooking shelter, a stocked trout pond, and mini-golf; unserviced sites $15, hookups $20.

The **MacEachern Tea House** (4719 50th Ave., 780/352-8308), built by one of the district's early pioneers, is a distinctive two-story green-and-yellow building. It's open for breakfast, lunch, and afternoon tea. Everything served is made on the premises, including delicious cheesecakes ($4 per slice). It's open Mon.–Sat. 9 A.M.–5 P.M. Other restaurants can be found along all main routes into town.

Information

The **Tourist Information Centre** (4910 55th St., 780/352-4636) is open in summer daily 9 A.M.–5 P.M.

CAMROSE

Camrose, 40 kilometers east of Wetaskiwin, is a town of 14,000 that has greatly benefited from the oil-and-gas boom yet retains its agricultural base. The area was first settled by Scandinavians, primarily Norwegians, in the late 1800s. As a tribute to their success in breaking the land and developing the community, a 10-meter Viking longship is on display in the **Bill Fowler Centre** (5402 48th Ave.), overlooking Mirror Lake. A **Tourist Information Centre,** 780/672-4217, is also in the Fowler Centre. It's open in summer daily 9 A.M.–9 P.M., the rest of the year Mon.–Fri. 8:30 A.M.–4:30 P.M.

Sights

One of western Canada's most recognizable breakfast cereals is Sunny Boy, manufactured in

Camrose by **Prairie Sun Grains** (4601 51st Ave., 780/672-3675). Tours are given and are not very official; call ahead or just roll up and you'll be taken through each process of the 50-year-old operation, then given some samples to try. The **Camrose & District Museum** (53rd St. at 46th Ave., 780/672-3298) presents a working model of a steam threshing machine and many other outdoor displays; it's open in summer daily 10 A.M.–5 P.M.

Big Valley Jamboree

Since 1992, Camrose has hosted the Big Valley Jamboree, one of North America's largest gatherings of country-music superstars. All of the action takes place during the first weekend of August, a holiday weekend, at the Exhibition Grounds east of Camrose. In addition to the main stage, live performances take place in the massive beer garden and on a smaller indoor stage. Between acts, there are rodeo performances, a midway, a trade show, and lots of drinking and dancing. Most fans camp out, with one area set aside especially for families. Daily passes are approximately $60, and a three-day weekend pass goes for $150. Call 780/672-0224 or 888/404-1234, www.bigvalleyjamboree.com.

Accommodations

The **Camrose Motel** (6116 48th Ave., 780/672-3364) has newly renovated rooms, each with a microwave and a small fridge; $38 single, $48 double. The much larger **Quality Inn** (3911 48th Ave., 780/672-7741) has large rooms, a café, a restaurant, and a lounge. Rates are $55 single, $60 double. **Valleyview Campground** has pow-

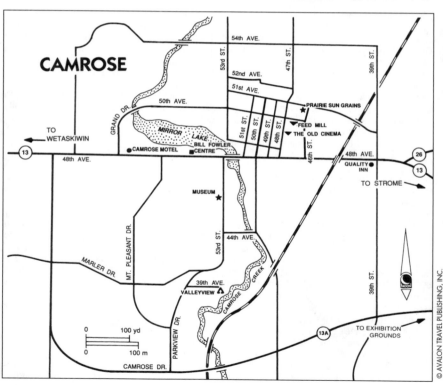

ered sites, showers, a kitchen shelter, and firewood. Sites overlook the ski hill and ski jump, and a trail links the campground to Mirror Lake. Unserviced sites are $10, powered $12. To get there, follow 53rd Street two kilometers and turn left on 39th Avenue.

Food

The **Feed Mill** (4919 47th St., 780/672-9502) is in an historic building downtown. The relaxed atmosphere and excellent food are popular with locals and visitors alike. The menu is fairly standard and the prices are good; entrées range $9.75–15. It's open daily 11 A.M.–10 P.M. Downtown, a two-tiered movie theater has been transformed into a unique restaurant called the **Old Cinema** (4917 48th St., 780/672-4809). Downstairs is a lounge and stage where live entertainment is presented on weekends. The dining area is upstairs on the balcony, surrounded in greenery. Expect to pay $20 for a three-course meal.

HIGHWAY 13 EAST

This part of Alberta is dominated by the **Battle River,** which flows from Pigeon Lake, in the foothills west of Wetaskiwin, through heavily developed agricultural land to Wainwright, then into Saskatchewan, where it drains into the North Saskatchewan River. Buffalo herds once congregated along the banks of the river, drawing Cree from the north and Blackfoot from the south, who fought over the right to hunt them—hence the river's name.

In **Strome,** the **Sodbuster's Museum** (Main St., 780/376-3688) is dedicated to the ingenuity of pioneer families who claimed homesteads in the region. The museum also has various Indian artifacts and a six-meter-long chunk of petrified wood. It's open in summer daily 9 A.M.–4 P.M. Continuing east, Highway 13 descends to the Battle River and **Hardisty,** which is home to a feedlot with the capacity to feed 15,000 cattle. **Hardisty Lake,** at the west edge of town, is stocked with rainbow trout and has a beach, a golf course, and a campground with hookups; $12–18 per night.

From Hardisty, the highway continues east through **Amisk** (a nearby Hutterite colony welcomes visitors) to **Czar** and the **Prairie Panora-**ma **Museum,** 780/857-2155, which is known throughout the land for its collection of more than 1,000 salt and pepper shakers; open Sunday 2–6 P.M.

The small town of **Provost** is 20 kilometers from the Alberta/Saskatchewan border. Ten kilometers south of town is **St. Norbert's Church,** a magnificent Gothic structure built in 1926.

HIGHWAY 14 EAST

Miquelon Lake Provincial Park

Originally a bird sanctuary, this 906-hectare park lies 30 kilometers north of Camrose on Highway 833. It is part of the 650-square-kilometer Cooking Lake Moraine, a hummocky, forested region dotted with lakes that extends north to Elk Island National Park. At the end of the last Ice Age, as the sheet of ice that covered much of the continent receded, it occasionally stalled, as it did in this area. Chunks of ice then broke off and melted, depositing glacial till in mounds. Between the mounds are hollows, known as kettles, that have filled with water. The **Knob and Kettle Trail System** starts behind the baseball diamond and is a series of short interconnecting trails through this intriguing landscape. Being heavily wooded, the area attracts many birds and animals; most ponds house a resident beaver family, and moose and deer can often be seen feeding at dawn and dusk. The main body of water is fed by underground springs and has no streams running into it. This means that the level of the lake in summer largely depends on winter snowfall, which, in recent years, has been low. During summer, rangers conduct guided hikes (Thursday at 7 P.M. and Sunday at 10 A.M.) and present evening shows in the amphitheater (Friday and Saturday at 8 P.M.). A visitors center is open in summer Wed.–Sun. 1–5 P.M. The campground has showers, kitchen shelters, and firewood; unserviced sites $22, powered sites $25. For more information on the park, or to reserve a campsite, call 780/672-7274.

Parkland Natural Area, west of the provincial park and 12 kilometers north of Highway 14, hosts a similar ecosystem of aspen interspersed with ponds.

Tofield

Western Canada's only shorebird reserve, **Beaverhill Natural Area,** is located 10 kilometers east of Tofield. Beaverhill Lake, with its unspoiled islands and rich marshes, is a haven for more than 250 species of birds. Many species use the lake as a stopover on their migratory path, attracting birders from around Canada during spring and fall. The natural area is relatively undeveloped. At the entrance to the town of Tofield is the **Beaverhill Lake Nature Centre,** 403/662-3191, an interpretive center with maps of the area and bird checklists. It's open in summer Mon.–Fri. 10 A.M.–6 P.M., Saturday noon–5 P.M., Sunday 1–4 P.M. A paved road from Tofield becomes a gravel drive four kilometers from town and ends at **Beaverhill Bird Observatory,** operated by the Edmonton Bird Club; biologists and club members are often present and are happy to answer questions. Before the road turns to gravel, you'll see a turnoff to the north (left). At the end of this road, a short trail leads to **Francis Viewpoint** and a bird blind on the lakeshore. On the eastern shore of the lake is another undeveloped area with access to a beach. Walking north along the beach, you can see pelicans, cormorants, and swans on **Pelican Island.** Farther north are the **Dekker Islands,** another nesting area for a variety of bird species.

With all of this great bird-watching, you'd expect a bird-related celebration at some point, and Tofield doesn't disappoint. The last weekend of April is the **Snow Goose Festival,** a celebration of the town's ornithological neighbors.

The **Beaverhill Motel,** 403/662-3396, has basic rooms for $45 single or double. The closest campground is in Ryley, east of town (free), or at **Ministik Recreation Area,** on the highway 24 kilometers west of town (much nicer, $9).

Ryley

If you need an excuse to stop in Ryley, visit **George's Harness & Saddlery,** 403/663-3611, a working museum that produces saddles, chuckwagon harnesses, and other equine accessories. Most artifacts are made with antique tools and stitching machines. The goings-on in the large workshop are visible from the shop, but if George isn't busy filling orders, he'll happily show you around. The store is on the main street; closed Sunday.

Viking

Southeast of Viking in a farmer's field are the **rib stones,** two stones carved with a design resembling bison ribs that have been dated at 1,000 years old. The stones held special significance for generations of Plains Indians, whose lives revolved around the movement of bison herds. They believed that by conducting certain ceremonial rites and by leaving gifts of beads or tobacco around the stones, their luck in hunting would improve. The site is not well marked. Fourteen kilometers east of Viking on Highway 14 is an historical marker. A little farther east is a gravel road to the south; follow this road 1.5 kilometers to Highway 615, turn east (left), then take the first gravel road to the south (right) and follow it for 2.5 kilometers to a low knoll surrounded by fields. A provincial historic cairn marks the site.

Wainwright

Best known for its large combined forces base, Wainwright is the last town along Highway 14 before Saskatchewan. The military's **Camp Wainwright** is on the site of what once was Buffalo National Park, the site of probably the most unusual chain of events ever to take place in a Canadian national park. Originally created in 1908 to protect 3,000 plains bison, **Buffalo National Park** was also home to elk, moose, and deer. Experiments within the park cross-bred bison with cattle, trying to create a more resilient farm stock. Meanwhile, bison parts were sold for pemmican. All that may seem odd enough to begin with, but then a Hollywood film crew paid officials to stampede a herd of bison and slaughter part of the herd for a movie scene. Shortly afterward, the bison were struck by tuberculosis and were secretly shot, along with every ungulate in the park. This sad and sorry story ended with the land being handed over to the Department of National Defence. Today it is Canada's second-largest military training facility, able to house 15,000 troops at one time. On its 400 square kilometers are 22 weapons ranges, two airfields, and a small herd of bison, which can be viewed in **Bud Cotton Buffalo Paddock** beside the base's main gate. The base is two kilometers south of town along 1st Street. The **Wainwright Museum,** 403/842-3115, is a restored Canadian National Railway station at the end of Main

Street, with displays on the railway and the ill-fated national park. Open daily 9 A.M.–5 P.M. A local restaurant, the **Honey Pot** (825 2nd Ave., 780/842-4094) is worthy of a mention. It has been serving hungry locals and travelers alike for more than two decades. The menu is fairly standard—steaks, salads, and pastas—but all are delicious and well-priced.

Dillberry Lake Provincial Park

This park is on the Alberta/Saskatchewan border, 50 kilometers southeast of Wainwright in the transition zone between aspen parkland and prairie. Of the many lakes within the park, Dillberry is the largest. It's surrounded by sandy beaches and low sand dunes (the biggest dunes are at the southeastern end of the lake), and its clear spring-fed waters are good for swimming. The aspen that do grow around the lake are somewhat stunted, a result of having adapted to the windy environment of the prairie. The diverse habitat creates excellent bird-watching opportunities—140 species have been recorded. The park's 200-site campground is situated right by the best beach and has showers, kitchen shelters, and firewood; unserviced sites $15, powered sites $17. For more information on the park, or to reserve a site, call 403/858-3824.

KAREN MCKINLEY

EDMONTON
INTRODUCTION

Edmonton, Alberta's capital, sits in the center of the province, surrounded by the vast natural resources that have made the city unabashedly wealthy. It's a vibrant cultural center and a gateway to the north, but its reputation as a boomtown may be its defining characteristic. Boomtowns are a phenomenon unique to the West—cities that have risen from the surrounding wilderness, oblivious to hardship, pushed forward by dreams of the incredible wealth to be made overnight by pulling riches from the earth. Most boomtowns disappear as quickly as they rise, but not Edmonton. The proud city saw not one, but three major booms in the 20th century and has grown into one of the world's largest northerly cities. Its population has mushroomed 800 percent in 50 years to 660,000, making it the fifth-largest city in Canada. Although Calgary is the administrative and business center of the province's billion-dollar petroleum industry, Edmonton is the technological, service, and supply center.

The **North Saskatchewan River Valley** winding through the city has been largely preserved as a 27-kilometer greenbelt of parks—the largest urban park system in Canada. Rather than the hodgepodge of slums and streets you might expect in a boomtown, the modern city of Edmonton has been extremely well designed and well built, with an eye toward the future. The downtown area sits on a spectacular bluff overlooking the river valley park system. Silhouetted against the deep-blue sky, a cluster of modern glass-and-steel highrises makes a dynamic contrast to the historic granite Alberta Legislature Building and the lush valley floor below.

Edmonton is home to the University of Alberta, and it's hosted events such as the 1978 Commonwealth Games, 1983 World University Games, and 1996 World Figure Skating Championships, and is hosting the 2001 World Championships in Athletics. So it comes as no surprise that Edmonton has some of Canada's best cultural facilities. Each week during summer, a festival of some sort takes place within the city. But the city's biggest attraction is the ultimate shopping mecca, **West Edmonton Mall,** the world's largest shopping and amusement complex.

Getting Oriented

Highway 2 from Calgary enters Edmonton from the south and divides just north of Gateway Park Tourist Information Centre. At that point, it becomes known as **Calgary Trail.** Northbound, Calgary Trail is also known as **103rd Street,** whereas southbound it's **104th Street.** From the south, you can get to West Edmonton Mall and Highway 16 West, without going through downtown, by taking **Whitemud Drive.** Whitemud crosses the North Saskatchewan River southwest of downtown. From the Whitemud Drive intersection, Calgary Trail continues north through **Old Strathcona,** crossing the North Saskatchewan River directly south of downtown.

The **Yellowhead Highway** passes through the city east to west, north of downtown. To get downtown from the east, take 97th Street. From downtown, Jasper Avenue changes to Stony Plain Road as it heads west, eventually joining Highway 16 at the city's western limits.

Since the early 1900s, Edmonton streets have been numbered. Avenues run east to west, numbered from 1st Avenue in the south to 259th Avenue in the north. Streets run north to south, numbered from 1st Street in the east to 231st Street in the west. Even-numbered addresses are on the north sides of the avenues and west sides of the streets. The center of the city is crossed by both 101st Street and 101st Avenue, the latter having retained its original name of **Jasper Avenue.**

When vast outlying areas were annexed by the city in 1982, new additions had to be made to the street-numbering system. First Street was renamed Meridian Street and 1st Avenue was renamed Quadrant Avenue. The entire existing city now lies within the northwest quadrant, allowing for easy numbering of new streets as the city grows to the south and east.

HISTORY

For at least 3,000 years, natives came to the river valley where Edmonton now stands, searching for quartzite to make stone tools. They had no knowledge of, or use for, the vast underground resources that would eventually cause a city to rise from the wilderness.

Fort Edmonton

European fur traders, canoeing along the North Saskatchewan River, found the area where Edmonton now stands to be one of the richest fur-bearing areas on the continent. Large populations of beavers and muskrats lived in the surrounding spruce, poplar, and aspen forest. In

Fort Edmonton, on the bank of the North Saskatchewan River, 1902

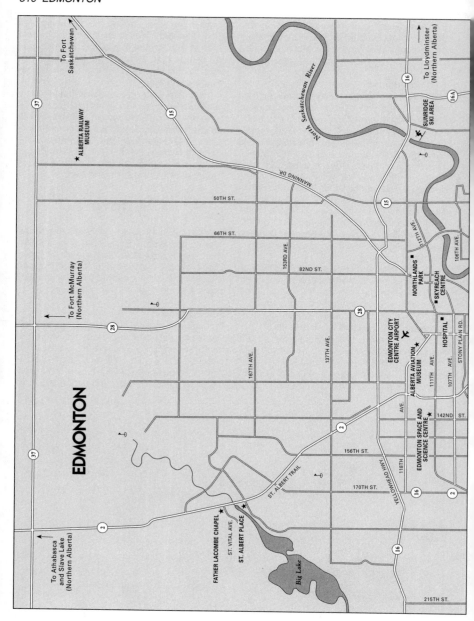

EDMONTON

To Fort
Saskatchewan

To Lloydminster
(Northern Alberta)

37

15

ALBERTA RAILWAY MUSEUM

North Saskatchewan River

MANNING DR.

16

16A

SUNRIDGE SKI AREA

50TH ST.

15

112TH AVE.

106TH AVE.

66TH ST.

153RD AVE.

82ND ST.

NORTHLANDS PARK

SKYREACH CENTRE

To Fort McMurray
(Northern Alberta)

28

28

EDMONTON CITY CENTRE AIRPORT

HOSPITAL

STONY PLAIN RD.

167TH AVE.

137TH AVE.

ALBERTA AVIATION MUSEUM

111TH AVE.

107TH AVE.

2

AVE.

EDMONTON SPACE AND SCIENCE CENTRE

142ND ST.

156TH ST.

ST. ALBERT TRAIL

118TH

YELLOWHEAD HWY.

170TH ST.

16

2

37

To Athabasca
and Slave Lake
(Northern Alberta)

2

FATHER LACOMBE CHAPEL

ST. VITAL AVE.

ST. ALBERT PLACE

16

Big Lake

215TH ST.

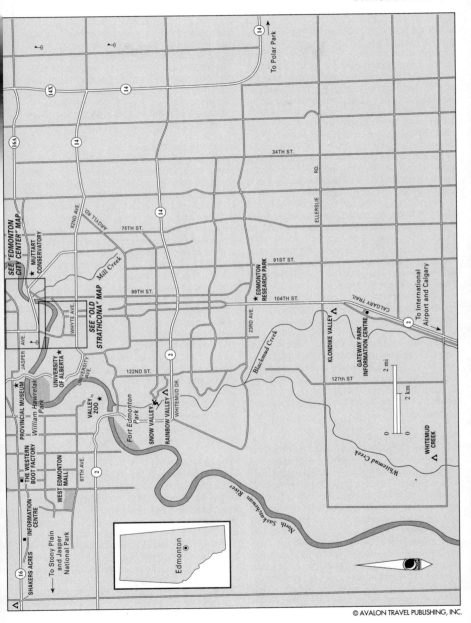

© AVALON TRAVEL PUBLISHING, INC.

1795, William Tomison, a Scotsman, built a sturdy log building beside the North West Company's Fort Augustus. He named it Fort Edmonton after an estate owned by Sir James Winter Lake, deputy governor of the Hudson's Bay Company. Both forts stood on the site of the present Legislature Building grounds. It was an ideal location for trading. Cree and Assiniboine could trade beaver, otter, and marten pelts in safety, without encroaching on the territory of fierce Plains Indians, such as the Blackfoot. Yet the fort was far enough south to be within range of the Blackfoot—peaceable when outside their own territory—who came north to buy muskrat, buffalo meat, and other natural resources, which they later traded with Europeans.

After 100 years, the fur trade ended abruptly. Many of the posts throughout the West were abandoned, but Edmonton continued to be an important stop on the route north. Goods were taken overland from Edmonton to Athabasca Landing, where they were transferred to barges or steamers and taken north on the Athabasca River. Around this time, there was an increased demand for grains, and improving technology made agriculture more viable. This opportunity attracted settlers, who arrived through the 1880s to farm the surrounding land. Edmonton suffered a setback when the Canadian Pacific Railway (CPR) chose a southerly route through Calgary for the TransContinental Railway. A branch built by the Calgary and Edmonton Railway Company arrived in 1891, but it ended on the south side of the North Saskatchewan River, at Strathcona.

The Klondike Gold Rush

The most common images of the Klondike Gold Rush in the Yukon are of miners climbing the Chilkoot or White Pass trails in a desperate attempt to reach Dawson City. Often for financial reasons, various other routes were promoted as being superior. The merchants of Edmonton led a patriot cry to try the "All-Canadian Route," which would allow prospectors to buy their supplies in a Canadian city rather than in Seattle. The proposed route followed the Athabasca Landing Trail north to Athabasca, continued by boat down the Athabasca, Slave, and Mackenzie rivers to just south of the Mackenzie Delta, and ended with a short over-

land trip to the goldfields. The route was impractical and very difficult. Approximately 1,600 people were persuaded to attempt the route. Of these, 50 died, many turned back, and only 700 reached the Yukon. None reached the goldfields before 1899, when the main rush was over, and few, if any, found gold. This slim connection to the gold rush is now celebrated in the annual **Edmonton's Klondike Days,** much to the displeasure of Yukoners.

Selecting the Capital

The provinces of Alberta and Saskatchewan were both inaugurated on September 1, 1905. Because Regina had been the capital of the Northwest Territories, it was only natural that it continued as the capital of Saskatchewan. The decision about Alberta's capital did not come as easily, however. The Alberta Act made Edmonton the temporary capital, but it had plenty of competition. Other contenders were Athabasca Landing, Banff, Calgary, Cochrane, Lacombe, Red Deer, Vegreville, and Wetaskiwin. Each town thought it had a rightful claim: Banff because it could be fortified if war ever broke out, Vegreville for the clean air and a climate free of chinook winds. But the strongest claims were from the citizens of Calgary, who believed their city to be the financial and transportation center of the province. Heated debates on the subject took place in the Canadian capital of Ottawa and among rival newspaper editors, but Edmonton has remained the capital to this day. In 1912, Edmonton merged with Strathcona, giving the city a total population of 55,000. For the next 35 years, the city grew and declined according to the fortunes of agriculture.

Oil and a Growing City

Fur was Edmonton's first industry and coal was its second. Commercial coal-mining operations began as early as 1880, with mining concentrated in three areas of the city. The last of more than 150 operations closed in 1970, and much of the coal seam remains unmined below the downtown area. But Edmonton's future lay not in coal, but oil. Since the discovery of "black gold" in 1947 at nearby Leduc, Edmonton has been one of Canada's fastest-growing cities. The building of pipelines and refineries created many jobs, and the city became the center of western

Canada's petrochemical industry. As demand continued to rise, hundreds of wildcat wells were drilled around Edmonton. Farmers' fields were filled with derricks, valves, and oil tanks, and by 1956, more than 3,000 producing wells were pumping within 100 kilometers of the city.

Edmonton experienced the same postwar boom of most major North American cities, as a major population shift from rural areas to the city began. By 1956, Edmonton's population had grown to 254,800, doubling in size since 1946. A 20-square-kilometer area east of the city was filled with huge oil tanks, refineries, and petrochemical plants. Changes were also taking place within the city as the wealth of the oil boom began to take hold. Restaurants improved and cultural life flourished. The city's businesses were jazzed up, and the expanding business community began moving into the glass-and-steel skyscrapers that form the city skyline today. Also important are the various service industries; West Edmonton Mall alone employs 22,000 people.

2000 and Beyond

Although the original boom is over, oil is still a major part of the city's economy. Planned developments in the surrounding service area total approximately $40 billion this decade, with Edmonton benefiting directly from spin-off infrastructure. More than $3 billion is being spent on oil sands development in the next five years, with a new pipeline and processing facilities being built in the city. In addition to oil-related companies, Edmonton's low cost of living is attractive to many companies. Economic Development Edmonton, www.ede.org, is a city-sponsored department that promotes the city to the world. One of its innovations is the sprawling **Edmonton Research Park,** on the southern outskirts, which has become a focal point for up-and-coming information technology and science companies. One of the tenants is the Edmonton Advanced Technology Centre, where young upstart companies can sign monthly leases and share resources such as printing services, meeting rooms, and administrative support.

SIGHTS

DOWNTOWN

Looking at Edmonton's dynamic skyline, it's hard to believe that just 100 years ago the main drag was lined with dingy saloons and rowdy dance halls. Since those heady days, the city has seen many ups and downs—its present look is a legacy of the 1970s oil boom. The well-planned city center, on the northern bank of the North Saskatchewan River, is a conglomeration of skyscrapers that seemingly rose overnight when oil money flooded the city. The downtown core is fairly compact and is within walking distance of many hotels, the bus depot, and the train station. **Jasper Avenue** (101st Ave.) is downtown's main thoroughfare, lined with restaurants and shops. At the east end of Jasper Avenue is the **Shaw Conference Centre,** a glass-and-steel building that seemingly clings to the wall of the river valley. The Pedway level of this building is home to Economic Development Edmonton, which supplies general tourist information and maintains brochure stands across the floor. One block

north is the large and popular **Eaton Centre** shopping complex. On 102nd Street is the 36-story ManuLife Place, Edmonton's tallest building. A few blocks east is the **Edmonton Civic Centre,** comprising the provincial government buildings, including the futuristic City Hall, which opened in August 1992. (The streets immediately east of 97th Street are a skid row with sleazy bars and suspicious-looking characters—not the place to linger at night.)

Throughout all of the development, several historic buildings managed to survive. Many can be seen along **Heritage Trail,** a route taken by early fur traders that linked the old town to Fort Edmonton. Today the trail begins at the Convention Centre, at the corner of Jasper Avenue and 97th Street, and ends at the legislature grounds. The route is easy to follow—the sidewalk is paved with red bricks and lined with period benches, replica lampposts, and old-fashioned street signs.

Edmonton Civic Centre

This complex, in the heart of downtown, occupies six square blocks and is one of the city's

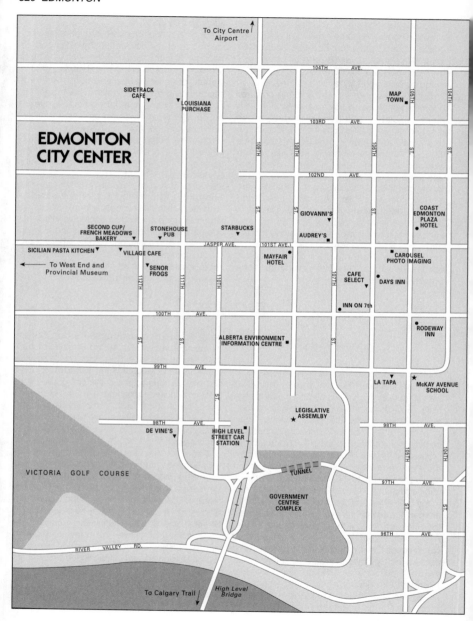

EDMONTON CITY CENTER

To City Centre Airport

104TH AVE.

MAP TOWN

SIDETRACK CAFE

LOUISIANA PURCHASE

103RD AVE.

102ND AVE.

COAST EDMONTON PLAZA HOTEL

GIOVANNI'S

AUDREY'S

SECOND CUP/ FRENCH MEADOWS BAKERY

STONEHOUSE PUB

STARBUCKS

SICILIAN PASTA KITCHEN

VILLAGE CAFE

JASPER AVE.

(101ST AVE.)

MAYFAIR HOTEL

CAROUSEL PHOTO IMAGING

To West End and Provincial Museum

SENOR FROGS

CAFE SELECT

DAYS INN

INN ON 7th

100TH AVE.

RODEWAY INN

ALBERTA ENVIRONMENT INFORMATION CENTRE

99TH AVE.

LA TAPA

McKAY AVENUE SCHOOL

98TH AVE.

DE VINE'S

LEGISLATIVE ASSEMLBY

98TH AVE.

HIGH LEVEL STREET CAR STATION

VICTORIA GOLF COURSE

TUNNEL

97TH AVE.

GOVERNMENT CENTRE COMPLEX

96TH AVE.

RIVER VALLEY RD.

To Calgary Trail

High Level Bridge

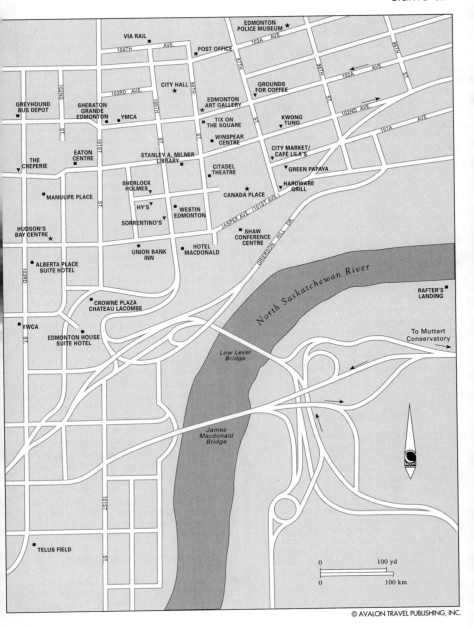

VIA RAIL

EDMONTON
POLICE MUSEUM ★

104TH AVE.

103A AVE.

POST OFFICE

103RD AVE.

CITY HALL ★

EDMONTON
ART GALLERY

GROUNDS
FOR COFFEE

102A AVE.

GREYHOUND
BUS DEPOT

SHERATON
GRANDE
EDMONTON

YMCA

TIX ON
THE SQUARE

KWONG
TUNG

102ND AVE.

THE
CREPERIE

EATON
CENTRE

STANLEY A. MILNER
LIBRARY

WINSPEAR
CENTRE

CITY MARKET/
CAFÉ LILA'S

101A AVE.

CITADEL
THEATRE

GREEN PAPAYA

MANULIFE PLACE

SHERLOCK
HOLMES

CANADA PLACE ★

HARDWARE
GRILL

HY'S

WESTIN
EDMONTON

JASPER AVE. (101ST AVE.)

HUDSON'S
BAY CENTRE ★

SORRENTINO'S

SHAW
CONFERENCE
CENTRE

UNION BANK
INN

HOTEL
MACDONALD

North Saskatchewan River

RAFTER'S
LANDING

ALBERTA PLACE
SUITE HOTEL

CROWNE PLAZA
CHATEAU LACOMBE

To Muttart
Conservatory

YWCA

EDMONTON HOUSE
SUITE HOTEL

Low Level
Bridge

James
Macdonald
Bridge

Moon

TELUS FIELD

0   100 yd

0   100 km

© AVALON TRAVEL PUBLISHING, INC.

showcases. Within its limits are the Stanley A. Milner Library, the Edmonton Art Gallery, Sir Winston Churchill Square, City Hall, the Law Courts Building, the Convention Centre, and the performing arts community's pride and joy, the magnificent Citadel Theatre and adjacent Winspear Centre.

The **Edmonton Art Gallery** (northeast of Sir Winston Churchill Square on 99th St., 780/472-6223) houses an extensive collection of 4,000 modern Canadian paintings as well as historical and contemporary art in all media. Various traveling exhibitions are presented throughout the year. The exhibit *From Sea to Sea: The Development of Canadian Art* catalogs the entire history of the country's art through well-designed displays. The gallery is open Mon.–Wed. and Friday 10:30 A.M.–5 P.M., Thursday 10:30 A.M.–8 P.M., and Sat.–Sun. 11 A.M.–5 P.M. Admission is adults $4, seniors and children $2, free on Thursday after 4 P.M.

City Hall, built on the site of the old city hall, is designed to be the centerpiece of the Civic Centre. The main public areas are located on the main floor. Tours of City Hall leave from the main lobby Monday, Wednesday, and Friday at 10:30 A.M. and 2:30 P.M. Immediately behind this area is the City Room, the building's main focal point. Its ceiling is a glass pyramid that rises eight stories. To the east are displays cataloging the city's short but colorful history.

THE PEDWAY SYSTEM

The pedway system is unique and necessary this far north. It's a complex system of enclosed walkways linking office buildings, hotels, plazas, the Civic Centre, and public transportation stops. Using the pedways, you can get virtually anywhere downtown, without ever having to step outside into the elements. At first it all seems a bit complicated, but if you're armed with a map, the system soon becomes second nature. Pedways are below, above, or at street level, and the excellent signage makes it easy to find your way. The walkways are spotlessly clean, well lit, and relatively safe, although you wouldn't want to loiter around the Central Light Rail Transit (LRT) Station at night.

Chinatown

An elaborate gateway designed by a master architect from China welcomes visitors to where Edmonton's small Chinatown *used* to be. The gate spans 23 meters across 102nd Avenue (also known as Harbin Rd.) at 97th Street. Eight steel columns painted the traditional Chinese color of red support it. Stretched across the center of the arch's roof is a row of ornamental tiles featuring two dragons, the symbol of power in China. The 11,000 tiles used in the gate were each handcrafted and glazed in China. In the last few years, Chinatown has moved up the road a few blocks. The archway now leads into an area of cheap boardinghouses and deserted parking lots but forms a colorful break from the pawnshops of 97th Street.

Edmonton Police Museum

This museum is located on the second floor of the Police Service Headquarters (9620 103A Ave., 780/421-2274). Displays of uniforms, photographs, and equipment tell the story of the Royal Canadian Mounted Police (originally called the North West Mounted Police) and the now-defunct Alberta Provincial Police, who existed from 1917–1932. The museum is open Mon.–Sat. 9 A.M.–3 P.M. Admission is free.

Hotel Macdonald

This hotel overlooking the river valley (10065 100th St.) has long been regarded as Edmonton's premier luxury accommodation. For many years, it was the social center of the city. It was built in 1915 by the Grand Trunk Railway in the same chateau style used for many of the Canadian Pacific hotels across the country. After closing in 1983, plans to tear it down were aborted. After $28 million was spent on refurbishing it, the hotel reopened, as grand and elegant as ever. The main lobby has been totally restored and opens to the Confederation Lounge and The Library, a bar overlooking the river that has the feel of an Edwardian gentlemen's club. Ask at the reception desk for a map of the hotel.

Edmonton Public Schools Archives and Museum

Built in 1904, **McKay Avenue School** (on the Heritage Trail, 10425 99th Ave., 780/422-1970) is Edmonton's oldest standing brick schoolhouse.

It was the venue of the first two sittings of the provincial legislature in 1906. The building contains reconstructions of early classrooms and of the historic legislature assembly. Edmonton's first schoolhouse, a single-story wooden building dating to 1881, lies in back of the grounds, looking much as it would have to 19th-century students. Admission to both is free. It's open the same hours as early students attended, Tues.–Fri. 12:30–4 P.M., as well as Sunday 1–4 P.M.

Alberta Legislature Building
Home of the provincial government, this elegant Edwardian building overlooking the North Saskatchewan River Valley is surrounded by 24 hectares of formal gardens and manicured lawns. It officially opened in 1912 and, for many years, stood beside the original Fort Edmonton. Today it is one of western Canada's best examples of architecture from that era. Its 16-story vaulted dome is one of Edmonton's most recognizable landmarks. Many materials used in its construction were imported: sandstone from near Calgary; granite from Vancouver; marble from Quebec, Pennsylvania, and Italy; and mahogany from Belize. The interior features a wide marble staircase that leads from the spacious rotunda in the lobby to the chamber and is surrounded by stained-glass windows and bronze statues.

Immediately north of the Legislature Building, beyond the fountains, is the **Legislative Assembly Interpretive Centre**, 780/427-7362, which recounts the development of Alberta's political history and serves as the starting point for free tours of the Legislature Building. Tour hours in summer are weekdays 9 A.M.–3 P.M. and weekends noon–4 P.M., the rest of the year weekdays noon–4:30 P.M. and Sunday noon–5 P.M.

High Level Bridge
This bridge crosses the North Saskatchewan River at the bottom end of 109th Street. It was built in 1913, linking the new capital to Strathcona. The bridge is 775 meters long and 53 meters above the river. It has been used as a tramway, a railway, a sidewalk, and a roadway. The rail line was in use until 1951, but in 2000 a local historical society began running a

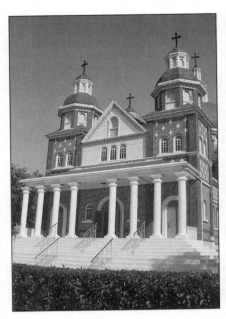

St. Josephat's Ukrainian Catholic Cathedral

scheduled street car over the bridge. It runs from adjacent to the Grandin Light Rail Transit (LRT) Station across the bridge to as far south as Old Strathcona. The service operates 15 and 45 minutes past the hour Sun.–Fri. 11 A.M.–4 P.M., Saturday 9 A.M.–4 P.M. and costs just $3 one-way.

In 1980, the **Great Divide Waterfall** was added to the bridge. When turned on, a curtain of water higher than Niagara Falls cascades down along the entire length of the bridge. It usually operates during special events such as Edmonton's Klondike Days. For operating times, call 780/496-8416.

Ukrainian Sights
The **Ukrainian Canadian Archives and Museum** (9543 110th Ave., 780/424-7580) exhibits artifacts from the lives of Ukrainian pioneers in Canada and has one of the largest archives in the country. It's open year-round Tues.–Fri. 10 A.M.–5 P.M., Saturday noon–5 P.M. Admission is

by donation. Edmonton has several Ukrainian churches. One of the most impressive is **St. Josephat's Ukrainian Catholic Cathedral** (97th St. at 108th Ave.), which is well worth a look for its elaborate decorations and pastel wall paintings. In the same vicinity is the **Ukrainian Bookstore** (10215 97th St., 780/422-4255).

SOUTHSIDE

Muttart Conservatory

Nestled in the valley on the south side of the North Saskatchewan River are four large pyramid-shaped greenhouses that make up the Muttart Conservatory (9626 96A St. off 98th Ave., 780/496-8755). Three of the greenhouses contain the flora of specific climates. In the arid pyramid are cacti and other hardy plants found in desertlike conditions. The tropical pyramid holds a humid jungle, one of North America's largest orchid collections, and colorful and raucous exotic birds, who live among the palms. The temperate pyramid features plant species from four continents, none of which would grow naturally in Edmonton's harsh environment. The contents of the fourth pyramid change with the season but always feature colorful floral displays such as red, white, and yellow poinsettias at Christmastime. Take bus number 45 or 51 south along 100th Street to get to the conservatory. It's open year-round Sun.–Wed.

11 A.M.–9 P.M., Thurs.–Sat. 11 A.M.–6 P.M. Admission is adults $4.75, seniors $3.75.

Edmonton Queen

The *Edmonton Queen* is a 58-meter-long paddlewheeler that cruises along the North Saskatchewan River from Rafter's Landing, near Muttart Conservatory and across the river from the Shaw Conference Centre. Cruise options include a one-hour afternoon trip (departs 3 P.M. and 5 P.M.; $10), a lunch cruise (noon; $18.95 includes lunch); and a dinner cruise (6:30 P.M.; $43.95 includes dinner). To get to Rafter's Landing, take 98th Avenue east along the south side of the river, 780/424-2628.

John Walter Museum

This historic site located near the Kinsmen Sports Centre consists of three houses—dating from 1875, 1884, and 1900—that were built by John Walter for his family. The first house was a stopping point for travelers using Walter's ferry service to cross the river. Walter also opened a carriage works, a lumber mill, and a coal mine, and at one time even built a steamship. For a time, the area was known as Walterdale, but with the completion of the High Level Bridge, the need for a ferry service ended. Today, all that remains are Walter's houses. Each house holds exhibits corresponding to the period of its construction and depicts the growth of Edmonton and the importance of the North Saskatchewan River.

Muttart Conservatory

ALBERTA TOURISM

The buildings are open only in summer, Sunday 1–4 P.M., but the grounds are pleasant to walk through at any time. The museum is at 10627 93rd Avenue. From downtown, take 101st Street south down Bellamy Hill and cross the river at the Walterdale Bridge. On foot, allow 30–60 minutes. By bus, jump aboard number 43 west along 102nd Avenue or south along 103rd Street. For further information, call 780/496-4852.

Rutherford House

Designated as a Provincial Historic Site, this elegant Edwardian mansion was built in 1911 for Alexander C. Rutherford, Alberta's first premier. The Rutherford family lived in this house for 30 years. It was then used as a University of Alberta fraternity house before being restored to its original condition and furnished with antiques from the Edwardian period. You can wander throughout the two-story house and ask questions of the costumed interpreters. The covered sunporch operates as a tearoom in summer (Wed.–Sun.), serving lunch ($8) and afternoon tea (from $5), using historical recipes from 1915 or earlier. The house is open in summer daily 10 A.M.–6 P.M., the rest of the year Tues.–Sun. noon–5 P.M. It's located on the University of Alberta campus (11153 Saskatchewan Dr., 780/427-3995). Admission is $2. The easiest way to get there by public transport is on the LRT from downtown.

Fort Edmonton Park

An authentic reconstruction of the early trading post from which Edmonton grew is only a small part of this exciting park, Canada's largest historic park. From the entrance, a 1919 steam locomotive takes you through the park to the Hudson's Bay Company Fort, which has been built much as the original fort would have looked in 1846—right down to the methods of carpentry used in its construction. Outside the fort is 1885 Street, re-creating downtown Edmonton between 1871 and 1891 when the West was opened up to settlers. The street is lined with wooden-facaded shops such as a bakery, a blacksmith, and Egges Stopping House (where there is always a game of horseshoes going on). As you continue down the road, you round a corner and are on 1905 Street, in the time period 1892–1914, when

the railway had arrived and Edmonton was proclaimed provincial capital. **Reed's Tea Room,** near the far end of the street, serves English teas and scones from 12:30–5 P.M. in a traditional atmosphere. By this time, you're nearly on 1920 Street, representing the years 1914–1929—a period of social changes when the business community was developing and the city's industrial base was expanding.

A constant variety of activities is offered; a weekly program is available from the main entrance or by calling 780/496-8787. An authentic streetcar travels the park, picking up passengers along the way. You can take a wagon ride or a pony ride, or rent a canoe.

The park is located in the North Saskatchewan River Valley off the Whitemud Freeway near Fox Drive. By public transport, take the LRT to University Station, then bus number 32, 39, or 139. It's open May–June Mon.–Fri. 10 A.M.–4 P.M. and Sat.–Sun. 10 A.M.–6 P.M., July–Sept. daily 10 A.M.–6 P.M., closed in winter except for special events (such as sleigh rides) over the Christmas break. Admission is adults $6.75, seniors $5, children $3.25. For more park information, call 780/496-8787.

John Janzen Nature Centre

Beside Fort Edmonton Park (use the same parking lot) is John Janzen Nature Centre, which has hands-on exhibits, displays of local flora and fauna—both dead and alive—and a four-kilometer self-guided interpretive trail that leads through the river valley and loops back to the center. In one room, various natural environments have been simulated with displays of frogs, fish, snakes, salamanders, and a working beehive made from glass. Throughout the year, special events are held, films are shown, and Sunday nature walks are conducted. The center is open year-round Mon.–Fri. 9 A.M.–4 P.M., longer hours and weekends in summer. Admission is $1. For more information, call 780/496-2939.

Valley Zoo

Across the river from Fort Edmonton Park is the city zoo (end of Buena Vista Rd., off 142nd St., 780/496-6911), which holds approximately 350 animals, representing all seven continents. It is designed mainly for kids, with a petting zoo, camel and pony rides, paddleboats, a miniature train, and cut-out storybook characters. The zoo is open daily May–June 10 A.M.–6 P.M., July–Aug. 10 A.M.–9 P.M., the rest of the year noon–4 P.M. To get there by bus, take number 12 from west along 102nd Avenue to Buena Vista Road and walk 1.5 kilometers down to the park. On Sunday, buses leave on the hour from the University Transit Centre and go right to the zoo. Admission is adults $5.50, seniors and children $3.75.

OLD STRATHCONA

When the Calgary and Edmonton Railway Company completed a rail line between the province's two largest cities, it decided to end it south of the North Saskatchewan River and establish a townsite there, rather than build a bridge and end the line in Edmonton. The town was named Strathcona, and it grew to a population of 7,500 before merging with Edmonton in 1912. Because of an early fire-prevention bylaw, buildings were built of brick. Today many still remain, looking much as they did at the turn of the 20th century. Old Strathcona is Edmonton's best-preserved historical district. In addition to the old brick buildings, the area has been refurbished with brick sidewalks and replica lampposts. The commercial core of Old Strathcona is centered along Whyte (82nd) Avenue west of the rail line. More than 75 residential houses built before 1926 are scattered to the north and west of Whyte Avenue.

Across from the rail line is the **Strathcona Hotel** (corner of 103rd St. and Whyte Ave.), one of the few wood-framed buildings surviving from the pre-1900 period. Before Strathcona had permanent churches, congregations worshiped in the hotel, and during Prohibition it was used as a ladies' college. The two blocks east of the hotel are lined with cafés and restaurants, used bookstores, and many interesting shops. One of these, and one of Old Strathcona's oldest businesses, is the **Hub Cigar and Newsstand** (10345 82nd Ave., 780/439-0144), which stocks more than 10,000 different newspapers and magazines from around the world. One block north is the **Old Strathcona Farmer's Market** (on 83rd Ave.), with plenty of fresh produce,

crafts, and homemade goodies for sale. It's open year-round Saturday 8 A.M.–3 P.M. and in summer Tuesday and Thursday noon–4 P.M. Within walking distance of Whyte Avenue are several small museums detailed as follows.

The best way to get to Old Strathcona from downtown is aboard the **High Level Street Car,** which runs from the west side of the Alberta Legislature Building to the 104th Street and 85th Avenue intersection on Old Strathcona. It departs downtown 15 and 45 minutes past the hour Sun.–Fri. 11 A.M.–4 P.M., Saturday 9 A.M.–4 P.M.; $3 one-way. From the station, wander north four blocks to the **Caboose Tourist Information Centre** at the end of the rail line, or south to bustling Whyte Avenue.

Many of the historic buildings have plaques at street level, but the brochures *A Walk through Old Strathcona* and *Historical Walking and Drivng Tour: Strathcona,* which are available at the information center, make a stroll much more interesting. For more information on the district, contact Old Strathcona Foundation, 4th Floor, 10324 82nd Avenue, Edmonton, Alberta T6E 1Z8, 780/433-5866.

C&E Railway Museum
Strathcona's original railway station was located just north of the CPR station. It was later moved farther along the line, then demolished, and replaced with a partial replica that houses a railway museum. The museum (10447 86th Ave., 780/433-9739) relives the days of steam engines and settlers, when people streamed into the newly opened Canadian West from around the world. It's open in summer Tues.–Sat. 10 A.M.–4 P.M.; admission by donation.

Telephone Historical Centre
This museum (10437 83rd Ave., 780/441-2077) catalogs the history of telecommunications in Edmonton from the introduction of telephones in 1885 to the present. It is housed in Strathcona's original telephone exchange and has many hands-on exhibits, including an early switchboard where you can make your own connections. Current technology is also displayed with exhibits of digital switching, fiberoptic cables, a talking robot, and cellular phones. A multimedia presentation in the small **Alex Taylor Theatre** traces telecommunications technology from

DETAIL

ATHABASCA BOOKS

HUB CIGAR AND NEWSSTAND

CHAPTERS
DA-DE-O

JULIO'S BARRIO MEXICAN RESTAURANT

SECOND CUP

BAGEL TREE

WEE BOOK INN

STRATHCONA HOTEL

WHYTE AVE. (82ND AVE.)

BLOCK 1912

GREENWOOD'S

PRINCESS THEATRE

ALHAMBRA BOOKS

SHERLOCK HOLMES PUB

105TH ST.

104TH ST.

103RD ST.

102ND ST.

0   50 yds

0   50 m

North   High Level Bridge

Saskatchewan

Walterdale Bridge

River

0   200 yds

0   200 m

SASKATCHEWAN DR.

JOHN WALTER MUSEUM ★

KINSMEN SPORTS CENTRE

RUTHERFORD HOUSE ★

UNIVERSITY OF ALBERTA

CABOOSE INFORMATION CENTRE

87TH AVE.

112TH ST.

86TH AVE.

YARDBIRD SUITE

C&E RAILWAY MUSEUM ★

OLD STRATHCONA

85TH AVE.

110TH ST.

108TH ST.

106TH ST.

105TH ST.

104TH ST.

103RD ST.

HIGH LEVEL STREET CAR STATION

101ST ST.

111TH ST.

109TH ST.

107TH ST.

84TH AVE.

83RD AVE.

WALTERDALE PLAYHOUSE

FARMER'S MARKET

102ND ST.

TELEPHONE HISTORICAL CENTRE ★

MANDARIN RESTAURANT

THE VARSCONA HOTEL

O'BYRNE'S IRISH PUB

TRACK AND TRAIL

WHYTE AVE. (82ND AVE.)

PARLIAMENT CLUB

SEE DETAIL

To The Unheardof

81ST AVE.

BJARNE'S BOOKS

CAFE LA GARE

HOSTEL

COOK COUNTY SALOON

© AVALON TRAVEL PUBLISHING, INC.

Looking west along Whyte Ave. in 1903, the large building on the right is the Strathcona Hotel, which still stands.

PROVINCIAL ARCHIVES OF ALBERTA

its earliest days. The center is open Mon.–Fri. 10 A.M.–4 P.M., Saturday noon–4 P.M. Admission is $2.

WEST OF DOWNTOWN EDMONTON

From the city center, Jasper Avenue (101st Ave.) goes west through the **West End**—where many residential and commercial buildings date from the boom years of 1912–1914—and continues to **Glenora,** one of the city's oldest and most sought-after neighborhoods. Many streets are lined with elegant two-story mansions from the early 1900s. The neighborhood fountain in Alexander Circle (103rd Ave. and 133rd St.) is the center of the area.

Provincial Museum of Alberta

The Provincial Museum (12845 102nd Ave., 780/453-9100) overlooks the river valley in the historic neighborhood of Glenora. It is one of Canada's largest (18,800 square meters) and most popular museums. Exhibits catalog one billion years of natural and human history. In the Habitat Gallery, Alberta's four natural regions—mountain, prairie, parkland, and boreal forest—are re-created with incredible accuracy. The Natural History Gallery explains the forces that have shaped Alberta's land, describes the dinosaurs of the Cretaceous period and mammals of the Ice Age (such as the woolly mammoth), and displays a large collection of rocks and gems. Another section, the Syncrude Gallery of Aboriginal Culture, details Alberta's indigenous peoples, from their arrival 11,000 years ago to the way in which their tra-

ditions live on today through thousands of artifacts, Aboriginal interpreters, and audiovisual presentations. Other sections tell the story of the province's earliest explorers and the settlers who came from around the world to eke out a living in the harsh environment. The Bug Room, another favorite, displays insects dead and alive from around the world. The museum is well known for hosting traveling exhibits, making repeat visits worthwhile. The museum also has a gift shop and a café. It's open year-round, daily 9 A.M.–5 P.M. Admission is $6.50. To get there, take bus number 1, 2, or 10 along Jasper Avenue; or bus number 115, 116, or 120 west along 102nd Avenue.

The museum houses the **Provincial Archives,** containing photographs, maps, government records, and other documents pertaining to Alberta's history. The archives are open to the public Tues.–Sat. 9 A.M.–5 P.M.; for more information, call 780/427-1750.

In front of the museum is the **Government House,** 780/427-2281, an impressive three-story sandstone structure built in 1913 for Alberta's lieutenant governor, who would entertain guests in the lavish reception rooms or in the surrounding gardens. The building was later used as a hospital, then restored to its former glory in the 1970s. Free tours are offered each Sunday afternoon 1–4:30 P.M. through summer.

Alberta Aviation Museum

This museum, adjoining Edmonton City Centre Airport (11410 Kingsway Ave., 780/453-1078), dates to World War II, when the hangars held British aircraft involved in training programs. Today the hangars contain restored aircraft, including a favorite of early Canadian bush pilots—the Fairchild 71-C. One of the most recently completed projects was the on-site restoration of a World War II de Havilland Mosquito. Admission is adults $6, seniors and children $5. Open Mon.– Sat. 10 A.M.–4 P.M.

Edmonton Space and Science Centre
Completed in 1984, this multipurpose complex, in Coronation Park (11211 142nd St., 780/451-3344), is one of Edmonton's major attractions and most recognizable landmarks. In the main rotunda, displays are spread over three levels. They include a look into the future of communications; a ham radio station hooked up to similar stations around the world; a weather display that includes an audiovisual of the deadly tornado that hit Edmonton in the summer of 1987; the Challenger Centre, which allows you to make a simulated mini-mission through the universe; the **Margaret Zeidler Star Theatre,** where laser light shows are presented daily noon–7 P.M. with a different show each hour; an interactive Eye-lusions exhibit; the Universe Gallery, where a chunk of the moon is displayed; Discoveryland, especially for kids; a room with 20 computer terminals linked to the Internet; and ever-changing science and technology exhibits. In the adjacent North Gallery, Sport II gives you the chance to try your hand at a variety of sports, including wheelchair racing. Also in the complex are an IMAX theater, a café,

and a science shop. A day pass (adults $7, seniors $6, children $5) includes admission to all galleries and theater presentations. The complex is open daily 10 A.M.–9:30 P.M.

The **IMAX Theatre** presents spectacular video productions—seemingly always of an interesting nature—projected onto a 13- by 19-meter screen; adults $8, seniors and children $7 for the theater only; $12 and $11, respectively, for admission to one IMAX feature and the other displays. Laser light shows featuring music of the world's most popular bands are presented each evening at 8 P.M., with three later shows on Friday and Saturday nights; $7–11 per show.

Beside the complex is an **observatory,** which is open to the public daily 1–5 P.M. then 8 P.M.–midnight (weather permitting) for star-, moon-, and planet-gazing; no charge.

By bus, from downtown, take number 5 or 22 west along Jasper Avenue to Westmount Station and hoof it through Coronation Park or transfer to bus number 96.

WEST EDMONTON MALL

Feel like a trip to the beach to do some sunbathing and surfing? Would you like to play a round of golf? How about a submarine trip through a coral reef? Do you like eating at Parisian cafés? Does watching a National Hockey League team in training seem like a good

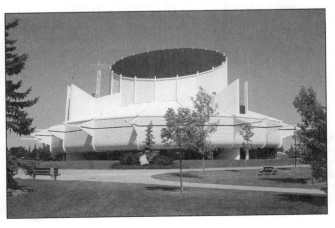

Edmonton Space and
Science Centre

way to spend the afternoon? Do the kids like dolphin shows? And at the end of the day, would you like to sink into a hot tub, surrounded by a lush tropical forest? All of these activities are possible under one roof at West Edmonton Mall, the largest shopping and indoor amusement complex in the whole world. Calgary may have the greatest *outdoor* show on earth, but Edmonton has what can surely be billed as the greatest *indoor* show on earth, a place that attracts eight million people annually. Much more than an oversized shopping mall, Edmonton's top tourist attraction is a shop-and-play four-season wonderland, where many visitors check into the 355-room luxury Fantasyland Hotel, stay a weekend, and never set foot outside the mall's 58 entrances.

WEST EDMONTON MALL TRIVIA

West Edmonton Mall is:
- the world's largest shopping and amusement complex, encompassing 483,000 square meters (that's equivalent to 48 city blocks)

West Edmonton Mall has:
- over 800 stores
- over 100 eateries
- 58 entrances
- 19 movie theaters
- 325,000 light bulbs
- five postal codes
- the world's largest car park (parking for 20,000 vehicles)
- the world's largest indoor amusement park
- the world's largest water park, covering two hectares and containing 50 million liters of water
- the world's largest indoor lake (122 meters long)
- the world's only indoor bungee jump
- more submarines than the Canadian Navy

West Edmonton Mall:
- cost over a billion dollars to construct
- employs 15,000 people
- uses the same amount of power as a city of 50,000
- attracts 20 million people a year (nearly 55,000 per day)

Shopping is only one part of the mall's universal appeal. Prices are no less than anywhere else in the city, but the experience of having more than 800 stores (including more than 200 women's-wear stores, 35 men's-wear stores, and 55 shoe shops) under one roof is unique.

Aside from the shops, many other major attractions fill the mall. **Galaxyland Amusement Park** is the world's largest indoor amusement park, with 27 rides, including "Mindbender"—a fourteen-story, triple-loop roller coaster (the world's largest indoor roller coaster)—and "Drop of Doom," where you're strapped into a cage, hauled up thirteen stories, then dropped, free falling back to earth in seconds. Admission is free, but the rides cost money. A Galaxyland day pass, allowing unlimited rides, is adults $24.95, families $59.95, and seniors and children $18.95.

In the two-hectare **World Waterpark,** you almost feel as though you're at the beach: the temperature is a balmy 30°C, and a long, sandy beach (with special nonslip sand), tropical palms, colorful cabanas, a beach bar, and waves crashing on the shore all simulate the real thing. The computerized wave pool holds 12.3 million liters of water and is programmed by computer to eject "sets" of waves at regular intervals. Behind the beach are 22 water slides that rise to a height of 26 meters. The World Waterpark also has the world's only indoor bungee jump, **Blue Thunder Bungee** ($69.95 including general waterpark access; $24.95 for an additional jump), three whirlpools, and a volleyball court. On the second floor of the mall is a water park viewpoint. Admission to World Waterpark is adults $24.95, families $59.95, seniors and children $18.95.

At the same end of the mall as World Waterpark is the world's largest indoor lake and a series of attractions, known collectively as **Deep Sea Adventure.** You can gawk at the area along its entire 122-meter length from either the main or second floor of the mall. The most dominant feature of the lagoon is a full-size replica of Christopher Columbus's flagship, the *Santa Maria.* It was built in False Creek, Vancouver, and shipped across the Rockies to its new indoor home. You can descend into the depths in one of four self-pro-

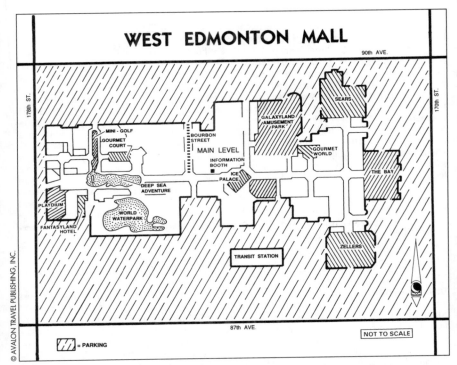

pelled submarines cruising the lake, passing 200 different types of marine life, including real coral (adults $9.95, families $24.95, seniors and children $5). The lake is also the site of regular dolphin shows ($3, or watch from above for free), scuba-diving courses, canoe rentals, and an underwater aquarium with seals, penguins, and sharks ($6). Beyond the Deep Sea Adventure is the **Playdium,** 780/444-7529, opened in 2000 as part of the mall's Stage IV development. This state-of-the-art entertainment center offers more than 150 attractions, from "reality" sports to test your athletic prowess against the professionals to a "Speed Zone," which is filled with the latest racing games. It's open 10 A.M.–midnight.

Other major attractions in the mall include **Xorbitor,** a hydraulic capsule that simulates on-screen movements ($7 per ride); **Professor WEM's Adventure Golf** (adults $7.50, se-

niors and children $5); **SkyRange,** an enclosed, rooftop golf driving range; and, smack in the middle of the mall, the newly renovated **Ice Palace.** This NHL-size skating rink is the second home of the Edmonton Oilers, who occasionally practice here. It's open to the public year-round; adults $4.50 per session, seniors and children $2, skate rentals $3.

Other sights include an aviary with various exotic birds, a Chinese pagoda that was hand-carved by four generations of the same family, replicas of the British crown jewels, bronze statues commissioned especially for the mall, and a couple of aquariums. Two theme streets, **Europa Boulevard** and the glitzy New Orleans–style **Bourbon Street** hold some of the mall's 110 restaurants and eateries.

Shopping hours vary seasonally but are generally Mon.–Fri. 10 A.M.–9 P.M., Saturday 10 A.M.–6 P.M., and Sunday noon–5 P.M. Hours of the various attractions and restaurants vary. Many restaurants stay open later, and the nightclubs stay open to the early hours of the morning.

The mall is on 170th Street, between 87th and 90th avenues. Parking is usually not a problem, but finding your car again can be, so remember which of the 58 entrances you parked near (a parking lot along 90th Ave. and 175th St. is designated for RVs). From downtown, take bus number 12, 115, or 10. On the Main Level, 50 meters west toward the World Waterpark, is a small **information booth,** open regular shopping hours, that can supply maps and answer all commonly asked questions. When your legs tire, **scooter rentals** are available (on the opposite side of the Ice Palace from the information booth); $5.50 for the first hour, $3.25 for each additional hour. For more information, contact West Edmonton Mall at 780/444-5200 or 800/661-8890, www.westedmontonmall.com.

DEVON

Devonian Botanic Garden
These gardens developed by the University of Alberta are located southwest of the city and five kilometers north of the small town of Devon, which was named for the Devonian rock formation in which nearby oil strikes were made during the late 1940s. The 70-hectare site has been developed around the natural contours of the land. The highlight is the **Kurimoto Japanese Garden,** one of the world's northernmost authentic Japanese gardens. The various natural elements are complemented by an ornamental gate, an arched bridge, and decorative lanterns. Other features are the large Alpine Garden, with examples of plants from mountainous regions; the Herb Garden, where in August the aroma is almost overpowering; the Peony Collection, which is at its most colorful in July; a greenhouse filled with plants unique to the Southern Hemisphere; and the Native People's Garden, which is surrounded by water and showcasing plants used by the native people of Alberta. The gardens are open May–Sept. daily 10 A.M.–7 P.M., the rest of the year weekends only 11 A.M.–4 P.M. Admission is adults $5.75, seniors $4.75, children $3.50. For more information, call 780/987-3054.

STONY PLAIN

Multicultural Heritage Centre
The streets of Stony Plain, west of the city, which was homesteaded before 1900, are lined with historic buildings, but the best place to learn more about the community's history is at this provincial historic site (5411 51st St.). On the grounds, the town's first high school houses a museum, a craft store, a library and archives, a candy store, and the **Homesteader's Kitchen—** a basement restaurant serving pioneer-style home-cooked meals at reasonable prices. Housed next door, in the historic residence of an early pioneer, is the **Oppertshauser House,** Alberta's first rural public art gallery. Admission to both buildings is free. The center, 780/963-2777, is open year-round Mon.–Sat. 10 A.M.–4 P.M. and Sunday 10 A.M.–6:30 P.M.

ST. ALBERT

The city of St. Albert (pop. 46,000)—northwest of Edmonton along the St. Albert Trail—is one of Alberta's oldest settlements but has today become part of Edmonton's sprawl. Albert Lacombe, a pioneering western Canadian priest, built a mansion overlooking the Sturgeon River in 1861, when Fort Edmonton was only a small trading post. A sawmill and gristmill were constructed, and by 1870, St. Albert was the largest agricultural community west of Winnipeg.

Sights
Father Lacombe's first log chapel, built in 1861, had a brick structure built around it in 1927. It was used as a museum until the mid-1970s, when it was declared a Provincial Historical Site and restored to its original appearance. The **Father Lacombe Chapel** (west of Hwy. 2 on St. Vital Ave., 780/427-3995) is open in summer daily 10 A.M.–4 P.M. Admission is $2. Beside the chapel is a cast-iron statue of Father Lacombe that was made in France and brought to Canada in 1929. Also on Mission Hill is the **Vital Grandin Centre,** an imposing three-story structure built in 1887 as a hospital.

In stark contrast to the historic buildings overlooking the Sturgeon River is City Hall in **St.**

Albert Place on St. Anne Street, a contoured brick building designed by Douglas Cardinal. Inside is the **Musée Heritage Museum,** 780/459-1528, with displays telling the story of St. Albert's history and the people who made it happen. It's open in summer daily 9:30 A.M.–5 P.M., the rest of the year Tues.–Sun. noon–5 P.M.

The **Tourist Information Centre** is in a large, modern building beside Highway 2 on the south side of St. Albert (you can't miss it coming into the city from the south), 780/459-1724. It's open year-round Mon.–Fri. 8 A.M.–5 P.M., Sat.–Sun. 10 A.M.–5 P.M. To reach the city from downtown Edmonton, take the St. Albert bus east along 102nd Avenue.

FORT SASKATCHEWAN AND VICINITY

In 1875—long after the fur-trading post of Fort Edmonton had been established—the North West Mounted Police (NWMP) marched north from Fort Macleod and established its northern divisional fort on the North Saskatchewan River, 30 kilometers northeast of Fort Edmonton. In the ensuing years, Fort Saskatchewan has grown into a large residential center, right at Edmonton's doorstep. To reach the town, take Highway 15 (Manning Dr.) out of Edmonton. Make your first stop the **Tourist Information Centre,** which is housed in the railway station (10030 99th Ave., 780/998-4355).

Fort Saskatchewan Museum and Historic Site

The site of the original fort overlooks the river from along 101st Street in downtown Fort Saskatchewan. A jail and courthouse replaced the original fort in 1909. The jail was demolished in 1994, but the two-story, red-brick courthouse still stands and now serves as a museum cataloguing the history of the site and the NWMP. Various other historic buildings have been moved to this picturesque site, including a restored log homestead, a blacksmith shop, and a one-room schoolhouse. A cairn marking the site of the NWMP guard room has been built from stones used in the original structure. Admission is $2. It's open July–Aug. daily 10 A.M.–6 P.M., the rest of the year Mon.–Fri. 11 A.M.–3 P.M. For more information, call 780/998-1750.

The NWMP warden's house was replaced by one for the jailer in 1909, and this building now serves as the **Warden's Art Centre and Tea Rooms** (10006 101st St., 780/998-4694). It's open Tues.–Sun. 11 A.M.–9 P.M.

Alberta Railway Museum

If antique railway memorabilia interests you, consider stopping at this museum, a short detour from Highway 15 to Fort Saskatchewan. Or take 97th Street (Hwy. 28) north to Namao, turn east on Highway 37 for seven kilometers, then south on 34th Street for two kilometers. It is well signposted from both directions. Featuring Canada's largest collection of Northern Alberta Railway (NAR) equipment, this museum also has rolling stock from the Canadian National Railway (CNR) and the CPR. More than 70 locomotive, passenger, and freight cars from 1877–1950 are displayed. Also exhibited are various railway artifacts, equipment, and machinery. Admission is adults $4, seniors $2.50, children $1.25, and train rides ($2) are offered on long weekends. The museum, 780/472-6229, is open in summer Tues.–Sun. 10 A.M.–6 P.M.

RECREATION

OUTDOOR ACTIVITIES

River Valley Park System

One of the first things you'll notice about Edmonton is its large amount of parkland. The city has more land set aside for parks, per capita, than any other city in Canada. Most parks interconnect along the banks of the North Saskatchewan River and in adjoining ravines, encompassing 7,400 hectares and comprising the largest stretch of urban parkland in North America. Within these parks are picnic areas, swimming pools, historic sites, golf courses, and many kilometers of walking and biking trails. The map *Cycle Edmonton,* available from Tourist

Information Centres, details all routes and trail lengths. One of the larger individual parks is **William Hawrelak Park,** west of the university along Groat Road. A one-way road loops through the park, circling a manmade lake with paddle boats and fishing, passing many quiet picnic areas and an outdoor amphitheater that hosts a wide range of summer events. **River Valley Cycle** (9124 82nd Ave., 780/465-3863) rents mountain bikes for $7.50 per hour, $30 per day, and leads guided tours during summer. **Sport & Ski Rentals** (6430 104th St., 780/435-7547) also rents bikes at similar rates.

Swimming

Edmonton's outdoor swimming season lasts approximately three months beginning at the end of May. Of the five outdoor pools owned by the city, the one in **Queen Elizabeth Park** is in a particularly picturesque location among poplar trees and with a view of the city skyline over the river; access is from 90th Avenue. Another pool, close to the city center, is in **Mill Creek Park,** north of Whyte Avenue (82nd Ave.) on 95A Street. Admission to all outdoor pools is $4. When the weather gets cooler, or to take advantage of more facilities, head to one of the city's many indoor pools, where admission includes the use of saunas, a hot tub, weight rooms, and water slides. The most famous of these is **World Waterpark** in the West Edmonton Mall, which has 22 water slides, a wave pool, a nonslip sandy beach, and a bungee jump (additional cost); admission is adults $24.95, families $59.95, seniors and children $18.95. Swimming events of the 1978 Commonwealth Games were held at the **Kinsmen Sports Centre** (9100 Walterdale Hill, 780/496-7300), in Kinsmen Park on the south bank of the North Saskatchewan River. Admission of $4.75 includes use of the pools, fitness center, sauna, and jogging track. The cafeteria here has reasonably priced meals. For information on all outdoor and indoor pools, call the Swim Line at 780/428-7946.

Golfing

Edmonton has so many golf courses that you could play a different one each day for a month. Three are within a three-iron shot of the city center, whereas others are located along the North Saskatchewan River Valley and throughout outlying suburbs. Canada's oldest municipal course is the **Victoria Golf Course,** which is still owned and operated by the city. This 18-hole course is only a little more than 6,000 yards in length but is made challenging by narrow fairways and smallish greens. It's located just west of the Legislature Building along River Road, 780/496-4710. Greens fee is $28. Slightly longer and situated on a sweeping bend of the river is the **Riverside Golf Course** (8630 Rowland Rd., 780/496-8702). Also owned by the city, this course also has greens fee of $28. West of the city, in Spruce Grove, is **The Links** (Calahoo Rd., 780/962-4653), a well-maintained course with rolling fairways and large greens; $36. **Kinsmen Pitch & Putt** is located behind the Kinsmen Sports Centre, a tree-covered area directly across the North Saskatchewan River from downtown; 18 holes $12, seniors $8. For tee times, call 780/432-1626.

Ballooning and Skydiving

Recreational and competition ballooning is popular in Edmonton throughout the year. One company offering flights is **Windship Aviation** (5615 103rd St., 780/438-0111). Flights depend entirely on weather conditions. Launch sites and landing sites change with the wind direction; the grounds of Muttart Conservatory are most often used for launching. Flight time is 60–90 minutes, and the $175 cost includes transportation back to the launch site, a celebration drink on landing, and a framed picture of your flight.

Edmonton Skydive Centre (10588 109th St., 780/444-5867) does its jumping from the small airport at Westlock, 85 kilometers north of the city. Experienced skydivers pay approximately $20–25 per jump, depending on the altitude; $35–39 with gear rental. A six-hour training program for first-timers includes a jump from 1,200 meters and costs $135. These courses begin each Saturday and Sunday at 9 A.M.

Climbing

The **Vertically Inclined Rock Gym** (8523 Argyll Rd., 780/496-9390) is Edmonton's best such facility, with a total of 2,000 meters of climbing wall. A day pass costs $15, equipment rental an additional $8. Climbing instruction courses are offered from $35 per person. It's open Monday 4–11 P.M., Tues.–Sat. 11 A.M.–11 P.M., Sunday noon–8 P.M.

Downhill Skiing and Snowboarding
The closest major alpine resort is Marmot Basin, in Jasper National Park, but Edmonton has three small lift-serviced hills within the city limits and one just outside. All are great for beginners but won't hold the interest of other skiers or snowboarders for very long. The **Edmonton Ski Club** (9613 96th Ave., 780/465-0852) runs the hill closest to the city. It's on the south side of the North Saskatchewan River, facing downtown. Lift tickets are $15 midweek, $17 on weekends. It's open from December to early March, Mon.–Thurs. 9 A.M.–9 P.M., Fri.–Sun. 9 A.M.–5:30 P.M. To get there, follow signs to the Muttart Conservatory. Southwest of downtown, where Whitemud Drive crosses the river, is **Snow Valley,** which has a chairlift, a T-bar, a rope tow, and a small snowboarding park. Lift tickets are $17, and seniors ski for just $6 for a full day. Hours are weekdays 9:30 A.M.–9:30 P.M., weekends 9 A.M.–6 P.M. For information, call 780/434-3991. **Sunridge Ski Area,** 780/449-6555, is east of downtown and has four lifts. Tickets are $17 per day, $13 half day. It's open Mon.–Fri. 9:30 A.M.–9:30 P.M., Sat.–Sun. 9:30 A.M.–5 P.M. To get there, follow the Yellowhead Highway to 17th Street, then turn south and follow the signs. **Rabbit Hill** is south of Edmonton, 780/955-2440. Take Calgary Trail south to Nisku, then follow the signs west for 13 kilometers. The hill has a chairlift, two T-bars, and four rope tows. Snowboarders are catered to with a half pipe and small terrain park. Lift tickets are adults $24, seniors and children $16. It's open Mon.–Fri. 10 A.M.–9:30 P.M., Sat.–Sun. 9 A.M.–6 P.M.

Cross-Country Skiing
The River Valley Park System provides ample opportunity for cross-country skiing. More than 75 kilometers of trails are groomed from December to early March. The most popular areas are in William Hawrelak Park, up Mill Creek Ravine, and through Capilano Park. For details of trails, pick up the brochure *Cross-country Ski Edmonton* from Tourist Information Centres or call 780/493-9000 and enter the code 3446. The **Kinsmen Sports Centre** has cross-country ski

rentals; $10 for two hours, or $15 per day, including boots and poles. **Sport & Ski Rentals** (6430 104th St., 780/435-7547) has similar packages for $12 per day and $25 for three days.

SPECTATOR SPORTS

Ice Hockey
Alberta's first major-league hockey team was the Alberta Oilers, who played in both Calgary and Edmonton. The team finally settled in Edmonton permanently for the 1973–1974 season. During the 1980s, when Wayne Gretzky was leading the **Edmonton Oilers,** the NHL's Stanley Cup resided just as permanently in Edmonton, "City of Champions." Since 1988, when Gretzky was sold to the L.A. Kings, the team has met with mixed success. For most of the 1990s, talk on the streets has been about the politics and viability of the team rather than its performances on the ice. Home games are played September–April in the Skyreach Centre adjacent to **Northlands Park** (7300 116th Ave., 780/471-2191 or Ticketmaster 780/451-8000, www.edmontonoilers.com). Tickets cost $15–60.

Baseball
The **Edmonton Trappers** are a successful farm team for the Anaheim Angels. They play in the AAA, Pacific Coast League, which they won in 1997. Home games are played April to early September at **Telus Field,** close to downtown at 10233 96th Avenue (John Ducey Way). General admission is $7.75, or you can sit in the main grandstand for $10.75; for details, call the club at 780/414-4450 or Ticketmaster at 780/451-8000.

Football
The **Edmonton Eskimos** have a distinguished record in the Canadian Football League (CFL), having won the Grey Cup 11 times—including five straight (1978–1982)—since joining the league in 1910. "Eskimos" was originally an insult, given to the team by a Calgary sportswriter in the team's early days, but the name stuck. Since 1948, the team has played in, and won, more Grey Cup games than any other team in the league. Two former Albertan premiers, Peter Lougheed and Don Getty, once starred for the team. The "Esks" play late June to November

at Commonwealth Stadium (9021 111th Ave., 780/448-3757 or 800/667-3757, www.esks.com). Tickets are $20–36.

Horse Racing
Harness racing takes place at Northlands (7300 116th Ave., 780/471-7379) from spring to mid-December. Thoroughbred racing takes place throughout summer at the same track. Racing is generally Wednesday and Friday at 6 P.M. and on weekends at 1 P.M. During Edmonton's Klondike Days, a full racing program is presented. General admission is $2.50, $4 for the Clubhouse.

ARTS AND ENTERTAINMENT

For details on theater events throughout the city, a listing of art galleries, what's going on where in the music scene, cinema screenings, and a full listing of festivals and events, pick up a free copy of *See Magazine* or *Vue Weekly*. Both are published every Thursday and are available all around town. Tickets to most major performances are available in advance from **Ticketmaster** (780/451-8000, www.ticketmaster.ca). Once you've arrived in Edmonton, head down to **Tix on the Square,** at street level of Chancery Hall (across from Sir Winston Churchill Square) for half-price tickets.

Art Galleries
Scattered throughout the city are commercial art galleries, many of which exhibit and sell Canadian and native art. A group of galleries close together on Jasper Avenue between 123rd and 124th streets downtown form what is known as **The Gallery Walk.** Other galleries of note include **Northern Images** (in West Edmonton Mall, 780/444-1995), with a good collection of native and northern arts and crafts, and **Bearclaw Gallery** (10403 124th St., 780/482-1204), which is closed Sunday.

Theater
Edmonton's 14 professional theater companies present productions at various locations all year long. For most companies, September–May is the main season.

The **Citadel** (9828 101A Ave., 780/425-1820 or 888/425-1820) is Canada's largest theater facility, taking up an entire downtown block. From the outside, it looks like a gigantic greenhouse; one entire side is glass, enclosing a magnificent indoor garden complete with a waterfall. The complex houses five theaters: the Maclab Theatre showcases the work of teens and children; the Rice Theatre features mainly experimental and innovative productions; Zeidler Hall hosts films, lectures, and children's theater; Tucker Amphitheatre presents concerts and recitals, and often puts on small lunchtime stage productions; and Shoctor Theatre is the main stage for the Citadel's long-running subscription program ($18–40 per production). Tickets are available from the Citadel Box Office.

The **Phoenix Theatre** company (9638 101A Ave., 780/429-4015) typically stages powerful and thought-provoking productions at the Kaasa Theatre in the University of Alberta's Jubilee Auditorium. Its season runs September–June. For tickets, call Ticketmaster, 780/451-8000. For slightly more adventurous productions and occasional international imports, see what's going on at the **Northern Light Theatre** (11516 103rd St., 780/471-1586). Tickets are $10–20. Edmonton's oldest theater is the **Walterdale Playhouse** (10322 83rd Ave., 780/439-2845), located in the heart of Old Strathcona, which presents historical and humorous material throughout the year. Ticket prices begin at $8. **Jagged Edge** is a small-time theater company with performances in the Edmonton Centre (10205 101st St., 780/463-4237), especially for the lunchtime crowd (Tues.–Fri. 12:10–1 P.M.). The show costs $8 and lunch is available for an additional $5.

Celebrations, in the Oasis Entertainment Centre (102-13103 Fort Rd., 780/448-9339), is a popular interactive dinner theater; the ticket price of $40–50 includes dinner. Open Wed.–Sun., reservations necessary, no jeans allowed, and you must be seated by 6 P.M. **Jubilations** (in West Edmonton Mall, 780/484-2424) is another such dinner theater, combining music and comedy. Shows start at 6:30 P.M.; from $40.

Music and Dance
The newest addition to Edmonton's theater district is the magnificent **Winspear Centre** (corner of 99th St. and 102nd Ave.), a venue renowned as an acoustic wonder that is also capable of producing high-quality amplified sound. It is

home to the **Edmonton Symphony Orches-tra,** 780/428-1414, and attracts a wide variety of national and international musical acts, ranging from choirs to classical performers. Tickets generally go for $26–35. Contact the Box Office at 780/428-1414 or 800/563-5081.

Both the **Edmonton Opera,** 780/429-1000, and the **Alberta Ballet,** 780/428-6839, perform at the Jubilee Auditorium in the University of Alberta (11455 87th Ave.) between October and March. For performance dates and ticket information, call the box office numbers or Ticketmaster, 780/451-8000.

Cinemas

Famous Players cinemas are located throughout the city, including 10233 Jasper Avenue, 780/428-1307; 2950 Calgary Trail S, 780/436-6977; and in West Edmonton Mall, 780/444-2400. The historic **Princess Theatre** (10337 82nd Ave., Old Strathcona, 780/433-0728) is an old-time movie house showing revivals, experiments, and foreign films. **Metro Cinema** has recently moved from Canada Place to Zeidler Hall in the Citadel Theatre on 101A Avenue. It shows classics, imports, and brave new films. The **Garneau Theatre** (8712 109th St., 780/433-0728) features mostly foreign films and those that have gained acclaim at film festivals.

Casinos

Casinos in Alberta are strange places. They are all privately owned and lack the glamour of Las Vegas, and all the profits must go to charity. They offer blackjack, roulette, baccarat, Red Dog, and Sic Bo—no slot machines. **Casino A.B.S.** has a location at 10549 102nd Street, 780/424-9467, and **Casino Palace** is in West Edmonton Mall by entrance 45, 780/444-2112.

Bars and Nightclubs

The **Sidetrack Café** (10333 112th St., 780/421-1326) is central to downtown, serves excellent food, and presents live entertainment nightly from 9 P.M. Shows change dramatically—one night it might be stand-up comedians, the next a blues band, then jazz—and the only thing you can rely on is that it will be busy. Monday is usually comedy night and Sunday variety night. Cover charges vary, $3–8 is normal. Downtown, the **Sherlock Holmes** (10012 101A Ave.,

780/426-7784) serves a large selection of British and Irish ales and is the place to head for on St. Patrick's Day (March 17). The rest of the year, drinkers are encouraged to join in nightly sing-alongs with the pianist. Sherlock Holmes also has locations in Old Strathcona (10341 82nd Ave., 780/433-9676) and along West Edmonton Mall's Bourbon Street, 780/444-1752. Old Strathcona is also home to **O'Byrne's Irish Pub** (10616 82nd Ave., 780/414-6766), where Celtic bands often play. **The Rose and Crown** (10235 101st St., 780/441-3036), in the Sheraton Grande, is another English-style pub with a great atmosphere and evening sing-alongs. The **Stonehouse Pub,** a few blocks west of downtown (11026 Jasper Ave., 780/420-0448), has an outdoor patio, plenty of pool tables, and big-screen TVs.

The **Cook County Saloon** (8010 103rd St., 780/432-2665) is consistently voted Canada's Best Country Nightclub by the Canadian Country

Head to the Cook County Saloon for live country music

Music Association. Its mellow honky-tonk ambience draws crowds, and Canadian and international performers play here. Free two-step lessons are offered on selected weeknights, and on Friday and Saturday nights the action really cranks up, with live entertainment and a DJ spinning country Top 40 discs. On these two nights, the cover is $6 after 8 P.M. Other country nightclubs are **Longriders Saloon** (11733 8th St.), where grassroots country bands perform; the often-rowdy **Mustang Saloon** (16648 109th Ave., 780/444-7474); the trendy **Nashville's Electric Roadhouse** (West Edmonton Mall, 780/489-1330); and **Rock 'n Rodeo,** south of downtown (5450 Calgary Trail, 780/437-9185). Beyond West Edmonton Mall is **Cowboys** (10102 180th St., 780/481-8739), with a Western theme but attracting a young, frat-like crowd with theme nights, popular promotions, white-hatted and scantily clad shooter girls, and a huge dance floor.

Top 40 and dance nightclubs change names, reputations, and locations regularly, but some are reliable fixtures. **Chase Nightclub,** downstairs in the Scotia Centre (10060 Jasper Ave., 780/426-0728), plays Top 40 and is one of the busiest clubs in the city. **Club Malibu** attracts the under-25 crowd to its locations at 10310 85th Avenue, 780/432-7300, and in West Edmonton Mall. An older crowd gathers at the **Urban Lounge** (8111 105th St., 780/439-3388), with live music nightly. **Barry T's Grand Central Station** (6111 107th St., 780/438-2582) plays a unique mix of Top 40 and country.

If you're into Gothic, punk, and hip-hop, head downtown to the **Crystal Lounge** (10336 Jasper Ave., 780/426-7521) or the **Likwid Lounge** (10161 112th St., 780/413-4578). In Old Strathcona, the **Parliament Club** (10551 82nd Ave., 780/434-5366), which opened in the fall of 2000, is the latest hotspot for disco, funk, and dance music.

Jazz and Comedy

The Edmonton Jazz Society is based at the **Yardbird Suite** (10203 86th Ave., 780/432-0428). Live jazz fills the air October–May nightly 10 P.M.–2 A.M. Tuesday night jam sessions are $2, other nights admission is $5–18. Friday is nonsmoking night. The **Full Moon Folk Club,** 780/438-6410, sponsors visiting performers at a variety of venues; tickets are well priced at approximately $15.

At **Yuk Yuk's Komedy Kabaret** (West Edmonton Mall, 780/481-9857), show times vary, but they generally offer two shows nightly Thursday–Saturday. Sunday is variety night, and Wednesday is amateur night. Tickets are $7–14.

SHOPPING

Plazas and Malls

Naturally, any talk of a shopping trip to Edmonton includes West Edmonton Mall, the world's largest shopping and amusement complex; the mall is covered under **Sights,** earlier in this chapter. Downtown's major shopping centers are **Eaton Centre, Edmonton Centre,** and **ManuLife Place.** Apart from **West Edmonton Mall** (at 87th Ave. and 170th St.), other malls are located along Stony Plain Road, Calgary Trail South, and north of the city at 137th Avenue and 66th Street (Londonderry Mall).

Camping Gear and Western Wear

Mountain Equipment Co-op, a Canadian outdoor equipment cooperative similar to R.E.I. in the United States, is located west of the provincial museum (12328 102nd Ave., 780/488-6614). Across the railway tracks from Old Strathcona is **Track 'n' Trail** (10148 82nd Ave., 780/432-1707), which carries a wide variety of camping and climbing gear. In the same general area is **Totem Outdoor Outfitters** (7430 99th St., 780/432-1223), with more of the same as well as kayaks, canoes, and some used gear. West of downtown is the large **Campers Village** (10951 170th St., 780/484-2700), with camping equipment, fishing tackle, books, boots, and scuba diving equipment. **Budget Sports Rentals** (6504 104th St., 780/434-3808) rents backpacks, tents, sleeping bags, and canoes.

Alberta's largest supplier of Western wear is **Lammle's,** 780/444-7877, with four outlets through the city, including two in West Edmonton Mall. The **Western Boot Factory** (10007 167th St., 780/489-0594) stocks thousands of styles of cowboy boots. You can't miss it because out front is the world's largest cowboy boot. This store has another location at 3414 Calgary Trail N, 780/435-3702. High-quality boots are also sold by **Diablo Boots** (3440 Calgary Trail N, 780/435-2592).

FESTIVALS AND EVENTS

Spring
The **Alberta Book Festival**, 780/426-5892, held in mid-March, is a three-day event with public workshops, readings, book signings, and a small midway. Many of the events are held in the Convention Centre. The rodeo season kicks off at Northlands Park the third weekend of March with Cody Snyder's **World Champion Bull Bustin'**, 780/471-7210. The **International Children's Festival**, 780/459-1692, takes place the weekend closest to June 1 in the Arden Theatre, St. Albert. Acts from around the world include theater, music, dance, storytelling, and puppetry.

The **Dreamspeakers Festival**, 780/451-5033, held on the last weekend of May, celebrates the art, culture, and filmmaking of the First Nations People—the native Canadians.

Edmonton's Klondike Days
This 11-day event beginning on the third Thursday of each July celebrates a somewhat infamous chapter in Edmonton's history. In 1898, when the rush to the Yukon goldfields was in full swing, city merchants persuaded approximately 1,600 miners that the best route north was to Edmonton and north along the Mackenzie River. The route turned out to be an impractical and difficult one. Few of the miners made it, many died trying, and when they reached the Klondike, the rush was nearly over. Today, that rush for gold is relived on the streets of the city. Events include a massive parade through downtown, an 1890s-style he-man contest at Hawrelak Park, the Sourdough River Race down the river, nonstop entertainment on downtown streets, and a bathtub road race that always gets a laugh. Edmonton's finest restaurants offer samples of their cuisine in a Taste of Edmonton, and each morning, throughout the city, pancake breakfasts are given away. At Northlands Park (7300 116th St.) is the Edmonton's Klondike Days Exposition, open every day, featuring a midway, Klondike Days Casino, a British Pavilion, free concerts, racing pigs, vaudeville shows, thoroughbred racing, and a crafts and country fair. This is the city's biggest annual event, attracting approximately 750,000 visitors, so be prepared for big crowds everywhere. For more information, contact Edmonton's Klondike Days, 780/423-2822, www.northlands.com.

World Championships in Athletics
The **World's**, which is the third-largest sporting event (only the Summer Olympic Games and soccer's World Cup are bigger) in the world, come to Edmonton August 3–12, 2001. Sports stars from 200 countries will compete in 46 running, jumping, and throwing events, with the epicenter of the action at the 60,000-seat Commonwealth Stadium, which was built for the 1978 Commonwealth Games. This is the first time that the World's have taken place in North America, ensuring an excellent following in Canada and the United States, but organizers have created extra interest through several unique features, such as having the men's marathon end in the stadium during the Opening Ceremony. In addition to the 1,600 competitors, an estimated 500,000 spectators are expected to attend over the 10 days. It is also estimated that the event will attract a television audience of more than four billion viewers. For further information and tickets, call 780/821-2001 or 877/240-2001, www.2001 .edmonton.com. The games are organized by the International Amateur Athletic Federation, www.iaaf.com.

Other Summer Festivals
During the last week of June, **Jazz City International**, 780/433-3333, is held at various indoor and outdoor venues. Many foreign stars make special appearances. **The Works: A Visual Arts Celebration**, 780/426-2122, features art exhibitions on downtown streets, in parks, and in art galleries for two weeks from late June. For 10 days in early July, the streets and parks come alive during the **International Street Performers Festival**, 780/425-5162, with almost 1,000 performances by magicians, comics, jugglers, musicians, and mimes. Fifty outdoor ethnic pavilions at Hawrelak Park are just a small part of **Heritage Days**, 780/488-3378, which is held on the August long weekend. Visitors to

the festival have the opportunity to experience international singing and dancing, arts-and-crafts displays, costumes, and cuisine from than 60 cultures. During the **Edmonton Folk Music Festival** (780/429-1999, www.efmf. ab.ca), held on the second weekend of August, Gallagher Park comes alive with the sound of blues, jazz, country, Celtic, traditional, and bluegrass music. Tickets are cheaper if bought in advance.

Quickly becoming one of the city's most popular festivals is **The Fringe,** 780/448-9000, a 10-day extravaganza that begins on the second Friday in August. It is held throughout Old Strathcona, in parks, on the streets, in parkades, and in the area's historic restored theaters. With more than 1,200 performances and a crowd of half a million (in 2000) watching on, the festival has become North America's largest alternative-theater event, attracting artists from around the world. Tickets are generally inexpensive.

Symphony under the Sky, 780/428-1108, held on the weekend closest to August 31, is the last gasp in Edmonton's busy summer festival schedule. Led by the Edmonton Symphony Orchestra, this five-day extravaganza of classical music takes place in William Hawrelak Park.

Fall and Winter
Farmfair International (780/471-7210 or 800/800-7275, www.northlands.com) showcases some of North America's best livestock through sales and auctions, but exhibits, a trade show, the judging of Miss Rodeo Canada, and thousands of farm animals draw in casual visitors. The fair takes place in Northlands Park the second week of November. That same week, the Skyreach Centre hosts the **Canadian Finals Rodeo.** This $500,000 event is the culmination of the year's work for Canada's top 10 money-earning cowboys and cowgirls in the six traditional rodeo events. The action takes place Wed.–Sun. at 7 P.M. and 1 P.M. Sunday. Purchase tickets ($20–35) through Ticketmaster, 780/451-8000, www.ticketmaster.ca.

The city celebrates the end of the year during the **First Night** festival, 780/448-9200, an alcohol-free celebration in Gallagher Park.

ACCOMMODATIONS

Nearly all of Edmonton's best hotels are located downtown. Other concentrations of motels can be found along Calgary Trail (south from downtown) and scattered along Stony Plain Road in the west. The towns of Leduc and Nisku have several motels close to Edmonton International Airport. Other options include many bed-and-breakfasts, a centrally located hostel, and camping (just five minutes from downtown, or in campgrounds west, east, or south of the city).

DOWNTOWN

$50–100
Generally, the least expensive downtown hotels lie just a few blocks from the core of the city. One of the best values is the **Mayfair Hotel,** five blocks west of the Hudson's Bay Centre (10815 Jasper Ave., 780/423-1650 or 800/463-7666). Rooms, each with a coffeemaker and cable TV, are $55 single, $60 double, which includes a light breakfast in the downstairs restaurant. Four other motels within this price range stand within a few blocks of the Mayfair Hotel. The least expensive is the **Rodeway Inn** (formerly the Garden City Hotel, 10425 100th Ave., 780/423-5611 or 888/384-6835), which has recently been renovated but is still well-priced at $58 single, $64 double. The **Days Inn** (10041 106th St., 780/423-1925 or 800/267-2191) is newly renovated and with large, comfortable rooms from $59 single, $66 double. The **Inn on 7th** (10001 107th St., 780/429-2861 or 800/661-7327, www.innon7th.com) features 173 rooms, a small fitness room, free parking, and rates from $75 single, $85 double.

The newly renovated **Coast Edmonton Plaza Hotel** (10155 105th St., 780/423-4811 or 800/268-8998, www.coasthotels.com) features an indoor pool, a brand-new exercise room, laundry service, a lounge, and a restaurant. Rates start at $89 single or double on weekends—one of the best values of Edmonton's downtown hotels.

If you plan to be in the city for a few days and want to cook your own meals, suite hotels (also called apartment hotels) offer a good value. The **Alberta Place Suite Hotel** (10049 103rd St., 780/423-1565 or 800/661-3982, www.albertaplace.com) is one of the best values. The 86 suites are large, and each has a well-equipped kitchen. Continental breakfast and daily papers are complimentary, and Jasper Avenue is only half a block away. Rates start at $90 single or double for a one-bedroom suite.

$100–150

the **Edmonton House Suite Hotel** (10205 100th Ave., 780/420-4000 or 800/661-6562, www.edmontonhouse.com) is more expensive than Alberta Place, but each of the 300 rooms has a balcony with views of the valley or the city, and there's an indoor pool, a fitness room, a guest lounge and reading room, and shuttle service to West Edmonton Mall; $110–160 single or double.

The recently renovated **Howard Johnson Plaza Hotel** (10010 104th St., 780/423-2450 or 800/446-4656, www.hojo.com) has an indoor pool and a variety of shops and restaurants along a covered arcade; $109 single, $119 double.

Formerly part of the Hilton chain, the **Sheraton Grande Edmonton** (10235 101st St., 780/428-7111 or 800/263-9030, www.sheratonedmonton.com) is in the financial district, linked to other buildings by the Pedway system. In each of the 313 elegantly furnished rooms, you'll find marble tabletops, walnut furniture, brass trimmings, and a bay window. Other hotel facilities include an indoor pool, an exercise room, a Starbucks coffee shop, and a British-style pub. Rooms are priced from $145 single or double.

$150–200

If you're looking for accommodations in this price category, it's very hard to do better than the **Union Bank Inn** (10053 Jasper Ave., 780/423-3600 or 888/423-3601, www.unionbankinn.com) for value, charm, and location. The inn is in a restored 1911 bank building in the heart of the city. The new owners have transformed the historic building into a luxurious boutique hotel, featuring a fireplace, down comforters, and bathrobes in each of 14 tastefully decorated rooms. The rates of $165–185 per room also include a cooked breakfast, a wine-and-cheese tray presented to guests each evening, and free parking.

The **Hotel Macdonald** (10065 100th St., 780/424-5181 or 800/441-1414) is an Edmonton landmark that was originally part of the Canadian Pacific hotel chain (along with the Palliser Hotel in Calgary and the Banff Springs Hotel in Banff) but is now part of Fairmont Hotels and Resorts, www.fairmont.com. The 198 smallish rooms are decorated with a subtle elegance, and the hotel has an excellent restaurant, a health club, and a beautiful lounge overlooking the river valley. Rates start at $179 single, $189 double, but deals are offered, including a weekend package ($149 double per night), a bed-and-breakfast package for guests over 60 ($132 single or double), and upgrade packages, including suite accommodation with all the trimmings (from $309 double).

Part of the Eaton Centre is the **Delta Edmonton Centre Suite Hotel** (10222 102nd St., access it from 103rd Ave., 780/429-3900 or 800/268-1133, www.deltahotels.com), with a private lounge for guests. Rates for one of the 169 luxuriously appointed rooms start at $169 and rise to $285 for a two-room suite.

Renovated in 1998, the 24-story **Crowne Plaza Chateau Lacombe** (10111 Bellamy Hill, 780/428-6611 or 800/661-8801, www.chateau-lacombe.com) sits on Bellamy Hill, and its unusual cylindrical design distinguishes it against the skyline. The Chateau Lacombe features a fitness center, boutiques, a cocktail lounge, and a revolving restaurant; $160 single or double (during summer, rooms are often advertised for less than $100, including breakfast).

More than $200

Joined to the Pedway system and very central, but still affording great river views, is the 20-story **Westin Edmonton** (10135 100th St., 780/426-3636 or 800/228-3000, www.westin.ab.ca). The 413 rooms are large and luxurious; $225 single, $235 double, but weekend package deals are almost half-price. Hotel facilities include a large pool, an exercise room, and one of Edmonton's best restaurants.

HOTELS AND MOTELS IN OTHER PARTS OF THE CITY

Calgary Trail

Calgary Trail is an extension of Highway 2 as it enters the city from the south. The following motels are listed from south to north. At the southern city limits and just north of Gateway Park, two inexpensive motels are on the west side of the highway. The best value of these is the **Ellerslie Motel** (1304 Calgary Trail S, 780/988-6406), where rooms are basic but clean and comfortable, some rooms have kitchenettes, and there's a laundry room; $35 single, $40 double. Next door, the **Chateau Motel** (1414 Calgary Trail S, 780/988-6661) offers similar rates.

Continuing north, the next motel you'll encounter on Calgary Trail northbound is the **Trailway Motel** (3815 Calgary Trail N, 780/435-3863), where the rooms have been recently renovated; $44 single, $50 double. Next door is the **Derrick Motel** (3925 Calgary Trail N, 780/438-6060), which is similarly priced.

As you drive north along Calgary Trail, it's impossible to miss the 11-story, pastel-colored **Delta Edmonton South** (4404 Calgary Trail N, 780/434-6415 or 800/661-1122, www.deltahotels.com) towering over the major intersection with Whitemud Drive. Guests are offered a wide variety of facilities and services, including an indoor pool, airport shuttles, and valet parking. Rates start at $110 single or double. Adjacent to the Delta is the **Coast Terrace Inn** (4440 Calgary Trail N, 780/437-6010 or 888/837-7223, www.coastterraceinn.com), another 200-room-plus, full-service hotel; from $104 single or double. Continuing north, the **Holiday Inn The Palace** (4235 Calgary Trail N, 780/438-1222 or 800/565-1222) resembles a modern Banff Springs Hotel from the road. This place features 137 large rooms surrounding a tropical atrium with restaurant and lounge; from $98 single or double.

The **Cedar Park Inn** (5116 Calgary Trail N, 780/434-7411 or 800/661-9461) is a Best Western property with a symmetrical design. Rooms are spacious and reasonably comfortable. Guest facilities include a pool and an exercise room. Rates are $89 single, $99 double. Behind this property is the **Southbend Motel** (5130 Cal-

gary Trail N, 780/434-1418), where guests have access to the recreation facilities at the Cedar Park Inn; $49 single, $54 double.

One of the city's finest accommodations is **The Varscona,** situated in the heart of Old Strathcona (10620 82nd Ave., 780/434-6111 or 888/515-3355, www.varscona.com). The 89 guest rooms are spacious and elegantly furnished with king-sized beds. Rates of $159 single, $169 double include parking, a light breakfast, a daily newspaper, and a wine and cheese tasting each evening.

Northwest of Downtown

Back in the days when the City Centre Airport was a major northern hub, surrounding motels did a roaring trade. Today, with the airport handling mostly charter flights and the city sprawl now extending west along Stony Plain Road, these motels offer good-value rates just a stone's throw from downtown. One of the best is the **Chateau Louis** (11727 Kingsway Ave., 780/452-7770 or 800/661-9843, www.chateaulouis.com). It looks like nothing special from the road, but the spacious rooms are well equiped with everything from VCRs to microwaves. Also on site is a restaurant and a lounge. Rates are from just $79 single or double. Also on the Kingsway is the **Ramada Hotel** (11834 Kingsway Ave., 780/454-5454 or 888/747-4114, www.ramada.ca), $89 single or double.

You'll find a bunch of inexpensive motels along 111th Avenue just west of the Edmonton Space and Science Centre. The best value of these is the **Aladdin Motel** (15425 111th Ave., 780/484-0071 or 888/484-0071). Each of 37 rooms has a small fridge and a microwave; $45 single, $55 double.

Fantasyland Hotel

Within West Edmonton Mall is the 355-room Fantasyland Hotel (17700 87th Ave., 780/444-3000 or 800/661-6454, www.westedmontonmall.com), famous for theme rooms that attract folks from around the world. No catching a cab back to your hotel after a day of shopping here—just ride the elevator to the room of your wildest fantasy. The lavish marble-floored lobby and two life-size lion statues surrounded by glittering lights are only a taste of what's to come upstairs.

Each floor has a theme: the choice is yours—

Hollywood, Roman, Polynesian, Victorian, African, Arabian, Igloo, Canadian Rail, or Truck—where you can slumber in the bed of a pickup truck. Each theme is carried out in minute detail. The Polynesian room fantasy, for example, begins as you walk along a hallway lined with murals depicting a tropical beach, floored with grass matting. You'll walk through a grove of palm trees before reaching your room. In the room, an enormous hot tub is nestled in a rocky grotto, and the bed is shaped like a warrior's catamaran, with a sail as the headboard.

All of this elaborate escapism comes at a cost, with the theme rooms ranging $225–265 per night. Regular guest rooms—without hot tubs and mirrors on the ceiling—are $148 per night. Despite the price, the theme rooms are very popular and are booked full far in advance, so make reservations early.

Vicinity of West Edmonton Mall
In the summer of 2000, the **West Edmonton Mall Inn** (17504 90th Ave., 780/444-9378 or 800/737-3783, www.westedmontonmall.com) opened across the road from the mall. Owned by the same company as the mall, it features 88 well-appointed rooms, each with two comfortable beds, coffeemakers, and Sony Playstations; from $120 single or double.

The next nearest accommodations are strung out to the north along Stony Plain Road. One of these, the three-story **West Harvest Inn** (17803 Stony Plain Rd., 780/484-8000 or 800/661-9993, www.westharvest.com), offers 160 well-appointed air-conditioned rooms; from $79 single or double. Two blocks toward the city is the **Sandman Hotel West Edmonton** (17635 Stony Plain Rd., 780/483-1385 or 800/726-3626, www.sandman.ca), which has recently been renovated and holds an indoor pool, a sauna, and a 24-hour restaurant; $82–92 single, $87–107 double.

North of Stony Plain Road is the **Mayfield Inn** (16615 109th Ave., 780/484-0821 or 800/661-9804, www.mayfield-inn.com), a large complex with 327 rooms, exercise facilities, an indoor pool, a squash court, a restaurant, a lounge, and mall shuttles. Rates range $95–115 single or double, which includes a cooked buffet breakfast.

If you're on a budget and want to stay out by the mall, consider the **Yellowhead Motor Inn,** farther north still (15004 Yellowhead Trail, 780/447-2400 or 800/661-6993), where rooms go for $59 single, $69 double.

BED-AND-BREAKFASTS

B&Bs start at $40 single, $50 double and are scattered throughout the city. Tourist Information Centres keep current listings, or check the back of the *Accommodations* guide.

La Boheme (6427 112th Ave., 780/474-5693) is located in the historic Gibbard building, which originally held Edmonton's first luxury apartments. Today, the La Boheme restaurant downstairs is one of the city's best, and several upstairs rooms have been refurnished and are run as a B&B. The building is certainly charming, right down to its creaky floors. Each of the simply furnished rooms has a kitchenette. Rates are $60–80 single or double.

On the other side of downtown, close to the Provincial Museum, is the **Glenora B&B Inn** (12327 102nd Ave., 780/488-6766). The building that houses this bed-and-breakfast was built as a commercial enterprise in 1912 and has been completely renovated with the guest rooms above a street-level café, restaurant, and wine shop. The rooms have shared or private bathrooms. Rates start at $60 single, $75 double.

HOSTELS AND YMCA

If you've stayed at the **Edmonton International Hostel** in the past, and found it crowded, cramped, and a long way from anywhere, you'll be pleasantly surprised to know that it has moved across the city to much larger premises in the heart of Old Strathcona (10647 81st Ave., 780/988-6836 or 877/467-8336). The building may seem a little clinical at first, but that feeling goes away when you begin to take advantage of the facilities offered. The lounge area is spacious and comfortable, and there's a quiet and private backyard, plenty of space in the kitchen, and off-street parking. Throughout summer, various trips and barbecues are put on, and a desk is set up in the lounge to take bookings for local sights and recreation. Rates are $17 for members of Hostelling International and $22 for nonmembers. From the Greyhound bus depot, walk two blocks east to 101st Street, catch the number 7 Belgravia or number 9 Southgate bus south. Get off at 82nd Avenue, then walk two blocks east and one south, and you're there.

The **YMCA** has an outstanding location, right downtown (10030 102A Ave., 780/421-9622). The rooms are small and sparsely furnished and are available to men, women, couples, and families. Also here are a café and fitness center. Rooms are $36 single, $58 double. The **YWCA** (10305 100th Ave., 780/429-8707) is for women only and has an exercise room and café. Dorm beds are $16.50, private rooms $45.

CAMPGROUNDS

The best camping within the city limits is at the **Rainbow Valley Campground** (13204 45th Ave., 780/434-5531 or 888/434-3991, www. snowvalley.ab.ca). The location is excellent and, as far as city camping goes, the setting is pleasant. Facilities include showers, a laundry room, a barbecue grill, and a cooking shelter. In summer, all sites are full by midday, and phone reservations aren't taken. Grassed tent sites are $15, powered sites $18. To get there, turn south off Whitemud Freeway at 119th Street, then take the first right and follow it into the valley. It's open April 15 to September 30.

South

If you're coming into the city from the south, take Ellerslie Road west from Highway 2 to access the **Klondike Valley Campground** (1660 Calgary Trail SW, 780/988-5067). Located along Blackmud Creek at the southern edge of the city limits, this sprawling campground offers all facilities. Walk-in tent sites are $16, hookups $21–24. In the same general area, although a little farther west, is the **Whitemud Creek Golf and RV Park** (3428 156th St., 780/988-6800,

www.whitemudcreek.com). The 41 fully serviced sites are bunched together in the middle of a nine-hole golf course, which is adjacent to a pleasant little creek. Facilities include a stocked trout pond, modern washrooms, a laundry room, and a clubhouse restaurant. All sites are $25 (no tents). To get there, follow Ellerslie Road three kilometers west from Highway 2, then take 127th Street for three kilometers south, then 41st Avenue for three more kilometers west.

In the town of Devon, a 20-minute drive southwest of the city, is the **River Valley Lions Campground,** 780/987-4777, which lies alongside the North Saskatchewan River and beside a golf course. Sites are $13–21. To get there from Highway 2, take Highway 19 west; from out near West Edmonton Mall, take Highway 60 south from Highway 16.

West

Continue west from West Edmonton Mall to **Shakers Acres** (21530 103rd Ave., 780/447-3564), on the north side of Stony Plain Road. Unserviced sites are $15 and hookups are $19–23. Farther out, in Spruce Grove, is the **Glowing Embers Travel Centre** (26309 Hwy. 16, 780/962-8100). All facilities are modern, and although tents are allowed, they may look out of place among the satellite-toting RVs; all 273 sites are $22.

East

The **Half Moon Lake Resort** (21524 Hwy. 520, 780/922-3045) is situated on the shore of a shallow lake, 30 kilometers from Edmonton. It has a large area set aside for tents ($15) and RVs and trailers ($19–21), but the emphasis is mainly on activities such as fishing, swimming, canoeing, boating, and horseback riding. To get there from downtown, head east on 82nd Avenue to Highway 21, three kilometers east of Sherwood Park, then south to Highway 520, then 10 kilometers east.

FOOD

Eating out in Edmonton used to be identified with the aroma of good ol' Alberta beef wafting from the city's many restaurants, but things are changing. Today, 2,000 restaurants offer a balance of international cuisine and local favorites in all price brackets. From the legendary home-style cooking of Barb and Ernie's to the historic elegance of Madison's Grill, there's something to suit everyone's taste and budget. Restaurants are concentrated in a few main areas. Downtown in the plazas are food courts that fill with office workers, shoppers, and tourists each lunchtime. This part of the city also has some of Edmonton's finest dining establishments. Old Strathcona offers a smorgasbord of choices, with cuisine from all corners of the world. Southbound and northbound along Calgary Trail are family restaurants, buffets, and inexpensive steakhouses.

DOWNTOWN

Coffeehouses
Zenari's in ManuLife Plaza East (10180 101st St., 780/423-5409) is a trendy lunchtime deli hangout known for its variety of sandwiches and freshly prepared soups, as well as coffees from around the world, ground fresh to order. It's closed on Sunday. Near the sights around Edmonton Civic Centre, **Grounds for Coffee** (10247 97th St., 780/429-1920) occupies a good location. In addition to coffee, patrons enjoy sandwiches, ice cream, and the daily newspapers. One block toward the city center, overlooking Churchill Square is **Coffee Mania**, in the Chancery Hall building (corner of 102A Ave. and 99th St.). It's part of Tix on the Square, which sells discounted theater tickets, and it has a few outdoor tables in a shaded courtyard. Eleven **Grabbajabba** cafes are spread throughout the city, including downtown at 10020 101A Avenue, 10250 101st Avenue, and 11210 Jasper Avenue. Near the Jasper Avenue outlet, west of downtown, are a string of other cafés, including the ever-popular **Second Cup**, at number 11210. Next door is the **French Meadows Bakery** (11212 Jasper Ave.), with a few tables separated

from the busy sidewalk by a low partition. **Starbucks** is on the corner of Jasper Avenue and 109th Street.

Cheap Eats
Most of the city's downtown highrises have food courts on their lower levels, where lunch dishes offered by many ethnic outlets begin at approximately $3. For the widest choice, try the food courts in the Eaton Centre, Edmonton Centre, or Canada Place.

If you're staying in one of the city's suite hotels or camping and want to try some Alberta beef without eating out, head to **Queen City Meats** (11104 102nd Ave., 780/426-2575), a specialty butcher open Mon.–Wed. 8 A.M.–6 P.M., Thurs.–Fri. 8 A.M.–8 P.M., Saturday 8 A.M.–6 P.M. Another outlet of fresh produce is **City Market**, near the Chinatown Gate on 97th Street, which sells bakery items, fruits and vegetables, and a variety of meat cuts.

Many of the least expensive restaurants downtown lie in the vicinity of 97th Street. Beside the City Market is **Café Lila's** (10153 97th St., 780/414-0627), which offers lunch dishes ranging from $3–6 in a diner-style atmosphere. Beyond the Chinatown archway is **Kwong Tung** (9630 102nd Ave., 780/424-1595), the only Chinatown restaurant that's made an effort to reflect Chinese architecture (and even then, it's rather ordinary). Stick to the set menus, from $8.25 per person. The **Green Papaya** (9663 101A Ave., 780/420-1008) is a more modern Indonesian/Thai restaurant with most main dishes less than $15. Like most downtown restaurants, Kwong Tung and Green Papaya are closed Sunday.

Surrounded by the city's highest highrises is the **Sherlock Holmes** (10012 101A Ave., 780/426-7784), a charming English-style pub with a shingled roof, whitewashed walls with black trim, and a white picket fence surrounding it. At lunchtime, it is packed with the office crowd. Try traditional British dishes such as Mrs. Hudson's Steak and Kidney Pie ($8), ploughmans ($8.50), liver and onions ($8.50), or fish and chips ($8.50), washed down with a pint of English ale or Guinness stout. It's open Mon.–Sat. from 11:30 A.M.

Canadian

The area along 97th Street has always been Edmonton's own little skid row, but this is changing. Now, it's home to the **Hardware Grill** (9698 Jasper Ave., 780/423-0969), one of the city's finest restaurants. Located at the street level of an early 1900s red-brick building, the white linen and silver table settings contrast starkly with the restored interior. The menu features dishes using a wide variety of seasonal Canadian produce, including pork, lamb, beef, venison, and salmon, all well prepared and delightfully presented. All lunches are less than $15, and dinner entrées run $23–35. The **Harvest Room,** in the Hotel Macdonald (10065 100th St., 780/429-6424), features a menu of Canadian specialties, including Alberta beef, to $32. High tea is served each summer afternoon (make reservations for weekend sittings); $18 per person includes a hotel tour. High tea is also served around the corner at **Madison's Grill,** in the Union Bank Inn (10053 Jasper Ave., 780/423-3600), with a patio and stylish Heritage-themed décor. Throughout the rest of the day, a seasonal menu is offered, using mostly Canadian produce prepared in European style. It's open daily for breakfast, lunch, and dinner, for Sunday brunch, and for high tea each afternoon.

La Ronde (10111 Bellamy Hill, 780/428-6611), atop the Crowne Plaza Chateau Lacombe, is the city's only revolving restaurant. The Canadian-inspired menu features delicacies such as salmon, pheasant, and Alberta beef; main dishes range from $15–27. It's open daily for dinner and for Sunday brunch.

Steakhouses

One of Canada's most renowned steakhouses, **Hy's** (10013 101A Ave., 780/424-4444) is probably also one of Canada's most expensive. The elegant setting, centered around a Tiffany-style skylight, is the perfect place for a splurge. The house specialty is New York strip steaks ($26); only the chicken dishes are less expensive. Also offered is a three-course table d'hôte for $47. It's open for lunch Mon.–Fri. and dinner nightly except Sunday. The **Carvery of Edmonton,** in the Westin Edmonton (10135 100th St., 780/426-3636), is another popular steakhouse at the top end of the market.

Mexican

Downtown's lone Mexican restaurant, **Senor Frogs** (10045 109th St., 780/429-3764), attracts a young crowd with loud music, trendy décor, and meal and drink specials, and is easily spotted by its distinctive medieval-looking facade.

Italian

Among the dozens of Italian restaurants in the city, one of the most popular is **Sorrentino's,** with six city locations including downtown at 10162 100th Street, 780/424-7500, and at 10844 95th Street, 780/425-0960, with the latter in an Italian-dominated area and featuring a cappuccino bar and cigar room. The décor at all locations is stylish, with a great Old World Italian charm. Pastas range from $11–14.50, and the rack of lamb, at $19, is the most expensive dish on the regular menu.

Giovanni's is half a block from Jasper Avenue (10130 107th St., behind Audrey's bookstore, 780/426-2021). This modern Italian restaurant is housed in a distinctive Tuscany-style building with a large tiled patio out front. Inside, the tables are well spaced, and diners look through the restaurant to an open kitchen. The menu is typically modern Italian, with pastas from $13 and specialty dishes from $14.50. It's open weekdays for lunch and Mon.–Sat. for dinner.

The **Sicilian Pasta Kitchen,** located on the western outskirts of downtown (11239 Jasper Ave., 780/488-3838), has a bright, breezy atmosphere, an open kitchen, and a bar. Main dishes at lunch average $8, at dinner $11–18.

Other European Restaurants

As you descend the stairs to **The Creperie** below the Boardwalk Market (10220 103rd St., 780/420-6656), a great smell, wafting from somewhere in the depths of this historic building, hits you in the face. It takes a minute for your eyes to adjust to the softly lit dining area, but once you do, its inviting French provincial atmosphere is apparent. Entrée crepes begin at $8.50, including rice and vegetables. Dessert crepes begin at $5. It's open weekdays for lunch and daily for dinner.

La Tapa (10523 99th Ave., 780/424-8272) is a modern, upbeat Spanish eatery in a restored two-story house. There are approximately 20 tapas to choose from, but I found it difficult to go past the *paella* ($18), a rice-based stew of meats and seafood. The wine list includes many Spanish wines, and Spanish beer is also offered.

Oysters at Midnight

Cafe Select (10018 106th St., 780/423-0419), nestled below a parkade just off Jasper Avenue, gives the first impression of being an upscale, trendy eatery, and to a degree it is. The restaurant is elegant, soft music is played, and a bunch of intellectuals sip wine and eat oysters until two in the morning. But the food is well priced ($10–15 for pasta, steak, or fondue dishes), and no one seems to mind if you stick to just coffee and dessert. Try the chocolate torte ($5.50). The café is open daily until 2 A.M. (midnight on Sunday).

WEST END

De Vine's

This popular eatery is located in a refurbished house overlooking the North Saskatchewan River (9712 111th St., 780/482-6402). Small groups of tables are located in various rooms throughout the house; many tables have river views. Upstairs is a lounge with some outside tables. The menu features lots of Canadian produce prepared in European-influenced dishes. The wide variety of entrées ($11–18) should suit everyone's taste, and you'd better save room for a piece of chocolate-glazed pecan pie ($4.50). De Vine's is open daily 11 A.M.–11 P.M.

A Southern Delight

Louisiana Purchase (10320 111th St., 780/420-6779) serves Cajun and Creole cuisine without overdoing the blackened bit. All the fish and meat are carefully trimmed, doing away with the fat that is so much a part of Southern cooking. Prices are reasonable; entrées begin at $8.50. Open Mon.–Fri. 11:30 A.M.–1 A.M. and Saturday 5 P.M.–midnight, Sunday 5–10 P.M.

Sidetrack Cafe

Directly behind Louisiana Purchase is the Sidetrack Cafe (10333 112th St., 780/421-1326). In addition to some of the city's best live entertainment, the café has a reputation for excellent food. Big, hearty breakfasts cost $4–7.50. Soups, salads, burgers, sandwiches, pizza, and world fare are all on the menu. The soup-and-sandwich lunch deal includes a bottomless bowl of soup. Dinners are served 5–10 P.M. and include such delicacies as Buffalo Meatloaf ($9.50). The café is open Mon.–Fri. from 7 A.M. and on weekends from 9 A.M.; expect a wait for a table for Sunday brunch (10 A.M.–2 P.M.) and most nights.

OLD STRATHCONA

This historic suburb south of downtown offers Edmonton's largest concentration of cafés and restaurants. There's a great variety of choices, and because it's a popular late-night hangout, many eateries are open to the wee hours.

Coffeehouses

The cavernous **Block 1912** (10361 82nd Ave., 780/433-6575) offers a great variety of hot drinks, cakes, pastries, and healthy full meals in an inviting atmosphere, which includes several comfortable lounges. Newspapers from around the world are available. Across the road, the **Bagel Tree** (10354 82nd Ave., 780/439-9604) offers deli treats such as antipasto, hummus, dips, and sandwiches to eat in or go. **Cafe La Gare** (10308 81st Ave., 780/439-2969) is beside Calgary Trail South on one of the busiest sidewalks in Old Strathcona, making it a prime people-watching location. It is bright, airy, gets the morning sun, and is nonsmoking. The **Second Cup** (10402 82nd Ave., 780/439-8097) occupies the prime spot at a busy intersection. Continuing west, upstairs in the Chapters bookstore (10504 82nd Ave., 780/435-1290) is a relaxing café away from the hustle and bustle of Whyte Avenue.

Mexican and Cajun

Julio's Barrio Mexican Restaurant (10450 Whyte Ave., 780/431-0774) is a huge restaurant decorated with earthy colors and Southwestern-style furniture and has a true south-of-the-border ambience. The menu is appealing but limited. If you just want a light snack, try the warm corn chips with Jack cheese and freshly made Ultimate Salsa for $5.25. Main meals are $9–15. Open daily until midnight.

Da-de-o (10548 Whyte Ave., 780/433-0930) is styled on a 1950s diner in New Orleans. The menu features traditional Cajun cuisine, including

Po 'Boys—Southern-style sandwiches using French bread and fillings such as blackened chicken and catfish—as well as *gumbos* (fritters), a delicious chick-pea salad, buckwheat crepes, and many other Southern delights. It's open 11:30 A.M.–midnight. This place attracts a wide cross-section of Old Strathcona residents, such as students and artists; it can get pretty loud when the jukebox is cranked up.

A Chinese Favorite
West of Old Strathcona, toward the University of Alberta, is **Mandarin Restaurant** (11044 82nd Ave., 780/433-8494), consistently voted as having the best Chinese food in the city, but you'd never know by looking at it. It's informal, noisy, family-style dining, and the walls are plastered with sporting memorabilia donated by diners. Most dishes are from northern China, which is known for traditionally hot food, but enough Cantonese dishes are offered to please all tastes. Expect to pay $20 per person for a three-course meal. It's open Mon.–Fri 11:30 A.M.–2 P.M. and daily for dinner from 4:30 P.M.

The Unheardof
Located a few blocks east of the railway tracks, in a renovated shop, is one of Edmonton's most popular restaurants, The Unheardof (9602 82nd Ave., 780/432-0480). The main dining room is filled with antiques, and the tables are set with starched-white linen and silver cutlery. The menu changes weekly, featuring fresh game, homemade chutneys, and relishes during fall, and chicken and beef dishes the rest of the year. Desserts such as Grapefruit Cheesecake with Grand Marnier top off your meal. The food is absolutely mouthwatering. Hours are Tues.–Sat. 5:30–8:30 P.M. Reservations are essential. At the side of the building is The Unheard of Deli, offering casual fare throughout the day.

OTHER PARTS OF THE CITY

Barb and Ernie's: A Local Legend
It's hard to believe that here in the cultural capital of Canada, getting a table at this restaurant sandwiched between auto-body shops and backing onto an abandoned rail line nearly always entails a wait. But such is the case at Barb and Ernie's (9906 72nd Ave., 780/433-3242), an unpretentious southside restaurant with vinyl seats, silver chrome chairs, and photos of Ernie with his hockey heroes. The home-style cooking is hearty and reasonably priced. Ernie will always make you feel welcome. Breakfast is the busiest time of day; omelettes begin at $4.50, and weekend breakfast specials are $5. The rest of the day, hamburgers begin at $2.50, main meals such as roast duck with red cabbage run approximately $12. It's open Mon.–Fri. 6 A.M.–8 P.M., Sat.–Sun. 9 A.M.–8 P.M.

Sawmill Restaurant
The menu at this popular south-of-the-river eatery, The Sawmill Restaurant (4745 Calgary Trail N, 780/436-1950), will suit everyone. An array of seafood, beef, chicken, and pasta dishes (from $14) is complemented by one of the city's best small salad and oyster bars. Most tables are partitioned from each other, and the restaurant is filled with antiques and greenery. The pub next door has live entertainment Thur.–Sat. The Sawmill is open Mon.–Thurs. 11:30 A.M.–2:30 P.M. and 4:30–10 P.M., Fri.–Sat. until midnight, and for Sunday brunch 10:30 A.M.–2 P.M.

La Boheme
La Boheme (6427 112th Ave., 780/474-5693) seems a little out of place, being in the same part of town where Wayne Gretzky made the Edmonton Oilers famous. But here just a five-minute drive east of the city center is one of Edmonton's best restaurants. The restaurant is an ever-changing gallery of French prints. Fresh flowers are placed on every table, the windows are bordered by lace curtains, and above are Edwardian tin ceilings. The classic French menu features fresh game; appetizers begin at $4 (for the thick, healthy soups) or $5 (for the salads); entrées are $11–25. The six-course table d'hôte is $33 per person. The restaurant is open daily 11:30 A.M.–10:30 P.M.

Buffet
Everything a buffet lacks in atmosphere, it usually makes up for in value. Out near the Edmonton Space and Science Centre is the Chinese buffet **Foody Goody** (13310 111th Ave., 780/488-4343). A huge restaurant with more

than 100 choices, Foody Goody features all of the usual Chinese fare, as well as fried chicken, pizza, and a wide variety of desserts, including a dozen or so flavors of ice cream. Dinner is more expensive but includes salmon, roast beef, and mussels or prawns. The food is very hot, so take only small portions (easier said than done). Weekdays the lunch buffet is $6.50, dinner $11, weekend brunch $8, and weekend dinner $12.50. Drinks are extra, but wine and beer are well priced. It's open daily 11 A.M.–10 P.M., closed 3–4 P.M. to prepare for the evening rush.

Cheesecake Cafe
Anyone with a sweet tooth would be proud to be seen at this restaurant. The long, well-presented menu is fine, and many diners come for the main meals, but the main meals here are really the desserts. A cabinet is filled with mouthwatering cheesecakes (from 4.25 per slice) and foot-high cakes that come in all imaginable flavors ($4.75 per slice). Like all of the good spots in town, expect a wait during the usual busy periods. It's open daily 11 A.M.–11 P.M., until 1 A.M. Fri.–Sat. The café's two locations are 17011 100th Avenue, 780/486-0440, and just off Calgary Trail S at 10390 51st Avenue, 780/437-5011.

Greek
A city favorite since the 1970s, **Syrtaki Greek Island Restaurant** (16313 111th Ave., 780/484-2473) is bright and airy, with four split-level dining areas, whitewashed walls, and a colorful Greek village mural encompassing one wall. A belly dancer shimmies up the aisles on Friday and Saturday nights. The extensive menu features dishes from northern Greece and Crete, with entrée prices ranging from $9–17.50. Combination platters for two begin at $25. It's open weekdays for lunch and dinner Mon.–Sat.

TRANSPORTATION

GETTING THERE

Air
Edmonton International Airport (YEG; www.edmontonairports.com) is 29 kilometers south of the city center along Calgary Trail (Hwy. 2). The airport is undergoing massive extensions, with the new terminal that opened in 2000 doubling its size. It includes modern lounge areas, more eating facilities, and a public viewing area. On the **arrivals** level is a small information booth; open year-round, daily 7:30 A.M.–11:30 P.M. Also at the airport are car-rental desks, hotel courtesy phones, a restaurant, and a currency exchange. The **Sky Shuttle**, 780/465-8515, departs the airport for downtown hotels every 20 minutes (every 30 minutes on weekends) on three different routes. One-way to downtown is $11, round-trip $18. The cab fare to downtown is set at $29 one-way. Parking is $1 for 30 minutes to a maximum of $10 for any 24-hour period. Long-term parking is available at other places nearby as well. For a regular-size car, **Airport Parking,** 780/890-7690, charges $7 per day, $34 per week, and $98 per month.

Airlines operating out of the International Airport include **Air Canada,** 780/423-1222 or 888/247-2262; **Air B.C.,** 780/423-1222 or 888/247-2262; **Canada 3000,** 780/425-3000 or 888/816-1168; **Delta,** 800/221-1212; **First Air,** 800/267-1247; **Horizon,** 780/547-9308 or 800/547-9308; and **WestJet,** 800/538-5696.

Before May 1996, domestic flights were routed through Edmonton Municipal Airport, north of downtown. After a few years, the renamed **Edmonton City Centre Airport** has begun to take in the flights of smaller scheduled airlines as well as chartered and private aircraft. Scheduled flights include **Air Miskisew,** 780/414-1029, from Fort McMurray; **Northern Sky,** 800/668-4037, from Grande Prairie; and **Peace Air,** 800/513-3060, from north British Columbia.

A $10 Airport Improvement Fee is built into all tickets for flights departing the international airport.

Rail
The **VIA Rail station** is located close to the city center, downstairs in the CN Tower (10004 104th Ave., 800/561-8630, www.viarail.ca). The ticket office is generally open 8 A.M.–3:30 P.M., later when trains are due. Trains leave Vancouver

(1150 Station St.) and Prince Rupert three times weekly for the grueling 23.5-hour trip to Edmonton (via Jasper), continuing on the Canadian route to the eastern provinces. Before paying full price for your ticket, inquire about off-season discounts (up to 40 percent) and the Canrailpass.

Bus

The **Greyhound bus depot** (10324 103rd St., 780/421-8899 or 800/661-8747, www .greyhound.ca) is within walking distance of the city center, the VIA Rail station, and many hotels. A cab to Edmonton International Hostel from the depot is $18. Within the depot is an A&W Restaurant, a small paper shop, a cash machine, and large lockers ($2). The depot is open 5:30 A.M.–midnight. Buses leave daily for all points in Canada, including Vancouver (15–17 hours, $119.43 one-way), Calgary (3.5 hours, $37.12), and Jasper (4.5 hours, $49.43). No reservations are taken—just turn up, buy your ticket, and hop aboard. Discounts apply if tickets are bought seven days in advance. For extensive travel, the Canada Coach Pass is a good deal (see **Getting There** in the On the Road chapter).

   Red Arrow buses leave Edmonton five to seven times daily for Red Deer ($23) and Calgary ($38) and once daily for Fort McMurray ($49). Buses leave Edmonton from the Howard Johnson Plaza Hotel (10014 104th St.) and on southbound runs pick up at the Cedar Park Inn (5116 Calgary Trail). For more information, call 780/424-3339 or 800/232-1958.

GETTING AROUND

Bus

The **Edmonton Transit System** (ETS) operates an extensive bus system that links the city center to all parts of the city and many major sights. Not all routes operate on Sunday. For many destinations south of the North Saskatchewan River, you'll need to jump aboard the Light Rail Transit (LRT) to the University Transfer Point. Bus fare anywhere within the city is $1.65 during peak hours (5–9 A.M. and 3–6 P.M.), $1.40 at other times; exact fare only. Transfers are available on boarding and can

be used for additional travel in any direction within 90 minutes. A day pass good for one day's unlimited travel is $4.50. For more information and passes, go to the Customer Services Outlet at the Churchill LRT Station on 99th Street (weekdays 8:30 A.M.–4:30 P.M.). For route and schedule information and a list of locations where day passes are sold, call 780/496-1611.

Light Rail Transit

The LRT has 10 stops (Canada's smallest subway system) running east-west along Jasper Avenue (101st Ave.), south to the University, and northeast as far as Whitemud Park. The LRT runs underground through the city center, connecting with many Pedways. Travel between Grandin and Churchill is free Mon.–Fri. 9 A.M.–3 P.M. and Saturday 9 A.M.–6 P.M. LRT tickets are the same price as the bus, and tickets, transfers, and day passes are valid for travel on either the LRT or the bus system.

High Level Street Car

A great way to travel between downtown and Old Strathcona is on the High Level Street Car. Trains and trams originally traveled this historic route over the High Level Bridge, but today a restored street car makes the journey from the west side of the Alberta Legislature Building to Old Strathcona every 15 and 45 minutes past the hour Sun.–Fri. 11 A.M.–4 P.M., Saturday 9 A.M.–4 P.M.; $3 one-way.

Passengers with Disabilities

Edmonton Transit operates the Disabled Adult Transit System (DATS), 780/496-4570, which provides access to various points of the city for physically disabled passengers who are unable to use the regular transit system. The door-to-door service costs the same as Edmonton Transit adult tickets. Priority is given to those heading to work or for medical trips. A Pedway Information Sheet, detailing accessibility, is available from City Hall or by calling 780/424-4085.

Taxi

The standard flag charge for cabs is $2.25 plus approximately $1.40 per kilometer, but most companies have flat rates for major destinations within the city. Major companies are **Checker Cabs,**

780/484-8888; **Alberta Co-op Taxi Line,** 780/425-8310; **Skyline Cabs,** 780/468-4646; and **Yellow Cab,** 780/462-3456.

Car Rental

If you've just arrived in Edmonton, call around and compare rates. Lesser-known agencies are often cheaper, and all rates fluctuate with the season and demand. Many larger agencies have higher rates for unlimited mileage and built-in drop-off charges to nearby centers. All agencies provide free pickup and drop-off at major Edmonton hotels and have outlets at the airport. Rental agencies are **Avis,** 780/423-2847 or 800/879-2847; **Budget,** 780/448-2000 or 800/268-8900; **Discount Car Rentals,** 780/448-3888 or 800/263-2355; **Dollar,** 780/413-8929 or 800/800-4000; **Enterprise,** 780/424-1105 or 800/325-8007; **Hertz,** 780/423-3431 or 800/263-0600; **National,** 780/422-6097 or 800/387-4747; **Rent-A-Wreck,** 780/414-6662 or 800/327-0116; and **Thrifty,** 780/428-8555 or 800/367-2277.

Tours

If you are short on time, or just want to see Edmonton's major attractions, **Royal Tours** has just the answer. The three-hour Capital Tour (Provincial Museum, University of Alberta, river valley, downtown, and West Edmonton Mall; $28) and four-hour Historical Tour (Legislature Building, river valley, and Fort Edmonton Park; $31) leave between 8:30 and 9:30 A.M. from all major hotels. Tours operate mid-May through October. For more information and ticketing details, call 780/435-6069. **Nite Tours,** 780/453-2134, offers theme tours—such as comedy, country, dance, and pub crawls—of the city's nightlife in English double-decker buses; $20 per person.

SERVICES AND INFORMATION

SERVICES

The main **post office** is downtown at 9808 103A Avenue. Public Internet access is free at all city libraries, or you can pay approximately $5 for 30 minutes downtown at the **Bohemia Cyber Café** (11012 Jasper Ave., 780/429-3442). In West Edmonton Mall, head to **Bytes Internet Café** (Bourbon St., 780/444-7833). Main branches of most banks in the downtown area will handle common foreign-currency exchange transactions. The **Thomas Cook Foreign Exchange,** 780/448-3660, is at 10165 102nd Street in ManuLife Place. **Currencies International,** 780/484-3868, is located in West Edmonton Mall at entrance nine beside the Fantasyland Hotel lobby. Edmonton International Airport has a foreign exchange on the departures level. **Carousel Photo Imaging** (10525 Jasper Ave., 780/424-7161) develops print film in an hour and E6 slide film in five hours; it's open Mon.–Fri. 7 A.M.–5:30 P.M. and Saturday 10 A.M.–4 P.M.

On the west side of the city is **LaPerle Homestyle Laundry** (9756 182nd St., 780/483-9200), which is handy to the hotels in the area and with large washers and dryers for sleeping bags. **The Laundry** (10808 107th Ave., 780/424-8981) is closer to downtown. The **Soap Time Laundromat** (7626 104th St., 780/439-3599) is open until 11:30 P.M.

Emergency Services

For medical emergencies, call 911 or one of the following hospitals: **Grey Nuns Community Hospital** (corner of 34th Ave. and 66th St., 780/450-7000); **Northeast Community Health Centre** (14007 50th St., 780/472-5000); **Royal Alexandra Hospital** (10240 Kingsway Ave., 780/477-4111); **University of Alberta Hospital** (8440 112th St., 780/407-8822). For the **Edmonton Police,** call 780/945-5330.

BOOKS AND BOOKSTORES

Downtown Bookstores

Audrey's (10702 Jasper Ave., 780/423-3487) has the city's largest collection of travel guides, western Canadiana, and general travel writing on two vast floors. Open Mon.–Fri. 9 A.M.–9 P.M., Saturday 9:30 A.M.–5:30 P.M., Sunday noon–5 P.M. **Map Town** (10344 105th St., 780/429-2600) stocks the provincial 1:50,000 and 1:250,000 topographical map series along with city maps, world maps, Alberta wall maps, travel guides, atlases, and a huge selection of specialty maps. It's open Mon.–Fri. 9 A.M.–6 P.M., Saturday 10 A.M.–2 P.M.

Old Strathcona Bookstores

Old Strathcona is an excellent place for browsing through used bookstores. **Wee Book Inn** (10310 82nd Ave., 780/432-7230) is the largest and stocks more recent titles and a large collection of magazines. **Alhambra Books** (upstairs at 10309 82nd Ave., 780/439-4195) specializes in Canadiana and has an extensive collection of Albertan material, including pamphlets and newspapers. **Athabasca Books** (8228 105th St., 780/431-1776) stocks mostly history and literature books. **Bjarne's Books** (10533 82nd Ave., 780/439-7123) has older books, including a large selection of hard-to-find western Canadiana and Arctic region material. The **Edmonton Bookstore,** west toward the university (11216 76th Ave., 780/433-1781), also has a large stock of out-of-print books from the region.

Old Strathcona's lone new-book stores are **Greenwood's** (10355 82nd Ave., 780/439-2005), which stocks a lot of everything, and **Chapters** (10504 82nd Ave., 780/435-1290).

Chapters

These are the new mega-bookstores that have sprung up in recent years in major cities, with each of the Edmonton stores boasting more than 100,000 titles, long hours (generally daily 9 A.M.–11 P.M.), and an in-store café. Aside from the Old Strathcona location listed previously, Chapters is at 3227 Calgary Trail S, 780/431-9694, and in West Edmonton Mall, 780/431-9694.

Libraries

The Edmonton Public Library System has 13 libraries spread throughout the city. The largest is the **Stanley A. Milner Library** (7 Sir Winston Churchill Square, 780/496-7000). It's open Mon.–Fri. 9 A.M.–9 P.M., Saturday 9 A.M.–6 P.M., and Sunday 1–5 P.M. This large, two-story facility, connected to the downtown core by Pedways, is a great place to spend a rainy afternoon. It carries newspapers, magazines, and phone books from all corners of the globe, as well as rows and rows of western Canadiana. Throughout the week, author readings take place on the main level. Other locations are **Jasper Place Library,** 9010 156th Street; **Millwoods Library,** 2331 66th Street; **Strathcona Library,** 8331 104th Street (closed Wednesday); and **Highlands Library,** 6710 118th Avenue.

INFORMATION

Edmonton Tourism has information centers at three locations in the city. The largest is in Gateway Park, south of town on Calgary Trail (Hwy. 2). Within this complex, you'll find interpretive displays on the oil industry as well as direct-dial phones for Edmonton accommodations; open in summer daily 8 A.M.–9 P.M., the rest of the year Mon.–Fri. 8:30 A.M.–4:30 P.M. and Sat.–Sun. 9 A.M.–5 P.M.

The most central source of tourist information is on the Pedway Level of the Shaw Conference Centre (9797 Jasper Ave.); staff here at the Economic Development Edmonton office maintain a brochure stand across from their office. On the arrivals level of the Edmonton International Airport is a small booth open year-round daily 7 A.M.–11 P.M. A seasonal center operates at 19001 Stony Plain Road. It's open summer only daily 9 A.M.–5 P.M. For more information on the city, contact Edmonton Tourism, 9797 Jasper Avenue, Dept. MM2000, Edmonton, Alberta T5J 1N9, 780/496-8400 or 800/463-4667, www.tourism.ede.org. Another good website, updated daily with a wide variety of information, is www.foundlocally.com/edmonton.

An excellent source of information on Alberta's provincial parks, forest reserves, and other protected areas is the **Alberta Environment Information Centre,** north of the Legislature Building at 9920 108th Street, 780/422-2079, www.gov.ab.ca/env. It's open Mon.–Fri. 8:15 A.M.–4:30 P.M.

KAREN MCKINLEY

NORTHERN ALBERTA

The northern half of Alberta, from Highway 16 north to the 60th parallel, is a sparsely populated land of unspoiled wilderness, home to deer, moose, coyotes, foxes, lynx, black bears, and the elusive Swan Hills grizzly bear. For the most part, it is heavily forested, part of the boreal forest ecoregion that sweeps around the Northern Hemisphere, broken only by the Atlantic and Pacific oceans. Much of the world's boreal forest has been devastated by logging, but in northern Alberta, a good portion of the land is muskeg—low-lying bogs and marshes that make logging difficult and expensive. Only a few species of trees are adapted to the long, cold winters and short summer growing seasons characteristic of these northern latitudes. Conifers such as white spruce, black spruce, jack pine, fir, and larch are the most common.

This vast expanse of land is relatively flat, the only exceptions being the Swan Hills—which rise to 1,200 meters—and, farther north, the Birch and Caribou mountains. The Athabasca and Peace river systems are the region's largest waterways. Carrying water from hundreds of tributaries, they merge in the far northeastern corner of the province and flow north into the Arctic Ocean. A third major watercourse, the North Saskatchewan River, flows east from the Continental Divide, crossing northern Alberta on its way to Hudson Bay. Alberta's earliest explorers arrived along these rivers, opening up the Canadian West to the trappers, missionaries, and settlers who followed.

Northeast of Edmonton is the Lakeland region, where many early fur-trading posts were established. From there, Highway 63 heads north through boreal forest to Fort McMurray, an isolated city of 40,000, 450 kilometers north of its closest sizable neighbor, Edmonton. Oil is Fort McMurray's raison d'être—oil sands, to be precise. The Athabasca Oil Sands are the world's largest such deposit. To extract just 33 billion barrels will take 500 years at current extraction rates.

North-central Alberta extends from Edmonton's outer suburbs north to the towns of

See color map of Northern Alberta, page xii–xiii.

Athabasca and Slave Lake, which are jumping-off points into the vast boreal forest. This area is a paradise for bird-watchers because it's at the confluence of three major flyways.

West of Edmonton, the Yellowhead Highway climbs into the Canadian Rockies, passing through Hinton, a town surrounded by natural wonders. From Hinton, travelers can continue on Highway 16 into Jasper National Park, or take Highway 40 northwest to Willmore Wilderness Park, a park usually ignored by tourists in favor of the neighboring national parks to the south. Continuing north on Highway 4, you come to Grande Prairie, one of northern Alberta's largest cities and a regional agriculture and service center. The Peace River Valley, north of Grande Prairie, leads travelers into the Northwest Territories via the Mackenzie Highway (Highway 35), which parallels the Peace and Hay rivers.

With few regular "sights," northern Alberta receives fewer tourists than the rest of the province. Those who do venture north find solitude in a vast, untapped wilderness with abundant wildlife and plenty of recreation—lakes and rivers to fish, historic sites to explore, rivers to float on, and gravel roads to drive just for the sake of it.

LAKELAND

Highway 16, east from Edmonton, follows the southern flanks of a region containing hundreds of lakes formed at the end of the last Ice Age by a retreating sheet of ice nearly one kilometer thick. From its headwaters beneath the Columbia Icefield on the Continental Divide, the **North Saskatchewan River** flows east through Edmonton and the Lakeland region before eventually draining into Hudson Bay.

History buffs appreciate the legacies of early white settlers that dot the landscape here—restored fur-trading posts, missions, and the Ukrainian Village near Vegreville. Other visitors are attracted by the region's vast areas of unspoiled wilderness, including seven provincial parks. Anglers will feel right at home among the area's countless lakes, and wildlife-watchers are drawn to Elk Island National Park, which rivals Tanzania's Serengeti Plain for the population densities of its animal inhabitants.

The region's major population centers are Lloydminster (250 kilometers east of Edmonton), Canada's only town in two provinces; St. Paul, which has the world's only UFO landing pad; and Cold Lake, at the edge of the boreal forest, surrounded by vast reserves of untapped oil.

The bison was once king of the plains.

ELK ISLAND NATIONAL PARK

Heading east from Edmonton on Highway 16, you'll soon come to Elk Island National Park. This small, fenced, 194-square-kilometer park preserves a remnant of the transitional grassland ecoregion—the aspen parkland—that once covered the entire northern flank of the prairie. It's also one of the best spots in Alberta for wildlife watching; with approximately 3,000 large mammals, the park has one of the highest concentrations of big game in the world.

The park was originally set aside in 1906 to protect a herd of elk; it's Canada's only national park formed to protect a native species. The elk here have never been crossbred and are probably the most genetically pure in the world. In addition to approximately 1,600 elk, resident mammals include moose, two species of bison, white-tailed and mule deer, coyotes, beavers, muskrats, mink, and porcupines. The many lakes and wetland areas in the park serve as nesting sites for waterfowl, and approximately 230 species of birds have been observed here.

A mosaic of mixed-wood forest—predominantly aspen and balsam poplar—covers the low, rolling Beaver Hills, slowly taking over the grassland. One slow-moving stream winds its way through the park, and many shallow lakes dot the landscape.

Park entry for one day is adults $4, seniors $3 to a maximum of $8 per vehicle; an annual permit for Elk Island is $28 per person to a maximum of $50; and a Great Western Pass, valid for all Alberta and British Columbia national parks, is $35 per person to a maximum of $70.

Bison in the Park

Two different species of bison inhabit the park,

and to prevent interbreeding, they are separated. All bison on the north side of Highway 16 are **plains bison,** whereas those on the south side are **wood bison.**

Before the late 1700s, 60 million plains bison lived on the North American plains. In less than a century, humanity brought these shaggy beasts to the brink of extinction. By 1880, incredibly, only a few hundred plains bison remained. A small herd, owned by ranchers in Montana, was brought north in 1907. They were held at what was then Elk Island Reserve until

Buffalo National Park (since closed) at Wainwright was fenced. When it came time to move the animals from Elk Island, some couldn't be found, and today's herd descended from those well-hidden progenitors. A small part of the herd is kept in a large enclosure just north of the Park Information Centre, whereas others roam freely through the north section of the park. Today they number approximately 630 within the park.

The wood bison, the largest native land mammal in North America, was thought to be extinct for many years —a victim of hunting, severe winters, and interbreeding with its close relative, the plains bison. In 1957, a herd of 200 was discovered in the remote northwestern corner of Wood Buffalo National Park. Some were captured and transported to the Mackenzie Bison Sanctuary in the Northwest Territories and to Elk Island National Park. The herd at Elk Island has ensured the survival of the species, and today it is the purest herd in the world. It is used as breeding stock for several captive herds throughout North America. To view the herd of 420, look south from Highway 16 or hike the Wood Bison Trail.

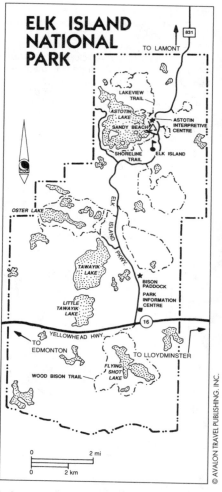

Hiking

Twelve trails, ranging in length from 2.5 to 18.6 kilometers, cover all areas of the park and provide excellent opportunities to view wildlife. A park information sheet details each one. Make sure to carry water with you, though, because surface water in the park is not suitable for drinking. The paved **Shoreline Trail** (three kilometers one-way) follows the shore of Astotin Lake from the golf course parking lot. The **Lakeview Trail** (3.3 kilometers round-trip) begins from the northern end of the recreation area and provides good views of the lake. Hike this trail in the evening for a chance to see beavers. The only trail on the south side of Highway 16 is the **Wood Bison Trail** (18.6 kilometers roundtrip), which has an interpretive display at the trailhead. In winter, the trails provide excellent cross-country skiing and snowshoeing.

Other Recreation and Events

Canoes, rowboats, sailboards, and small sailboats can be rented at Astotin Lake. **Elk Island Golf Course,** an interesting nine-hole layout, is located beside Astotin Lake. Greens fee is $28 for 18 holes; call 780/998-3161 for reservations.

In summer, an array of interpretive talks and walks are held at various locations; ask for details at the Park Information Centre or Astotin Interpretive Centre. Late July brings the **Buffalo Chip Flip Contest** to nearby Lamont, where contestants throw the organic Frisbees and win prizes for accuracy and distance.

Practicalities

The **Sandy Beach Campground** is the only overnight facility within the park. It has firepits, picnic tables, flush toilets, and showers; $14 per night plus $4 for a firewood permit. This facility is open in summer only; the rest of the year, primitive camping (no water, chemical toilets) is available at the boat-launch area. A concession selling fast food and basic camping supplies operates May–October at Astotin Lake, and the golf course has a restaurant, 780/998-3161. The closest motel is five kilometers north of the park in Lamont; **Archie's Motel** (5008 49th Ave., 780/895-2053 or 888/895-2227) charges $40 single, $50 double.

The **Park Information Centre,** 780/992-5790, is located less than one kilometer north of Highway 16 on the Elk Island Parkway; it's open in summer Mon.–Sat. 10 A.M.–6 P.M., Sunday 8 A.M.–8 P.M. The **Astotin Interpretive Centre,** 780/992-6392, farther along the parkway, has a sundeck with telescopes for wildlife viewing, shows a park audiovisual presentation, has interpretive programs, and is the trailhead for a short walk; open in summer Thurs.–Mon. noon–6 P.M. Another source of information is the park radio station (1540 AM). For further information on the park, write to Superintendent, Elk Island National Park, R.R. No. 1, Site 4, Fort Saskatchewan, Alberta T8L 2N7, www.parkscanada.gc.ca.

EAST ALONG THE YELLOWHEAD HIGHWAY

Blackfoot Recreation Area

South of Elk Island National Park is the 97-square-kilometer Cooking Lake–Blackfoot Recreation Area. It is an integrated resource management unit, meaning that it can be used for many purposes, including grazing, mineral exploration, hunting, and recreation. It is part of the massive Cooking Lake Moraine, formed during the last Ice Age as the retreating sheet of ice stalled for a time, leaving mounds and hollows that have since filled with water. Large natural areas of wetland and forest provide habitat for abundant wildlife, including moose, elk, white-tailed deer, coyotes, beavers, and more than 200 species of birds. Much of the well-posted trail system is for hik-

ers only, but some parts are open to horses and mountain bikes. The **Blackfoot Staging Area,** off Highway 16, is the trailhead for a good selection of short hiking trails, but to really get into the heart of the area, head south along the southwestern border of Elk Island National Park to three other staging areas.

Ukrainian Cultural Heritage Village

This site, located 50 kilometers east of Edmonton, is a realistic replica of a Ukrainian settlement, common in the rural areas of east-central Alberta at the turn of the 20th century. The first, and largest, Ukrainian settlement in Canada was located in this region. Driven from their homeland in Eastern Europe, Ukrainians fled to the Canadian prairies where, for many years, they dressed and worked in the ways of the Old World. These traditions are kept alive at the heritage village. Special events are held on the second Sunday in June, the second Sunday in August, and the last Sunday in August. It's open in summer daily 10 A.M.–6 P.M. Admission is $7. For more information, call 780/662-3640.

Vegreville

Although first settled by French farmers from Kansas, this town of 5,200 is best known for its Ukrainian heritage. Today Vegreville's biggest attraction is the world's largest *pysanka,* a giant, traditionally decorated Ukrainian Easter egg at the east end of town. It measures eight meters long, weighs 2,270 kilograms, and can turn in the wind like a giant weathervane.

Vegreville celebrates its multicultural past on the Canada Day (July 1) weekend with the **Ukrainian Pysanka Folk Festival.**

Vermilion

The reddish-colored iron deposits in a nearby river gave this town of 4,200 at the junction of highways 16 and 41 its name. **Vermilion Provincial Park** is one of only two urban-area provincial parks in Alberta. The park encompasses 771 hectares of aspen parkland and grassland along the banks of the Vermilion River (access is from the end of 62nd St.), an ancient glacial meltwater channel. To date, 20 species of mammals and 110 species of birds have been documented here. The park also has 15 kilometers of hiking trails and a campground.

the world's largest pysanka—a Ukranian Easter Egg

The **Vermilion Heritage Museum** (50th Ave., 780/853-6211) features a pioneer home, an extensive photographic collection, and native artifacts; it's open in summer daily 10 A.M.–5 P.M. Across from the town office is a cast-iron mill wheel, one of the only relics retrieved from the Frog Lake Settlement after the massacre in 1885 (see **Frog Lake Massacre**).

LLOYDMINSTER

North America has several "twin cities" that straddle borders (such as Minneapolis and St. Paul), but Lloydminster is the only one that has a single corporate body in two provinces (or states, depending on the case). Approximately 60 percent of the city's 18,500 residents live on the Alberta side, separated from their Saskatchewan neighbors by the main street.

Lloydminster was settled in 1903 by 500 immigrants from Britain, who followed the Reverend George Lloyd to the site of Lloydminster in search of good agricultural land. The community thrived, and when the provinces of Alberta and Saskatchewan were created out of the Northwest Territories in 1905, the town was divided by the new border, which ran along the fourth meridian. It functioned as two separate communities until 1930, when community leaders requested that the two halves be amalgamated into the City of Lloydminster. Farming and cattle ranching form the base of the regional economy, although oil and natural gas play an important role in the city's future.

Sights
The **Barr Colony Heritage Cultural Centre** (in Weaver Park on Highway 16, 306/825-5655) houses the Richard Larsen Museum featuring a collection of artifacts and antiques used by early settlers. Also here, the Imhoff Art Gallery contains more than 200 works of early-1900s artist Count Berthold Von Imhoff. In an adjoining wing is a taxidermy display. The center is open in summer daily 10 A.M.–8 P.M., the rest of the year Wed.–Sun. 1–5 P.M.; admission $3.

The 81-hectare **Bud Miller Park** (south of Hwy. 16 along 59th Ave., 780/875-4497) offers several nature trails winding around a two-hectare lake and through stands of aspen. Canada's largest sundial, a tree maze, formal gardens, an arboretum, a nature center, and boat rentals can also be found here. The park is open year-round daily 7 A.M.–11 P.M.

Events
On the second weekend of July, Lloydminster hosts **Colonial Days**. Its **Heritage Day Festival** takes place in mid-August, and the last week of October is the **Canadian Cowboys Association Rodeo Finals**.

Accommodations
Motels are located along Highway 16 (44th St.), mostly on the Alberta side of the border. The **Cedar Inn Motel,** on the Saskatchewan side (4526 44th St., 306/825-6155), is the least expensive at $32 single, $38 double. Also on the Saskatchewan side of the border, but a better value, is the **Good Knight Inn** (4729 44th St., 306/825-0124), where each of the 37 rooms is air-

conditioned and has a coffeemaker, a small fridge, and a microwave; $40 single, $50 double. The **Tropical Inn** (5621 44th St., 780/825-7000 or 800/219-5244, www.tropicalinns.com) is a large hotel, with a choice of dining facilities, an indoor pool and water slides, and 150 basic rooms from $52 single, $56 double. The **West Harvest Inn** (5614 44th St., 780/875-6113 or 800/661-7221) offers similar facilities but is more expensive; $65 single, $70 double.

Weaver Park Campground (behind the Barr Colony Centre, 780/825-3726) has showers and a grocery store; unserviced sites $11, powered sites $16. Much nicer is **Rolling Green**

Fairways, 780/875-4653, located two kilometers west of the city on Highway 16, then one kilometer north. Facilities include showers, a laundry room, and an adjacent golf course; tents $10, hookups $16–18.

Food

The **Teahouse Antiques and Collectibles,** 306/825-9498, is located on the south side of Highway 16, just east of the border post. The teahouse was built in 1942 and is surrounded by well-established gardens. Afternoon tea and light lunches are served April–Dec. Tues.–Sat. 10 A.M.–6 P.M. At the opposite end

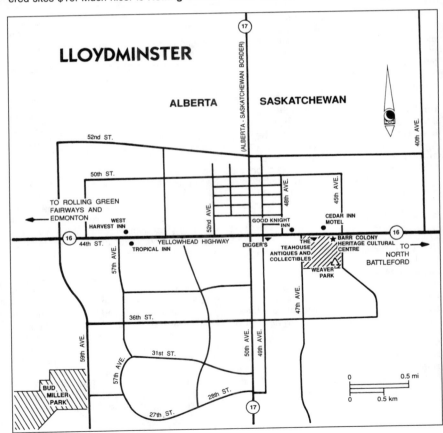

LIVING IN LLOYDMINSTER

Living in a town in two provinces can be confusing. The liquor store on the Alberta side is always busier—Alberta's booze is cheaper—except, of course, during one of Alberta's all-too-frequent beer strikes, when the Saskatchewan store gets the trade. The minimum drinking age is 19 in Saskatchewan, but 18-year-olds can just cross the road into Alberta to drink. The minimum wage is higher in Saskatchewan and vacations are longer, but income tax is higher. In theory Saskatchewan retailers charge five percent provincial sales tax on many goods, unless of course you can prove they will be used or consumed outside of the province. Telephones are serviced by an Albertan company. Power is supplied by two companies; those on the Alberta side get a rebate. Albertans pay a monthly fee for health care, even though the hospital is in Saskatchewan. The best strategy might be to live in Alberta and work in Saskatchewan; houses on the Alberta side are up to 30% more expensive, but the province has lower taxes, and with a job in Saskatchewan—where the benefits are better—you'd come out in front eventually.

of the cholesterol scale is **Digger's Roadhouse** (4301 49th Ave., 306/825-7979), where, although it may seem so at first, you don't have to wear a cap saying "I Love My Mother-in-law" to be served promptly.

Information
The **Saskatchewan Visitor Reception Centre** (beside the Barr Colony Centre, 306/825-5488) has information on the town but is mainly a source of information for those heading east; open in summer daily 8 A.M.–8 P.M. A **Travel Alberta Information Centre,** for those entering the province from the east, is located one kilometer east of town on the north side of the highway; it's open mid-May to mid-June daily 9 A.M.–6 P.M. and through summer daily 8 A.M.–7 P.M.

HIGHWAY 28 TO ASHMONT

Highway 28 leaves Edmonton heading north through the suburbs. After a series of 90-degree turns—first one way, then the other, then back again—it comes to **Waskatenau,** where it straightens out to pursue an easterly heading toward Cold Lake.

Long Lake Provincial Park
During the last Ice Age, the low-lying area occupied by this 764-hectare park was part of a deep glacial meltwater channel. Today it's surrounded by boreal forest, although aspens predominate in the park because of fires over the years. Fishing is great here because the main body of water holds some lunker northern pike, as well as perch and walleye. Right on the lake is a 220-site campground with flush toilets, showers, a grocery store, and canoe rentals; unserviced sites $13; powered sites $15. To get there from Highway 28, head north from Waskatenau on Highway 831 for 48 kilometers.

Immediately to the south of the park is the **White Earth Valley Natural Area,** a 2,055-hectare tract of land set aside to protect the habitat of the abundant wildlife and waterfowl.

Smoky Lake
Named for a lake 93 kilometers west of St. Paul, where natives once rested and smoked pipes during hunts, this small town is home to the **Great White North Pumpkin Fair & Weigh-off,** an annual competition to find the world's largest pumpkin. Weigh-offs are held the same weekend at select locations around the world, with the winner from Smoky Lake winning $1,400 and a trophy and the world's heaviest winning US$2,000. But don't waste time scanning the vegetable section at your local supermarket for a winner; you'll need a pumpkin weighing at least 340 kilograms (750 pounds) to take the day at Smoky Lake (the world record is 513 kilograms). For those who don't consider size important, there's always a prize for the ugliest pumpkin (officially, only "aesthetically challenged" pumpkins can be entered, appeasing the politically correct) and the pumpkin that's traveled the farthest. Celebrations take place the first weekend of October out at the agricultural complex at the junction of highways

28 and 855. The official weigh-in takes place on Saturday at noon and is followed by a pig roast and, on Sunday, the Pumpkin Classic Golf Tournament. For details, call 780/656-3674.

Victoria Settlement

Victoria Settlement is 21 kilometers south and east of Smoky Lake, on the north bank of the North Saskatchewan River. Founded as a mission in 1862, the settlement originally consisted of a small house, a church, and a school. In 1864, the Hudson's Bay Company established a fur-trading post at the site. The clerk's 1864 log house still stands, 100 years after the last beaver pelt changed hands. The trading post closed in 1897 and was abandoned until the early 1900s, when groups of Ukrainian settlers moved to the area and the settlement became known as Victoria-Pakan. When the railway bypassed the settlement in 1918, businesses moved north to Smoky Lake, and the area was abandoned once again. The Pakan Church is open in summer daily 10 A.M.–8 P.M. and presents a short slideshow about the settlement. Paved trails lead to the clerk's house, to the river (where traders came ashore), and to the site of the McDougall Mission and the graves of the founder's three daughters. Picnic tables are set among broad maple trees, which were planted during the fur-trading days. For more information on the site, call 780/645-6256.

From Victoria Settlement, you can continue south on Highway 855, which eventually intersects Highway 16 west of Vegreville. Along the way, you'll pass by **Andrew,** home of the world's largest mallard duck. Be careful not to rip your jeans climbing the fence to touch it.

East to Ashmont

East from Smoky Lake, Highway 28 passes **Vilna**—home of the world's largest mushrooms—and skirts many lakes with excellent swimming, fishing, and boating. **Garner Lake Provincial Park,** four kilometers north of Spedden, is a 74-hectare park with a sandy beach and fishing for northern pike, perch, and pickerel; camping is $13. At **Ashmont,** highways 28 and 28A split, with Highway 28 dipping south to St. Paul and 28A continuing east to Bonnyville and Cold Lake (see **Northeast toward Cold Lake**).

SOUTHEAST TO ST. PAUL AND BEYOND

St. Paul

This town of 5,000 gets very few visitors from outer space. Ordinarily, that wouldn't be surprising, except that here they are encouraged to drop by. You guessed it (or maybe you didn't), St. Paul has the world's only UFO landing pad—a raised platform beside the main road forlornly waiting for its first visitor. The town's origins date to 1896, when Father Albert Lacombe, the famed Western missionary, established a settlement where Métis people—who had been largely ignored by the government during treaty talks—could live and learn farming skills. Lacombe extended an open invitation to all Métis in western Canada, but fewer than 300 responded. After 10 years of hardship, he opened the settlement to whites, attracting people from many cultures. The town's diverse background is cataloged at the **St. Paul Culture Centre** (4537 50th Ave., 780/645-4800); open in summer Mon.–Fri. 8:30 A.M.–4:30 P.M. The **Old Rectory** (5015 47th St.) looks much as it would have when it was built in 1896. At the south end of town (head down 47th St.) is **Upper Therien Lake.** More than 200 species of birds have been recorded around this and other nearby lakes. A large stretch of land along Lakeshore Drive has been set aside as a park with picnic shelters and paths leading out to the lake.

King's Motel (5638 50th Ave., 780/645-5656 or 800/265-7407) has good rooms for $40 single, $50 double. The **Municipal Campground** (55th St. at 49th Ave.), which has showers, is located a short walk from the golf course; unserviced sites $9, powered sites $12. **Westcove Municipal Recreation Area,** 16 kilometers north of St. Paul, 780/645-6688, is beside a beach on the shore of Vincent Lake and has all facilities; unserviced sites $8, powered sites $10.

Corfou Restaurant (5010 50th Ave., 780/645-2948) has a pleasant atmosphere and is managed by a friendly character. Pasta and other southern European dishes range from $8–15; seafood and grills start at $10 but tend to be smaller portions. The **Tourist Information Centre** (50th Ave. at 53rd St., 780/645-6800) is a raised, circular structure behind the UFO landing pad; if approaching from outer space, look for the green flashing light on top. Hours are daily 9 A.M.–5 P.M.

Twenty-eight kilometers east of St. Paul, Highway 28 makes a 90-degree left turn at its junction with Highway 41 and resumes its northeasterly course toward Cold Lake. Those heading back to Highway 16 can turn right at this junction and either beeline directly south on Highway 41 to Vermilion or wind around the backwoods to Lloydminster, taking in the following sights.

Fort George/Buckingham House

Nine kilometers south of Highway 28 is the junction of highways 41 and 646 at **Elk Point** (look for a large mural outlining the history of the area along 50th Avenue and an 11-meter statue of explorer Peter Fidler at the north end of town). Turn left (east) onto Highway 646, and soon you'll come to Fort George and the Buckingham House.

The site of these two fur-trading posts on the north bank of the North Saskatchewan River, 13 kilometers east of Elk Point, has been designated a Provincial Historical Site. In 1792, soon after the North West Company had established Fort George, the Hudson's Bay Company followed suit a few hundred meters away with Buckingham House. Both posts were abandoned in the early 1800s and have long since been destroyed; depressions in the ground, piles of stone, and indistinct pathways are all that remain. Above the site is an interpretive center with audio and visual presentations explaining the rivalry between the two companies and the history of the forts. Interpretive trails lead from the center down to the river. It's open mid-May to September daily 10 A.M.–6 P.M. Admission is $3. For more information, call 780/724-2611.

Whitney Lakes Provincial Park

Whitney, Ross, Laurier, and Borden lakes are the namesake attractions at this 1,490-hectare park on Highway 646. The fishing is excellent in all lakes but Borden. Because the park is located in a transition zone, plant, mammal, and bird species are diverse. A mixed forest of aspen, white spruce, balsam poplar, and jack pine grows on the uplands, whereas black spruce and tamarack grow in lower, wetter areas. Beavers are common—look for their ponds on the north side

of Laurier Lake. Other resident mammals include porcupines, white-tailed deer, coyotes, and, during berry season, black bears. Birds are abundant, especially waterfowl and shorebirds. A 1.5-kilometer interpretive trail starts at the day-use area at the northeast corner of Ross Lake. Fishing is best for northern pike, perch, and pickerel.

Within the park are two campgrounds totaling more than 200 sites. **Ross Lake Campground** has 149 powered sites on six short loops around the south and eastern shore of the lake. Coin-operated showers are located between loops A and B. Whitney Lakes Campground is smaller and has no showers but does have power hookups. A trail along the shore links both campgrounds. All sites are $18.

Vast reserves of salt, west of Whitney Lakes, are harvested by the **Canadian Salt Company,** based at Lindbergh. Hour-long tours of the factory are available on weekdays 9 A.M.–3 P.M.; call ahead to 780/724-3745.

Frog Lake Massacre

OnApril 2, 1885, a band of Cree led by Chief Big Bear massacred nine whites in a remote Hudson's Bay Company post on Frog Lake. It was an act of desperation on the part of the Cree. The great buffalo herds had been devastated, and the fur trade was coming to an end. Big Bear had been forced into signing land treaties to prevent his people from starving. Life on reserves didn't suit the nomadic Cree, and they yearned to return to the old ways. Exactly what sparked the massacre remains unknown, but word of confrontations farther east may have encouraged the Cree. Historians believe the natives originally planned to take hostages, but when Tom Quinn, the post's Indian agent, refused native orders, a shooting spree took place.

The site is marked by a small graveyard and a series of interpretive panels outlining the events leading up to the massacre. To get there from Whitney Lakes, continue east on Highway 646 to its junction with Highway 897. Follow 897 north to the small hamlet of **Frog Lake.** At the Frog Lake General Store, head east for three kilometers to a slight rise, then south at the crest.

To Lloydminster

From Frog Lake, get back on Highway 646 and follow it east to Highway 17 at the native community of **Onion Lake.** Highway 17 parallels the border 26 kilometers south to Lloydminster.

NORTHEAST TOWARD COLD LAKE

Highway 28A
Highway 28A leaves Ashmont and bisects Upper and Lower Mann lakes (best fishing is in Upper Mann Lake on the *south* side of the road).

Twenty-five kilometers farther east is a turnoff to **Glendon.** Glendon's claim to fame takes the cake, or actually the pyrogy—it has the world's largest pyrogy. This indigestible part of the Ukrainian diet (something like boiled potato, or onion-filled ravioli) can be sampled next to Pyrogy Park in the Pyrogy Park Cafe, opposite the Pyrogy Motel on Pyrogy Drive.

Bonnyville
Originally called St. Louis de Moose Lake, this town of 5,000 is an agriculture center surrounded by many good fishing and swimming lakes, including **Moose Lake,** to the west, and **Muriel Lake,** to the south. The town is situated on the north shore of **Jessie Lake,** where more than 300 species of waterfowl and shorebirds have been recorded. Spring and fall are the best viewing times, although many species are present year-round, nesting in the marshes and aspen parkland surrounding the lake. Numerous viewing platforms, linked by the **Wetlands Nature Trail,** are scattered along Lakeshore Drive and Highway 41.

All of Bonnyville's tourist facilities, including motels, are located along the main highway. The **Tourist Information Centre,** 780/826-7807, is at the west end of town. It's open in summer Mon.–Sat. 10 A.M.–8 P.M., Sunday 10 A.M.–5 P.M.

Moose Lake Provincial Park
Moose Lake is a large, shallow body of water between highways 28A and 660. One of Alberta's earliest trading posts was built in 1789 on the shore of Moose Lake by Angus Shaw, of the North West Company. All that remains of the post is a pile of rocks and a depression just west of Moose Lake River (which forms the park's western boundary). In 1870, a smallpox epidemic wiped out the local Cree—they're buried on the west side of Deadman's Point.

Access to the lake is possible from many directions, but the 736-hectare provincial park is on the lake's north shore. All but Deadman's Point has been affected by fire and is reforested with jack pine and dense forests of aspen and birch. Ground squirrels and coyotes are common, and black bears occasionally wander through. The park's namesake, however—moose—are long gone. The lakeshore is a good place to explore, with trails leading either way from the day-use area to good sandy beaches. Another trail leads to the tip of Deadman's Point and to a bog that is home to many species of birds. Fishing in the lake is best for northern pike, perch, and walleye. The small campground has 59 sites on two loops, both of which have access to the beach; unserviced sites $15, powered sites $18.

COLD LAKE

At the end of Highway 28, a little less than 300 kilometers northwest of Edmonton, is Cold Lake (pop. 12,000). In 1997, the administration of three existing towns—Cold Lake, Grand Centre, and Medley—amalgamated, but only seven kilometers separates what are now known as North Cold Lake and South Cold Lake, but still collectively referred to as simply Cold Lake. The area you'll want to visit is North Cold Lake, on the south shore of Alberta's seventh-largest lake. This historic town has a large marina and is close to Cold Lake Provincial Park. The town that is still marked on most maps as "Medley"—now part of South Cold Lake—is, in fact, only the name of the post office at **Canadian Forces Base Cold Lake**—Canada's largest jet-fighter base, whose training range occupies a large tract of wilderness to the north. More than 5,000 military personnel and their families live on the base. The other part of South Cold Lake is a large service and residential area formerly known as Grand Centre. At the town's main intersection is a CF-104 Starfighter donated by the base in recognition of the ties between the communities.

Generations of Chipewyan Indians hunted and trapped in the area, and both major fur-trading companies had established posts on the lake, but the population didn't boom until after World War II. In 1952, Canadian Forces Base (CFB) Cold Lake was established. The base continues to expand, but the area's future economic growth is tied to its large deposits of oil sands.

Cold Lake Oil Sands

The heavy oil found northwest of Cold Lake is similar to that of the Athabasca Oil Sands at Fort McMurray, but the extraction process is different. The oil-rich sands lie in a 50-meter-thick band nearly a half kilometer underground, making surface mining impractical. Instead, steam is pumped into the reservoir, thinning out the tarlike bitumen, which is then pumped to the surface and piped to Edmonton. This process, known as cyclic-steam simulation, is still in its developmental stages and is very expensive, but many of the major players in the North American oil market have leases around Cold Lake.

Alberta's Seventh-Largest Lake

Cold Lake is part of what was once a much larger lake, a remnant of the last Ice Age. Today

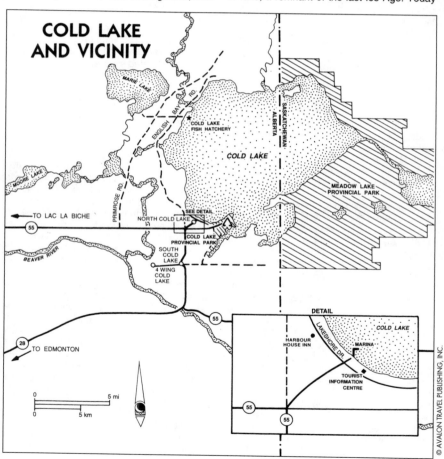

© AVALON TRAVEL PUBLISHING, INC.

the lake is approximately 22 kilometers wide, 27 kilometers long, has a surface area of 370 square kilometers, and reaches depths of 100 meters. Its surface is frozen for five months of the year and doesn't break up until early May; the tackle shop at the marina has a sheet pinned to the wall showing breakup dates for the last 50 years. Fishing in the lake is best for northern pike, lake trout, and walleye.

North Cold Lake, on the south shore, is the center of most activity on the lake. The marina at the end of the main street, 780/639-3535, rents boats and fishing tackle; four-meter boats with small outboard engines are $10 per hour and $70 per day. **Hook, Line, and Sinker Fishing Tours,** 780/594-3474, offers varying packages in a modern 5.5-meter fishing boat. Charters are from $15 per person per hour for two people, but it's least expensive for four, when a full day of guided fishing is a reasonable $55 per person. The best beaches are on the northwestern shore of the lake at **English Bay. Kinosoo Beach,** along Lakeshore Drive, is also popular.

The **Cold Lake Fish Hatchery,** 780/639-4087, is one of five facilities in Alberta where fish hatched at Calgary's Sam Livingston Fish Hatchery are raised to stock lakes throughout the province. It's open for self-guided tours daily 10 A.M.–3 P.M. To get there, take Highway 55 eight kilometers west of Cold Lake, then Primrose Road 15 kilometers north, then head two kilometers east.

Cold Lake Provincial Park

This 399-hectare park is located on a low isthmus of land east of town along 16th Avenue. Although the beaches are much nicer on the northwestern shore of the lake, fishing is excellent here, and the park holds many interesting places to explore. A diversity of plant species grows in the park, thanks to its location in a transition zone between boreal forest and aspen parkland. Balsam fir and white spruce dominate the northern end of the peninsula, whereas stands of aspen and birch can be found to the south. The dominant natural feature of the park is **Hall's Lagoon,** on the northwest side of the isthmus. The lagoon is very shallow, and thick vegetation lines its banks. This is the best place for viewing birdlife. More than 40 species of mammals also inhabit the area, including

muskrats, mink, water shrews, and moose. Within the park are many short hiking trails, most radiating from the campground and day-use area. The campground has coin-operated showers, firewood sales, a beach, summer interpretive programs, and is open year-round; unserviced sites $13, powered sites $15.

Call of the Wild Horn Music Festival

Each year, on the first weekend of September at a time when thousands of birds are migrating over Cold Lake and fall colors are at their most spectacular, the town hosts a weekend-long festival of horn music. Festivities include performances—by solo artists as well as groups—and a dinner featuring the best in local game. A package, including all events, accommodations, and meals, is $160 single, $220 double. For details, call 780/840-8000.

Accommodations

On the shore of Cold Lake North, a short stroll from town, is the **Harbour House Inn** (615 Lakeshore Dr., 780/639-2337), one of Alberta's finest bed-and-breakfasts. Each of the 11 rooms is tastefully decorated in a unique theme. The Hearts Afire room is decorated in pastel colors and has a lake view, a fireplace, a bath, and a magnificent mahogany canopy bed that you need a stepping stool to get into. Rooms range $60–80 single, $70–100 double; you'll need reservations in summer. Also in Cold Lake North is the **Frontier Motel** (1002 8th Ave., 780/639-3030), with rooms for $40 single, $50 double. In Cold Lake South, the **Imperial Motor Inn,** 780/594-7133, features 72 large, well-furnished rooms, as well as a restaurant, a lounge, and a nightclub. Rates start at $48 single, $55 double.

Along 1st Avenue, past Kinosoo Beach, is the **Cold Lake Municipal Campground,** 780/639-4121, a resort-style place where most sites are taken by families who stay the summer; unserviced sites $11, powered sites $13, lakefront sites with power $15. Other options are located east at **Cold Lake Provincial Park** and west along Highway 55, where numerous gravel roads head north to primitive campgrounds (kitchen shelters, firewood, pit toilets); the best of the bunch is at **English Bay** on the northwest shore of Cold Lake.

Food
Harbour House Inn, along Lakeshore Drive, has an adjoining teahouse that is open each afternoon with a changing menu of mouthwatering desserts to accompany tea and coffee. In Cold Lake South, the **Imperial Dining Room** (in the Imperial Motor Inn, 780/594-7133) has a large family-style restaurant that is open for breakfast, lunch (buffet), and dinner.

Services and Information
Greyhound buses depart daily from the Cold Lake South depot (5504 55th St., 780/594-2777) for the five-hour run to Edmonton. In Cold Lake North, the **post office** is at 913 8th Avenue. The only **laundromat** is at the Husky gas station in Cold Lake South. The **Cold Lake Health Centre** is at 314 25th Street, through Cold Lake North to the west, 780/639-3322.

Cold Lake North has a small **information center** in an A-frame building on Lakeshore Drive; open in summer daily 9 A.M.–8 P.M., 780/639-2999 or 800/661-8747.

LAC LA BICHE

The historic town of Lac La Biche (pop. 2,600) is located on the southern flanks of the boreal forest, 225 kilometers northeast of Edmonton. The town itself has little of interest, but nearby you'll find a restored mission, two interesting provincial parks, many excellent fishing lakes, one of northern Alberta's finest golf courses, and a gravel road that may, or may not, get you to Fort Mc-Murray.

The town lies on a divide that separates the Athabasca River System, which drains into the Arctic Ocean, from the Churchill River System, which drains into Hudson Bay. The historic Portage La Biche, across this strip of land, was a vital link in the transcontinental route taken by the early fur traders. Voyageurs would paddle up the Beaver River from the east to Beaver Lake and portage the five kilometers to Lac La Biche, from where passage could be made to the rich fur-trapping regions along the Athabasca River. In 1798, David Thompson built Red Deer Lake House for the North West Company at the southeast end of the lake. Soon after, Peter Fidler built Greenwich House nearby for the Hudson's

Bay Company. By the early 1820s, this northern route across the continent was virtually abandoned for a shorter route along the North Saskatchewan River via Edmonton House.

Lac La Biche Mission
The mission was established beside the Hudson's Bay Company post in 1853 and was moved to its present site, 11 kilometers northwest of Lac La Biche, in 1855. It became a base for priests who had missions along the Athabasca, Peace, and Mackenzie rivers and was used as a supply depot for voyageurs still using the northern trade route. The parish expanded, adding a sawmill, a gristmill, a printing press, and a boat-building yard. Today, the original buildings still stand, and services take place each Sunday in the church. A free, guided tour takes one hour, or you can wander around the buildings yourself. It's open in summer daily 10 A.M.–6 P.M.; for more information, call 780/623-3274.

Practicalities
La Biche Inn (101st Ave., 780/623-4427 or 888/884-8886) has a restaurant and a nightclub where the disc jockey sits in a big rig; $54 single, $60 double. The closest campgrounds are east and north of town in the two provincial parks (see following section). **Spruce Point Resort,** 780/623-3930, is a full-service RV park on Beaver Lake, three kilometers east and nine kilometers south of town; sites are $14–16. One block west of the Almac Motor Inn is a small **Tourist Information Centre,** 780/623-4804. It's open in summer daily 10 A.M.–6 P.M.

VICINITY OF LAC LA BICHE

Sir Winston Churchill Provincial Park
Located on the largest of nine islands in Lac La Biche, this unique 239-hectare park was linked to the mainland in 1968 by a 2.5-kilometer causeway. A road around the island leads through a lush, old-growth coniferous forest. The trees on the island are much larger than those found on the mainland as a result of little disturbance from people and no major fires in more than 300 years. As they come to the end of their 65-year lifespan, the aspen and poplar that dominate younger boreal forests are replaced by balsam

fir. Many fir trees are 150 years old and reach a height of 23 meters. Along the loop road, short trails lead to sandy beaches (the best on the northeast side of the island), marshes rich with birdlife, and a bird-viewing platform where a mounted telescope lets you watch white pelicans and double-crested cormorants resting on a gravel bar. A campground with showers is located on the south side of the island; $11.

Lakeland Provincial Park

Encompassing 60,000 hectares of boreal forest that is mostly in its natural state, this park and an adjacent recreation area are a wildlife-watcher's paradise that includes 11 major lakes.

black bear

Deer, moose, beavers, red foxes, lynx, coyotes, a few wolves and black bears, and more than 200 species of birds can be spotted in the area. A colony of great blue herons, Alberta's largest wading bird, lives at **Pinehurst Lake,** 27 kilometers off Highway 55. Fishing in the lakes is excellent for northern pike and walleye. Those with their own canoes can get out on the water for a real wilderness experience.

Campgrounds are located at **Pinehurst, Ironwood, Seibert,** and **Touchwood lakes.** Each site has pit toilets, kitchen shelters, and firewood sales; $9–13 per night. Several routes access the two areas; head east from Lac La Biche or north from Highway 55.

FORT MCMURRAY AND VICINITY

This city of 39,000, 450 kilometers north of Edmonton, has grown around the Athabasca Oil Sands, the largest deposit of oil in the world and more than all of the proven reserves of Saudi Arabia, the United States, and Western Europe combined. The oil is not conventional oil but a heavy oil, commonly called bitumen. Extracting it is expensive, and once on the surface, it must be chemically altered to produce a lighter, more useful oil. This process, in stark contrast to other operations where the oil is simply brought to the surface and shipped or piped around the world, requires an enormous amount of machinery and labor.

Fort McMurray is a long drive from anywhere else and has little of interest except for the mining operation, but it is surrounded by a wilderness that would be difficult to access without the services of the city.

To Fort McMurray

For many years, the only way to get to Fort McMurray was by airplane or the Muskeg Express, a rail service to Edmonton. Today, a paved highway (Hwy. 63), as good as any in the province, has replaced the rail line. It parallels, but never crosses, the Athabasca River, which cuts deeply into the boreal forest, covering the entire northern

half of the province. From its southern terminus (at the junction of Hwy. 55, between Lac La Biche and Athabasca) to Fort McMurray, only two small communities hug the highway. The first is **Wandering River,** a small lumber and service town with gas, a motel, and a 24-hour restaurant. The Alberta Forest Service maintains campgrounds 13, 58, and 76 kilometers north of Wandering River. Each has a water source, pit toilets, kitchen shelter, and firewood; $7 per night. Along the route are many roadside fens and areas ravished by fire, where the cycle of natural reforestation has just begun.

Mariana Lake, a little more than halfway to Fort McMurray, has the same services as Wandering River. Just south of town is **Mariana Lake Recreation Area,** which, although beside the highway, has a good campground; also $7 per night.

History

In 1870, Henry Moberly opened a trading post on the Athabasca River and named it after the chief factor of the Hudson's Bay Company, William McMurray. The post quickly gained popularity as a transportation hub and for trading with Cree and Chipewyan natives. The natives first reported oil oozing from the sand here, but it took

FORT McMURRAY

TO FORT McKAY

THICKWOOD BLVD.

63

FORT McMURRAY

ATHABASCA RIVER

MISKANAW GOLF COURSE

MacDONALD ISLAND

CLEARWATER RIVER

SEE DETAIL

MAIN ST.

RED ARROW

FRANKLIN AVE.

PARK PLAZA MALL

ABASAND DR.

HOSPITAL

HOSPITAL ST.

CENTENNIAL DR.

TOLEN DR.

GREYHOUND BUS DEPOT

KEYANO COLLEGE

HERITAGE PARK

63

BEACON HILL DR.

CENTENNIAL PARK

GREGOIRE DR.

MACKENZIE PARK INN

BEST CANADIAN MOTOR INN

ALBERTA FORESTRY RANGER STATION

VISITORS BUREAU

OIL SANDS DISCOVERY CENTRE

SAWRIDGE HOTEL

MACKENZIE BLVD.

TO AIRPORT AND ROTARY PARK CAMPGROUND

TO GREGOIRE LAKE P. P. AND EDMONTON

63 69

DETAIL

63

MACDONALD AVE.

MORRISON ST.

FRAZER AVE.

PODOLLAN INNS

FRANKLIN AVE.

MAIN ST.

MANNING AVE.

OIL CAN TAVERN

TWIN PINE MOTOR INN

CEDAR STEAK HOUSE

NOMAD INN

BIGGS AVE.

GARDEN CAFE

LIBRARY

POST OFFICE

HARDIN ST.

PETER POND SHOPPING CENTRE

63

TRAVELODGE HOTEL

0   0.5 mi

0   0.5 km

© AVALON TRAVEL PUBLISHING, INC.

a long time for anyone to gain commercial success from extracting it. For the first half of the 20th century, the town experienced little growth. But in 1964, the first oil-sands plant was built, and 10 years later a second company began operation. Between 1974 and 1994, the population mushroomed from 1,500 to 36,000 as personnel from around the world came to work at the plants, attracted by high wages. At first the population was young and transient; they made their money and left. But today the city has an air of permanence about it. As new subdivisions are carved into the boreal forest, suburbs of respectable three-bedroom homes are springing up, and downtown looks similar to hundreds of midsize cities across Canada. The city is now part of the Region of Wood Buffalo, North America's largest municipality at 67,104 square kilometers.

Athabasca Oil Sands

Only 800 billion barrels of conventional crude oil are known to remain on this planet, but trapped in the Athabasca Oil Sands surrounding Fort McMurray are an estimated 1.3 trillion barrels of bitumen. As conventional crude-oil reserves are depleted, the sands will become essential to the world's future energy needs. At current production rates (250,000 barrels a day or 25 percent of Canada's total daily oil production), it will take 500 years to extract just 3 percent of the deposit.

As the name implies, the deposits are of highly compacted sand containing heavy oil or bitumen. The oil-rich sand is found both close to the surface—beneath a layer of clay and silt—and deeper down, requiring a more expensive extraction technique. Rather than being drilled for oil, the sands are mined. Once on the surface, hot water and steam are used to separate the sand from the bitumen, which is then diluted with naphtha to make it flow more easily. The bitumen is heated to 500°C, producing vapors that, when cooled, condense at three levels. The sulfur and the gases produced during the process are all drawn off and put to use, but the liquid products are the most precious. By blending them and increasing the hydrogen content of the mix to make it "lighter," a high-quality synthetic crude oil is produced. This oil is piped to Edmonton and distributed around North America for use in cars, airplanes, and derivative products such as plastics.

Three companies are involved in mining the oil sands. **Suncor Energy,** the smallest of the three, began production in 1967 after taking over the company that had initiated mining in the area three years earlier. The Suncor operation became the world's first commercially successful oil-sands plant. It is currently expanding its operation, with long-term predictions that it will have increased its production to 400,000 barrels per day by 2008. Established in 1978, **Syncrude,** the world's largest producer of synthetic crude oil, is also expanding its Fort McMurray operations. The company is spending $8 billion to increase production to 220,000 barrels daily by 2002. A third company, **Albian Sands,** is in the process of constructing a site near the Muskeg River. This operation is slated to begin operating sometime late in 2002. Both operations and the Albian Sands site are located north of Fort McMurray. The size of the machinery used to scrape off the surface layer of muskeg and excavate the oil sands below it is mind-boggling. Syncrude's walking draglines are the largest pieces of land-bound machinery in the world. Each moves slowly, dropping buckets as large as a two-car garage into the ground and dragging them back on a boom the length of a football field. The process continues around the clock, with a constant stream of 170-ton heavy haulers taking the overburden to reclamation sites and the oil sands to conveyor belts bound for the processing plants. The three oil sands companies, along with major players in the industry, have collaborated on a development proposal that guarantees a combined regional investment of $33 billion over the next 25 years.

SIGHTS

Oil Sands Discovery Centre

For an insight into the history, geology, and technology of the Athabasca Oil Sands mining process, head to this large interpretive center at the south end of the city (on the corner of Hwy. 63 and Mackenzie Blvd.). Start your visit by watching *Quest for Energy,* a multimedia, big-screen presentation about the industry that has grown around the resource. The center houses an interesting collection of machinery and has interactive displays, hands-on exhibits, and interpretive presentations. Outside is the Industrial Equipment Garden, where an older-style bucket-wheel excavator and other machinery are displayed. To move the excavator to this site, it had to be disassembled, with some sections requiring a 144-wheel, 45-meter-long trailer for the 45-kilometer trip from the mine. The center is open in summer daily 10 A.M.–6 P.M., the rest of the year Tues.–Sun. 10 A.M.–4 P.M. Admission is $3.50. For information, call 780/743-7167.

Syncrude/Suncor Plant Tours
Touring the oil-sands plants is the best way to experience the operation firsthand. Syncrude is the larger, more imposing operation of the two, but it imposes more rules and keeps you farther from the action; tours depart July–Aug. Wed.–Sat. at 9 A.M. The Suncor tour gives you a better feel for the sheer size of the equipment; tours depart mid-June–August Sun.–Tues. at 1 P.M. Both tours are operated by the Fort McMurray Visitors Bureau and depart from the Oil Sands Discovery Centre. Tour cost is adults $15, seniors $12.50; reservations are essential and can be made at the Visitors Bureau or by calling 780/791-4336 or 800/565-3947. The visitors bureau has put together some accommodation/tour packages that are an excellent deal.

To Fort McKay
Fort McKay is a small native settlement on the west bank of the Athabasca River. The town itself has little of interest (and no services), but the drive out to the end of Highway 63 is pleasant and gives you a chance to view the mining operations, albeit at a distance. Make your first stop at the 30-kilometer mark, where a short trail leads through reclaimed land to the manmade **Crane Lake.** Continuing north, the **Oil Sands Viewpoint,** 40 kilometers from Fort McMurray, looks out over tailing ponds and reclaimed land from the Suncor operation. Immediately north is an 83-hectare plot of reclaimed Syncrude land that is now home to a heard of wood bison. The road then continues toward Fort McKay along a causeway over **Mildred Lake,** Canada's largest reservoir.

Five kilometers farther north, the road forks.

To the left is Fort McKay, and to the right Highway 63 crosses the Athabasca River and continues 10 kilometers to a dock. Here, supplies such as petroleum and building materials are loaded onto barges and transported downstream (north) to the communities of Fort Chipewyan, Uranium City, and Fond-du-lac on Lake Athabasca.

This is the end of the summer road. Between December and March, a winter road is built over the frozen muskeg and river 225 kilometers to Fort Chipewyan and up the Slave River to Fort Smith in the Northwest Territories.

Heritage Park
A two-hectare village, Heritage Park (1 Tolen Dr., 780/791-7575) is made up of historic buildings linked by a boardwalk and houses artifacts that reflect the importance of fishing, trapping, and transportation to the city. Other displays include boats used on the river, a Northern Alberta Railway passenger car, and an early log mission, while another tells the story of local bush pilots. The park is open in summer Mon.–Fri. 10 A.M.–5 P.M., Sat.–Sun. noon–5 P.M., the rest of the year Mon.–Fri. 8:30 A.M.–4:30 P.M. Admission is $2.

Gregoire Lake Provincial Park
Southeast of the city 34 kilometers is Gregoire Lake, the only accessible lake in the Fort McMurray area. The 690-hectare park on the lake's west shore is a typical boreal forest of mixed woods and black-spruce bogs. Many species of waterfowl nest on the lake, and mammals such as moose and black bears are relatively common. Some short hiking trails wind through the park, and canoes are rented in the day-use area.

Farther around the lake is the small community of **Anzac;** many people camp free on the beach here.

RECREATION AND EVENTS

Hiking
An extensive network of trails links downtown to all parts of the city, the Athabasca River, small parks, and picnic areas; ask for a map at the visitors bureau. A self-guided interpretive trail

demonstrating forestry management practices begins at the Alberta Forestry Ranger Station across the highway from the Fort McMurray Visitors Bureau.

Wilderness Tours

Majic Country Wilderness Adventures, 780/743-0766, offers tours from Fort McMurray. The most popular outings are the jet-boat tours to a wilderness camp along the river for fishing or bird-watching. Three-night packages, including accommodations, transportation, and meals, start at $350 per person. Other options include overnight horseback-riding trips, fishing and sightseeing charters on the Athabasca River, and floats by canoe down the Clearwater River. Another local operator is **Points North Adventures,** 780/743-9350.

Other Recreation

More than 60 sports, ranging from scuba diving to skydiving, are organized locally. The **Miskanaw Golf Course,** 780/790-1812, on MacDonald Island, north of downtown, is a challenging 6,650-yard layout with plenty of hazards. Green fees are $30. The **Fort McMurray Golf Club,** on the north side of the Athabasca River (off Thickwood Blvd., 780/743-5577), is a new course that was carved out of the forest. Greens fee is $33.

The **MacDonald Island Recreation Complex,** 780/791-0070, north of downtown, has a modern exercise room, tennis courts, squash courts, and a swimming pool; it's open daily 8 A.M.–11 P.M.

Entertainment and Events

Fort McMurray has more than 20 bars and lounges. The legendary **Oil Can Tavern** (10007 Franklin Ave., 780/743-2211) occasionally presents live entertainment but is best known as a hard-drinking pub. At the **Mackenzie Park Inn** (424 Gregoire Dr., 780/791-4770), a DJ plays country tunes Tuesday–Saturday. The inn also has an outside deck area. The **Keyano Theatre** (Keyano College at 8115 Franklin Ave., 780/791-4990) puts on a season of live performances September–March, with top country and pop acts appearing throughout the year.

MacDonald Island comes alive with highland dancing, pipe bands, a tug-o-war, and caber-tossing on the middle weekend of June during the **Highland Games. Canada Day** is celebrated on MacDonald Island with multicultural performers and ethnic foods. At **Heritage Park** on the second Sunday of each month, you'll find a barbecue and displays of pioneer arts and crafts. **Heritage Day,** the first Monday in August, is also celebrated at the park. A **Beerfest** takes place on MacDonald Island on the last Saturday in July; many out-of-town musicians perform in an outdoor concert. The end of summer is celebrated during the **Blueberry Festival,** the first weekend of summer.

ACCOMMODATIONS AND CAMPING

$50–100

Fort McMurray's least expensive accommodation is the older-style **Twin Pine Motor Inn** (downtown at 10024 Biggs Ave., 780/743-3391). The 42 basic rooms are air-conditioned and guests have use of a laundry facility; $52 single, $64 double. The **Best Canadian Motor Inn** is four kilometers south of downtown toward the visitors center (385 Gregoire Dr., 780/791-4646); $55 single, $65 double. The best value in this price range is the **Mackenzie Park Inn,** across the road from the Best Canadian (424 Gregoire Dr., 780/791-7200 or 800/582-3273). It features a good restaurant, a lounge, and an indoor swimming pool; from $87 single or double. Back downtown, the **Nomad Inn** (10006 MacDonald Ave., 780/791-4770 or 800/661-5029, www.nomadinn.com) has well-kept rooms and a restaurant and a lively bar; from $99 single or double includes a light breakfast.

$100–150

The largest accommodation in the city, with 190 rooms, is the **Sawridge Hotel** (530 Mackenzie Blvd., 780/791-7900 or 800/661-6567, www.sawridge.com), which is geared for business travelers, with a business center, a small indoor pool, and a choice of dining facilities; from $95 single, $100 double. The **Travelodge Hotel,** is in a prime downtown location (9713 Hardin St., 780/743-3301 or 888/799-7663). Formerly the Peter Pond Hotel, it has recently undergone a facelift, with all 134 rooms completely renovated. Guest facilities include a fitness room,

Smitty's restaurant, and a pub. Rates are from $105 single or double, which includes a daily paper. **Podollan Inns** (10131 Franklin Ave., 780/790-2000 or 888/448-2080) is a new downtown hotel. The 54 rooms are large and well-appointed, many with king-size beds and kitchens; from $99 single, $109 double.

Campgrounds

Two campgrounds are located south of the city limits. The **Rotary Park Campground,** 780/790-1581, 11 kilometers south, offers showers, cooking facilities, and powered sites and is open year-round; all sites are $14. The park is signposted but easy to miss; turn east along Highway 69 and look for the entrance to the left. **Fort McMurray Centennial Park** (9909 Franklin Ave., 780/799-5832) doesn't have showers or hookups but is along Highway 63, closer to the city. Sites are $9.

FOOD

The **Peter Pond Shopping Centre** has a fast-food court, which is the least expensive place to go for a meal. Also downtown is **Mitchell's Café and Gifts,** housed in a heritage building (10015 Main St., 780/743-1665). It's open 10 A.M.–5 P.M., serving light meals in a relaxing, informal atmosphere. **Mapletrees Restaurant,** in the Mackenzie Park Inn (424 Gregoire Dr., 780/791-7200), serves well-prepared dishes at reasonable prices and offers the best Sunday brunch buffet in town ($11). Daily dinner specials, which include soup or salad, run approximately $10; open daily 6 A.M.–11 P.M. For steaks, try the **Cedar Steak House** (10021 Biggs Ave., 780/743-1717), where entrées start at $12. The **Garden Cafe** (9924 Biggs Ave., 780/791-6665) is bright, full of greenery, and always busy; it's open 24 hours.

TRANSPORTATION

Getting There
Although the road out of Fort McMurray is excellent and always seems to be busy, many people prefer to fly. The **airport** is located nine kilometers south, then six kilometers east of downtown. **Air B.C.,** 780/790-1373 or 800/332-1080, flies daily to Edmonton. A cab from the airport to downtown runs approximately $20.

Greyhound (8220 Manning Avenue, 780/791-3664) has services three times daily to Edmonton. **Red Arrow** (8217 Franklin Ave., 780/791-2990 or 800/232-1958) offers a more luxurious service than Greyhound, with fewer stops, more legroom, and free coffee and snacks. Either way, it's a five-hour trip to Edmonton.

Getting Around
Diversified Transportation (460 MacAlpine Crescent, 780/743-4157) operates a transit service around town and to outlying suburbs; $1.10 per sector. From downtown, a cab costs $8 to the Oil Sands Discovery Centre and $18 to the airport. Taxi companies include **Sun Taxi,** 780/743-5050; and **United Class Cabs,** 780/743-1234. The following car rentals are available in town, and all have airport counters: **Avis,** 780/743-4773; **Budget,** 780/743-8215; **Hertz,** 780/743-2894; and **National,** 780/743-6393.

SERVICES AND INFORMATION

The **post office** is at 9702 Hardin Street. **D' Laundromat** is in the Park Plaza Mall on Franklin Avenue; open daily 8 A.M.–10:30 P.M. **Fort McMurray Public Library** is housed in a large, rust-colored building (9907 Franklin Avenue, 780/743-7800); open Tuesday 10 A.M.–5 P.M., Wednesday 1–9 P.M., Thurs.–Sat. 10 A.M.–5 P.M., Sunday 1–5 P.M. **Fort McMurray Regional Hospital** is at 7 Hospital Street, 780/791-6161. For the **RCMP,** call 780/799-8888.

Fort McMurray Visitors Bureau (780/791-4336 or 800/565-3947, www.visitors.fortmcmurray.com) is south of downtown, just north of the Oil Sands Discovery Centre. In addition to having a wealth of information on the city, it represents many northern fly-in fishing lodges and offers overnight accommodation packages. It's open May–Aug. Mon.–Fri. 9 A.M.–7 P.M. and Sat.–Sun. 10 A.M.–7 P.M., the rest of the year Mon.–Fri. 9 A.M.–5 P.M.

FORT CHIPEWYAN

When the North West Company established a post on the west shore of Lake Athabasca in 1788, what is now Alberta was a wild land with no white settlers. Today, Fort Chipewyan (pop. 1,200), on the site of the original trading post (225 kilometers north of Fort McMurray), holds the title of Alberta's most remote community. In summer, the only access is by river or air. After the winter freeze settles in, a winter road connects the community to the outside world. For fur traders, Fort Chip, as it's best known, was the ideal location for a post. The confluence of the Athabasca and Peace rivers was nearby, and to the north were the Slave and Mackenzie rivers. It became a way station for some of Canada's great explorers—Alexander Mackenzie, David Thompson, Simon Fraser, and Sir John Franklin—who rested and replenished supplies at the post.

Things to See and Do
Perched on a south-facing slope overlooking the lake, the town itself is not particularly inspiring but is a good base for trips into nearby Wood Buffalo National Park and fishing on the lake and nearby rivers. In town is the **Bicentennial Museum** (Mackenzie Avenue, 780/697-3844), modeled on the original fur-trading post. The second floor is dedicated to the fur trade, where-

as the lower floor catalogs the native history of the region, the Royal Canadian Mounted Police (RCMP), and local industries. Open year-round Mon.–Fri. 11 A.M.–5:30 P.M., Sat.–Sun. 1–5 P.M.

Athabasca Delta Interpretive Tours, P.O. Box 178, Fort Chipewyan, Alberta T0P 1B0, 780/697-3521, operates a lodge on Jackfish Lake that is reached by a short boat ride from Fort Chip. The emphasis is on the traditional lifestyle of the local Dene people; activities include wilderness trips, fishing, wildlife viewing, and native cooking. Rates are $160 per person per day or $1,570 for a seven-day package departing from Fort McMurray.

Practicalities
The only accommodation in town is the **Fort Chipewyan Lodge** (P.O. Box 347, Fort Chipewyan, Alberta T0P 1B0, 780/697-3679 or 888/686-6333). The lodge has 10 basic but comfortable rooms and a spectacular view over the lake. Rates are $85 single, $95 double, but many package deals, including meals and tours into the delta, are offered. The closest camping is 17 kilometers northeast of town at **Dore Lake.** The lodge has a lounge restaurant, or you can grab light snacks at the **Athabasca Café,** 780/697-3737.

Contact Air, 780/697-3753, departs twice daily from Fort McMurray for Fort Chipewyan. If you are up in Fort Smith (Northwest Territories), there are two options for visiting Fort

PROVINCIAL ARCHIVES OF ALBERTA

Originally, fur-trading posts were heavily foritfied, hence the name "fort." Later, the fortifications were no longer necessary, but the name stuck. Today the names of many northern towns reflect this early heritage.

Chipewyan. **Northwestern Air,** 867/872-2216, has scheduled flights between the two towns for approximately $100 each way, or you can take a five-hour tour from Fort Smith with **Big River Air,** 867/872-3030, for $260. Between mid-December and mid-March, a winter road constructed from Fort McMurray to Fort Smith passes through Fort Chip and is passable by two-wheel-drive vehicles; call 780/697-3778 for road conditions.

NORTH-CENTRAL ALBERTA

The area immediately north of Edmonton is a varied region that extends north out of the provincial capital's suburbs through rich agricultural land and into the wilderness of the boreal forest. The **Athabasca River** flows southwest to northeast through the region. It is linked to Edmonton by Highway 2, which follows the historic Athabasca Landing Trail—a supply route used by early explorers and traders for travel between the North Saskatchewan and Athabasca river systems. From Athabasca, Highway 2 heads northwest to the city of Slave Lake, on the southeast shore of Lesser Slave Lake. From there, it continues along the lake's southern shore to High Prairie and into the Peace River Valley. Other major roads in the region include Highway 18, which runs east-west through the southern portion of the region and through the farming and oil towns of Westlock and Barrhead; Highway 33, which climbs into the Swan Hills, home to a subspecies of the now-extinct plains grizzly bear; and Highway 43, the main thoroughfare northwest from Edmonton to Grande Prairie. Adventurous souls driving to the Northwest Territories will want to travel the Bicentennial Highway (Highway 88) at least one-way. This gravel road opens up a remote part of the province that is otherwise accessible only by floatplane.

EDMONTON TO ATHABASCA

From downtown Edmonton, Highway 2 (called the St. Albert Trail in the vicinity of Edmonton) heads north into a once-forested land, which is now heavily developed as farm and ranch country. The first town north of the city limits is **Morinville,** a farming community founded by French and German settlers more than 100 years ago. **St. Jean Baptiste Church,** built by the town's founders, is an imposing structure that has been declared a Provincial Historical Site. **Heritage Lake,** at the junction of Highways 2 and 642, is a popular recreation and camping area.

Athabasca Landing Trail

The Athabasca Landing Trail was an historic trade route plied first by indigenous people and later used by the Hudson's Bay Company to carry goods between Fort Saskatchewan and Athabasca. Bits and pieces of the original trail can still be seen today, interspersed among the small towns and hamlets east of Highway 2. Travelers wandering through this area will find a variety of other sights in addition to the old trail.

At one time, the trail passed through **Gibbons,** a small town of 2,800 on the banks of the Sturgeon River. Sites of interest here include **Gibbons Anglican Church,** whose unique interior is shaped like a ship, and **Sturgeon River Historical Museum,** located in Oliver Park, which features a two-story log house. The museum is open in summer daily noon–8 P.M. Golfers should head to one of Northern Alberta's finest courses, **Goose Hummock Golf Resort,** four kilometers north of town, 780/921-2444, which features water hazards on 15 of the 18 holes. Green fees are $35 ($22 after 4 P.M.).

Old St. Mary's Ukrainian Catholic Church is located 1.5 kilometers west of the hamlet of **Waugh.** It was the first church of its denomination to be built north of Edmonton and is located adjacent to the original trail. The trail disappears north of Highway 18, but historic markers and buildings are accessible by following gravel roads east through **Tawatinaw** and **Rochester** (look for historic markers and log buildings on the roadside approaching the crest of the first ridge east of these towns).

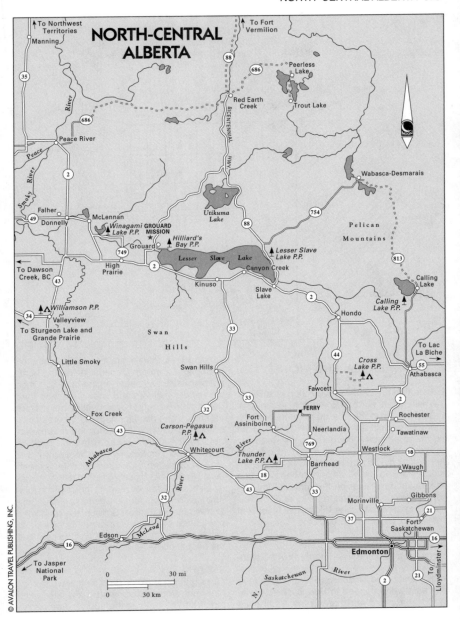

NORTH-CENTRAL ALBERTA

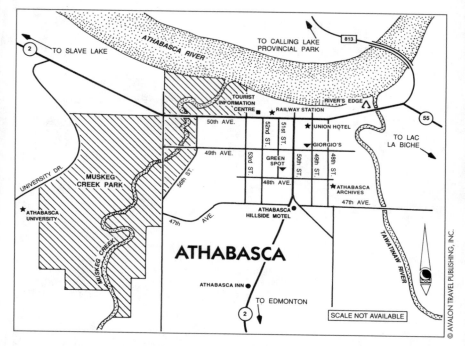

© AVALON TRAVEL PUBLISHING, INC.

ATHABASCA AND VICINITY

Located on the banks of the Athabasca River, 147 kilometers north of Edmonton, this town of 2,300 was probably the most famous of the many communities that formed vital links to the north. *Athabasca* (Where There are Reeds, in the language of the Cree) is on a gently sloping hill on the river's south bank ,with the steep-sided Muskeg Creek Valley on one side and the Tawatinaw River on the other. Many historic buildings still stand in town, and the surrounding area is pristine wilderness, excellent for fishing, boating, and camping.

History

Athabasca Landing was founded by the Hudson's Bay Company in 1874 on the southernmost bend of the Athabasca River. Goods from the east were shipped to Fort Saskatchewan and transported north along the Athabasca Landing Trail, from where they were distributed throughout northern Canada. A thriving boat-building business began at the landing. Once the paddlewheelers and scows reached their destination along the river system, many were broken up and used for housing, whereas others were loaded with furs for the return journey. Passengers who boarded the paddlewheelers from the landing were from all walks of life—traders, trappers, land speculators, settlers, North West Mounted Police (NWMP), geologists, missionaries, and anyone looking for a new life and adventure in Canada's great northern wilderness. Robert Service, the renowned poet, lived at Athabasca Landing for a time; much of his early work was about trappers and the people of the Athabasca River.

Sights

Although the Hudson's Bay Company buildings have long since disappeared, many later buildings from the days of the paddlewheelers remain. On the riverfront is the railway station, circa 1912. Next to it is a 1915 steam engine. The Union Hotel, overlooking the river, was built in 1913. Behind it, up the hill on 48th Street, is an old brick schoolhouse, also built in 1913. Next door is the library. 780/675-2735. that houses the **Athabasca Archives,** a comprehensive collection of photographs and newspapers. It's open Tuesday and Thursday noon–4 P.M.

Muskeg Creek Park, on the west side of town, offers hiking trails and good fishing during spring. The creek flows through a heavily forested ravine into a floodplain, then drains into the Athabasca River. Wildlife abounds, berry picking is good in late summer, and cross-country skiing trails are laid in winter. Access to the park is from the elementary school on 48th Avenue.

Athabasca University has a 12,000-square-meter facility on a 180-hectare site, with a staff of more than 500, a library with 100,000 books, an extensive art collection, a fitness facility, and an annual budget exceeding $22 million—but no on-campus students. It's one of the largest correspondence universities in North America, open to students regardless of their geographical location or previous academic levels. The 14,000 enrolled students work from home, communicating with their tutors by mail, phone, fax, and e-mail. The campus is open to the public and has some unique artworks commissioned especially for the building. For more information, or to arrange a tour, call 780/675-6111, www.athabascau.ca.

Accommodations and Food

Several motels are located on Highway 2, south of town. Try the **Athabasca Hillside Motel** (4804 46th Ave., 780/675-5111), with good views of the river and kitchenettes in each of the 17 rooms; $44 single, $49 double. The **Athabasca Inn** (5211 41st Ave., 780/675-2294 or 800/567-5718) is larger, with 65 spacious rooms, a health club, a restaurant, and a lounge; $89 single, $99 double. The **River's Edge Campground,** on 50th Avenue where the Tawatinaw River drains into the Athabasca, is the site of the original landing; unserviced sites $9, powered sites $14. It has showers.

The **Green Spot** (4820 51st St., 780/675-

3040) serves breakfast for approximately $5 and sandwiches, hamburgers, and other dishes the rest of the day. **Giorgio's** (4901 49th St., 780/675-5418) is a pizza, pasta, and steak place; the pizza is especially well priced.

Services and Information

Greyhound (4902 50th Ave., 780/675-2112) stops three times daily downtown on its run between Edmonton and Fort McMurray. The **Tourist Information Centre** (beside the railway station on 50th Avenue, 780/675-2055) is open mid-May to mid-September daily 10 A.M.–6 P.M.

Calling Lake Provincial Park

Lying along the south shore of one of Alberta's larger lakes, this 741-hectare park is on Highway 813, 55 kilometers north of Athabasca. A boreal forest of aspen surrounds the lake, giving way to a marshy area nearer the shore. Look for deer, moose, and black bears, as well as the occasional white pelican and blue heron. Fishing for northern pike, walleye, perch, and whitefish is the park's main attraction, although swimming and canoeing on the lake are also possible. Camping in the small campground is $13.

From the park, Highway 813 follows the east shore of Calling Lake to a hamlet of the same name. The road turns to gravel and continues 130 kilometers north to **Wabasca-Desmarais,** a native settlement between South and North Wabasca lakes, then loops back and follows the Willow River for much of the way to Lesser Slave Lake. This is a remote region of Alberta, and services are few and far between, but wildlife is abundant and fishing is excellent in the many roadside lakes and rivers.

Amber Valley

This small hamlet just east of Athabasca was first settled in 1910 by 200 blacks from Oklahoma. They moved from their homeland to escape racial persecution, led north by 22-year-old Jefferson Davis Edwards. The prejudice continued in Alberta, with locals suggesting they should head south because the climate wouldn't suit them. Despite the hard times, the community thrived and remained virtually all black. Since World War II, the population has declined, and today only a few black families remain.

ATHABASCA TO SLAVE LAKE

From Athabasca, Highway 2 heads northwest to Slave Lake, passing many summer communities along the shores of **Baptiste** and **Island Lakes,** both of which have good fishing for northern pike; their campgrounds are inexpensive. This section of the highway is known as the **Northern Woods and Water Route.** Just before **Hondo,** the route intersects Highway 44, which heads south 106 kilometers to Westlock and Highway 18. At Hondo, 72 kilometers from Athabasca, Highway 2A leads to **Fawcett Lake,** known for its good walleye fishing. At the lake are two campgrounds, cabins, and boat rentals.

SLAVE LAKE

The town of Slave Lake (pop. 6,500) is located on the southeastern shore of **Lesser Slave Lake,** 250 kilometers northwest of Edmonton. It began as an important staging point for steamboat freight and passengers heading for the Peace River Country and Yukon goldfields. The arrival of a rail line in 1914 meant a boom time for the fledgling community and the beginning of a lumber industry that continues today. In 1935, disastrous floods destroyed many of the buildings on the main street. Following that debacle, the town was relocated, 3.5 kilometers to the south. Only a few foundations remain of the original settlement. Today the town has little to interest visitors, but Lesser Slave Lake has some of the best fishing in the province, with northern pike to nine kilograms, walleye to four kilograms, whitefish to 2.5 kilograms, and yellow perch to one kilogram—enough to make any self-respecting fisherman quit his job, pack the rod and reel, and head north.

But Isn't Slave Lake in the Arctic?
Well, no, but an explanation is in order. Lesser Slave Lake is one of *two* Slave Lakes in northwestern Canada. Both lakes are at the same longitude, but they're about 600 kilometers apart as the crow flies. The bigger one—the one that many people *think* is in the Arctic—is north of Alberta in the Northwest Territories (but still south

of the Arctic Circle). The smaller, more southerly of the two is here in northern Alberta. Both are named after the Slavey Indians who traveled south up the Athabasca River from the big Slave Lake to the smaller Slave Lake on hunting and fishing expeditions. In early writings, and on maps, both lakes were denoted as Slave Lake. This led to confusion, especially because both were in what was then the Northwest Territories. To remedy the problem, the larger, northern body of water was renamed Great Slave Lake, and its Albertan counterpart, Lesser Slave Lake. Lesser Slave Lake is the third largest lake in Alberta (only lakes Athabasca and Claire are larger) and the largest accessible by road. It is 90 kilometers long, 20 kilometers wide, has an area of 1,150 square kilometers, and is relatively shallow, especially along the south shore, where deltas have formed from the many northward-flowing Swan Hills watersheds.

And Why Are So Many Things Named "Sawridge"?
The original settlement on Lesser Slave Lake was named Sawridge, for the jagged range of hills to the north. Many prominent residents didn't like the name, so in 1922, they changed it to Slave Lake, but the original name lives on. Today it's the name of the local Indian band and a creek flowing through town, and many local businesses use the name as well.

Lesser Slave Lake Provincial Park
At this 7,290-hectare park north of town, you'll find a campground, long sandy beaches, unique sand dunes, and wetland and boreal forest habitats supporting diverse wildlife. Offshore is **Dog Island,** the lake's only island, home to a pair of bald eagles, pelicans, and other shorebirds. North of the Lesser Slave River are many access roads leading to **Devonshire Beach,** a seven-kilometer stretch of sandy beach popular for sunbaking and swimming. The sunsets from this beach are spectacular (at the north end is a viewing platform). The **North Shore,** to the north of Devonshire Beach, has a picnic area and provides access to the 23-kilometer **Freighter Lakeshore Trail,** which runs the entire length of the park. North Shore beaches are nonexistent, but a gravel road heading back toward Devonshire leads to a quiet one.

The **Gilwood Golf Club,** 780/849-4389, with a challenging nine-hole course, is also on the North Shore. Greens fee are $16.50 per round. At the north end of the park, a steep eight-kilometer road leads through a dense forest of lodgepole pine to the plateau-like summit of 1,030-meter Marten Mountain. The views are spectacular from this vantage point 500 meters above the lake. A 2.8-kilometer trail from the summit winds through an old-growth forest of balsam fir that has escaped major fires. The trail ends up at **Lily Lake,** a small, secluded lake (stocked with rainbow trout) from where Lily Creek flows into Lesser Slave Lake.

Fishing

Although fishing from the lake's edge and in nearby rivers can be productive, the big ones are hooked out on the lake, where pike grow to nine kilograms and walleye to four kilograms. Sawridge Recreation Area, on the Caribou Trail, rents small motorboats for $20 per hour, $50 half day, or $100 full day. Ask at the information center for a list of local fishing guides.

Pilots at **Slave Air,** 780/849-5353, based at the airport in town, will fly you to their favorite fishing lakes. Orloff Lake is a half hour to the east and has a campsite (flight is $245 for up to five people), and God's Lake is one hour north

Fishing in Northern Lakes is nearly always productive.

ALBERTA TOURISM

(flight is $480). If the pilot knows that the fishing is good, he won't charge you ground time.

Accommodations

The **Highway Motor Inn,** on Highway 2 by the Tourist Information Centre (600 14th Ave. SW, 780/849-2400 or 888/848-2400), has 75 basic rooms for $58 single, $68 double. The **Sawridge Hotel** (200 Main St. S, 780/849-4101 or 800/661-6657, www.sawridge.com) has rooms in an older section ($60 single, $65 double) and larger ones in a new wing ($65 single, $75 double), as well as a café, a lounge, and a restaurant. Just down Main Street is the **Northwest Inn** (801 Main St., 780/849-3300 or 888/849-5450), which offers an exercise room and an indoor pool; $69 single, $75 double.

Worth the drive 30 kilometers west of Slave Lake is the **Canyon Creek Hotel,** 780/369-3784, in a small village of the same name. It's the only accommodation right on Lesser Slave Lake, and although basic, it's comfortable and clean. Out front is a sandy beach, and meals are available. Rates are $45 single, $55 double, which includes breakfast.

Lesser Slave Lake Provincial Park's **Marten River Campground** (at the extreme northern end of the park) has coin-operated showers, a beach, and a summer interpretive program; unserviced sites $15, powered sites $17. Immediately north, outside the park boundary, is the **Diamond Willow Resort,** 780/849-2292, a private campground with coin showers, a grocery store, a pitch-and-putt golf course, and a nature trail; unserviced sites $13.50, powered sites $17. **Sawridge Recreation Area,** in town, is used mainly by noisy families who stay the entire summer. Sites here are $13–15 per night.

Food

The **Sunrise Cafe** in the Sawridge Hotel, 780/849-4101, serves a good lunch buffet with a wide selection of dishes; $7.95. Also in the hotel is the **Sweet Grass Cafe,** 780/849-4101, a casual dining room with bright décor and a great atmosphere. Expect to pay $6–8 for lunch and a few dollars more for the pasta, ribs, steak, and chicken on the dinner menu. Right downtown is **Joey's Incredible Edibles** (101 3rd Ave. NW, 780/849-5577), which isn't that incredible but has a fairly standard menu of pasta, chicken, and beef from $10 at dinner. The **Sawridge Truckstop** (on the corner of Highway 88 and Caribou Trail NE, 780/849-4030) is just that—a truckstop with vinyl seats, hearty meals, inexpensive prices, and waitresses as busy as Beirut bricklayers. It's open 24 hours.

Services and Information

The **Greyhound** bus depot, 780/849-4003, is in the Sawridge Truckstop on Highway 88 at the east end of town. The **post office** is on 2nd Street NE. **Allarie Cleaners** (116 3rd Ave. NE) is open 8:30 A.M.–10 P.M.

The **Tourist Information Centre** (off Highway 2, west of Main Street, 780/849-4611 or 800/267-4654) is open May–Sept. daily 10 A.M.–6 P.M.

Bicentennial Highway

This 430-kilometer road (also known as Hwy. 88) connects Slave Lake with Fort Vermilion to the north and is an excellent alternative to the Mackenzie Highway for those traveling in that direction. It was renamed and renumbered to commemorate the bicentenary of Fort Vermilion in 1988. Services (gas, rooms, and restaurant) are available at the only community along the road, **Red Earth Creek**—a semipermanent oil-fields town 130 kilometers north of Slave Lake. From there, Highway 686 heads east to **Peerless** and **Trout Lakes,** named for the excellent fishing, and west to the town of Peace River.

At Red Earth Creek, the Bicentennial Highway becomes a gravel road and parallels the Loon and Wabasca rivers, following the eastern flanks of the **Buffalo Head Hills.** Seventy kilometers from Fort Vermilion, a turnoff to the west leads to **Wadlin Lake,** home to one of Alberta's four colonies of white pelicans. They nest on an island during summer, migrating south to the Gulf of Mexico each winter. The island is a Prohibited Access Wildlife Area, and the birds should not be disturbed during the breeding season because they are prone to abandoning their nests if approached. The lake has good fishing for northern pike and whitefish, and a primitive campground with sites for $10 a night.

(For Fort Vermilion, see **The Peace River Valley,** later in this chapter.)

TO THE PEACE RIVER

From Slave Lake, Highway 2 follows the southern shore of Lesser Slave Lake past the small resort towns of Widewater and Canyon Creek. Take the turnoff to Wagner to follow the historic route to High Prairie along the lake. Mink farming was big business in the early 1900s, and many mink cages remain, scattered along the shore. The hotel at Canyon Creek was once a fish hatchery where fish were raised as food for the mink. At **Kinuso** there is a museum with a stuffed grizzly bear that stands more than 2.5 meters tall; the museum is open Mon.–Fri. 10 A.M.–4 P.M. A little farther along the highway, a nine-kilometer gravel road leads to a marina, camping, and a beach at 144-hectare **Spruce Point Park,** 780/775-2117.

Grouard

A town of 400 on Buffalo Bay near the west end of Lesser Slave Lake, Grouard grew up around the St. Bernard Mission, founded in 1884 by Father Emile Grouard. The town was destined to become the center of the north. It had a few thousand people and a rail line on the way, when, because of an unfortunate set of circumstances, everything changed. A sample of water from a nearby lake was sent to the railway headquarters to ensure that it was fit for the steam engines. Along the way it was either dropped, lost, or emptied and replaced by a sample of water from muskeg wetland. The new sample was tested and found to be of poor quality. The proposed route for the railway changed, and the once-thriving town collapsed. **Grouard Native Cultural Arts Museum,** 780/751-3915, is dedicated to promoting a better understanding of North American native cultures through exhibition of native arts, crafts, and historic artifacts. It's open in summer daily 10 A.M.–4 P.M. in the Moosehorn Lodge Building of the Alberta Vocational College.

Hilliard's Bay Provincial Park is 13 kilometers east of Grouard on the northwest shore of Lesser Slave Lake. It is a 2,330-hectare park with mixed woods, two sandy beaches, and a one-kilometer spit framed by a stand of gnarled paper birches. The **Boreal Forest Interpretive Trail** meanders through a forest habitat, where many species of mammals are present—look for tracks along the top of the ridges at the east end of the park. The campground has showers, kitchen shelters, and firewood; sites are $13–15 a night.

Shaw's Point Lakeside Resort, 780/751-3900, is a full-service campground located just outside the provincial park. It caters mainly to families and fishing enthusiasts. Facilities include showers, a laundry room, a general store, two marinas, boat launches, and boat rentals; unserviced sites $15, powered sites $17.

High Prairie

This town of 2,900 near the west end of Lesser Slave Lake hosts the **Golden Walleye Classic** the third week of August. It is North America's richest catch-and-release walleye tournament, boasting $130,000 in prize money. Walleye fishing is not the world's most exciting spectator sport, but amateur anglers are welcome to enter. For details, call 780/523-3505.

The **High Prairie and District Museum** (in the library on 53rd Ave., 780/523-2601) has some material on the early settlement of Grouard. Open Tues.–Sat. 11:30 A.M.–5 P.M.

High Prairie Lions Campground, at the east end of town, has showers; unserviced sites $10, powered sites $14. The **Tourist Information Centre** is open in summer daily 9 A.M.–5 P.M.

Winagami Lake Provincial Park

Winagami Lake, north of High Prairie on Highway 749, is ringed by a riot of paper birch, aspen, balsam fir, and poplar trees. The park is on the lake's eastern shore and is an excellent place for bird-watching; two platforms have been built for this purpose (the best time of year is May–June). The day-use area has been planted with ornamental shrubs, and a short hiking trail leads along the lakeshore. The campground has pit toilets, firewood, and kitchen shelters; unserviced sites are $15, powered sites $18.

The **Winagami Conservation Area,** located along the northeastern arm of the lake (turn off nine kilometers south of McLennan), is also good for bird-watching. It's undeveloped except for a few short trails.

McLennan

Known as the "Bird Capital of Canada," this town of 1,000 is located on **Kimiwan Lake** at the confluence of three major bird migration paths—the Mississippi, Pacific, and Central. An estimated 27,000 shorebirds and 250,000 waterfowl reside or pass through here; more than 200 different species are sighted annually. An excellent interpretive center overlooking the lake has information on the many species sighted and comprehensive bird lists; it's open in summer daily 10 A.M.–7 P.M. From the center, a boardwalk leads through a wetland area to a gazebo and a bird blind. Panels along the boardwalk provide pictures and descriptions of commonly sighted species. For more information, write to P.O. Box 606, McLennan, Alberta T0H 2L0, 780/324-2004.

Continuing West

The small hamlet of **Donnelly,** 14 kilometers west of McLennan, is best known for the annual **Smoky River Agriculture Society Fair** held on the first weekend of August. The fair features home cooking, a parade, demonstrations of country skills, a country-style beauty contest (the best-looking tractor wins), and the highlight of the weekend—the Antique Tractor Pull.

From west of Donnelly, Highway 2 heads north 63 kilometers to the town of Peace River. Highway 49 continues west to Spirit River and the turnoff to Grande Prairie. The first town along this route is **Falher,** known as the "Honey Capital of Canada." One million bees in 25,000 hives produce 2.5 million kilograms of honey annually. Naturally, this industry has created a need for the town to construct the world's largest honey bee, which is located in a small park on Third Avenue. At the east end of town are two strange-smelling alfalfa-processing plants. The alfalfa is dehydrated and pressed into pellets—more than 50,000 tons annually. You can watch all the action from across the road.

HIGHWAY 18 WEST

Seventy-three kilometers north of Edmonton on Highway 2, Highway 18 heads west through some of Canada's most productive mixed farming land. Major crops include wheat, barley, oats, canola, and hay. Livestock operations include cattle, hogs, poultry, dairy cows, and sheep; the area is home to several large feedlots and Alberta's two largest livestock auctions. At the junction of highways 2 and 18, a gravel road leads north to **Nilsson Bros. Inc.,** Canada's largest privately owned cattle exchange. Live auctions are held in summer on Tuesday and Thursday mornings, more often the rest of the year. Buyers come from throughout North America, but anyone is welcome to attend. The auctioneer is lightning fast—Alberta's best beef cattle are sold hundreds at a time by gross weight. The facility is open every day; ask to have a look around. The staff restaurant, open for an hour at lunchtime, serves hearty meat-and-potato meals for a reasonable price. Just don't ask for lamb. For details and auction times, call 780/348-5893.

Westlock

Westlock is an agricultural service center 11 kilometers west of Highway 2 and 84 kilometers north of Edmonton. The small **District Museum** is at 10216 100th Street, 780/349-2887 (open Fri.–Sun. 1–5 P.M.), and a private museum is on the south side of Highway 18, just west of town. Look for colorful wooden animals alongside the road, and head down the driveway to a collection of antiques gathered over many years by the friendly owner.

One of the best-value motels in the entire province is the **Southview Motel** (9919 100th St., 780/349-2700), which has 14 rooms with baths, kitchens, and cable TV for $39 single,

$42 double and is only a one-hour drive from West Edmonton Mall.

Highway 44 North

From Westlock, it is 106 kilometers north along Highway 44 to Hondo, halfway between Athabasca and Slave Lake. Along the way are two worthwhile detours. **Long Island Lake Municipal Park** (go 22 kilometers north from Westlock, then turn right at Dapp Corner and follow the signs) is a recreation area with fishing, swimming, canoeing, and camping; sites are $10. Farther north, near the hamlet of Fawcett, is a turnoff to 2,068-hectare **Cross Lake Provincial Park.** Deer and moose are common here, and in late summer black bears often feed among the berry patches. The shallow lake is good for swimming, canoeing, and fishing for northern pike. The campground has pit toilets, firewood sales, kitchen shelters, coin-operated showers, and a concession; unserviced sites are $13, powered sites $15.

FATHER ALBERT LACOMBE

Dressed in a tattered black robe and brandishing a cross, Father Albert Lacombe, known to natives as "the man with the good heart," dedicated his life to those with native blood—to the Assiniboine, Blackfoot, Cree, and, in particular, to the Métis. His travels, mainly associated with northern Alberta, took him as far south as Calgary, but his reputation extended to every corner of the province. He was a spokesman for the church, an effective influence on government policies, and, most importantly, he had a hand in just about every advance in the often-tense relationship between warring tribes and white men.

Father Lacombe originally came to what is now Alberta in 1852 to serve the Métis and natives who had moved to Fort Edmonton. In his time there he founded missions at what are now St. Albert and Brosseau. After a short stint in Manitoba, he returned as a traveling missionary, instigating Canada's first industrial school for natives. He also mediated a dispute between the C.P.R. and angry leaders of the Blackfoot over rights to build a rail line through a reserve, and he wrote the first Cree dictionary. The trust he built up with native leaders was great; during one rebellion of the Blackfoot Confederacy, it is

PROVINCIAL ARCHIVES OF ALBERTA

claimed that his influence prevented the slaughter of every white man on the prairies.

Barrhead and Vicinity

Continuing west on Highway 18 takes you to Barrhead, an agriculture and lumber town of 4,100 located 1.5 hours northwest of Edmonton. **Barrhead Museum** (along Highway 33 at 57th Avenue, 780/674-5203), with displays depicting the town's agricultural past, is north of downtown. The museum is open in summer Mon.–Sat. 10 A.M.–4 P.M., Sunday 1–4 P.M. The town's symbol is the great blue heron; you can see a model of one at the top end of 50th Street, or head out to Thunder Lake Provincial Park for the chance to see a real one. The biggest event of the year is the **Wildrose Rodeo Association Finals** in mid-September.

An interesting loop drive from Barrhead is to take Highway 769 north to **Neerlandia** (settled by the Dutch in 1912 and named after their homeland), the small hamlet of **Vega**, and the Athabasca River. The river crossing is on the **Klondike Ferry**, one of the province's few remaining ferries. The next community along this route is **Fort Assiniboine**, which was a vital link in the Hudson's Bay Company chain of fur-trading posts. The original fort was built in 1824, making it one of the oldest settlements in Alberta. Although furs were traded at the fort, its main role was as a transportation link across the then-uncharted wilderness. A reconstruction of the original fur-trading post is located in the center of town; open in summer daily 1–5 P.M. From Fort Assiniboine, it is 38 kilometers southeast back to Barrhead, completing the loop, or 62 kilometers northwest to Swan Hills.

Thunder Lake Provincial Park

Colonies of great blue herons reside at this 208-hectare park 21 kilometers west of Barrhead on Highway 18. The park is on the northeast shore of shallow Thunder Lake, set among stands of aspen and balsam fir. Bird-watching, especially for waterfowl, is excellent; look for herons on the islands in the quiet northwest corner of the lake. Grebes and black terns are also common. The lake's water level is artificially controlled to prevent flooding of cottages and beaches. This control results in poor fishing, although the lake is stocked annually with northern pike and perch. Three short hiking trails begin from the day-use area, including one along the lakeshore that links to three other

trails originating from the campground. The campground is beside the beach and is open year-round. It has pit toilets, coin-operated showers, a concession, firewood sales, kitchen shelters, and canoe rentals; unserviced sites are $15, whereas powered sites, found on Loop A, are $18.

SWAN HILLS

The town of Swan Hills (pop. 2,000) is in the hills of the same name 100 kilometers northwest of Barrhead. The hills were named, according to Indian legend, for giant swans that nested in a nearby river estuary. Oil was discovered in 1957, and the town grew quickly thereafter. Today, five major companies extract 260,000 barrels of oil and 250 million cubic meters of gas daily from 2,000 wells. North of town is the world's most modern special-waste treatment plant, which treats material that cannot be disposed of in a landfill, incinerator, or sewage system. Corrosive, combustible, and environmentally unfriendly materials such as lead, mercury, and pesticides are broken down into nontoxic compounds and either burned off or safely stored. Up to 55,000 tons of waste are treated annually. Tours of the plant are available; call 780/333-4197 for details. The surrounding hills are wetter than the Canadian Rockies foothills, creating a unique environment of rainforest, boreal, and subarctic zones. The best place to observe this blend is at **Goose Mountain Ecological Reserve,** 24 kilometers west of town. Hiking and fishing are popular activities throughout the hills; the easiest area to access is **Krause Lake Recreation Area,** south of town. Old logging roads crisscross the entire region, making exploration easy, with a full tank of gas and a map from the Alberta Forest Service Office. Moose, deer, and coyotes are common, whereas the **Swan Hills grizzly bear,** a subspecies of the now-extinct plains grizzly, is rare.

The **Grizzly Trail** (Highway 33), linking Barrhead and Swan Hills, offers two interesting stops along its route. **Trapper Lea's Cabin** is 30 kilometers southeast of Swan Hills. It consists of two buildings constructed on the trapline of the "Wolf King of Alberta," the man who trapped the most wolves in the province during the early 1940s. Five kilometers farther south is a highway rest area from where a three-kilometer trail leads to the geographic center of Alberta. Follow the brown and yellow signs along an old seismic road to the center, indicated by an orange marker.

Accommodations and Food

Swan Hills has several motels, but each is usually full with work crews. Try the **Derrick Motor Inn**, 780/333-4405, in the plaza; $45 single, $50 double. Instead of staying at the unappealing campground in town, head 30 kilometers southeast to Trapper Lea's Cabin ($7), 15 kilometers north to Chrystina Lake Provincial Recreation Area ($7), or 16 kilometers south to Freeman River ($9). The best place to get a meal in town is the **Swan Palace Restaurant** in the plaza, 780/333-4892.

Information

The **Tourist Information Centre** is on Highway 33, opposite the Grizzly Motel; open in summer daily 9 A.M.–5 P.M. For a good map of the surrounding area, go to the **Natural Resources Service** (4831 Plaza Ave., 780/333-2229).

Carson-Pegasus Provincial Park

This 1,178-hectare park is located on the southern edge of the Swan Hills, 49 kilometers south of the town of Swan Hills and 30 kilometers north of Whitecourt. Because of its location in a transition zone, it contains forest typical of both the foothills (lodgepole pine and spruce) and the boreal forest (aspen, poplar, birch, and fir). More than 40 species of mammals have been recorded here, including deer, moose, and black bear. The epicenter of the park is McLeod Lake, where the fishing is excellent for rainbow trout (stocked annually) and the day-use area offers canoe, rowboat, and motorboat rentals ($6, $7, and $11 per hour, respectively) and a sandy beach. Northern pike, perch, and whitefish are caught in Little McLeod Lake. The general store sells groceries, fishing tackle, bait, and hot food, and has a laundry room; it's open in summer daily 9 A.M.–9 P.M. The campground has flush toilets, showers, firewood sales, kitchen shelters, and an interpretive theater; unserviced sites $15, powered sites $17. For reservations, call 780/778-2664.

WHITECOURT

Whitecourt (population 7,700) sits at the confluence of the Athabasca, McLeod, and Sakwatamau rivers on Highway 43, 177 kilometers northwest of Edmonton and 341 kilometers southeast of Grande Prairie. Highway 32 also passes through town; Swan Hills is 74 kilometers north, and the Yellowhead Highway is 72 kilometers south. If you're coming in from the southeast, you'll pass a strip of motels and restaurants before descending to the Athabasca River and the older part of town, off to the right. Many of Whitecourt's earliest settlers were Yukon-bound in search of gold when they reached this lushly forested region and decided to settle here instead. To them, the area held plenty of opportunities that wouldn't require an arduous trek to the Klondike. When the railroad arrived, so did many homesteaders. They took to cutting down trees to sell for firewood and railroad ties. Thus began Whitecourt's lumber industry; today the town is the "Forest Centre of Alberta."

The **Tourist Information Centre** is by the traffic lights at the top of the hill, 780/778-5363; it's open in summer daily 8 A.M.–7 P.M., the rest of the year Mon.–Fri. 9 A.M.–5 P.M.

Sights

The two-story **Forest Interpretive Centre** (on the south side of town, 780/778-2214) is dedicated to Alberta's forest industry. Displays recreate forest environment and a logging camp, and a series of hands-on, interactive exhibits describe every aspect of the industry. The center also holds the town's information center. It's open in summer daily 9 A.M.–6 P.M. Industrial tours are run by the interpretive center Mon.–Fri. in summer. Each of the four tours is to a forestry-related industry—a pulp mill, a newsprint plant, a sawmill, and a medium-density fiberboard plant. The **E.S. Huestis Demonstration Forest,** five kilometers north of Highway 43 on Highway 32, contains several stages of forest development. A seven-kilometer road leads through various ecosystems, including an old-growth coniferous forest and a deciduous forest, and past aspen and spruce cut blocks, a beaver dam, and an exotic plantation. Each site has interpretive signs; additional information is available from the Forest Interpretive Centre.

Medi-save Drugs, in Valley Centre Mall on 51st Street, has North America's longest suspended railway, a large display of Coca-Cola memorabilia, a fudge machine, and a 1950s-style diner.

Accommodations and Food

Most of Whitecourt's dozen motels are on Highway 43 as it enters town from the southeast. The best value of the bunch is the **Glenview Motel,** 780/778-2276, which charges $47 single, $52 double. The **Green Gables Inn,** 780/778-4537, at the top end of the scale, has large, modern rooms and a good restaurant; $64 single, $69 double. The **Lions Club Campground,** at the south end of the service strip, is set in a heavily forested area and has a laundry and showers; unserviced sites $10–13, powered sites $15. On the opposite side of town, one kilometer along Highway 43, is the full-service **Sagitawah Tourist Park,** 780/778-3734. Sites with hookups are $17–19. Camping is also possible at **Carson-Pegasus Provincial Park,** 30 kilometers north of Whitecourt on Highway 32.

Mountain Pizza & Steak House, 780/778-3600, has great pizza from $7.75 and broiled steaks from $14. The restaurant in the **Quality Inn** (5420 47th Ave., 780/778-5477) serves an excellent rib-eye steak for $15; open for lunch and dinner daily.

HIGHWAY 43 WEST

From Whitecourt, Highway 43 continues northeast to **Fox Creek,** a small town surrounded by a wilderness where wildlife is abundant and the fishing legendary. If you don't believe the local fishing stories, head to the Home Hardware Store to see a 12-kilogram northern pike caught in a nearby lake. **Smoke** and **Iosegun lakes** are two of the most accessible and offer excellent fishing for northern pike, walleye, perch, and whitefish. Both lakes have primitive camping.

Moose are abundant between Fox Creek and **Little Smoky,** 47 kilometers northwest, from where gravel roads lead to small lakes. This area is not noted for fossils, but a few years back, a mammoth tusk was found in Waskahigan River, west of Little Smoky.

Valleyview

Valleyview is an agricultural and oil-and-gas center that also serves travelers who pass through heading north to the Northwest Territories and west to Alaska. It is also one of the largest towns in Alberta without a pioneer museum. Instead, it has the **Text Garden** (beside the Four Seasons Flower Centre at 4909 50th St., 780/524-3872), a series of miniature gardens with paths, benches, and a small chapel. Open daily 10 A.M.–6 P.M.

The town's four motels fill up each night with road-weary travelers. The **Horizon Motel,** 780/524-3904 or 888/909-3908, expanded to 89 rooms in 1999. The 45 new rooms are air-conditioned, spacious, and modern ($65 single, $78 double), whereas those in the old wing are basic but also large ($55 single, $64 double). The **Lions Den Campground** is on Highway 34, just west of Highway 43, and has showers, but with only 20 sites fills up quickly each summer evening; $12 per night. **Sherk's RV Park,** 780/524-4949, is a full-service campground on the south side of town (head west from Esso); tent sites $13, full hookups $19. The large **Tourist Information Centre,** five kilometers south of town in a shaded rest area, is open in summer daily 8 A.M.–9 P.M.

Sturgeon Lake

Sturgeon Lake, west of Valleyview, is known for its excellent northern pike, perch, and walleye fishing and two interesting provincial parks. Located along the south side of the lake is the **Sturgeon Lake Indian Band Reserve,** whose members are from the Cree Nation. Although many Cree still pursue a traditional lifestyle, the band has built, of all things, a chopstick factory, from where the finished product is exported throughout the world, including to China.

Williamson Provincial Park is only 17 hectares but has a sandy beach, good swimming, and a campground with flush toilets and showers; unserviced sites $13, powered sites $15.

Young's Point Provincial Park, on the lake's northwest shore, tripled in size to more than 3,100 hectares in 1998. Here you'll find good bird-watching for forest birds and waterfowl, and good fishing among the dense aquatic growth close to the shore. Much of the park is forested with a blend of aspen, white spruce, and lodgepole pine. Porcupines, deer, and coyotes wander the woods here, and if you're lucky, you might see red foxes, lynx, and black bears. Hiking trails begin at the day-use area and lead along the lake and to an active beaver pond. The campground has flush toilets, showers, and is near a sandy beach; unserviced sites $13, powered sites $15.

WEST OF EDMONTON

From the provincial capital, the Yellowhead Highway (Hwy. 16) heads west through a region of aspen parkland and scattered lakes to the Canadian Rockies foothills and the border of Jasper National Park. The region's other main thoroughfare, Highway 40, spurs north off the Yellowhead Highway to Grande Cache and Willmore Wilderness Park. An area of frenzied oil activity during the early 1970s, the region west of Edmonton is the center for a large petroleum industry, as well as for farming, coal mining, forestry, and the production of electricity. The major service centers are Edson and Hinton, both on the Yellowhead Highway.

FROM EDMONTON TOWARD HINTON

Long after leaving Edmonton's city limits, the Yellowhead Highway is lined with motels, industrial parks, and housing estates. The towns of Spruce Grove and Stony Plain flash by, and farming begins to dominate the landscape.

Wabamun and Nearby Lakes

Wabamun is the name of a town, lake, and provincial park 32 kilometers west of Stony Plain. The skyline around Wabamun Lake is dominated by high-voltage power lines coming from the three coal-fired generating plants that supply more than two-thirds of Alberta's electrical requirements. Fuel for the plants is supplied by nearby mining operations—the largest coal extraction sites in Canada. Tours of the plants, mines, and the relocated hamlet of **Keephills** can be arranged through TransAlta Utilities, 780/498-7020 (Edmonton).

Wabamun Lake Provincial Park is on Moonlight Bay at the lake's eastern end. The fishing is good for northern pike (especially in fall), a manmade beach is the perfect spot for a swim, and the hiking trail is a good spot for wildlife viewing. Two geothermal outlets create a perfect environment for waterfowl in winter; expect to see up to 40 species at each site. The easiest outlet to get to is at the end of the wharf. The park campground has almost 300 sites, but because of its proximity to Edmonton is very busy on weekends. Facilities include coin-operated showers, firewood sales, kitchen shelters, and a concession; unserviced sites $17 per night, powered sites $19.

On the west side of Wabamun Lake is the busy resort community of **Seba Beach.** Canoes, paddleboats, and fishing boats can be rented from the main pier. **Shadybrook Campground,** 780/797-5433, south of town and close to the beach, is a good place to escape the mob. It has showers and groceries and is close to the lake for fishing; unserviced sites $17, with power and water $19. North of the Yellowhead Highway are other lakes good for swimming, boating, and fishing, including **Lac Ste. Anne.**

Pembina River Provincial Park and Vicinity

The Pembina River Valley is the first true wilderness area west of Edmonton. The small towns of Entwistle and Evansburg straddle either side of the valley where the park lies. The only structures you'll see in this 167-hectare park are an old single-lane road bridge and the concrete foundations of what once was a railroad trestle. White spruce and aspen blanket the park and provide a habitat for many mammals, including beavers, mule deer, white-tailed deer, and moose. Fishing in the river is particularly good for northern pike and walleye, and those who don't fish might appreciate the deep swimming hole behind a weir, or the hiking trails in the northern part of the park. The campground, on the eastern side of the river, has flush toilets,

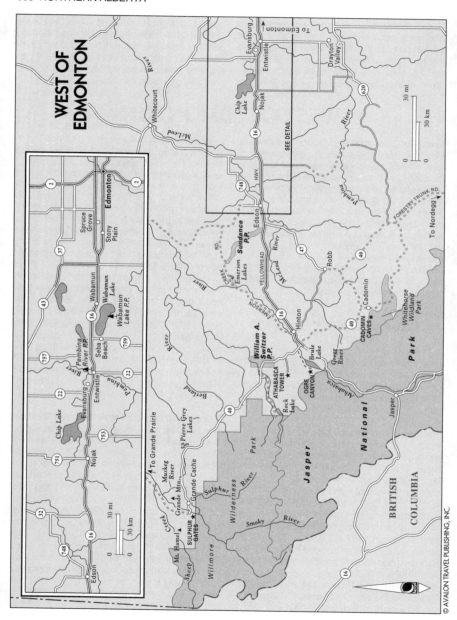

WEST OF
EDMONTON

© AVALON TRAVEL PUBLISHING, INC.

kitchen shelters, and firewood sales; unserviced sites $13, powered sites $16.

Highway 16 bypasses **Entwistle,** but the town's main street is worth a look for its historic buildings. Out on the highway are all the services you'll need: motels (from $45 single, $55 double), restaurants, gas, and, of course, mini-golf.

Continuing west on Highway 16 toward Edson, you'll pass **Chip Lake,** interesting primarily for the scatological story behind its name. It used to be called Buffalo Chip Lake, but the name was shortened for aesthetic reasons.

Edson

The site of today's town of Edson was once the starting point of a trail early settlers used to access the Peace River Valley to the north. Later, the site was picked as a divisional point of the Grand Trunk Pacific Railway, and the town sprang up around it. Today this town of 7,500, located 199 kilometers west of Edmonton, relies on natural resource–based industries such as forestry and oil-and-gas to fuel its economy.

The **Galloway Station Museum** is in the RCMP Centennial Park (5433 3rd Ave.). The museum houses artifacts reflecting the importance of transportation and industry to the town's growth. Also on display in the park are a restored 1917 caboose and a 1964 Lockheed jet. The museum is open in summer daily 10 A.M.–4:30 P.M. Admission is $1.

Most motels are along 2nd Avenue (heading east) and 4th Avenue (heading west). **Castle Motel** (5604 4th Ave., 780/723-3279) is the best value at $38 single, $50 double.

The **Lions Park Campground,** 780/723-3169, at the east end of town, has treed sites far enough from the highway to be relatively quiet. Facilities include extra hot (and fast) showers and plenty of free firewood, which is just as well because you need a bonfire to cook anything on the oversized fire rings; unserviced sites $12, powered sites $15. Primitive campgrounds are signposted east and west of town; most are a short drive from Highway 16 along gravel roads and have a water source, pit toilets, and firewood.

Ernie O's (4340 2nd Ave., 780/723-3600) is one of the best places in town to eat breakfast ($4–7). Nightly specials are $10. **Mountain Pizza & Steakhouse** (5102 4th Ave., 780/723-3900) is a classy pizza joint where the food and prices are excellent. The Mountain Extra Special Pizza ($16) is worth the extra bucks.

The **Tourist Information Centre** is in the RCMP Centennial Park (5433 3rd Ave., 780/723-4918). It's open in summer daily 8 A.M.–7 P.M., the rest of the year weekdays 9 A.M.–5 P.M.

Sundance Provincial Park

As an alternative to taking Highway 16 west from Edson to Hinton, consider the Emerson

Emerson Lakes

Creek Road, which links the two towns, running north of and parallel to Highway 16. The road passes through the 3,712-hectare Sundance Provincial Park, protecting a variety of interesting geological features and the picturesque Emerson Lakes. (Emerson Creek Road is maintained primarily as a logging road, so drive with care and yield to trucks—yellow signs along the road are not kilometer markers.) From Edson, take 51st Street north from Highway 16 for 32 kilometers, turning left (to the west) at the Silver Summit ski area sign; this is Emerson Creek Road, and from this point it's 83 kilometers to Hinton. The two picturesque Emerson Lakes, between signs 53 and 52, were formed as the sheet of ice from the last Ice Age receded. A 5.7-kilometer (90-minute) round-trip trail winds around the lakes to an old trapper's cabin and past some active beaver dams. The lakes are stocked with brook trout and Sundance Creek with rainbow and brown trout. A small campground at the lakes has sites with no services for $9. In the west of the park, between signs 18 and 19, a short trail follows **Canyon Creek** to a point where it cascades dramatically into a series of canyons.

If you're traveling west to east, the access point in Hinton is a little more difficult to find. To get there, take Switzer Drive north from Highway 16, turn left (north) at the traffic light, then at the junction of West River Road, take the right (to the east) fork through the gates to the Hi-Atha lumberyards. This road then crests at another sawmill; take the left (to the north) fork down to a bridge over the Athabasca River and follow this road until Emerson Creek Road is signed to the right.

HINTON

Located on the south bank of the Athabasca River and surrounded in total wilderness, this town of 10,000, located 287 kilometers west of Edmonton, makes an ideal base for a couple of days' exploration. It's also only 75 kilometers from Jasper, but before speeding off into the mountains, take time out to explore Hinton's immediate vicinity. To the south are well-maintained roads leading into the historic Coal Branch; to the north are lakes, streams, canyons, hoodoos, and sand dunes. The town has some interesting sights, and the motels and restaurants have prices you'll appreciate after spending time in Jasper.

Hinton began as a coal-mining and forestry town. These industries still play a major role in the town's economy, although the town now also benefits from being an important service along the Yellowhead Highway.

On the campus of the **Environmental Training Centre** (1176 Switzer Dr., 780/865-8200), you'll find a small museum dedicated to the history of forestry in the province. It's open year-round, weekdays 8:30 A.M.–4:30 P.M. Outside, the **Forestry School Trail**—a 1.5-kilometer interpretive path—winds around the perimeter of the school, passing various forest environments, an old ranger's cabin (get a key from the main office), Edna the erratic,(a huge boulder carried far from its source during the last ice age), and a viewpoint with magnificent views of the Athabasca River Valley and Canadian Rockies. If you're interested in seeing aspects of the forestry industry up close, **Weldwood** offers summer tours of its sawmill (Mon.–Thurs. at 9:30 A.M.) and pulp mill (Mon.–Fri. at 1:30 P.M.). Book tours at 780/865-8586.

Accommodations

The strip of motels, hotels, restaurants, fast-food places, and gas stations along Highway 16 reflects the importance of Hinton as a service center. The cost of motel rooms here is considerably less than in Jasper, one hour west, making the town an ideal alternative for budget-conscious travelers. The **Pines Motel** (beside the golf course, 780/865-2624) has the least expensive rooms in town at $55 single or double. The dowdy-looking **Big Horn Motel** (beside the Husky gas station, 780/865-1555) has surprisingly good rooms, some larger than others; $70 single, $75 double, kitchenettes an extra $10. The **Tara Vista Motel,** 780/865-3391 or 800/661-7651, with the best views in town, is $84 single, $89 double.

The **Holiday Inn Hinton** (780/865-3321, www.hintonholidayinn.com) has a restaurant, an outdoor heated pool, and a fitness room with a hot tub. The 104 rooms are well furnished and equipped with everything from hairdryers to Sony Playstation games; from $79 single, $89 double. The **Best Western White Wolf Inn** (west of town on Hwy. 16, 780/865-7777 or 800/220-7870) features a hot tub, an exercise room, and large, modern rooms for $95 single, $99 double. Hinton's newest accommodation is the **Ramada Limited & Suites,** 780/865-2575, which features 55 comfortable rooms and a gym; $96 single or double includes a light breakfast.

The **Black Cat Guest Ranch,** 780/865-3084 or 800/859-6840, is a mountain retreat west of Hinton. All of the rooms have private baths and views of the mountains. Horseback riding is available during the day, and in the evening, guests can relax in the large living room or hot tub. Meals are included in the rates of $133 single, $168 double. To get to the ranch, take Highway 40 north for six kilometers, turn left to Brûlé and continue for 11 kilometers, then turn right and follow the signs.

Hinton Campground (813 Switzer Dr.) has flush toilets, kitchen shelters, and firewood; $14 per night. A much nicer alternative is to stay at a forest service campground (Emerson Lakes or along the Coal Branch Rd.) or in William A. Switzer Provincial Park toward Grande Cache.

Food

Apart from the fast-food restaurants that line the highway from one end of town to the other, Hinton has little to offer the hungry traveler. The **Husky Restaurant,** as usual, serves filling meals at good prices; open 24 hours. If gas-station dining isn't your style, try the **Greentree Restaurant** in the Holiday Inn. A Continental breakfast is $4, the lumberjack breakfast of steak, bacon, eggs, and hotcakes is $10. Lunch specials are $5.50–8 and dinner specials start at $10. Also in the Holiday Inn is the elegant **Fireside Dining Room,** 780/865-3321. Along the same strip is the **Eagle Steakhouse** (343 Gregg Ave., 780/865-4074), renowned for Alberta beef and also serving chicken and pasta dishes for $13–19 in a comfortable setting; open daily from 4 P.M. **Rancher's** (in the Hill Shopping Centre, 780/865-4129) serves hearty Canadian fare at reasonable prices (from $9 for a dinner entrée).

Services and Information

The **Greyhound bus depot** (128 North St., 780/865-2367) is served daily by buses from Edmonton and Jasper. **National** car rental has an office in the Holiday Inn, 780/817-2662. For **Mountain Taxis,** call 780/865-1889.

The **post office** is on Parks Street. The **Koin Spin and Dry Laundromat** is at 220 Pembina Avenue. The **Tourist Information Centre** is on Gregg Avenue, which parallels the highway, 780/865-2777; open in summer daily 8 A.M.–7 P.M., the rest of the year weekdays 8 A.M.–4 P.M.

THE COAL BRANCH

An area of heavily forested foothills south of Hinton has been the scene of feverish coal-mining activity for 90 years. Most of the mines, along with the towns of Mountain Park, Luscar, Leyland, Coal Spur, and Mercoal, have been abandoned. Two mines still operate, and two towns have survived, although the populations of **Cadomin** and **Robb** have dwindled to approximately 100 residents apiece. This area, so rich in history, is also a wilderness offering hiking, fishing, and spectacular views of the Canadian Rockies. The best way to access the region, known as the Coal Branch, is via Highway 40. The active mines are Cardinal River Coal's pit-mining operation and another at Gregg River. A viewpoint overlooks one of the largest pits. Look for bighorn sheep, oblivious to the rumbling trucks below, at natural salt deposits on the cliff above the viewpoint. If you're interested in touring the mines, contact the information center in Hinton, 780/865-2777. The tours are free, and take up most of the day, departing by bus from Hinton on Tuesday, Thursday, and Friday. A packed lunch is included.

From the junction beyond the mines, a spur branches south to Cadomin and Whitehorse Wildland Park; on your return trip, you can take Highway 40 northeast to Highway 47, passing through the coal-mining hamlet of Robb and rejoining Highway 16 just west of Edson. This 250-kilometer loop through the Coal Branch takes at least one day.

Cadomin

This remote little hamlet—once a town of 2,500—is kept alive by Genstar Cement's Cadomin Quarry, just to the north of town. From the highway, **Cadomin Caves** can be seen in the mountain face west of town, and its "giant's staircase" comes into view. These caves are the best known and most accessible in Alberta. The trail begins two kilometers south of Cadomin, climbing 350 vertical meters in two kilometers to the mouth of the cave. Anyone serious about exploring the caves can find out more from the Tourist Information Centre in Hinton. Cadomin has a motel (780/692-3663), a restaurant, and a general store.

Whitehorse Wildland Park

This 17,500-hectare area of wilderness lies south and west of Cadomin, adjacent to Jasper National Park. Highway 40 south from Cadomin enters the park after three kilometers and crosses Whitehorse Creek after another two kilometers. A trail from this creek crossing leads 10 kilometers up the Whitehorse Creek Valley to **Whitehorse Falls,** another four kilometers to **Whitehorse Pass,** then continues to Miette Hot Springs in Jasper National Park, a total of 40 kilometers one-way. Also at the creek crossing, nestled below a sheer rock wall, is a campground; $9 per night.

Continuing south through the park, Highway 40 climbs above the treeline and passes what's left of **Mountain Park,** once a thriving community of 1,000 connected by rail to Coal Spur to the east. The mine at Mountain Park closed in 1950, and residents dismantled their houses and moved to new locations. Today all that remains is a cemetery, some foundations, and remnants of the narrow-gauge railway.

From here, the road continues climbing to the Cardinal Divide (the division between the Athabasca River System, which flows north, and the North Saskatchewan River System, which flows east), more than 2,000 meters above sea level. This magnificent ridge extends as far as the eye can see to the east and west. No trails are marked in this remote corner of the park, but walking through the treeless alpine landscape is possible in either direction.

HIGHWAY 40 TO GRANDE CACHE

Take divided Highway 16 west out of Hinton and, before you know it, Highway 40 spurs north, passing the following sights, reaching Grande Cache after 142 kilometers.

Ogre Canyon

This unique natural feature, between **Brûlé Lake** and the front ranges of the Canadian Rockies, was created by underground streams that dried up, creating sinkholes. Huge chunks of the treed surface above have dropped down, just like an elevator. In most cases, the trees have continued growing, their tops barely reaching the level of the surrounding ground. Between the canyon and the lake is an old packhorse trail that switchbacks steeply up a hill (look for it near the CPR tunnel). At the top of the ridge, a cairn marks the boundary of Jasper National Park. The trail continues into a lush valley and to a hidden stream that cascades into a canyon below. A dry gully of eroded rock, across the canyon, marks the stream's former route. Camping is possible at Brûlé Lake, although there are no facilities. To get to Ogre Canyon, head north of Highway 16 on Highway 40 and take the first left after crossing the Athabasca River. Continue through Brûlé; the road is rough but passable and ends by Brûlé Lake. The canyon, at the base of the cliffs, is obvious.

Athabasca Tower

Fire towers are spread at regular intervals throughout the foothills. The Athabasca Tower is one of the few that can be reached by a two-wheel-drive vehicle. The access road turns west off Highway 40, 14 kilometers north of Highway 16. The gravel road passes a Nordic center and finishes at the tower. Before attempting to climb the structure, holler for the warden or call 780/865-2400 in advance. The 360-degree view from the 15-meter tower is fantastic. Anyone who doesn't like heights can appreciate the view from a platform a little farther up the road. This is also a popular hang-gliding spot—many record-breaking flights have been made here, thanks to the updrafts that sweep through the valley.

William A. Switzer Provincial Park

This 2,688-hectare park, in the foothills 26 kilometers northwest of Hinton on Highway 40, encompasses a series of shallow lakes linked by Jarvis Creek. Most of the park is heavily forested with lodgepole pine, spruce, and aspen. The northern section, however, is more wide open, and elk, moose, and deer can often be seen grazing there. An ill-fated attempt at beaver ranching was made in the 1940s (cement lodges built for the purpose can be seen near Beaver Ranch Campground). Soon after, Entrance Provincial Park was established and renamed Switzer in 1958. The lakes are excellent for canoeing, bird-watching, and wildlife viewing, but fishing is considered average. Highway 40 divides the park roughly in two, with many access points. From the south, the first road loops around the west side of Jarvis Lake, passing a pleasant picnic area and camping before rejoining Highway 40. At the north end of Jarvis Lake is Kelley's Bathtub day-use area, where a short trail leads to a bird blind. The roads leading into the northern section of the park lead past various hiking trails, three more day-use areas, and three campgrounds.

The main campground is on **Gregg Lake**. It offers 164 sites, coin-operated showers, kitchen shelters, an interpretive theater, and winter camping; unserviced sites $16–18, powered sites $21. In the same vicinity are **Graveyard/Halfway** and **Cache campgrounds,** where sites range $12–14 per night. In the south of the park is **Jarvis Lake Campground;** $14. For more information on the park, call 780/865-5600.

Roughly in the middle of the park is the **Blue Lake Adventure Lodge** (780/865-4741 or 800/582-3305, www.bluelakelodge.com), comprising chalets and cabins in a forested setting and adjacent to Blue Lake. The emphasis is on activities, with canoes, kayaks, mountain bikes, and fishing tackle for rent as well as nearby hiking trails, a spa and sauna, and a game room. Rates for the smallest cabins are $75, those

with two rooms are $105, and the more luxurious chalets are $120. Meal and accommodation packages run $70–90 per person per day. Open year-round.

On to Grande Cache

From Switzer park, it is 118 kilometers to Grande Cache. A 32-kilometer gravel spur to **Rock Lake,** a staging area for hikes into Jasper National Park and a worthwhile destination in itself, is 15 kilometers north of William A. Switzer Provincial Park. Ever since a Hudson's Bay Company post was established at the lake, the area has drawn hikers and anglers, attracted by mountain scenery, the chance of viewing abundant big game, excellent fishing for huge lake trout, and the remote location. Hiking trails lead around the lake and three kilometers to the remote northern reaches of Jasper National Park. Fortunately, you don't have to travel far to appreciate the rugged beauty of the lake and surrounding mountainscapes. The large campground has kitchen shelters, firewood, and pit toilets; sites are $15 per night.

From Rock Lake Road, Highway 40 continues to climb steadily, crossing Pinto Creek and Berland River (small campground), then following Muskeg River for a short while. Continuing north, the road then passes **Pierre Grey Lakes,** a string of five lakes protected as a provincial recreation area. The lakes lie in a beautiful spot, with birdlife prolific and the waters stocked annually with rainbow trout. From the boat launch, a rough trail leads 1.6 kilometers along the lakeshore to the site of a trading post. Camping is $14 per night.

GRANDE CACHE

Grande Cache is a remote town of 4,400, located 450 kilometers west of Edmonton and 182 kilometers south of Grande Prairie. The surrounding wilderness is totally undeveloped, offering endless opportunities for hiking, canoeing, kayaking, fishing, and horseback riding. Immediately to the south is Willmore Wilderness Park, an unspoiled region of snowcapped mountains, rivers, and more than 700 kilometers of hiking trails. The town is located on the side of Grande Mountain above the Smoky River. This

river flows from its source in Jasper National Park through Willmore Wilderness Park and north, through the valley in which Grande Cache lies, to the Peace River, whose waters drain into the Arctic Ocean.

History

The first Europeans to explore the area were fur trappers and traders. They cached furs near the site of the present town before taking them to major trading posts. At one point, there was a small trading post on a lake south of town, remains of which can still be found.

Grande Cache is a planned town. Construction started in 1969 in response to a need for services and housing for miners and their families working at the McIntyre Porcupine Coal Mine. The town was developed 20 kilometers south of the mine to maintain a scenic environment.

Grande Cache Tourism and Interpretive Centre

This center is outstanding, not just considering the size of the town that it represents, but for the wealth of information contained within it. It's easy to spend at least one hour in the two-story complex, with displays that include information about the human history of the region, the local industry, taxidermy, tree identification, and Willmore Wilderness Park. Other features include an information desk, a gift shop,

Pleasant stretches of beach line the shore of Grande Cache Lake.

and a large deck from where views extend across the Smoky River Valley to the highest peaks of the Canadian Rockies. It's open in summer daily 9 A.M.–7 P.M., the rest of the year Mon.–Fri. 8:30 A.M.–4:30 P.M. Call 780/827-3300 or 888/827-3790 for details or for general information on the Grande Cache area.

WILLMORE WILDERNESS PARK

To the west and south of Grande Cache is Willmore Wilderness Park, 4,600 square kilometers of foothill and mountain wilderness accessible only on foot, horseback, or, in winter, skis. It is totally undeveloped; the trails that do exist are not maintained, and in most cases are those once used by trappers. The park is divided roughly in half by the Smoky River. The area west of the river is reached from Sulphur Gates. The east side is far less traveled—the terrain is rougher and wetter.

The park is made up of long, green ridges above the treeline and, farther west, wide passes and expansive basins along the Continental Divide. Lower elevations are covered in lodgepole pine and spruce, whereas at higher elevations the cover changes to fir. The diverse wildlife is one of the park's main attractions; white-tailed and mule deer, mountain goats, bighorn sheep, moose, elk, caribou, and black bears are all common. The park is also home to wolves, cougars, and grizzly bears.

The easiest access to the park is from Sulphur Gates Provincial Recreation Area, six kilometers north of town off Highway 40. From there, follow a gravel road the same distance farther in. Even for those not planning a trip into the park, the cliffs at **Sulphur Gates** (formerly known as Hell's Gate) are only a short walk. These 70-meter cliffs are at the confluence of the Sulphur and Smoky rivers. The color difference between the glacial-fed Smoky River and spring-fed Sulphur River is apparent as they merge. One of the most popular overnight trips is to Clarke's Cache, an easy 16-kilometer hike to the remains of a cabin where the original Grande Cache fur caches were made.

Anyone planning an extended trip into the park should be aware that no services are available within the park, most trails are unmarked,

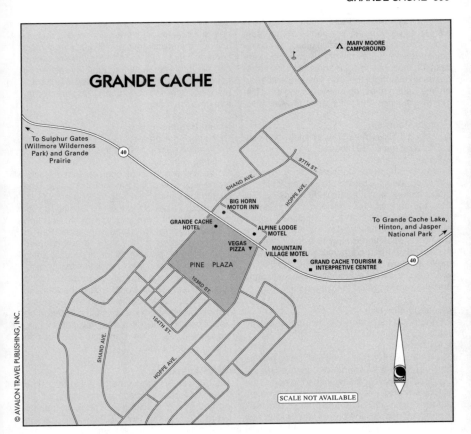

GRANDE CACHE

To Sulphur Gates
(Willmore Wilderness
Park) and Grande
Prairie

40

MARV MOORE
CAMPGROUND

97TH ST.

SHAND AVE.

HOPPE AVE.

BIG HORN
MOTOR INN

GRANDE CACHE
HOTEL

ALPINE LODGE
MOTEL

VEGAS
PIZZA

MOUNTAIN
VILLAGE MOTEL

PINE PLAZA

GRAND CACHE TOURISM &
INTERPRETIVE CENTRE

To Grande Cache Lake,
Hinton, and Jasper
National Park

40

103RD ST.

104TH ST.

SHAND AVE.

HOPPE AVE.

SCALE NOT AVAILABLE

© AVALON TRAVEL PUBLISHING, INC.

and certain areas are heavily used by horse-packers. Three outfitters—**Sherwood Guides and Outfitters,** 780/922-2266; **U Bar Enterprises,** 780/827-3641; and **Wild Rose Outfitting,** 780/693-2296—offer pack trips into the park; expect to pay approximately $150 per person per day, all-inclusive. Shorter trips are also offered, from $15 per hour, but these don't actually enter the park. Information and topographical maps are available from the **Natural Resources Service** office (Shand Ave., Grande Cache, 780/827-3356) or in advance from Alberta Environment, Main Floor, 9945 108th Street, Edmonton, Alberta T5K 2A6, 780/944-0313, www.gov.ab.ca/env.

HIKING AND OTHER RECREATION

The main attraction of the Grande Cache area is the great outdoors, and recreational opportunities around Grande Cache are almost unlimited, but unlike the national parks to the south, commercialism is almost nonexistent, so you're basically by yourself. Two local companies, **Taste of Wilderness Tours,** 780/827-4250, and **Wild Blue Yonder,** 780/827-5450 or 888/511-0298, offer guided hiking, canoeing, rafting, or just about any kind of adventure recreation you can dream up.

Hiking is excellent both inside and outside

Willmore Wilderness Park—many short trails lead to lakes or along the banks of mountain rivers. Climbing the surrounding peaks usually requires at least a half day of walking, and to access the most spectacular areas of Willmore requires an overnight trip. The Tourism and Interpretive Centre has brochures detailing local hiking opportunities. Following are a few favorites.

Grande Mountain
- Length: 3.5 kilometers (90 minutes) one-way
- Elevation gain: 730 meters
- Rating: moderate

The town of Grande Cache sits on the southern shoulder of Grande Mountain, which, at 2,000 meters, is not particularly imposing. But from the summit, the view across the Smoky River Valley to the Canadian Rockies is spectacular. The trail follows a power line the entire way to the peak and is easy to follow. To get to the trailhead, head northwest of town one kilometer and turn right at the cemetery gate. Park, walk along the road to the power line, veer right, and start the long slog to the summit.

Muskeg Falls
- Length: 1.5 kilometers (30 minutes) one-way
- Elevation gain: minimal
- Rating: easy

The trailhead for this pleasant, easy hike to Muskeg Falls is 16 kilometers east of Grande Cache. The gravel parking lot on the north side of Highway 40 is easy to miss. It's two kilometers before the airport. The first half of the trail, through lodgepole pine and aspen, is relatively flat. The trail then forks; to the right is the preferred route, which takes you to the top of the falls, whereas to the left the trail descends steeply to below the falls. In both cases, the trail can be wet and slippery, so stay away from the edge.

Mount Stearn
- Length: 6.5 kilometers (3 hours) one-way
- Elevation gain: 1,000 meters
- Rating: difficult

A good option for a day trip for fit hikers is to the 2,013-meter summit of Mt. Stearn from a trailhead 3.5 kilometers along the access road to Sulphur Gates. The trail begins by climbing alongside a stream through montane, then sub-alpine forest, and then through open meadows before reentering the forest and forking and rejoining. The official trail then climbs steeply and continuously to Lightning Ridge (10 kilometers one-way), but an easier summit is reached by heading up through the grassed slopes to a summit knob, 6.5 kilometers and 1,000 vertical meters from the road.

Mount Hamel
- Length: 7.5 kilometers (3–3.5 hours) one-way
- Elevation gain: 1,110 meters
- Rating: difficult

Mount Hamel is the peak north of Grande Cache on the west side of the Smoky River Valley. The hike to the summit is a long haul up an old logging road. To get to the trailhead, drive 10 kilometers north of town on Highway 40 and turn west at the far end of a grassy meadow. Park in an area just before the road enters the forest. Start hiking up the road to the right, past a "No Trespassing" sign. Take a left at the first junction, from where the road quickly switchbacks to the right. The road climbs slowly around the southern and western flanks of the mountain. From the summit, where there is a cabin, the 360-degree view is breathtaking. On a clear day, Mt. Robson, the highest peak in the Canadian Rockies, can be seen to the south.

Other Recreation
The many rivers that come churning out of the Canadian Rockies provide some exciting kayaking and rafting possibilities. The most popular rivers are Muskeg River (Class I–II), Sheep Creek (Class III–V), and the Smoky River (Class I–II). The first two rivers flow into the Smoky, which can be navigated on a multiday trip to Grande Prairie, Peace River, or even to Inuvik and the Arctic Ocean.

For those who don't need an adrenaline rush to enjoy themselves, the lakes to the east of town are good for exploring by canoe and harbor large populations of waterfowl. These same lakes are good for fishing, with rainbow and brook trout, whitefish, and arctic grayling commonly caught. The only lake with any kind of facilities is **Grande Cache Lake,** five kilometers southeast of town, which has a pleasant picnic area overlooking a beach. Boating, canoeing, and windsurfing are popular on these lakes, but you'll need your own equipment. Grande Mountain is a popular spot for hang-gliding, or you can go mountain biking on the maze of trails in the region.

The **Grande Cache Golf and Country Club,** 780/827-5151, is only nine holes, but you'll want to go around twice, however badly you're playing, because the scenery is distracting to say the least; greens fee is $22.

The whole town celebrates **Coal Dust Daze** in June, a jet-boat race thunders through in July, and a hang-gliding competition and mountain-bike race take place in September.

PRACTICALITIES

Accommodations
Room rates in this mountain hideaway are surprisingly inexpensive, but because fewer than 250 rooms are available in the whole town, reservations should be made in advance. On the highway through town, the **Big Horn Motor Inn,** 780/827-3744, is the best value. Each room has a small fridge, some have kitchenettes, and a laundry room and a restaurant are on the premises; $40–50 single, $50–60 double. Also along the highway are the **Alpine Lodge Motel,** 780/827-2450, $50 single, $60 double; and the **Mountain Village Motel,** 780/827-2453, which charges the same for basic but modern rooms. Overlooking the plaza is the **Grande Cache Hotel** (780/827-3377, www.grandecachehotel.ab.ca), which has 44 standard rooms and a few suites, a restaurant, and a lounge with country bands on weekends; $65 single, $69 double.

Campgrounds
The only camping right in town is at the **Marv Moore Campground,** 780/827-2404, which has semiprivate, well-shaded sites and showers, kitchen shelters, and firewood; unserviced sites $13, hookups $15. It's at the north end of town on Shand Avenue beside the golf course. Alberta Environment campgrounds are spaced at regular intervals along the entire length of Highway 40. Of special note are **Grande Cache Lake,** five kilometers south of town, which has good swimming, canoeing, and fishing ($10); **Sulphur Gates Provincial Recreation Area,** north of town, which makes a good base for exploring Willmore Wilderness Park ($10); and **Smoky River Campground,** 20 kilometers north of town, which has powered sites ($7–10).

Food
On a clear day, the view from the **Family Restaurant** (in the Grande Cache Hotel, 780/827-3377) is worth at least the price of a coffee. Soup and sandwich lunch specials are approximately $6, and pizza and pasta dishes start at $8. The **High Country Restaurant,** also in the hotel, opens at 5 P.M.; dinner entrées range from $12–16, and on Friday night there's a prime rib buffet. At the back of the hotel is **Rockies Bar and Grill,** with a regular bar menu and occasional live music. **Vegas Pizza and Spaghetti House** (207 Pine Plaza, 780/827-5444) is an inexpensive place to go for a meal; portions are large and the atmosphere pleasant.

Services and Information
A contract carrier for **Greyhound** runs a daily service between Hinton and the Alpine Lodge, 780/827-3411. Once you're in town, you're by yourself—there's no local bus or taxi service.

The **post office** is in the plaza, as is a **laundromat** (beside IGA). **Home Hardware,** in the Pine Plaza, stocks camping and fishing gear. The **Grande Cache Tourism and Interpretive Centre** (see previous entry), at the southern approach to town, 780/827-3300 or 888/827-3790, is a great source of local information. The **Natural Resources Service** is at the corner of Shand Avenue and 97th Street, 780/827-3626.

TO GRANDE PRAIRIE

From Grande Cache, a 181-kilometer gravel road follows the Smoky River out of the foothills and into the wide valley in which Grande Prairie lies. Along the route are service campgrounds and good opportunities for wildlife viewing. A worthwhile detour is **Musreau Lake,** where you'll find good fishing, cabins for rent ($40 per night; 780/532-1261), and camping.

GRANDE PRAIRIE AND VICINITY

Grande Prairie, a city of 35,000, is in a wide, gently rolling valley surrounded by large areas of natural grasslands. Edmonton is 460 kilometers to the southeast, while Dawson Creek (British Columbia) and Mile Zero of the Alaska Highway are 135 kilometers to the northwest. Grasslands are something of an anomaly at such a northern latitude. To the south and west are heavily forested mountains, and to the north and east are boreal forests and wetlands. But the grasslands here, *la grande prairie,* provided the stimulus for growth in the region. Although so many of Alberta's northern towns began and grew as trading posts beside rivers, Grande Prairie grew as a result of the land's agricultural potential.

In the late 1800s, when the first settlers began making the arduous journey north to Peace River Country, the area had no roads and no communication to the outside world. Families had to be entirely self-sufficient. But that didn't deter the first immigrants from journeying through 300 kilometers of dense forests and boggy muskeg to the prairie, which was isolated from southern farmland but highly suited to agriculture. When the Grand Trunk Pacific Railway reached Edson, to the south, settlers arrived over the **Edson Trail.** When the railway arrived from Dunvegan in 1916, the settlement—then on the floodplains of Bear Creek—boomed. The population continued to climb slowly but steadily until 1976, when the discovery of Alberta's largest gas reserve nearby boosted it to more than 20,000. Now the largest city in northwestern Alberta, Grande Prairie is a major service, cultural, and transportation center.

SIGHTS

Although malls, motels, restaurants, and other services are spread out along Highway 2 west and north of town, the center of the city has managed to retain much of its original charm. A short walk west of downtown on 100th Avenue is **Bear Creek,** along which most of Grande Prairie's sights lie.

Grande Prairie Museum
Located in Muskoseepi Park and overlooking Bear Creek, this excellent museum, 780/532-5482, houses artifacts from the area's early development, a natural history display, and dinosaur bones from a nearby dig site. Historic buildings outside include a church, a schoolhouse, a blacksmith shop, and a fire station. It's open in summer daily 10 A.M.–6 P.M., the rest of the year Sunday 1–5 P.M.; admission $2. The easiest access from downtown is east along 102nd Avenue.

Muskoseepi Park
Muskoseepi (Bear Creek, in the Cree language) is a 446-hectare city park. The valley through which Bear Creek flows has always been used for recreation and is now preserved as a natural area within the city limits. At the north end of the park is the **Bear Creek Reservoir,** the focal point of the park. Here you'll find an interpretive pavilion, a heated outdoor pool, tennis courts, mini-golf, and canoe rentals ($7 per hour; 780/539-9397). Grande Prairie's main information center is also located here. From the lake, 40 kilometers of hiking and biking trails follow both sides of Bear Creek to the city's outer edge.

Overlooking the reservoir (access from the Hwy. 2 bypass) is **Grande Prairie Regional College.** Designed by renowned architect Douglas Cardinal, the flowing curves of this brick building are the city's most distinctive landmark.

Prairie Art Gallery
Housed in the original Grande Prairie High School (10209 99th St., 780/532-8111), this large facility has three main galleries displaying permanent and temporary exhibitions of work by artists from throughout Canada. It's open year-round Tues.–Fri. 10 A.M.–6 P.M., Sat.–Sun. 1–5 P.M.

Kleskun Hill Natural Area
Kleskun Hill, 20 kilometers east of Grande Prairie along Highway 34, is the most northern badlands in North America. Approximately 70 million

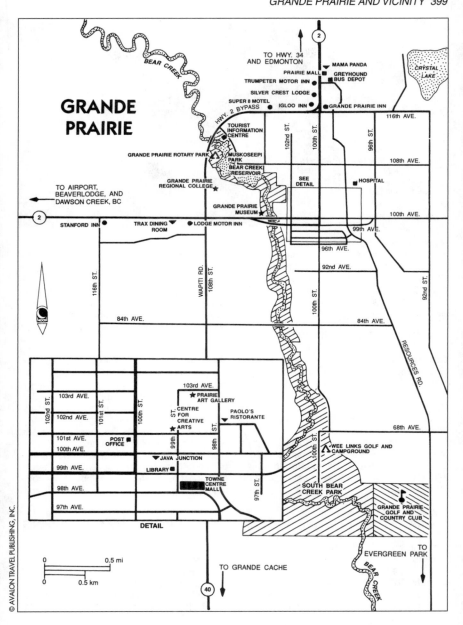

GRANDE PRAIRIE

BEAR CREEK

TO HWY. 34 AND EDMONTON

CRYSTAL LAKE

MAMA PANDA
PRAIRIE MALL
GREYHOUND BUS DEPOT
TRUMPETER MOTOR INN
SILVER CREST LODGE
SUPER 8 MOTEL
IGLOO INN
GRANDE PRAIRIE INN

HWY. 2 BYPASS

TOURIST INFORMATION CENTRE
GRANDE PRAIRIE ROTARY PARK
MUSKOSEEPI PARK
BEAR CREEK RESERVOIR

116th AVE.
108th AVE.

102nd ST.
100th ST.
96th ST.

SEE DETAIL

HOSPITAL

GRANDE PRAIRIE REGIONAL COLLEGE

GRANDE PRAIRIE MUSEUM

TO AIRPORT, BEAVERLODGE, AND DAWSON CREEK, BC

100th AVE.

STANFORD INN
TRAX DINING ROOM
LODGE MOTOR INN

99th AVE.
96th AVE.
92nd AVE.

116th ST.
WAPITI RD.
108th ST.
100th ST.
92nd ST.

84th AVE.

RESOURCES RD.

DETAIL

103rd AVE.
102nd AVE.
101st AVE.
100th AVE.
99th AVE.
98th AVE.
97th AVE.

102nd ST.
101st ST.
100th ST.
99th ST.
98th ST.
97th ST.
100th ST.

PRAIRIE ART GALLERY
CENTRE FOR CREATIVE ARTS
PAOLO'S RISTORANTE
POST OFFICE
JAVA JUNCTION
LIBRARY
TOWNE CENTRE MALL

68th AVE.

WEE LINKS GOLF AND CAMPGROUND

SOUTH BEAR CREEK PARK

GRANDE PRAIRIE GOLF AND COUNTRY CLUB

0   0.5 mi
0   0.5 km

TO GRANDE CACHE

40

TO EVERGREEN PARK

BEAR CREEK

Glen Leslie Church, 22 km east of Grande Prairie, is typical of wooden churches that dotted the rural landscape of Alberta earlier this century.

years ago, the land around these parts was a river delta, which today rises 100 meters above the surrounding prairie. Plant species normally associated with southern latitudes, such as prickly pear cactus, are found here. The only facility is a picnic area at the south end.

RECREATION AND EVENTS

Golfing
Grande Prairie has several challenging and well-maintained golf courses. Greens fee ranges from $21–38. My favorite is the 6,450-yard-long **The Dunes,** on the Wapiti River seven kilometers south of the city, 780/538-4333 or 888/224-2252. It features two distinct "nines," the first with tree-lined fairways, the second, wide open in the style of a Scottish links course. Also south of the city are the **Grande Prairie Golf and Country Club,** 780/532-0340, and the **Bear Creek Golf Club,** 780/538-3393.

Theater
Two theaters offer performances September–April. The **Grande Prairie Little Theatre,** based at the newly renovated Second Street Theatre (10130 98th Ave., 780/538-1616), is small, but all productions are popular. The **Grande Prairie Regional College Theatre,** 780/539-2911, hosts amateur dramas as well as touring performers and country-music stars.

Events
Evergreen Park, south of downtown, is a 200-hectare site that hosts many of the city's larger events, including a farmers' market each Saturday during summer, horse racing, demolition derbies, and fall harvest festivals. The weekend closest to May 31 is **Stompede,** a gathering of North America's best cowboys and chuckwagon drivers. On the Canada Day long weekend, **Bud Country Fever** hits the city. This large gathering of country music stars from Canada and the United States attracts thousands of fans. The regional fair, with a livestock show, chuckwagon races, and a midway, is the last weekend of July. For further information on these events, call the park administration at 780/532-3279. Muskoseepi Park hosts the **Highland Games** on the second weekend of June.

Grande Prairie's climate is perfect for **hot-air ballooning,** and every couple of years the city plays host to a national or international competition.

ACCOMMODATIONS AND CAMPING

Hotels and Motels
All motels are located west and north of downtown along Highway 2; the first two listed are to the west, whereas the remainder line the northern approach to the city. The **Lodge Motor Inn** (10909 100th Ave., 780/539-4700 or 800/661-

7874), has medium-size rooms, and even though they are fairly basic, they provide a good value at $54 single, $68 double. A few blocks farther west, the **Stanford Inn** (11401 100th Ave., 780/539-5678 or 800/661-8160, www.stanfordinn.net) is a large 206-room complex, with newly renovated rooms, a restaurant, and a bar. Rates are also reasonable at $65 single, $70 double.

One of Grande Prairie's least expensive motels is the **Silver Crest Lodge,** north of downtown (11902 100th St., 780/532-1040 or 800/422-7791), which charges $52 single, $55 double. The **Grande Prairie Inn** (11633 Clairmont Rd., 780/532-5221 or 800/661-6529) is a full-service hotel right at the Highway 2 bypass. Facilities include an indoor pool, two restaurants, a lounge, and a nightclub; $72 single, $78 double. Newest of the city's accommodations is the **Super 8 Motel** (10050 116th Ave., 780/532-8288 or 800/800-8000, www .super8.com), featuring an indoor pool and water slide, a laundry facility, and a free Continental breakfast. Rooms here are a good value at $79-89 single or double. The **Trumpeter Motor Inn** (12102 100th St., 780/539-5561 or 800/661-9435) is part of the Travelodge chain. It has 118 rooms, a good restaurant, and an indoor pool, but is a bit overpriced at $79 single, $89 double.

Campgrounds
The **Grande Prairie Rotary Park** (along the Highway 2 bypass, 780/532-1137) overlooks Bear Creek and is a short walk from downtown through Muskoseepi Park. It has showers and a laundry room but few trees; tent sites are $12, RVs and trailers $17-20 (no reservations taken). At the south end of town, along 68th Avenue, is the **Wee Links Golf & Campground,** 780/538-4501, at a pitch-and-putt golf course; $15-17.

OTHER PRACTICALITIES

Food
Downtown is **Java Junction** (9931 100th Ave., 780/539-5070), a small coffee shop with friendly staff; coffee and a muffin is $2.50, and soup, sandwich, and coffee is $6. **Trax Dining Room**

(11001 100th Ave., 780/532-0776) is open daily 6 A.M.-11 P.M. and has good breakfasts from $5 and lunch and dinner from $9. This joint is always busy. **Mama Panda** (12309 100th St., 780/538-1600) is a reasonable buffet restaurant, although the choice of hot dishes is not great; lunch is $7.50, dinner $10-12. **Paolo's Ristorante** (9728 Montrose Ave., 780/539-7400) has a warm, cozy atmosphere and reasonably priced traditional Italian cuisine ($12-18.50). **The Golden Inn** (11201 100th Ave., 780/539-6000) opens at 5:30 A.M. and is popular for breakfast. The Grande Prairie Inn (11633 Clairmont Rd., 780/532-5221) holds two eateries: the **Drake's Nest Café** offers a daily buffet lunch for $8.50, whereas the more upscale **La Provence** offers a French-influenced menu. The cafeteria in Grande Prairie Regional College has inexpensive meals from $4.

Transportation
Grande Prairie Regional Airport is two kilometers west of downtown, then north along Airport Road. It is served by **Air B.C.,** 888/247-2262, which has daily flights to Edmonton International Airport, and **Northern Sky,** 800/668-4037, which has daily flights to Edmonton City Centre Airport.

The **Greyhound bus depot** (9918 121st Ave., 780/539-1111 or 800/661-8747) has a café and lockers. Buses leave four times daily to Edmonton ($51.28 one-way), once daily to Peace River ($17.32), and twice daily to Dawson Creek in British Columbia ($14.98).

For a taxi, call **Prairie Cabs,** 780/532-1060, or **Swan Taxi,** 780/539-4000.

Other Services
The **post office** is at 10001 101st Avenue. **Towne Centre Laundry** is in the Towne Centre Mall on 99th Avenue. **Queen Elizabeth II Hospital** is at 10409 98th Street, 780/538-7100.

Information
The **Grande Prairie Public Library** (9910 99th Ave., 780/532-3580) is an excellent facility open Tues.-Thurs. 10 A.M.-9 P.M., Fri.-Sat. 10 A.M.-6 P.M., and Sunday 1-5 P.M.

The **Tourist Information Centre** is off the Highway 2 bypass and overlooks Bear Creek Reservoir, 780/539-7688. Staffed by friendly volunteers, it's open in summer daily 8:30 A.M.-8:30

GRANDE PRAIRIE / UPPER PEACE RIVER VALLEY

© AVALON TRAVEL PUBLISHING, INC.

P.M. Every Monday, Tuesday, and Thursday at 7 P.M., the center offers a short, guided bus tour of the city, pointing out mainly civic sights, but it's an interesting way to get an overview of the city.

VICINITY OF GRANDE PRAIRIE

Saskatoon Island Provincial Park

For thousands of years, natives have come to this area to collect, as the name suggests, saskatoons (the "Island" part of the name dates to the 1920s, when much of what is now protected was an island, in a shallow body of water that has since disappeared). These sweet, purple-colored berries are still abundant and cover nearly one-third of the 102-hectare park. Late July and August are the best times for berry picking, although park rangers don't encourage the activity. **Little Lake,** with its abundant aquatic vegetation, provides an ideal habitat for **trumpeter swans,** North America's largest waterfowl. This park is one of the few areas in Canada where the majestic bird can be viewed during the nesting season. Vegetation in the park is classified as northern aspen parkland, the only park in Alberta to represent this biome.

The campground has showers, groceries, a food concession, and mini-golf, and is beside a beach; unserviced sites are $13, powered sites $16. The park is 19 kilometers west of Grande Prairie on Highway 2, then three kilometers north.

Beaverlodge and Vicinity

This small town, 40 kilometers west of Grande Prairie along Highway 2, is a northern agricultural center at the gateway to **Monkman Pass,** a pass through the Canadian Rockies found earlier in the 20th century. The only access to the pass is by four-wheel-drive vehicle. **Beaverlodge Hotel** houses a collection of more than 20,000 historical artifacts, including a mechanical stuffed animal.

Two kilometers west from Beaverlodge, the **South Peace Centennial Museum,** 780/354-8869, started as a farmer's hobby and has grown into a working museum cataloging the agricultural history of Alberta, with displays housed in 15 buildings. It's open in summer daily 10 A.M.–6 P.M.; admission is $3. On **Museum Day,** the third Sunday of July, all of the farm machinery is started up and operated.

Sexsmith

North of Grande Prairie, the small town of Sexsmith—once known as the "Grain Capital of the British Empire"—has undergone extensive restoration. Its main street is now a pleasant place to stop, with most businesses fronted by early-1900s–style facades. One block off the main street is the **Sexsmith Blacksmith Shop,** 780/568-3668, a working shop restored to its original 1916 condition. Inside the log structure are more than 10,000 artifacts, including caches of moonshine, which were hidden in the log walls to prevent detection by the North West Mounted Police (NWMP). The shop is open in summer Mon.–Fri. 9:30 A.M.–4:30 P.M., Sat.–Sun. 10 A.M.–4 P.M.

From Sexsmith, Highway 2 climbs slowly through a mixed-wood forest connecting the Saddle Hills, to the west, and the Birch Hills, to the northeast. After crossing a low, indistinguishable summit, the road begins descending into the Peace River Valley.

THE PEACE RIVER VALLEY

From its source in the interior of British Columbia, the Peace River has carved a majestic swath across the northwestern corner of Alberta's boreal forest. Explorers, trappers, settlers, and missionaries traveled upstream from Fort Chipewyan on Lake Athabasca and established trading posts along the fertile valley and surrounding plains. The posts at Fort Vermilion and Dunvegan have slipped into oblivion and are now designated as historical sites, but the town of Peace River has grown from a small post into an agriculture and distribution center that serves the entire Peace River region. The river—so named because on its banks peace was made between warring Cree and Beaver Indians—and the surrounding land are often referred to as Peace Country. This moniker is a throwback to the 1930s, when the government refused to build a rail link and many local residents favored seceding from Alberta and creating their own country.

UPPER PEACE VALLEY

The Upper Peace Valley extends 230 kilometers from the Alberta/British Columbia border to the town of Peace River. From Highway 49, on the south side of the river, and highways 64 and 2 on the north side, roads lead down to the river and nine recreation and camping areas, initially developed for the bicentennial of Alexander Mackenzie's historical passage to the Pacific Ocean. The best way to start a visit to the region is to stop at **Rycroft,** at the junction of Highways 2 and 49. **Courtesy Corner,** 780/765-3730, an enormous red-and-white tepee situated right at the highway junction, houses an information center and sells local arts and crafts; open in summer daily 9 A.M.–8 P.M.

Moonshine Lake Provincial Park and Vicinity

More than 100 species of birds and, in winter,

high concentrations of moose call Moonshine Lake Provincial Park home. Occupying 1,080 hectares 42 kilometers west of Rycroft, the park is best known for its rainbow trout fishing. Some people claim that the lake is named for the moon's reflection on its still water, although it more likely came from a fellow who sold moonshine to travelers en route to Dawson Creek. Campsites are scattered among stands of aspen, poplar, and white spruce, and all have showers, flush toilets, kitchen shelters, a concession, and firewood; unserviced sites $13, powered sites $16.

From south of the park, Highway 49 continues 54 kilometers to the Alberta/British Columbia border and another 19 kilometers to Dawson Creek at Mile Zero of the Alaska Highway. **Cotillion Park,** on the southern banks of the Peace River, is accessible along 35-kilometer Pillsworth Road (Hwy. 719), eight kilometers from the border. Many large mammals frequent this secluded park, and sandstone cliffs here have been eroded into strange-looking pinnacles called hoodoos. Camping, with showers, is $11.

Historic Dunvegan

As Highway 2 descends into the Peace River Valley from the south, it crosses Alberta's longest suspension bridge at Dunvegan—a point that was the site of many trading posts and a mission. On the east side of the road is a large **interpretive center,** 780/835-5244, featuring displays that tell the story of Dunvegan and its role in the early history of northern Alberta. The center is open May–Sept. daily 10 A.M.–6 P.M. On the riverbank are the restored church and rectory of the St. Charles Roman Catholic Mission, circa 1885 (look for the gnarled maple tree, planted by early missionaries, behind the mission site). A gravel road leads under the bridge to the site of the original settlement, **Fort Dunvegan,** which was built as a trading post for the North West Company in 1805, and in use until 1918. Behind the site, hidden in the trees, is a white Hudson's Bay Company factor's house. Also on the west side of the bridge is a truck farm that dates back more than 100 years.

A small provincial park on the east side of the bridge has a 67-site campground; unserviced sites $13, powered sites $15. Downstream from the fort is the **Dunvegan Tea Room,** 780/835-4459, in an old greenhouse, which, naturally, means it's a well-lit place and surrounded by plenty of greenery.

Highway 64

From **Fairview,** 26 kilometers northeast of Dunvegan, Highway 64 heads north then west, roughly following the Peace River into British Columbia. To the west, on the banks of the Peace River, are two campgrounds that form part of the Upper Peace Valley Recreation Area. **Pratt's Landing** is along Highway 682, and to the north, at the mouth of Montagneuse River, is **Carter Camp.** Back on Highway 64 is the town of **Hines Creek** and its **End of Steel Museum and Heritage Park,** 780/494-3522, featuring a caboose, a church, a trapper's cabin, and a Russian pioneer home; open in summer, Mon.–Fri. 9 A.M.–5 P.M., weekends 1–7 P.M. From Hines Creek, it is 98 kilometers to the British Columbia border.

PEACE RIVER

From all directions, the final approach into the town of Peace River is breathtaking. This town of 6,800 straddles the majestic Peace River below the confluence of the Smoky and Heart rivers. Alexander Mackenzie was one of the earliest white men to visit the region. He established a post, named Fort Forks, on the south bank of the river, upstream of the present town. From here, after the winter of 1792–1793, he completed his historic journey to the Pacific Ocean and became the first person to cross the North American continent north of Mexico. The first permanent settlers were missionaries who, apart from their zealous religious work, promoted the region for its agricultural potential and as a service center and distribution point for river transportation. When the rail link with Edmonton was completed in 1916, land was opened for homesteading, and settlers poured into town. The farming traditions they began continue on.

Sights

Many historic buildings line the main street (100th St.), and many have plaques with historical facts. The wide street is typical of early

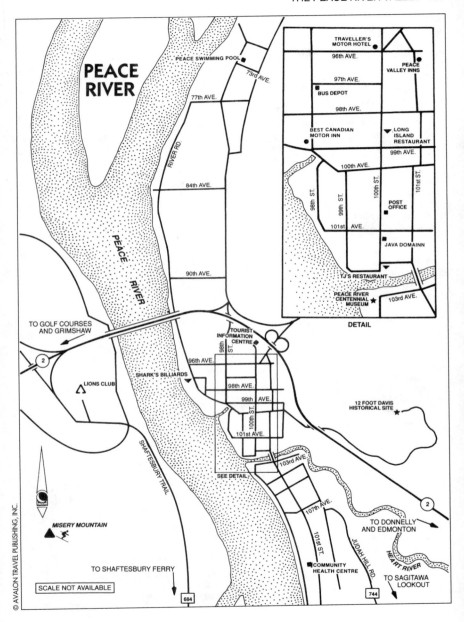

PEACE RIVER

PEACE SWIMMING POOL

73rd AVE.

RIVER RD.

77th AVE.

84th AVE.

90th AVE.

PEACE RIVER

TO GOLF COURSES
AND GRIMSHAW

2

LIONS CLUB

SHARK'S BILLIARDS

TOURIST
INFORMATION
CENTRE

98th ST.

96th AVE.

98th AVE.

99th AVE.

100th ST.

101st AVE.

SHAFTESBURY TRAIL

MISERY MOUNTAIN

MOON

SCALE NOT AVAILABLE

TO SHAFTESBURY FERRY

684

SEE DETAIL

103rd AVE.

107th AVE.

101st ST.

COMMUNITY
HEALTH CENTRE

JUDAH HILL RD.

744

12 FOOT DAVIS
HISTORICAL SITE

TO DONNELLY
AND EDMONTON

2

HEART RIVER

TO SAGITAWA
LOOKOUT

DETAIL

TRAVELLER'S
MOTOR HOTEL

96th AVE.

97th AVE.

BUS DEPOT

98th AVE.

PEACE
VALLEY INNS

BEST CANADIAN
MOTOR INN

LONG
ISLAND
RESTAURANT

99th AVE.

100th AVE.

98th ST.

99th ST.

100th ST.

101st ST.

101st AVE.

POST
OFFICE

JAVA DOMAINN

TJ'S RESTAURANT

PEACE RIVER
CENTENNIAL
MUSEUM

103rd AVE.

© AVALON TRAVEL PUBLISHING, INC.

boomtowns in that its width allowed wagons to turn around. At the southern end of the street, across the mouth of the Heart River, is the **Peace River Centennial Museum** (10302 99th St., 780/624-4261), which has displays on native clothing, the fur trade, early explorers, and the development of the town, and an extensive photo collection and archives. It's open in summer daily 9 A.M.–5 P.M.; admission is $3.

Two spots near downtown afford excellent views of the Peace River and the valley through which it flows. To access the closest, take 100th Avenue under Highway 2 and follow this winding road to its end, or, alternatively, take 101st Street south to 107th Avenue, which links up with Judah Hill Road. This road passes **Sagitawa Lookout**, from where you can see the town, the valley, and the confluence of the Peace and Smoky rivers.

On the west side of the river is the site of **Shaftesbury**, a settlement that grew around an Anglican mission founded in 1887. From the site, Highway 684 follows the historic Shaftesbury Trail—used for hundreds of years by natives, explorers, traders, missionaries, and Klondikers—to Blakely's Landing from where the **Shaftesbury Ferry** now crosses the river all summer, daily 7 A.M.–midnight.

Recreation and Events

The nine-hole course at **Peace View Golf & Country Club,** 780/624-1164, is along Weberville Road, west of town. Farther west is the **Mighty Peace Golf and Country Club,** 780/332-4653, an 18-hole championship course; greens fee $27.50. The **Peace River Swim-**

ming Pool (9810 73rd Ave., 780/624-3720) opens for public swimming each day; $4.50.

Misery Mountain, 780/624-4881, off Highway 684, is visible from most points in town. It's the largest nonmountain ski area in Alberta, with a vertical rise of 160 meters. Although the lifts don't operate in summer, views from the summit are well worth the one-hour walk from the base area. In winter, lifts run on Friday night and all weekend. Lift tickets are $15.

The second weekend of July, the **Peace Festival** brings a parade, street performances, and a rock concert to town. The **Lobster Fest** in mid-September centers around a feast of East Coast lobster, as well as an outdoor concert and various family activities. Fall is welcomed with **Bullorama,** a two-day rodeo on the last weekend of September at the Kinsmaen Arena.

Accommodations

The least expensive accommodation in town is the **Best Canadian Motor Inn** (9810 98th St., 780/624-2586 or 888/700-2264); $49 single, $54 double. Kitchenettes are an extra $8. The following two motels are at the north end of downtown but are still within walking distance of shops and restaurants. **Peace Valley Inns** (9609 101st St., 780/624-2020 or 800/661-5897) is beside a 24-hour Smitty's Restaurant; from $53 single, $58. One block west (9510 100th St., 780/624-3621 or 800/661-3227), is the **Traveller's Motor Hotel,** which has a sauna, a restaurant, a lounge, and more than 140 rooms at $55–75 single or double. Peace River's newest accommodation is the **New Western Budget Motel** (7701 100th Ave., 780/624-3445); $60 single, $65 double.

Before 1916, Peace River had no rail line and was just one of many remote posts throughout the north.

TWELVE-FOOT DAVIS

Pathfinder, pioneer, miner, trader. He was every man's friend and never locked his cabin door.

This fitting tribute adorns the headstone of Twelve-Foot Davis, one of the early pioneers of the Peace River Country.

Born Henry Fuller Davis in Vermont in 1820, Twelve-Foot was not a giant of a man. In fact, he was short. But he got his name from a claim he staked in the Cariboo goldfields in British Columbia. He noticed that two very successful claims had a 12-foot strip between them, so he staked the area and made a fortune. Continuing north, he arrived in the Peace River Country in the 1870s, opening up trading posts as far apart as Hudson's Hope (British Columbia) and Fort Vermilion, but spending most of his later years running a post at Dunvegan. He died at Grouard in 1900, and in response to his dying wishes, he now lies buried high above his beloved river (access from 100th Ave., and under Hwy. 2).

The **Lions Club Campground** (on the west side of the river, 780/624-2120) has well-shaded sites, showers, a laundry room, and groceries; unserviced sites $12, hookups $14–18. Other campgrounds include **Tangent Park,** beside the Shaftesbury Ferry south of town; at both golf courses (west of town); and west of town off Highway 2 at **Queen Elizabeth Provincial Park.**

Food

If you're looking for just coffee or a light meal, a pleasant choice is **Java Domain** (10107 100th St., 780/624-5557), a city-style coffeehouse. Restaurant choices are limited. Try busy **TJ's Restaurant** (10011 102nd Ave., 780/624-3427), where the Chinese dishes are better than the Canadian and there's generally a daily pasta special. Especially delicious is the Seafood Hotpot, $15. Offering a similar menu is the **Long Island Restaurant** (9809 100th St., 780/624-9220), where a buffet is served weekdays lunchtime and Fri.–Sun. evenings. **Alexander's,** in the Traveller's Motor

Hotel (9510 100th St., 780/624-3621), also offers a weekday lunchtime buffet, a seafood dinner buffet October–April on Friday, and a regular menu the rest of the week. In the same hotel is a café open from 5:30 A.M. Along River Road is **Shark's Billiards & Sports Lounge,** 780/624-5007, which offers meals at lunch and dinnertime.

Transportation and Tours

The **airport,** 13 kilometers west of town, is served by **Air Canada,** 888/247-2262, and **Peace Air,** 780/563-3060. The **Greyhound** bus depot (9801 97th Ave., 780/624-2558) is downtown with daily services to Edmonton, Grande Prairie, and Hay River in the Northwest Territories. For **Peace River Taxi,** call 780/624-3020. Departing at 2 P.M., **Peace Island Tours** operates jet-boat trips 60 kilometers down the Peace River to a 14-hectare island with log cabins. The seven-hour Supper Cruise is $72 per person, whereas the overnight journey, including three meals, the boat ride, and lodging, is $130 per person. For more information, call 780/624-4295.

Services and Information

The **post office** is at 10031 100th Street. The **Peace River Community Health Centre** is at 10915 99th Street, 780/624-7500. For the **RCMP,** call 780/624-6611. The Mighty Peace Tourist Association operates a **Tourist Information Centre** in the old Peace River railway station at the top end of 100th Street (behind KFC), 780/624-2044; it's open in summer daily 10 A.M.–6 P.M.

MACKENZIE HIGHWAY

Named for 18th-century explorer Alexander Mackenzie, this route, also known as Highway 35, extends from Grimshaw, 24 kilometers west of Peace River, for 473 kilometers north to the Northwest Territories. It passes through a vast, empty land dominated by the Peace River and a seemingly endless forest of spruce, poplar, and jack pine. The main population centers are Manning and High Level. Along the way are many stump-filled fields, carved out of the boreal forest by farmers who, for the last 100 years, have eked out a living from some of the world's northernmost farmland. The only access to the Peace River is at Notikewin Provincial Park and at **Tompkin's Landing,** a ferry crossing east of Paddle Prairie.

When you're through exploring this wild northland, you have two alternatives to backtracking along Mackenzie Highway. One is to continue into the Northwest Territories and complete what is known as the **Deh Cho Connection,** which links the Mackenzie with the Liard and Alaska highways—an 1,800-kilometer loop that finishes in Dawson Creek, British Columbia. The other option is to follow Highway 58 east from High Level and head south on the Bicentennial Highway 430 kilometers to Slave Lake.

Grimshaw

Best known as Mile Zero of the Mackenzie Highway, this town of 2,700 has grown around the railway as a farming center. For many years after the railway arrived, it was a jumping-off point for farmers, trappers, and homesteaders in Peace Valley Country. Camp at nearby Queen Elizabeth Provincial Park (see following section) or continue 11 kilometers north to **Bear Creek Golf Course,** where camping with hookups and showers is $15.

Lac Cardinal

North of Grimshaw, on the eastern shore of Lac Cardinal, is **Queen Elizabeth Provincial Park.** The lake is very shallow, and no streams flow from it. This creates an ideal habitat for many species of waterfowl. Beavers, moose, and black bears are also present. The camping area has pit toilets and kitchen shelters; unserviced sites $13, powered sites $20, which includes one bundle of firewood. Immediately south of the park is **Lac Cardinal Regional Pioneer Village,** 780/332-2030, featuring a large outdoor collection of memorabilia from the Peace River region. It's open in summer Fri.–Sun. 3–7 P.M.

To Manning

From Grimshaw, it is 40 kilometers north to the small hamlet of **Dixonville.** Here you'll find a trading post and the turnoff to Sulphur Lake (55 kilometers northwest along Highway 689), where camping is available.

A homestead built by a Latvian settler in 1918 is located three kilometers south of **North Star,** on the old Highway 35. It has been declared a Provincial Historical Site, and although it's locked, you can look in the windows and see homemade wooden beds and a sauna, and appreciate the work that went into the hand-hewn log buildings.

Manning

As the highway descends into the picturesque Notikewin Valley, it passes through the relatively new town of Manning. Formerly called Aurora, this town of 1,200 is a service center for the region's agricultural and petroleum industries. At the south end of town, one kilometer east on Highway 691, is the excellent **Battle River Museum,** 780/836-2374, which has a large collection of antique wrenches, taxidermy (including a rare albino moose), carriages and buggies, farm machinery, a birch necklace carved out of a single piece of wood, and a collection of prehistoric arrowheads—ask to see the one embedded in a whalebone. The museum is open in summer daily 10 A.M.–6 P.M.

Manning Motor Inn, 780/836-2801, is at the south end of town and has a restaurant; $59 single, $71 double. **Manning Municipal Campground** is immediately west of the Tourist Information Centre in a shaded spot beside the Notikewin River. The campground is small (10 sites), but has showers and powered sites; $10. It is also possible to camp at the golf course, north of town, which offers powered sites ($10 per night) and a restaurant. The **Tourist Information Centre,** 780/836-3606, is on the main street in an old hospital building; open from May to mid-September daily 9 A.M.–5 P.M. Next to the information center is an old hospital dating to 1937. It has recently been opened as an art gallery, 780/836-2969; open Mon.–Sat. 10 A.M.–5 P.M.

Notikewin Provincial Park

Twenty-one kilometers north of Hotchkiss, Highway 692 turns east off Highway 35 and leads to Notikewin Provincial Park, a 970-hectare preserve at the confluence of the Notikewin and Peace rivers. The 30-kilometer road to the park is partly paved and occasionally steep. In *Notikewin* (battle, in the Cree language), a stand of 200-year-old spruce presides over Spruce Island, at the mouth of the Notikewin River. The island also supports an abundance of ostrich ferns growing to a height of two meters. Beavers, mule deer, moose, and the occasional black bear can be seen in the area. Bird species are diverse and include sandhill cranes, which rest at the mouth of the Notikewin River on their southern migration in September. The river offers good fishing for gold-eye, walleye, and northern pike. Camping is $9.

If you're looking for a spot to camp without detouring from Highway 35, continue 23 kilometers north to **Twin Lakes,** where camping is also $9. Take time to walk the three-kilometer (50-minute) circuit around the larger of the two lakes—it's a typical environment of boreal forest, and it has been unaffected by fire or deforestation for more than 80 years.

A Short Detour

The largest of eight Métis settlements established throughout the province during the 1930s is **Paddle Prairie,** 65 kilometers north of Twin Lakes. From 10 kilometers north of here, a gravel road (Hwy. 697) leads east to the Peace River and Tomkin's Landing and one of only eight ferry crossings in the province (operates in summer, daily 24 hours). It then continues to La Crete and Fort Vermilion, crosses the Peace River, and intersects Highway 58, which heads west, rejoining the Mackenzie Highway at High Level.

La Crete (pop. 1,400) has grown into an agricultural center on the northern fringe of the continent's arable land. Most residents are Mennonites who moved to the region in the 1930s. They are from a traditional Protestant sect originating in Holland, whose members settled in remote regions throughout the world and established self-sufficient agricultural lifestyles, in hopes of being left to practice their faith in peace. On the streets and in the local restaurants, you'll hear their language, *Plattdeutsch* (Low German), which is spoken by Mennonites throughout the world.

To the southeast of this flat, prairielike area, the Buffalo Head Hills rise almost 700 meters above the surrounding land. The only way into the hills is along an 18-kilometer gravel road that spurs east from Highway 697 approximately 18 kilometers south of La Crete. To the west, an eight-kilometer road from town leads past a golf course to one of the Peace River's many natural sandbars, and to Etna's Landing where there is good swimming.

Fort Vermilion

This town of 800, on the south bank of the Peace River, 40 kilometers north of La Crete and 77 kilometers east of High Level, vies with Fort Chipewyan as the oldest settlement in Alberta. It was named for the red clay deposits present in the banks of the river. The first trading post here was established a few kilometers downstream of present-day Fort Vermilion by the North West Company in 1788. Trade with the Beaver, Cree, and Dene was brisk, and by 1802 the Hudson's Bay Company had also established a post. In 1821, the companies merged, and in 1830 they moved operations to the town's present site. The area's agricultural potential gained worldwide attention when locally grown wheat, transported along the river highway, won a gold medal at the 1876 World Fair in Philadelphia. For 150 years, supplies arrived by riverboat or were hauled overland from the town of Peace River. When the Mackenzie Highway was completed, the river highway became obsolete. The last riverboat arrived in Fort Vermilion in 1952, but not until 1974, when a bridge was built across the Peace River, was the town linked to the outside world. Many old buildings and cabins, in varying states of disrepair, still stand. Pick up a *Fort Vermilion Heritage Guide* from the Tourist Information Centre to help identify the many historical sites in town. The **Mary Batt & Son General Store** was constructed from logs removed from the 1897 Hudson's Bay Company post.

The **Sheridan Lawrence Inn**, 780/927-4400, is the only place to stay in town. Its 16 rooms go for $64 single, $72 double. It has a small restaurant, open from 7 A.M., with a Canadian and Chinese menu. Breakfast is reasonable at $6. The summer-only **Tourist Information Centre**, 780/927-3216, is in a dove-tailed log home built by hand in 1923. Open in summer daily 9 A.M.–5 P.M.

High Level

Named for its location on a divide between the Peace and Hay River watersheds, High Level (pop. 3,100), located 279 kilometers north of Grimshaw, is the last town before the Alberta/Northwest Territories border. It is a major service center for a region rich in natural re-sources. The town expanded during the oil boom of the 1960s and has prospered ever since. The grain elevators, serving agricultural communities to the east, are the northernmost in the world. Forestry is also a major local industry; the town boasts one of the world's most productive logging and sawmill operations, turning out more than 250 million board-feet of lumber annually.

Fortunately, much of the surrounding forest is safe from loggers; the 19-million-hectare **Footner Lake Forest** has poor drainage, forming major bogs and permafrost that make timber harvest commercially unviable. The forest encompasses the entire northern part of the province west of Wood Buffalo National Park.

Northeast of High Level are the **Caribou Mountains,** which rise to a plateau 800 meters above the Peace River. At that altitude, and being so far north, the fragile environment is easily disturbed. The mountains are blanketed in white spruce, aspen, and pine, and two lakes—Margaret and Wentzel—offer excellent fly-fishing. Northwest of High Level are the Cameron Hills and **Bistcho Lake** (where Albertan fish hatcheries harvest walleye spawn). The most accessible part of the forest is **Hutch Lake,** 32 kilometers north of town. The lake is surrounded by aspen and poplar and is the source of the **Meander River.** The dominant feature here is **Watt Mountain** (780 meters), which you can

AURORA BOREALIS

The aurora borealis, or northern lights, is an emotional experience for some, spiritual for others, and without exception is unforgettable—an exhibition of color that dances the sky like a kaleidoscope.

Auroral light is created through a complex process—a spontaneous phenomenon with no pattern and no "season"—that occurs within the earth's atmosphere and starts with the sun. Essentially a huge, atomic fusion reactor, the sun emits the heat and light that keep us alive, and also emits electronically charged ions that are thrust through space at high speeds. When these ions reach the earth's rarefied upper atmosphere—about 180 km above the earth's surface—they are captured by the earth's magnetic field and accelerated toward the poles. Along the way they col-lide with the atoms and molecules of the gases in the atmosphere, which in turn become temporarily charged or "ionized." This absorbed energy is then released by the ionized gases, often in the form of light. The color of the light varies from red to yellow to green, depending on the gas: nitrogen atoms produce a violet and sometimes red color, oxygen a green and, at higher altitudes, an orange.

Because the magnetic field is more intense near the north and south magnetic poles the lights are best seen at high latitudes. In northern Alberta the light show takes place up to 160 nights annually, with displays best north of Peace River. They generally start as a faint glow on the northeastern horizon after the sun has set, improving as the sky becomes darker.

see to the northwest of High Level. From Hutch Lake, a service road leads 10 kilometers to a lookout and 21 kilometers to a fire tower on the summit. The recreation area at the north end of the lake has a large picnic area, an interpretive trail, and camping. Maps are available at the Tourist Information Centre.

The only worthwhile sight in town is the **Mackenzie Crossroads Museum** (at the south entrance to town, 780/926-4811). Located in the tourist information center building, the museum is themed on a northern trading post, with interesting displays telling the human history of northern Alberta. In another room, the industries upon which High Level was built are described through photographs and interpretive boards. A three-dimensional map of northwestern Alberta gives a great perspective of this inaccessible part of the province. The museum is open in summer Mon.–Fri. 9 A.M.–9 P.M., Sat.–Sun. 10 A.M.–8 P.M., and the rest of the year Mon.–Sat. 9 A.M.–4:30 P.M.

Motel prices in High Level are just a warm-up for those in the Northwest Territories, so don't be surprised at $60 rooms that you'd prefer to pay $40 for. The motels in town are usually full throughout the year with work crews. The least expensive option is the **Family Motel**, 780/926-3395; $38 single, $45 double. The **Four Winds Hotel** (780/926-3736 or 888/449-4637, www .4windshotel.com) provides a good value. Each of the 75 air-conditioned rooms has a small fridge and a microwave, and guests have use of a laundry room; $48 single, $52 double. The **Best Canadian Motor Inn**, 780/926-2272, has recently undergone a total facelift, 76 rooms and the restaurant included, to make it the most comfortable accommodation in High Level; rates are $68 single, $78 double. A free municipal campground is 400 meters east of town on Highway 35 (but it's pretty grotty), and a primitive campground lies farther north at **Hutch Lake Recreation Area**, $9 per night. **Aspen Ridge Campground**, 780/926-4540, three kilometers south of town, is privately owned and has coin showers and a laundry; unserviced sites $13, hookups $15–20.

The **Family Restaurant**, 780/926-3111, in front of the Family Motel, offers a Chinese buffet lunch ($8) and a regular dinner menu with main meals from $10. Another Chinese place is the **Canton Restaurant** (100th Ave., 780/926-3053); the combo dinners seem like a good deal, but portions are small, so stick to the main meals. The restaurant in the Sunset Motor Inn serves dishes starting at $10, including a salad bar (which also offers soup and fresh fruit). Also here is a lounge and a nightclub that are open Friday and Saturday nights with occasional live bands.

Footner Lake Airport, north of town, is served by **Northern Sky,** 780/926-3672 or 800/668-4037, from Edmonton's City Centre Airport. Buses depart daily from the **Greyhound** bus depot (10101 95th St., 780/926-3233) for Peace River, continuing to Edmonton, and northbound buses terminate at Hay River.

The post office, banks, library, and several laundromats are located on 100th Street. The large **Tourist Information Centre,** 780/926-4811, is at the south end of town. It's open in summer Mon.–Fri. 9 A.M.–9 P.M., Sat.–Sun. 10 A.M.–8 P.M., and the rest of the year Mon.–Sat. 9 A.M.–4:30 P.M.

Rainbow Lake

Rainbow Lake is an oil field community of 1,100, located 141 kilometers west of High Level along Highway 58. The town grew around oil-and-gas exploration during the 1960s, and today a pipeline links it to Edmonton. Vast reservoirs of these resources still lie underneath the ground, untapped until oil prices rise. **Husky Oil Operations** offers tours of its plant; call ahead at 780/956-8000 for details. The town has a golf course, two motels, and two restaurants. A campground 24 kilometers southwest of town on the Buffalo River has a few primitive sites, which are free. The other option is **Rainbow Lake Recreation Area**, 48 kilometers south of town, where there's a beach with swimming, fishing, and campsites for $9.

Hay-Zama Lakes

This complex network of lakes, marshes, and streams is one of Canada's largest freshwater wetlands. It covers 800 square kilometers and is home to more than 200 species of birds. It's also the main source of the Hay River, which flows north to Great Slave Lake. This fragile ecosystem, 160 kilometers northwest of High

Level, is relatively remote and would have remained that way except for the large reservoirs of oil that lie beneath its surface. Oil and birds do not mix, but drilling has gone ahead, and the small community of **Zama City,** north of the lakes, has grown around the drilling project. The town is also the southern terminus for an interprovincial pipeline from the oil fields at Norman Wells (in the Northwest Territories). Strict environmental guidelines mean that most of the mining activity takes place during winter, after the many thousands of geese, ducks, and other shorebirds have migrated south. Although no roads or camping areas are designated around the lakes, many gravel roads used by the natives and oil-exploration personnel lead through the area.

The Border or Bust

From High Level, it is 191 kilometers to the Alberta/Northwest Territories border. The road follows the Meander River to a town of the same name at the confluence of the Hay River, which then parallels the border. The settlement of **Meander River** is on a Dene Tha Indian Reserve and is noted for its many local artists. Watch for the local rabbit population living beside the road. North of the community, where the highway crosses the Hay River, a gravel road leads 63 kilometers to the oil town of Zama City. Campgrounds are located north of Meander River and just south of the small community of **Steen River,** a base for forest-fire–fighting planes. Alberta's northernmost community is **Indian Cabins,** 14 kilometers from the border. The cabins that gave the town its name are gone, but a traditional native cemetery with spirit houses covering the graves is located 200 meters north of the gas station. In the trees is the scaffold burial site of a child whose body was placed in a hollowed-out log and hung between the limbs of two trees.

NORTHWEST TERRITORIES

TERRITORIES

AND

NUNAVUT

KAREN MCKINLEY

INTRODUCTION

As the world's last great wilderness frontiers slowly disappear, Canada's vast northlands—the Northwest Territories and Nunavut—remain relatively untouched, unspoiled, and uninhabited. Once these lands were home only to small populations of indigenous Dene and Inuit people who had adapted to the harsh environment. But explorers, whalers, missionaries, and governments eventually found their way here, bringing rapid changes to native lifestyles. Today, travelers, adventurers, writers, artists, and scientists come in search of the territories' unlimited opportunities for naturalist and wilderness pursuits.

Within the region's borders are two of the world's 10 largest lakes, one of the world's longest rivers, a waterfall twice the height of Niagara, two UNESCO World Heritage Sites, five national parks, the glaciated peaks of Baffin and Ellesmere islands, and an amazing abundance of wildlife.

THE LAND

The two territories' 3.4 million square kilometers take up one-third of Canada—an area almost half the size of the United States, with a population of only 64,500, just 0.2 percent of Canada's total population. Its borders stretch from the 60th parallel to the 84th, and from the Yukon to Davis Strait (just 50 kilometers from Greenland)—more than 3,200 kilometers in each direction. Aside from political divisions, the land can be divided into two regions: below the treeline and above it. The treeline is marked on most Canadian maps as a single line that snakes from the southern reaches of Hudson Bay northwest to the Mackenzie Delta near Inuvik. The "line" provides a rough idea of where the boreal forest stops and the treeless tundra starts. But the actual transition takes place gradually across many kilometers and varies in latitude depending on the topography and climate of the particular area.

Apart from the **Mackenzie Mountains,** which form the Northwest Territories/Yukon border, the dominant natural feature of the mainland is the glacially scarred bedrock of the Canadian Shield. As ice from four or five ice ages receded north, it scoured the bedrock, carving hundreds of depressions—now lakes—and creating meltwater streams that today flow throughout the land. In the west is the **Mackenzie River,** the 10th-longest river in the world. North and east of the Mackenzie River Valley, the land is relatively flat. Only lakes, rivers, and low rolling hills break the monotonous landscape, which ends at the west coast of Hudson Bay and, farther north, at the Arctic coast. The tidal zone here is devoid of sessile life, which would be crushed by annual movement of pack ice. North of the Arctic coast are the lower Arctic islands, which are generally less than 300 meters above sea level, their gently rolling landscapes broken only by occasional bluffs. Finally, to the northeast are the islands of the high Arctic, where you'll find the classic Arctic landscape of mountains, icefields, glaciers, and icebergs. Here sheer cliffs rise thousands of meters out of the ice-choked waters of **Baffin Bay,** incised by steep-walled fiords that end at massive glaciers spilling over from the inland ice cap.

Climate

In general, the human species lives in the middle latitudes and is accustomed to the particular set of natural phenomena common to those latitudes—the sun rises in the east each morning and sets in the west each evening; night follows day; vegetation is lush; and water most often occurs as a liquid. But here in the north, these comfortable patterns don't exist. In winter, the sun doesn't rise for days (or, in some places, even months), whereas in summer, it circles endlessly around the horizon. And for more than half the year, lakes, rivers, and the ocean aren't free-flowing water but solid ice.

The region's climate is harsh, but the image of the Canadian North being a land of eternal ice and snow is a misconception. During the summer months, from late May to September, the weather can be quite pleasant. Precipitation is slight, and the average July temperature in Yellowknife is 16°C—only five degrees cooler than Calgary. Farther north, the average July temperature in Inuvik is 13°C, and in Iqaluit 8°C. The highest temperature recorded in the region was 34°C in Kugluktuk (Coppermine); the lowest, –57°C in Inuvik. In January, Yellowknife's average of –28°C is colder than that of Iqaluit, –26°C.

Much of the north is covered by **permafrost**—ground with an average annual temperature below freezing. In much of the mainland, the topsoil melts each summer. This is known as an active layer of permafrost. But farther north, and in the Arctic archipelago, the ground remains continuously frozen in a layer two to 500 meters deep, which is called continuous permafrost.

Parks

Many of the region's most spectacular landscapes, wildlife concentrations, and sites of historical importance have been set aside as national, territorial, and historic parks. In the Northwest Territories, national parks include **Wood Buffalo,** south and west of Fort Smith, and the second-largest national park in the world; **Nahanni,** in the rugged Mackenzie Mountains; **Aulavik,** on Banks Island, representative of Canada's Arctic lowlands and supporting one of the world's greatest concentrations of musk oxen; and **Tuktut Nogait,** between Paulatuk and Kugluktuk, the breeding ground of the Bluenose caribou herd. Nunavut boasts three national parks, each unique, spectacular, and remote. **Auyuittuq** is in the rugged mountains of Baffin Island; **Sirmilik** protects the nesting grounds of millions of seabirds on Bylot Island and around Lancaster Sound; and **Quttinirpaaq** (formerly Ellesmere Island), the world's northernmost national park, lies at the tip of the North American continent. Proposals are currently under consideration to protect several additional areas as national parks, including the dramatic **East Arm of Great Slave Lake** and wildlife-rich **Wager Bay** on Hudson Bay. All of these parks have links on the Parks Canada website, www.parkscanada.gc.ca.

Territorial parks preserve and protect sites with historic or scenic value. The largest is **Katannilik,** stretching across Baffin Island's Meta Incognita Peninsula. The **Soper River** running through the park has been designated as a Canadian Heritage River.

Among the 17 migratory bird sanctuaries in the territories are **Queen Maud Gulf,** the world's largest such sanctuary, and **McConnell River,** where one million lesser snow geese gather during the fall migration. The **Thelon Game Sanctuary,** the only such area in Canada, is primarily for wildlife conservation but is also a popular area for wilderness river trips.

The Regions

In addition to dividing Canada's north into the Northwest Territories and Nunavut, the following sections break down the region even further.

The **Accessible North** is immediately north of Alberta and has a good road system linking Hay River, on the south shore of Great Slave Lake, to Fort Smith and Wood Buffalo National Park. Across the lake to the north is the territorial capital, **Yellowknife,** and the outlying Dene communities. The spectacular mountainous region in the southwest corner of the Northwest Territories, including Nahanni National Park, has been known as **Rivers of Myth, Mountains of Mystery** for many generations. These mountains and Great Slave Lake form part of the watershed that drains into the **Mackenzie River Valley.** The Mackenzie flows into the Arctic Ocean in the **Western Arctic,** north of Inuvik, at the end of North America's northernmost public road.

Nunavut encompasses three distinct areas. In the west is the **Arctic Coast,** a barren, treeless land where small Inuit communities rely on the abundance of marine mammals and arctic char for survival. Traditionally known as the **Keewatin,** the west coast of **Hudson Bay** is an area rich in human history and wildlife. Finally, Iqaluit, Nunavut's capital, and the mountainous islands of the eastern and high Arctic, including Baffin and Ellesmere, are covered under **Baffin and Beyond.**

FLORA

The Northwest Territories include two main biomes. The **subarctic** biome, below the treeline, is predominantly evergreens interspersed with tundra vegetation. Black spruce, white spruce, jack pine (the most northerly of the pines), and aspen are the most common trees found here. White birch is the only deciduous tree able to withstand the region's climate. Because of little precipitation and a short growing season (70–80 frost-free days annually), tree growth is slow and stunted, especially closer to the treeline.

Above the treeline, in an area of continuous permafrost, is the **arctic** biome—the tundra. Here a unique selection of vegetation has successfully adapted to the region's extreme seasonal changes of temperature and sunlight, as well as to its lack of precipitation (less than the Sahara Desert). Where water and wind have deposited soil, usually in depressions or along the banks of rivers, the vegetation is more varied.

Almost all plants are perennials, able to spring to life quickly after a winter of hibernation. Brightly colored flowers such as yellow arctic poppies, purple saxifrage, pink rhododendrons, and white heather carpet entire landscapes during the short summer. Willows are one of the few woody plants to survive on the otherwise treeless tundra; they're found across the Arctic mainland along with ground birch and Labrador tea. Other areas are almost completely devoid of soil, supporting little more than arctic ferns, lichens, and mosses. Low temperatures here restrict bacterial action, and as a result, the soil is lacking in nitrogen necessary for plant growth. Occasional oases of lush vegetation mark spots where the soil received a nitrogen boost—as from a rotting animal carcass or the detritus of an ancient Inuit campsite.

The sparse plantlife of the Arctic is inadequate as a human food source, but all of the region's plants are edible. A popular Inuit drink is made by boiling sorrel grass and adding sugar. When chilled, this concoction is cool and refreshing.

FAUNA

Species *diversity* in the Northwest Territories is relatively low compared to other parts of the world. Species *concentrations* here, however, are enormous, including some of the world's largest populations of caribou, musk oxen, polar bears, whales, and seabirds. The same species are found below the treeline in the Mackenzie River Basin as are found in the mountainous and northern parts of Alberta. Of note are the large populations of black bears and moose, which are especially prevalent along the Liard Highway; the Dall's sheep that roam the Mackenzie Mountains; and the hybrid bison of Wood Buffalo National Park.

Caribou

Caribou, standing 1.5 meters tall at the shoulder, seem ungainly but have adapted superbly to life in the Arctic. Those on the mainland normally live in small groups but congregate each fall for a migration west to the boreal forest. As many as 400,000 of the animals may band together into a single herd. Each spring the process is reversed as they head east to summer calving grounds, high above the treeline. Caribou are also found on islands of the Arctic archipelago, as far north as Ellesmere Island.

Grizzly Bears

Although there is only one species of grizzly bear—whether they are on the tundra of the Northwest Territories, on Alaska's Kodiak Island, or in the forests of northern Russia—populations in different parts of the world have each made unique adaptations to their particular environment. The grizzlies inhabiting lands north of the treeline feed mostly on the vegetation alongside Arctic streams but occasionally hunt down other animals. One grizzly was spotted hunting seals on pack ice north of Victoria Island, 500 kilometers north of the bears' usual range.

Musk Oxen

These shaggy beasts, hunted to near extinction by the turn of the 20th century, are now restricted to the Arctic archipelago and Thelon Game Sanctuary and number approximately 80,000. The image of them in a defensive circle, protecting the young from predators or the cold, is an endearing symbol of the north. Known to the Inuit as *oomingmak*, meaning "bearded one," they are covered with an underlayer of short, fine wool and a topcoat of shaggy hair up to 60 centimeters long. This gives the animals their characteristic prehistoric appearance and helps protect them from frequent blizzards and winter temperatures that in some areas average –30°C.

Polar Bears

Evolving from the grizzly bear 250,000–400,000 years ago, polar bears may weigh up to 600 kilograms and measure 3.5 meters from head to tail. Their most distinctive feature is a pure white coat, but they also have long bodies with large necks.

The bears' scientific name, *Ursus maritimus,* aptly describes their habitat, that of the permanent pack ice of the Arctic Ocean and the eastern coastline down to Hudson Bay. Polar bears are at home in the sea and have been known to swim hundreds of kilometers. Their most common hunting strategy is to wait at a hole in the ice, days at a time, for a seal that needs to take a breath.

Whales

Only three of the world's 80 species of whales are widespread in the waters of the Canadian Arctic. Belugas—also called white whales for their coloring—are most common. They winter in the Bering Sea and off the west coast of Greenland and migrate to estuarine areas such as the Mackenzie Delta in the western Arctic for summer calving season. Bowheads were the most intensely hunted of all whales, mainly because of their slow speed and great yield of blubber. The bowhead weighs as much as 50,000 kilograms and may reach 20 meters in length. Two separate populations inhabit these waters—one spends summer in the Beaufort Sea, the other in Lancaster Sound and Davis Strait.

The narwhal got its name from the Old Norse word *nar* (corpse)—a reference to the whale's mottled gray color. Distinguished by an ivory tusk that spirals from the male's head—an extension of a tooth—the European legend of the unicorn was probably born from this mammal. It is one of the least understood of all whale species, wintering under the pack ice of Baffin Bay and the Davis Strait and migrating north in pods of up to 300 each spring. Its remarkable circulatory system allows it to dive to great depths without suffering from the bends upon surfacing.

A fourth species, the killer whale, is occasionally seen in the Beaufort Sea and Davis Strait.

Walruses

With their massive build and saberlike tusks, walruses present a formidable and intriguing sight. They spend the summer months sunning themselves on pack ice or on isolated shorelines, and they spend winter at the edge of the pack ice or at recurring polynyas in the high Arctic. Their main diet consists of mollusks, but they've also been known to eat fish and seals. Males can weigh up to 1,400 kilograms.

Seals

Five types of seals inhabit the Canadian Arctic. The most abundant, smallest, and most important to the Inuit are the ringed seals, the name referring to the cream-colored circular markings on their backs. The largest are the bearded seals, which weigh up to 250 kilograms and have facial whiskers resembling a beard. Harp seals are found primarily around the coastline of Baffin Island. In the early 1980s, they were the focus of an emotional campaign aimed at ending hunting of the species. Harbour seals and hooded seals, although common, are found only in Hudson Bay and the waters of Davis Strait.

Fish

Arctic grayling are found in all watersheds on the mainland and are particularly common in the Mackenzie River Basin. Inconnu, a member of the whitefish family, inhabit the Hay River and are occasionally caught in the Big Buffalo and Taltson rivers. Lake whitefish occur mainly in lakes and are bottom feeders. They are also the most valuable commercial fish in the territories; Great Slave Lake is the center of the industry. Pickerel, known as walleye in the south, inhabit small lakes in the southwest. Northern pike live around aquatic vegetation in slow-moving rivers and have been recorded weighing up to 18 kilograms. Lake trout (known affectionately as "lakers" in the north) are common in Great Slave and Great Bear lakes but also occur in fast-flowing rivers and small lakes.

The most dominant fish of the Arctic is the arctic char, a member of the salmon family. They weigh an average of three to four kilograms but can grow to seven. Char spend most of their life in the freshwater of inland lakes, but each summer they make a run to the ocean, returning after only a few weeks. They occur throughout the Arctic archipelago and in rivers and lakes along the coast.

Birds

Approximately 280 species of birds have been recorded in the territories, of which 70 nest exclusively north of the 60th parallel. These figures do no justice to the many millions of shorebirds, waterfowl, and seabirds that migrate north each spring to breed. Birds from six continents and 30 countries flock here each year, including species such as gulls, kittiwakes, terns, fulmars, eiders, and geese. Other species, such as ptarmigan and ravens, spend all year in the region. The winner for the longest migration goes to the arctic tern, which flies here from Antarctica. Many of Canada's endangered species spend summer here; the Ross gull prefers

Queen Maud Gulf, whereas the whooping crane, which was thought to be extinct for many years, nests in Wood Buffalo National Park.

HISTORY

Prehistory

Two distinct groups of natives lived in the Canadian north for thousands of years before European exploration was begun in the region. Approximately 15,000 years ago, at the end of the last Ice Age, a group of people migrated from Siberia across the Bering Strait, which was then solid ice, and fanned out across North and South America. At first, the northern extent of their range was limited by the polar ice cap, but as the ice cap retreated, the people spread north. Over the generations, some of them eventually found their way to the Mackenzie River Basin, where they lived as hunters and gatherers. These people were known as the *Dene* (The People).

The second group crossed the Bering ice bridge much later—approximately 10,000 years ago—and settled in Alaska. Eventually, people from this group would migrate across the Arctic coast in two major waves. The first wave occurred approximately 4,000 years ago when the people known as the **Dorset culture** began to move east. They lived in skin tents in summer and snow houses—previously unknown in Alaska—in winter. The second eastward migration, that of the **Thule culture,** occurred approximately 1,000 years ago and picked up elements of the Dorset culture, such as snow houses and intricate carvings, as it progressed. The Thule lived in semipermanent villages and specialized in hunting sea mammals. The Thule are ancestors of the Inuit.

European Contact

The first European contact with the Inuit was recorded by expeditions searching for the **Northwest Passage.** (Vikings probably encountered the Inuit earlier, but no written record is available to prove it.) European contact with the Dene occurred much later but was more extensive, and the results more dramatic. Many Dene died of diseases brought by the white settlers, and the Dene lifestyle changed forever as they gave up their nomadic existence to settle around trading

walrus

NWT ARCTIC TOURISM

posts. Rivalry between the Hudson's Bay Company and the North West Company pushed traders farther north in search of furs. By 1900, the whaling industry was in decline and the fur trade of the Mackenzie was finished, but posts remained throughout the north. In 1905, when the provinces of Alberta and Saskatchewan were created, administration of the Northwest Territories remained with Ottawa. Local issues were left to the Royal Canadian Mounted Police (RCMP), and the church was responsible for medical and education services.

The 20th Century

Although many Inuit and Dene continued a nomadic way of life into the 20th century, rapid changes were soon to come. The World War II–instigated construction of military installations such as airfields and Distant Early Warning Line stations created an economic boom and a wage economy for many natives, and the construction of schools and hospitals throughout the 1950s gradually led natives to move into towns.

Mining has played an important role in the development of the north since Martin Frobisher took 1,000 tons of fool's gold back to England in 1576. Mineral and oil exploration had taken place for decades, but the introduction of aircraft opened the north up for mining. In the last 60 years, versatile bush planes, which are capable of carrying heavy loads and landing on short strips, have contributed to continued northward expansion.

GOVERNMENT

The Northwest Territories and Nunavut are two of Canada's three territories (the other is the Yukon). Their governments are led by a commissioner with the advice of a legislative assembly. Unlike in Canada's provinces, the territories' natural resources are the sole responsibility of the federal government. The legislative assembly does not operate on a party system, and a majority of members are of Dene or Inuit descent.

ECONOMY

Those communities in the Northwest Territories that are accessible by road have a cost of living comparable to other areas of Canada, whereas those in more remote regions and in Nunavut are up to 100 percent higher. Most consumer goods are imported from other parts of Canada, and all transportation costs must be added. Higher prices are offset by higher wages (the Northwest Territories has Canada's highest average weekly earnings—approximately $700 per person), but visitors should arrive well prepared. The economies of both the Northwest Territories and Nunavut rely heavily on nonrenewable resources and less so on renewable resources. Although the federal and territorial governments are the largest employers, mining is the mainstay of their economies.

Mining

Apart from the government, mining is the largest employer, employing 10 percent of the total workforce alone and paying more than $100 million in wages annually. In addition to the money mining companies spend in the north, they pay the territorial governments millions in taxes and royalties, which helps the local economy. Eight mines produce more than $1 billion worth of minerals annually. The principal minerals extracted are zinc and gold, with yields totaling 25 percent and 10 percent, respectively, of all Canadian production. Although Yellowknife has two gold mines within its city limits, **Lupin,** on the barrenlands 400 kilometers northeast, is Canada's largest gold mine. Lupin and four other mines produce a total of 15,000 kilograms of gold annually, whereas Nunavut's two mines combined, at Nanisivik and on Little Cornwallis Island, extract 20,000 kilograms of silver, 32,000 tons of lead, and 176,355 tons of zinc.

Rumors of diamonds on the barrenlands had been rife for many years, but until 1991 no serious attempt was made to confirm the viability of mining the remote tract of land between Great Slave Lake and the Arctic Ocean. That summer and the following two summers, 13,000 claims were staked, totaling 11.8 million hectares. The rush confirmed that the gems were there, but extraction is a long and expensive process. On June 21, 1996, BHP Minerals, a subsidiary of BHP, one of the world's mining giants, was granted approval by an Environmental Assessment Review Panel to commence mining 300 kilometers northeast of Yellowknife at Lac de Gras. Established at a cost of $950 million, the mine employs more than 700 workers and revenue is $500 million annually (equivalent to the extraction of 9,000 carats—about five cupfuls—daily). In late 1998, a second diamond mine, Ekati, opened on the barrenlands, with a slightly lower extraction rate.

Although the approval of the territories' first diamond mine made headlines in June 1996, it was the end of an era at **Norman Wells,** on the Mackenzie River, when, after more than 70 years, the north's only producing oil field closed. But the oil under Norman Wells is only a tiny fraction of the vast reserves located in the Mackenzie Delta and islands of the high Arctic. In the future, as oil prices rise and supplies elsewhere in the world decline, extraction will become commercially viable.

Mineral exploration is also a major component of the economy. In 1993, $60 million was spent looking for diamonds alone, and BHP spent $170 million in the territories even before being granted approval to commence mining.

WHOOPING CRANES

The whooping crane, *Grus americana,* has become a symbol of human efforts to protect endangered species in North America. Whoopers, as they are commonly called, have never been prolific. Their naturally low reproduction rate, coupled with severe degradation of their habitat, caused their numbers at one point to dip as low as 21. This small flock wintered along the Texas coast in Aransas National Wildlife Refuge, but no one knew where their summer breeding grounds were. The last time infant whoopers had been seen in the wild was 1922, when a Saskatchewan game warden found a nesting couple and preserved a newly hatched chick for posterity. The mystery was solved in 1954 when a helicopter pilot spotted nesting whoopers in Wood Buffalo National Park. Ever since, a concerted effort has been made to increase their population, including an intense captive-breeding program. A count made in 1998 recorded the encouraging figures of 50 nesting pairs and a total population of 178 birds. The birds arrive in the park in late April, with some pairs nesting in the same area for up to 15 years. Each pair produces two eggs but raises only one chick, leaving the other to die. By late September the young chicks have learned to fly and the flock migrates south, taking 20-40 days to cover the 4,000 km to the Texas coast.

Other Industry

Fishing has long been important to the economy of Hay River, the territories' second-largest town. Commercial fishing began in 1945, when 10 companies had dozens of boats trawling the farthest reaches of Great Slave Lake. The industry continues to this day, with lake trout, inconnu, pickerel, whitefish, and northern pike transported from out on the lake to Hay River for packaging and processing.

Hunting and trapping had, until World War II, been the staple of the territorial economy; today they remain an important part of native lifestyle.

Tourism has grown quickly to become the second-largest slice in the Northwest Territories' economic pie. Its importance to the economy will continue to grow as more people become aware of the region's potential. Tourism is an untapped resource in Nunavut, and a large amount of money has been set aside to promote the new territory as a viable travel destination.

PEOPLE

The combined population of the Northwest Territories and Nunavut is 62,000, and it's been growing in recent years at 4 percent annually. Roughly half the population is of native descent. Three groups of indigenous Northerners inhabit the Northwest Territories. The Dene and Métis peoples are found along the Mackenzie River Basin, and the Inuit live in the western Arctic. The Inuit also account for most of Nunavut's population, with 18,000 of these Arctic dwellers living in the territory. Nonnatives number approximately 4,000 in Nunavut.

The native peoples of the Arctic are often called Eskimos. This term comes from the French *esquimau,* a word derived from the Algonquin *esquimantsic* (eater of raw fish). Although not derogatory, the natives of the Arctic feel it puts them in a poor light. They prefer to use more specific terms. The most widely used of these is Inuit, referring to those people of the Arctic coast and eastern Arctic regions of Canada. Inuvialuit refers to people of the Mackenzie Delta, and Inupiat and Yup'ik to those of the Alaskan coastlines.

Dene

The Dene (DEN-ay) people comprise seven groups—Chipewyan, Dogrib, Gwich'in, Hare, Loucheux, Nahanni, and Slavey—that are part of the Athabascan family. As ice from the last Ice Age receded, North American Indians whose ancestors had migrated from Siberia moved north in small groups. They were nomadic hunters whose survival depended on their ability to fish and hunt in a harsh environment. This pattern of life changed dramatically with the coming of Europeans; the old trading systems and nomadic lifestyles were given up for life in settlements around trading posts. Today many Dene live a traditional lifestyle, whereas others

The first bank in the NWT was erected at Fort Smith in the 1870s.

PROVINCIAL ARCHIVES OF ALBERTA

NUNAVUT

On 1 April 1999 the map of Canada was redrawn when Canada's third territory, Nunavut, was born. Nunavut, meaning "Our Land," encompasses the Keewatin, Arctic coast, and Baffin regions—over two million square km—and is home to 22,000 people, of whom 18,000 are Inuit. While native groups around the world dragged issues of land claims through courts, held demonstrations, and, in parts of Canada, took up arms, the Inuit led a low-profile 15-year campaign that on 9 July 1993 culminated in the passage in Canadian Parliament of the historic bill creating Nunavut. But Nunavut was a lot more than the world's largest land claim. It was an enormous step for the Inuit. Now they assume responsibility for a chunk of land twice as big as Ontario (Canada's largest province) and four times the size of Texas and have outright ownership of about 18% of the land, including subsurface mineral rights. The capital of the new territory is **Iqaluit**. The working language of the government is **Inuktitut**.

Although Nunavut was a victory for the Inuit, it hasn't automatically solved the many social problems experienced in the region—unemployment is three times the national average, and cost of living is twice the national average. Only 21 km of government-maintained roads cross the region, and only five percent of its population has completed high school. Nevertheless, after 100 years, the Inuit once again have control of their land.

have moved into a wage economy. All have developed influential political organizations such as the Dene Nation to seek increased control of their own affairs.

Métis
The Métis, numbering approximately 7,000 in the territories, are of mixed French Canadian and Cree or Dene descent. They were traditionally employed as workers for the major fur-trading companies and settled along the Mackenzie and Slave rivers in the 18th and 19th centuries. They were well suited for positions with trading companies because they were bilingual. The Métis were responsible for bringing commerce to the north, and they continue to play an integral role in the territories' commercial world. Like the Dene, culture plays an important role in their lives, and they have formed a political organization known as the Métis Nation.

Inuit
The Inuit live mainly above the treeline and along the coast. Their distant ancestors, the Thule, specialized in hunting whales. Although the Inuit's physical adaptation to Arctic conditions has been phenomenal, their recent Asian origins can be seen in the epicanthic eyefold. They are a short, stocky people, with small hands and feet. Their survival depended on insulated clothing and a diet high in saturated fats. Traditionally, the Inuit hunted marine mammals in the spring, moved inland to hunt caribou in summer, and spent fall preparing for the long winter. By the end of the 1800s, they had developed a dependence on white man's goods, brought by whalers. Diseases devastated their numbers in the 1940s, and when the fur-trading economy collapsed, the federal government began settling the Inuit in communities. Today, most Inuit still have strong ties to the land, living a traditional lifestyle of hunting and fishing. They are also heavily involved in their own political and economic future, having successfully negotiated the world's largest land claim.

RECREATION

Although the vast wilderness of the Canadian north is the perfect destination for adventure, the climate can be unpredictable, severe, and dangerous for the ill-prepared. Help may be hundreds of kilometers away; you must be able to take care of yourself. Before setting out, you should file travel plans with local authorities. In some areas, you are required to travel with a local guide, and these arrangements should be made well in advance. The **Canadian Polar Commission** was established in the early 1990s to promote polar research and exploration. This group produces a wide variety of literature and is a good source of information for anyone planning a high arctic expedition. Contact the commission at Suite 1710, Constitution Square, 360 Albert Street, Ottawa, Ontario K1R 7X7, 613/943-8605, www.polarcom.gc.ca.

Hiking

For all the wilderness in the north, opportunities for extended hikes along established trails are limited. The **Canol Heritage Trail** is a 372-kilometer hike from the Northwest Territories/Yukon border to the Mackenzie River along a service road established in World War II. The most popular area for wilderness hiking is **Auyuittuq National Park** on Baffin Island. Exploring either of these areas requires much advance planning and a big budget. **Katannilik Territorial Park,** near Kimmirut, also has excellent hiking. **Northwinds Arctic Adventures** (867/979-0551 or 800/549-0551, www.northwinds-arctic.com) is a well-respected Northern adventure company with hiking trips to Auyuittuq and Quttinirpaaq national parks.

Canoeing and Kayaking

Several adventure outfitters offer white-water trips down some of the territories' most exciting rivers. For those with experience in both river *and* wilderness travel, there are some excellent opportunities for extended river trips. The legendary **Nahanni River** is at the top of many people's to-do list. It provides unrivaled wildlife viewing, the excitement of fast-flowing water, and beautiful scenery. Other popular rivers include the **Burnside,** which bisects the vast barrenlands; the **Coppermine,** which combines isolation, wildlife, and history; the **Thomsen,** the world's northernmost navigable river; and the **Soper,** on Baffin Island. All of these rivers are run by outfitters. Experienced paddlers who can handle the challenging logistics can organize their own expedition and save some money.

Whitney & Smith (P.O. Box 2097, Banff, Alberta T0L 0C0, 403/678-3052, www.legendaryex.com) features sea-kayaking adventures through the high Arctic. Led by trained biologists, the trips offer the unique perspective of viewing marine mammals from sea level. Most trips depart from Resolute, with other trips including an expedition searching out musk oxen on Banks Island. **Canadian River Expeditions** (P.O. Box 1023, Whistler, British Columbia V0N 1B0, 604/938-6651 or 800/898-7238, www.canriver.com) has an eight-day trip in mid-June to Lancaster Sound on Baffin Island. From an onshore base camp, sea kayaks are used to search out marine mammals congregating at the retreating floe edge.

Peter Clarkson, 867/777-2594, rents canoes for travel along the Mackenzie River and central Arctic. He has canoes in Inuvik, Norman Wells, and Cambridge Bay but can help with logistics for canoe drop-offs just about anywhere. The rate of $240 per week includes life jackets, paddles, and spray jackets. Peter also sells used canoes and buys them from paddlers pulling off the Mackenzie River at Inuvik.

Fishing

The Northwest Territories has countless rivers, streams, and lakes teeming with fish that are both exciting to catch and delicious to eat. Inland lakes and rivers are the domain of trophy-size lake trout, arctic grayling, pickerel (walleye), and northern pike (jackfish). Great Bear Lake holds world records in *every* class of lake trout and arctic grayling (including a 34.5-kilogram lake trout). The arctic char, caught in rivers, lakes, and the open ocean of the Arctic coast and Arctic archipelago, is famous as a fighting fish and as an acclaimed Northern delicacy. The Northwest Territories also holds the overall world record for this species; an arctic char weighing a whopping 14.7 kilograms was caught in the Tree River.

Plummer's Arctic Lodges (950 Bradford St., Winnipeg, Manitoba R3H 0N5, 204/774-5775 or 800/665-0240, www.plummerslodges.com) operates fishing lodges on Great Slave and Great Bear lakes and on the Tree River. Rates including charter flights from Winnipeg or Edmonton, professionally equipped boats, accommodations, and all meals start at US$1,995 for three days, US$2,495 for four days, and US$3,195 for seven days.

Before going fishing, you'll need a license, which is available from sport stores, co-ops, and outfitters. A three-day license costs $15 for Canadians, $30 for nonresidents. An annual license is $20 or $40, respectively. A separate license is required for fishing in national parks. For the *Northwest Territories Sport Fishing Guide,* write Resources, Wildlife, and Economic Development, Suite 101, Diamond Plaza, 5204 50th Avenue, Yellowknife, Northwest Territories X1A 1E2, www.rwed.gov.nt.ca.

ACCOMMODATIONS AND FOOD

Indoor Accommodations
Every community has at least one hotel, which is often run by the local native co-op. Prices in Yellowknife and southern towns begin at approximately $100 single or double for a basic room. Farther north, and in those communities without road access, prices are generally quoted per person and include meals. (Often, the hotel offers the only restaurant in town.) In smaller communities, you will be asked to share your room if it's busy, and it is standard practice to accept. Bed-and-breakfasts, starting at $55 single, $65 double, operate in Yellowknife, Inuvik, and Iqaluit.

Campgrounds
Camping is the only way to stay cheaply in the north. Territorial campgrounds are spaced at regular intervals along the road system. Some are very basic, whereas others—usually those on the outskirts of towns—have showers. Most have bug-proof kitchen shelters. They are $12–15 per night. Payment is often on an honor system. Many of the more remote communities have an area designated for campers, often a short walk from the airport. Always make a point of asking at the hamlet office before pitching a tent away from a designated area. In national parks and other wilderness areas, campers should practice no-trace camping and pack out all rubbish. North of the treeline, there is no source of firewood (although driftwood can often be found on beaches). This means that a lightweight campstove is indispensable. White gas, known as naphtha in the north, is not allowed on scheduled flights but is available in most Northern stores and co-ops. If it's late in the season, call ahead to check availability because some communities receive supplies only once a year.

Food
Part of the Northern experience is tasting local foods. Most restaurants serve these dishes when availability allows. Favorites are musk ox, caribou, and arctic char, all of which can be bought as jerky or, from meat co-ops, as steaks. When meals are part of an accommodations package, they are usually served cafeteria-style and offer little or no choice. For a true Northern experience, have a meal at the **Wild Cat Cafe** in Yellowknife or **To Go's** on Inuvik's main drag.

GETTING THERE

Air
The main air route into the Northwest Territories is from Edmonton or Calgary, in Alberta, to the capital Yellowknife, from where easy connections can be made throughout the north. Airlines flying this route are **Air Canada** (403/265-9555 or

Floatplanes are an integral mode of transportation in the north.

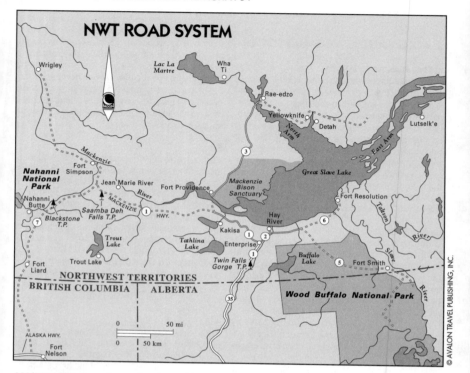

888/247-2262, www.aircanada.ca), and **First Air** (613/839-3340 or 800/267-1247, www.firstair.ca), with First Air also providing scheduled flights between Whitehorse (Yukon) and Yellowknife as well as onward connections. **Air North** (867/668-2228 or 800/661-0407, Canada, or 800/764-0407, U.S., www.airnorth.yk.net) provides a link from Alaska and the Yukon to Inuvik.

For destinations in Nunavut, **First Air** (867/979-8333 or 800/267-1247, www.firstair.ca) flys at least once daily to Iqaluit from Edmonton (with connections through Yellowknife), Ottawa, and Montreal; and to Rankin Inlet from Winnipeg. From Montreal and Great Whale River, **Air Inuit**, 514/636-9445, flies to Iqaluit via Sanikiluaq (Belcher Islands) and Cape Dorset.

For those keen on circumpolar travel **First Air** flies to Iqaluit from Sondre Stromfjord and Nuuk (Greenland) twice weekly. This could, con-ceivably, be linked with an **SAS** flight from Copenhagen or an **Icelandair** flight from New York or Luxembourg via Reykjavik. The best people to contact for travel in this part of the world are at **Arctic Experience** (29 Nork Way, Banstead, Surrey SM7 1PB, England, tel. 01737-218800, www.arctic-discover.co.uk). Greenland's tourism website is www.greenland-guide.dk.

Bus

From Edmonton, **Greyhound**, 780/421-4211, or, in Canada only, 800/661-8747, www.greyhound.ca, goes as far north as Hay River ($167.82 one-way), just over the Northwest Territories border.

Car

Driving is the most popular way to come north. The main route is the **Mackenzie Highway,** which begins northwest of Edmonton at Grimshaw. From Grimshaw, the road is paved beyond the 60th parallel to Hay River. From there, gravel highways lead east to Fort Smith and Wood Buffalo National Park, northwest to Yellowknife, and west to Fort Simpson. A loop known as the **Deh Cho Connection** can be made by taking the **Liard Highway** from southeast of Fort Simpson, south to Fort Nelson (British Columbia), and back to Edmonton. The other route north is the **Dempster Highway** from Dawson City (Yukon) to Inuvik in the western Arctic. This is the northernmost public road on the continent.

GETTING AROUND

Air
In many cases, the only way to get from place to place is by plane. If you are flying into Yellowknife or Iqaluit, make reservations for all further flights before coming north; this works out much cheaper than buying flight sectors separately. If round-trip tickets are bought 14 days in advance and you meet certain requirements, they will be similar in price to one-way tickets bought on the spot. Student standby tickets (anyone under 25) save 30–60 percent off regular ticket prices. Officially, stops are not permitted on regular fares, but if you buy the tickets in the north and have some skill at negotiation, you may be able to work something out.

Since the demise of Canadian Airlines in 2000, the air travel scene has changed greatly throughout Canada, and especially in the north. There are now only two major carriers serving the Northwest Territories and Nunavut: **NWT Air,** a carrier for Air Canada (888/247-2262, www.aircanada.ca), and **First Air** (613/839-3340 or 800/267-1247, www.firstair.ca), but word has it that these two airlines will merge in the future. First Air has been serving the north for more than 50 years, with scheduled services to 28 northern towns. Although based in Ottawa, First Air's hub is Iqaluit, from where flights radiate to all Nunavut communities and across to the Northwest Territories. Each of these airlines has affiliated connector airlines serving smaller communities. **Air Nunavut,** 867/979-4018, operates services around the Baffin region.

Bus
Frontier Coachlines, 867/874-2566, continues to Fort Smith and Yellowknife from Hay River (the end of the line for Greyhound).

Car Rental
Car-rental companies with offices in Yellowknife include **Budget,** 867/920-4719; **National,** 867/873-2911; and **Rent-A-Relic,** 867/873-3400. Budget also has rentals available in Hay River, 867/874-2808.

INFORMATION

Money
All prices quoted in this book are in the local currency, **Canadian dollars.** As this book went to press, one American dollar would buy you $1.47 Canadian. Banks are located in all major centers, and you should check with hotels and outfitters before expecting them to accept U.S. dollars or credit cards. The Northwest Territories and Nunavut are liable to the same taxes as Alberta, including the 7 percent Goods and Services Tax (GST), which applies to all goods and services, including hotel accommodations.

Road Information
For information on highways through the Accessible North section, call 867/874-2208 or 800/661-0750. For information on the Dempster Highway, call 867/777-2678 or 800/661-0752. For ferry information, call 800/661-0751. If you plan a trip north during spring or fall, call ahead to confirm dates of river crossing closures at freeze-up and breakup.

Tourism Information
For detailed information on accommodations and outfitters in the Northwest Territories, write **NWT Arctic Tourism,** P.O. Box 610, Yellowknife, Northwest Territories X1A 2N5, 867/873-7200 or 800/661-0788, www.nwttravel.nt.ca. For the same information on Nunavut, contact **Nunavut Tourism,** P.O. Box 1450, Iqaluit, Nunavut X0A 0H0, 867/979-6551 or 800/491-7910, www.nunatour.nt.ca.

NORTHWEST TERRITORIES
THE ACCESSIBLE NORTH

Whether it's your first time or your 40th, crossing the 60th parallel marks the beginning of a new adventure. And the adventure starts in the most accessible section of the territories, sandwiched between the Alberta/Northwest Territories border and Great Slave Lake. It's a vast expanse of spruce, poplar, and aspen forests, stunted in growth by the harsh climate and scarred by wildfires that sweep unforgivingly through the region every few years. Two of North America's largest rivers, the **Slave** and **Mackenzie,** flow through the area en route to the Arctic Ocean. Many of their smaller tributaries are perfect for wilderness canoe trips and offer streamside hiking and some of the world's best fly-fishing. To the north lies **Great Slave Lake,** named for the Slavey Dene who have trapped and fished along its southern shores for thousands of years. This vast inland sea of freshwater is the world's 10th-largest lake. It covers an area of 28,438 square kilometers and is 456 kilometers long. It is also the world's sixth-deep-est lake (615 meters), meaning that water temperatures remain cold year-round and ice is present for at least five months of the year. The lake remains frozen long after the rivers flowing into it have broken up, creating an annual cycle of flooding at rivermouths.

The region's main communities are Hay River, on the south shore of Great Slave Lake, and Fort Smith, the gateway to Wood Buffalo National Park, the second-largest national park in the world. Paved and improved gravel roads link the two towns and continue around the west and north sides of Great Slave Lake to the territorial capital, Yellowknife.

60TH PARALLEL TO HAY RIVER

The wood-and-stone structure marking the 60th parallel is a welcome sight after the long drive north through Alberta up the Mackenzie Highway. North of the border, the highway number

ARCTIC OCEAN

NORTHWEST TERRITORIES

NORTH MAGNETIC POLE ★

ALASKA

Banks Island

Aulavik National Park

Melville Island

BEAUFORT SEA

Sachs Harbour

0   300 mi
0   300 km

ARCTIC CIRCLE

Herschel Island

Amundsen Gulf

Holman

NUNAVUT

Tuktoyaktuk

TREELINE

Victoria Island

Aklavik

Inuvik

8

Cambridge Bay

Fort McPherson

Tsiigehtchic

Paulatuk

Tuktut Nogait National Park

Colville Lake

DEMPSTER HWY

5

Kugluktuk

Umingmaktok

Dawson City

YUKON TERRITORY

Fort Good Hope

Copermine River

NUNAVUT

Norman Wells

Deline

Great Bear Lake

1

2

Canol Heritage Trail

Port Radium

Back River

ALASKA HWY

4

6

Ross River

Tulita

Burnside River

Thelon Game Sanctuary

Mackenzie Mountains

Wrigley

Rae Lakes

Snare Lake

2

6

TREELINE

Thelon River

Whitehorse

4

60th PARALLEL

1

Wha Ti

Mackenzie River

Nahanni National Park

Fort Simpson

Yellowknife

Watson Lake

Nahanni Butte

3

Great Slave Lake

Lutselk'e

Fort Liard

Liard Hwy

1

BRITISH COLUMBIA

Hay River

1

5

Liard River

97

To Grimshaw (Northern Alberta) and Edmonton

MACKENZIE HWY

Fort Smith

To Prince George, B.C. and Edmonton

Fort Nelson

97

Fort Liard

Wood Buffalo National Park

SASKATCHEWAN

35

ALBERTA

© AVALON TRAVEL PUBLISHING, INC.

changes from 35 to 1, and the road follows the Hay River 118 kilometers to Great Slave Lake. This stretch is known as the **Waterfalls Route,** for the impressive falls along the way.

Just beyond the border is the **60th Parallel Visitors Centre,** 867/920-1021, which is well worth a stop just to have a chat with the friendly hosts. The center offers maps and brochures, camping permits, fishing licenses, and displays of local arts and crafts. And the coffeepot is always on, accompanied by freshly made scones, if you're lucky. Behind the center is the **60th Parallel Campground,** a small facility overlooking the Hay River; $12. The Visitors Centre is open May to mid-September daily 9 A.M.–9 P.M.

Twin Falls Gorge Territorial Park

North of the border, the Hay River has carved a deep gorge into the limestone bedrock. Punctuating the river's flow are two dramatic waterfalls that formed a major barrier for early river travelers, forcing a portage along the west bank. Encompassing both falls, and the equally impressive **Escarpment Creek,** is Twin Falls Gorge Territorial Park. From the first day-use area, a short trail leads to a viewing platform overlooking **Alexandra Falls,** where the peat-colored Hay River tumbles 34 meters. **Louise Falls,** three kilometers downstream, is not as high, but its intriguing steps make it just as interesting. A walking trail through jack pine, aspen, and white spruce links the two sets of falls. Escarpment Creek (also known as Twin Falls Creek) flows into the Hay River four kilometers downstream and has some smaller falls worthy of the short walk. **Louise Falls Campground** has water, pit toilets, and bug-proof kitchen shelters; $12.

Enterprise

After completion of the Mackenzie Highway in 1948, two gas stations opened here, marking the beginning of this small community of 55 residents. The community had hoped to become a transportation hub for freight heading north, but nothing materialized. Today, with a gas station, a restaurant, a few motel rooms, and a highway-maintenance depot, it just manages to hang on. East of the highway are excellent views of the Hay River Gorge. Gas and food are available at **Winnie's,** 867/984-3211.

HAY RIVER

This town of 3,600 lies 127 kilometers north of the border, 1,070 kilometers north of Edmonton, and 500 kilometers from the territorial capital of Yellowknife. Hay River is a vital transportation link for waterborne freight bound for communities along the Mackenzie River and throughout the western and central Arctic. Within the town limits, several distinct communities surround the delta, which was formed where the Hay River flows into Great Slave Lake. Most modern development, including motels, restaurants, and government offices, is located in **New Town,** on the west bank of the Hay River. A bridge links New Town to **Vale Island,** where the airport, campground, and excellent beaches are located. Also on the island are the communities of **Old Town,** which was partially destroyed by flooding in 1963, and **West Channel Village,** which grew around the commercial fishing industry. Across the mouth of Hay River is the **Hay River Dene Reserve,** the only Indian reserve in the Northwest Territories. Farther upstream are **Delancey Estates,** a modern subdivision, and **Paradise Gardens,** where at a wide, sweeping curve of the river the particularly rich soil has sprouted the territories' largest truck-farm operation. Follow a gravel road down to this small community, 24 kilometers south of Hay River, to a sign advertising fresh produce. Look around for the Greenfields, who will be in their extensive gardens, toiling away as they have done for years. Many of their customers come from Hay River, although any self-respecting Yellowknife resident returning from a trip south stops by for the freshest and best-priced produce north of the 60th parallel.

History

For thousands of years, Slavey Dene inhabited the area. Their nomadic lifestyle required no permanent settlements. Rival fur-trading companies had opened posts along the Hay River as early as 1806, but the Hudson's Bay Company didn't build their post on the east bank at the river's mouth until 1868. It closed after 10 years of poor trade. Soon after, Chief Chatla of the Slavey Dene constructed some log cabins

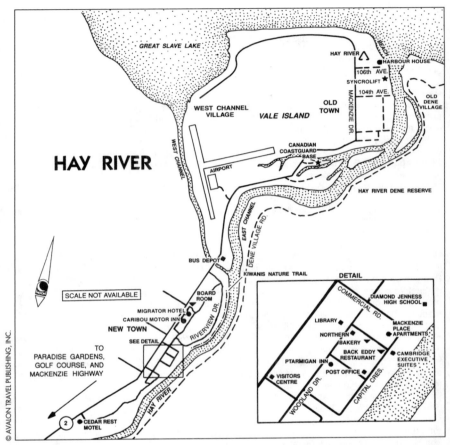

near the defunct post and asked church officials to build a small mission to serve his people. The community grew, and by the turn of the 20th century had a school, a boatyard, and vegetable gardens. The traditional transportation route north to Slave Lake, along the Athabasca and Slave rivers and through Fort Smith, was superseded in 1939 by an overland route from Grimshaw, following the west bank of the Hay River to Vale Island at the mouth. Before long, the west side of the island was crisscrossed with streets lined with shops, and the waterfront was alive with tugs and

barges being loaded with goods for the long trip north.

In 1945, Great Slave Lake was opened to commercial fishing, and a community known as West Channel Village was established on the west side of the island. Fishing soon became the town's leading industry, with 10 companies and eight processing plants harvesting up to eight million tons of fish annually, including the whitefish for which Great Slave Lake is renowned. Vale Island was once linked to the mainland by a causeway that was removed each spring to prevent flooding during breakup.

But in 1963, the causeway was left in place, and the fast-flowing Hay River, which breaks up well before the lake, flooded much of the island. As a result, the town was moved to the mainland, and a permanent bridge was built over the channel.

New Town Sights

With the opening of the Pine Point Mine and arrival of the railway in the 1960s, and general economic growth of the western Arctic in the 1970s, the new townsite grew rapidly. In anticipation of further growth, the 17-story **Mackenzie Place Apartment Building** was constructed in the center of town. Ask for a key at the manager's office (second floor) and ride the claustrophobia-inducing elevator to the roof, from where panoramic views of the Great Slave Lake, Hay River, and the boreal forest extend to the horizon. The **Diamond Jenness High School,** on Riverview Drive, was named for a famed Northern anthropologist and is undoubtedly the town's most unique structure. It was designed by Douglas Cardinal, an Albertan architect whose distinctive work is found throughout that province. Its curved walls alone would have made it a Northern landmark, but the choice of color for the entire exterior was left to the students—and they chose purple! (it's known to the kids as the "Purple People Eater"). Behind the school, the **Kiwanis Nature Trail** leads along the west bank of the Hay River (look for fossils) to various signposted points of interest, then across Highway 2 and along the West Channel to Great Slave Lake.

Vale Island

The boarded-up shopfronts, dusty streets, and empty houses of Vale Island belie the activity that still takes place along the waterfront. The port facilities are the closest to the western and central Arctic and have been used as a transportation hub for the Canol Project and construction of the Distant Early Warning Line stations. The large **Canadian Coast Guard Base** is responsible for all search-and-rescue operations in the western Arctic. And the facilities of the **Northern Transportation Company Ltd.** (NTCL), a large shipping concern, include shipyards, a dry dock, freight-storage areas, and a syncrolift—a hydraulic device that removes vessels from the water for easy maintenance (it's one of only four in Canada; it can be seen to the right along 106th Ave.).

From Old Town, Mackenzie Drive—the island's main thoroughfare—continues past a popular swimming beach and a radio observatory before it dead-ends in **West Channel Village.** This once-prosperous fishing community is a shadow of its former self because processing is now done at the Freshwater Fish Marketing Board Plant in New Town.

Hay River Dene Reserve

Across East Channel from Vale Island is the site of Hay River's first permanent settlement. To get there, backtrack to the Fort Smith turnoff and head north (turn left) shortly after crossing the Hay River. Dene Village Road follows the river to New Indian Village (pop. 250), which, through the work of a dedicated Band Council, has a school, new houses, a grocery store, and scheduled bus service to Hay River. Also here is the **Dene Cultural Institute,** 867/874-8480, which is dedicated to preserving Dene culture through interpretive displays and cultural programs. It's open in summer Mon.–Fri. 9 A.M.–5 P.M., with a special event scheduled every Friday afternoon. The road continues through the community to the original site of the village. Here you will see early churches and the remains of the Hudson's Bay Company post, sitting in mute testimony to the two major influences on early life in the north.

Recreation

The beaches of Vale Island are very popular during summer, even if the water may be a little cold for most. The best beach is at the end of 106th Avenue; those farther around the island are quieter. Anglers will find plentiful northern pike and pickerel in the Hay River.

Located 13 kilometers south of town is the territories' finest **golf course,** 867/874-6290. It has nine holes with grassed fairways, artificial greens, a driving range, and a superbly crafted log clubhouse (well worth a look, even for non-golfers). A round of golf (18 holes) is $24, or play all day for $30. The course also has a driving range, and club rentals are available. The clubhouse is used as a base for cross-country skiers who set tracks around the course in winter.

Festivals and Events

The **Kamba Winter Carnival,** held during the first weekend of March, celebrates the end of winter with various traditional Northern events. **Jet boat races** on the Hay River in late May attract a surprising number of competitors. **Heritage Days,** in mid-June, celebrates the fishing industry with displays, a parade, a concert on the school grounds, and a food festival. With the best golf course in the north, it's natural that the town is host to many tournaments throughout the summer. The most important of these is the **NWT Open** on the Labour Day weekend in September. This fully sanctioned event attracts golfers from throughout the north, but everyone is welcome to enter. The entry fee of $75 includes greens fee and two evening meals. Book well in advance; 867/874-6290.

Accommodations

Motels are spread out along the highway through New Town. The least expensive of these options, but located a couple of kilometers from downtown, is the **Cedar Rest Motel,** 867/874-3732, a place that looks half finished, with a massive gravel parking lot out front; $70 single, $75 double. The **Caribou Motor Inn,** 867/874-6706, has rooms for $80 single, $90 double; similar in standard is the **Migrator Hotel,** 867/874-6792, $80 single, $90 double. One step up, with a restaurant and a lounge, is the **Ptarmigan Inn,** 867/874-6591 or 800/661-0842, in the center of town, with rooms for $115 single, $130 double. The **Cambridge Executive Suites** (31 Capital Dr., 867/874-2233) is Hay River's most luxurious accommodation. Each of the one- and two-bedroom suites has a kitchen and a private balcony; $125–140 per night.

Harbour House (106th St., 867/874-2233) is an inexpensive alternative to the motels. Although located away from downtown, it has an excellent location overlooking Vale Island's best beach. The rate of $60 single, $70 double includes breakfast.

Hay River Campground, on Vale Island, is a short walk from the beach and seven kilometers from downtown. The sites are private, a few have power, and all have picnic tables and fire rings. It's open mid-May to mid-September; $12–15. South of town is the **Paradise Garden Campground,** 867/874-4422, which has showers and an enclosed cooking shelter with a woodstove. The camping area is operated by farmers whose delicious vegetables are a welcome and inexpensive addition to any meal; unserviced sites $12, powered sites $15.

Food

Worth the effort to find is **Back Eddy Restaurant,** 867/874-6680. It's above Rings Drug Store on Capital Crescent. Meals are served in the lounge or, for families, in a separate dining area. The menu features pickerel and whitefish, fresh from the lake. Expect to pay $7–12 for lunch and a few dollars more for dinner. Closed Sunday. **The Keys,** 867/874-6781, in the Ptarmigan Inn, is popular with locals, especially at lunchtime, but it can get very smoky. Beside Northern, the **Hay River Bakery,** 867/874-2322, has a wide variety of cakes and pastries and is a good place for an inexpensive lunch. Meals at the **Board Room,** 867/874-2111, are also well priced; Chinese combos are $9, burgers from $6.50, and main dishes approximately $11–14. The restaurant is a pleasant place, with new furniture and a glass-enclosed section that catches the afternoon sun. It's located on the road toward Old Town and open daily from 11 A.M.

The **Freshwater Fish Marketing Corporation** (1 Birch Rd., 867/874-6630) handles fish from the commercial boats working Great Slave Lake but has a small on-site retail outlet that is open to the public.

Transportation

Hay River Airport is located on Vale Island, a $10 cab ride from town. During freeze-up and breakup of the Mackenzie River, road traffic through to Yellowknife is blocked, and Hay River Airport becomes the center of frenzied activity; freight and passengers arriving by road from the south transfer to planes for the short hop over Great Slave Lake. **Buffalo Air Express,** 867/874-3333, and **Northwestern,** 867/669-7606, fly daily between Hay River and Yellowknife. Local flightseeing is done by **Landa Aviation,** 867/874-3500. A flight over the Hay River Delta and Louise and Alexandra Falls costs $45 per person, three-person minimum; flights to view bison in Wood Buffalo National Park are $120 per person.

The bus depot is at the south end of Vale Island. **Greyhound** departs daily for Edmonton (16 hours). Connecting with the Greyhound services is **Frontier Coachlines**, using the same depot. Buses run to Yellowknife and Fort Smith. For all bus times, call 867/874-6966, or 800/661-8747 in Canada only.

Services and Information
The **post office** is located on Capital Crescent. Just around the corner, at the base of Mackenzie Place Apartment Building, is a **laundromat**; open daily 8 A.M.–8 P.M. The **NWT Centennial Library**, opposite Northern (Woodland Dr., 867/874-6486), is headquarters for the Northwest Territories library system. Books are transported by road, air, and sea to 18 other libraries, including those in the most remote communities. The library has a reasonable selection of books and magazines, including material on the north; open Mon.–Thurs. 10 A.M.–5 P.M., Fri.–Sat. 7–9 P.M. **Snowy Owl Books** is downtown (4 Courtoreille St., 867/874-2714). The **hospital** is at 3 Gaetz Drive, 867/874-7100. The **Visitors Centre**, 867/874-3180, at the south entrance to town, has bundles of literature and books to read, leads guided walking tours, and the coffeepot is always on; open mid-May to mid-September daily 9 A.M.–9 P.M.

TO FORT SMITH

The 270-kilometer road linking Hay River to Fort Smith (Hwy. 5) is paved for the first 60 kilometers then turns to improved gravel. No services are available along this route. The road bisects a typical boreal forest of stunted spruce and aspen. Jack pine dominates areas scorched in a disastrous fire that consumed 160,000 hectares in 1981. The fire burned for three months, and pockets continued to smolder under the snow until the following spring. Visible to the north along the paved section of road is a rail bed used by the Great Slave Lake Railway to link the now-abandoned mine at Pine Point to Roma, Alberta, 680 kilometers to the south. A gravel road to the north, 49 kilometers from Highway 2, leads two kilometers to **Polar Lake**, a camping and picnic area developed by the old community of Pine Lake.

The lake is stocked with rainbow trout and has good bird-watching around the shoreline. Camping is $5, picnicking $3. Eleven kilometers farther, the road divides: the right fork continues to Fort Smith, the left to Pine Point and Fort Resolution.

Pine Point
Early prospectors interested in gold and silver largely ignored the area east of Hay River. But in 1951, Pine Point Mines Ltd., owned by Cominco, began extracting lead and zinc from an open-pit mine at a site known as Pine Point. In 1965, the Great Slave Lake Railway was built, linking the mine to outside markets. With production on the increase, a town was built, at one time boasting more than 2,000 residents. Low lead and zinc prices, coupled with rising operational costs, forced Cominco to close the mine in 1988. One of the lease conditions was that Cominco was to restore the land to its original condition when it left. As a result, the whole town—a school, a hospital, a supermarket, and hundreds of houses—had to be moved. After standing empty for a few years, the buildings were moved to various locations throughout the north. Today all that remains are tailing piles from the mine, paved streets, sidewalks, and an overgrown golf course.

Fort Resolution
This historic community of 500 is located in a forested area on the southeastern shore of Great Slave Lake at the end of Highway 6, approximately 170 kilometers east of Hay River. The original fort, built by the North West Company in 1786, was to the east, on the Slave River Delta. When the post was moved, a Chipewyan Dene settlement grew around it, and in 1852 Roman Catholic missionaries arrived, building a school and a hospital. A road connecting the town to Pine Point was completed in the 1960s, and today the mainly Chipewyan and Métis population relies on trapping and a sawmill operation as its economic base.

Walking tours through town can be arranged through the Community Office on the main road. Also ask here about walking along the lakeshore to the site of the original fort. The town is a good jumping-off point for exploring the spectacular East Arm of Great Slave Lake.

Res Delta Tours, 867/394-3141, offers a variety of excursions including 2.5-hour birdwatching tours of the delta ($60 per person) and overnight trips along the East Arm and to Fort Smith.

Fort Resolution has no motels, but Stan Hunter, 867/394-4451, has opened four rooms to guests; $125 per person includes breakfast. Camping is 24 kilometers southwest, where the highway crosses the Little Buffalo River. Or you could camp down a gravel road just west of town where there appears to have been a campground at one time. Also in town is a gas station, a café, and a community hall, where evening meals are served for reasonable prices.

Continuing to Fort Smith on Highway 5

From the Fort Smith/Fort Resolution junction, 60 kilometers east of Hay River, it is 210 kilometers southeast to Fort Smith. For much of the way, the highway is paralleled by power lines. A hydroelectric plant was built on the Taltson River, east of Slave River, in the 1960s to provide electricity to Pine Point. Now it runs well below capacity, supplying towns in the Big River region. Many of the power line's towers are capped by masses of sticks and twigs—the nesting sites of ravens. Twenty-seven kilometers from the Fort Resolution junction is a 13-kilometer road to **Sandy Lake,** which has a good beach, swimming, and fishing for northern pike, but no camping.

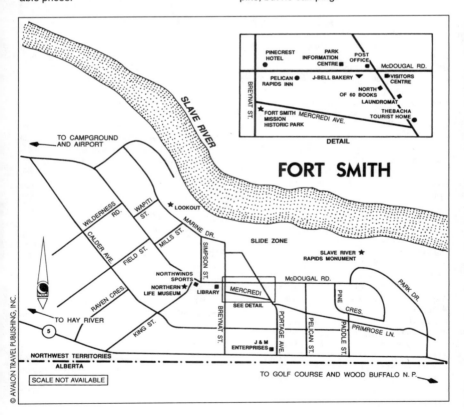

Fort Smith Mission Historical Park

The road then enters Wood Buffalo National Park, the largest national park in North America. Five kilometers beyond the park entrance sign is the **Angus Fire Tower.** Behind the tower is one of many sinkholes found in the northern reaches of the park. This example of karst topography occurs when underground caves collapse, creating a craterlike depression. This one is 26 meters deep and 40 meters across. The next worthwhile stop is at **Nyarling River,** 14 kilometers farther east. The dried-up riverbed is actually the path of an underground river, hence the name *Nyarling* (Underground, in the Slavey language).

Little Buffalo Falls Territorial Park
As the highway continues east, it enters an area where the Precambrian Shield is exposed, making for a rocky landscape where stunted trees cling to shallow depressions that have filled with soil. After crossing the Sass River, the road passes an area of shallow lakes and marshes where whooping cranes—one of North America's rarest birds—make their nests. As the road crosses Little Buffalo River, it leaves the park. To the north, an access road leads to several small waterfalls in Little Buffalo Falls Territorial Park. This was only a small part of an enormous area that was affected by fire in 1981. An interpretive trail follows the cycle of regeneration from stands of aspen and spruce to jack pine, whose seeds are released at high

temperatures. Near the end of the access road is a campground with pit toilets, a kitchen shelter, and firewood; $12.

FORT SMITH

Until 1967, this town of 2,500 on the west bank of the Slave River was the territorial capital. It still functions as an administrative center for various governmental offices and is the educational center for the western regions of the Northwest Territories, with students studying at one of three northern campuses of Aurora College. But Fort Smith's glory days are over. The transportation routes on which the town was built have long since been abandoned, and the governmental hierarchy that once resided here is long gone. Rapids in the Slave River—the Dene name for the area is *Thebacha* (Along the Rapids)—are the nesting grounds of white pelicans, a unique location considering its northern latitude and the pelicans' ability to raise young among the fast-flowing waters of the river.

History
The town was established because of the formidable rapids. The Slave River was a vital link for all travelers heading north, but rapids here and upstream necessitated a 25-kilometer portage around them. In 1872, the Hudson's Bay Company opened a post, later known as

Fort Fitzgerald, at the southern end of the rapids. Two years later, the company established a fort near the northern end of the portage route, at Fort Smith. Occasionally, the brave attempted to run the rapids. In 1876, five paddlers for the North West Company successfully negotiated the three upstream sets but then misinterpreted instructions and perished on the rapids in front of Fort Smith. Their misfortune won't be forgotten; these rapids are now known as Rapids of the Drowned. Around this time, sternwheelers began replacing the slower and more cumbersome voyageur canoes and larger York boats. Red River carts, drawn by oxen, replaced human portagers, and were in turn replaced by tractors in 1919. By this time, Fort Smith had become the administrative center of the Northwest Territories. It remained so until 1967, when an all-weather road was built from Peace River to Hay River and through to Yellowknife, and river transportation slid into oblivion.

Sights

Most people who venture to Fort Smith do so to visit Wood Buffalo National Park, although it is possible to spend a day sightseeing in town. Back in the 1920s, when Fort Smith was capital of the Northwest Territories, administrative duties fell to the local bishop, whose house and gardens are now part of **Fort Smith Mission Historic Park,** at the corner of Mercredi Avenue and Breynat Street. Declared a Territorial Historic Park in 1991, it's an ongoing restoration project; at this stage, interpretive signs explain the various buildings, and gardens are planted for each summer. The **Northern Life Museum** (110 King St., 867/872-2859) is shaped like a fort and houses a large collection of artifacts from the days of the fur trade, as well as mushing equipment, Inuit carvings, the first printing press in the north, and displays on bison; open in summer daily 1–5 P.M. At the end of Breynat Street, signs indicate the **slide zone,** where many of Fort Smith's riverfront buildings stood before a devastating landslide destroyed them in 1968. Continue downstream and onto Marine Drive to the **Slave River Lookout,** a gazebo with a telescope through which you can watch the pelicans. Overlooking the rapids (the view is slightly marred by trees) is the **Slave River Rapids Monument,** which is dedicated to the explorers and riverboat guides of the 1800s who courageously tackled the river. To get there, follow McDougal Road east through town and turn left on Park Drive; the monument is off to the left in the trees.

Fort Fitzgerald, 25 kilometers upstream of Fort Smith, was once a hive of activity at the beginning of the north's most notorious portage. Today, all that remains along with a small population are abandoned houses, a deserted mission, and, down on the river, rotting docks.

Rather than portaging the rapids, some brave souls attempted to run them in scows.

Recreation and Tours

Pelican Rapids Golf and Country Club, 867/872-4653, through town to the southeast, has been carved out of the forest by the town's surprisingly large golfing population. It has grassed fairways and oil-soaked greens. The year's biggest tournament is the 54-hole Merchants Classic Golf Tournament, held during the August long weekend. Everyone is welcome to enter, and a great time is had by all. Regular greens fee is $15 per day. The clubhouse has rentals, but for all your other golfing needs, you should head to **Northwind Sports** (182 McDougal Rd., 867/872-5660). This shop also stocks fishing tackle and camping gear. Fort Smith has grown into a legendary whitewater kayaking destination since it hosted the Canadian Championships in 1994. Some sets of rapids on the Slave River have yet to be run, but you'll need to be totally self-sufficient to tackle them.

Accommodations and Food

The least expensive motel is the **Pinecrest Hotel** (163 McDougal Rd., 867/872-2320); $80 single, $90 double. Much nicer is the **Pelican Rapids Inn** (152 McDougal Rd., 867/872-2789), with large rooms for $110 single or double, $15 extra for kitchenettes; call in advance because this place fills up fast. Another option is the **Thebacha Tourist Home** (53 Portage Ave., 867/872-2060), which offers four rooms, breakfast, and the use of a kitchen for $75 single, $90 double.

The only campground close to town is the **Queen Elizabeth Campground,** located four kilometers west toward the airport; turn north on Teepee Trail Road. Sites cost $12 per night and are spread out and private, with pit toilets and cooking shelters. Showers and flush toilets are available in the warden's compound. Alternatives are **Thebacha Campground,** 16 kilometers west of Fort Smith on Highway 5, or **Pine Lake,** 60 kilometers south in Wood Buffalo National Park.

The **J-Bell Bakery** (corner of McDougal Rd. and Portage Ave.) is always my first stop in Fort Smith to hear the latest gossip, to see if anyone wants to go golfing, and, most important, to enjoy the best breakfast in town. The bakery also serves hot and cold lunches and great pastries.

Transportation

The **airport** is located five kilometers west of town along McDougal Road. **Northwestern,** 867/872-2216, flies daily between Fort Smith and Yellowknife. This company also operates a scheduled air service to and from Fort Chipewyan. **Frontier Coachlines,** 867/872-2031, runs a passenger service between Fort Smith and Yellowknife. **J & M Enterprises** (Portage Ave., 867/872-2221) is open daily 8 A.M.–midnight and has a mechanic, a car wash, and car rentals. For a taxi, call **Portage Cabs** at 867/872-3333.

Information

Mary Kaeser Library is located at 170 McDougal Road, 867/872-2296, and **North of 60 Books,** across from the Visitors Centre, 867/872-2606, offers a great selection of books, maps, and souvenirs. The **Fort Smith Visitors Centre** is on Portage Road, 867/872-2515. It's open mid-May to mid-September 10 A.M.–10 P.M.

WOOD BUFFALO NATIONAL PARK

The sheer size of Wood Buffalo National Park, the second-largest national park in the world (the largest is in Greenland), can be overwhelming at first. With few conventional "sights," many first-time visitors leave disillusioned. The park really is a place where you must stop, pause, and take it all in. Throughout this 45,000-square-kilometer chunk of boreal forest, boreal plains, shallow lakes, and bogs flow two major rivers—the Peace and Athabasca. These drain into **Lake Claire,** forming one of the world's largest freshwater deltas. The Peace-Athabasca Delta is a mass of confusing channels, shallow lakes, and sedge meadows, surrounded by a wetland that is a prime wintering range for bison, rich in waterfowl, and home to beavers, muskrats, moose, lynx, wolves, and black bears. From the delta, the Slave River, which forms the park's eastern boundary, flows north into Great Slave Lake.

Probably best known for being the last natural nesting habitat of the rare whooping crane, the park is also home to the world's largest free-roaming herd of bison. It has extensive salt plains and North America's finest example of gypsum

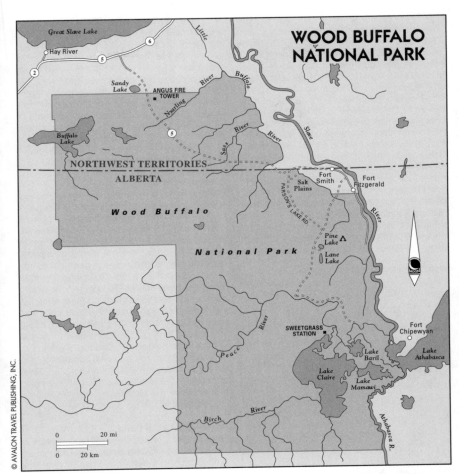

WOOD BUFFALO
NATIONAL PARK

karst topography—a phenomenon created by underground water activity. For all of these reasons, and as an intact example of the boreal forest that once circled the entire Northern Hemisphere, the park was declared a UNESCO World Heritage Site in December 1983.

On the surface, Wood Buffalo epitomizes everything that a national park should be—little development and stable wildlife populations—so it is ironic that the park has faced ongoing problems with diseased bison and clear-cut log-

ging, and currently faces the prospect of a collapse of the entire delta ecosystem because of a dam built more than 1,000 kilometers away. But let's start at the beginning.

Bison: The Good Times and the Bad

Wood Buffalo National Park was created by the Dominion Government in 1922 to protect 1,500 wood bison that were scattered throughout the region. At the time, the wood bison—a larger subspecies of plains bison—were being heavily hunted, and their future was in jeopardy. In the years that followed, their numbers were supplemented with nearly 6,000 plains bison from Buffalo National Park near Wainwright, in Alberta. Unfortunately, the imported plains bison were carrying tuberculosis and brucellosis, which have remained in the park's now-hybrid population of bison for 70 years. In the early 1950s, large-scale bison roundups took place in the Sweetgrass area of the delta, and many diseased bison were slaughtered. Park administrators set up a small settlement at Sweetgrass and constructed more than 30 kilometers of corrals to hold the diseased animals. The last slaughter took place in 1967, and the corrals were last used in 1976 to vaccinate the bison against anthrax—an infectious disease that can kill bison in a few days. For the most part, these diseases lie dormant in the ecosystem; bison generally show no outward effects of illness, and the diseases are not easily transmitted to humans. In late 1990, an Environmental Advisory Board recommended that the entire bison population be slaughtered, eradicating the diseases once and for all. No action was taken, and in 1995 a five-year Bison Research and Containment Program was initiated, from which a long-term management program will be developed. For the bison themselves, life goes on; each spring, hundreds of calves are born, and bison numbers remain steady at just less than 3,000. No cases of disease transfer to humans have been reported in the park's history.

Timber Berth 408

Logging in most national parks would raise a few eyebrows; clear-cut logging of a 500-square-kilometer old-growth spruce forest would create a furor; and, if foreign interests were involved, you'd think there would be a riot—but not in Wood Buffalo. For the last 30 years, several companies have held leases to harvest timber in "Timber Berth 408," a remote region of the park along the Peace River. Throughout the years, many infractions were made on the leases, but they were always extended. The final lease was held by Canadian Forest Products Ltd. (Canfor), whose logging operations feed a sawmill in High Level owned by Diashowa Canada Co. Ltd., a Japanese multinational corporation. On March 7, 1991, the operation was shut down after further lease violations. No further logging has taken place within the park, and reforestation is being planned for the near future.

Peace-Athabasca Delta

For thousands of years, the silt-laden waters of the Peace and Athabasca rivers flowed into Lake Claire, forming a delta rich in vegetation that provided diverse habitats for larger mammals and a traditional hunting ground for Chipewyan and Cree natives. Each spring, a natural cycle of flooding took place when the Peace River broke its banks, replenishing sloughs and marshes. This cycle created hundreds of square kilometers of wetland, vital to the millions of birds that use the delta as a stopover on their annual migratory path and to the fur-bearing mammals whose survival depends on this annual cycle.

That age-old natural cycle was broken in the 1980s by the construction of the WAC Bennett

The bison is North America's largest land mammal.

Dam on the Peace River more than 1,000 kilometers upstream in British Columbia. Since the river has been dammed, the flow has been regulated and the flood-cycle ended. Now the delta is slowly drying up. Protein-rich sedges along the sloughs have been replaced by silverweed and thistle, and large areas of once-rich marshland are now dried-up mudflats, seriously affecting the wintering range of bison. In an attempt to return the delta to its natural state, several groups, including the federal government and local native associations, came together for the Peace-Athabasca Delta Technical Studies, a management program that culminated in the artificial flooding of a small section of the delta during the breakup of 1996. Adding to the tarnished image of the park are worries about water contamination from mills upstream on the Peace and Athabasca rivers and the threat of a dam being constructed on the Lower Slave River, which would flood northern sections of the park, including the salt plains.

Whooping Cranes: A Park Success Story

In 1954, when a flock of 21 whooping cranes was discovered nesting in the park, the species was on the verge of extinction. Today, the population of the highly publicized and heavily studied flock has increased to more than 170, more than half the number that remain worldwide (most of those remaining are in captivity). The birds nest in a remote area of marshes and bogs in the northern reaches of Wood Buffalo far from human contact. They stand 1.3 meters, have a wing span of 2.4 meters, and are pure white, with long black legs. They are often confused with the slightly smaller, reddish-brown-colored sandhill crane, which is common in the park.

Salt Plains

The expansive salt-encrusted plains located in the northeast of the park are one of Wood Buffalo's dominant natural features. Underground water flows through deposits of salt left behind by an ancient saltwater ocean, emerging in the form of salt springs. Large white mounds form at their source, and where the water has evaporated the ground is covered in a fine layer of salt. The best place to view this phenomenon is from the **Salt Plains Overlook,** 35 kilometers west of

Fort Smith, then 11 kilometers south on Parson's Lake Road. The panoramic view of the plains is spectacular from this spot, but **Salt Plains Trail** (one kilometer each way), which leads to the bottom of the hill, is well worth the effort. If you decide to go beyond the trail, take your shoes and socks off (squishing through the mud is good fun, and you'll appreciate clean shoes back at the car). The salt attracts many mammals, including bison, wolves, foxes, and black bears. Their tracks can often be seen in the mud, along with those of various birds that feed on the aquatic vegetation unique to the plains.

Gypsum Karst

A gypsum bedrock underlies many areas of the northeast corner of the park. Gypsum is a soft, white rock that slowly dissolves in water. Underground water here has created large cavities beneath this fragile mantle. This type of terrain is known as karst, and this area is the best example of karst terrain in North America.

As the bedrock continues to dissolve, the underground caves enlarge, eventually collapsing under their own weight, forming large depressions known as **sinkholes.** The thousands of sinkholes here vary in size from a few meters to 100 meters across. The most accessible large sinkhole is behind the Angus Fire Tower, 150 kilometers west of Fort Smith. The short **Karstland Trail,** which begins behind the Salt River Picnic Area, 24 kilometers south of Fort Smith, passes several smaller sinkholes. The **North Loop Trail,** which starts as part of the Karstland Trail but branches right, off the gravel trail, is a longer hike through typical gypsum karst terrain, ending on the main road a short walk from the picnic area. The total loop is nine kilometers; allow 2.5 hours. **Pine Lake,** 60 kilometers south of Fort Smith, is a sinkhole that formed beneath the water table. This deep, clear lake is excellent for canoeing and fishing. A trail follows the southern shore or you can continue south to **Lane Lake,** a 6.5-kilometer (one-way) hike.

Sweetgrass

The Peace-Athabasca Delta is in a remote part of this remote park and is rarely visited. Getting to the delta requires some planning because no roads access the area. The most popular visitor destination on the delta is **Sweetgrass Station,** located 12 kilometers south of the Peace River. The site is on the edge of a vast meadow that extends around the north and west shore of Lake Claire, providing a summer range for most of the park's bison. The corrals at Sweetgrass Station were built in 1954 to help the fight against diseased bison. Although now abandoned, facilities remain to vaccinate the herd if the need ever arises. A cabin with bunks and a woodstove is available for visitors to the area at no charge, although reservations at the park information center are required. The cabin is an excellent base for exploring the meadows around Lake Claire and viewing the abundant wildlife. Drinking water can be obtained from Sweetgrass Creek but should be filtered and boiled.

The easiest access is with **Northwestern Air,** 867/872-2216, which charges approximately $340 each way for two people and their gear. This company, along with **Big River Air,** 867/872-3030, also offers flightseeing over the area from $55 per person for 35 minutes. The other, more complicated way to access Sweetgrass is by canoe, paddling down the Peace River to Sweetgrass Landing, from where it's a 12-kilometer hike or a five-kilometer portage and easy float down Sweetgrass Creek to the station. Getting out requires a pickup by floatplane from Fort Smith or boat operator from Fort Chipewyan.

Park Practicalities

Park headquarters (the Federal Building in Fort Smith at 126 McDougal Rd.) houses the excellent **Park Information Centre,** 867/872-7900, which offers current park information, a short slideshow, and an exhibit room. The center is open in summer Mon.–Fri. 8:30 A.M.–5 P.M. and Sat.–Sun. 10 A.M.–5 P.M., the rest of the year Mon.–Fri. only. Another small park office, 780/697-3662, is located in Fort Chipewyan. It has an interesting exhibit on the Peace River and is open year-round Mon.–Fri. 8:30 A.M.–5 P.M.

The park's only developed facilities are at **Pine Lake,** 60 kilometers south of Fort Smith. The lake has a campground with pit toilets, covered kitchen shelters, and firewood; sites $10. On a spit of land jutting into the lake beyond the campground is a picnic area with bug-proof shelters. The park staff presents a summer interpretive program at various locations; check the schedule at the park information center or on the campground notice board.

For further information, write to Superintendent, Wood Buffalo National Park, P.O. Box 750, Fort Smith, Northwest Territories X0E 0P0, www.parkscanada.gc.ca. Seven 1:250,000 topographic maps are needed to cover the entire park. Order copies through any specialty map shop or at North of 60 Books in Fort Smith, 867/872-2606.

Lady Evelyn Falls

HAY RIVER TO YELLOWKNIFE

Yellowknife, located on the north shore of the Great Slave Lake, is a long 480-kilometer haul from Hay River, through a monotonous boreal forest of spruce, poplar, and jack pine. The trees diminish in size as the road heads north. The gravel road is slowly being replaced, but it will be many years before the territorial capital is linked to the outside world by a paved road. Twice a year, for three to six weeks in spring and again in late fall (at breakup and freeze-up, respectively, of the Mackenzie River), the road to Yellowknife is not passable (call 800/661-0751 for closure dates).

Lady Evelyn Falls
From Enterprise, south of Hay River, Highway 1 heads northwest, coming to Lady Evelyn Falls after 53 kilometers. These falls, where the wide **Kakisa River** cascades off a 15-meter escarpment, are easily accessible from the highway, seven kilometers down a gravel road. A short trail leads from the day-use area down to a platform overlooking the falls. A path continues upstream past a different view of the falls to a miniature version of the larger falls downstream. The falls are part of a territorial park that has a campground with pit toilets, bug-proof kitchen shelters, and firewood; sites $12.

Kakisa
Kakisa is a small Slavey community on Kakisa Lake at the end of the Lady Evelyn Falls access road. It was established in 1962 when the community, then located farther south on Tathlina Lake, moved to have access to the newly constructed highway. Kakisa has no services, although the lake is known for good pickerel and whitefish fishing.

Fort Providence
Eighty-five kilometers from Enterprise, the highway forks: to the left, Highway 1 continues west to Fort Simpson, and to the right, Highway 3 heads north toward Yellowknife. Highway 3 crosses the Mackenzie River, via a ferry (operating 6 A.M.–midnight), 24 kilometers from the junction. Across the river and just up the highway, a spur road leads eight kilo-

meters to the Slavey Dene community of Fort Providence (population 650), perched high above the river on its steep northern bank. A Roman Catholic mission was established here in 1861, attracting natives from nearby communities. The mission continued to play an important role in the area, encouraging agriculture and operating a school. Some of the town's older residents can speak French, a legacy of the French-speaking Catholic missionaries who taught at the school. Local artisans are known for moose-hair tufting and intricate porcupine-quill weaving. On the riverfront is a **visitors center,** and farther along, historical markers honor the roles played by Alexander Mackenzie and the church in the region's history. Fishing in the Mackenzie River is excellent, with catches of northern pike up to 12 kilograms—ask a local where the best spots are. You can rent a boat, organize river tours, and book cabin accommodations through **Aurora Sport Fishing,** 867/699-3551. The **Snowshoe Inn,** 867/699-3511, on the riverfront, has basic rooms; $90 single, $110 double. Out on the highway, you'll find the **Big River Service Centre,** 867/699-4301, a gas station, a café with reasonable food, and a few motel rooms in ATCO trailers for $65 single, $80 double. The café is open until 10 P.M. and the gas station until midnight. A **campground** is located along the Fort Providence access road; sites $10.

Mackenzie Bison Sanctuary
Many years after the wood and plains bison in Wood Buffalo National Park had interbred, a small herd of pure wood bison was found in a remote corner of the park. In 1963, 18 of these animals were moved to the northwest side of Great Slave Lake. The herd has now grown to 2,000, occupying an area of approximately 10,000 square kilometers. The region between the highway and Great Slave Lake is a bison sanctuary, although their range extends well beyond these boundaries. The animals were thought to be disease-free, but in August 1993 an outbreak of anthrax killed more than 100 bison before it was quelled.

Rae-Edzo
Rae-Edzo, 214 kilometers north of Fort Providence, is the largest Dene community in the

Northwest Territories, with a population of 1,500 Dogrib Dene. Dogrib have hunted and trapped in the area for centuries, but a permanent settlement wasn't established until 1852, when Dr. John Rae—an early explorer who had adopted the Indian way of life—built a Hudson's Bay Company post nearby. Soon after, the post was moved to the present site of Rae on Marian Lake, an extension of the North Arm of Great Slave Lake.

The Dogrib were severely affected by measles, tuberculosis, and influenza—diseases brought by traders and explorers. The spread of disease was exacerbated by the poor drainage at Rae, which caused sanitation problems that continue to affect the community. By the 1940s, the Dogribs' survival was in doubt. In 1965, the government began developing a new townsite, Edzo, closer to the highway. The school at Rae was closed, and a new one opened at Edzo.

Today, most of the people continue living at Rae, where the water access is better for fishing and hunting, whereas the government buildings are up on the highway at Edzo.

The 10-kilometer side trip to Rae is worth taking. The resilient community is perched on a rocky outcrop jutting into **Marian Lake.** The main road through town leads to a small island, where the rocky beaches are littered with boats, fishing nets, and dogs tied up waiting for snow. Apart from the snowmobiles, the village looks much as it did 100 years ago. In Rae, the **Jeik'o Motel,** 867/392-6184, offers 12 double rooms, with use of a kitchen and laundry room; $80 single, $120 double.

North of Rae-Edzo are the remote communities of Wha Ti (formerly Lac La Martre), Rae Lakes, and Snare Lake, accessible only by plane from Yellowknife (see **Vicinity of Yellowknife,** page 451).

YELLOWKNIFE AND VICINITY

Built on dreams, perseverance, and the ingenuity of a small group of pioneers who came in search of gold, the territorial capital of Yellowknife has grown into a modern urban center of 17,500. Its frontier-town flavor and independent spirit distinguish it from all other Canadian cities. It's the northernmost city in Canada, the *only* city in the Northwest Territories, and the only predominantly nonnative community in the territories. Located on the North Arm of the Great Slave Lake, the city clings precariously to the ancient, glacial-scarred rock of the Canadian Shield. Edmonton is 1,524 kilometers south by road, 965 kilometers by air. The Arctic Circle is 442 kilometers north. At first, Yellowknife looks little different from other small Canadian cities, but unique contrasts soon become apparent. Some residents write computer programs for a living, whereas others prepare caribou hides; architect-designed houses are scattered among squatters' log cabins; and the roads are seemingly always under repair, a legacy of permafrost. To the Dene, Yellowknife is known as *Som bak'e* (Place of Money).

History

Samuel Hearne dubbed the local Dene natives the Yellowknife for the copper knives they used.

Their numbers were devastated by disease and by warring with the Dogrib, who had traditionally hunted in the area. Miners on their way to the Klondike were the first to discover gold in the area, but they didn't rush in to stake claims because of the area's remote location and the difficulty of extracting the mineral from the hard bedrock. But as airplanes began opening up the north, the area became more attractive to gold-seekers. Hundreds of claims were staked between 1934 and 1936, and a boomtown sprang up along the shore of Yellowknife Bay. Very few struck it rich, but the rush continued until World War II, with miners coming north in scows, barges, floatplanes, and a sternwheeler that plied the lake from Fort Smith. After the war, growth continued, and soon the original townsite around the bay was at full capacity. A new town, just up the hill, was surveyed, and by 1947. the city center of today began taking shape. In 1967, a road was completed to the outside, and the city came to rely less on air travel. The city was named territorial capital the same year. As the white-collar population grew, houses went up and more sophisticated services became available. Although the federal and territorial governments are Yellowknife's biggest employers,

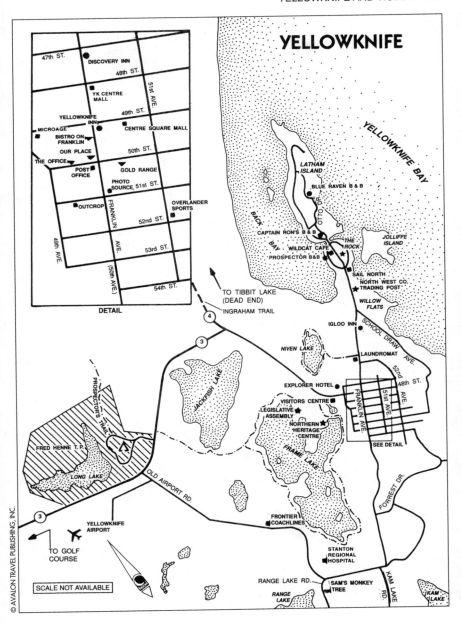

YELLOWKNIFE

DETAIL

47th ST.
DISCOVERY INN
48th ST.
51st AVE.
YK CENTRE MALL
49th ST.
YELLOWKNIFE INN
MICROAGE
BISTRO ON FRANKLIN
CENTRE SQUARE MALL
OUR PLACE
50th ST.
THE OFFICE
POST OFFICE
GOLD RANGE
PHOTO SOURCE, 51st ST.
FRANKLIN AVE.
OUTCROP
OVERLANDER SPORTS
52nd ST.
49th AVE.
53rd ST.
(50th AVE.)
54th ST.

YELLOWKNIFE BAY

LATHAM ISLAND
BLUE RAVEN B & B
BACK BAY
OTTO DR.
JOLLIFFE ISLAND
CAPTAIN RON'S B & B
WILDCAT CAFE
THE ROCK
PROSPECTOR B&B
SAIL NORTH
NORTH WEST CO. TRADING POST
WILLOW FLATS

TO TIBBIT LAKE (DEAD END)
INGRAHAM TRAIL
4
3

IGLOO INN
SCHOOL DRAW AVE.
NIVEN LAKE
LAUNDROMAT
52nd AVE.
JACKFISH LAKE
EXPLORER HOTEL
48th ST.
FRANKLIN AVE.
51st AVE.
VISITORS CENTRE
LEGISLATIVE ASSEMBLY
PROSPECTOR'S TRAIL
NORTHERN HERITAGE CENTRE
SEE DETAIL
FRED HENNE T.P.
LONG LAKE
FRAME LAKE
OLD AIRPORT RD.
FORREST DR.
3
TO GOLF COURSE
YELLOWKNIFE AIRPORT
FRONTIER COACHLINES
STANTON REGIONAL HOSPITAL
KAM LAKE RD.
SCALE NOT AVAILABLE
RANGE LAKE RD.
SAM'S MONKEY TREE
RANGE LAKE
KAM LAKE

several producing gold mines have kept the economy alive.

In early 1991, a general downturn in the price of gold, along with union demands for better and safer conditions, led to a general strike that became the most vicious in Canada's history. The strike was violent from the start, with security guards protecting the mine and scab workers, brawls in bars, and daily battles at the picket line. The strike's darkest hour was the morning of September 18, 1992, when a bomb planted by a striking miner exploded 150 meters underground, killing nine miners. It was the worst crime in Canadian labor history. The strike continued for another 18 months.

SIGHTS

Prince of Wales Northern Heritage Centre

The entire history of the territories is cataloged at this modern facility on the shore of Frame Lake. The South Gallery displays a collection of Dene, Métis, and Inuit artifacts. The North Gallery catalogs the arrival of European explorers, miners, and missionaries and their impact on the environment. The Aviation Gallery presents a realistic display of a bush pilot and his plane and a wall of fame for the pilots who helped open up the north. Also here is a live hookup to the traffic controllers at Yellowknife Airport. The center houses the Northwest Territories Archives of maps, pho-

tographs, books, and manuscripts available for public examination. A library stocks 6,000 historical and fictional books on the north. The center, 867/873-7551, is open in summer daily 10:30 A.M.–5:30 P.M., the rest of the year Tues.–Fri. 10:30 A.M.–5 P.M. and Sat.–Sun. noon–5 P.M.

Legislative Assembly of the Northwest Territories

Opened in the fall of 1993 on the shore of Frame Lake, this building is the heart of territorial politics and the first permanent home for the legislature. At a cost of $25 million, it was designed to blend in with the surrounding landscape and made use of Northern materials. Through the front doors of a massive glass-walled facade is the Great Hall, topped by skylights and lined with the artwork of Angus Cockney. The building's centerpiece is the circular Chamber, in which the members of the legislative assembly sit facing the Speaker. Behind the Speaker stretches a massive zinc-plated mural of a Northern landscape. The building is open Mon.–Fri. 7 A.M.–6 P.M., Sat.–Sun. 10 A.M.–6 P.M. One-hour tours are offered in summer Mon.–Fri. at 10:30 A.M., 1:30 P.M., and 3:30 P.M. as well as Sunday at 1:30 P.M. For details, call 867/669-2300.

Old Town

From the city center, Franklin Avenue (50th Ave.) descends a long, dusty hill to Yellowknife's Old Town. In the 1930s, the first log and frame build-

The eclectic housing along Ragged Ass Road is a reminder of the city's earliest days.

ings were erected at this site. Along the narrow streets, Quonset huts, original settlers' homes, converted buses, old boats, and tin shanties look incongruous in a Canadian capital city. Some of the most unusual housing is in **Willow Flats,** east of Franklin Avenue. **Ragged Ass Road,** named for a mine claim, has the most unusual houses, many posting signs telling the story of the building. Across Franklin Avenue is **Peace River Flats,** where a few original buildings remain. Farther north along Franklin Avenue is an area known simply as **The Rock,** for the huge chunk of Canadian Shield that towers above the surrounding landscape. At the top of The Rock is the **Pilot's Monument,** dedicated to the bush pilots who opened up the north. At the corner of Pilots Lane and Wiley Road is **Weaver & Devore,** an old-time general store selling just about everything. Many of their larger orders have to be flown in to buyers scattered throughout the north. Farther around Wiley Road, overlooking Back Bay, is the **Wildcat Cafe,** one of the city's landmarks. East of The Rock, in Yellowknife Bay, is **Jolliffe Island,** once a fuel depot but now a residential area. The homes are reached by boat or canoe in summer and by road in winter. At the north end of The Rock, a causeway, built in 1948, connects **Latham Island** to the mainland. At the south end of the island are floatplane bases where the constant buzz of small planes taking off and landing symbolizes the north.

Fred Henne Territorial Park
Forest-encircled **Long Lake,** opposite Yellowknife Airport, is used by visitors mainly for the excellent camping facilities, but it's also a good example of the wilderness surrounding the city. The four-kilometer-loop **Prospector's Trail,** which begins from the campground, is a good way to experience the unique landscape. You can hike to the park from the city center along the trails around **Frame Lake.**

Ingraham Trail
Apart from Highway 3 from the south, the Ingraham Trail (Hwy. 4 East) is the only route out of the city. It then crosses the Yellowknife River and passes **Prosperous, Pontoon,** and **Prelude lakes,** each with day-use areas and great for fishing, boating, and swimming. Continuing east, the road parallels the **Cameron River,** 48

kilometers from Yellowknife. Trails lead down to the riverbank, and waterfalls dot the route. The road ends at **Tibbit Lake,** 71 kilometers from Yellowknife.

Detah
This community, originally a seasonal fish camp for the Dogrib Dene, is located east of Yellowknife across Yellowknife Bay. As Yellowknife grew, the Dogrib people settled here permanently to take advantage of the growing services of the new city, while maintaining a traditional way of life. Today the 180 residents continue a lifestyle of fishing, hunting, and trapping.

RECREATION

Hiking
Hiking trails exist around Frame and Niven lakes, but the best way to truly appreciate the city's unique surroundings is with **Cygnus Ecotours,** 867/873-4782. Led by Jamie Bastedo, author of the book *Shield Country,* there are various tour options, the least strenuous being a 3.5-hour stroll around Frame Lake learning about the formation of the Canadian Shield, its plant and bird life, and the area's traditional owners. The cost is $42 per person, which includes a light snack.

Fishing and Boating
The brochures of many fishing-charter operators fill the Northern Frontier Regional Visitors Centre, but **Bluefish Services,** 867/873-4818, offers the widest range of fishing opportunities, including fishing for arctic grayling from local river banks, chasing northern pike out on North Arm, and trawling the deepest parts of Great Slave Lake for massive lake trout. Rates are from $65 per person for four hours and $105–160 for a full day. **Enodah Wilderness Travel** (P.O. Box 2382, Northwest Territories X1A 2P8, 867/873-4334, www.enodah.com) has a lodge on Trout Rock, a two-square-kilometer island 30 kilometers west of Yellowknife that was once the site of a Dogrib community; three-day fishing trips start at $675 per person.

Sail North (P.O. Box 2496, Yellowknife, Northwest Territories X1A 2P8, 867/873-8019) charters boats. Motorboats start at $20 per hour for a four-meter boat ($100 per day) and $80 per hour for a 12-meter boat. Per week, the same boats are $500–2,500. Sailboats ranging eight to 13 meters rent for $185–549 per day or $735–2,699 per week and are a great way to explore the hundreds of uncharted bays on the East Arm. You can sail yourself or hire a skipper ($85 extra per day). Houseboats are similarly priced, but because they are slower than sailboats, a few are based on the East Arm (transfers are $300 each way).

Canoeing and Kayaking

One block from the main drag is **Overlander Sports** (5103 51st Ave., 867/873-2474), renting canoes for $20 for four hours, the perfect length of time to explore nearby Jolliffe Island and its surrounding waters. For those interested in longer trips, canoes are $30 per day. Opportunities for kayaking around Yellowknife are more limited, although some interesting opportunities exist along the Cameron River, which is accessed from the Ingraham Trail (see previous section). Overlander Sports rents single kayaks ($25 for four hours, $50 per day, and $200 per week) as well as doubles ($40 for four hours, $75 per day, and $260 per week) and folding kayaks ($150 per week, $500 per month).

Golf

The **Yellowknife Golf Course** is located west of downtown along Highway 3, 867/873-4326. The "greens" of this course used to be oil-soaked sand but were recently replaced by artificial grass in the mid-1990s, and the course was extended to 18 holes in 1999. One thing that hasn't changed is the rock and gravel fairways. Each shot must be hit from a small mat that players carry around the course; greens fee is $25. Aside from the unique playing conditions, facilities are similar to those at any regular golf course: a pro shop with rentals, a driving range, a restaurant, and a beer cart, of course. Also look for some great photos of the course's early days in the clubhouse. The course is only open May to mid-Sept.; the rest of the year, golfers head to **Forty Below Golf,** a virtual-reality golf course in Stanton Plaza Mall (Old Airport Rd., 867/669-7529).

Entertainment

Entertainment at the **Gold Range Hotel** (5010 50th St., 867/873-4441), best known as the "Strange Range," is like no other in the country.

Don't be put off by the unusual characters, hundreds of empty beer glasses, and bouncers with legs like tree trunks; it isn't as rowdy as it seems. There's live entertainment on weekends, including one bloke who, in the winter months, rides 50 kilometers on his snowmobile from his remote trapper's cabin to perform. If you like to mix with the locals, this is the place to do it, and you may help them claim the title for highest beer sales per capita in Canada; so far they run only second. On Franklin Avenue, **The Gallery,** 867/873-2651, also has live entertainment but is rougher.

Shopping

Yellowknife has many arts-and-crafts shops, but the best place for browsing is the **North West Co. Trading Post** (5005 Bryson Dr., 867/873-8064). The store sells native arts, warm clothing, Northern literature, and tacky souvenirs. It's a replica of trading posts that once dotted the north; open daily 10 A.M.–9 P.M. For limited-edition prints, paintings, and carvings from throughout the north, head to **Northern Images** in the YK Centre Mall (4801 Franklin Ave., 867/873-5944). **Overlander Sports** (5103 51st Ave., 867/873-2474) and **Wolverine Sports Shop** (Centre Square Mall, 867/873-4350) both stock a wide range of outdoor equipment and clothing.

Festivals and Events

Not many visitors are around for the **Caribou Carnival,** held during the third weekend in March. Events include bingo on ice and log-sawing, flour-packing, igloo-building, and dog-mushing, and a tent village is set up on the frozen surface of Frame Lake. The weekend closest to Summer Solstice (June 21) is **Raven Mad Daze,** featuring street entertainment and a midnight-sun golf tournament (this event is popular with visitors, so make reservations in advance, 867/873-2386). The **Midnight Sun Festival,** starting in late June, combines **Summerfest**—a 10-day celebration of performing arts at the Northern Arts & Culture Centre, 867/669-9826—with visual and performing arts at venues throughout Yellowknife. The festival culminates in **Folk on the Rocks,** held during the third weekend of July, which takes place on the shore of Long Lake and attracts Northern and Southern performers of folk, reggae, and Inuit music. The **Commissioner's Cup Race,** held during the last weekend of August, is a yacht race from Yellowknife across Great Slave Lake and back again. Call 867/873-8019 for entry details. The **Far North Film Festival** is held during the second weekend of November.

ACCOMMODATIONS AND CAMPING

$50–100

The only accommodations within the city limits less than $100 are at bed-and-breakfasts. Ask at the Visitors Centre for a current list of B&Bs, or contact the following. **The Prospector** (3506 Wiley Rd., 867/920-7620) is in a prime position overlooking Back Bay down the hill from downtown in Back Bay. The rooms each have private bathrooms and are decorated with Northern art. Along the front of the second-floor rooms is a wide balcony overlooking the water, and the guest lounge is stocked with Northern reading material, videos, and maps. Rates range from $90–150 single or double. **Captain Ron's** (8 Lessard Dr., Yellowknife, Northwest Territories X1A 2G5, 867/873-3746), overlooking the floatplane base, has four rooms, a sundeck, a library, and a guest lounge; $80 single, $95 double. The **Blue Raven B&B** (37B Otto Dr., Yellowknife, Northwest Territories X1A 2T9, 867/873-6328), on top of a hill on Latham Island, overlooks Great Slave Lake; $70 single, $80 double.

Of the many wilderness lodges surrounding the city, the only one accessible by road is the **Prelude Lake Lodge** (P.O. Box 447, Yellowknife, Northwest Territories X1A 2N4, 867/920-4654). It's 32 kilometers east of town along the Ingraham Trail and offers cabins beginning at $75. Motor boats and canoes are available for rent and fishing is good in the lake.

$100–150

Yellowknife's least expensive motel is the **Igloo Inn** (4115 Franklin Ave., P.O. Box 596, Northwest Territories X1A 2N4, 867/873-8511), halfway to Old Town; $94 single, $99 double, extra for kitchenettes. The only other motel in this price category is the **Discovery Inn** (4701 Franklin Ave., P.O. Box 784, Northwest Territories X1A 2N6, 867/873-4151), which is simply furnished, with older-style rooms and a bar downstairs; from $130 single or double.

$150–200

The **Yellowknife Inn** (P.O. Box 490, Yellowknife, Northwest Territories X1A 2N4, 867/873-2601 or 800/661-0580) is located right in the center of the city at 5010 49th Street. Each room has a minibar and is well decorated. Guests have use of a health club, laundry facilities, and an airport shuttle; $150 single, $165 double. The **Explorer Hotel** (47th Street, Postal Service 7000, Northwest Territories X1A 2R3, 867/873-3531 or 800/661-0892) is an eight-story luxury hotel with 128 air-conditioned rooms, many with views of Old Town and the rolling tundra beyond; $158 single, $172 double.

Campgrounds

The city's only campground is at **Fred Henne Territorial Park**, 867/920-2472, across from the airport and a one-hour walk from downtown. Facilities include bug-proof kitchen shelters, woodstoves, showers, and some powered sites; $12–15 per night. Along the Ingraham Trail, at Reid Lake, and at Prelude Lake are primitive campgrounds. All three sites are open late May–September.

FOOD

The **Red Apple** in the Discovery Inn, 867/873-2324, opens at 6 A.M. and is a popular spot for breakfast. It also serves a variety of dishes starting at $8 the rest of the day. Farther out is **Sam's Monkey Tree** (483 Range Lake Rd., 867/920-4914), a good, clean, family-style restaurant. **L'atitudes**, in Centre Square Mall below the Yellowknife Inn, 867/920-7880, is a stylish, dimly lit restaurant open daily for breakfast and lunch and Thurs.–Fri. until 9 P.M. Cooked breakfasts are $6.25, and the rest of the day main meals start at $10.

McDonald's and **KFC** (once voted the national dish of the Northwest Territories) have two and one franchises, respectively, each in Yellowknife, and here in the north, take-out really means take-out; when people from outlying communities visit the capital, they often take a large supply home with them to microwave. KFC has even developed special boxes that fit under airplane seats.

Northern

Head down the hill from the city center to enjoy Northern cuisine and typically hospitable Northern atmosphere at any of the following restaurants. The **Wildcat Cafe** (3904 Wiley Rd., 867/873-8850) has been famous since it was opened by Willy Wiley and Smoky Stout in 1937, becoming the first place in Yellowknife to sell ice cream. The café closed its doors in 1959 but reopened with some remodeling in 1977. The distinctive Northern feel hasn't been lost—log walls, wooden tables, a sloping floor, and a congenial atmosphere are part of the charm. It only has a few tables and is perpetually full, so chances are you'll end up sharing a table. The blackboard menu changes daily but features mostly Northern dishes from $14. It's open in summer only, Mon.–Sat. 7 A.M.–10 P.M., Sunday 10 A.M.–10 P.M. Opposite the Wildcat is the **Prospector's Bar and Grill** (3506 Wiley Rd., 867/920-7620), featuring a hearty fish chowder using Northern fish such as pickerel, whitefish, and char ($7), and many other Northern specialties less than $25 for an entrée. The **Trapper's Cabin** (4 Lessard Dr., 867/873-3020) is Northern in name only, but after a few hours' sightseeing through Old Town, it's a great spot to stop for a coffee and light snack.

Other Restaurants

Several upscale restaurants in Yellowknife serve Northern specialties. Small and dimly lit, **The Office** (4915 50th St., 867/873-3750) serves delicious arctic char and other seasonal game from $20. **Bistro on Franklin** (4910 Franklin Ave., 867/873-3991) is similarly priced but with a more intimate atmosphere. **Our Place** (in the 50/50 Mini Mall Building on Franklin Ave., 867/920-2265) is a well-decorated cocktail lounge serving meals.

TRANSPORTATION

Air

Yellowknife Airport, five kilometers west of the city along Highway 3, is the hub of air travel in the Northwest Territories. It is open daily 24 hours, has an inexpensive café (5:30 A.M.–10 P.M.), a bar, lockers, and rental cars. **First Air,** 867/669-

8500 or 800/267-1247, uses Yellowknife as its western hub, with flights arriving and departing daily from Edmonton, Whitehorse, Inuvik, and all Nunavut communities. Other scheduled airlines flying to Yellowknife include **Air Tindi,** from communities around Great Slave Lake and Fort Simpson, 867/669-8200; **Buffalo Air Express,** from Hay River and Fort Simpson, 867/873-6112; **Great Bear Aviation,** from communities along the Mackenzie River, 867/873-3626; **Northwestern,** from Fort Smith and Hay River, 867/669-7606; and **North-Wright Air,** from communities along the Mackenzie River, 867/920-4287.

Bus

Frontier Coachlines (328 Old Airport Rd., 867/874-2566) offers bus service five times weekly from Hay River to Yellowknife ($69 one-way), with connections from there to Greyhound's other Canadian services.

Getting Around

Arctic Frontier Carriers, 867/873-4437, operates the **Public Transit System** along two routes, including out to the campground and airport, Mon.–Fri. and with a limited Saturday service. Flag charge for a cab is $2.75, then it's $1.65 for every kilometer. To the campground is $11, to the airport $12.50; call **City Cab,** 867/873-4444, or **Sunshine Taxi,** 867/873-4414. Rental-car agencies include **Budget,** 867/920-2776; **National,** 867/920-2970; **Rent-A-Relic,** 867/873-3400; **Thrifty,** 867/669-9277; and **Yellowknife Motors,** 867/873-4414. Rates start at $45 per day and $210 per week for a small car, plus 20 cents per kilometer. **Overlander Sports** (5103 51st Ave., 867/873-2474) rents bikes for $7 per hour and $28 per 24 hours.

City Tours

Raven Tours, 867/873-4776, runs a three-hour Yellowknife Sightseeing Tour that takes in all the sights of New Town, Old Town, Latham Island, and a sled-dog kennel; $20 per person. The tour departs Mon.–Sat. at 1:15 P.M. from the Visitors Centre. The company also offers guided hikes to Cameron River Falls ($38 per person), a two-hour lake cruise ($24 per person), and flightseeing (from $55 per person).

SERVICES AND INFORMATION

Services
The **post office** is at 4902 50th Street. **Microage** (4817 49th St., 867/920-5263), open Mon.–Fri. 8:30 A.M.–5:30 P.M., Saturday noon–5 P.M., has public Internet access. The **Arctic Laundromat** (4310 Franklin Ave.) is open daily 8:30 A.M.–11 P.M. **Henry's Camera and Photo Lab** (Centre Square Mall, 867/873-2389) develops film in one hour and has a limited range of camera supplies. On the main drag, **Yellowknife Foto Source** (5005 Franklin Ave., 867/873-2196) has the same services.

Stanton Regional Hospital is on Old Airport Road at Range Lake Road, 867/920-4111. For the **RCMP**, call 867/669-5100.

Books and Bookstores
Yellowknife Public Library is on the second floor of Centre Square Mall (5022 49th St., 867/920-5642). Although small, it has newspapers from throughout Canada, lots of literature on the north, and public Internet access. It's open year-round Mon.–Thurs. 10 A.M.–9 P.M., Fri.–Sat. 10 A.M.–6 P.M. **Yellowknife Book Cellar** (Panda II Mall, 867/920-2220) has a wide selection of Northern and Canadian literature. The north's biggest publisher, **Outcrop** (4920 52nd St., 867/920-4343 or 800/661-0861), has back issues of *Up Here* for sale and catalogs of all books they publish.

Tourist Information
The **Northern Frontier Regional Visitors Centre** overlooks Frame Lake (4807 49th St., 867/873-4262 or 877/881-4261, www .northernfrontier.com). It is stocked with brochures on everything you'll need to know about Yellowknife, historic photographs, and interesting displays. It's open in summer Mon.–Fri. 8:30 A.M.–6 P.M. and Sat.–Sun. 9 A.M.–5 P.M., the rest of the year Mon.–Fri. 8:30 A.M.–5:30 P.M. and Sat.–Sun. noon–4 P.M.

VICINITY OF YELLOWKNIFE

Within a 250-kilometer radius of Yellowknife are five communities accessible only by air, or in the case of Reliance and Lutselk'e, by boat. Each receives few casual visitors, and if you plan to stay overnight, you should reserve accommodations before arriving. **Air Tindi,** 867/669-8200, flies to each of the communities. Fares range $100–135 each way.

Lutselk'e
Formerly known as **Snowdrift,** this community of 200 Chipewyan Dene is located on a peninsula extending into the East Arm of Great Slave Lake. The Hudson's Bay Company established a post here in 1925, which quickly attracted Chipewyan families from the surrounding area. Nearby you'll find some excellent fishing and sheer cliffs that drop into the lake. **Snowdrift Co-op Hotel** (General Delivery, Lutselk'e, Northwest Territories X0E 1A0, 867/370-3511) has three rooms, each with shared bath; $115 per person.

Wha Ti
Wha Ti (Marten Lake) was formerly known as **Lac La Martre** and is a community of 400 Dogrib Dene on the southeast shore of a shallow lake 160 kilometers northwest of Yellowknife. A North West Company trading post was established on the lake in 1793. Today, the community functions much as it did then, relying on the area's abundant fish and mammals to provide a subsistence lifestyle. **Meni Khon Hotel** (General Delivery, Wha Ti, Northwest Territories X0E 1P0, 867/573-3381) has 10 rooms for $185 per person per day inclusive of meals, as well as a lodge on the northeast shore of the lake.

Rae Lakes
This community, 170 kilometers north of Yellowknife, was used as an outpost for hunting by the Dogrib Dene until recently. It is located on the shore of a lake that is part of a chain between Great Slave and Great Bear lakes. Permanent facilities and new housing have kept the population at approximately 220. **Gameti Motel** (General Delivery, Rae Lakes, Northwest Territories X0E 1R0, 867/997-3031) has eight rooms with private baths, and the staff can organize fishing trips; rooms are $160 per person inclusive of meals.

Snare Lake

Until recently, this community was, like Rae Lakes to the west, an outpost for hunters of the Dogrib Dene. The community of 100 is located east of Rae Lakes. Accommodations are offered in four rooms at **Snare Lake Hotel** (General Delivery, Snare Lake, Northwest Territories X0E 1W0, 867/713-2700). Rates are $185 per person per day, including meals. The hotel organizes fishing and wildlife-viewing trips for guests.

RIVERS OF MYTH, MOUNTAINS OF MYSTERY

Tucked into the southwest corner of the territories—between the Mackenzie River to the north and east and the Yukon Territory and British Columbia to the south and west—is a wild, uninhabited, roadless land of jagged peaks, thundering rivers, a waterfall twice the height of Niagara, and pristine lakes so full of fish that you'll need to bait your hook behind a tree. Not only is it one of North America's most remote mountain regions, it is one of the least understood. Scientists have only recently begun to unravel the mysteries of the strikingly varied landforms within Nahanni National Park, a UNESCO World Heritage Site. The region's history is equally mysterious. A little-known band of Indians once lived here, high in the mountains, and were feared by the Slavey Dene who lived along the Liard and Mackenzie rivers. Legends of lost gold mines, tropical valleys, and headless bodies have been luring adventurers to the area for more than 100 years. The first white men to travel up the South Nahanni River were fur trappers and missionaries. Those who managed to return brought back stories that helped create the region's mythical allure. Today, visitors from around the world come to paddle down the South Nahanni (Canada's finest wilderness river), climb in the Cirque of the Unclimbables, or just fly into this spectacular part of the world. But with names on the map like Headless Creek, Deadmen Valley, Hell's Gate, Funeral Range, Devils Kitchen, Broken Skull River, and Death Canyon, you'd better tell someone where you're going before heading out.

Nahanni National Park is visited by fewer than 1,500 people each year. Roads have replaced rivers as transportation routes through much of the region, but communities built around fur-trading posts still remain. The Mackenzie Highway, which begins in northern Alberta, ends 427 kilometers west of Hay River in Fort Simpson, the main jumping-off point for wilderness trips into the Nahanni and beyond.

Saamba Deh Falls Territorial Park

From the Yellowknife junction, the Mackenzie Highway continues west through a typical northern boreal forest, crossing many small creeks along the way. Approximately 136 kilometers from this junction, the road crosses **Trout River,** which flows alongside Saamba Deh Falls Territorial Park. The falls are directly downstream from the road bridge and are easily accessible from the day-use area. Here, the river is forced through a narrow gorge, exploding into the deep pond below. The one-kilometer hike upstream from the day-use area to **Coral Falls,** named for the abundant marine fossils found in the surrounding limestone banks, is a worthwhile side trip. Most common are crinoids and brachiopods that are approximately 400 million years old (Late Devonian period). The trail is well defined at first, then climbs steeply, making getting down to the river level in one piece rather interesting. The alternative is to scramble down along the river as soon as the trail begins climbing. The **Visitors Centre** has a small fossil display and free coffee. Across the parking lot is a TV room where the friendly staff can put on videos pertaining to the region's natural and human history; it's open mid-May to mid-September daily 8 A.M.–8 P.M. The park also has a small campground with showers, bug-proof kitchen shelters, and well-maintained sites for $12 per night.

From here, the Mackenzie Highway continues in a northwesterly direction to a junction with the Liard Highway, which heads south to Fort Liard and into British Columbia. Past the junction 46 kilometers, it crosses the Liard River by ferry and, 16 kilometers farther, ends in Fort Simpson. The ferry operates late May to late October daily 8 A.M.–11:45 P.M.

ALBERT FAILLE

Each break-up from 1916 to 1961, Albert Faille left Fort Simpson by scow in a feverish, determined quest for the elusive Nahanni gold. Some said it was sheer lunacy, others said a waste of time. But his relentless obsession and exploits against insurmountable odds created the Faille legend, which has become synonymous with the Nahanni.

Of Swiss descent, Faille was born in Minnesota. He was one of the earliest men to tackle the river alone, and at the time, the first to winter there in seven years. He built a cabin at the mouth of the Flat River, but it was at Murder Creek, upstream from the cabin, that Faille believed his fortune in gold lay. At times he'd be given up for dead, and rumors and tales would begin to unfold—but then he would turn up at Fort Simpson for supplies. He spent most winters in a small cabin that still stands today, overlooking the Mackenzie River in Fort Simpson. He died there in 1974. His scows still lie out front, ready for break-up and another attempt for the elusive key to finding gold. His final trip is documented by a 1961 National Film Board production that can be seen in the Fort Simpson and Blackstone visitor centers.

Trout Lake

This small community (pop. 100) was established in the late 1960s as a permanent base for the Slavey Dene who had hunted, trapped, and fished in the area for thousands of years. It's located in a heavily wooded area where the Island River drains into Trout Lake, approximately 100 kilometers east of Fort Liard. The community's only link to the outside world is by charter flight from Fort Liard or Fort Simpson or by a winter road from the Mackenzie Highway, just east of Saamba Deh Falls Territorial Park. With a name like Trout Lake, it's not surprising that the fishing is excellent, especially for lake trout, pickerel, and whitefish. The best spot is at the lake's northern end, where the Moose River flows into the lake. The main problem with coming here to fish is that you reach your daily limit too quickly. The local Dene band runs a fishing lodge nine kilometers from the community. The

Lake trout inhabit the aptly named waters of Trout Lake.

lodge costs $160 per person per day including guided fishing, lunch, and use of kitchen facilities. Boat rentals are also available. For more information, call the band office at 867/695-9800. **Deh Cho Air,** 867/770-4103, in Fort Liard, flies to Trout Lake and offers day trips to the lake for $195 per person.

Jean Marie River

The Slavey Dene of this small community (pop. 50) still hunt, trap, and fish for a living in the old way but are best known for their moose-hair tufting and porcupine-quill work, which can be purchased in Fort Simpson and Yellowknife. This community is situated at the confluence of the Jean Marie and Mackenzie rivers with no summer road access, and the residents travel downstream to Fort Simpson to trade and buy supplies. No visitor services are available, but those en route down the Mackenzie are always welcome to drop in. Fort Simpson is 68 kilometers downstream, along a section of river dotted with islands.

FORT SIMPSON

Best known as one of the jumping-off points for Nahanni National Park, the town of Fort Simpson (pop. 1,000) is at the confluence of two major rivers—the Liard and Mackenzie—and at the western terminus of the Mackenzie Highway. Throughout summer, the town is a hive of activity, a constant buzz of floatplanes taking off to remote fly-in fishing lakes, groups of Gore-Tex–clad adventurers from around the world checking their equipment before heading off for the adventure of a lifetime down the South Nahanni River, and the occasional canoe-load of paddlers stopping in on their way to the Arctic Ocean. The town provides a good base for exploring the region—whether by car, plane, boat, or on foot. Wildlife is abundant, and the lakes and rivers teem with fish.

History

A permanent settlement was not established at this strategic location until 1815, after Alexander Mackenzie had paddled by on his way to the Arctic

Ocean. Originally known as "Fort of the Forks," it was built by North West Company in 1804 but was renamed Fort Simpson in 1821. In addition to being an important fur-trading post, it was a stopping point for barges plying the Mackenzie River loaded with supplies, fuel, and furs. Missions were established in 1858 and 1894, and the area's potential for agriculture began to be realized. The government operated an experimental farm here for years, but it was closed in 1969 when a highway linking Fort Simpson to the outside was completed and importing food overland became practical. During the 1960s, the town became a base for oil exploration along the Mackenzie Valley and an administrative center for the territorial government.

Around Town

At one time, the town's main street was Mackenzie Drive, along the riverfront. But when the highway was completed, many buildings were moved closer to it. Now most town services are located along 100th Street. At the south end of Mackenzie Drive is an area known as "The Flat," where many people lived until severe flooding in 1963 forced relocation of homes. The large tepee and other structures here, known as the **Papal Grounds,** were built for a visit by Pope John Paul II on September 20, 1987. Walking north from here along Mackenzie Drive, a sternwheeler on the riverbank soon comes into view. Built in 1920, this boat was one of many that plied the Mackenzie River. Also here is a small monument noting the importance of the river in the town's history. Across the road is the site of the Hudson's Bay Company post; the only original building remaining is the company's outhouse. Continuing farther along the river, you pass the sites of an Anglican church, the Royal Canadian Mounted Police (RCMP), an early hotel, the Power Corporation building, and the cabin of Nahanni legend **Albert Faille.** Faille wintered here between his goldseeking trips. Peering through the windows and marveling at the wooden scows laying in the yard gives you some insight into the life of this amazing man, particularly if you've watched the National Film Board documentary about him shown at the Visitors Centre. Faille is buried behind the post office on 100th Street. North along Mackenzie

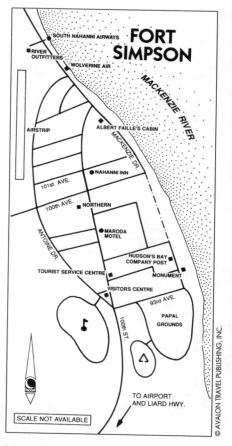

Drive, at the far end of the airstrip, is the staging area for the four outfitters operating trips down the South Nahanni River.

Recreation

Many local lakes have great fishing. **McGill Lake** and **Mustard Lake** are two of the many fly-in spots with trophy-size northern pike, pickerel, lake trout, and arctic grayling. Contact **Cherokee Enterprises,** 867/695-2712, for guided river fishing. If you've never gotten hooked on fishing, perhaps golf sounds better. Down by the entrance to town on Antoine Drive is the local golf course, which was recently expanded from six to nine holes and with no clubhouse or rentals, but the local golfing population is proud of it.

Accommodations and Food
Along the road into town is **Bannockland Inn** (P.O. Box 656, Northwest Territories X0E 0N0, 867/695-3337). It's the home of long-time Northerners, the Sibbestons, who have opened six rooms to visitors. Each room has private facilities, and rates include a cooked breakfast and airport transfers; $80 single, $105 double. Rooms in both of Fort Simpson's hotels are little more than basic. The **Maroda Motel** (P.O. Box 250, Fort Simpson, 867/695-2602) charges from $100 single, $115 double. Some of the 15 rooms have kitchenettes. The 34-room **Nahanni Inn** (P.O. Box 248, 867/695-2201) has a coffee shop (open daily at 8 A.M.) and dining room; $105 single, $115 double. Both accommodations are within walking distance of everything. On the road to the Papal Grounds is **Fort Simpson Campground.** The sites ($8 per night) provide ample privacy, and a large supply of firewood is available. On the Yellowknife side of the ferry is another primitive campground. Anyone heading into the Nahanni with a river outfitter may pitch a tent at the airstrip compound for free, but you need to ask permission first.

For breakfast, everyone heads to the coffee shop in the Nahanni Inn, but it's nothing special. Northern has a take-out outlet for Pizza Hut and KFC specialties.

Transportation
The main airport is 12 kilometers south of town ($15 in a cab, 867/695-2777). Two airlines fly to Fort Simpson, both from Yellowknife (all connections from the south are through the territorial capital). **Buffalo Air Express,** 867/874-3333 or 800/465-3168, a connector airline for Air Canada, flies from Yellowknife Monday, Wednesday, and Friday at 10:10 A.M. **First Air,** 867/695-2020, stops at Fort Simpson on its run between Yellowknife and Whitehorse. The floatplane base is along Mackenzie Drive at the north end of town.

Services and Information
Groceries and basic camping supplies are available from **Northern,** but you should stock up in Hay River. On 97th Avenue is a **bank** (C.I.B.C.); on 100th Street are a **post office,** a **liquor store** (with a ration system in effect), and a **gas station.**

At the south entrance to town is an excellent **Visitors Centre,** 867/695-3182. Inside is a recreation of the original Hudson's Bay Company post and some interesting historical displays. Don't miss the 1961 National Film Board documentary on Nahanni legend Albert Faille, which is shown, along with others, in the theater; open May 15 to September 15 daily 8 A.M.–8 P.M. Diagonally opposite the Visitors Centre is the **Tourist Service Centre,** with coin showers, a car wash, and a laundromat. You could also use the laundry facilities in the apartment block on 101st Avenue.

LIARD HIGHWAY

Although this highway, which follows the Liard River Valley from Fort Simpson to Fort Nelson (British Columbia), was officially completed in 1984, it wasn't marked on most maps until the late 1980s and didn't really become an all-weather gravel highway (read: passable) until the early 1990s. From the Mackenzie Highway, southeast of Fort Simpson, to Fort Nelson is 394 kilometers of relatively straight road through a boreal forest of spruce, aspen, and poplar. Wildlife along this route is abundant; chances are you'll see moose and black bears, especially at dawn and dusk. The only services are at Fort Liard.

Lindberg Landing
Although the highway parallels the Liard River, access to the water is limited. One of the first landings is 100 kilometers south of the Mackenzie Highway at the home of Ed and Sue Lindberg, who provide accommodations and have an amazingly diverse vegetable garden. Ed Lindberg's father, Ole, arrived from Sweden in the mid-1920s and was the first permanent settler along the river. The service offered by the Lindbergs is excellent for those beginning or ending a journey down the South Nahanni River. Local air charter companies (see "Your Own Whitewater Expedition" in "Nahanni National Park") will pick you up at the landing and drop you upriver, allowing you to float back to Lindberg Landing farm and finish your trip with

a bed, a beer, and a shower. Reservations for rooms are essential; no walk-ins. Dinner, bed, and breakfast is $80 per person. Or rent one of the two rustic cabins, which sleep four, for $80. For bookings, contact P.O. Box 28, Fort Simpson, Northwest Territories X0E 0N0; by phone, call the operator and ask for Pointed Mountain Channel JR3-6644. From the north, Lindberg Landing is marked by a small sign in a tree. If you pass Blackstone Territorial Park, you missed it.

Blackstone Territorial Park
Just south of the Lindberg's homestead, where the Blackstone River drains into the Liard River, a small territorial park has been established at a site known as **Blackstone Landing.** A Visitors Centre overlooks the river, and from there a short trail leads along the river to a trapper's cabin. The campground has flush toilets, showers, and two bug-proof, woodstove-equipped kitchen shelters hidden among the trees. Sites cost $12 per night. Black bears are common, so keep your food securely stored. The Visitors Centre has interesting displays on the area's history, a good selection of videos, and information on Nahanni National Park (although registering for a trip into the park must be done in Fort Simpson); open mid-May to mid-September daily 8 A.M.–8 P.M.

From the park, Fort Liard is 114 kilometers farther south. The highway crosses many small creeks, passes the winter road to Nahanni Butte, and affords views of the Liard Range to the west. Approximately 68 kilometers south of Blackstone Territorial Park is a winter road that was cut through the muskeg to the now-abandoned Paramount Mine, on the opposite side of the Liard River. It is a pleasant one-kilometer hike (15 minutes each way) down to the river.

Save a moose, honk your horn.

Nahanni Butte
Named for the steeply sided butte across the South Nahanni River, this small Slavey Dene community of less than 100 is located across the Liard River from the highway. Although you can drive to it in winter, the rest of the year it is accessible only by plane or boat. The town is fairly modern. It was established by the government to house a group of once-nomadic natives who, at times, traded with the Tahltan and Tlingit of the Pacific coast. For many years, Nahanni National Park headquarters was here, and a small office still operates in summer for "checking-out" after a river trip. Most paddlers stop by anyway because the town is in a picturesque setting and holds an interesting log church and log school. Accommodations are at **Nahanni Butte Inn** (P.O. Box 149, Fort Simpson, Northwest Territories X0E 0N0, 867/602-2002), which offers eight beds in four rooms; $110 per person. The inn is a new addition to a small general store, which constitutes the only other services available.

FORT LIARD

Best known as the "Tropics of the North," this town of 400 is set among a lush forest of poplar and birch on the banks of the Liard River. The southern location, warm climate, and rich soil mean that residents are able to grow a variety of vegetables. Log homes and green gardens make the six-kilometer detour from the Liard Highway worthwhile.

The North West Company established a post in 1807 where the Petitot River drains into the Liard, but abandoned the site after many of the residents were massacred by natives. In 1821, after the company merged with the Hudson's Bay Company, the post reopened, but trade was continually disrupted by warring native tribes. Until the 1960s, most of the Dene inhabitants spent winter away from Fort Liard, and modern development didn't begin until the highway opened to Fort Nelson. Traditional lifestyles are still important to residents, nearly all of whom spend time trapping, hunting, fishing, and making clothing and crafts.

Birchbark Baskets

The women of Fort Liard are famous for these baskets, made for storing food, collecting berries, carrying supplies, or even boiling water. Birch is abundant in the area and has a remarkably pliable nature, ideal for bending and sewing. The bark contains a natural wax, making it not only rot-resistant but also waterproof. Baskets are still made in the long, tedious process handed down from generation to generation. They are sewn together with specially prepared roots and decorated with porcupine quills. If you are unable to afford a soapstone carving from Cape Dorset, these baskets are a good second choice for a Northern souvenir. They are available from the small gift store on Fort Liard's main street, or in Fort Simpson and Hay River.

Practicalities

The small but well-maintained **Hay Lake Campground** has pit toilets, firewood, and drinking water. It's along the Fort Liard access road; sites are $12 per night. Accommodations above the **Liard Valley General Store,** 867/770-4441, sleep 24 in 12 basic rooms, for $90 single, $100 double, $120 and $130, respectively, for a kitchenette. Back out on the highway is a gas station that is open 7 A.M.–11 P.M.

   Deh Cho Air (P.O. Box 78, Fort Liard, Northwest Territories X0G 0A0, 867/770-4103) flies from Fort Liard into Nahanni National Park, and to Trout Lake for legendary fishing.

NAHANNI NATIONAL PARK

Through this rugged land of mountains flows one of the most spectacular, wildest, and purest stretches of white-water in the world—the South Nahanni River. Protecting a 300-kilometer stretch of this remote river is 4,766-square-kilometer Nahanni National Park, which boasts some of the world's most breathtaking, unde-

veloped mountain scenery. The park holds North America's deepest river canyons and a waterfall twice the height of Niagara. It's home to legends of deadly Indian tribes and hapless prospectors whose bodies turned up headless. The roadless park is a vast wilderness inhabited only by bears, mountain goats, Dall's sheep, caribou, moose, and wolves, and is accessible only by air or water.

   The best way to really experience the park is on a one- to three-week canoe or raft trip down the river, offered by four outfitters. However you decide to visit the park, whether with an outfitter, on your own carefully prepared expedition, or even just on a daylong flightseeing trip, the adventure will remain with you for the rest of your life.

Of Myths and Legends

Slavey Dene, who lived on the lowlands along the Mackenzie and Liard rivers, feared a mysterious group of Indians living high in the Mackenzie Mountains. The mountain people, who became known as the *Nahanni* (The People Who Live Far Away), would travel down the South Nahanni River each spring in boats up to 20 meters long. The boats were constructed of moosehide stretched over a spruce frame. Upon arrival at the trading post, the Indians would dismantle the boats, trading furs and the moosehides before returning on foot to the mountains.

   Circa 1900, a Nahanni Indian arrived at the trading post with a chunk of quartz bearing gold. That got some people's attention. In 1905, Willie and Frank McLeod began prospecting tributaries of the Flat River in search of an elusive mother lode. Three years later, their headless bodies were discovered at the mouth of what is now known as Headless Creek; for many years thereafter, the entire valley was called Deadmen Valley. Very quickly, stories of gold mines, murder, lush tropical valleys, and a tribe of Indians dominated by a white woman became rampant. These stories did nothing but lure other prospecting adventurers to the valley—Jorgenson, Shebbach, Field, Faille, Sibbeston, Kraus, and Patterson. Many died mysteriously: Jorgenson's skeleton was found outside his cabin, his precious rifle gone; Shebbach died of starvation at the

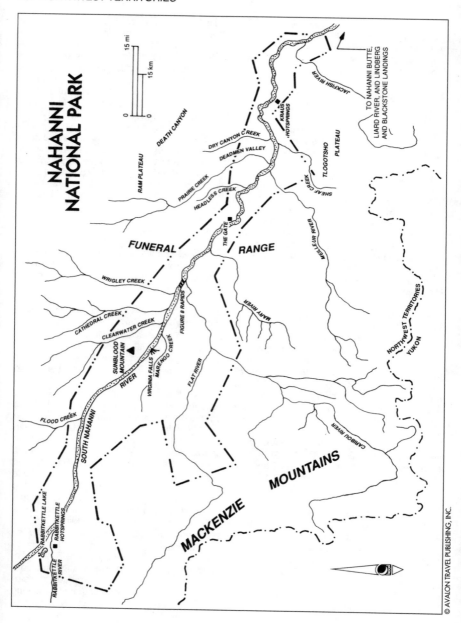

NAHANNI NATIONAL PARK

© AVALON TRAVEL PUBLISHING, INC.

mouth of Caribou Creek; the body of Phil Powers was discovered in his burned-out cabin; Angus Hall just plain disappeared.

The Land

The **Mackenzie Mountains** rise abruptly from the lowlands west of the Mackenzie River. The headwaters of the **South Nahanni River** are high in these mountains, northwest of the park along the Northwest Territories/Yukon border. Flowing in a roughly southeasterly direction for 540 kilometers, it drains into the Liard River, a major tributary of the Mackenzie River. The South Nahanni, cut deeply into the mountains, is known as an "antecedent"; that is, it preceded the mountains. It once meandered through a wide-open plain. As uplift in the earth's surface occurred, the river cut down through the rising rock strata and created the deep, meandering canyons present today.

Tufa Mounds

One of the most remarkable geological formations in the park occurs at **Rabbitkettle Hotsprings,** a seven-kilometer hike from Rabbitkettle Lake. Two flat-topped mounds, the larger 27 meters high and 60 meters wide, are composed entirely of tufa. A rocklike substance, tufa is formed when dissolved minerals, in this case mainly calcium carbonate, rise to the earth's surface as a thermal spring, radiating outward and forming a series of terraces known as rimstone dams. These tufa mounds are approximately 10,000 years old and are the largest in Canada. The delicate surface, sculptured into intricate patterns, is easily damaged; therefore, hikers heading here must be accompanied by a warden, who is stationed at Rabbitkettle Lake.

Virginia Falls

From their highest point, these falls on the South Nahanni River drop 92 meters. Water from the South Nahanni River cascading over the escarpment is separated on one side by a great pinnacle of rock. The smaller side of the falls is 55 meters. A 1.3-kilometer portage on the south side of the river follows the path previously taken by the river. The falls have migrated upstream through gradual erosion, creating Fourth Canyon.

Virginia Falls

Fourth, Third, Second, and First Canyons

These four canyons, immediately downstream of Virginia Falls, form one of the most extensive canyon systems north of the 60th parallel. The canyon walls are up to 1,200 meters high and 19 kilometers long. At **The Gate,** a sharp turn through the Third Canyon, the river flows through a narrow gap where the canyon walls rise 460 meters. Between Second and First canyons is a wide floodplain where **Prairie Creek** drains into the South Nahanni River. From this area, **Tlogotsho Plateau** dominates the southern skyline. First Canyon has the highest walls, almost vertical and towering 1,000 meters above the river—not a place for the claustrophobic. Throughout the canyons are four sets of rapids, including **Figure Eight Rapids,** best known for producing waves up to 1.5 meters high.

Flat River

Running the Flat River is for experienced whitewater enthusiasts only. It is a 125-kilometer run from the start at **Seaplane Lake,** just outside the park boundary, to the river's confluence with the South Nahanni River between Fourth and Third canyons. Along its course, the Flat River spews through a series of chutes and ledges known as Cascade-of-the-Thirteen-Steps rapids (Class VI) and passes several 15-meter limestone hoodoos. Most of the prospecting in the area took place along the banks of this river. At the rivermouth is a pile of logs, the remains of a cabin built by Albert Faille. Also at this site is a cabin built by Fred Sibbeston, who wintered here in 1944 with his wife, mother, and five children.

Kraus Hotsprings

These hot springs, just downstream of First Canyon, are named for Gus and Mary Kraus, who lived here on and off between 1940 and 1971. Bubbling up through fine mud, the hot springs remain at a constant temperature of 35°C year-round. Sulphuric acid is formed when hydrogen sulfide in the water comes into contact with oxygen in the air. The acid erodes any tufa that forms, and, more important for those planning a relaxing soak, it produces a strong rotten-egg smell. Many exotic plants thrive here, a legacy of the Krauses' garden.

Running the South Nahanni with an Outfitter

For most people, whether experienced canoeists or never-evers, the advantages of a trip down the South Nahanni River with a licensed outfitter far outweigh the disadvantages. Outfitters must have a license to operate guided river trips. Each of the two outfitters recommended offer trips of varying lengths—three weeks from Moose Ponds, two weeks from Rabbitkettle Lake, or eight to 12 days from Virginia Falls. Itineraries are worked out so that no more than four to seven hours per day are spent on the river, leaving plenty of time for hiking, exploring, and viewing wildlife. Craft used are either rafts, 5.5-meter canoes, or longer voyageur-type canoes. The small canoes hold two people and are generally for those with some previous paddling experience. Inflatable rafts are great if you want to lay back and relax as you float down the river under a guide's supervision. Only Nahanni River Adventures offers trips in the voyageur canoes, which are 10 meters long and seat eight, including a guide. They are an excellent compromise, offering the stability of a raft, but with the feeling of canoeing; you can paddle as much, or as little, as you like.

Prices between operators vary little and are generally $2,400–4,000. Some offer a small discount for those with their own tent, whereas others charge more for those without. Check whether the price includes the Goods and Services Tax (GST, 7 percent). Most important, talk to each outfitter (they all love "their" river, so getting them to talk is no problem). Guided trips operate mid-June to early September, and many dates fill up fast. The staging area for all commercial outfitters is the north end of the old airstrip in downtown Fort Simpson.

For details, contact **Nahanni River Adventures** (P.O. Box 4869, Whitehorse, Yukon Y1A 4N6, 867/668-3180 or 800/297-6927, www.nahanni.com), or **Nahanni Wilderness Adventures** (Box 4, Site 6, R.R. 1, Didsbury, Alberta T0M 0W0, 403/637-3843 or 888/897-5223, www.nahanniwild.com).

Your Own White-water Expedition

Experienced white-water enthusiasts planning their own trip down the Nahanni have four main components to organize: permits and fees, transportation into the park, transportation down the river, and supplies.

Permits and Fees: Because of the high number of visitors using the river, a reservation and fee system has been implemented. Two nonguided parties are allowed to start out each day, with a maximum of two nights at Virginia Falls. For those beginning their river trip upstream of Virginia Falls, their allotted time starts when they reach the falls. An annual Backcountry User Fee of $100 covers registration and camping fees. For all of the relevant forms and further information, call park headquarters at 867/695-3151 or visit the website at www.parkscanada.gc.ca/nahanni.

Entering the Park: Most expeditions begin from Virginia Falls. Floatplanes land upstream from the falls, from where, in readiness for the trip downstream, a steep portage must be made to the base of the falls. To prevent the cost of an air charter at the end of your trip, it is best to pull out along the Liard River at Blackstone or Lindberg Landing, a full day's paddle downstream of the park boundary.

Four charter companies take paddlers into the park. They use three different types of planes: Cessna 185s, capable of carrying two passengers, a canoe or kayak, and gear to a total of 500-600 pounds; Beavers, capable of carrying four passengers, two (nesting) canoes, and gear to a total of 1,000–1,200 pounds; and Twin Otters, which can carry six passengers, three (nesting) canoes, and gear to a total of 1,500 pounds. **Deh Cho Air,** 867/770-4103, leaves from Fort Liard, but charter rates include van transportation from Blackstone Landing back to Fort Liard. Charter rates in the Cessna 185 are to Virginia Falls, $750; Rabbitkettle Lake, $1,050; Moose Ponds, $1,500; and Glacier Lake, $1,100. This company has recently come under new management, and in the process expanded its services to include canoe and equipment rentals. Air mileage from Fort Simpson is longer and, therefore, more expensive, but the town has more services than Fort Liard, including canoe rentals, restaurants, motels, groceries, and an airport with connections to the outside world. Three companies fly into the park from Fort Simpson: **Wolverine Air,** 867/695-2263; **Simpson Air,** 867/695-2505; and **South Nahanni Airways,** 867/695-2007. Among the three companies, they run a variety of aircraft; rates according to destination are Virginia Falls, $960 in the Cessna and $1,200 in the Beaver; Rabbitkettle Lake, $1,250 and $1,650; Moose Ponds, $1,750 and $2,250; and Glacier Lake, $1,420 and $1,700.

A few years ago, I picked up a guy who'd just come down the river and was hitchhiking back to Watson Lake from Blackstone Landing. He'd started at Moose Ponds, which is closer to Watson Lake (Yukon) than any Northwest Territories community, therefore chartering a plane from Watson Lake cost less, but it seemed an inconvenient way to save a couple hundred bucks.

Down the River: The river can easily be divided into four sections. From Moose Ponds to Rabbitkettle Lake takes three to five days and includes a 60-kilometer stretch of rapids. From Rabbitkettle Lake to Virginia Falls is a two- to three-day float down one of the river's easier stretches. After a short but steep portage around the falls, there is a three- to four-day paddle through spectacular canyon scenery with many sets of rapids to an area known as "The Splits."

Here the river flows into a broad floodplain, passing the community of Nahanni Butte and draining into the Liard River. Allow two days to get to Blackstone Landing from The Splits. The entire trip from Moose Ponds can be done in less than two weeks, but allow extra days for hiking, exploring, or just relaxing.

Most people choose canoes for the trip, although kayaks and inflatable rafts are also feasible. Whatever craft you decide to use will need a spray deck, and all gear should be securely waterproofed. **Deh Cho Air, Nahanni River Adventures,** and **Nahanni Wilderness Adventures** rent canoes ($35–40 per day) and rafts ($160 per day). All rentals should be organized well before the summer season begins.

Supplies: Charter operators have reasonably generous load limits, allowing you to take plenty of food. But no amount of food can substitute for good prior planning; a crate of oranges picked up on the way through British Columbia's Okanagan Valley or vegetables from Paradise Gardens, near Hay River, all help make the trip more enjoyable—and oranges float if they go overboard. Both Fort Liard and Fort Simpson have a small grocery store, but don't count on finding your favorite brand of anything, especially at your favorite price. Stock up on plenty of bug repellent, bring lots of film, and if you bring a video camera, don't forget extra batteries because you'll be hundreds of miles from the nearest power source.

Hiking

Renowned for its river running, the park also has some fantastic hiking opportunities. Apart from the portage route around Virginia Falls, the park has no developed trails. **The Cirque of the Unclimbables,** near the Yukon border, is a spectacular arc of sheer-walled rock rising almost 1,000 meters. It is a mecca for rock climbers from around the world but is in a nearly inaccessible part of the Logan Mountains. Most climbers access the region by helicopter from Watson Lake or hike in from Glacier Lake, on a tributary of the South Nahanni River. **Rabbitkettle Hotsprings** is a seven-kilometer hike from Rabbitkettle Lake, a staging area where floatplanes drop river runners off. Most guided trips allow time for a hike to these amazing tufa mounds. All hikers heading to the hot springs must be accompanied by a park warden based at the lake.

The eight-kilometer hike to the summit of **Sunblood Mountain** from Virginia Falls is one of the park's most popular hikes. Breathtaking views of the surrounding mountainscape and the river below are afforded from the top. **Marengo Falls**, four kilometers from Virginia Falls, is another popular destination. Farther downstream, the **Tlogotsho Plateau** is reached by an 18-kilometer trek up Sheaf Creek; the **Ram Plateau** is accessible along Deadmen Valley; and six kilometers up **Dry Canyon Creek** is a much smaller tundralike plateau.

Flightseeing
Getting into the park for just the day is problematic but well worth the effort and cost. Typically, charter operators fly to Virginia Falls, with two hours on the ground. If you have three or more people in your group, there are no problems; just call each operator for the best quote (or get the staff at Fort Simpson Visitors Centre to do it for you). Groups of less than three have the choice of chartering an entire plane (from approximately $800) or waiting around for other interested parties to turn up. Each of the air charter companies can tailor flights to suit your needs. By waiting around until the plane is full, or by booking in advance, you have more of a chance of keeping the cost down. **Deh Cho Air,** 867/770-4103, charges $300 for a one-hour flight into the southern end of the park, or $720 for a half-day trip including time on the ground at Virginia Falls; maximum three people. From Fort Simpson, **Wolverine Air,** 867/695-2263; **Simpson Air,** 867/695-2505; and **South Nahanni Airways,** 867/695-2007, all fly into the park for flightseeing, from $300 per person for a six-hour trip.

Camping
Campsites along the river should always be chosen on alluvial fans or sandbars at the mouths of tributaries. Primitive campsites are located at Rabbitkettle Lake, Virginia Falls, and Kraus Hotsprings. **Virginia Falls** is a good base if you don't plan on a trip down the river (two-night maximum). **Deh Cho Air** offers an overnight package from $340 per person round-trip, but you'll need six people to get this rate. All campers should register at park headquarters in Fort Simpson.

More Information
A lot has been written about the Nahanni, both the natural and human history. One well-known book is *The Dangerous River* (1990) by R.M. Patterson. Patterson is one of the river's legendary figures, and he spent many years in Nahanni Country with Albert Faille. Another storyteller and writer, Dick Turner, homesteaded for many years beside the Lindbergs on the Liard River. He is best known for his book *Nahanni* (1975), describing his life trapping and hunting in the Mackenzie Mountains. *Nahanni: River of Gold, River of Dreams* is a contemporary look at the river through yarns told by one of the river's most experienced guides, "Nahanni" Neil Hartling of Nahanni River Adventures. *National Geographic* published an article about the river in September 1981.

The outfitters on the river are experts in their own right and can answer many of your questions long before you arrive. For specific information on the park, contact Superintendent, Nahanni National Park, P.O. Box 348, Fort Simpson, Northwest Territories X0E 0N0, 867/695-3151, www.parkscanada.gc.ca/nahanni. **Park Headquarters,** once located in Dick Turner's old cabin at Nahanni Butte, is now in Fort Simpson. Head there for further information and to pick up trip permits. The Fort Simpson Visitors Centre has park displays as well as relevant videos and books for visitor use. The same service on a smaller scale is offered at Blackstone Territorial Park.

MACKENZIE RIVER VALLEY

Between the treeless barrenlands and the jagged peaks of the Mackenzie Mountains flows one of the world's mightiest rivers—the Mackenzie. The river begins at Great Slave Lake and flows in a northwesterly direction 1,800 kilometers to the Arctic Ocean, draining one-fifth of Canada in the process. In places, it is three kilometers across. The lowlands of the wide valley flanking the river are covered in a boreal forest of black spruce, tamarack, and paper birch, with an understory of moss and lichens, high bush, cranberry, and blueberry. East of the river is 31,400-square-kilometer Great Bear Lake, the eighth-largest lake in the world.

For thousands of years, the North Slavey Dene lived along the *Deh Cho* (Big River) hunting, fishing, and trapping. In 1789, Alexander Mackenzie became the first European to travel the river, which now bears his name. After his reports of rich fur resources reached the outside, the North West Company established fur-trading posts along the river. The Dene, who were originally nomadic, settled at the trading posts, forming small communities. In addition to these native settlements, communities along the river today include old fur-trading posts and the modern oil and government towns of Norman Wells and Inuvik, respectively. North of Fort Simpson and south of the Arctic Circle are four riverside communities: Wrigley, Tulita (formerly Fort Norman), Norman Wells, and Fort Good Hope. The only community on Great Bear Lake is Déline (formerly Fort Franklin), a base for fishing trips. Just north of the Arctic Circle, east of the Mackenzie River, is Colville Lake, famous for its world-class artists. The only road into the region begins at Fort Simpson and extends north to Wrigley. In winter, this road continues to Norman Wells along the frozen river and ends at Fort Good Hope. In summer, the only highway is the Mackenzie River, along which tugs and barges carry freight to and from Hay River. Ambitious hikers in the area can attempt the challenging 372-kilometer Canol Heritage Trail, which begins across the river from Norman Wells and heads deep into the rugged Mackenzie Mountains.

Traveling the Mackenzie River

Paddlers in canoes and kayaks set out along the river every summer with the Arctic Ocean in their sights. The entire trip, from Fort Providence to Tuktoyaktuk, is 1,800 kilometers but can be broken up into shorter sections. Generally, the river has no rapids and is more of a paddle than a float, but strong winds and sudden storms can create dangerous high waves. Advance planning is required because communities are generally at least 200 kilometers apart. The prime canoeing season on the river is late June–August. This leaves little time for a long trip, but the days are generally sunny, with up to 24 hours of daylight. The RCMP should be informed of your plans and approximate arrival times. Boats along the river generally keep an eye out for paddlers and pull alongside for a chat. Communities along the river all have grocery stores, but prices are high. Wherever you decide to end the trip (Inuvik is a popular destination), you must organize with an airline to get the canoe back to civilization or be prepared to sell it in the north. Peter Clarkson, 867/777-2594, buys and sells canoes from his base in Inuvik and can arrange canoe dropoffs along the Mackenzie River.

If you're really adventurous, the **Rat River Route** may be to your liking. This entails pulling out of the Mackenzie River north of Tsiigehtchic, portaging 75 kilometers up the Rat River to MacDougall Pass, paddling the Bell River to the Porcupine River, and then into the Yukon River into Alaska. Good luck.

Once a year, the **Norweta,** a small cruise boat, sails from Yellowknife to Inuvik on a 10-day (one-way) journey, staying in Inuvik for a week and then returning to Yellowknife the following week. The cost of the all-inclusive trip is $3,795 per person one-way for a cabin with two berths or $5,195 single occupancy. For more information, write the Whitlock Family, P.O. Box 2216, Yellowknife, Northwest Territories X1A 2P6, 867/873-2489 or 877/874-6001.

Wrigley

In 1994, a summer road was completed to the town of Wrigley, 225 kilometers northwest of

Fort Simpson. It is the first section of an all-weather road planned to eventually extend to Inuvik. From **Ndulee Ferry Crossing** (daily 9–11 A.M. and 2–8 P.M.), 84 kilometers out of Fort Simpson, the road passes through thick boreal forest on the way to Wrigley.

Most of the community's 160 residents are Slavey Dene who live a semitraditional lifestyle, having settled in the area since the North West Company's Fort Alexander opened at the mouth of the Willow Lake River in 1817. Over the next 150 years, the community moved several times. The present community of Wrigley sits at the site of an airstrip built during World War II. Opposite Wrigley is *Roche qui-Trempe-à–L'eau* (The Rock that Plunges into the Water). It's an isolated hill that has been eroded away by the river on one side, creating a sheer cliff that drops 400 meters into the water below. Peregrine falcons are occasionally seen swooping down on cliff swallows that nest here.

The **Petanea Co-op Hotel** (General Delivery, Wrigley, Northwest Territories X0E 1E0, 867/581-3121) has five rooms with a shared bath for $180 per person per day with three meals. Ask here about boat rentals. The hotel also has a small coffee shop and a dining room that opens in the evening. Camping anywhere along the river is allowed.

NORMAN WELLS

Residents were expecting the news, but on June 15, 1996, the official announcement was made that the oil wells and refinery that had been the lifeblood of Norman Wells were to close. Their closure is only a page in Norman Wells's fascinating history, however. The town is best known by adventurers for the Canol Heritage Trail, a wilderness trek following a route punched through the Mackenzie and Selwyn mountains to transport oil to Alaska. It is also a good staging area for trips into the surrounding mountains, along the many rivers, or to world-class fly-in fishing lodges.

History
Unlike other settlements along the Mackenzie River, Norman Wells did not originate as a trading post but owes its existence to oil. Oil seeps along the riverbank were known to the Dene, who named the area *Le Gohlini* (Where the Oil Is). Alexander Mackenzie reported oil in the area in 1789 on his historic voyage to the Arctic Ocean. But the first well, "Discovery," wasn't drilled until 1919, and it didn't become productive until 1932. Increased mining activity in the western Arctic and a change from woodburning riverboats to those using petroleum-based fuel meant that demand for oil quickly grew. Despite the ill-fated Canol Project (see following section), oil production at Norman Wells' oil fields continued to increase to a maximum production of 10 million barrels per year from a field tapped by 160 wells. It was a unique field, and the infrastructure will remain for many years. Six manmade islands in the middle of the Mackenzie River, directly offshore from town, allowed oil extraction to continue throughout breakup and freeze-up of the river. Today, Norman Wells (pop. 500) remains as a firefighting base, a transportation hub, and a regional government center.

Canol Project
The large U.S. military force present in Alaska during World War II needed oil to fuel aircraft

brave adventurers paddling down the MacKenzie River

and ships, which were in place for expected Japanese attacks. The strategically located Norman Wells oil fields were chosen as a source of crude oil, with little regard for the engineering feat needed to build a pipeline over the Mackenzie Mountains. To this day, it remains one of the largest projects ever undertaken in northern Canada. More than $300 million was spent between 1942 and 1945, employing 30,000 people who laid 2,650 kilometers of four- and six-inch pipeline and 1,600 kilometers of telephone lines, and built a road over some of North America's most isolated and impenetrable mountain ranges. Conditions were terrible; makeshift camps housed thousands of men, temperatures dipped to –40°C, and the isolation took its toll. Throughout the impossible terrain, thousands of tons of equipment was hauled, pump stations were installed, and camps were set up. Then, less than one year after its completion, the pipeline was quietly abandoned for less expensive oil sources elsewhere. In 1947, the pipeline was dismantled and sold. Today, the roadbed remains, strewn with structures, trucks, and equipment used in the project's construction.

Norman Wells Today

The **Norman Wells Historical Centre**, 867/587-2415, tells the story of the Canol Project through historical displays, photographs, artifacts recovered from along the road, and an excellent propaganda movie, which was commissioned to help finance the project. The center is officially open in summer daily 10 A.M.–10 P.M. Next door is an interesting church. Actually, the church is fairly normal, but the congregation is unique. Roman Catholics meet on one side, Protestants on the other. The center of town, a 20-minute walk from the airport, is a semicircle of semi-permanent buildings around a dusty parking lot. Also in town you'll find a bank, motels, restaurants, Northern, and a post office. Farther down the road is a small refinery and, overlooking the river, a gazebo from where the manmade islands can be seen.

Canol Heritage Trail

Considered by many to be one of the world's great wilderness hikes, the Canol is by no means typical. It follows the Canol Road from mile Zero (Canol Camp) on the west bank of the Mackenzie River across from Norman Wells, to mile 230 on the Yukon border—a distance of 372 kilometers (distances on the trail are in miles, a legacy of imperial measurement). Hiking the entire trail takes three to four weeks. Following the road causes little problem, but the logistics of getting to the beginning of the trail, arranging food drops, crossing rivers, and returning to Norman Wells require much planning. Every year, a few hikers attempt the entire length of the trail, whereas many others opt for a shorter section. The trail has been done on horseback, motorcycle, mountain bike, and all-terrain vehicle, but walking is the most popular and reliable method.

The most popular jumping-off point is Norman Wells, from where you can charter a plane or helicopter and be dropped as far along the trail as desired. From the Yukon side, you can drive from Ross River to mile 208. Many hikers organize food drops with charter operators in Norman Wells to help ease the load.

All bridges along the route have been washed out, making many river crossings necessary. The most difficult of these is the **Twitya River** at mile 131. This fast-flowing, cold (3–4°C) river is approximately 50 meters wide and up to five meters deep. Inner tubes purchased in Norman Wells (ask at Esso Resources) are a popular way of floating gear across, but check that they inflate before hitting the trail. The general consensus among those who have tried it is that the crossing is easier upstream of the old bridge. With two or more persons facilitating the endeavor, a length of rope can be strung across the river for ferrying packs across. Along the length of the trail are many Quonset huts used during construction of the road. Many are uninhabitable, but others have bunk beds and cookstoves.

Frank Pope, 867/587-2285, organizes transportation to either end of the trailhead and is a wealth of information about the trail.

Accommodations and Food

Located in the center of town, the **Rayuka Inn** (P.O. Box 308, 867/587-2354) charges $105 single, $120. Across the dusty parking lot is the **Yamouri Inn** (P.O. Box 268, Norman Wells, Northwest Territories X0E 0V0, 867/587-2744), which has a bar, a coffee shop, and a restaurant; $110 single, $130 double. Closer to the airport is the 20-room **Mackenzie Valley Hotel**

(Bag Service 1250, 867/587-2511); $109 single, $139 double. The town has no developed campgrounds; pitching your tent beside the Mackenzie River is an accepted practice (but don't leave valuables in it). The cheapest place to eat is the coffee shop or dimly lit cocktail lounge in the Yamouri Inn.

Transportation
Norman Wells has an impressive three-story airport complete with an observation deck and revolving baggage claim—not bad for a town of 500 people. It is a one-kilometer walk into town. **North-Wright Air,** 867/587-2333, has daily flights from Yellowknife to Norman Wells, continuing north to Inuvik, and flies from Norman Wells to all Mackenzie River communities.

OTHER COMMUNITIES

Tulita
Formerly known as Fort Norman, the Slavey Dene of this small community (pop. 300) have known it as *Tulita* (Where the Two Rivers Meet) for many years. Its strategic location where the **Great Bear River** joins the Mackenzie River has made it a transportation hub since the days of Sir John Franklin. Upstream five kilometers are the **Smoking Hills,** where an exposed seam of coal burns permanently. The first trading post was built here in 1810. An Anglican church, built of squared logs and dating to the 1860s, sits on the riverbank, beside the Hudson's Bay Company post. Many houses have colorful tepees in their yards, which are used for drying and smoking fish. The tepees provide a stark contrast to the modern school and the now-defunct Norman Wells–Zama pipeline, which passes through the outskirts of the community. The Great Bear River is navigable for its 128-kilometer distance into Great Bear Lake, with the exception of one set of rapids, which can easily be portaged. The river's clear, aqua-colored waters provide excellent fishing for arctic grayling. The **Fort Norman Lodge** (P.O. Box 117, Tulita, Northwest Territories X0E 0K0, 867/588-3320) has eight rooms with single and double beds, all with a shared bathroom and kitchen. Meals can also be arranged in the dining room. Rates are $149 single, $199 double

per night. **North-Wright Air,** 867/587-2333, flies daily between Tulita and Norman Wells.

Déline
Formerly known as Fort Franklin, *Déline* (Flowing Water) is on the Keith Arm of **Great Bear Lake,** at the outlet where the Great Bear River begins flowing west to the Mackenzie River. The population is about 550. A North West Company trading post opened here in 1810 but closed soon after. It was reopened by the Hudson's Bay Company in 1825 as a winter home and supply depot for Sir John Franklin, who led several expeditions to the Arctic in search of the Northwest Passage. Then it was abandoned again. With the discovery of pitchblende ore at Port Radium in the 1920s, traffic on the lake and river increased, and a small community grew. Today, the Slavey Dene of Déline live a traditional lifestyle, trapping, fishing, and making crafts, including moccasins for which they are well known. The tepee-shaped church is worth visiting, and the hike along the shore of Great Bear Lake offers rewarding vistas and passes several historic sites.

The **Turili Inn** (Box 144, Déline, Northwest Territories X0E 0G0, 867/589-4722) is a modern accommodation with eight self-contained rooms for $135 per person including breakfast. Groceries and crafts are available at **Northern. North-Wright Air,** 867/587-2333, flies daily between Norman Wells and Déline.

Where the Big One Won't Get Away
Great Bear Lake is one of the world's best freshwater fishing lakes, and it has the records to prove it. This lake holds world records for *all* line classes of lake trout; the overall world record, caught in 1993, weighed in at a whopping 34.5 kilograms and measured more than one meter. The lake also holds world records for most classes of arctic grayling, including the overall record. Around the lake are small fishing lodges offering all-inclusive packages. The best of these are run by **Plummer's Arctic Lodges** (950 Bradford St., Winnipeg, Manitoba R3H 0N5, 204/774-5775 or 800/665-0240, www.plummerslodges.com), which operates three lodges around the lake. Accommodations, all meals, guides, professionally equipped boats, and round-trip air charters from Winnipeg or Yel-

lowknife are included in the package; US$3,795 for seven days.

Fort Good Hope

Overlooking the Mackenzie River and flanked by boreal forest, this Slavey Dene community of 550 is located on the east bank of the Mackenzie River, just south of the Arctic Circle and approximately 193 kilometers downstream of Norman Wells. A trading post established here in 1805 by the North West Company attracted not only the Slavey Dene but also the Inuit, who lived in the Mackenzie Delta. During the 1860s, Father Emile Petitot, a well-known Northern missionary, constructed **Our Lady of Good Hope Church,** which has been declared a National Historic Site. The church's interior is decorated in ornate panels and friezes painted by Petitot, depicting aspects of his travels and life in the north.

One of the highlights of a trip to Fort Good Hope is visiting **The Ramparts,** where 200-meter-high cliffs force the Mackenzie River through a 500-meter-wide canyon. Although the cliffs continue for many kilometers, the most spectacular section is upstream of town and can be reached on foot or by boat. Arrange boat rentals and tours through the **Ramparts Hotel** (General Delivery, Fort Good Hope, Northwest Territories X0E 0H0, 867/598-2500). This hotel overlooks the river and has a restaurant with a simple menu, at Northern prices; expect to pay $15–25 for a main meal. Rooms are $110 per person. Inquire at the hotel for boat tours to the Ramparts, river fishing, and transfers to a tent camp on the Hume River. **North-Wright Air,** 867/587-2333, flies daily from Norman Wells to Fort Good Hope.

Colville Lake

This community of 50 North Slavey Dene, located just north of the Arctic Circle on the southeast shore of Colville Lake, was established in 1962 when a Roman Catholic mission was built. It is the territories' only community built entirely from logs. The largest building is the church, which supports a bell weighing 454 kilograms. The mission was built by Father Bern Will Brown, who has now left the church and is one of the north's most respected artists. His paintings, which depict the lifestyle of Northerners, are in demand across North America. Brown is also the host at **Colville Lake Lodge,** which combines excellent fishing for lake trout, arctic grayling, northern pike, whitefish, and inconnu, with a small museum highlighting life in the north. The lodge also has an art gallery, boat and canoe rentals, and common kitchen facilities. It is located in the town of Colville Lake. For more information, write to Bern Will Brown, Colville Lake via Norman Wells, Northwest Territories X0E 0L0, 867/709-2500. **North-Wright Air,** 867/587-2333, flies Saturday between Colville Lake and Norman Wells.

WESTERN ARCTIC

The far northwestern corner of the territories, where the mighty Mackenzie River drains into the Arctic Ocean, is linked to the outside world by the Dempster Highway, the continent's northernmost public road. The region, which is located entirely above the Arctic Circle, encompasses the Mackenzie River Valley and the vast barrens flanking the Arctic Ocean.

The **Mackenzie Delta,** a 90-kilometer-long and 60-kilometer-wide twisted maze of channels, is one of the world's greatest waterfowl nesting grounds and is home to muskrats, beavers, and marten, the mainstay of an early fur-trading economy. In the vicinity of the delta live red foxes, lynx, wolves, black bears, and moose. Many wood-land and barrenground caribou migrate through the region in early spring and fall; the Porcupine herd, named for the Porcupine River, migrates as far as Alaska. Arctic foxes inhabit the Arctic coast, whereas the king of the land, the grizzly bear, lives on the tundra. Banks Island has the world's largest population of musk oxen, which are protected by a national park. Beluga whales spend summer in the shallow waters around the delta and can be viewed from the air or in a boat. Hundreds of thousands of birds migrate to the delta each spring; among them are swans, cranes, hawks, bald eagles, and peregrine falcons.

At the end of the Dempster Highway is the region's largest community, Inuvik, a planned government town. Aklavik, west of Inuvik on a low area of land in the middle of the delta, was officially moved to Inuvik, but its residents stayed. Tuktoyaktuk is a "must-see" for those who want to dip their toes in the Arctic Ocean. To the east is Paulatuk, a traditional Inuvialuit community known for its excellent arctic char fishing, as well as its proximity to Tuktut Nogait National Park, the home range of the Bluenose caribou herd. The community of Sachs Harbour, on Banks Island, is a good base for exploring Aulavik National Park. To the east is massive Victoria Island. Most of the island is part of Nunavut, except for the western corner, where the community of Holman lies.

DEMPSTER HIGHWAY

This 741-kilometer highway, which begins east of Dawson City in the Yukon, is the only road leading into the western Arctic. It ends at Inuvik, but from November to late March you can drive on a winter road across the frozen Mackenzie Delta all the way to Tuktoyaktuk on the Arctic Ocean.

Finished in 1978 after nearly 20 years of work, the highway stretches through some of North America's most inhospitable terrain. It was named after RCMP Inspector W.J.D. Dempster, who was sent to look for the "Lost Patrol"—a team of Mounties who disappeared near Fort McPherson during the winter of 1910–1911. (He found them, but they were dead.) Driving the Dempster Highway should not be taken lightly. Services are few and far between, and the gravel road has a reputation for shredding tires. Always carry spare gas and tires, have plenty of water, and be prepared to drive slowly. Many large mammals are seen from the highway, but the most impressive sight is the **Porcupine caribou herd,** which migrates through the area each spring and fall.

The **Dempster Highway Visitors Centre** in Dawson City (on Front St., across the road from the Dawson Visitors Centre, 867/993-6167) is a good place to head before commencing the long drive north. It's open mid-May to mid-June Mon.–Fri. 8:30 A.M.–5 P.M. and through summer daily 9 A.M.–9 P.M.

The Dempster Highway crosses the **Arctic Circle** at kilometer 403, then climbs into the Richardson Mountains. The Continental Divide, at kilometer 471, marks the Yukon/Northwest Territories border. West of the divide, water flows to the Pacific Ocean; east-side waters end up in the Arctic Ocean. The highway then descends to the **Peel River,** which can be crossed by ferry from mid-June to October and by an ice bridge most of the rest of the year. No crossings are possible during freeze-up and breakup. For ferry updates, call 867/777-2678 or 800/661-0752.

Fort McPherson

After crossing the Peel River, the highway soon comes to Fort McPherson, a Gwich'in Dene community on the river's east bank, 550 kilometers from Dawson City. They live at the eastern edge of their territory and have strong links to the Yukon and Alaska. A Hudson's Bay Company post was established here in 1840, and in 1852 a nearby Dene village was moved to Fort McPherson, away from the annual flooding that occurred at lower elevations. An RCMP post here became an important center for annual patrols throughout the western Arctic. On December 21, 1910, a patrol led by Inspector Fitzgerald left for Dawson City from here. The four members perished on the return trip, just one day short of Fort McPherson. An account of their journey is found in Dick North's *Lost Patrol.* The patrolmen are buried on the banks of the Peel River, and a monument stands in their memory. Beside the monument, in a log cabin, is a small **Visitors Centre** open through summer daily 9 A.M.–9 P.M. Well worth a visit is the **Fort McPherson Tent and Canvas,** 867/952-2179, a thriving local business producing high-quality backpacks, tote bags, and tents; open Mon.–Fri. 9:30 A.M.–5 P.M. Abe Wilson, 867/952-2363, is a knowledgable local who offers sightseeing and fishing trips along the Peel and Rat rivers.

Stay at **Bell River Bedrooms** (P.O. Box 420, Fort McPherson, Northwest Territories X0E 0J0, 867/952-2465), where the rates of $115 per person include a self-serve breakfast. In **Nitainlaii Territorial Park,** 10 kilometers south of town, camping is $12 per night.

Tsiigehtchic

One hour's drive (58 kilometers) north of Fort McPherson is another ferry crossing, this time over the Mackenzie River (mid-June to October, 9 A.M.–midnight). Here, at the confluence of the Mackenzie and Arctic Red rivers, a small mission was established in 1868, followed soon after by a Hudson's Bay Company post. For hundreds of years, it has been a popular fishing spot for the Dene, and traditional fishing camps still operate on the river; look for fish being prepared and dried by the ferry landings. Until 1996, the community was known as **Arctic Red River**; however, the traditional name is *Tsiigehtchic* (Mouth of the Iron-colored River). The most recognizable landmark is a red-roofed mission church built in 1931 that stands on a small rise overlooking the river. The town has few services and may or may not have gas, so fill up in Fort McPherson for the 180-kilometer run to Inuvik. To visit the community, which is off the main ferry route, you must tell the ferry operators, who will happily make the detour for you.

South of Tsiigehtchic is the **Peel River Preserve.** High in the Mackenzie Mountains, this habitat is home to Dall's sheep, moose, lynx, woodland caribou, and grizzly bears. It is accessible only by traveling up either the Arctic Red or Peel rivers.

The last worthwhile stop before Inuvik and the end of the road is **Gwich'in Territorial Park.** This 8,800-hectare park extends from the Dempster Highway to the east bank of Campbell Lake, encompassing typical delta landscape.

INUVIK

You must see Inuvik with your own eyes to believe it, and then you may still doubt what you see: brightly painted houses on stilts, a monstrous church shaped like an igloo, metal tunnels snaking through town, and a main street where businesses have names such as Eskimo Inn, 60 Below Construction, and Polar TV. Inuvik marks the end of the Dempster Highway, as far north as you can drive on a public road in North America, which is reason enough for many visitors to make the trek to town. If you've come up from Calgary, you will have driven 3,560 kilometers, from Seattle 4,030 kilometers, from Los Angeles 6,100 kilometers, or from New York 7,600 kilometers.

Inuvik is obviously a planned community, transformed from some architect's drafting board into full-blown reality high above the Arctic Circle. All aspects have been scientifically planned, right down to the foundations—all structures sit on piles of rock, ensuring stability in the permafrost and preventing heat from turning the ground into sludge.

History
In 1954, the Canadian government decided to build an administrative center for the western Arctic. The traditional center was Aklavik, located in the middle of the Mackenzie Delta. But because Aklavik had continual problems with erosion and flooding, and offered little room for expansion, a new site was decided on. The location chosen was a large, level area alongside the East Channel of the Mackenzie River, 200 kilometers north of the Arctic Circle, 50 kilometers east of Aklavik, and just below the treeline. *Inuvik* (Place of Man, in Invialuktun) was the first planned Canadian town above the Arctic Circle. By the summer of 1961, most of the major construction was completed.

Today, Inuvik serves not only as a government headquarters but also as a transportation hub and oil-and-gas exploration base. The Canadian Armed Forces station, which closed in 1986, has been converted to the Aurora Campus of Arctic College. The town's population of 3,200 consists of an equal mix of Dene/Métis, Inuvialuit (Mackenzie Inuit), and nonnative people. The nonnative population rises and falls with the fortunes of the oil and gas industries. Current proposals to tap the vast reserves of natural gas under the Mackenzie Delta would push the town's economy out of the doldrums and bring increased wealth to the region.

Sights
It is easy to spend a whole day walking around town, checking out the unique considerations involved in living at a latitude of 68°N. *Utilidors,* for example, snake around town, linking businesses and houses and passing right through the middle of the schoolyard. These conduits contain water, heat, and sewerage pipelines and are raised above the ground to prevent problems associated with permafrost. Inuvik's most famous landmark is **Our Lady**

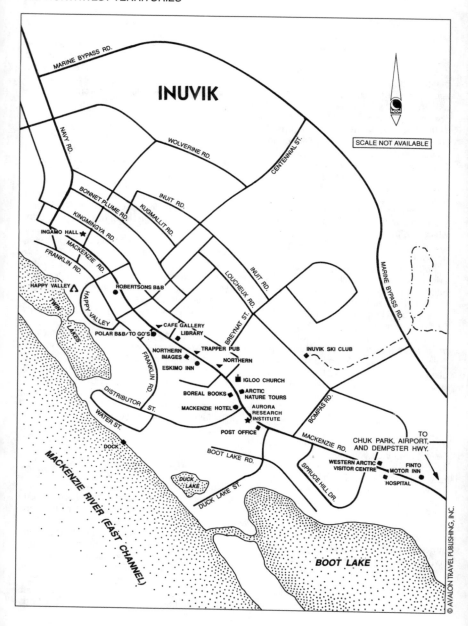

INUVIK

MARINE BYPASS RD.

NAVY RD.

WOLVERINE RD.

CENTENNIAL ST.

MOON

SCALE NOT AVAILABLE

BONNET PLUME RD.

KINGMINGYA RD.

INUIT RD.

KUGMALLIT RD.

INGAMO HALL ★

MACKENZIE RD.

FRANKLIN RD.

LOUCHEUX RD.

INUIT RD.

MARINE BYPASS RD.

HAPPY VALLEY

ROBERTSONS B&B

TWIN LAKES

HAPPY VALLEY

CAFE GALLERY

BREYNAT ST.

INUVIK SKI CLUB

POLAR B&B/TO GO'S

LIBRARY

NORTHERN IMAGES

TRAPPER PUB

ESKIMO INN

NORTHERN

FRANKLIN RD.

IGLOO CHURCH

BOREAL BOOKS

ARCTIC NATURE TOURS

DISTRIBUTOR ST.

MACKENZIE HOTEL

AURORA RESEARCH INSTITUTE

BOMPAS RD.

WATER ST.

POST OFFICE

MACKENZIE RD.

TO CHUK PARK, AIRPORT, AND DEMPSTER HWY.

DOCK

BOOT LAKE RD.

WESTERN ARCTIC VISITOR CENTRE

FINTO MOTOR INN

DUCK LAKE

SPRUCE HILL DR.

HOSPITAL

DUCK LAKE ST.

MACKENZIE RIVER (EAST CHANNEL)

BOOT LAKE

© AVALON TRAVEL PUBLISHING, INC.

of **Victory Church,** commonly known as the **igloo church** for its distinctive shape. The church, located on Mackenzie Road, is not always open; ask at the rectory for permission to enter. The interior is decorated with a series of paintings by Inuvialuit artist Mona Thrasher, depicting various religious scenes. A few blocks to the east is the **Aurora Research Institute,** 867/777-3298, one of three support facilities for scientific projects throughout the Arctic. It's open year-round Mon.–Fri. 9 A.M.–5 P.M. West along Mackenzie Road is **Ingamo Hall,** a three-story structure built with more than 1,000 logs. This far north, trees are not large enough for construction, so the logs, cut from white spruce, were transported by barge down the Mackenzie River. The best views of the delta are, naturally, from the air, but the next best thing is to climb the 20-meter-high observation tower in **Chuk Park,** six kilometers south of downtown.

Tours

It seems that everyone who visits Inuvik takes at least one tour, whether it is around town, on the delta, or to an outlying community. **Arctic Nature Tours** (beside the igloo church on Mackenzie Rd., 867/777-3300, www.arcticnaturetours.com) offers an extensive variety of tours; those that require flying include transportation from town out to the airport. The town tour lasts approximately two hours, taking in all the sights; $25 per person. Tours to Tuktoyaktuk and Aklavik start at $120 (see following entry). Arctic Nature Tours also offers trips to remote **Herschel Island** located in the Beaufort Sea. The island was a major whaling station during the early 1900s, but today only ruins remain. This trip is especially good for bird-watchers because more than 70 avian species have been recorded on the island. The flight to the island passes **Ivvavik National Park** in the northern Yukon, providing opportunities to see musk oxen, caribou, and grizzly bears. A two-hour stay on the island costs $275 per person, including the 90-minute (each way) flight. Overnight stays begin at $550 per person.

Midnight Express Tours, 867/777-4829 or book through Arctic Nature Tours at 867/777-3300, are a great way to experience the vastness of the delta. A three-hour cruise to the bush camp of an Inuvialuit elder, where tea and bannock is served, costs $45 per person. Evening tours on the river, including a traditional Northern meal, cost $75. Also offered are fishing trips, naturalist tours, or a boat trip to Aklavik or Tuktoyaktuk returning by plane.

Recreation

The town has no set hiking trails, but in summer you can hike along the tracks used by cross-country skiers in winter. Two trails—four and six kilometers—begin from the ski club on Loucheux Road, opposite the elementary school. They may be muddy, so plan accordingly. The treeline passes invitingly close to town to the east. Look for trails leading in that direction out by Marine Bypass Road and Long Lake. Another option is to walk around Boot Lake.

Paddling the length of the Mackenzie River is the stuff legends are made of, but it's also possible to experience the river just for a day. Peter Clarkson, 867/777-2594, rents canoes for $35 per day and can provide drop-offs near the airport, the perfect starting point for a leisurely paddle back to Inuvik. If you're planning a longer trip through the western Arctic, canoes can be rented from $200 per week.

Drinking and Dancing

Inuvik's most famous nightspot is **The Zoo,** in the Mackenzie Hotel, where a colorful mixture of oil field workers, German backpackers, drunken Aussies, fur-coated southerners, pin-striped businessmen, and locals who've been kicked out of every other place in town converge to listen to the best music the 1980s had to offer or some band that lost its way down in Whitehorse and wound up in Inuvik. There's no cover charge, and things usually end at approximately 2 A.M. Also in the Mackenzie Hotel is the more mellow **Brass Rail Lounge,** where the bar is covered in roofing materials—a legacy of the owner's profession before becoming involved in the hotel business. If the bar's quiet, the owner will join you in sampling his specially imported German liqueur, which is kept behind the bar for when outsiders drop by. The **Sly Fox** in the Eskimo Inn is a locals' hangout, as is the **Mad Trapper Pub** across the road, where local musicians jam on Saturday afternoons at 4 P.M., hoping one day to play at the Zoo.

Festivals and Events

After a month of darkness, the first day that the sun rises above the horizon is celebrated with the **Inuvik Sunrise Festival** (January 5–6). Although the sun actually rises at about 1:30 P.M. on the 6th, there's a parade the day before, as well as ice-skating and a fireworks display at Twin Lakes. Summer Solstice in June is celebrated by **Midnight Madness,** although because the sun doesn't set for a month, the actual date of the festival is of little importance. Celebrations on the weekend closest to the solstice include traditional music and dancing and a feast of lobster imported from the east coast for the occasion. The **Great Northern Arts Festival,** held during the third week of July, features demonstrations, musical performances such as Inuit drumming, displays, and sales of Northern art. On the second weekend of October, street dances, parades, Northern games, and traditional foods highlight **Delta Daze.**

Accommodations

Each of Inuvik's three motels has a coffee shop, a restaurant, and basic rooms with private baths. The **Mackenzie Hotel** (185 Mackenzie Rd., P.O. Box 1618, Inuvik, Northwest Territories X0E 0T0, 867/777-2861) is the nicest accommodation and is located in town. Rooms with shared baths are $115 single, $130 double, those with private bathrooms go for $135 single, $150 double. Also in town is the 74-room **Eskimo Inn** (133 Mackenzie Rd., P.O. Box 1740, 867/777-2801 or 800/661-0725); $115 single, $125 double. On the way to the airport is the **Finto Motor Inn** (288 Mackenzie Rd., P.O. Box 1925, 867/777-2647 or 800/661-0843), which has a good view of the delta; $120 single, $140 double.

A few locals run bed-and-breakfasts, which are less expensive than the motels and provide a good way to meet the locals. Accommodations at **Polar B&B** (P.O. Box 1393, Mackenzie Rd., 867/777-2554) are comfortable, with a shared bathroom, kitchen, laundry, and lounge with television. Rates are $75 single, $85 double, which includes a voucher for a meal at the adjacent To Go's restaurant. Another good choice, **Robertson's B&B** (41 Mackenzie Rd., P.O. Box 2356, 867/777-3111), is close to downtown, and its large outdoor deck offers a great view of the delta; $80 single, $90 double.

Happy Valley Campground is located on a bluff overlooking the delta. It has 20 private, unserviced sites and a gravel parking area for RVs and trailers that need power. Facilities include flush toilets, showers, and firewood; unpowered sites $12, powered $15. Outside of town toward the airport is the **Chuk Park;** it's quiet but has limited facilities; $10.

Food

If you don't mind your wallet taking a battering, the thing to do this far north is to sample local fare such as musk ox, caribou, and arctic char. The least expensive way to do this is at **To Go's** (71 Mackenzie Rd., 867/777-3030), which has a few tables and a take-out menu. Caribou burgers and musk ox burgers ($5.50) are the same price as regular hamburgers but cheaper than mushroom burgers. Pizza starts at $10; extras such as musk ox are $2, and the Northern Pizza—with the works—is $17. It's open daily until 4 A.M. Across the road is the **Cafe Gallery** (84 Mackenzie Rd., 867/777-2888), a city-style coffeehouse with decent coffee and muffins and a selection of local artwork down the back. The coffee shop in the **Mackenzie Hotel,** which opens at 7 A.M., is the most popular breakfast hangout, but it can get smoky. The **Green Briar Dining Room,** 867/777-2414, also in the Mackenzie Hotel, serves a good selection of Northern cuisine (starting at $13.95 for a caribou burger); open Tues.–Sat. from 6 P.M. The **Peppermill Restaurant,** 867/777-2999, in the Finto Motor Inn, offers much of the same; try caribou steaks smothered in blueberry sauce (made from locally picked blueberries), $20.50. The town's only supermarket is at 120 Mackenzie Road, open daily 10 A.M.–midnight. Prices aren't as high as you might expect.

Getting There

Mike Zubko Airport, named for an early Arctic aviator, is small but always busy, thanks to its status as the hub of air transport in the western Arctic. A cab to the airport, 12 kilometers south of town, is $32 for one or two passengers, $38 for three, and $46 for four. **NWT Air,** 867/777-2341 or 800/661-0789, and **First Air,** 867/777-2341 or 800/267-1247, fly into Inuvik daily from Yellowknife. Sit on the left side of the plane for views of the Mackenzie Mountains. From Edmonton, the least expensive high-season fare is $786 round-trip. **Air North,** 867/668-2228 or 800/661-0407, flies into Inuvik from Dawson City, with connections from Whitehorse, Fairbanks, and Juneau. **North-Wright Air,** 867/587-2333, flies from Norman Wells to Inuvik. **Arctic Wings,** 867/777-2220, has scheduled flights to Aklavik and Tuktoyaktuk. **Aklak Air,** 867/777-3777, flies from Inuvik to all western Arctic communities.

Getting Around
For a taxi, call 867/777-5050 or 777-2244. The cabs don't have meters because fares are set: $5 anywhere around town, $32–46 to the airport, and $320 to Tuktoyaktuk on the winter road.

Services
The **post office** is at 817 Mackenzie Road. **Northern Images** (upstairs at 115 Mackenzie Rd., 867/777-2786) has a fantastic collection of paintings and sculptures from throughout the territories. The **hospital** is on the east end of town, 867/777-2955. For the **RCMP,** call 867/777-2935. The local newspaper is the *Inuvik Drum,* which is published each Thursday.

Information
The **Inuvik Centennial Library,** 867/777-2749, located in the center of town, has a fairly extensive collection of Northern books and literature; open Monday and Friday 2–5 P.M. and Tues.–Thurs. 10 A.M.–9 P.M. The **Boreal Book-** **store** (181 Mackenzie Rd., 867/777-3748) has a large selection of Northern material, both new and used, as well as relevant topographical maps and marine charts.

The **Western Arctic Visitor Centre** is at the entrance to town, a 10-minute walk from downtown (867/777-4727, www.inuvik.net). This modern facility features displays on the people of the north, details on each of the western Arctic communities, and all the usual tour information. It's open in summer daily 9 A.M.–8 P.M. Out back, a trail leads through a re-creation of an Inuvialuit whaling camp and a Gwich'in fishing camp. For road and ferry information, call 867/777-2678 or 800/661-0752.

AKLAVIK

Theoretically, this community in the middle of the Mackenzie Delta was abandoned more than 35 years ago, but don't tell that to the 700 Dene and Inuvialuit who call Aklavik home. The Hudson's Bay Company post, established here in 1918, became the trading and transportation center of the muskrat-rich Mackenzie Delta. River erosion and surface instability seriously threatened the physical existence of the town, so the federal government decided to relocate it to the East Channel, 58 kilometers west. The planned town of Inuvik serves the purpose of the government well, but for many delta old-timers,

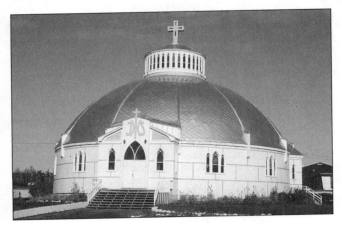

igloo church

living in a town that sprang from the muskeg isn't their cup of tea. In fact, since Inuvik was established in 1961, this ramshackle community, cut off from the outside world, has reported steady population increases.

Wooden sidewalks, a legacy of Aklavik's one-time importance, link the Hudson's Bay Company post and a mission church (now a small museum) to newer structures, built before the big move east was announced. Many large houses still stand, testimony to the fortunes made by prosperous traders in days gone by. Trails lead in all directions from town, inviting the curious to explore this small delta island. The most popular attraction is the grave of **Albert Johnson,** "The Mad Trapper of Rat River," who sparked the north's most famous manhunt.

Tours and Transportation
Most people arrive in Aklavik as part of a tour from Inuvik, with **Arctic Nature Tours,** 867/777-3300. On clear days, the 20-minute flight is awe-inspiring. The company offers flights to Aklavik with a one-hour town tour ($160), but a better way to experience the delta is by boat. To boat one-way then fly the other is $175. Tours that combine Aklavik and Tuktoyaktuk begin at $240. **Aklavik Tours,** 867/978-2527, operates a water taxi service between Aklavik and Inuvik.

If you would like to spend more time in town, scheduled flights leave daily from the airport with **Aklak Air,** 867/777-3777, and **Arctic Wings,** 867/777-2220. Arctic Nature Tours can usually arrange cheaper flights and advise on accommodation in the small hotel in Aklavik. Between December and March, a winter road is constructed between Inuvik and Aklavik; Arctic Wings operates a winter-only bus service between the two communities for $45 each way.

TUKTOYAKTUK

Most travelers, not satisfied with driving to the end of the road, hop aboard a small plane in Inuvik for the flight along the Mackenzie Delta to Tuktoyaktuk, a small community perched precariously on an exposed gravel strip on the Beaufort Sea. Although it would be a harsh and unforgiving place to live, a visit to "Tuk," as it is sensibly known, is a delightful eye-opener. The community is spread out around **Tuktoyaktuk Harbour** and has spilled over to the gravel beach, where meter-high waves whipped up by cold Arctic winds roll in off the Beaufort Sea and thunder up against the shore. The most dominant natural features of the landscape are **pingos,** massive mounds of ice forced upward by the action of permafrost. The mounds look like mini-volcanoes protruding from the otherwise flat environs. The ice is camouflaged by a natural covering of tundra growth, making the pingos all the more mysterious. Approximately 1,400 pingos dot the coastal plain around Tuk, one of the world's densest concentrations of these geological wonders peculiar to the north. **Ibyuk,** visible from town, is the world's largest pingo; it's 30 meters tall and has a circumference of 1.5 kilometers.

History
This area was traditionally the home of Karngmalit, or Inuvialuit, who lived along the coast in small family camps hunting beluga whales. Earlier in the 20th century, an epidemic of influenza wiped out more than half of their people. As Herschel Island lost importance as a base for whaling in the Beaufort Sea, the Hudson's Bay Company opened a post at the safe harbor of Tuk in 1937. Reindeer herding was attempted in the late 1930s, with animals brought over from Scandinavia. Today, a large herd of these mammals—the same species as the indigenous caribou but a little smaller—live in the area. A Distant Early Warning Line station was constructed in 1955. Although the residents harvest fish, seals, and whales, most wage earners are land based, involved in government, transportation, and tourism. The town is also a base for oil and gas exploration in the Beaufort Sea.

Around Town
Most visitors see Tuk from the inside of a transporter van driven by accommodating locals who never tire of the same hackneyed questions about living at the end of the earth. The bus stops at *Our Lady of Lourdes,* once part of a fleet of vessels that plied the Arctic delivering supplies to isolated communities. Here also are two mission churches built in the late 1930s. A stop is also made at the Arctic Ocean, where you are encouraged to dip your toes in the water or go for a

THE MAD TRAPPER OF RAT RIVER

For seven long weeks, ravaged by brutal winter temperatures, hunger, and exhaustion, a man whose identity remains a mystery to this day led Mounties on an astonishing chase through the Arctic. No one quite knows what instigated the murderous events of the winter of 1932, nor from where the mad, mysterious trapper came. Natives knew him as "the man who steals gold from men's teeth"; they were afraid of him and rumors surfaced that he was a notorious Chicago gangster.

In 1931 a man going by the name Albert Johnson arrived in Fort McPherson. He first raised a few eyebrows by purchasing unusually large amounts of ammunition and supplies with a fistful of notes. Then he left for the Rat River region to build a small cabin that doubled as an impregnable fortress—evidence that from the start he anticipated trouble. Answering complaints of a strange white man interfering with traplines, Constable King went to question Johnson. Instead of answers, King was met with a bullet.

A seven-man posse, carrying 20 pounds of dynamite, came from Aklavik to bring the gunman in. For 15 hours Johnson withstood the mounted siege, finally forcing the posse to retreat. Johnson fled, heading west. In temperatures that dipped below -40° C, and with meager supplies, four Mounties took up the chase. Four times Johnson repelled them with gunfire, killing a Mountie in the process. It became obvious to the Mounties that, against incredible physical hardships, Johnson was attempting to cross the mountains to Alaska. His cunning kept him alive for seven weeks, long enough for "Wop" May, a famed bush pilot, to be summoned. Surrounded by 17 men and with Wop May circling overhead in a plane loaded with bombs, Johnson never had a chance. His death ended the north's most notorious manhunt but was the beginning of the mystery—just who was the Mad Trapper of Rat River?

beach, climbing a nearby pingo, and checking out the well-equipped ocean port.

Practicalities

Tuk is the most popular flightseeing destination from Inuvik, and a variety of trips are offered by the two tour operators in Inuvik. Trips start at $160, which includes the return flight (worth the price alone) and a tour of the town. The flight into Tuk is breathtaking—the pilots fly at low altitudes for the best possible views. For those who wish to spend longer in Tuk (there are enough things to do to hold your interest for at least one day), both companies offer extended tours, including a visit community's unique cool room, for $180 per person. For tour details, contact **Arctic Tour Co.,** 867/977-2230 or **Arctic Nature Tours,** 867/777-3300. Tour operators use the services of **Arctic Wings,** 867/777-2220, and **Aklak Air,** 867/777-3777, which also have daily scheduled flights ($220 round-trip). **Ookpik Tours and Adventures,** 867/977-2399, take independent visitors on boat trips to the pingos and fishing, as well as dog-sledding in winter.

The **Hotel Tuk Inn** (P.O. Box 193, Tuktoyaktuk, Northwest Territories X0E 1C0, 867/977-2381), and the **Pingo Park Lodge** (Bag 6000, 867/977-2155) are of an acceptable Northern standard. Prices start at $130 single, $160 double, and both have dining facilities. Winnie and Roger Gruben of the Arctic Tour Co., 867/977-2230, offer three guest rooms that share a bathroom. The boarding price can be combined with a tour to cut costs. Arctic Nature Tours offers a package of airfare, one night's accommodation, and a town tour for $340 per person. Camping is allowed; the beach is a favorite place to pitch tents, but check the weather forecast (867/777-4183) before putting too much faith in your trusty canvas companion. **Northern,** for groceries, and a **post office** are located by the public dock. Crafts are available in a small store next to *Our Lady of Lourdes.*

PAULATUK

Meaning "Place of the Coal" in the local language, Paulatuk is a small Arctic community, with a population of 190 Inuvialuit who live a traditional lifestyle of hunting, trapping, and

swim if you really want to impress the folks back home. (Tuk is actually on the Beaufort Sea, an arm of the Arctic Ocean, but who's telling?) For a few extra bucks, you are given some time to explore on your own, including walking along the

fishing. A Roman Catholic mission and trading post, established in 1935, attracted Inuvialuit families from camps along the Arctic coast. Their descendants continue living off the abundant natural resources. The community is located on a sandy strip of land between the Beaufort Sea and an inland lake along a rugged stretch of coastline, 400 kilometers east of Inuvik. To the northeast are the **Smoking Hills,** seams of coal, rich with sulfide, that were ignited centuries ago and still burn today, filling the immediate area with distinctively shaped clouds of smoke.

The Hornaday, Horton, and other rivers whose headwaters are north of Great Bear Lake drain into the ocean near Paulatuk, providing unparalleled opportunities for extended white-water trips (experienced paddlers only).

Sprawling across Parry Peninsula, to the west of Paulatuk and partly within Nunavut, is 16,340-square-kilometer **Tuktut Nogait National Park,** the major staging area for the 125,000-strong **Bluenose caribou herd,** which migrates across the north. The park is also renowned for its diversity of birds of prey. For more information, visit www.parkscanada.gc.ca. The coastal cliffs of **Cape Parry Bird Sanctuary** are a nesting site for rare murres. In spring, local outfitters will take you far out onto the pack ice of **Amundsen Gulf** in search of polar bears.

Practicalities

The only accommodation in town is the **Paulatuk Hotel** (General Delivery, Paulatuk, Northwest Territories X0E 1N0, 867/580-3027), with eight rooms with a shared bath and a small restaurant; $125 per person. You can camp along the beach, but ask at the hamlet office before pitching your tent. The only scheduled flights to Paulatuk are on **Aklak Air,** 867/777-3777, leaving Inuvik on Tuesday and Friday. Check with Inuvik tour operators for cheaper deals.

BANKS ISLAND

Banks Island is one of the best places in the western Arctic for viewing wildlife, especially musk oxen. Approximately 60,000 (half the world's population and the largest concentration) of these shaggy beasts call the park home.

Other wildlife includes foxes, polar bears, and wolves. The island is separated from the mainland by **Amundsen Gulf** and from Victoria Island by the **Prince of Wales Strait** and is the most westerly island in the Canadian Arctic archipelago. Throughout the barren, low, rolling hills that characterize this island flow some major rivers, including the **Thomsen,** the northernmost navigable river in Canada. **Aulavik National Park** protects the river and 12,300 square kilometers of its watersheds. To get to the park, you need to charter a plane in Inuvik.

Sachs Harbour (Ikaahuk)

The only permanent settlement on Banks Island is Sachs Harbour, situated at the foot of a low bluff along the southwest coast, 520 kilometers northeast of Inuvik. An abundance of white foxes had attracted Thule people to the island for centuries, and early Arctic explorers such as Beechley and McLure had charted the island. In the late 1920s, three Inuvialuit families settled permanently in what is now known as Sachs Harbour. The island has always been regarded as one of the finest trapping areas in the Canadian Arctic, and the people who lived here were able to afford such luxuries as washing machines and holidays to Aklavik. The town of 150 remains relatively self-sufficient. The first weekend of May is the **White Fox Jamboree,** a three-day festival of traditional Northern games, food, and dance.

Practicalities

The least expensive way to visit Sachs Harbour is on a tour organized by **Arctic Nature Tours,** 867/777-3300. Airfare from Inuvik and a town tour is $399 per person, but this tour leaves only if at least four people are interested. Another tour includes airfare, two nights' accommodations, meals, and tours by boat and all-terrain vehicle to see local wildlife populations, including musk oxen, for approximately $1,000 per person. This tour departs every Thursday regardless of numbers. Accommodations on this tour are at **Kuptana's Guesthouse** (General Delivery, Sachs Harbour, Northwest Territories X0E 0Z0, 867/690-4151). Rates are $175 per person, including three meals. Facilities for the five rooms are shared, but each room has a television. The owners offer tundra tours for $50 per person for half a day out on the water or tundra (for both guests and nonguests). Camping along the beach should be okay, but check first with the hamlet office. The town has no restaurants, only a small co-op grocery store (closed Sunday). **Aklak Air,** 867/777-3777, has a twice-weekly scheduled flight to Sachs Harbour from Inuvik. This flight is used by Arctic Nature Tours, so inquire about cheaper fares.

HOLMAN (ULUQSAQTUUQ)

Most of Victoria Island, separated by the Prince of Wales Strait from Banks Island, falls within Nunavut. The exception is the island's western corner, including Diamond Jenness Peninsula, where the community of Holman (pop. 360) lies. Holman is on a gravel beach at the end of horseshoe-shaped Queens Bay and is surrounded by steep bluffs that rise as high as 200 meters.

Copper Inuit had traditionally wintered on nearby Banks Island and spent summer hunting caribou on Victoria Island. But when a Hudson's Bay Company post that had been on Prince Albert Sound was moved to what is now Holman in 1939, the Inuit began to settle around it. As they moved to the post, they were taught printmaking by a missionary, Reverend Henri Tardi, who had come to the settlement as an oblate missionary. To this day, printmaking is a major source of income for the community, as are trapping and hunting.

The area is renowned for arctic char and trout fishing. **David Kanayok Outfitting** (General Delivery, Holman, Northwest Territories X0E 0S0, 867/396-3401) is the best way to get among the fish. This outfitter also takes visitors to Holman's original townsite and on wildlife-viewing trips out on the tundra. Holman has a golf course, the northernmost in the world. Playing a round of golf here is really something to tell the folks back at the country club about; for the record, the course is at a latitude of 70 degrees 44 minutes North. In mid-July, the course hosts the **Billy Joss Open,** attracting sports celebrities from as far away as the United States; call 867/396-3080 for entry details.

Practicalities

Holman's only hotel is the **Arctic Char Inn** (P.O. Box 64, Holman, Northwest Territories X0E 0S0, 867/396-3501). Rates are $180 per person, including meals. The town has no established campgrounds, but many locals camp at Okpilik Lake. If you'd like to be closer to town, ask at the hamlet office for the best place to pitch a tent. Meals are available at the Arctic Char Inn and groceries across the road in **Northern.** Local arts and crafts are available in the Arctic Char Inn or at the **Co-op.**

The only scheduled flights into Holman are three times weekly from Yellowknife with **First Air,** 867/396-3063 or 800/267-1247. **Arctic Nature Tours,** based in Inuvik, 867/777-3300, combines Holman and Sachs Harbour in a day trip for $540 per person if enough people (at least four) are interested.

NUNAVUT
ARCTIC COAST

Imagine a strip of coastline that stretched from San Diego to Seattle with an offshore island the size of California and a total population that would fit easily into a couple of jumbo jets; without traffic lights, power lines, road systems, or McDonald's, and a complete absence of trees. Such is the Arctic coast. For nine months of the year, it is a cold, frozen land where it seems that no lifeforms could possibly exist. Then, during the short Arctic summer, the land comes alive. Its rivers provide what many adventurers regard to be the ultimate canoe trips, naturalists and photographers are drawn by the abundant wildlife-viewing opportunities, and anglers from around the world arrive, hoping to catch the most prized of all Northern fish, the delicious arctic char.

Lowland arctic makes up the bulk of the region, including the Arctic coast mainland and lower Arctic islands such as King William, Prince of Wales, and Victoria (the world's 12th-largest island). It is a land of low, rolling hills, scoured by glacial ice during the last Ice Age, deeply incised by meltwater streams, and scattered with shallow lakes. Boothia Peninsula, in the east part of the region, is a classic example. This northernmost point of mainland on the continent is a bleak, barren land that is rarely penetrated, even by the Inuit.

For centuries, Copper and Netsilik Inuit spent summer traveling the length of the Arctic coast, fishing and hunting seals and caribou. They moved as the seasons dictated and had no permanent settlements. As the quest for a northwest passage to the Orient heated up, the Hudson's Bay Company began establishing posts at remote locations throughout the region. These posts attracted the nomadic Inuit, whose lifestyle began to change as a result. The posts formed the basis of today's six Arctic coast communities. In many, the characteristic red-and-white-trimmed Hudson's Bay Company buildings still stand, as do stone churches that were built by missionaries.

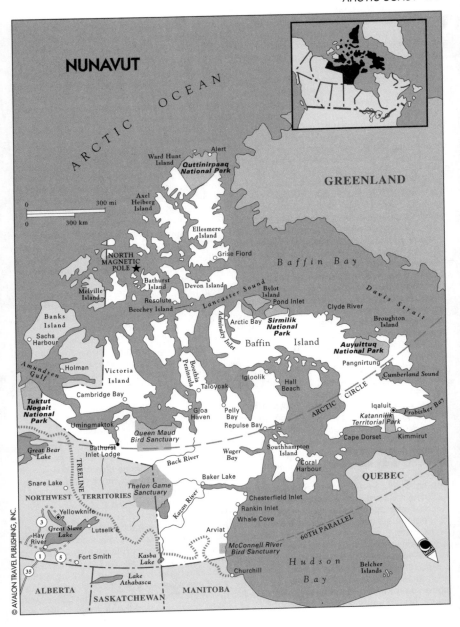

NUNAVUT

ARCTIC OCEAN

GREENLAND

0   300 mi
0   300 km

Ward Hunt
Island

Alert
*Quttinirpaaq
National Park*

Axel
Heiberg
Island

Ellesmere
Island

Grise Fiord

Baffin Bay

NORTH
MAGNETIC
POLE ★

Bathurst
Island

Devon Island

Bylot
Island

Pond Inlet

Clyde River

Davis Strait

Broughton
Island

Melville
Island

Resolute

Beechey Island

Lancaster Sound

Arctic Bay

*Sirmilik
National
Park*

Banks
Island

Baffin   Island

*Auyuittuq
National Park*

Sachs
Harbour

Amundsen
Gulf

Holman

Admiralty Inlet

Boothia
Peninsula

Igloolik

Hall
Beach

Pangnirtung

Cumberland Sound

ARCTIC CIRCLE

Victoria
Island

Cambridge Bay

Taloyoak

*Tuktut
Negait
National
Park*

Gjoa
Haven

Pelly
Bay

Umingmaktok

Repulse Bay

Iqaluit

*Katannilik
Territorial Park*

Frobisher Bay

Kimmirut

Bathurst
Inlet Lodge

Queen Maud
Bird Sanctuary

Back River

Wager
Bay

Cape Dorset

Great Bear
Lake

Southampton
Island

Coral
Harbour

QUEBEC

Snare Lake

TREELINE

Thelon Game
Sanctuary

Baker Lake

Kazan River

Chesterfield Inlet

NORTHWEST
TERRITORIES

Yellowknife

Great Slave
Lake

Lutselk'e

Rankin Inlet

Whale Cove

Arviat

60TH PARALLEL

3

Hay
River

1   5

Fort Smith

Kasba
Lake

McConnell River
Bird Sanctuary

Churchill

Hudson

Bay

Belcher
Islands

35

Lake
Athabasca

ALBERTA

SASKATCHEWAN

MANITOBA

© AVALON TRAVEL PUBLISHING, INC.

All communities, except Pelly Bay, rely on supplies barged down the Mackenzie River from Hay River once a year. Otherwise, the only links to the outside world are by plane. Scheduled flights from Yellowknife serve all communities except Bathurst Inlet, where charter flights bring guests into one of the world's premier naturalist lodges. For whatever reason you visit this fascinating region, it is important to be prepared. Each community has a hotel serving meals, but reservations should be made well in advance. Groceries and basic camping supplies are available in all communities, but there are no banks.

CAMBRIDGE BAY (IKALUKTUTIAK)

Cambridge Bay is located on the southeast coast of 212,688-square-kilometer **Victoria Island,** Canada's second-largest island. A busy administrative center for the western section of Nunavut, it lies 1,300 kilometers west of Nunavut's capital, Iqaluit. The Inuit name for the bay is *Ikaluktutiak* (good fishing place). For hundreds of years before European arrival, Copper Inuit gathered here in summer to take advantage of the abundant caribou and seals and to fish for arctic char. These people fashioned tools and implements from copper, hence the name Copper Inuit. Doctor John Rae, who visited the bay in 1851 in search of the Franklin Expedition, was one of many Arctic explorers who stopped to rest in its sheltered waters.

The Hudson's Bay Company established a trading post on the bay in 1921 and bought Roald Amundsen's schooner *Maud* as a supply ship. After being used for many years, the ship fell into disrepair and sank in the bay. It is still visible from the shores of Old Town, resting in the shallow waters of Cambridge Bay. A stone church, built by Anglican missionaries in the 1920s, is a Cambridge Bay landmark.

The landscape surrounding the bay is barren, but the summit of 220-meter **Mt. Pelly,** a 15-kilometer (each way) hike from town, affords a panoramic view and a chance to spot musk oxen. Another interesting destination is **Greiner Lake,** 10 kilometers northwest of town, where more than 50 species of birds have been reported. In town, the **Ikaluktutiak Co-op** operates a fishery that is a major supplier of arctic char to the rest of Canada, and **Kitikmeot Meats** processes caribou and musk ox. Both plants are open to visitors, selling smoked arctic char and musk ox jerky, respectively.

The **Arctic Coast Visitors Centre,** 867/983-2224, has interesting displays on all coastal communities and a library, and offers a brochure of a self-guided interpretive walk through town; open May–Sept. daily 9 A.M.–5 P.M.

Practicalities
Campers can pitch tents along the shoreline, as long as they're out of sight of the community, or five kilometers from town at **Freshwater Creek.** For those wanting to stay indoors, the choices are **Ikaluktutiak Hotel–Inns North** (P.O. Box 38, Cambridge Bay, Nunavut X0E 0C0, 867/983-2215), $115 per person and $50 per person extra for meals; **Enokhok Inn** (P.O. Box 103, 867/983-2444), with self-contained units, each with a kitchenette, $125 per person; and the newest accommodation, **Arctic Islands Lodge** (P.O. Box 1031, 867/983-2345), where each room has a private bath, and a restaurant and laundry facility are on the premises, $180 per person includes meals. Meals are available in the hotels, groceries from **Northern.**

First Air, 867/983-2599 or 800/267-1247, has six flights per week from Yellowknife. If you are planning to visit Arctic coast communities east of Cambridge Bay, First Air provides connections.

KUGLUKTUK

Formerly known as Coppermine, *Kugluktuk* (Place of Rapids, pop. 1,200) lies at the mouth of one of North America's finest wilderness rivers. It is located 600 kilometers north of Yellowknife on **Coronation Gulf,** a vital link in the Northwest Passage.

History
Historians believe that Inuit fished at the mouth of the Coppermine River for more than 4,000 years before Samuel Hearne arrived there on July 14, 1771. The Hudson's Bay Company had sent Hearne to find the source of the copper that traders were starting to bring into posts farther east. When Hearne and his Chipewyan Dene guides neared the rivermouth, they en-

countered a party of Copper Inuit. Relations between the Dene and Copper Inuit had traditionally been tense, and as the result of an argument, the Inuit were massacred. Hearne named the site of the tragedy Bloody Falls, now a popular hike from Coppermine. As the great inland caribou herds began to decline in number, the Inuit spent more time near the coast hunting sea mammals. In 1927, a Hudson's Bay Company post was established at the rivermouth, followed by an Anglican mission and a Royal Canadian Mounted Police (RCMP) outpost in 1932, and a weather station in 1937. Today, fishing and hunting play an important role in the local economy, as do oil-and-gas exploration and tourism.

Coppermine River

The Coppermine River makes for one of North America's classic paddling trips, combining tundra wilderness with unparalleled opportunities for viewing moose, wolves, caribou, grizzly bears, and musk oxen. A sense of history prevails—after all, it's the same route north taken by Hearne, Franklin, and Hood. The headwaters of this remote river are below the treeline at a series of joined lakes, 360 kilometers north of Yellowknife. The 325-kilometer float from the headwaters to Coppermine takes a minimum of 10 days, but most people allow time for tundra hikes, arctic char fishing, and relaxing. The river flows primarily through tundra, but the valley is characteristically lushly vegetated, creating prime habitat for larger mammals. Hawks, falcons, and eagles nest in the cliff faces along the route. The only portage is at Bloody Falls, 16 kilometers from the ocean. For those planning their own expedition, **Air Tindi,** 867/669-8200, provides charter flights for the 360 kilometers from Yellowknife to the river's headwaters.

Things to Do around Town

Although most keen naturalists are drawn to nearby Bathurst Inlet Lodge (see following entry), the immediate vicinity of Coppermine provides many opportunities for wildlife viewing. The best way to get a feel for the area is by hiking along one of the numerous trails that radiate from town. The trail to **Bloody Falls** is less than 20 kilometers one-way, but the going can get rough. Chances are you'll want to make numerous

stops, both to search out routes through the many swampy sections of the trail and to admire the colorful tundra vegetation. Rewards along the way are ample, however, and none more so than the final destination where the Coppermine River plunges into a narrow canyon. Most hikers opt to camp here overnight. Other possible hikes include walking along the beach west of town to **Expeditor Cove** or climbing the rocky ridge above the garbage dump road for a view of town and the ocean. **Aime's Arctic Tours,** 867/982-5724, organizes fishing trips to nearby islands and up the Coppermine River for arctic char. Inquire at the **Hunters and Trappers Organization,** 867/982-3903, by the recreation center for other outfitters. The year's biggest festival is **Nattik Frolics,** at the end of April, which includes traditional Northern sports and other not-so-traditional events such as poker and snowmobile races. A **fishing derby,** 867/982-4471, held during the first weekend of September attracts arctic char enthusiasts from throughout the north.

Practicalities

The **Coppermine Inn** (P.O. Box 282, Coppermine, Nunavut X0E 0E0, 867/982-3333) is in the center of town. Guests have a choice of motel rooms or self-contained units; $125 per person. Breakfast, lunch, and dinner are $15, $20, and $30, respectively, and should be booked in advance. Nonguests may also eat here but should book meals one day in advance. The **Enokhok Inn** (P.O. Box 162, 867/982-3197) has three rooms for $170 per person, which includes meals. **Northern,** 867/982-4171, just up from the dock, sells groceries and souvenirs, and usually has white gas (check supplies before flying in). The town has a **post office, a library,** and a **craft shop,** but no bank.

The airport is a short two-kilometer walk from town and is served by **First Air,** 867/982-3208 or 800/267-1247, from Yellowknife.

BATHURST INLET

Bathurst Inlet, 210 kilometers east of Coppermine, is the name of an expansive bay, an abandoned Hudson's Bay Company post, and a popular naturalist lodge. The Hudson's Bay

Company established a trading post on the southwest side of the inlet at the mouth of the **Burnside River** in the 1930s. Various Inuit had inhabited the Bathurst Inlet area for thousands of years, but the post, along with others along the rugged coastline, was the first permanent settlement. In 1964, the post moved across the inlet and 120 kilometers north to Bay Chimo. Four years later, it closed for good. The small Inuit community here, now known as ***Umingmaktok*** (Place of Many Musk Oxen, pop. 50), continues to prosper and is one of the North's more traditional communities. Residents are noted for their crafts, which can be bought at Bathurst Inlet Lodge.

Bathurst Inlet Lodge

Glenn Warner, a former Mountie, and his wife Trish bought the various Hudson's Bay Company buildings at the mouth of the Burnside River and in 1969 opened what has evolved into the north's most renowned naturalist lodge. Most of the original buildings remain—as a lounge, a dining room, and guest rooms for up to 25 visitors at a time. But it is not the quaint red-and-white-trimmed buildings that attract people from around the world. Rather, it is the chance to become immersed in the fascinating natural world of the Arctic, with a soft bed and a hot shower at the end of each day. One of the beauties of the lodge, apart from its magnificent setting, is the diversity of things to see and do in the surrounding area. The *Arctic Queen,* a pontoon boat, cruises the inlet in search of ringed seals and musk oxen grazing on the shore. Bird-watchers will be captivated by the seabirds and shorebirds that spend summer in the area. Local Inuit families, who have become part owners of the lodge, teach guests their own interpretation of the land's natural history. And there's plenty of time for fishing, photography, hiking, or just soaking up the scenery.

Rates for the lodge include charter flights from Yellowknife, seven nights' accommodations at the lodge, all meals, guided day trips (except flightseeing, $200), and a traditional drum dance on your final night. Essentially, all you have to do is get to Yellowknife. Cost is $3,420 out of Yellowknife. The floatplane leaves from Back Bay in Old Town Yellowknife at 3618 McAvoy Road. For more information, contact Bathurst Inlet Lodge, P.O. Box 820, Yellowknife, Northwest Territories X1A 2N6, 867/873-2595, www.bathurstinletlodge.com.

GJOA HAVEN (URSUQTUQ)

Gjoa Haven (pop. 850) is the only settlement on **King William Island,** which is separated from the mainland by the narrow Simpson Strait. The island had long been the traditional territory of the Netsilik Inuit, who were expert seal hunters. Early explorers named it King William

caribou

J. PETERSON/NWT ARCTIC TOURISM

Land, mistakenly thinking that it was part of the mainland. The island has been the scene of much conjecture ever since the disappearance of Sir John Franklin, one of many explorers sent to find the elusive Northwest Passage. One of the Franklin Expedition's main mistakes was underestimating the Netsilik, whose advice could have prevented the tragedy. Roald Amundsen made no such mistakes on his 1903–1906 expedition. After spending two winters on King William Island learning from the Netsilik, at a harbor he named after his ship *Gjoa*, he went on to become the first person to successfully navigate the Northwest Passage. Today, the location of what Amundsen called "the finest little harbor in the world" is home to approximately 700 Inuit who live a traditional lifestyle—hunting, fishing, and making crafts such as wall hangings and soapstone carvings. The well-marked **Northwest Passage Interpretive Trail** tells the story of the search for the passage and the part Gjoa Haven played in it. The trail is three kilometers long and can be boggy early in the summer. Ask at the hamlet office, 867/360-7141, just up from Northern, for an interpretive brochure explaining the historical importance of sites along the trail. Apart from the excellent arctic char fishing, Gjoa Haven is a good base for sled dog trips across Rae Strait to Taloyoak. The end of winter is celebrated with the **Qavvarrik Carnival,** which takes place on the still-frozen bay in front of the community in late May. The carnival features events for everyone—an egg toss, a blindfolded sled race, and a harpoon throw, just to name a few—all with small cash prizes. For outsiders, winning the weightlifting competition will cause some problems because first prize is a 44-gallon drum of fuel!

Practicalities

The **Amundsen Hotel** (P.O. Box 120, Gjoa Haven, Nunavut X0E 1J0, 867/360-6176) has 19 rooms for $150 per person plus $60 per person for meals. The small restaurant is open to nonguests, but reservations should be made in advance. For groceries, head to **Northern**, and for local crafts to the **Co-op**, behind the hotel.

The only scheduled air service to Gjoa Haven is with **First Air**, 867/360-6612 or 800/267-1247, via Cambridge Bay from Yellowknife.

TALOYOAK

Formerly known as Spence Bay, this Inuit community of 650 lies in low, rolling hills and is surrounded by fish-filled lakes. It is located on the west side of an isthmus linking the mainland to **Boothia Peninsula.** The tip of this peninsula, 250 kilometers north of Taloyoak at Bellot Strait, is the northernmost point of mainland North America. Spence Bay was named by John Ross, a British explorer who wintered in the area in the early 1830s. Taloyoak, its Inuit name, refers to a caribou blind built by early natives to corral and kill caribou. The Netsilik Inuit traveled great distances through the region—hunting, trapping, and trading. By following Inuit directions, John Ross escaped certain death after becoming icebound. His abandoned vessel, a paddle-steamer, the first such boat to be used for Arctic exploration, was a source of wood and iron to the Inuit for many years. It is interesting that Ross was able to accurately pinpoint the magnetic North Pole to a spot along the southwestern coast of Boothia Peninsula. The pole, which annually moves 25 kilometers north and six kilometers west, has since moved many hundreds of kilometers to a point northwest of Resolute.

A permanent settlement was not established at Spence Bay until 1947, one of the only safe harbors on the west coast of Boothia Peninsula. Local Inuit artisans are known for their stuffed "packing dolls" of animals such as whales and seals. At the mouth of the harbor stand the distinctive red-and-white Hudson's Bay Company buildings. A short hike leads to a stone caribou blind. It is also possible to travel overland to **Fort Ross,** or 80 kilometers north to **Thom Bay,** where the *Victory* was abandoned by Ross in 1929. Inland are lakes where the local Inuit travel each summer to fish.

Practicalities

The **Co-op Hotel** (General Delivery, Taloyoak, Nunavut X0E 1B0, 867/561-5803) has rooms with shared facilities for $110 per person. Meals are an extra $50 per person per day. The **Boothia Inn** (P.O. Box 18, 867/561-5300) has rooms for $170 per person, including meals. A semi-official camping area is near an old mission church, west of the post office. Meals are available at the Paleajook Hotel but should be booked in advance. Groceries and limited camping supplies are available at **Northern** or the **Co-op.** Ask at the Hunters and Trappers Organization, 867/561-5066, for locally harvested food such as arctic char and caribou. The community also has a **post office** and a **medical center** but no bank.

The small airport, within walking distance of town, is served by **First Air,** 867/561-5400 or 800/267-1247, from Yellowknife. First Air also flies between Taloyoak and Iqaluit twice weekly; the Tuesday flight is a real milk run with seven stops. **Lyall's Taxi and Cartage,** 867/561-6363, operates a cab service.

PELLY BAY (ARVILIQJUAT)

Pelly Bay is a Netsilingmiut Inuit community of 500 located 177 kilometers southeast of Taloyoak. The community is named for Sir Henry Pelly, an early governor of the Hudson's Bay Company. It grew around a Roman Catholic mission established in 1935. The mission's founder, Father Henri, was the only *qallunaaq* (nonnative) to reside here for many years. Today, the residents of Pelly Bay continue to fish and hunt as they have for generations. The town's location deep in Pelly Bay makes accessibility for barge traffic nearly impossible and gives the town the distinction of having the highest cost of living of any community in the North.

A stone church located on the road to the dock, built by Father Henri, houses a small museum. In the immediate vicinity of the community are some interesting sites. On top of a nearby hill is a unique cross built out of empty gasoline drums by early missionaries. Also close to town are several *inukshuks* and scraps of metal from the fuselage of a U.S. plane. Hikes lead along the rocky shoreline, inland to fishing lakes, and to archaeological remains of Inuit camps. Seals and, occasionally, narwhals are seen in the bay. The Inuit name for Pelly Bay is *Arviliqjuat* (Place of the Bowhead Whale), but those magnificent creatures are long gone.

Practicalities
The lack of tourist facilities here is more than made up for by the friendliness of the locals. The **Inukshuk Inn** (General Delivery, Pelly Bay, Nunavut X0E 1K0, 867/769-7211) has 11 rooms with shared facilities, a TV room, and a small restaurant, and can book tours through local outfitters; $125 per person, meals are $50 per day. Meals in the restaurant are provided by prior arrangement only, whether a guest or not. Groceries are available at **Koomiut Co-op,** next door to the hotel. The town has no bank, and alcohol is not allowed. Ask at the co-op about campsites close to town.

First Air, 867/769-7505 or 800/267-1247, flies into Pelly Bay three times weekly from Yellowknife via Coppermine.

KEEWATIN

The Keewatin stretches along the west coast of Hudson Bay from north of Churchill, Manitoba, to the Melville Peninsula and west to the heart of the barrenlands. Each summer, vast herds of caribou migrate across the region to their calving grounds. Wolves, foxes, and grizzlies are scattered throughout the region, while musk oxen graze in small herds in the Thelon Game Sanctuary. Polar bears migrate along the coastal regions and are best viewed at Wager Bay. The thousands of lakes and rivers dotting the region are alive with fish; arctic char is dominant, but huge lake trout and whitefish also inhabit all lakes large enough not to freeze to the bottom. Whaling took place throughout the Arctic, but Hudson Bay was

affected more than anywhere. All species were hunted to near extinction during this period, and today whales exist in only a small fraction of their former numbers. The most common sea mammal here is the ringed seal, which spends summer basking on the shoreline or ice floes.

Dorset and Thule cultures inhabited the region for thousands of years before European whalers arrived, but the latter people had the most dramatic effect on animal populations. Trading posts, built to support the whaling industry, attracted the Inuit, and in time, communities developed around them. Rankin Inlet is the largest of seven communities and the transportation hub of the Keewatin.

RANKIN INLET (KANGIQTINQ)

Rankin Inlet is the communication, administrative, and transportation center of the Keewatin region. It is located on rocky terrain, west of where the Meliadine River drains into Rankin Inlet, approximately 25 kilometers from Hudson Bay. It wasn't established until 1955, when the North Rankin Nickel Mine opened. A Hudson's Bay Company store, hospital, homes, three churches, and a school were soon added to the mine structures as many Inuit moved to the area seeking a wage. In 1958, the Department of Indian Affairs, appalled at the living conditions of the nomadic Inuit, set up a relocation program, moving them to **Itivia**, one kilometer southeast of Rankin Inlet. Here the government constructed huts, a school, and a store. Because of a depletion of ore, the mine closed in 1962 and the population dipped to 350. Itivia was deemed a failure soon after. An arts-and-crafts manufacturing program was the turning point in Rankin Inlet's fortunes. Although recovery has been slow, the population has increased to 2,000, and today the streets are the typical Northern clutter of weathered buildings joined by a net of electrical wires. The Keewatin's only paved road links downtown to the airport.

Around Town

The **North Rankin Nickel Mine** is located on a gravel hill overlooking the harbor and town. Al-though it has been closed since 1962, much of the machinery remains, slowly rusting away and leaving a graphic memory of the eastern Arctic's first mine. Across the road from the mine site is a commercial fish-processing plant where arctic char is prepared for shipment south. From the mine site, the road continues down to the harbor, where there's a dock and a small fleet of fishing boats. On the opposite side of town, near the Matchbox Gallery, a one-kilometer trail leads to Itivia. Little remains of the settlement, but from the site there is a good view of the Barrier Islands. An important archaeological site is located eight kilometers north of town, where the Meliadine River drains into Hudson Bay. The area was never particularly good for hunting but was used for centuries as a seasonal fishing camp. Many stone tent rings, foundations of semi-subterranean houses, and several graves can be found in the area. Interpretive signs explain this history. The road to the site is used by locals going fishing, so if you walk, you may be able to hitch a ride along the way.

Marble Island

Lying 40 kilometers east of Rankin Inlet is an island where many dramas have played out over the years. The lineaments are simple; it is a barren island dominated by slabs of cream-colored quartzite protruding from an otherwise featureless terrain. European traders and explorers probably landed on the island as early as the 1600s. In 1721, Captain James Knight and his crew were searching for the Northwest Passage when his two ships were wrecked on a shallow bar at the east end of the island. Everyone made it ashore, and a stone house was built to winter in. One by one, they perished, waiting for a rescue that never came. During the late 1800s, the island was used as a wintering site for whalers. Today it is regarded as a mystical place; Thule camps can be seen, along with the remains of Knight's house and the site of an open-air theater, used by the whalers for entertainment.

Accommodations and Food

Rankin Inlet's two accommodations are located in the center of town and should be able to organize transportation from the airport if you book a room in advance. The **Nanuq Inn** (P.O. Box 175, Rankin Inlet, Nunavut X0C 0A0,

ESKIMO ICE CREAM

Recipes vary from region to region depending on the ingredients available. This version is from the eastern Arctic and, once started, must be completed without interruptions.

Pound an amount of seal fat until soft, then melt over low heat until there is a thick layer of grease on the base of the pot. Grind up dried arctic char roe and berries, then stir slowly into the melted fat; make sure the temperature remains low—a guide is to keep the mixture at a temperature that is not too hot to touch. Add salt to taste. If the mixture congeals, water will soften it up. Freeze the mixture, then serve with bread or meat.

867/645-2513) has 10 rooms with cable TV in each and shared bathrooms. The inn also has a coffee shop, a dining room, and a lounge; $125 per person. The **Siniktarvik Hotel** (P.O. Box 190, 867/645-2807) is larger, and each of the 65 rooms has a private bath, and a restaurant and lounge is available for guests. Rates are $160 per person.

Northern has a good range of groceries and a snack bar serving fast food (closes at 5 P.M.). Dining in the two hotel restaurants is expensive, but not outrageously so.

Transportation

Rankin Inlet is the transportation hub of the Keewatin. **First Air,** 867/645-3445 or 800/267-1247, flies in from Yellowknife five times weekly and from Winnipeg three times weekly, with connecting flights through to Iqaluit. For a cab, call 867/645-2411 or 867/645-2892.

Services and Information

The **post office** is behind the Siniktarvik Hotel; the only bank is a C.I.B.C. in the Kissarvik Co-op. A small **visitors center,** 867/645-5091, in the Siniktarvik Hotel, features Inuit displays and details of the Knight Expedition and has local crafts for sale.

WHALE COVE (TIKIRARJUAQ)

Whale Cove's Inuit name is *Tikirarjuaq* (Where Many People Arrive), a reference to the whalers, trading ships, and Inuit who stopped here. This small community of 300 is located 80 kilometers south of Rankin Inlet, on a peninsula where the Wilson River drains into Hudson Bay. The area was explored in 1613 by Captain Thomas Button, and from the early 1700s onward, Hudson's Bay Company traders regularly visited the area. The community wasn't officially established until 1959. At this time, the federal government began moving Caribou Inuit to the coast, where they adapted their hunting and fishing skills to the abundant coastal resources.

The community has little to offer in the way of tourist facilities but provides a unique opportunity to view the traditional Inuit lifestyle, including women scraping caribou skins and fishermen returning with their daily catches. On one side of

town are large tanks, which are filled each summer with fuel for the winter. On the other side is a small dock and a beach. The beach is lined with freighter canoes, engines, and the ubiquitous snowmobile. Behind town is **Whale's Tail Monument,** built in 1967 to celebrate the community's link to the ocean. A rough trail leads to this viewpoint. Other trails lead inland to several lakes, the deeper ones supporting lake trout and whitefish.

Practicalities

The **Issatik Hotel** (Whale Cove, Nunavut X0C 0J0, 867/896-9252) is in the center of town and has six rooms, each with a private bathroom; $200 per person per day includes three meals. Ask at the hamlet office next door about camping; 867/896-9961. A **grocery store** and **post office** are located by the fish plant opposite the waterfront. The only scheduled flights to Whale Cove are with **Calm Air,** 867/896-9310, from Rankin Inlet.

ARVIAT

For many centuries, Arviat (formerly known as Eskimo Point), located 240 kilometers southwest of Rankin Inlet, was a summer camp for Pallirmiut Inuit who came to the coast to hunt seals. They spent the rest of the year inland, but during their time in the area in the late 1600s, they made contact with traders from Churchill. A Hudson's Bay Company post was established in 1921, followed by Roman Catholic and Anglican missions. Inuit were attracted to the settlement for food, medicine, and trade goods. During the 1940s and 1950s, the migration patterns of the caribou changed and their numbers declined, causing great hardship for the remaining inland Inuit, who were relocated to Arviat by the Canadian government. Today, this community of 1,500 still largely depends on hunting, trapping, and fishing for its livelihood.

To the south is the **McConnell River Bird Sanctuary,** a 330-square-kilometer area of wetlands and tidal flats that is a breeding ground for 250,000 lesser snow geese and a staging area for one million birds each fall. For boat transfers to the sanctuary or to good fishing areas, call the hamlet office, 867/857-2841.

DAN HERINGA/NWT ARCTIC TOURISM

Inukshuks *were built by the Inuit as a navigation aid on the featureless turndra.*

pany didn't establish a post on the Keewatin coast, at Chesterfield Inlet, until 1912. The community, which is situated on a gravel strip of land overlooking the inlet, has several historic buildings, including the impressive three-story **St. Theresa Hospital,** circa 1931.

Tours of the community, three-day tours up the inlet to archaeological sites, and five-day tours up the coast to Cape Fullerton (the site of the eastern Arctic's first RCMP post, which has been restored to its original condition) can be booked through the local hamlet office, 867/898-9063.

Practicalities

The only tourist services are at the **Tangmavik Hotel** (P.O. Box 500, Chesterfield Inlet, Nunavut X0C 0B0, 867/898-9190); $185 per person includes three meals.

Calm Air, 867/898-9103, has daily flights from Rankin Inlet.

BAKER LAKE (QAMANITTUAQ)

Baker Lake or *Qamanittuaq* (Far Inland, pop. 1,300), located west of Chesterfield Inlet, is the only inland Inuit community. Rankin Inlet is located 260 kilometers to the east and, surprisingly, the geographical center of Canada is located a few kilometers to the northeast. The community is a good jumping-off point for sightseeing in Thelon Game Sanctuary or canoeing the various wilderness rivers to the south and west.

The local population is thought to have descended from a group of Inuit of the Thule culture who migrated onto the barrenlands to hunt caribou. Before the Hudson's Bay Company established a post in 1916 on an island in the lake, few whites had ventured into the area. The post moved to the present site in 1936, and the community has been steadily expanding since. Local Inuit are renowned for their art, much of which reflects the importance of the caribou herds. Their artworks can be viewed at the **Jessie Oonark Ltd. Arts and Crafts Centre,** 867/793-2428.

Accommodations

The two accommodations are the **Baker Lake Lodge** (P.O. Box 239, Baker Lake, Nunavut X0C 0A0, 867/793-2905) and the much larger (25

Practicalities

Padlei Inns North (P.O. Box 90, Arviat, Nunavut X0C 0E0, 867/857-2919) has 10 rooms, a lounge, and a laundry facility; $175 per person includes three meals.

Calm Air, 867/857-2997, flies daily from Rankin Inlet.

In town is the **Margaret Aniksak Visitors Centre,** 867/857-2366, with a tour-booking service and displays of local archaeological sites.

CHESTERFIELD INLET (IGLULIGAARJUK)

This community of 290 north of Rankin Inlet was an important medical and educational center for the eastern Arctic until the government helped other communities develop their own facilities. Although much whaling activity took place in Hudson Bay in the 1700s, the Hudson's Bay Com-

rooms) **Iglu Hotel** (P.O. Box 179, 867/793-2801). Both charge $180 per person, including meals. Camping is possible along the lakeshore, but check with the hamlet office before pitching a tent.

Services and Information
Calm Air, 867/793-2873 or 800/839-2256, has flights daily from Rankin Inlet into Baker Lake; $212 one-way, $238 14-day APEX round-trip.

Limited groceries and camping supplies are available at **Northern.** The **Visitors Centre,** 867/793-2456, is down beside the beach in the original 1936 Hudson's Bay Company trading post, which has been restored. Bookings can be made here for local tours.

Thelon Game Sanctuary
This 67,340-square-kilometer sanctuary was established in 1927 to conserve wildlife. Its dominant natural feature, the **Thelon River,** begins from 200 kilometers east of Great Slave Lake and is the largest unaltered watershed emptying into Hudson Bay. The river flows through a wide valley, surrounded in barrenlands yet lined with stands of spruce, protected from the elements by the valley wall. The Beverly caribou herd—numbering approximately 380,000—migrates through the sanctuary. Other mammals present are wolves, musk oxen, moose, wolverines, foxes, lynx, and grizzly bears. Rare raptors, such as the peregrine falcon, nest in the sanctuary, along with 10,000 Canada geese.

The Thelon River has been designated as a Canadian Heritage River, not only for its abundant wildlife and natural heritage but also for the unique wilderness recreation it offers. Canoeing is by far the most popular activity. Although it is possible to begin a canoe trip from the Upper Thelon or Hanbury rivers, strenuous portages are required to do so. The most popular put-in point is at the confluence of these two rivers, from where it is 300 kilometers to Beverly Lake or an extra 100 kilometers of open-water paddling to the community of Baker Lake.

Great Canadian Ecoventures (P.O. Box 2481, Yellowknife, Northwest Territories X1A 2P8, 867/920-7110 or 800/667-9453, www.thelon.com) offers a variety of popular Dance with the Wildlife tours through the sanctuary, hosted by experts in various fields of study, which search out wolves, caribou, and musk oxen. These trips are especially popular with photographers. Costs are $4,300 single, $3,500 double for eight days, which includes charter flights from Yellowknife. The company also outfits experienced travelers for a week-long trip to a remote spot along the Thelon River; $2,800 per person includes the use of a base camp, air transfers from Yellowknife, and a boat.

REPULSE BAY (NAUJAT)

Although Repulse Bay was used as a refuge for whaling ships, a permanent settlement wasn't established until 1962. The community of 560 is located right on the Arctic Circle, at the south side of an isthmus between the Gulf of Boothia and Hudson Bay. The community sits on sloping land, overlooking Repulse Bay, and with steep coastline cliffs on either side. The bay is good for **whale-watching,** especially in August when belugas and narwhals can often be seen from the shoreline. Contact the local Hunters and Trappers Organization, 867/462-995, for details of outfitters offering fishing trips or tours up the coast to either **Harbour Island**—the site of an old whaling camp—or a stone house built in 1846 by explorer John Rae.

Practicalities
The **Naujat Inns North Hotel** (General Delivery, 867/462-4304) has private bathrooms and a TV room; $180 per person includes three meals. **Calm Air,** 867/462-4091, flies three times weekly between Rankin Inlet and Repulse Bay.

Wager Bay
Isolated, rugged terrain and a rich food base contribute to make Wager Bay—which penetrates 150 kilometers into the Arctic tundra south of Repulse Bay—prime habitat for a wide variety of land and sea mammals. This abundance of wildlife has led to proposals that the bay and a wide strip around its perimeter be designated as a national park. The south shore is one of the Arctic's major polar bear denning sites. Ice floes, which remain in the bay until midsummer, make hunting ringed seals easy for the bears. Seals, in turn, are attracted by healthy populations of arctic char. On the land, caribou graze on the tundra throughout sum-

mer, attracting wolves and wolverines. In contrast to other flatter areas of the barrenlands, the landscape surrounding the bay features 500-meter cliffs (prime nesting sites for the rare gyrfalcon), waterfalls cascading down glacially carved rock, and rocky crests, with sweeping panoramas of the bay.

The closest community to Wager Bay is Repulse Bay, 160 air kilometers northeast and much farther by boat, making it too far for Inuit hunters. The **Sila Lodge** (774 Bronx Ave., Winnipeg, Manitoba R2K 4E9, 204/949-2050 or 800/663-9832), located on the shoreline, is the only accommodation in the bay. The cost of staying at the lodge is, as you'd expect, very expensive, more than $4,000 for one week.

CORAL HARBOUR (SALLIQ)

Coral Harbour (pop. 670) is the only community on 40,663-square-kilometer **Southampton Island,** a large island of low, rolling hills that rises from the waters of the north end of Hudson Bay. One of the Arctic's most intriguing tragedies occurred in 1902–1903 on its shores, when the last remaining Sallirmiut Inuit mysteriously died. The Hudson's Bay Company established a post on **Coats Island** to the south, to serve fleets of whalers. In 1927, it was moved to the head of South Bay on Southampton Island to serve the Inuit who had been moved to a newly established Anglican mission. The community today is traditional, relying heavily on the abundance of sea mammals in the immediate vicinity.

Coral Harbour is the best jumping-off point for trips to the large walrus colonies in the region; the animals gather in the thousands along the coast and on Coats and Depot islands. Other mammals often seen are polar bears and ringed and bearded seals. Also on Southampton Island is the **Harry Gibbons Bird Sanctuary,** a nesting site for various species of geese, including 200,000 lesser snow geese. Within hiking distance of Coral Harbour are the spectacular **Kirchoffer Falls** and various historic and prehistoric sites. Trips to these sights, as well as to Native Point (see following entry), can be arranged through the Hunters and Trappers Organization, 867/925-8875.

The Mystery of the Sallirmiut

Arctic historians engage in much speculation as to who the Sallirmiut were and what caused their demise. But it is known that in the winter of 1902–1903, after surviving on a bleak and inhospitable spit of land for many hundreds of years, they all died. They may have descended from the Dorset culture, who disappeared elsewhere in the north approximately 700 years ago, or from the Thule, who had evolved into the Inuit culture found elsewhere in the Canadian Arctic. Whoever their ancestors were, this splinter group settled at **Native Point,** 60 kilometers southeast of the community of Coral Harbour, and remained in near-total isolation, culturally distinct from the rest of the world. They lived a Stone Age existence until that fateful winter earlier this century, building homes from stone, sod, and whalebone, and hunting sea mammals with flint-headed weapons. Their demise was probably caused by contact with a whaling fleet that transmitted a disease such as dysentery or smallpox, killing off the entire Sallirmiut population in one long winter. The following year, visitors to the settlement found bodies everywhere, with dogs being the only sign of life.

The site, a two-hour boat trip from Coral Harbour, attracts few visitors. But walking around the 100 or so houses with sun-bleached bones scattering the rocky ground provokes feelings of veneration for a now-extinct culture that, after surviving unbelievable natural hardships, was wiped out by fellow humans.

Practicalities

The only accommodation at Coral Harbour is **Leonie's Place Hotel** (P.O. Box 29, Coral Harbour, Nunavut X0C 0C0, 867/925-9751), which has six double rooms; $190 per person includes three meals. Ask at the hamlet office about camping.

Calm Air, 867/925-9767, flies three times weekly from Rankin Inlet to Coral Harbour.

BAFFIN AND BEYOND

Baffin Island, the surrounding administrative region, and the islands of the high Arctic sit atop the continent of North America—a vast, rugged, virtually uninhabitable, and relatively unexplored part of the world that has only recently been viewed as a viable travel destination. Within this area are endless opportunities for adventure travel, whether it's hiking in two of the world's most remote national parks, canoeing a Canadian Heritage River, climbing the towering peaks along the spectacular fjords of North Baffin Island, or making the ultimate trip—to the North Pole. If you're looking for something equally satisfying but less challenging, you can visit the many prehistoric Thule sites, chase the legend of the ill-fated Franklin Expedition, view the abundant sea mammals from the safety of a boat, visit islands that are home to millions of seabirds, learn more about the Inuit culture by visiting the 14 communities, and, yes, you too can visit the North Pole, with a champagne lunch thrown in.

Baffin Island is the world's sixth-largest island (after Australia, Greenland, New Guinea, Borneo, and Madagascar) at 507,500 square kilometers. Most of the island is lowland Arctic, made up of gently rolling hills, rarely rising more than 700 meters above sea level and broken only occasionally by a rocky headland or bluff. The southern end of the island is made up of three distinct peninsulas, two of which are separated by Frobisher Bay where Iqaluit, the capital of Nunavut, lies. In lower-central Baffin Island, northwest of Iqaluit, is the **Great Plain of the Koukdjuak,** which rose so quickly from the surrounding sea that colonies of seals became landlocked in two large lakes and have evolved into freshwater mammals. The northeastern coast of Baffin Island, from Cumberland Peninsula to Bylot Island, is the mountainous Arctic. Here, glaciated peaks rising more than 2,000 meters are incised by steep-sided fiords cutting deeply into the land. Auyuittuq National Park, on Cumberland Peninsula, is the most accessible part of this spectacular region and attracts hikers and mountaineers from around the world.

IQALUIT

Pronounced ee-ka-loo-EET, *Iqaluit* (pop. 4,300—60% Inuit) was the natural choice for the capital of Nunavut because it had always filled the role of the government, transportation, and administrative center for all eastern Arctic communities. Although most people who live here earn a wage, Iqaluit is still relatively traditional. Known as Frobisher Bay until 1987, the terrain on which the community is built is uninspiring, a glacially scoured landscape of rocky ridges and exposed bedrock. The land is dotted with many lakes, the coastline with many islands. It is located on Koojesse Inlet at the northwest head of **Frobisher Bay** on southern Baffin Island. The national capital, Ottawa, lies 2,080 kilometers south, and Yellowknife is 2,260 kilometers to the west.

History
The first recorded contact the local Inuit had with Europeans was in 1576 when Sir Martin Frobisher entered the bay that now bears his name. He was searching for the Northwest Passage. Instead, he found ore samples that he mistakenly thought were gold. He returned with 15 ships and had established a camp before the mistake was realized. Although whalers frequented the area in the 18th and 19th centuries, the community didn't take hold until after the construction of the north's largest U.S. Air Force base in 1942. The Hudson's Bay Company established a post, and in 1959 the federal government moved its regional headquarters to the townsite.

Sights
The best place to begin a visit to this area is at the **Baffin Regional Visitor Information Centre,** in the **Unikkaarvik Building** on the beach at the southeast end of town, 867/979-4636. The staff supplies brochures and maps and can arrange trips with local outfitters. (You'll need a map; although there are street signs, no one uses them.) Also here is a life-size marble carv-

ing of an Inuit drum dancer and a model of the inside of a Thule sod house. The building also houses the offices of Nunavut Tourism and a library stocked with polar-related literature. Next door, housed in a restored Hudson's Bay Company post, is the **Nunatta Sunakkutaangit Museum,** 867/979-5537, housing a collection of Thule and Inuit prehistoric and historic artifacts, a flora and fauna display, and lots of interesting historic photographs. It's open Tues.–Sun. 1–5 P.M. Farther along the beach is a sod house. Behind the visitors center is the Arctic Ventures gift shop and, farther up the hill, a lookout and another gift shop. From this gift shop, a gravel road leads five kilometers east to **Apex,** a residential part of Iqaluit. Before Apex, a road leads to some historic Hudson's Bay Company buildings.

Most businesses, including the airport, are located to the west of the visitors center. A 15-minute walk south from the airport brings you to the **Sylvia Grinnell Territorial Park,** 148 hectares of rolling Arctic tundra. More than 160 species of plants have been recorded in the park, and the cliffs there provide excellent views across the bay. A trail leads up the Sylvia Grinnell River, past a traditional fishing spot, but the going is rough.

Qaummaarviit Historic Park

Twelve kilometers west of Iqaluit near Peale Point, a small island (connected to the mainland only at low tide) has been inhabited intermittently for almost 1,000 years. The Thule, who migrated from Alaska, settled on the island for the abundance of both sea and land mammals in the vicinity. More than 3,000 tools and 20,000 bones have been discovered. Today, a series of boardwalks leads through the sod houses on the south end of the island and through a shallow valley to graves and tent rings.

Outfitters

To get to Qaummaarviit you'll need to use the services of an outfitter. Both **Qairrulik Outfitting** (P.O. Box 863, Iqaluit, Nunavut X0A 0H0, 867/979-6280) and **Northwinds Arctic Adventures** (P.O. Box 849, 867/979-0551) offer trips to the island; $100–150 per person includes a bannock meal. You can also charter a boat from either company for fishing, whale-watching, or visiting fossil beds.

Events

Toonik Tyme, a weeklong festival at the end of April, is a celebration of spring with traditional Inuit games, a snowmobile race to Kimmirut, harpoon throwing, igloo building, and a community feast.

Accommodations

Iqaluit has four hotels, a couple of B&Bs, and a campground. **Toonoonik Hotel–Inns North** (P.O. Box 1859, Iqaluit, Nunavut X0A 0H0,

Travel by dog team is a unique way to visit the sights around Iqaluit.

WOLFGANG WEBER/NWT ARCTIC TOURISM

867/979-6733) features good views but has small rooms; $125 single, $145 double. Other choices are the **Regency Frobisher Inn** (P.O. Box 610, 867/979-2222), which has a good restaurant, $140 single, $150 double; the **Discovery Lodge Hotel** (P.O. Box 387, 867/979-4433), the pick of the bunch, $165 single or double; and the **Navigator Inn** (P.O. Box 158, 867/979-6201), located across the road from the Discovery, $155 single, $170 double. **Accommodations By the Sea** (P.O. Box 341, 867/979-6074) is a bed-and-breakfast in Apex, five kilometers east of town. Facilities include a kitchen and a laundry room. Rates include a cooked breakfast and transportation from the airport; $95 single, $120 double.

Camping is available at the **Sylvia Grinnell Territorial Park,** a 15-minute walk ($5.50 taxi ride) from the airport. The park's facilities include tent platforms, foul-weather shelters, pit toilets, and fire rings.

Food

Coffee shops are located in **Northern** and the **Navigator Inn,** 867/979-6201, and a small bakery is located in the Astro Hill Complex. For something more substantial, the Navigator Inn is a favorite, especially on Saturday for a pizza buffet. The rest of the week, arctic char and caribou are served, and there's a good salad bar. For dessert, fresh fruit is flown in and delicious chocolate crepes, made in-house, are served. The **Granite Room** (in the Discovery Lodge Hotel, 867/979-4433) features a nightly table d'hôte menu featuring local specialties such as Cumberland Sound scallops, seal, and shrimp served in season. The Regency Frobisher Inn offers a weekday lunch buffet.

Transportation

The distinctive yellow air terminal, a short walk from downtown Iqaluit, is a Northern landmark. The airport is always busy and handles 10,000 take-offs and landings per year. It is a hub for **First Air,** 867/979-8333, which flies to Iqaluit from Ottawa, Montreal, Yellowknife via Resolute or Rankin Inlet, and Winnipeg via Rankin Inlet. First Air also links Iqaluit to all Nunavut communities, and to Sondre Stromfjord and Nuuk, in Greenland. **Air Nunavut,** 867/979-4018, has scheduled flights to all communities in

the south of Baffin Island. It also has flightseeing from $100 per person for a 30-minute tour.

A cab anywhere in town costs $4; out to the campground it's $5.50; 867/979-5333 or 867/979-5222.

Services and Information

Iqaluit has a post office, banks, one-hour photo developing, a hospital, and an indoor pool. The massive **Northern** store sells everything from camping gear to fresh cakes and pastries. **Baffin Regional Visitor Information Centre,** 867/979-4636, has all the information you'll need for touring through the Baffin region; open year-round Mon.–Fri. 10 A.M.–noon and 1–7 P.M., Sat.–Sun. noon–7 P.M.

KIMMIRUT

Kimmirut (Looks Like a Heel, for the spit of land on which it lies) is a community of 400 that was known as **Lake Harbour** until 1996. It's located on the south coast of **Meta Incognita Peninsula** 120 kilometers south of Iqaluit, overlooking a picturesque harbor. The peninsula is separated from the mainland of northern Quebec by the Hudson Strait. From the low peaks of this peninsula flows the Soper River, one of the world's great wilderness canoeing rivers. Jutting westward are the low-lying wetlands of **Foxe Peninsula.** In spring, the nearby floe edge is a good place to view sea mammals.

The anchorage of Lake Harbour was the most important on South Baffin Island for whaling ships. The Hudson's Bay Company opened a post in 1911, and during World War II, a radio station was set up. Although most of the population moved to Iqaluit in the 1960s, the local Inuit population of 350 remains steady—hunting, fishing, and carving local soapstone, distinguished by its apple-green color.

A limestone outcrop, located immediately to the east, has good views. A variety of geological formations and flora can be found close to town. To the northwest is a chain of lakes, including **Shoogle Lake,** which has a 60-meter waterfall at its far end. Many of the lakes offer excellent fishing for landlocked arctic char. **Mayukalik Outfitting** (P.O. Box 99, Kimmirut, Nunavut X0A 0N0, 867/939-2355) takes boat trips around the harbor, to 3,500-year-old archaeological sites at McKellar Bay and Cape Tanfield, and trips into the open water in search of sea mammals. It also rents canoes and other gear for trips down the Soper River.

Practicalities
The **Kimik Hotel** (P.O. Box 69, 867/939-2093) has eight rooms with private bathrooms; $185 per person includes three meals. Although the community has no established campgrounds, the beach is only a short walk from the airport and, with advance bookings, you can eat at the hotel. White gas and groceries are available at the co-op.
   First Air, 867/939-2250 or 800/267-1247, serves Kimmirut three times weekly from Iqaluit.

Katannilik Territorial Park
The watershed of the **Soper River** is protected by this 1,269-square-kilometer park that spans the Meta Incognita Peninsula from the waters of Frobisher Bay to the community of Kimmirut (formerly Lake Harbour) near Hudson Strait. The Soper River has carved out a deep valley near **Mt. Joy** (610 meters) and becomes wider and shallower as it flows through low-lying wetlands to the south. To the east, the peninsula is nearly devoid of vegetation, but the river valley is carpeted in colorful wildflowers and is lined with willow bushes. The most common mammals are arctic foxes and arctic hares. A herd of 3,000 caribou grazes throughout the area. Ermines and lemmings are also present. Just upstream from **Fleming Hill** is one of the world's few deposits of high-quality lapis lazuli. Four kilometers north of Kimmirut is **Soper Lake.** At the southern outlet are meromictic (reversing) falls where water drains out of the lake at low tide and pours back in again at high tide. At the north end of the lake is **Soper Falls.**
   The easiest way to explore the park is on foot from Kimmirut. Two designated landing strips can be accessed by Twin Otter or helicopter from Iqaluit from where you can hike to Kimmirut. The third, and most challenging, option is to charter a boat in Iqaluit and be dropped at the northeast corner of the park. The hike from there to Kimmirut would be 120 kilometers. Park information and trail maps are available at the Unikkaarvik Visitors Centre in Iqaluit

or from the park at P.O. Box 1000, Iqaluit, Nunavut X0A 0H0, 867/979-4636.

CAPE DORSET (KINGAIT)

For a community recognized around the world for fine arts and crafts, the cluster of weathered houses on a small island off the southwest coast of Baffin Island bears little resemblance to an art colony. *Kingait* (pop. 1,000) is named for the remains of an ancient people who flourished in the area between 1000 B.C. and A.D. 1000. The cape is actually an island, attached to the Foxe Peninsula of southwest Baffin Island only at low tide. The Hudson's Bay Company established a trading post at the cape in 1913, and in 1953, a nursing station was built to help avert diseases that had ravaged other communities. Also in this year, James Houston, an award-winning writer, and his wife arrived. They spent 10 years working with the local Inuit, encouraging the development of soapstone carving and printmaking. They also initiated the formation of the **West Baffin Eskimo Co-operative,** which has since gained international recognition for the artists it represents. Today the industry is worth $4 million annually, with 75 percent of the local residents earning all or part of their income from the production of art.
   Called soapstone, but really a form of serpentine, the soft rock used for carving is generally a mottled dark green. It is found 130 kilometers east of Cape Dorset at **Korak Inlet,** and many artists spend summer at this site. If you walk around the streets of Cape Dorset, you'll see artists at work, but to buy work, head to the co-op overlooking the bay, 867/897-8944. Also of interest are numerous Thule sites, including two within walking distance of the airport. **Mallikjuaq Island** can be reached on foot at low tide and has some high peaks offering good views and more archaeological sites, including a reconstructed sod house.

Practicalities
The **Kingnait Inn** (General Delivery, Cape Dorset, Nunavut X0A 0C0, 867/897-8863) has 17 rooms with private bathrooms; $190 per person includes three meals. No designated

camping areas exist, but anywhere out of sight of the community should be all right. Nonguests may eat at the hotel with advance reservations. The hotel also has take-out service.

The airstrip, within walking distance of the hotel, is served by **First Air,** 867/897-8938 or 800/267-1247, and **Air Nunavut,** 867/979-4018, from Iqaluit. These flights continue to Rankin Inlet. For a cab, call 867/897-8340.

BELCHER ISLANDS

Chances are, these islands will never make the cover of *Islands* magazine, nor will they ever be on the main tourist trail. But for those who seek them out, the enchanting lifestyle of the local Ungava Inuit and the absolute isolation the islands afford will be unforgettable.

The islands are spread over 5,000 square kilometers of southern Hudson Bay—low, barren, and windswept, with only one settlement, that of **Sanikiluaq** (pop. 630) on Flaherty Island. Although geographically and culturally removed from the rest of Nunavut, the islands are nevertheless politically a part, administered from Iqaluit 1,024 kilometers to the north.

Inuit migrated to the islands from northern Quebec 200 years ago, but with no airstrip, surrounded by shallow and treacherous waters, and a four-day kayak trip from the mainland, they remained almost forgotten.

The lack of land mammals meant that the Inuit had no source of furs for clothing. But living near one of the densest wildfowl nesting areas in Hudson Bay, the Inuit became one of the few peoples in the world to use feathered bird skins for clothing. Their tradition of making such clothing remains, although today they supplement their wardrobe with modern down-filled garb. The islanders are also known for their carvings of bird figures from dark green argillite.

Practicalities

The **Amaulik Hotel–Inns North** (Sanikiluaq, Nunavut X0A 0W0, 867/266-8821) is a new facility that opened in 1998. It has accommodations for 16 in eight rooms, each with a private bathroom; $150 per person. Breakfast, lunch, and dinner in the restaurant cost $10, $15, and $25 respectively. Camping is per-

mitted on a gravel beach along the north side of the harbor (but it can become windy). Access to the islands is by **Air Inuit,** 514/636-9445, from Montreal via Kuujjuarapik (Great Whale River).

HALL BEACH (SANIRAJAK)

Although part of the mainland, the flat, lowland region of Melville Peninsula, separated from Baffin Island by the narrow Fury and Hecla Strait, is part of the Baffin region. On its northeastern coastline are the communities of Hall Beach (pop. 540) and Igloolik, good bases for fishing trips or exploring Thule historic sites.

The Thule Inuit have hunted and fished on the peninsula for 7,000 years. A Distant Early Warning Line station, constructed in 1955, attracted the Inuit, who stayed and became dependent on a wage economy. A few years ago, when news reached the Inuit that the 20-meter radar screens were to be dismantled, they asked that the screens remain because they served as ideal landmarks on the otherwise featureless tundra. Their request was granted.

Hall Beach or *Sanirajak* (Flat Land) certainly isn't the place to come for scenery, but there is good arctic char fishing and viewing of sea mammals such as walrus and seals. Numerous archaeological sites are located in the area, including the Uglit Islands four kilometers offshore, where you'll find broken-down sod houses and gravesites. Between town and the airstrip are the remains of a whale, estimated to be 500 years old.

Practicalities

The **Co-op Hotel** (General Delivery, 867/928-8952) has five rooms, each with three beds; $185 per person including three meals. Ask here or at the hamlet office about camping.

First Air, 867/928-8927 or 800/267-1247, flies four times weekly between Iqaluit and Hall Beach.

IGLOOLIK (IGLULIK)

North of Hall Beach is Igloolik, which is large by Arctic standards (pop. 1,170), with the usual clutter of buildings. It is surrounded by low-lying topography and is a small island, separated from the mainland by Hector Strait. Archaeological sites on the island provide records of nearly unbroken habitation since 2000 B.C. Captain William Parry spent the winter of 1822–1823 on the island; the grave of one of his English sailors who died in the spring is located just outside town. Before the Hudson's Bay Company established a post in 1939, the Inuit had traveled to Pond Inlet and Repulse Bay to trade. Of the various Thule and Dorset sites, those at Ungalujat Point, 18 kilometers from Igloolik, including a ceremonial house, are the most interesting. In town, the **Nunavut Research Institute,** 867/928-8803, a large, mushroom-shaped building, is a government facility for public and private scientific research and a weather and seismic station. It also has a general Arctic reference section and small library.

Practicalities
The **Tujormivik Hotel** (P.O. Box 39, Igloolik, Nunavut X0A 0L0, 867/934-8814) is $195 per person per day, including three meals, usually local game or pastas in the evening. There is no set area for camping; ask at the hamlet office, 867/934-8830. For tours out on the tundra and ocean searching out sea mammals at the floe edge, contact the hamlet office, 867/934-8830, which can supply a list of local outfitters.

First Air, 867/934-8973 or 800/267-1247, flies between Iqaluit and Igloolik four times weekly.

PANGNIRTUNG (PANNIQTUUQ)

Pangnirtung (Lots of Caribou) sits in a spectacular setting, flanked by sheer cliffs rising almost 1,000 meters out of Pangnirtung Fjord. But most visitors come here on their way to somewhere even more awesome, Auyuittuq National Park (see following section).

The fjord was a base for whalers as early as 1840, but the Hudson's Bay Company didn't establish a trading post here until 1921, a decade after the decline of the whaling industry. Throughout the years, a community has grown, with Inuit from other areas moving here.

Although the Inuit have been strongly influenced by white settlers, many retain a traditional lifestyle.

Today, with a population of 1,300, "Pang," as it's best known, is Baffin Island's second-largest community.

Although the national park to the north is the main drawcard, the picturesque community is also worth exploring. The **Ukama Trail** follows a well-worn path from behind the arena along the west bank of the Duval River, passing numerous waterfalls; six kilometers (2.5 hours) one-way. Another trail, to the top of **Mt. Duval** (670 meters), begins near the campground and is seven kilometers (3–3.5 hours) each way. The views from the summit are spectacular, but the hike is strenuous.

Kekerten Historic Park
For nearly a century, hundreds of whaling ships plied the waters of the Baffin region. Instead of returning to their European or American ports, many wintered here at the end of the short summer season. This historic park, situated on

a small island 50 kilometers south of Pangnirtung, was one of two shore-based whaling stations in the eastern Arctic. The site has been partially restored; interpretive signs explain the importance of the artifacts and foundations that remain. The *Easonian,* a ship used to hunt beluga whales, burned in 1922 and is visible at low tide. From May to mid-June, access to the island is by snowmobile, and after mid-July by boat. **Alivaktuk Outfitting** (P.O. Box 3, Pangnirtung, Nunavut X0A 0R0, 867/473-8721) offers a 12-hour trip, including lunch, for $460 for two people. The price drops to $120 per person for a group of six.

Accommodations and Food
The **Auyuittuq Lodge** (P.O. Box 53, 867/473-8955) is located on a slight rise overlooking an old whaling station and the fjord. The 50 rooms with shared bath and laundry cost $135 per person, $75 extra for three meals. The rate includes airport transfers. **Pisuktinu Tungavik Territorial Campground** is located east of town over the Duval River, a 20-minute walk from the airport. The campground is free but has only pit toilets (ask at the Auyuittuq Lodge for showers). In bad weather, the Anglican Church, located behind Northern, opens its doors to campers. Groceries and white gas are available at **Northern,** 867/473-8935.

The dining room in the Auyuittuq Lodge offers fixed-price dinners for $35 per person, with arctic char served in season. Mealtimes are 7–9 A.M., noon–1 P.M., and 6–7 P.M.; reservations required. Near the airport is a snack bar.

Services and Information
The **airport** is located behind the main community and within walking distance of all services. **First Air,** 867/473-8771 or 800/267-1247, has six flights weekly from Iqaluit. Connections can also be made from Yellowknife, Ottawa, Montreal, and Winnipeg.

The **Angmarlik Interpretive Centre,** 867/473-8737, has information on the community, relics from whaling days, a small library, and Inuit elders on hand to interpret the area's natural history. The staff can also organize outfitters and trips to a char-fishing camp 20 kilometers from Pangnirtung; open in summer daily 9 A.M.–9 P.M.

AUYUITTUQ NATIONAL PARK

Auyuittuq (The Land That Never Melts) is a 21,000-square-kilometer wilderness of vast icefields, glacial lakes, some of the world's highest cliffs, and one long valley paralleled by peaks almost 3,000 meters high. The most popular trip within this totally undeveloped park is the hiking over **Akshayak Pass** (also called Pangnirtung Pass).

The Land
The park is part of a spine of mountains along the **Cumberland Peninsula,** which was formed by the same forces of Continental Drift that separated Baffin Island from Greenland. Draped over these mountains is the **Penny Ice Cap,** a sheet of ice up to 300 meters thick that covers 6,000 square kilometers. This icefield is drained on all sides by glaciers, slow-moving rivers of ice that have sculpted many of the park's features, including a 97-kilometer-long valley that cuts across Cumberland Peninsula. The highest elevation of the valley occurs midway along its length at Akshayak Pass (500 meters). From the pass, the **Weasel River** flows south to Summit Lake and South Pangnirtung Fjord, and the **Owl River** flows north into the Davis Strait. Along the southern half of the valley are mounts Asgard, Thor, and Overlord, steep granite peaks that attract climbers from around the world.

Flora and Fauna
Plantlife in the pass is best observed around summer solstice, when the ground is carpeted by masses of purple willow herbs, arctic poppies, and arctic willow. This sparse vegetation supports very few species of animals. The lemming is the most common mammal, although their numbers vary dramatically from season to season. Also common are the large arctic hare and the small arctic fox. Although the polar bear is essentially a seal hunter, it occasionally wanders inland to feed on berries. Caribou, which are rare in the pass but are occasionally seen in the northwest corner of the park, are hunted by wolves. Birds most commonly seen are ptarmigan, ravens, and snowy owls. The red-throated loon is also common

during the short nesting season. **Cape Searle,** adjacent to the park, is the breeding ground for 10,000 **northern fulmars.**

Practicalities

A trip to Auyuittuq requires advance planning, preparation, and, for those attempting the pass, experience in the wilderness. Hikers must ford swiftly flowing streams and negotiate ankle-wrenching slopes of glacial moraine. No services are available, and the barren land offers no trees to block the wind or provide firewood. Most trips begin with a boat or snowmobile trip (Pangnirtung Fjord is choked with ice until mid-July) from Pangnirtung to the **Overlord Warden Station** ($100 per person), where a campground is set among huge boulders. Many hikers travel only as far as Summit Lake, returning to Overlord the same way. This section of the trail is the most inspiring and crosses the **Arctic Circle,** which is flanked by the towering peaks of Mt. Odin to the west and Mt. Thor to the east. The second half of the valley is broader and less impressive, its terrain is more rugged, and it is traveled by fewer people. If you plan to hike the entire pass, you will have to prearrange a pickup on Broughton Island. Travel is by snowmobile or dogsled in early summer and by boat after mid-August. Although the most popular time of year for hiking is July and August, late June is good for the 24 hours of daylight.

Park Information Centres are located in Pangnirtung, 867/473-8828, and Broughton Island, 867/927-8834. The park-use fee is $15 per day; a three-night pass is $40, and an annual pass is $100. For further information, write Parks Canada, P.O. Box 353, Pangnirtung, Nunavut X0A 0R0, www.parkscanada.gc.ca/auyuittuq. Each center has topographical maps of the park ($10 each).

BROUGHTON ISLAND (QIKIQTARJUAQ)

On an island of the same name, this community of 500 Inuit adjoins an area rich with seals, whales, and polar bears. The community is located off the east coast of Baffin Island on a raised beach flanked by glaciated hills. It is a five- to six-hour trip from the terminus of the Ak-

shayak Pass hiking trail in Auyuittuq National Park, so many people spend time here. The community began when Inuit families were moved to the site to help construct a Distant Early Warning Line station in 1956. **Pikaluyak Outfitting** (General Delivery, Broughton Island, Nunavut X0A 0B0, 867/927-8316) has a 10-meter boat for drop-offs and pickups in Auyuittuq ($280 one-way for two people), or for viewing the abundant icebergs, sea mammals, and colonies of seabirds along the Baffin Island coast.

Practicalities

If you're planning a trip with Pikaluyak Outfitting, ask about its Quonset hut (no running water or electricity) for $35 per night. The **Tulugak Hotel** (P.O. Box 8, 867/927-8874) has nine rooms with private baths and is close to the airport; $175 per person includes three meals. The campground has running water and tent platforms and is one kilometer from the community. **Northern** sells groceries and white gas.

First Air, 867/927-8873 or 800/267-1247, flies six times weekly from Iqaluit to Broughton Island, with some flights stopping at Pangnirtung.

CLYDE RIVER (KANGIQLUGAAPIK)

This remote community is located on a floodplain, surrounded by mountainous scenery. It's near the mouth of the Clyde Inlet, a fjord that slices southwest into the mountainous east coast of Baffin Island. Most of the 700 residents of Clyde River live a traditional lifestyle of fishing and hunting. The site has never been a traditional hunting ground, but Inuit families moved here in the 1950s when the Hudson's Bay Company opened a post to take advantage of high seal prices.

Sawtooth Mountain, 25 kilometers from the community, is a good vantage point for viewing the surrounding peaks and bays. Unfortunately, reaching most other sights in the area requires the services of an outfitter. **Qullikkut Guides** (P.O. Box 29, Clyde River, Nunavut X0A 0E0, 867/924-6268) offers fishing and sightseeing trips. Rates are $275 per person per day by dog team and $300 per person by boat. At Cape Hewitt, 35 kilometers from town, are tent rings from the Thule culture; at Cape Christian is an abandoned U.S. Coast Guard station; and farther down the coast is **Isabella Bay,** a breeding ground for many of the world's remaining bowhead whales. These slow, copepod-eating whales were decimated by whalers in the 1800s, and their numbers have never recovered.

Practicalities

The **Qamaq Hotel** (General Delivery, 867/924-6201) charges $190 per person, including three meals. Meals are available at the hotel, and groceries from **Northern.**

From the airport four kilometers from town, **First Air,** 867/924-6365 or 800/267-1247, flies to and from Iqaluit.

POND INLET (MITTIMATALIK)

The first Europeans in the area, Robert Bylot and William Baffin, arrived in 1616, but the local Inuit, who have strong links to the Greenland Thule, hunted in the area well before then. The first permanent settlement on the southern shore of the Eclipse Sound was an RCMP post established in 1921. The community has grown to 1,100, mostly Inuit, living in a brightly colored clump of civilization overlooking Bylot Island.

The main attraction in the area is Sirmilik National Park, but hiking in the region is also good. **Mt. Herodier** (765 meters) is a 15-kilometer (one-way) hike from town, with only one difficult stream crossing.

Sirmilik National Park,

In late spring and early summer, the waterways of this newly established park host the highest concentrations of sea mammals in the eastern Arctic. Narwhal, beluga, and bowhead whales, polar bears, seals, and walruses can all be viewed from the floe edge or a boat. The park extends from Pond Inlet across the Eclipse Sound to **Bylot Sound** and north to Lancaster Sound. In summer, 50 species of birds nest on Bylot Island, including tens of thousands of murres and kittiwakes and most of the world's snow goose population. Also on the island are hoodoos, archaeological sites, and glaciated peaks rising to 2,000 meters. The park's main outfitter is **Polar Sea Adventures** (P.O. Box 60, Pond Inlet, Nunavut X0A 0S0, 867/899-

8870), which organizes snowmobile trips to the floe edge (the best time for wildlife viewing is early July, including the chance to see narwhals), dogsled trips around the sound, and boat trips to historic sites and over to Bylot Island. To get to the island by boat or snowmobile costs $400. This company also rents kayaks for $45 per day. For further park information, write Parks Canada, P.O. Box 353, Pangnirtung, Nunavut X0A 0R0, www.parkscanada.gc.ca.

Practicalities

The **Sauniq Hotel** (General Delivery, 867/899-8928) has 15 rooms, each with two single beds and a private bathroom; $250 per person per day includes three meals. The hotel has a gift shop selling carvings and can set up tours onto the sound. Salmon Creek, two kilometers west of town, has a campground with tent platforms. You can also pitch your tent on the beach just west of town. Meals are available with advance reservations at the hotel; groceries are available from **Northern.**

First Air, 867/899-8882 or 800/267-1247, flies daily between Iqaluit and Pond Inlet.

ARCTIC BAY AND VICINITY

The northern reaches of Baffin Island are made up of two peninsulas, Borden and Brodeur. These desolate plateaus of land are divided by **Admiralty Inlet,** the world's longest fjord and also one of the deepest. No one knows just how deep it is, but at one point its depth is so great that, combined with upwellings of water, currents, and tides, an expanse of water remains ice-free year-round. This phenomenon, which has intrigued scientists for decades, is known as a polynya. The only inhabited area is on Borden Peninsula.

Arctic Bay (Ikpiarjuk)

Arctic Bay (pop. 650) is surrounded on three sides by hills and on the fourth by Admiralty Inlet. The only road in the Baffin region connects the community to Nanisivik, to the east. The area has been occupied by nomadic Inuit hunters for almost 5,000 years. The first permanent settlement was a Hudson's Bay Company post established in 1924. Remains of prehistoric cultures can be found around the area, including at **Uluksan Point,** a low-lying area to the west of the community. To the east is a distinctive cairn, erected by the crew of a government steamer that wintered here in 1910–1911.

Lancaster Sound

Between the northern tip of Baffin Island and the rugged southern coast of Devon Island is Lancaster Sound, the eastern entrance to the **Northwest Passage** and the western extent of Sirmilik National Park (see Pond Inlet). Each year, tens of thousands of sea mammals migrate through this corridor, in turn attracting seabirds and polar bears. Each spring, they must wait at the floe edge that spans the sound, until the ice has broken up and they are free to travel through to the islands of the high Arctic. This spectacle of mammals and birds is the destination of a high Arctic expedition offered by **Niglasuk Co.** (Arctic Bay, Nunavut X0A 0A0, 867/439-9949). Four seven-night trips are undertaken each June, with a base camp established on the shoreline closest to the floe edge and daily trips made to view the wildlife. The cost is $3,650 per person from Arctic Bay. This tour books up months in advance. The company also offers shorter trips, including dog sledding, sea kayaking, and fishing.

Prince Leopold Island is a flat-topped, barren island of 85 square kilometers rising 300 meters from the waters northeast of Somerset Island. In summer, it supports four species of seabirds, who nest in the hundreds of thousands on the island's narrow ledges. The island has been designated as a migratory bird sanctuary.

Nanisivik

The infrastructure at Nanisivik, 21 kilometers east of Arctic Bay, has been in place since 1974. It serves the 300 workers who mine the silver, lead, and zinc deposits on the shore of Strathcona Sound. To protect against the high winds that howl through camp, all buildings have curved walls. Once extracted, ore is stored on the beach for summer shipment to European markets. No tours of the mine are offered, nor are any tourist services available.

The **Midnight Sun Marathon,** which takes place on the weekend closest to July 1, is the world's northernmost marathon. The race, which attracts marathoners from around the world, is run between Nanisivik and Arctic Bay; the most grueling event is 84 kilometers. For information, call 867/436-7502.

Practicalities

The **Enokseot Hotel** (P.O. Box 69, Arctic Bay, Nunavut X0A 0A0, 867/439-8811) charges $130 per person per night, with meals an extra $70 per person. The campground is at **Victor Bay,** five kilometers from the community ($10 in a taxi). These accommodations are handy if you'd

"Do you think we can tow it to Southern California?"

NWT ARCTIC TOURISM

like to visit Lancaster Sound without forking out for a seven-day trip. If that's the case, Niglasuk Co. can arrange travel to the floe edge ($450 per person per day). Food is available, cafeteria-style, at the hotel, and **Northern** has groceries.

The airport is at Nanisivik, 21 kilometers from Arctic Bay. Taxis meet all flights. **First Air,** 867/436-7481 or 800/267-1247, flies twice weekly from Iqaluit and from Yellowknife via Resolute.

RESOLUTE: GATEWAY TO THE HIGH ARCTIC (QAUSUITTUQ)

With a population of only 200, the small community of Resolute is an important jumping-off point for expeditions to the high Arctic. It also holds an important scientific research station and several excellent outfitters. The community is located on Resolute Bay on the south coast of **Cornwallis Island,** a low-lying island on the north side of the Northwest Passage.

William Parry was the first white man to report seeing the island, and in the 1850s, the island was the center of much activity during the search for the lost Franklin Expedition. In fact, the town was named after the HMS *Resolute,* one of the vessels involved in the search. An airfield established in 1947 as a weather station soon became the hub of air transportation in the high Arctic.

Since the late 1950s, Resolute has been the operations base for the **Polar Continental Shelf Project,** a program of Arctic research. The research center and a weather station at the airport are open for tours. Near the dock is a small aquarium stocked with local specimens. The surrounding hills, once under the sea, are full of fossils, and five kilometers west of the airport are Thule tent rings.

A Controversial Move

In 1953, Inuit families from Inukjuak, Quebec, and Pond Inlet were relocated to Cornwallis Island and Southern Ellesmere Island; more followed in 1955. At the time, the Department of Northern Affairs and National Resources claimed that the island was a land of plentiful resources and the move was for the good of the Inuit. More recently, it has been revealed that the people were moved to help reinforce Canada's right to sovereignty in the islands of the high Arctic. The full story is only just beginning to be revealed, but apparently, after the families were separated into two groups, they were left in a totally alien environment, with scant regard for their needs and feelings. With only a U.S. Forces garbage dump as a food source, they were lucky to survive. For 35 years, little was known about their plight, and they didn't receive government support and the promise of repatriation until 1988. After a two-year inquiry by the Royal Commission into Aboriginal Peoples, a report released in July 1994 concluded that "the relocation plan was an ill-conceived solution that was inhumane and damaging in its design and effects," and that "there was a significant lack of care and skill in various aspects of the project, including a severe shortage of clothing and bedding during the first winter, causing hardship and suffering." It also recommended that the Canadian government apologize and provide compensation.

Practicalities

The largest accommodation in Resolute is the **Narwhal Hotel** (P.O. Box 88, Resolute, Nunavut X0A 0V0, 867/252-3968), near the airport, which sleeps 45 in 30 rooms. Meals are served cafeteria-style, and the demands of government workers keep the standard of food high. The other choice is **Tudjaat Inns North** (General Delivery, 867/252-3900), offering seven rooms with shared bathrooms; $185 per person including meals. Camping is available at **Resolute Lake,** one kilometer from the airport, and at Mecham River, five kilometers farther. **Northern** and the **post office** are by the airport, and the accommodations and other services are in the Inuit village, eight kilometers away. The road has regular traffic, and commuting between the two is relatively easy.

Resolute is a long way from anywhere; in fact, London is closer than many U.S. cities. **First Air,** 867/252-3981 or 800/267-1247, has flights from Yellowknife and Iqaluit. **Kenn Borek Air,** 867/252-3845, and First Air, have aircraft for charter, with Kenn Borek Air offering scheduled flights from Resolute to Grise Fiord, Nanisivik, and Pond Inlet.

Devon and Beechey Islands

Devon Island, to the north of Baffin Island across **Lancaster Sound,** is a smaller version of its southerly neighbor. The eastern part of this 350-kilometer-long island is lowland arctic, whereas in the west, cliffs drop 1,000 meters into the ocean below. West of Cape Sparbo are the **Truelove Lowlands,** lake-strewn meadows that have been the scene of much Arctic research and are currently the site of a summer camp of the Arctic Institute of North America, based in Calgary.

Off the island's southwest coast is Beechey Island, where the Franklin Expedition wintered while searching for the Northwest Passage. Beechey is only an island at high tide; at low tide, a sandbar joins it to Devon Island. Graves and artifacts were found on one of the many gravel beaches on the north side of the island, partly explaining one of the Arctic's most famous sagas. Access is by snowmobile, boat, or chartered Twin Otter from Resolute, 80 kilometers away.

The Parry Islands

To the west of Resolute are **Little Cornwallis Island** and the uninhabited islands of **Bathurst** and **Melville,** collectively known as the Parry Islands. Little Cornwallis Island is home to Cominco's **Polaris Mine,** the northernmost metal mine in the world. It is a modern, year-round operation producing lead and zinc for European markets. The self-contained operation employs 200 people and even boasts an indoor pool.

Polar Bear Pass, on Bathurst Island, is an ecological reserve with high concentrations of land mammals and birds. Generally, it is visited only by Inuit hunting parties and scientific expeditions.

The **magnetic North Pole,** which is continually changing positions in a wobbly, circular motion, currently lies in the general area of **Cameron Island,** to the north of Bathurst Island. It was first located in 1831, when James Ross found his compass dipping downward on King William Island, just off the Arctic coast. The pole moves because of magnetic distortions caused by convection deep below the earth's crust. On the southwest coast of Cameron Island is **Bent Horn A-02,** an oil well operated by Panarctic Oils, a company that has been at

the forefront of high Arctic oil exploration since 1968. Oil produced here is so light that it can be used directly in diesel engines on site; the rest is shipped to Montreal.

ELLESMERE ISLAND

Ellesmere Island sits at the top of the North American continent, a wild, rugged landscape of steep-sided fjords and glaciers. At 212,688 square kilometers, it's the 10th-largest island in the world. It extends 800 kilometers from its southern coast and the picturesque community of Grise Fjord to above the 83rd parallel, and east to within 30 kilometers of Greenland. **Axel Heiberg Island,** to the west of Ellesmere and separated by narrow **Eureka Sound,** has peaks rising more than 1,000 meters. On the east coast of Axel Heiberg Island, across from **Eureka** (a high Arctic weather station), are the **Geodetic**

TO THE TOP OF THE WORLD

On 6 April 1909, an expedition led by American explorer Robert Peary—including four other men, five sledges, and 38 dogs—became the first to reach the geographic North Pole.

Every year audacious adventurers attempt to reach the pole under their own steam, with dogs, and on snowmobiles. But relative to the South Pole or the summit of Mt. Everest, the North Pole receives few visitors. From the most popular staging area, Ward Hunt Island, it's 772 km to the pole. Most expeditions spend at least two years in preparation, including a few months under Arctic conditions, and budget upward of $1 million. For less adventurous adventurers it's possible to get there on an organized trip in a couple of days, have a champagne lunch, and return to a warm bed at night. The least expensive option, without the trimmings, would be to get a group of six people together and charter a Twin Otter from **Bradley Air Service** in Resolute. The flight, with an overnight stop in Eureka, costs $26,000. **Quark Expeditions,** tel. (203) 358-9033 or (800) 356-5699, often charters a Russian icebreaker—complete with all the facilities of a top hotel and an onboard helicopter—for the long trip north; US$17,900 per person.

Hills. In the hills is a fossilized forest, the remains of thick forests that grew in a lush valley here 40 million years ago.

Grise Fjord (Aujuitittuq)

Overlooking Jones Sound and backed by the spectacular ice-capped peaks of southern Ellesmere Island, this small Inuit community of 150 has reached near-mythical status as North America's northernmost community. Here, at a latitude of 76°N, the sun dips below the horizon for 3.5 months each year, and the sound is ice-free only in August.

Otto Sverdrup coined the name *Grise* (Pig, in Norwegian) when he wintered here in 1899–1890. The community was born in 1953, when Inuit from Port Harrison and Pond Inlet were brought here as part of a relocation program. Today, the Inuit live a traditional lifestyle of hunting, trapping, and fishing. Although Resolute, 383 kilometers southwest, is the major hub of the high Arctic, Grise Fjord is used as a staging point for trips into the interior of Ellesmere Island and to Greenland, accessible by dogsled and snowmobile for six months of the year.

Grise Fjord Lodge–Inns North (General Delivery, Grise Fjord, Nunavut X0A 0J0, 867/980-9913) can organize outfitters for all seasons, has a recently refitted lodge ($195 per person, including three meals), and sells groceries.

Kenn Borek Air, 867/252-3845 in Resolute, flies between Grise Fjord and Resolute twice weekly.

Quttinirpaaq National Park

This 37,775-square-kilometer park is literally at the top of the world. It extends from a vast ice-field in the central part of Ellesmere Island to the northern coastline where the Grant Land Mountains drop dramatically into the Arctic Ocean. **Mt. Barbeau** (2,629 meters) is the highest peak in North America east of the Rockies. **Lake Hazen,** in the center of the park, is the most popular destination for backpackers. It is 80 kilometers long and the largest lake north of the Arctic Circle. The lake is a thermal oasis, attracting diverse species of birds and mammals during the short summer season. The park receives less than 100 millimeters of precipitation annually, making it one of the driest areas in the world. But where wind has deposited soil, pockets of lush vegetation manage to survive, and brightly colored arctic flowers soak up the sun's rays. The most common mammals here are foxes and hares, although Peary caribou, musk oxen, and wolves are also present. The park also provides suitable nesting habitat for 30 species of birds. The best place for viewing all wildlife is the Lake Hazen area.

The main access point is park headquarters at Tanquary Fjord, a five-hour flight in a chartered Twin Otter from Resolute. Both Resolute charter companies fly to the park, but it is very expensive—$27,000 round-trip for 10 people. You will need to be totally self-sufficient and prepared for all climatic conditions. From Tanquary Fjord, the hike to Lake Hazen is 130 kilometers, including one glacier crossing. For more information, write to Superintendent, Quttinirpaaq National Park, P.O. Box 353, Pangnirtung, Nunavut X0A 0R0, 867/473-8828, www.parkscanada.gc.ca.

Ward Hunt Island

North of the national park at the mouth of Markham Fiord is four-kilometer-long Ward Hunt Island. At 83° 5 minutes N, it's the northernmost point of land in North America. Therefore, it is the main staging point for land-based expeditions to the North Pole, 772 kilometers farther north.

Alert

The high Arctic weather station of Alert, 170 kilometers west of Ward Hunt Island, is the continent's northernmost occupied site and has been since 1950. The average high temperature in July is only 6.5°C. Temperatures in winter are not as harsh as you might expect, rarely dropping below –40°C, but the base is totally dark for four months of the year.

BOOKLIST

GEOGRAPHY, TRAVEL, AND RECREATION

Gadd, Ben. *Handbook of the Canadian Rockies.* Jasper: Corax Press, 1995. The latest edition of this classic guide is in color, and although bulky for backpackers to carry, it's a must-read for anyone interested in the natural history of the mountains.

Kane, Alan. *Scrambles in the Canadian Rockies.* Calgary: Rocky Mountain Books, 1992. Routes detailed in this guide lead to summits, without the use of ropes or mountaineering equipment.

Kariel, Herbert G. *Alpine Huts in the Canadian Rockies, Selkirks, and Purcells.* Canmore: Alpine Club of Canada, 1986. Covers the history of all huts in the Rockies, with current access routes and status and descriptions of nearby peaks to climb.

Kunelius, Rick, and Dave Biederman. *Ski Trails in the Canadian Rockies.* Banff: Summerthought, 1981. Detailed guide to cross-country skiing in all national parks of the Canadian Rockies.

MacDonald, Janice E. *Canoeing Alberta.* Edmonton: Lone Pine Publishing, 1985. Comprehensive guide to all navigable rivers in the province.

Patterson, Bruce. *The Wild West.* Canmore: Altitude Publishing, 1993. From the Calgary Exhibition and Stampede to the working ranches of Alberta's foothills, this book covers all aspects of life in the West.

Patton, Brian, and Bart Robinson. *The Canadian Rockies Trail Guide.* Banff: Summerthought, 2000. This regularly updated guide, first published in 1971, covers all hiking trails in the mountain national parks. Distances are measured accurately, and the two authors hiked all trails for this latest edition, so you can be confident of the book's accuracy.

Savage, Brian. *Ski Alberta.* Edmonton: Lone Pine Publishing, 1985. Comprehensive guide to cross-country ski trails across the province. Downhill ski areas are also detailed.

FLORA AND FAUNA

Alberta Forestry, Lands, and Wildlife. *Alberta Wildlife Viewing Guide.* Edmonton: Lone Pine Publishing, 1990. Describes where to see particular species of animals, with color photographs, small maps of certain areas, and best viewing seasons.

Federation of Alberta Naturalists. *The Atlas of Breeding Birds of Alberta.* Edmonton: Federation of Alberta Naturalists, 1992. Comprehensive study of all birds that breed in the province with easy-to-read distribution maps, details on nesting and other behavioral patterns, and color plates.

Foster, John E., Dick Harrison, and I.S. MacLaren, eds. *Buffalo.* Edmonton: University of Alberta Press, 1992. A series of essays by noted historians and experts in the field of the American bison, addressing their disappearance from the prairies, buffalo jumps, and current problems in Wood Buffalo National Park.

Gray, David R. *The Muskoxen of Polar Bear Pass.* Markham: Fitzhenry & Whiteside, 1987. A detailed yet entertaining look at the lives of one of North America's least understood mammals.

Herreo, Stephen. *Bear Attacks: Their Causes and Avoidances.* New York: Nick Lyons Books, 1985. Through a series of gruesome stories, this book catalogs the stormy relationship between people and bruins, provides hints on avoiding attacks, and tells what to do in case you're attacked.

Lauriault, Jean. *Identification Guide to the Trees of Canada.* Markham: Fitzhenry & Whiteside, 1989. Makes tree identification easy through drawings of leaves and maps detailing distribution of species.

National Wetlands Working Group. *Wetlands of Canada.* Ottawa: Sustainable Development Branch, Canada Wildlife Service, Conservation and Protection, Environment Canada, 1988. Each chapter deals with a region of Canada and its specific areas of wetland.

Nelson, Joseph S. *The Fishes of Alberta.* Calgary: University of Calgary Press, 1992. Describes 59 species of fish and provides maps of their distribution. Also looks at fish management and fishing in the province.

Scotter, George W. *Birds of the Canadian Rockies.* Saskatoon: Western Producer Prairie Books, 1990. Description of most-recorded species, including habitat and habits. Color photos.

Smith, Hugh C. *Alberta Mammals: An Atlas and a Guide.* Edmonton: Provincial Museum of Alberta, 1993. Written from a database accumulated by the author over 23 years as curator of mammalogy at the Provincial Museum, this book describes range, identifying characteristics, and habitat of each species, accompanied by full-page maps of their distribution.

Vacher, André. *Summer of the Grizzly.* Saskatoon: Western Producer Prairie Books, 1985. True story of a grizzly bear that went on a terrifying rampage near the town of Banff.

Whitaker, John. *National Audubon Society Field Guide to North American Mammals.* New York: Random House, 1997. One of a notable series of field guides produced by the National Audubon Society, this one details mammals through color plates and detailed descriptions of characteristics, habitat, and range.

Scotter, George W. *Wildflowers of the Canadian Rockies.* Edmonton: Hurtig Publishers Ltd., 1986. Color plates of all flowers found in the mountain national parks. Chapters are divided by flower colors, making identification in the field easy.

HISTORY

Fryer, Harold. *Ghost Towns of Alberta.* Langley, British Columbia: Stagecoach Publishing, 1976. Alberta's ghost towns are unlike those found in the western states of the United States. Many towns have slipped into oblivion, and this guide looks at more of these than you'd ever dreamed existed.

Hamilton, Jacques. *Our Alberta Heritage.* Calgary: Calgary Power Ltd., 1977. Available in one hardbound copy or as five softcover editions, each covering a different aspect of the province's history.

Jenness, Diamond. *The Indians of Canada.* Toronto: University of Toronto Press, 1977. Originally published in 1932, this is the classic study of natives in Canada, although his conclusion, that they were facing certain extinction by "the end of this century" is obviously outdated.

Jones, David. *Empire of Dust.* Edmonton: University of Alberta, 1987. Complete history of Alderston and the surrounding prairie; a sorry story of drought and the destruction it brings.

Lavallee, Omer. *Van Horne's Road.* Montreal: Railfare Enterprises, 1974. William Van Horne was instrumental in the construction of Canada's first transcontinental railway. This is the story of his dream, and the boomtowns that sprung up along the route. Lavallee devotes a section of the book to the crossing of Alberta and the enormous task faced by engineers when the rail line reached the Canadian Rockies.

MacGregor, James. *A History of Alberta.* Edmonton: Hurtig Publishers, 1981. Complete history of Alberta from a wild frontier to world leader.

McMillan, Alan D. *Native Peoples and Cultures of Canada*. Vancouver: Douglas & McIntyre, 1995. A comprehensive look at the archeology, anthropology, and ethnography of the native peoples of Canada. The last chapters delve into the problems facing these people today.

Newman, Peter C. *Company of Adventurers*. Markham: Penguin Books Canada, 1985. The story of the Hudson's Bay Company and its impact on Canada.

Sandford, R.W. *The Canadian Alps: The History of Mountaineering in Canada*. Canmore: Altitude Publishing, 1990. Complete human history of the Canadian Rockies from the earliest explorers to first ascents of major peaks.

Schäffer, Mary T.S. *A Hunter of Peace*. Banff: Whyte Museum of the Canadian Rockies, 1980. This book was first published in 1911 by G.P. Putnam & Sons, New York, under the name *Old Indian Trails of the Canadian Rockies*. Tales recount the exploration of the Rockies during the turn of the 20th century, with many of the author's photographs appearing throughout.

Smith, Cyndi. *Off the Beaten Track*. Jasper: Coyote Books, 1989. Accounts of women adventurers and mountaineers and their impact on the early history of western Canada.

Touche, Rodney. *Brown Cows, Sacred Cows*. Hanna: Gorman, 1990. The story of the development of the Lake Louise ski area as told by a former general manager.

United Western Communications. *Alberta in the 20th Century*. Edmonton: United Western Communications Ltd., 1991. Each volume of this series covers a decade in the history of Alberta through a comprehensive essay.

Woodman, David C. *Unravelling the Franklin Mystery*. Montreal: McGill-Queen's University Press, 1991. Many volumes have been written on the ill-fated Franklin Expedition. This one, using Inuit recollections, is among the best.

PALEONTOLOGY

Grady, Wayne. *The Dinosaur Project*. Toronto: Macfarlane, Walter, & Ross, 1993. Tells the story of paleontological expeditions to China and the Albertan badlands and how the work has enhanced our knowledge of dinosaurs and their movements between Asia and North America. Accounts of actual field trips are given as well as easy to read backgrounds on each area.

Gross, Renie. *Dinosaur Country*. Saskatoon: Western Producer Prairie Books, 1985. Describes Alberta's earliest inhabitants, their habitat, why they disappeared, and the history of dinosaur hunting in the province, including detailed coverage of Dinosaur Provincial Park.

Russell, D.A. *An Odyssey in Time: The Dinosaurs of North America*. Toronto: University of Toronto Press, 1989. Complete details of all known dinosaurs on the North American continent.

Spalding, David A.E. *Dinosaur Hunters*. Toronto: Key Porter Books, 1993. Tells the story of the men and women who have devoted their lives to the study of dinosaurs.

POLITICS AND GOVERNMENT

Bone, Robert. *The Geography of the Canadian North*. Toronto: Oxford University Press, 1992. An in-depth look at the role Canada's north has played and will play in the management of world resources, and the impact of self-government on the region.

Watkins, Ernest. *The Golden Province*. Calgary: Sandstone Publishing, 1980. A political history of Alberta from 1905, focusing on the Social Credit Party.

Wood, David G. *The Lougheed Legacy*. Toronto: Key Porter Books, 1985. Tells the story of Peter Lougheed's 14-year reign as premier of Alberta.

PERIODICALS

The Canadian Alpine Journal. Canmore, Alberta. Annual magazine of the Alpine Club of Canada, with articles from its members and climbers from around the world; www.alpineclubofcanada.ca.

Canadian Geographic. Ottawa. Bimonthly publication by the Royal Canadian Geographical Society pertaining to Canada's natural and human histories and resources.

Equinox. Markham, Ontario. This bimonthly publication looks at Canada's natural world and humanity's relationship with it.

Explore. Calgary. Bimonthly publication of adventure travel throughout Canada.

Up Here. Yellowknife. Magazine of life in Canada's north published by Outcrop Ltd. Eight issues annually.

FREE CATALOGS

Alberta Accommodation and Visitors' Guide. Alberta Hotel Association. Annually updated listing of all hotel, motel, and other lodging in the province. Available at all Tourist Information Centres or by calling 800/661-8888; www.alberta-accommodations.com.

Alberta Campground Guide. Alberta Hotel Association. Lists all campgrounds in the province. Available at all Tourist Information Centres or by calling 800/661-8888; www.alberta-campgrounds.com.

Tour Book: Western Canada and Alaska. Booklet available to members of the Canadian or American Automobile Association.

LITERATURE

Kroetsch, Robert. *Badlands.* Toronto: New Press, 1975. A fictional account of Alberta's first dinosaur hunters.

Marty, Sid. *Switchbacks: True Stories from the Canadian Rockies.* Toronto: McClelland & Stewart, 1999. This book tells of Marty's experiences in the mountains and of people he came in contact with in his role as a park warden. Along the way, he describes the way his experiences with both nature and fellow humans have shaped his views on conservation today.

Mowat, Farley. *Never Cry Wolf.* Toronto: McClelland and Stewart, 1990. This story of living with Arctic wolves on the Keewatin barrenlands is an international bestseller and has been made into a feature film.

Turner, Dick. *Nahanni.* Surrey, British Columbia: Hancock House, 1975. One of the north's most celebrated authors recounts stories of early life in the north and particularly on the South Nahanni River.

REFERENCE

Daffern, Tony. *Avalanche Safety for Skiers & Climbers.* Calgary: Rocky Mountain Books, 1992. Covers all aspects of avalanches, including their causes, practical information on how to avoid them, and a section on rescue techniques and first aid.

Gray, D.M., and D.H. Male. *Handbook of Snow.* Toronto: Pergamon Press, 1991. Comprehensive guide on everything you ever wanted to know about snow but didn't ask because no one else would have known either.

Hare, F.K., and M.K. Thomas. *Climate Canada.* Toronto: John Wiley & Sons, 1974. One of the most extensive works on Canada's climate ever written. Includes a chapter on how the climate is changing.

Interwest Publications. *The Atlas of Alberta.* Edmonton: Interwest Publications Ltd., 1984. Historical, resource, city, and town maps of Alberta.

Johnson, Leslie. *Basic Mountain Safety from A to Z.* Canmore: Altitude Books, 2000. Everything you need to know about safety in the mountains, including a large section on camping.

Karamitsanis, Aphrodite, Tracey Harrison, and Merrily K. Aubrey, eds. *Place Names of Alberta.* Calgary: University of Alberta Press, 1991. An ongoing toponomy project. Volume 1 alphabetically lists all geographic features of the mountains and foothills with explanations of each name's origin. Volume 2 does the same for southern Alberta's geographical features, while Volume 3 tackles northern Alberta.

Patterson, W.S. *The Physics of Glaciers.* Toronto: Pergamon Press, 1969. A highly technical look at all aspects of glaciation, why glaciers form, how they flow, and their effect on the environment.

Whyte Museum of the Canadian Rockies. *Guide to Manuscripts: The Fonds and Collections of the Archives, Whyte Museum of the Canadian Rockies.* Banff: Whyte Museum of the Canadian Rockies, 1988. This book makes finding items in the Whyte Museum easy through alphabetical lists of all parts of the collection.

Zuehlke, Mark. *Alberta Fact Book.* Vancouver: Whitecap Books, 1997. This very readable book gives details on hundreds of Alberta towns, sights, and historical events.

INDEXES
ACCOMODATIONS INDEX

RESTAURANT INDEX

MAIN INDEX

FISHING

GOLFING

general discussion 33
Billy Joss Open (Holman): 477
Blairmore: 165
Bragg Creek: 174
Calgary: 64-65
Canmore: 194-195
Cochrane: 173
Drumheller: 95
Edmonton: 331, 334
Elkwater: 137
Elk Island National Park (Lakeland): 356
Fort McMurray: 371
Fort Smith: 438
Gibbons: 374
Grand Prairie: 400
Grande Cache: 397
Grimshaw: 408
Hardisty: 311
Holman: 477
Jasper National Park: 280
Kananaskis Valley: 182
Lethbridge: 119
NWT Open (Hay River): 433
Peace River: 406
Raven Mad Daze (Yellowknife): 448
Red Deer: 305
Slave Lake: 379
Town of Banff: 224
Vale Island (Hay River): 432,
Waterton Lakes National Park: 150

303; Devonian Botanic Garden (Edmonton) 332; Devonian Gardens (Calgary) 59; Kurimoto Japanese Garden 332; Muttart Conservatory 324; Nikka Yuko Japanese Garden 118-119; Text Garden 386
Garner Lake Provincial Park: 361
gasoline: 46
geese: 14, 301, 419
Genesee Fossil beds: 298
Geodetic Hills: 501-502
geology: 4-6
George's Harness & Saddlery: 312
Germans: 27
Ghost Reservation Provincial Recreation Area: 173
Ghost River Wilderness Area: 179
ghost towns: 298

Giant Steps Waterfalls: 248
giardia: 47
Gibbons: 374
glaciation: 6, 179, 261
Glenbow Museum: 59
Glendon: 363
Glenora: 328
Goat Haunt, MT: 147, 149
Goat Lookout: 267
gold mining: 421, 444
golden eagles: 15, 265
Golden Walleye Classic: 382
gondolas: 245
Goods and Services Tax (GST): 38, 46-47
Goose Mountain Ecological Reserve: 384
Gooseberry Lake Provincial Park: 308
Gopher Hole Museum: 301
government: Alberta 24-25; NWT/Nunavut 420
Government House: 328
Grain Academy: 63
Grande Cache Lake: 396-397
Grande Cache: 393-397
Grande Prairie: 398-403
Grande Prairie Little Theatre: 400
Grande Prairie Museum: 398
Grande Prairie Regional Airport: 400
Grande Prairie Regional College Theatre: 400
Grande Prairie Regional College: 398
Great Bear Lake: 466
Great Bear River: 466
Great Divide Waterfall: 323
great horned owls: 14
Great Northern Arts Festival: 472
Great Plain of the Koukdjuak: 490
Great White North Pumpkin Fair & Weighoff: 360-361
greenhouses: 131
Gregoire Lake Provincial Park: 370
Greiner Lake: 480
Griffin Valley Ranch: 173
Grimshaw: 408
Grise Fjord: 502
grizzly bears: 11, 205, 418, 471, 481,
Grizzly Trail: 384
Grouard Native Cultural Arts Museum: 381
Grouard: 381
guest ranches: 29, 31
guns: 46
GuZoo Animal Farm: 300-301
Gwich'in Territorial Park: 469
gypsum karst: 441

HIKES

ABOUT THE AUTHOR 543

ABOUT THE AUTHOR

A ndrew Hempstead has spent many years exploring, writing about, and photographing western Canada. He has been writing since the late 1980s, when, after leaving a promising career in the field of advertising, he took off for Alaska, linking up with veteran travel-writer Deke Castleman to help research and update the fourth edition of *Alaska-Yukon Handbook.*

In addition to this book, he is the author of *Moon Handbooks: Canadian Rockies* and *Vancouver Handbook* (Moon Travel Handbooks/Avalon Travel Publishing); is co-author of *British Columbia Handbook* (Moon Travel Handbooks/Avalon Travel Publishing) and *Australia Handbook* (Moon Travel Handbooks/Avalon Travel Publishing)*;* and has contributed to subsequent editions of *Moon Handbooks: Alaska-Yukon* (Moon Travel Handbooks/Avalon Travel Publishing). Andrew has also traveled to New Zealand multiple times on assignment to write and photograph for Moon Travel Handbooks/Avalon Travel Publishing and The Guide Book Company. He is a contributing writer to *Road Trip USA* (Avalon Travel Publishing) and Microsoft's *Automap,* and his work has appeared in *National Geographic Traveler*. He has also traveled purely for pleasure throughout most of the United States, Europe, the South Pacific, and India.

When not working on his books, Andrew is happiest hiking, fishing, golfing, camping, and enjoying the simple pleasures in life, such as sitting on his deck with a nice cold beer and watching the sun set over the mountains. He calls Canmore, Alberta home.

AVALON TRAVEL

publishing

BECAUSE TRAVEL MATTERS.

AVALON TRAVEL PUBLISHING knows that travel is more than coming and going—travel is taking part in new experiences, new ideas, and a new outlook. Our goal is to bring you complete and up-to-date information to help you make informed travel decisions.

AVALON TRAVEL GUIDES feature a combination of practicality and spirit, offering a unique traveler-to-traveler perspective perfect for an afternoon hike, around-the-world journey, or anything in between.

WWW.TRAVELMATTERS.COM

Avalon Travel Publishing guides are available at your favorite book or travel store.

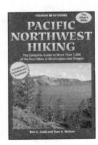

www.travelmatters.com

User-friendly, informative, and fun:
Because travel *matters.*

Visit our newly launched web site and explore the variety of titles and travel information available online, featuring an interactive *Road Trip USA* exhibit.

also check out:

www.ricksteves.com

The Rick Steves web site is bursting with information to boost your travel I.Q. and liven up your European adventure.

www.foghorn.com

Visit the Foghorn Outdoors web site for more information on the premier source of U.S. outdoor recreation guides.

www.moon.com

The Moon Handbooks web site offers interesting information and practical advice that ensure an extraordinary travel experience.

U.S.~METRIC CONVERSION

1 inch = 2.54 centimeters (cm)
1 foot = .304 meters (m)
1 yard = 0.914 meters
1 mile = 1.6093 kilometers (km)
1 km = .6214 miles
1 fathom = 1.8288 m
1 chain = 20.1168 m
1 furlong = 201.168 m
1 acre = .4047 hectares
1 sq km = 100 hectares
1 sq mile = 2.59 square km
1 ounce = 28.35 grams
1 pound = .4536 kilograms
1 short ton = .90718 metric ton
1 short ton = 2000 pounds
1 long ton = 1.016 metric tons
1 long ton = 2240 pounds
1 metric ton = 1000 kilograms
1 quart = .94635 liters
1 US gallon = 3.7854 liters
1 Imperial gallon = 4.5459 liters
1 nautical mile = 1.852 km

To compute celsius temperatures, subtract 32 from Fahrenheit and divide by 1.8. To go the other way, multiply celsius by 1.8 and add 32.

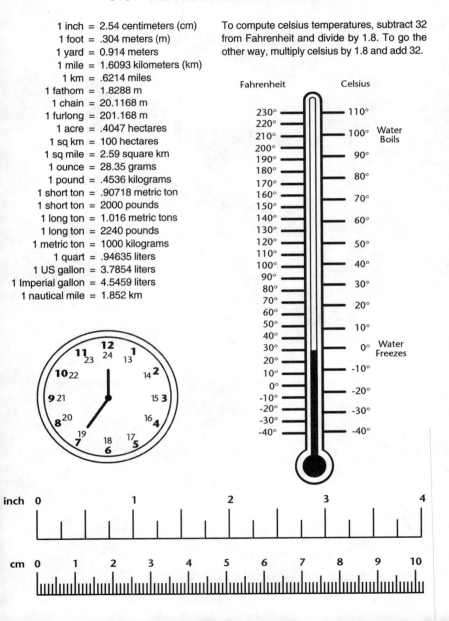

Will you have enough stories to tell your grandchildren?